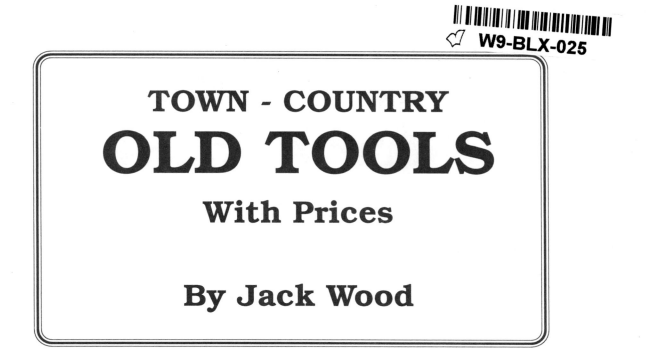

TOWN - COUNTRY
OLD TOOLS
With Prices

By Jack Wood

10th Printing 2005

© Copyright 1990

ISBN# 0-89145-417-9

Published By
L-W BOOKS
P.O. Box 69
Gas City, IN 46933

TABLE OF CONTENTS

LOCKS, KEYS, AND CLOSURES Starts After The Old Tools Index.

****Look to Index of Old Tools for Detailed Listings.

Foreword

The pricing in this book is only an opinion of the Editor. It is intended only as a guide. Prices vary so much from area to area, only an approximate price is given. Remember, the price of a collectible is what a collector is willing to pay.

Many of the pictures in this volume were taken with a pegboard background. All holes are 1 inch apart. This should make it very easy to measure all tools thus pictured.

Planes, Wood & Metal

Planes were the backbone of the carpenter's trade at the turn of the century and earlier. Many of the mouldings and trim were formed by using wood planes. Of all the various types of early tools, these are probably the easiest to find. They are still priced high because of the demand of collectors.

Cooper's Tools

Coopering or the making of wooden barrels is a very old trade. No doubt, barrels were made during the time of ancient Rome and Coopers have been high on the list of respected tradesmen. Cooper's tools are much harder to find than regular hand tools.

Axes, Hammers, Hatchets, Etc.

Some hand forged broad axes date into the middle 1700's. Their primary use was for straightened timbers. Although handle lenghths seem to be a matter of personal preference, shape and design of the head would determine the nation of origin or ancestry of the maker.

Blacksmith Tools

Since the founding of our nation, blacksmithing has been the most illustrated through books, poems, and songs. Truly, the village Smithy was a mighty man.

Braces, Bits, Hand Drills, Etc.

Drilling was important for fitting together early furniture, also in the construction of barns, houses, etc.

Draw Knives, Spoke Shaves

Wheel makers and carpenters made much use of the early draw knives and shaves.

Wrenches

Wrenches came into being early in the industrial revolution. The first ones were made by blacksmiths and later were manufactured in factories for use on new equipment then being invented.

CHAPTER I

Planes, Wood & Metal

Planes were the backbone of the carpenter's trade at the turn of the century and earlier. Many of the mouldings and trim were formed by hand using wood planes. Of all the various types of early tools, these are probably the easiest to find. They are still priced high because of the demand of collectors.

Molding Planes

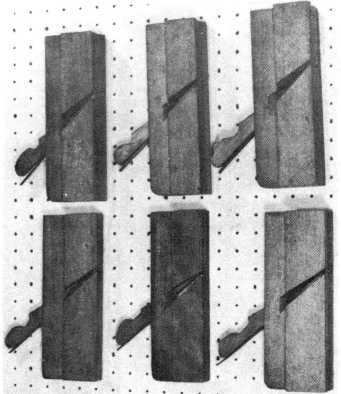

2 on Left Molding Planes
4 on Right Bannister Planes

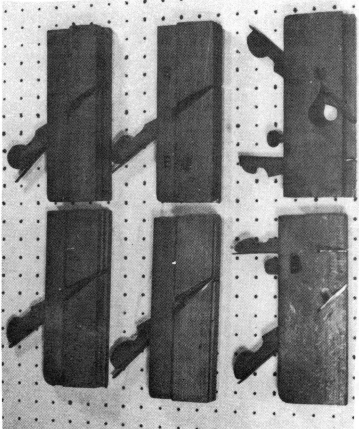

Molding Planes
Note — Lower Right is Back Side of Plane

2

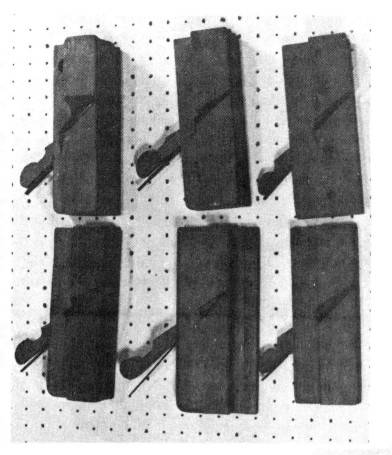

Molding Planes

Left, Plow Plane (Auburn Tool Co.)
Right, Tongue and Groove (Ohio Tool Co.)

Plow Planes
Top, Ohio Tool Co.
Bottom, John Bell, Phil.

Plow Planes

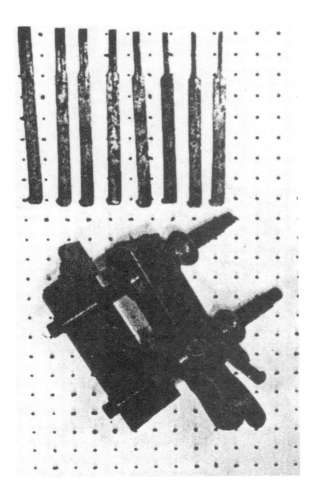

Plow Plane with Cutters, Ohio Tool Co.

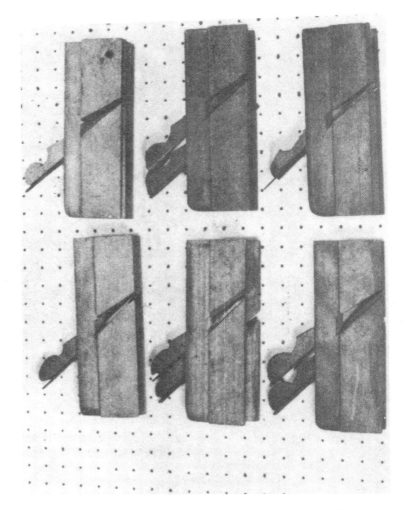

Round and Hollow Planes
Left to Right, Each Top & Bottom is a pair

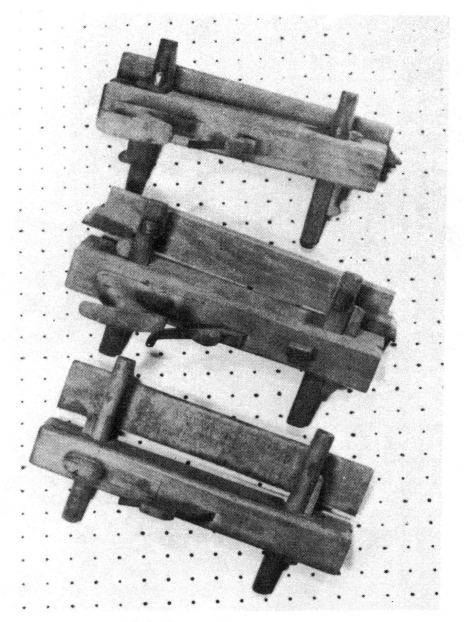

Groove Planes
Adjustable with wedged side-runners

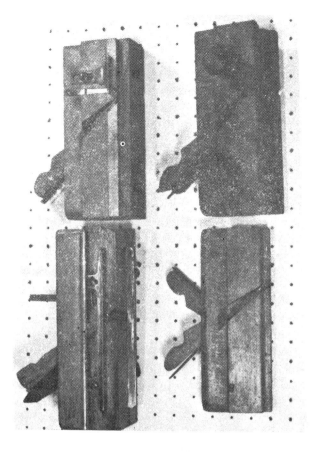

Top Left, Fillister Plane
Bottom Left, Tongue & Groove Comb.
Top Right, Smoothing Plane with side marker
Bottom Right, Adj. Molding Plane

Top Left, Smoothing Plane with side marker
Bottom Left, Fillister Plane
Top Right, Adj. Molding Plane
Bottom Right, Tongue and Groove Com.

Top, German Groove Plane
Bottom, Groove Plane-wedge Adj.

7

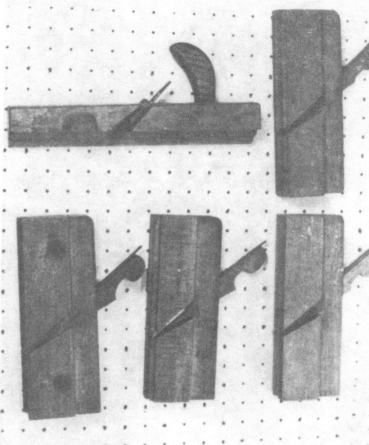

Top Left, Molding Planes

Top, Groove Plane
Center, Groove Plane
Bottom, Tongue Plane

8

Top, Tongue Plane
Center, Groove Plane
Bottom, Tongue Plane

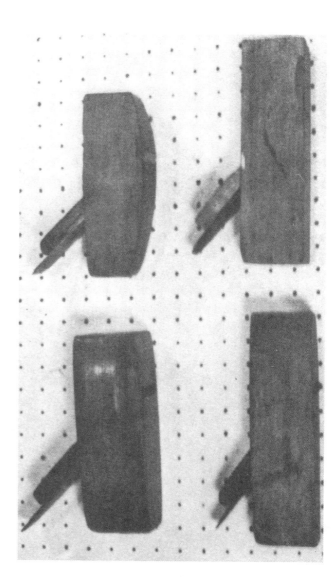

Jack Planes

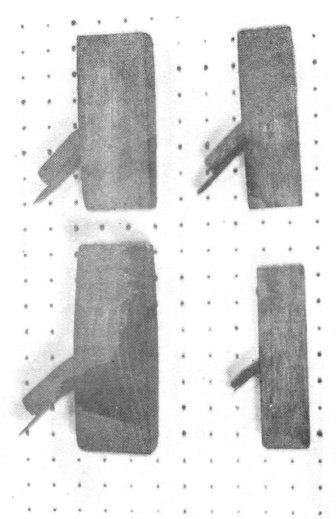

Jack Planes

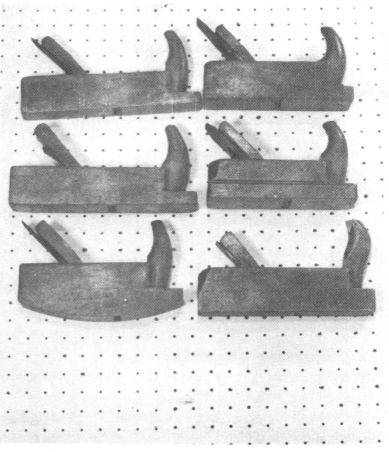

German Jack Planes (before 1900)
Horn Style Handle is Characteristic
of German Planes

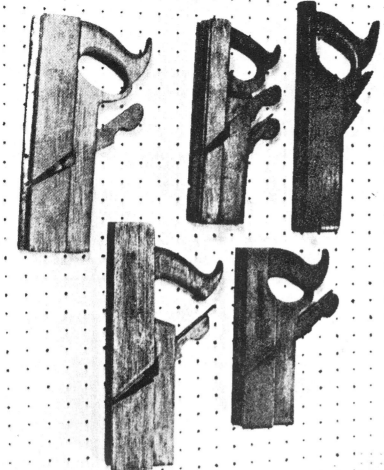

Top Left, Concave Plane
Top Center, Double Cutter Molding Plane
Top Right, Tongue Plane
Bottom Left, Tongue Plane
Bottom Right, Hollow Plane

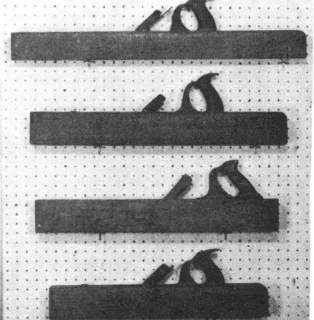

Running Planes
Top, 29″ Made of Curly Maple
Top Center, 25″ Curly Maple
Bottom Center, 24″ Looks German
Bottom, 22″ Curly Maple

BEADING, RABBET, AND SLITTING.

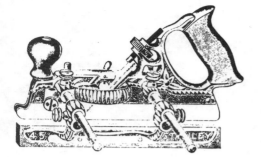

BULLNOSE PLOW, FILLETSTER AND MATCHING.

PATENT TONGUING AND GROOVING PLANE.

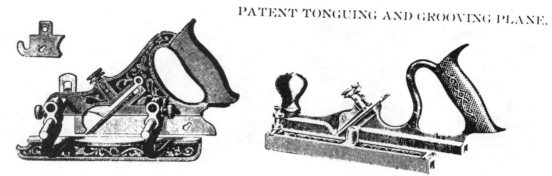

PLOW, FILLETSTER AND MATCHING.

PATENT DUPLEX RABBET PLANE AND FILLETSTER.

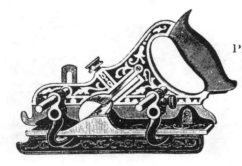

All planes are made of cast metal.

PATENT IMPROVED RABBET PLANE.

All planes made of cast metal.

Bailey's Patent Adjustable Planes.

Wood Planes.

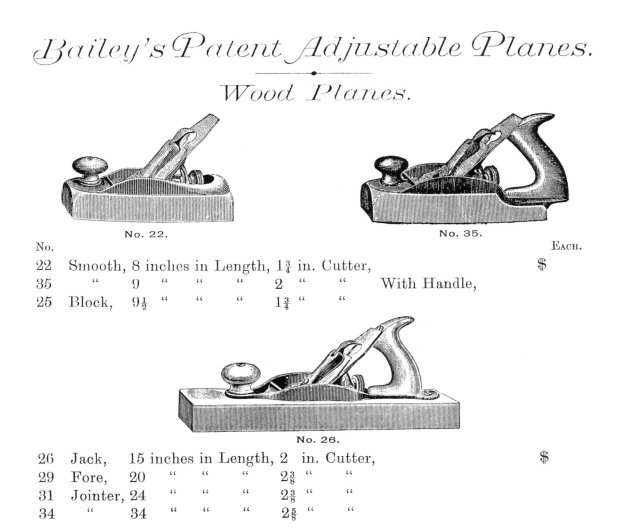

No. 22.   No. 35.

No.											Each.
22	Smooth,	8 inches in Length,	$1\frac{3}{4}$ in. Cutter,								$
35	"	9 " " "	2 " "				With Handle,				
25	Block,	$9\frac{1}{2}$ " " "	$1\frac{3}{4}$ " "								

No. 26.

26	Jack,	15 inches in Length,	2 in. Cutter,			$
29	Fore,	20 " " "	$2\frac{3}{8}$ " "			
31	Jointer,	24 " " "	$2\frac{3}{8}$ " "			
34	"	34 " " "	$2\frac{5}{8}$ " "			

Iron Planes.

No. 3.

3	Smooth,	8 inches in Length,	$1\frac{3}{4}$ in. Cutter,			$
4	"	9 " " "	2 " "			
5	Jack,	14 " " "	2 " "			
6	Fore,	18 " " "	$2\frac{3}{8}$ " "			
8	Jointer,	24 " " "	$2\frac{5}{8}$ " "			

ONE IN A BOX.

Bailey's Patent Adjustable Planes.

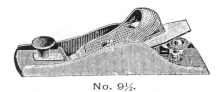
No. 9½.

No. 9¾.

No.		Each.
9½	Excelsior Block, 6 inches in Length, 1¾ in. Cutter, Adjustable,	$
9¾	" " " 7 " " " 1¾ " " " with Rosewood Handle.

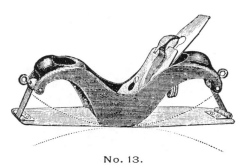
No. 13.

13 Circular, 1¾ inch Cutter, Adjustable, $

Miller's Patent Plows.

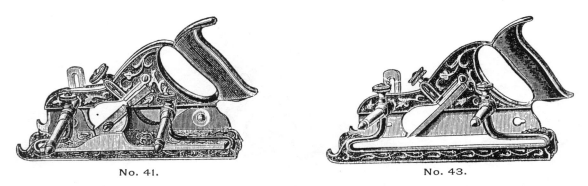
No. 41.   No. 43.

41 Iron Stock and Fence, Combined Plow, Fillister and Matching
      Plane, $
43 Iron Stock and Fence, Combined Plow and Matching Plane,

ONE IN A BOX.

Traut's Patent Plows.

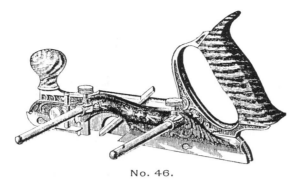

No. 46.

No.		Each.
46	Iron Stock and Fence, Adjustable Dado, Fillister, Plow, etc.,	$
47	" " " " " "	

Each Plow is complete with Plow Bits, Tonguing and Grooving Tools.

Patent
Tonguing and Grooving Planes.

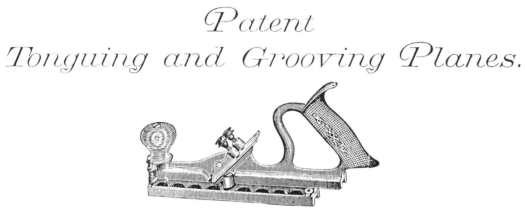

48   Iron Stock and Fence, including Tonguing and Grooving Tools, $

Bailey's Veneer Scrapers.

12   Adjustable Veneer Scraper, 3 inch Cutter $

PER DOZEN.

Cast Steel Hand Veneer Scrapers, 3 × 5 inch, $

ONE IN A BOX.

6

Bench Planes.

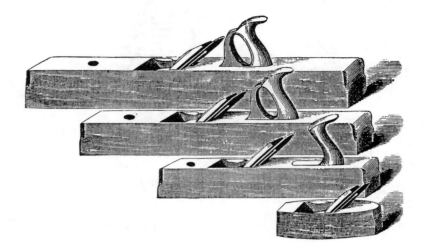

A. C. Bartlett's Ohio Planes.

Warranted Irons.

NO.	KIND.	DESCRIPTION.					EACH.
3	Smooth	Double Irons, Polished, Ebony Start, 2 to 2¼ in.					$0 90
5	"	"	"	"	"	" with Handle	1 75
10	Jack . . .	Single	"	"	"	" 16 in., 2 to 2¼ in.	75
13	" . . .	Double	"	"	"	" " "	1 00
19	Fore . . .	"	"	"	"	" 22 in., 2⅜ to 2⅝ in.	1 40
25	Jointer .	"	"	"	"	" 26 " 2½ to 2¾ in.	1 50
25	" .	"	"	"	"	" 28 " "	1 60
25	" .	"	"	"	"	" 30 " "	1 75

Eastern Planes.

NO.	KIND.	DESCRIPTION.					EACH.
6	Smooth	Double Irons, Polished Ebony Start, 2 to 2¼ in.					$0 90
12	Jack . . .	"	"	"	"	" 16 in., 2 to 2¼ in.	1 00
20	Fore . . .	"	"	"	"	" 22 " 2⅜ to 2⅝ in.	1 40
30	Jointer .	"	"	"	"	" 26 " 2½ to 2¾ in.	1 50

A. C. Bartlett's Ohio Planes.

No. 38½.

NO.	KIND.	DESCRIPTION.	EACH.
36	Tooth Plane	2¼ in., Cast Steel Iron,	$1 00
38½	Mitre "	1¾ in., " "	75

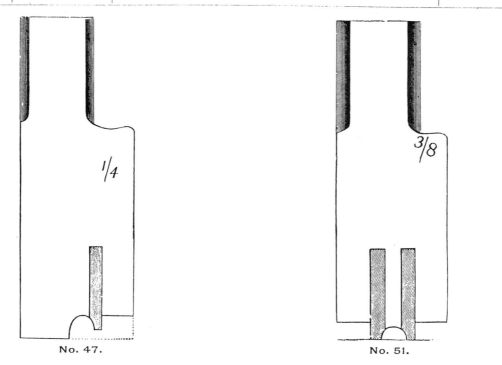

No. 47.   No. 51.

47	Side Beads..	Single, Boxed, ⅛ to ½ in.,	$0 50
"	" " ..	" " ⅝ to ¾ "	55
"	" " ..	" " ⅞ to 1 "	70
"	" " ..	" " 1¼ "	90
"	" " ..	" " 1½ "	1 00

51	Centre Beads	Double, Boxed, ⅛ to ½ in.,	$0 60
"	" "	" " ⅝ to ¾ "	65

A. C. Bartlett's Ohio Planes.

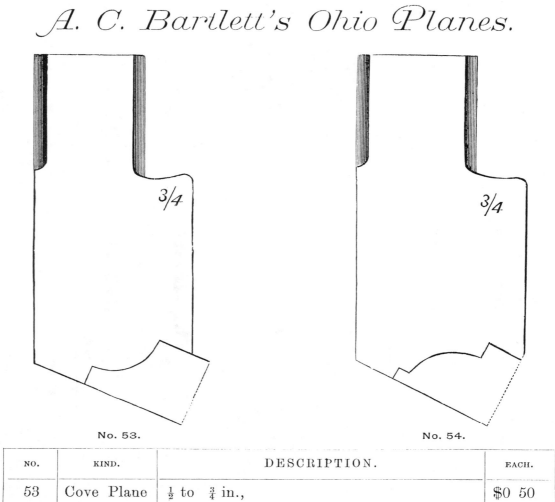

No. 53.   No. 54.

NO.	KIND.	DESCRIPTION.	EACH.
53	Cove Plane	$\frac{1}{2}$ to $\frac{3}{4}$ in.,	$0 50
"	" "	$\frac{7}{8}$ to 1 "	65

NO.	KIND.	DESCRIPTION.	EACH.
54	Scotia	Or Quarter Round, $\frac{3}{8}$ to $\frac{5}{8}$ in.,	$0 50
"	"	" " " $\frac{3}{4}$ to 1 "	65

No. 62.

62	Dados	Screw Stop, $\frac{1}{4}$ to 1 in.,	$1 50

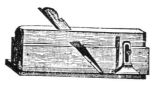

No. 67.

NO.	KIND.	DESCRIPTION.	EACH.
66	Fillister	With Cutter,	$1 25
67	"	" " and Brass Side Stop,	1 40
68	"	" " " " " " and Boxed,	1 85
69	"	" " " " Screw " " "	2 50

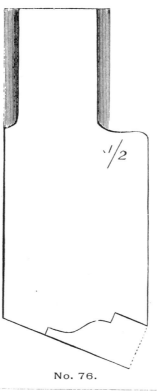

No. 76.

76	Roman Ogee	To work on Edge, ½ in.,	$0 75
"	" "	" " " " ⅝ to 1 in.,	85
"	" "	" " " " 1¼ in.,	90
"	" "	" " " " 1½ "	95

A. C. Bartlett's Ohio Planes.

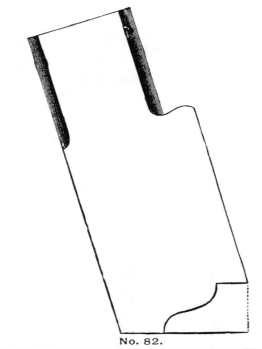

No. 82.

NO.	KIND.	DESCRIPTION.	EACH.
82	Roman Reverse Ogee	$\frac{3}{8}$ to $\frac{5}{8}$ in.,	$0 75
"	" " "	$\frac{3}{4}$ to 1 "	85
"	" " "	$1\frac{1}{4}$ "	1 00
"	" " "	$1\frac{1}{2}$ "	1 15

			PER PAIR.
92	Hollows and Rounds	1 to 6,	$0 75
"	" " "	7 to 9,	90
"	" " "	10 to 12,	1 10
"	" " "	Per Set of Nine Pairs, Nos. 1 to 9,	7 20

A. C. Bartlett's Ohio Planes.

No. 146.

NO.	KIND.			DESCRIPTION.	EACH.
146	Rabbet Plane, Skew..			$\frac{1}{2}$, $\frac{5}{8}$, $\frac{3}{4}$ in.,	$0 60
"	"	"	"	$\frac{7}{8}$, 1, 1$\frac{1}{4}$ "	65
"	"	"	"	1$\frac{1}{2}$ "	70
"	"	"	"	1$\frac{3}{4}$ "	80
"	"	"	"	2 "	90
149	"	"	"	with Handle & 2 Cutters, 1$\frac{1}{2}$, 1$\frac{3}{4}$, 2 in.	1 70

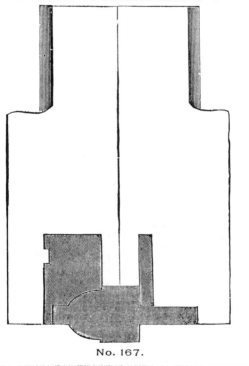

No. 167.

167	Sash Plane..	Screw Arms, Self-Regulating, Boxed, Gothic or Ogee,	$2 00
168	" " ..	Screw Arms, Self-Regulating, Dovetailed, Boxed, Bevel or Ovolo,	2 25
169	" " ..	Screw Arms, Self-Regulating, Dovetailed, Boxed, Gothic or Ogee,	2 25

A. C. Bartlett's Ohio Planes.

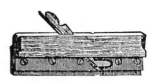

No. 99.

No. 113.

NO.	KIND.	DESCRIPTION.	PER PAIR.
99	Board Match	$\frac{3}{8}, \frac{1}{2}, \frac{5}{8}, \frac{3}{4}, \frac{7}{8}$, 1 in.,	$1 25
"	" "	Twin, $\frac{3}{8}, \frac{1}{2}, \frac{3}{4}, \frac{7}{8}$ in.,	1 25
"	" "	" 1 in.,	1 50
100	" "	Plated, $\frac{1}{2}$ to 1 in.,	1 50
101	" "	With Solid Handle, $\frac{1}{2}, \frac{3}{4}, \frac{7}{8}$, 1 in.,	2 00
102	" "	" " " Plated, $\frac{1}{2}$ to 1 in.,	2 25
106	Plank "	" Screw Arms,	3 50

			EACH.
113	Nosing Step	Two Irons, $\frac{3}{4}$ to $1\frac{1}{4}$,	$1 10
"	" "	" " $1\frac{3}{8}$ to $1\frac{1}{2}$,	1 20

Panel Plows.

117	Beech, 8 Irons, Screw Stop,		$4 50
119	" 8 " " " with Handle,		5 50
120	" 8 " " " "	Boxwood Fence,	5 85
123	" 8 " Boxwood Arms, "		6 75
124	" 8 " " " "	Boxwood Fence,	7 00
125	Applewood, 8 Irons, Screw Top, "	Boxwood Fence,	6 75
132	Box or Rosewood, 8 Irons, "		9 00
133	" " 8 " "	Ivory Tipped,	10 00

PLANES

WOOD BENCH PLANES

Our Wood Bench Planes are made of selected stock, and are cut with bottom of Plane to the heart of tree; this gives a hard sole to the Plane.

FITTED WITH SANDUSKY IRONS

No. 300. Smooth Plane, with 1½, 1¾, 1⅞, 2 inch iron..each **1.50**   No. 36. Tooth Plane, with 1⅞, 2, 2⅛ inch irons.....each **2.00**

If fitted with Buck Bros. irons, add 75 cents.

No. 1300. Jack Plane, 2⅛ or 2¼ inch iron.........each **1.85**   No. 1500. Cut Down Jack Plane, 2 or 2⅛ inch iron..each **2.25**

If fitted with Buck Bros. irons, add 75 cents.

No. 1900. Fore Plane, 22 inches long, 2¾ inch iron...each **2.75**
No. 2100. Fore Plane, cut down handle...each **3.00**

If fitted with Buck Bros. irons, add 75 cents.

G. A. R. CABINET JOINTERS

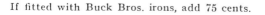

G. A. R. Cabinet Jointer Plane, 28 inches long, 2⅜ inch iron...each **3.50**
If fitted with Buck Bros. irons, add 75 cents.

GAGE SELF-SETTING PLANES

The Gage Self-Setting Wood Plane as made in Vineland, N. J., has recently been acquired by this company and the manufacture will be continued, as well as an additional line of Iron Planes of the same principle.

THE SELF-SETTING FEATURE lies in the fact that the plane iron, if taken out to be honed or sharpened, goes back in exactly the same position as before removal.

Likewise the plane cap, when taken out to allow removal of the cutter, goes back in its same position.

THE PLANE CAP (A) is the same in Iron and Wood Planes. The upper part is cast iron and has a steel bottom fastened to it by screws. The steel bottom may be so adjusted before the screws are set up so that, when the parts are all assembled in the plane, the steel cap so fits the cutting iron as to make it, either a single or double plane iron, as desired, for various kinds of work. The cap is black in cut.

THE PLANE IRON (B) shown in the cut consists of three pieces—the cutter, the adjustment slide fastened to the under side of the cutter (shown black), and the binder plate fastened above the cutter—all three being fastened by one screw.

THE ADJUSTMENT SLIDE (C) is machined on its sides to accurately fit the groove machined in the frog and is also machined to fit the adjusting screw, so that it is permanently fixed both side-ways and endwise. This is the same in both Iron and Wood Planes.

THE FROG in the wood plane is a part of an iron throat which fits into the plane wood and is there fastened by screws. (See cut.) This iron throat is adjustable as the plane bottom wears, thus eliminating any difficulty of the mouth wearing large. The bottom of this throat is ground a little rounding and may be set slightly below the plane bottom, which enables the plane to cut very fast with a fine shaving.

In the iron plane the Frog is fitted to the plane bottom and then permanently attached by screws and pin, so that a continuous cutter seat obtains clear to the plane mouth.

There is an endwise screw adjustment to the cutter in both the Iron and Wood Planes.

Cut to left shows iron frog part of plane body.
Cut to right, plane wood is black, showing how iron throat is set.

GAGE WOOD PLANES

No. G22.   10 inches long, 1¾ inch cutter...........each **3.65**

No. G35.   10 inches long, 2   inch cutter...........each **3.90**

No. G36.   10½ inches long, 2¼ inch cutter.........each **4.50**

No. G26.   14 inches long, 2   inch cutter...........each **4.25**

No. G28.   18 inches long, 2¼ inch cutter...........each **5.00**

No. G30.   22 inches long, 2¼ inch cutter...........each **5.25**

No. G31.   24 inches long, 2½ inch cutter...........each **5.75**

GAGE IRON PLANES

				Smooth Bottom	Corrugated Bottom
No. G3.	Smooth,	8¾ inches long, 1¾ inch cutter...each	**3.50**	3.75
No. G4.	Smooth,	9 inches long, 2 inch cutter...each	**3.90**	4.15
No. G5.	Jack,	15 inches long, 2 inch cutter...each	**4.35**	4.60
No. G6.	Fore,	18 inches long, 2¼ inch cutter...each	**5.65**	5.90
No. G7.	Jointer,	22 inches long, 2½ inch cutter...each	**6.50**	6.75

Specify whether Smooth or Corrugated bottom is wanted.

PLANES

WOOD MOLDING PLANES

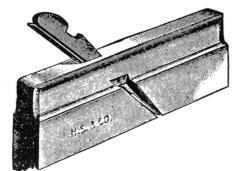

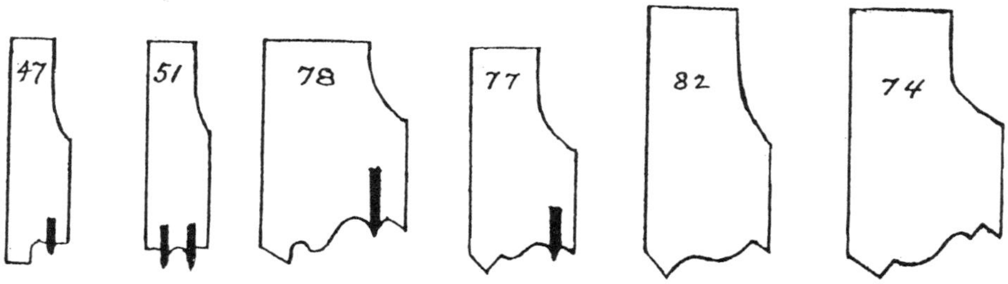

No. 47. Side Bead, ⅛, ³₁₆, ¼, ⁵₁₆, ⅜, ½ inch...each **1.00**

No. 51. Centre Bead, ⅛, ³₁₆, ¼, ⁵₁₆, ⅜, ½ inch...each **1.20**

For Boards, thickness, inches	½	¾	⅞	1
No. 78. Grecian O. G. and Bead.................................each	1.75	1.75	1.75	1.75
No. 77. Grecian O. G...each	1.50	1.50	1.50	1.50
No. 82. Roman Revease O. G......................................each	1.50	1.50	1.50	1.50
No. 74. Plain O. G..each	1.30	1.30	1.30	1.30

METAL WEATHER-STRIP PLANES
STEEL LINED

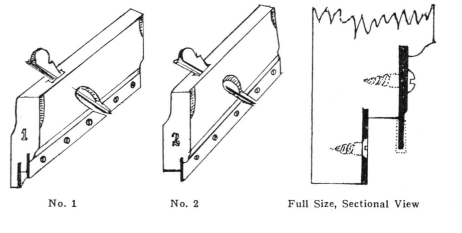

No. 1   No. 2   Full Size, Sectional View

No. 1 ....each **2.25**

No. 2 ....each **2.50**

PLANES

GERMAN SMOOTH PLANES

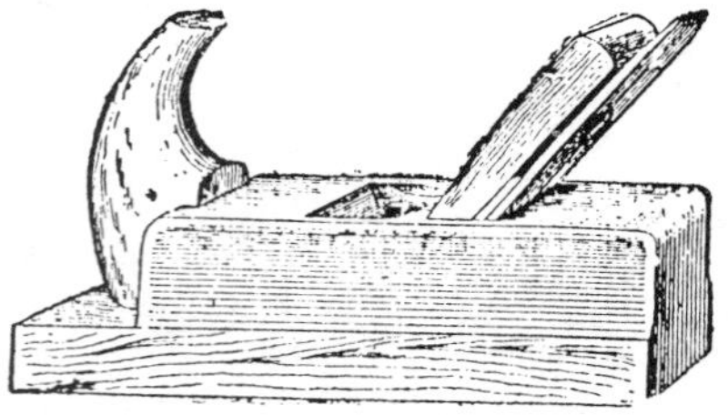

2 or 2⅛ inch iron.................................each **3.00**

GERMAN SCRUB PLANES

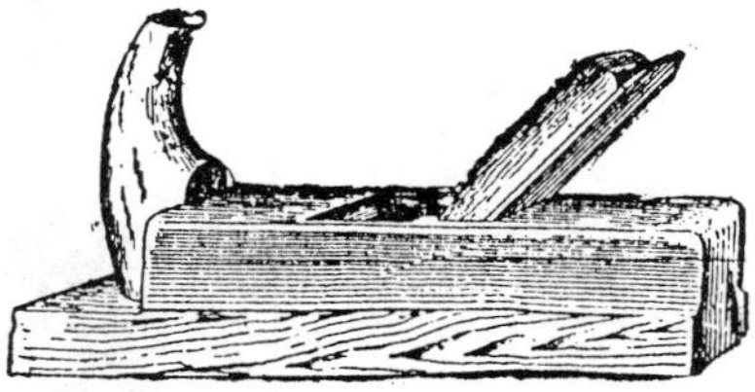

1¼ inch Round Nose Iron.

A GOOD PLANE FOR ROUGHING OUT

Each **2.00**

THESE GERMAN PLANES ARE MADE OF GERMAN WHITE BEECH

Nos. 146 AND 150—RABBET PLANES

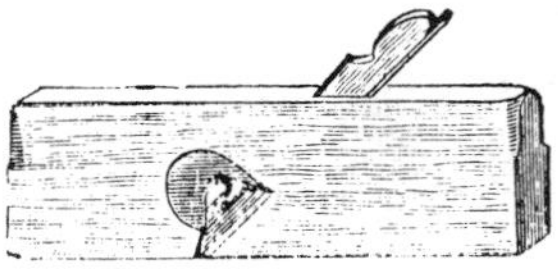

146 Is Skew Iron

150 Is Square Iron

Size, inches..................	¼	⅜	½	⅝	¾	⅞	1	1¼	1½	1¾	2
Each........................	**2.00**	**2.00**	**1.20**	**1.20**	**1.20**	**1.20**	**1.20**	**1.30**	**1.40**	**1.60**	**1.75**

G. A. R. JACK RABBET PLANE

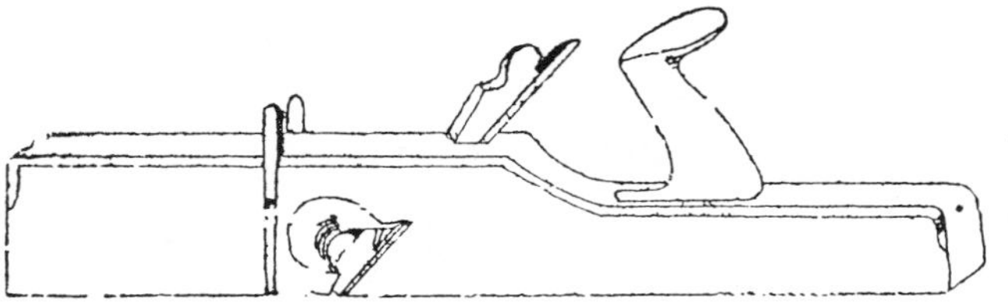

G. A. R. 16 inches in length, 1½ inch cutter..each **3.00**

No. 149. Side Handle, 15 inches long, 1½ inch cutter..each **3.30**

No. 60—DADO PLANES

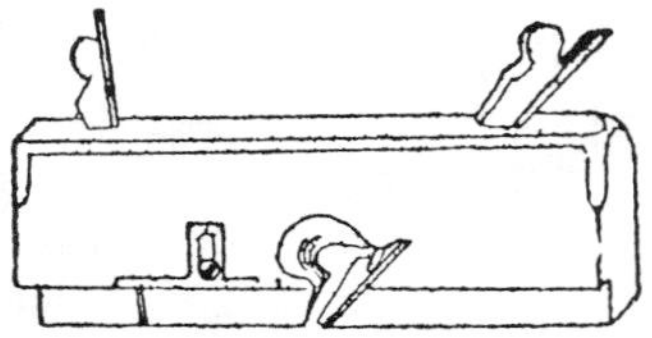

Sizes: ¼, ⅜, ½, ⅝, ¾, 13/16, ⅞ inches..each **2.30**

PLANES

HOLLOWS AND ROUNDS

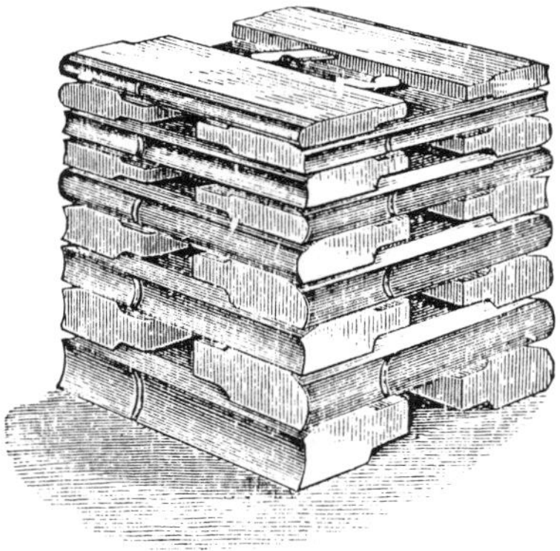

Per set of 9 pairs, Nos. 1 to 9, inclusive 15.00
Per pair, Nos. 1 to 6, inclusive 2.00
Per pair, Nos. 7, 8 and 9 .... 2.30
Per pair, Nos. 10, 11 and 12 .... 2.50

Size, inches	1	2	3	4	5	6	7	8	9	10	11	12
Numbers	5/16	7/16	9/16	11/16	13/16	15/16	1 1/16	1 3/16	1 5/16	1 7/16	1 9/16	1 11/16

MATCH PLANES

To Cut Tongue and Groove

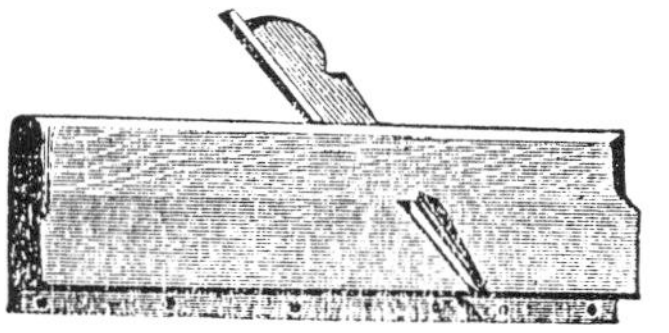

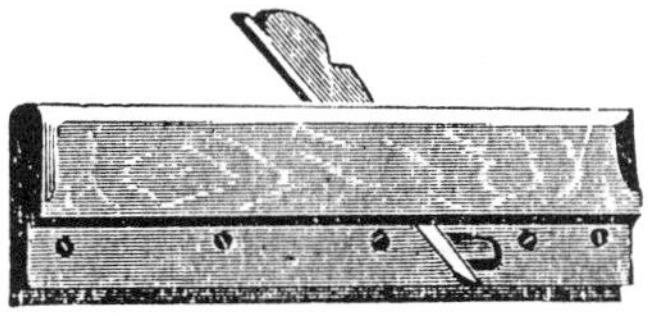

No. 99. 3/8, 1/2, 5/8, 3/4, 13/16, 7/8, 1 inch .... per pair **3.50**

No. 113—NOSING PLANE, DOUBLE IRON

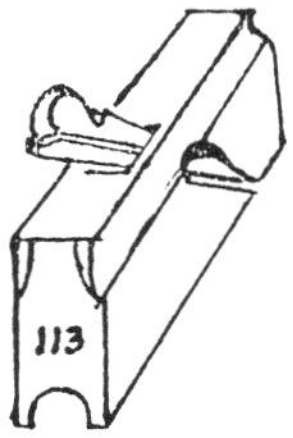

7/8, 1, 1 1/8, 1 1/4 inch.

Any size .... each **2.20**

T. RABBET PLANE

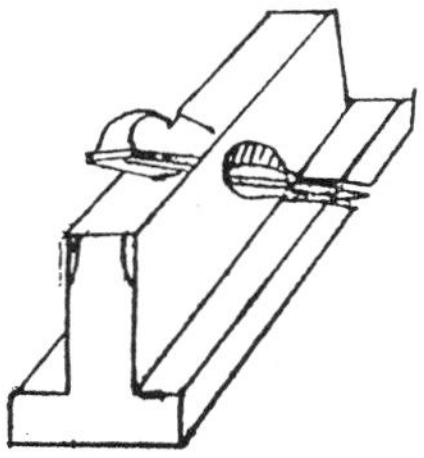

No. 045A. 1 1/2 inch wide, 5/8 inch deep, 3/8 inch off-set .... each **2.25**
No. 045B. 2 inch wide, 5/8 inch deep, 5/8 inch off-set .... each **2.25**

WOOD PLANES

BARTLETT'S BENCH

All Bartlett planes are fitted with superior irons, manufactured from best cast steel and fullv warranted.

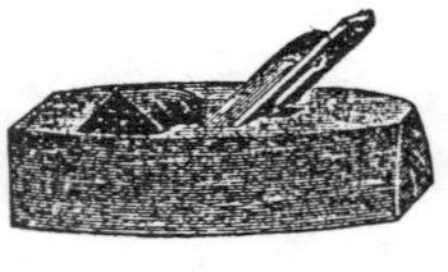

Smooth.

No. 03—8 in., 2 to $2\frac{1}{4}$ in. double iron, polished lignumvitae start, w't 2 lbs., each $2.50

ONE IN A PACKAGE

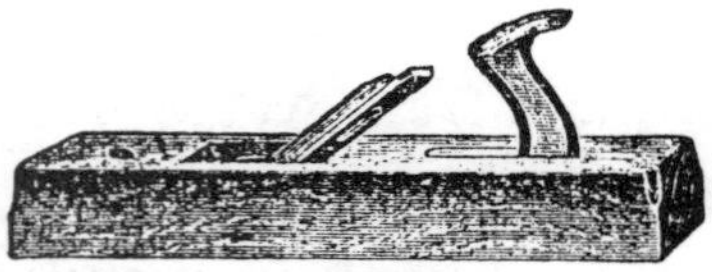

Jack.
Polished Lignumvitae Start.

No. 010—16 in., 2 to $2\frac{1}{4}$ in., **single** iron, w't $3\frac{1}{2}$ lbs. ....each $2.40

No. 013—16 in., 2 to $2\frac{1}{4}$ in., **double** iron, w't $3\frac{1}{2}$ lbs. ....each $2.80

ONE IN A PACKAGE

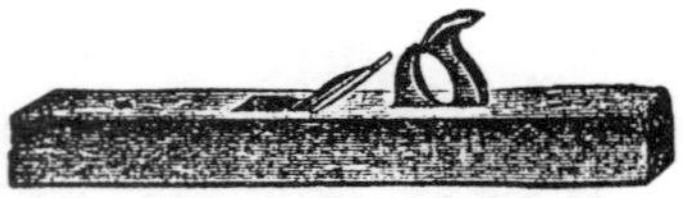

No. 019—22 in., fore, $2\frac{3}{8}$ to $2\frac{1}{2}$ in., double iron, polished lignumvitae start, w't $5\frac{1}{4}$ lbs. ......each $4.70

ONE IN A PACKAGE

OGONTZ BENCH

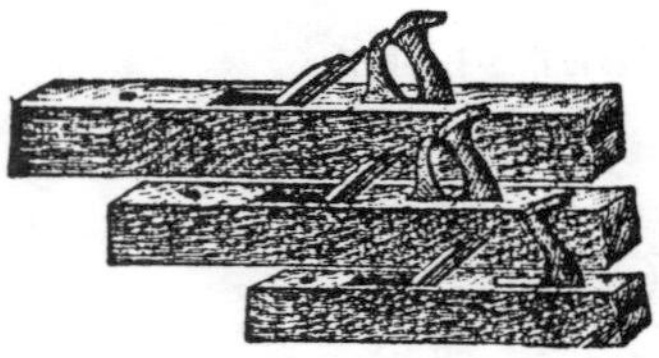

Double Iron, Polished Ebony Start.

8 in. Smooth, 2 to $2\frac{1}{4}$ in., w't 2 lbs., each $2.30

16 in. Jack, 2 to $2\frac{1}{4}$ in., w't $3\frac{3}{4}$ lbs., each $2.60

22 in. Fore, $2\frac{3}{8}$ to $2\frac{1}{2}$ in., w't 6 lbs., each $4.30

26 in. Jointer, $2\frac{1}{2}$ to $2\frac{5}{8}$ in., w't $7\frac{1}{2}$ lbs., each $4.60

ONE IN A PACKAGE

BARTLETT'S TOOTH

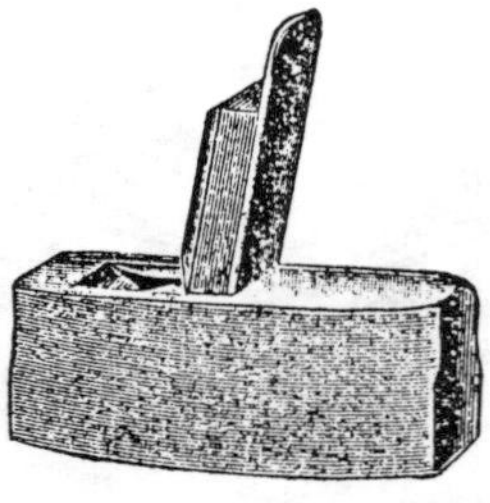

No. 36W—$2\frac{1}{8}$ in., cast steel iron, w't $1\frac{3}{4}$ lbs. ....each $2.70

ONE IN A PACKAGE

BARTLETT'S DADO

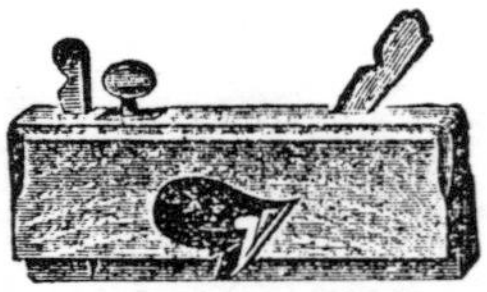

Specify size in ordering.

No. 62B—Screw top, sizes $\frac{1}{2}$, $\frac{3}{4}$ and $\frac{7}{8}$ in., w't 1 lb. ....each $4.00

ONE IN A PACKAGE

BARTLETT'S STEP NOSING

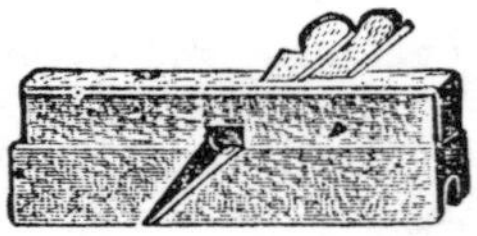

Specify size in ordering.

No. 113½—2 irons, sizes $1\frac{3}{8}$ **and** $1\frac{1}{2}$ **in.,** $1\frac{1}{4}$ **in.,** w't $1\frac{1}{4}$ lbs. ......each $3.00

No. 113½—2 irons, sizes $1\frac{3}{8}$ **and** $1\frac{1}{2}$ **in.,** w't $1\frac{1}{2}$ lbs. ....each $3.40

ONE IN A PACKAGE

BARTLETT'S BOARD MATCH

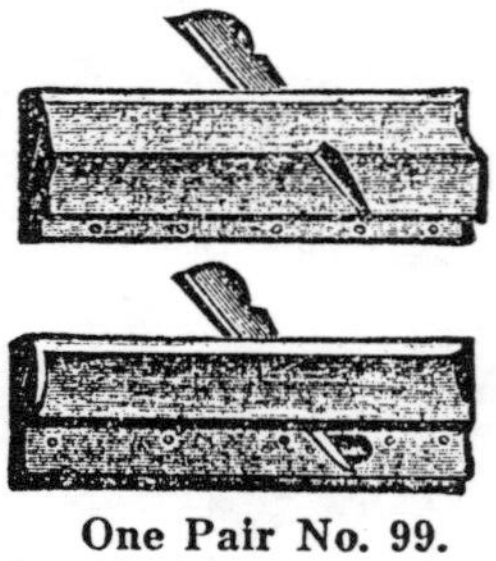

One Pair No. 99.

Specify size in ordering.

No. 199—Sizes $\frac{1}{2}$, $\frac{5}{8}$, $\frac{3}{4}$, $\frac{7}{8}$ and 1 in., w't $2\frac{1}{4}$ lbs. ....per pair $4.20

ONE PAIR IN A PACKAGE

BARTLETT'S SKEW RABBET

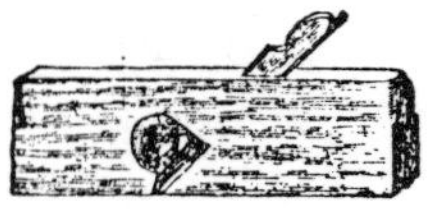

Specify size in ordering.

No. 146½—W't 14 oz.—

Size, in.	$\frac{1}{2}$	$\frac{5}{8}$	$\frac{3}{4}$	$\frac{7}{8}$	1
Each	$1.60	1.65	1.70	1.75	1.80

No. 146½—$1\frac{1}{4}$ in. w't $1\frac{1}{4}$ lbs., each $1.85

No. 146½—$1\frac{1}{2}$ in., w't $1\frac{1}{2}$ lbs., each $1.90

No. 146½—$1\frac{3}{4}$ in., w't $1\frac{3}{4}$ lbs., each $2.10

ONE PAIR IN A PACKAGE

BARTLETT'S JACK RABBET

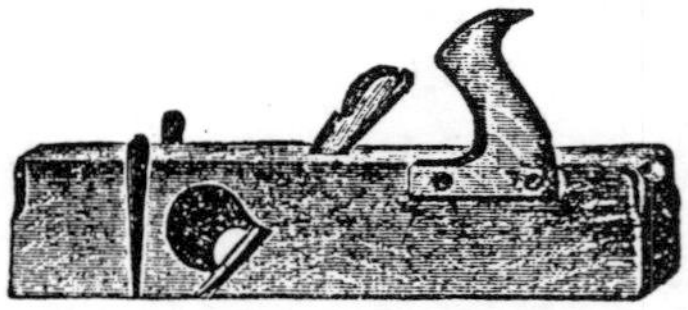

No. 149. Side Handle.
With 2 Cutters, Sizes $1\frac{1}{2}$, $1\frac{3}{4}$ and 2 in.
W't $2\frac{1}{4}$ Lbs.

Specify size in ordering.

No. 149—Center handle, each $4.70
No. 149—Side handle...each 5.20

ONE PAIR IN A PACKAGE

HORN SCRUB

This plane is imported from Germany where it is extensively used. It has a round nose iron and is especially useful for rough planing.

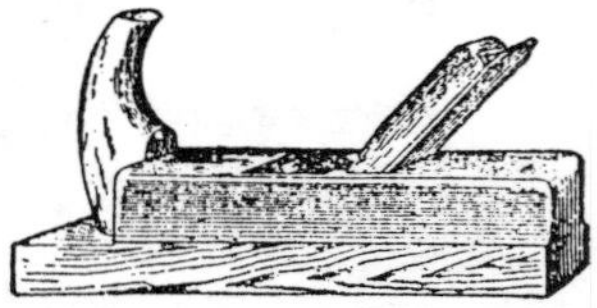

No. 500—9 in., $1\frac{1}{2}$ in. single iron, with horn, white hardwood nicely finished, w't $1\frac{1}{2}$ lbs., each $3.00

ONE IN A PACKAGE

Extra iron for No. 500, each $0.80

HORN SMOOTH

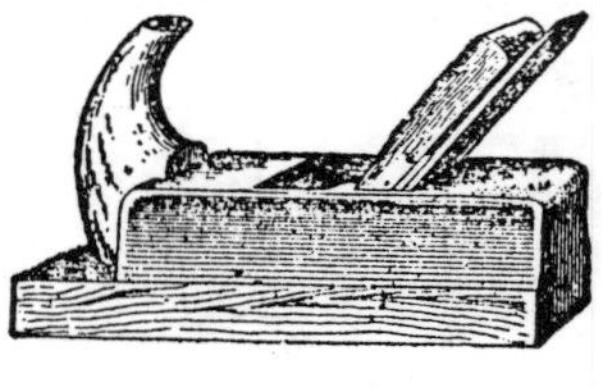

No. 400—$8\frac{1}{2}$ in., 2 in. double iron, with horn, white hardwood nicely finished, w't $2\frac{1}{2}$ lbs. ....each $4.50

ONE IN A PACKAGE

PLANE IRONS

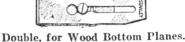

Single.

Width, in.	$1\frac{5}{8}$	$1\frac{3}{4}$	2
No. 60—Bailey, each	$0.70	.80	.85
No. 60R REVONOC. each	.70	.80	.85

Width, in.	$2\frac{1}{8}$	$2\frac{1}{4}$	$2\frac{3}{8}$	$2\frac{5}{8}$
No. 60—Bailey, each	$0.90	1.00	1.05	1.10
No. 60R REVONOC, each	$0.90	1.00	1.05	1.10

HALF DOZEN IN A BOX

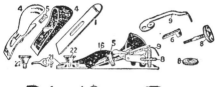

Double, for Wood Bottom Planes.

Width, in.	$1\frac{3}{4}$	2	$2\frac{1}{8}$
No. 65—Bailey, each	$1.25	1.45	1.50
No. 65R REVONOC, each	1.25	1.45	1.50

Width, in.	$2\frac{1}{4}$	$2\frac{3}{8}$	$2\frac{5}{8}$
No. 65—Bailey, each	$1.60	1.65	1.70
No. 65R REVONOC, each	1.60	1.65	1.70

Double, for Iron Bottom Planes.

Width, in.	$1\frac{3}{4}$	2	$2\frac{1}{4}$
No. 75—Bailey, each	$1.25	1.45	1.60
No. 75R REVONOC, each	1.25	1.45	1.60

Width, in.	$2\frac{3}{8}$	$2\frac{5}{8}$
No. 75—Bailey each	$1.65	1.70
No. 75R REVONOC each	1.65	1.70

HALF DOZEN IN A BOX

Block.

Irons, for Bailey planes, Nos. $9\frac{1}{2}$, $9\frac{3}{4}$, 15, $15\frac{1}{2}$ 16, 17, 18, 19 and 220, each $0.55

Irons, for REVONOC planes, Nos. $9\frac{1}{2}$R, $9\frac{3}{4}$R, 15R, $15\frac{1}{2}$R, 1600R, 1700R, 1800R, 1900R, 6500R, 2200R, each $0.55

Extra Caps and Levers, for Bailey planes, Nos. $9\frac{1}{2}$, $9\frac{3}{4}$, 15, $15\frac{1}{2}$ and 103, each $0.30

Extra Caps and Levers, for Bailey planes, Nos. 18 and 19...each $0.60

HALF DOZEN IN A BOX

Block.

Irons, for Bailey planes, Nos. 110 and 130, each $0.45

Irons, for REVONOC. planes, Nos. 102R, 103R ....each $0.30

Irons, for REVONOC planes, Nos. 110R and 1300R ....each $0.45

Extra Caps and Screws, for Bailey planes, Nos. 110, 220 and 130, each $0.30

Extra Caps and Screws for REVONOC planes, Nos. 110R to 1300R, each $0.30

No. 4—Extra Caps for Nos. 3, 4, 5, $5\frac{1}{2}$, 6 and 7 **Bailey** and REVONOC Planes ....each $0.80

HALF DOZEN IN A BOX

SIEGLEY SINGLE PLANE IRONS

Width, in.	2	$2\frac{1}{4}$	$2\frac{3}{8}$	$2\frac{1}{2}$
Each	$0.85	1.00	1.05	1.10

HALF DOZEN IN A BOX

PLANE PARTS

No.   1B—Plane iron.

No.   4B—Cap.

No.   5B—Cap screw.

No.   6B—Frog complete.

No.   7B—Adjusting lever.

No.   8B—Adjusting nut.

No.   9B—Lateral adjustment.

No. 12B—Knob.

No. 16B—Bottom—adjustable throat.

No. 18B—Detached side.

No. 21B—Eccentric plate.

No. 22B—Finger rest knob.

PLANE PARTS

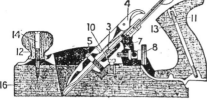

Sectional View of Bailey Wood Planes.

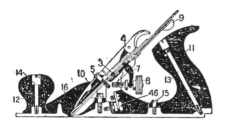

Sectional View of Bailey Iron Planes.

No.   1—Plane iron.

No.   2—Plane iron cap.

No.   3—Plane iron screw.

No.   4—Lever cap.

No.   5—Cap screw.

No.   6—Frog.

No.   7—"Y" adjustment.

No.   8—Brass adjusting nut.

No.   9—Lateral adjustment.

No. 10—Frog screw.

No. 11—Handle.

No. 12—Knob.

No. 13—Handle "bolt and nut."

No. 14—Knob "bolt and nut."

No. 15—Handle screw.

No. 16—Bottom.

No. 35—Top casting—wood plane.

An improvement has been made in the "Bailey" Iron Plane which necessitated a change in the construction of the Bottom and Frog, thereby making it impossible to use the new style Frog in an old style Bottom, or the old style Frog in a new style Bottom.

For a time an intermediate style was made having same Frog and Bottom as the latest design, except that there was no Frog adjusting screw, consequently no clip on the Frog.

The latest design Frog or Bottom will be furnished for both the intermediate and new style Planes.   If your Plane is of the intermediate pattern, remove the steel clip from the Frog and the parts will fit.

In order that we may fill your order correctly, kindly advise us which style Plane you have.

The difference in construction of the Frogs and Bottoms is very clearly shown in the illustration above.

OVB SELF-SETTING IRON PLANES
SMOOTH BOTTOM

The cutter irons are made from special high grade steel, are thin and easily kept in order.

The malleable Frog and Steel Cap reduce greatly the liability of breakage.

Handle and knob are made of highly finished, thoroughly seasoned rosewood. They are securely fastened to plane with steel rods that have brass screw heads. Trimmings are nickel plated and japanned, giving the planes a very fine finish throughout.

The principal features of this line of new Planes are the self-setting cutting iron, the rigidity with which this is held in place by the plane cap, thus preventing any chatter in Plane, the fine adjustments that can be made with cutter for all kinds of work and the few parts used in its construction, which make it almost entirley free from any costs for repairs.

The Planes are set for fine work when they leave the factory.

SMOOTH

No. 803 OVB—8¾ in. long, 1¾ in. cutter, w't each 3 lbs., each $5.40

No. 804 OVB—9 in. long, 2 in. cutter, w't each 3¼ lbs., each $5.90

JACK

No. 805 OVB—14 in. long, 2 in. cutter, w't each 4¼ lbs. ....each **$6.75**

FORE

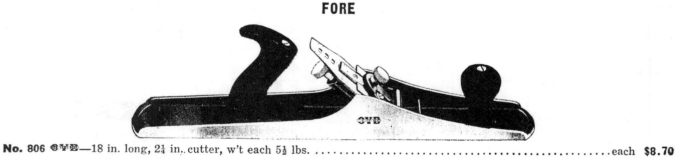

No. 806 OVB—18 in. long, 2¼ in. cutter, w't each 5½ lbs. ....each **$8.70**

JOINTER

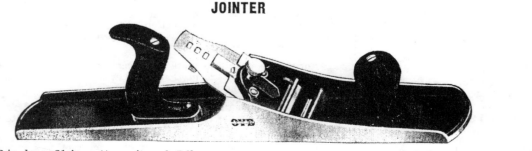

No. 807 OVB—22 in. long, 2½ in. cutter, w't each 7 lbs. ....each **$9.90**

ALL ABOVE ARE ONE IN AN ATTRACTIVE BOX

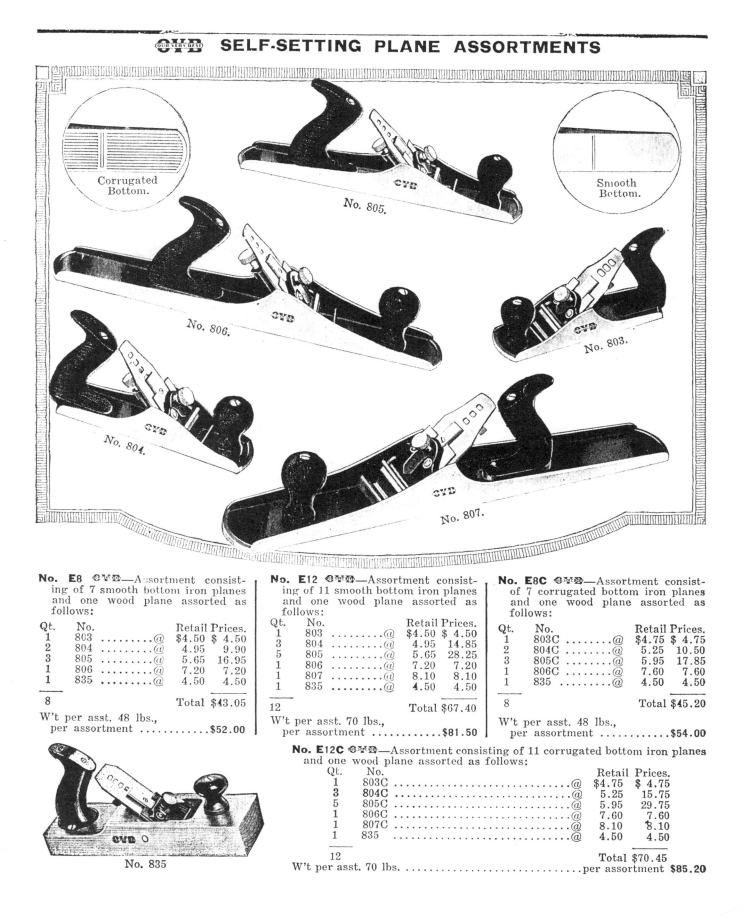

Corrugated Bottom.

Smooth Bottom.

No. 805.

No. 806.

No. 803.

No. 804.

No. 807.

No. 835

No. E8 OVB—Assortment consisting of 7 smooth bottom iron planes and one wood plane assorted as follows:

Qt.	No.		Retail Prices.	
1	803	........@	$4.50	$ 4.50
2	804	........@	4.95	9.90
3	805	........@	5.65	16.95
1	806	........@	7.20	7.20
1	835	........@	4.50	4.50
8			Total	$43.05

W't per asst. 48 lbs.,
   per assortment $52.00

No. E12 OVB—Assortment consisting of 11 smooth bottom iron planes and one wood plane assorted as follows:

Qt.	No.		Retail Prices.	
1	803	........@	$4.50	$ 4.50
3	804	........@	4.95	14.85
5	805	........@	5.65	28.25
1	806	........@	7.20	7.20
1	807	........@	8.10	8.10
1	835	........@	4.50	4.50
12			Total	$67.40

W't per asst. 70 lbs.,
   per assortment $81.50

No. E8C OVB—Assortment consisting of 7 corrugated bottom iron planes and one wood plane assorted as follows:

Qt.	No.		Retail Prices.	
1	803C	........@	$4.75	$ 4.75
2	804C	........@	5.25	10.50
3	805C	........@	5.95	17.85
1	806C	........@	7.60	7.60
1	835	........@	4.50	4.50
8			Total	$45.20

W't per asst. 48 lbs.,
   per assortment $54.00

No. E12C OVB—Assortment consisting of 11 corrugated bottom iron planes and one wood plane assorted as follows:

Qt.	No.		Retail Prices.	
1	803C	...............................@	$4.75	$ 4.75
3	804C	...............................@	5.25	15.75
5	805C	...............................@	5.95	29.75
1	806C	...............................@	7.60	7.60
1	807C	...............................@	8.10	8.10
1	835	...............................@	4.50	4.50
12			Total	$70.45

W't per asst. 70 lbs. ....per assortment **$85.20**

OVB SELF-SETTING WOOD PLANES

Wood planes are preferred by many because of being lighter in weight than the iron planes.

OVB Wood Planes are made of specially selected beechwood, thoroughly seasoned and dried.

The iron frog with adjustable throat will lengthen greatly the life of these wood planes, as this frog and throat can be moved up to permit the bottom of the plane to be trued up when worn.

The cutter iron can also be adjusted sidewise by loosening the small screw that holds the binder plate to cutter.

Keep cutter iron sharp and properly adjusted, and you will have a plane that is easy to push and will give the greatest satisfaction. In sharpening, care should be taken to keep the cutting edge straight and square with the edge of the cutter iron. Cutting iron can be adjusted sidewise by loosening the set screw that holds binder plate to top of cutting iron.

SMOOTH

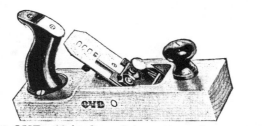 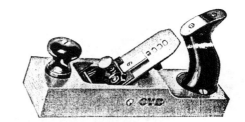

No. 835 OVB—10 in. long, 2 in. cutter, w't each 2¾ lbs.,
each **$6.70**

No. 822 OVB—10 in. long, 1¾ in. cutter, w't each 2½ lbs.,
each **$6.30**

JACK

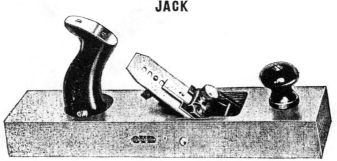

No. 826 OVB—14 in. long, 2 in. cutter, w't each 4 lbs. ....each **$7.30**

FORE

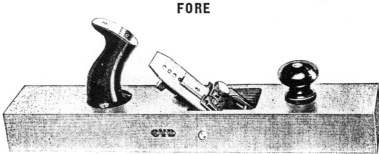

No. 828 OVB—18 in. long, 2¼ in. cutter, w't each 5½ lbs. ....each **$8.30**

JOINTER

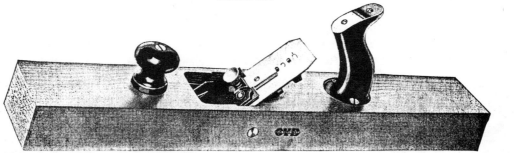

No. 830 OVB—22 in. long, 2½ in. cutter, w't each 6½ lbs. ....each **$8.90**

ALL ABOVE ARE ONE IN AN ATTRACTIVE BOX

OVB SELF-SETTING IRON PLANES
CORRUGATED BOTTOM

Corrugated bottom planes are preferred by many users, because of there being less friction from the bottom, runs a little lighter. They have the self-setting cutter iron made from special high grade steel.

The malleable Frog and Steel Cap reduce greatly the liability of breakage.

The Handle and Knob are made of highly finished, thoroughly seasoned rosewood. These are securely fastened to plane with steel rods that have brass screw heads. Trimmings are nickel plated and japanned. Plane is finely finished throughout.

The self-cutting feature lies in the construction of the plane iron. If taken out to be honed or sharpened, goes back in same position as before removal. The plane cannot chatter because the cutter iron is held rigid at the point by the cap; at the same time the cap screw used for tightening the cap is pressing against the binder plate on top of the cutter iron. This pressure against the binder plate holds the cutter firm its entire length.

SMOOTH

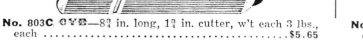 

No. 803C OVB—8¾ in. long, 1¾ in. cutter, w't each 3 lbs.,
each $5.65

No. 804C OVB—9 in. long, 2 in. cutter, w't each 3¼ lbs.,
each $6.20

JACK

No. 805C OVB—14 in. long, 2 in. cutter, w't each 4¼ lbs..each $7.10

FORE

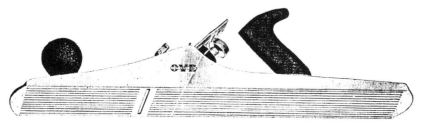

No. 806C OVB—18 in. long, 2¼ in. cutter, w't each 5½ lbs. ....each $9.10

JOINTER

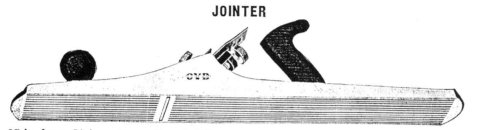

No. 807C OVB—22 in. long, 2½ in. cutter, w't each 7 lbs. ....each $10.40
ALL ABOVE ARE ONE IN AN ATTRACTIVE BOX

These Planes Are Guaranteed to be the Very Best Possible to Produce. The Materials Used Are the Highest Grade Obtainable. They Are Made by American Workmen of Skill and Experience. The Cutters on these Planes Are Made from Best English Crucible Cast Steel, Tempered in Oil, Hand Honed and Ready for Use, Are Extra Heavy, Being Almost Twice the Thickness Used on Other Makes, Making a Very Firm and Solid Cutting Edge, Which Prevents Chattering When Used on Hard Woods, and is a Marked Improvement. They Are Fully Warranted to Give Satisfaction.

ADJUSTABLE IRON

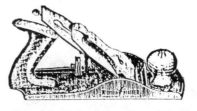

Bog Oak Stained Handle and Knob

No. 1002 Smooth, Length 7 in., Cutter 1⅝ in.........Each, $2.36
No. 1003 Smooth, Length 8 in., Cutter 1¾ in.........Each, 2.46
No. 1004 Smooth, Length 9 in., Cutter 2 in.........Each, 2.68

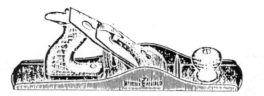

No. 1005 Jack, Length 14 in., Cutter 2 in.............Each, $3.06
No. 1006 Fore, Length 18 in., Cutter 2⅜ in............Each, 3.96

No. 1007 Jointer, Length 22 in., Cutter 2⅜ in........Each, $4.50
No. 1008 Jointer, Length 24 in., Cutter 2⅝ in.........Each, 5.36

WITH CORRUGATED BOTTOMS

o. 1003C Smooth, Length 8 in., Cutter 1¾ in.......Each, $2.46
o. 1004C Smooth, Length 9 in., Cutter 2 in.......Each, 2.68
o. 1005C Jack,   Length 14 in., Cutter 2 in.......Each, 3.06
o. 1006C Fore,   Length 18 in., Cutter 2⅜ in.......Each, 3.96
No. 1007C Jointer, Length 22 in., Cutter 2⅜ in.......Each, 4.50
No. 1008C Jointer, Length 24 in., Cutter 2⅝ in.......Each, 5.36

WOOD PLANES

No. 1023 Smooth, Length 9 in., Cutter 1¾ in., Bog Oak Stained Knob ....Each, $1.70

No. 1035 Smooth, Length 9 in., Cutter 2 in., Bog Oak Stained Handle and Knob......................Each, $2.06

Bog Oak Stained Handle and Knob

No. 1026 Jack,   Length 15 in., Cutter 2 in........ Each, $1.82
No. 1027 Jack,   Length 15 in., Cutter 2⅛ in.........Each, 2.06
No. 1028 Fore,   Length 18 in., Cutter 2⅛ in.........Each, 2.30
No. 1029 Fore,   Length 20 in., Cutter 2⅛ in.........Each, 2.36
No. 1031 Jointer, Length 24 in., Cutter 2⅜ in.........Each, 2.54
No. 1033 Jointer, Length 28 in., Cutter 2⅝ in.........Each, 2.76

ADJUSTABLE CIRCULAR PLANE

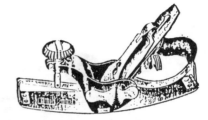

No. 1113 Improved, Cutter 1¾ in.....................Each, $3.60

The Flexible Steel Face can be Easily Set to Work an Arc of the Same Circle, Either Concave or Convex. Adjustment is Easy and Rapid.

One Plane in Plaid Covered

No. 1018   Length 6 Inches, Cutter 1¾
Inches .Each, $1.46
No. 1019   Length 7 Inches, Cutter 1¾
Inches .Each,   1.60
These Planes have the Knuckle Joint Lever.
Provided with Throat Adjustment by Means
of which Opening for Cutter may be Closed
or Enlarged. Nickel Trimmings.

Adjustable
No. 1009½   Length 6 Inches, Cutter
1¾ Inches . . . . .Each, $1.26

Screw Adjustment, Bog Oak Stained Knob.
No. 1220   Length 7 Inches, Cutter 1¾
Inches . . . . .Each, $0.84

With Bog Oak Stained Knob.
No. 1110   Length 7 Inches, Cutter 1¾
Inches . . . . .Each, $0.60

Adjustable.
No. 1103   Length 5½ Inches, Cutter
1¼ Inches . . . . .Each, $0.60

Not Adjustable.
No. 1102   Length 5½ Inches, Cutter
1¼ Inches . . . . .Each, $0.44

Without Handle.
No. 1101   Length 3 Inches Cutter 1
Inch .Each, $0.22

Low Angle.
No. 1060   Length 6 Inches, Cutter 1½
Inches . . . . .Each, $1.50
No. 1065   Length 7 Inches, Cutter 1¾
Inches . . . . .Each,   1.65
Nickel Trimmings. The Cutters are Set at
a Very Low Angle, which is a Great Advan-
tage when Working Across the Grain.

Double End, Bog Oak Stained Knob.
No. 1130   Length 8 Inches, Cutter 1¾
Inches .Each, $0.84
Two Slots and Two Cutter Seats, Reversing
Cutter and Lever, it can be Used Close up
Into Corners or Other Difficult Places.

RABBET PLANE AND FILLETSTER

No. 1078   Length 8½ Inches, Cutter 1½ Inches. . . . . . .Each, $1.96
This Plane has Two Cutter Seats. Inserting Cutter Into For-
ward Seat this Tool can be Used as Bull-Nose Rabbet. Arm is
Reversible, Making a Right or Left-hand Filletster.

BULL-NOSE RABBET PLANES

No. 1075   Length 4 Inches, Cutter 1 Inch. . . . . .Each, $0.64
For Fine Cabinet Work, this Plane will be Found Very Handy
and Useful.

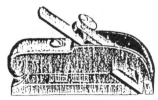

ADJUSTABLE VENEER SCRAPERS

No. 1012   Veneer Scraper, 3 Inch Cutter, Bog Oak Stai   Handle. . . . . .Each, $3.00
For Scraping Veneers and Cabinet Work. Its Pecu   Form is of Great Advantage. Can Also be Used as a Tooth Plane.
All Planes Sh   this Page Put up in Plaid Covered Boxes.

UNION ADJUSTABLE PLANES

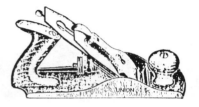

IRON

No. 3B   Smooth, 8 in. Long, 1¾ in. Cutter....Each, $3.00 **2.40**
No. 4B   Smooth, 9 in. Long, 2 in. Cutter....Each, 3.25 **2.60**
No. 4½B Smooth, 10 in. Long, 2⅜ in. Cutter....Each, 3.75 **3.00**

No. 5B   Jack, 14 in. Long, 2 in. Cutter........Each, $3.75 **3.00**
No. 6B   Fore, 18 in. Long, 2⅜ in. Cutter........Each, 4.75 **3.80**

No. 7B   Jointer, 22 in. Long, 2⅜ in. Cutter.......Each, $5.50 **4.40**
No. 8B   Jointer, 24 in. Long, 2⅝ in. Cutter.......Each, 6.50 **5.20**
One in a Box.

BLOCK PLANES
With Improved Throat Adjustment.
No. 9½B 6 in. Long, 1¾ in. Cutter.............Each, $1.60 **1.28**

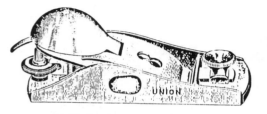

KNUCKLE JOINT LEVER
Nickel-plated Trimmings.
No. 138B Knuckle Joint Lever 6 in. Long, 1¾ in. Cutter ....Each, $1.85 **1.48**
No. 139B Knuckle Joint Lever 7 in. Long, 1¾ in. Cutter ....Each, 1.95 **1.56**
One in a Box.

WOOD BOTTOM

No. 23B Smooth, 9 in. Long, 1¾ in. Cutter.....Each, $2.00 **1.60**

No. 35B Smooth, 9 in. Long, 2 in. Cutter.......Each, $2.50 **2.00**
One in a Box.

No. 26B Jack,   15 in. Long, 2 in. Cutter......Each, $2.25 **1.80**
No. 27B Jack,   15 in. Long, 2⅜ in. Cutter......Each, 2.50 **2.00**
No. 28B Fore,   18 in. Long, 2⅜ in. Cutter......Each, 2.75 **2.20**
No. 29B Fore,   20 in. Long, 2⅜ in. Cutter......Each, 2.75 **2.20**
No. 30B Jointer, 22 in. Long, 2⅜ in. Cutter......Each, 3.00 **2.40**
No. 31B Jointer, 24 in. Long, 2⅜ in. Cutter......Each, 3.00 **2.40**
One in a Package.

No. 101B   No. 100B, With Handle
BLOCK PLANES
No. 101B 3 in. Long, 1 in. Cutter................Each, $0.25 **0.20**
No. 100B 3 in. Long, 1 in. Cutter, With Handle...Each, 0.33 **.27**

No. 102B, NON-ADJUSTABLE
No. 102B 5½ in. Long 1¼ in. Cutter............Each, $0.55 **$0.45**

No. 103, ADJUSTABLE
No. 103B 5½ in. Long, 1¼ in. Cutter...........Each, $0.70 **0.56**
One in a Box.

UNION IRON BLOCK PLANES

No. 110B

No. 110B Non-adjustable, 7 in. Long, 1¾ in. Cutter..Each, $0.70 **.56**

No. 120B

No. 120B Adjustable, 7 in. Long, 1¾ in. Cutter.....Each, $0.95 **.76**

No. 227

No. 227 Screw Adjustment, 7 in. Long, 1¾ in. Cutter,
....Each, $0.95 **.76**

No. 137

By Changing the Cutter and Lever from One Position to the Other, as Shown in the Cuts, it can be Used to Plane into Close Corners Which Cannot be Reached by the Ordinary Plane.

No. 137 Double End, 8 in. Long, 1¾ in. Cutter....Each, $1.00 **.80**

One in a Box.

WOOD BENCH PLANES

All Wood Bench Planes Have Cast Steel Double Irons, Polished Lignum-vitae Start.

No. 3 and 03

No. 3 First Quality Smooth, 8 in. Long, 2 to 2¼ in. Cutter ....Each, $0.90 **1.56**

No. 03 Ohio King, Smooth, 8 in. Long, 2 to 2¼ in. Cutter ....Each, .90 **1.36**

No. 05

No. 05 Ohio King, Handled Smooth, 10½ in. Long, 2 to 2¼ in. Cutter ....Each, $1.75 **2.70**

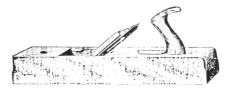

No. 13 and 013

No. 13 First Quality Jack, 16 in. Long; 2 to 2¼ in. Cutter ....Each, $1.00 **1.80**

No. 013 Ohio King Jack, 16 in. Long; 2 to 2¼ in. Cutter ....Each, 1.00 **1.50**

Nos. 19 and 019

No. 19 First Quality Fore, 22 in. Long, 2⅜ to 2½ in. Cutter ....Each, $1.70 **3.00**

No. 019 Ohio King Fore, 22 in. Long 2⅜ to 2½ in. Cutter ....Each, 1.70 **2.60**

No. 015

No. 015 Ohio King Razee Jack, 16 in. Long, 2 to 2¼ in. Cutter ....Each, $1.20 **1.80**

Nos. 25 and 025

No. 25 First Quality Jointer, 26 in. Long, 2½ to 2¾ in. Cutter ....Each, $1.80 **3.20**

No. 025 Ohio King Jointer, 26 in. Long, 2½ to 2¾ in. Cutter ....Each, 1.80 **2.80**

PLANES

STANLEY CURVE-RABBET PLANE

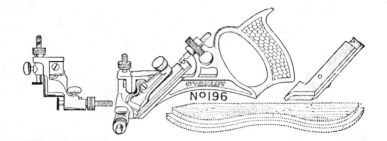

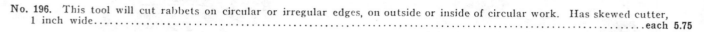

No. 196. This tool will cut rabbets on circular or irregular edges, on outside or inside of circular work. Has skewed cutter, 1 inch wide...each **5.75**

DOOR TRIM PLANE

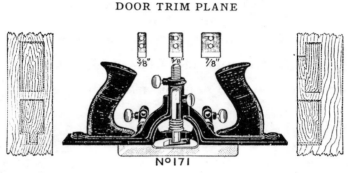

No. 171. This new Plane will make mortises for butts, face plates, strike plates, etc. Will cut to a depth of $\frac{5}{16}$ and a width of 3 inches...each **4.75**

SHOOT BOARD WITH PLANE

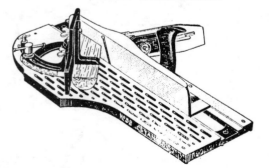

No. 52. 22 inches long. Plane 15 inches long, 2⅜ inch Cutter :...............................each **15.00**

PLANE ONLY

No. 51. 15 inches long, 2¼ inch Cutter.............each **6.50**

PLANES

PLOW PLANES

Made by Stanley

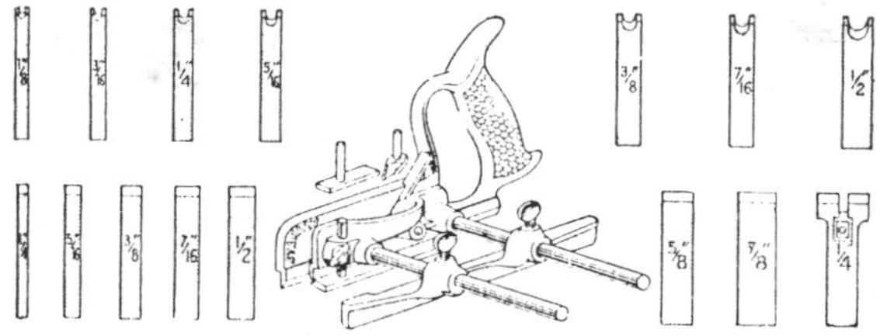

No. 50—9¼ inches long. Nickel Plated..each **6.50**

15 Cutters, as follows:

Plow and Dado—¼, 5/16, ⅜, 7/16, ½, ⅝, ⅞ in.
Beading—⅛, 3/16, ¼, 5/16, ⅜, 7/16, ½ in.
Tonguing—¼ in.

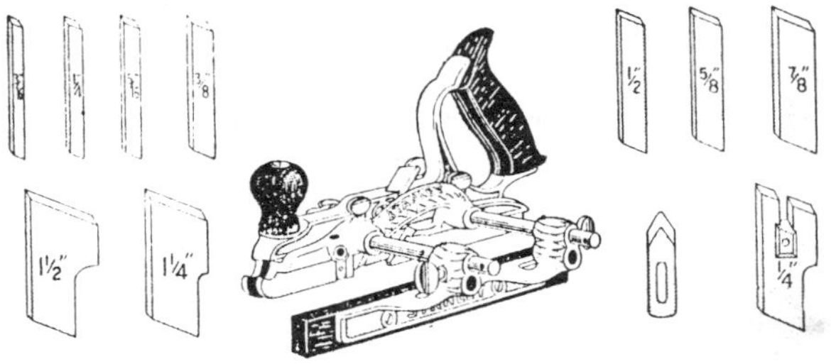

No. 46—10½ inches long. Nickel Plated..each **8.25**

12 Cutters, as follows:

Plow and Dado—3/16, ¼, 5/16, ⅜, ½, ⅝, 13/16, ⅞, 1¼ in.
Filletster—1½ in.
Tonguing—¼ in. and Slitter.

EDGE TRIMMING PLANE

No. 95

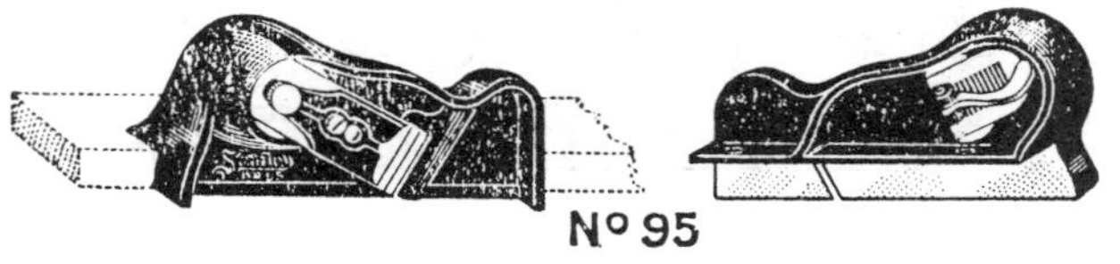

No. 95—6 inches long, Cutter ⅞ in. Designed for trimming ends of boards, such as siding, etc., for a close fit. There are screw holes in guide to which wood guides of various angles may be attached......................................each **1.75**

BLOCK PLANES

Made by Stanley

No. 60½

6 inches long, 1⅜ inch Cutter. Screw Adjustment. Adjustable Throat. Japanned Cap...............each 2.00

65½. 7 inches long, 1⅝ inch Cutter................each 2.20

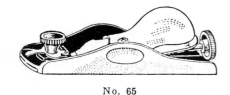

No. 65

7 inches long, 1⅝ inch Cutter. Screw Adjustment. Adjustable Throat. Nickeled Steel Cap...........each 2.50

Above plane has the new Unbreakable Cap.

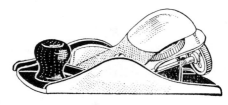

No. 140

No. 140. 7 inches long, 1⅝ inch Cutter set on Skew. One side of plane is removable, thus changing plane to a Rabbet Plane ....each 2.75

No. 130

8 inches long, 1⅝ inch Cutter. The Cutter may be reversed to opposite end of plane, making a plane for close up work..............................each 1.50

No. 131

8 inches long, 1⅝ inch Cutter. The entire Frog of plane may be reversed, throwing bit to Bull Nose End, making a plane for close up work..............each 2.25

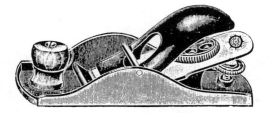

No. 1205

This plane is not a Stanley; it is a medium quality tool at a moderate price. Length 7 inches. Cutter, 1⅝ inch. Screw Adjustment.

Each 1.25

RABBET PLANES

Made by Stanley

No. 190. 8 inches long, 1½ in. Cutter............each **2.60**
No. 191. 8 inches long, 1¼ in. Cutter............each **2.50**
No. 192. 8 inches long, 1 in. Cutter............each **2.40**

No. 78. 8½ inches long, 1½ in. Cutter. With Adjustable Fence. Bit may be moved forward for close work ....each **2.75**

No. 289. 8½ inches long, 1¾ in. Cutter. With Adjustable Fence. Cutter is skewed, therefore plane cannot be used as Bull Nose. This plane is heavier than No. 78, shown above..........................each **3.25**

No. 278. 6¾ inches long, 1 in. Cutter. This plane will lie flat on either side and has Adjustable Fence. Front part can be detached for Bull Nose Work..each **3.25**

No. 75. Bull Nose. 4 inches long, 1 in. Cutter. Japanned Finish..each **.65**

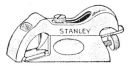

No. 90. Bull Nose. 4 inches long, 1 in. Cutter. Nickel Plated....each.. **3.50**

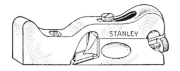

No. 92. 5½ inches long, ¾ in. Cutter ....each **3.50**

No. 93. 6½ inches long, 1 in. Cutter ....each **4.00**

No. 94. 7½ inches long, 1¼ in. Cutter ....each **4.65**

BLOCK PLANES

Made by Stanley

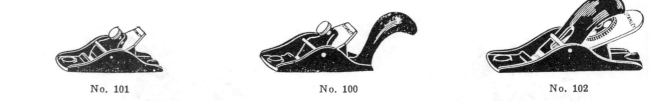

No. 101	No. 100	No. 102

3½ inches long, 1 inch Cutter....each **.35**   3½ inches long, 1 inch Cutter....each **.50**   5½ inches long, 1⅜ inch Cutter..each **.75**

No. 103   No. 110

5½ inches long, 1⅜ inch Cutter. Adjustable........each **.90**   7 inches long, 1⅝ inch Cutter.......................each **1.00**

No. 120

No. 203. 5½ inches long, 1⅜ inch Cutter. With Screw Adjustment ....each **1.35**

No. 220. 7 inches long, 1⅝ inch Cutter. With Screw Adjustment ....each **1.50**

7 inches long, 1⅝ inch Cutter. Adjustable.........each **1.40**

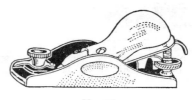

No. 9½   No. 18

6 inches long, 1⅝ inch Cutter. With Screw Adjustment and Adustable Throat.........................each **2.00**   6 inches long, 1⅝ inch Cutter. With Screw Adjustment and Adjustable Throat. Nickeled Steel Cap....each **2.40**

PLANES

BAILEY IRON PLANES

Made by Stanley

Smooth Bottom

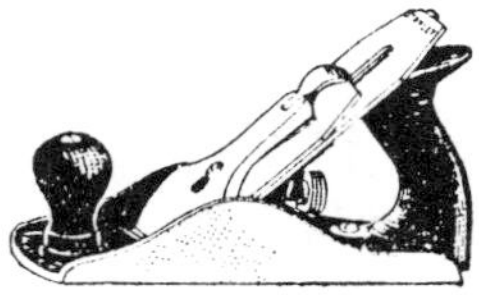

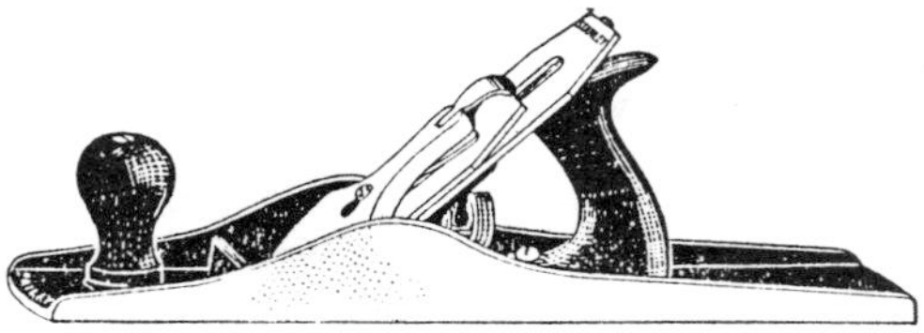

Corrugated Bottom

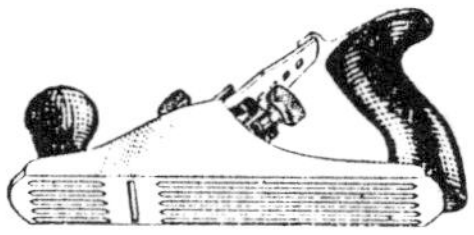

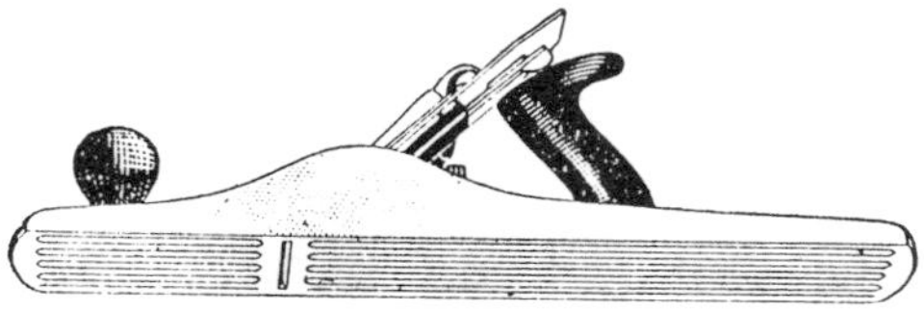

			Smooth Bottom	Corrugated Bottom
No. 1.	Smooth,	5½ inches long, 1¼ inch cutter......each	**2.50**	...
No. 2.	Smooth,	7 inches long, 1⅜ inch cutter......each	**2.75**	...
No. 3.	Smooth,	8 inches long, 1¾ inch cutter......each	**3.00**	**3.25**
No. 4.	Smooth,	9 inches long, 2 inch cutter......each	**3.50**	**3.75**
No. 4½.	Smooth,	10 inches long, 2⅜ inch cutter......each	**4.00**	**4.25**
No. 5.	Jack,	14 inches long, 2 inch cutter......each	**3.75**	**4.00**
No. 5¼.	Jack,	11½ inches long, 1¾ inch cutter......each	**3.50**	**3.75**
No. 5½.	Jack,	15 inches long, 2¼ inch cutter......each	**4.50**	**4.75**
No. 6.	Fore,	18 inches long, 2⅜ inch cutter......each	**5.00**	**5.25**
No. 7.	Jointer,	22 inches long, 2⅜ inch cutter......each	**5.50**	**5.75**
No. 8.	Jointer,	24 inches long, 2⅝ inch cutter......each	**6.75**	**7.00**

BAILEY WOOD PLANES

Made by Stanley

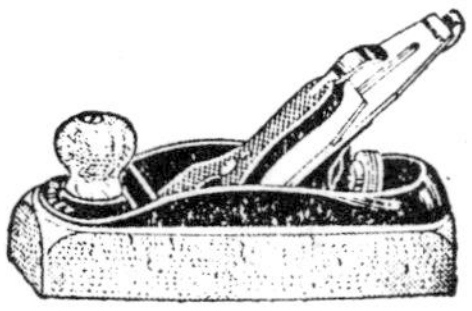

No. 22

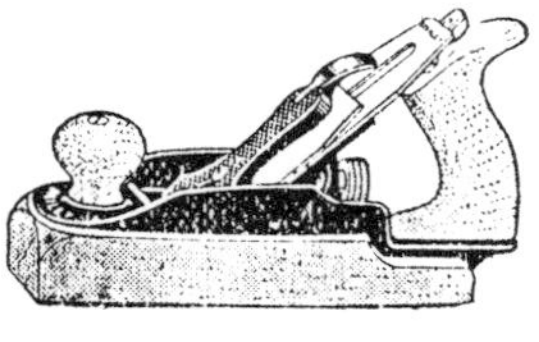

No. 35

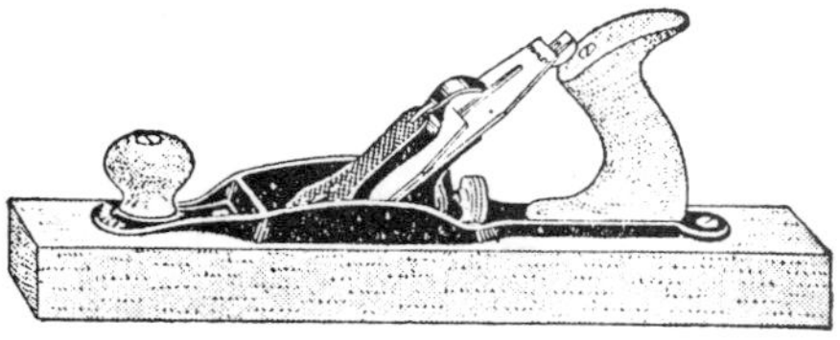

Nos. 26, 28, 31

No. 22.	Smooth,	8 inches long, 1¾ inch cutter......each	**2.75**
No. 35.	Smooth,	9 inches long, 2 inch cutter......each	**3.25**
No. 26.	Jack,	15 inches long, 2 inch cutter......each	**3.25**
No. 28.	Fore,	18 inches long, 2⅜ inch cutter......each	**3.75**
No. 31.	Jointer,	24 inches long, 2⅜ inch cutter......each	**4.00**
No. 32.	Jointer,	26 inches long, 2⅝ inch cutter......each	**4.50**

PLANES

SIDE RABBET PLANES

Made by Stanley

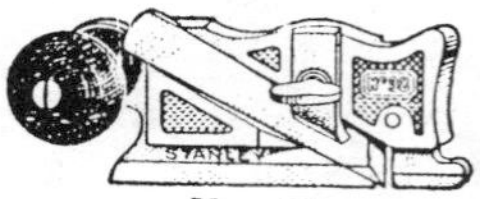

No. 98

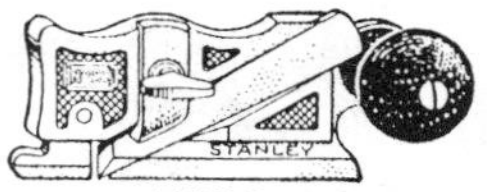

N°99

For side rabbeting in trimming dados, moldings and grooves of all sorts. A very convenient tool for Metal Weather Strip Work.

No. 98. Right Hand, 4 inches long, 1/2 in. Cutter.

No. 99. Left Hand, 4 inches long, 1/2 in. Cutter.
Each Plane **1.90**

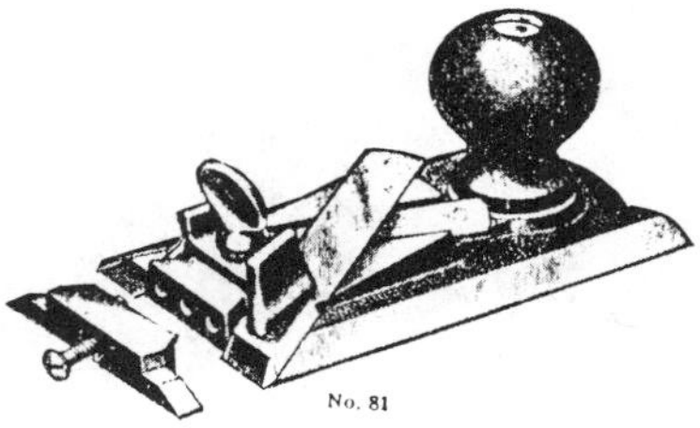

No. 81

No. 81. Double, Side Rabbet Plane. Either Right or Left hand. Size of plane, 2 1/4x4 1/4 inches. Cutter 1/2 in. wide......................................each **2.25**

IRON DADO PLANES

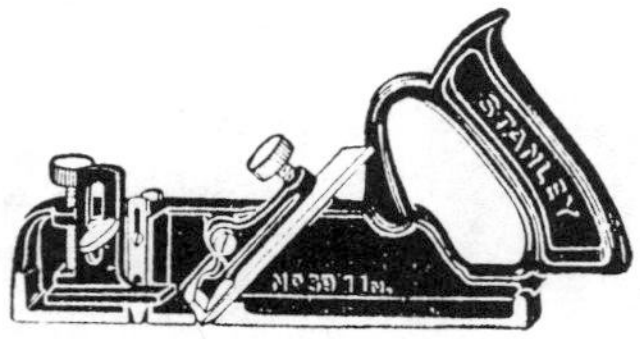

These Planes are 8 inches long

No. 39.	1/4 in. Cutter...............................each	**2.50**
	3/8 in. Cutter...............................each	**2.60**
	1/2 in. Cutter...............................each	**2.75**
	5/8 in. Cutter...............................each	**2.85**
	3/4 in. Cutter...............................each	**3.00**
	13/16 in. Cutter...............................each	**3.25**
	7/8 in. Cutter...............................each	**3.35**

SPECIAL DADO PLANE

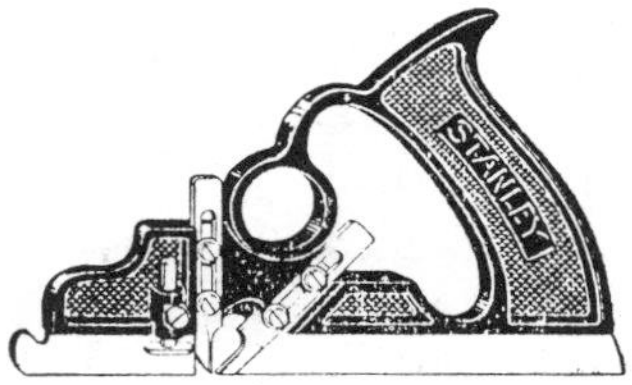

No. 239½. 7 1/2 inches long, 1/8 in. Cutter. For blind, wire grooving and other purposes where narrow groove is required. Has Side Fence same as a plow ....each **4.25**

CORE BOX PLANES

For making circular core boxes, either straight or tapered.

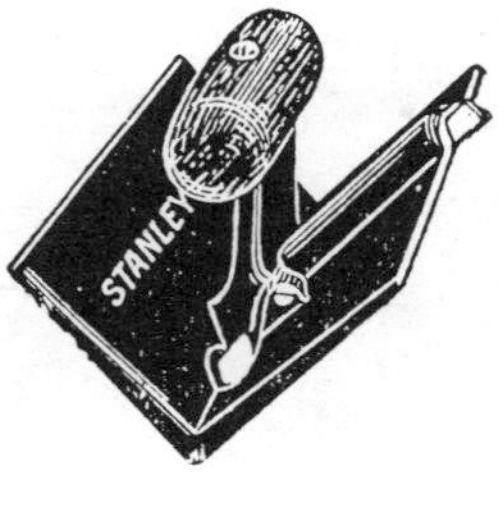

No. 56. 4 inches long, 3/8 in. Cutter. To work semi-circles 9/16 to 2 in...............................each **3.75**

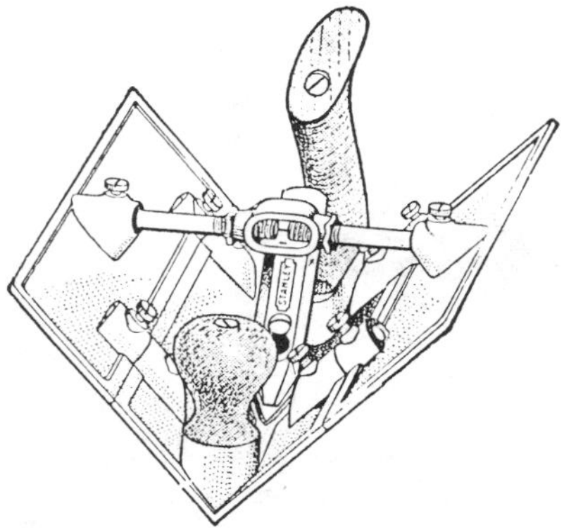

No. 57. 10 inches long, 7/8 in. Cutter. To work semi-circles 1 to 5 in...............................each **7.00**

No. 2. Additional sections. To work semi-circles 5 to 7½ in...pair **2.25**

PLANES

CARRIAGE RABBET PLANES
Made by Stanley

For Carriage or Wagon building, Mill work, or any heavy rabbet work.

No. 10½.   9 inches long, 2⅛ inch Cutter.........each **4.75**

No. 10.   13 inches long, 2⅛ inch Cutter.........each **5.25**

No. 10¼.   13 inches long, 2⅛ inch Cutter. With Advance Spurs ....each **6.50**

SCRUB PLANES

No. 40.   9½ inches long, 1⅛ inch round nose Cutter..each **2.00**

No. 40½.   10½ inches long, 1½ inch round nose Cutter..each **2.65**

JACK BLOCK-PLANE

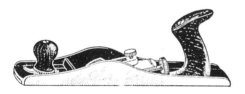

No. 62.   14 inches long, 2⅛ inch Cutter. For heavy work across the grain. For blocking large mitres. A good Box Makers' Plane.............................each **4.75**

BUTCHER BLOCK-PLANE

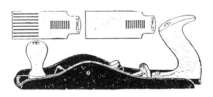

No. 64.   12½ inches long, 2 inch Cutter. Has additional grooved cutter blade for roughing off block before smoothing ....each **4.50**

CIRCULAR PLANES

No. 20.   10 inches long, 1¾ inch Cutter. Steel face may be curved for inside or outside work...........each **7.00**

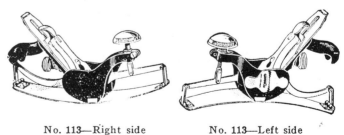

No. 113—Right side   No. 113—Left side

No. 113.   10 inches long, 1¾ inch Cutter. Has graduated scale for setting the face.........................each **6.50**

PLOW PLANES

Made by Stanley

No. 45. Seven Tools in one. Beading and Center Beading, Plow, Dado, Rabbet and Fillister, Match Plane, Sash Plane and Slitting Plane. Packed with 22 Cutters. All parts Nickel Plated ....each 12.00

EXTRAS FOR No. 45 PLANE

HOLLOWS AND ROUNDS

NOSING TOOL

		Per Set
No. 6.	Hollow and Round, work ¾ in. circle	2.35
No. 8.	Hollow and Round, work 1 in. circle	2.35
No. 10.	Hollow and Round, work 1¼ in. circle	2.50
No. 12.	Hollow and Round, work 1½ in. circle	2.50

No. 5N. Work 1¼ in. circle..........................per set 1.75

THE SIEGLEY PLOW

This Plane is a combination of a Carpenter's Plow and Dado with a Side and Center Beading Plane.

Each Plane is accompanied by 9 Plow Cutters (3/16, ¼, 5/16, 3/8, 7/16, ½, 5/8, ¾ and 7/8 inch).

Seven Beading Tools (⅛, 3/16, ¼, 5/16, 3/8 and ½ inch), a 7/8 inch Match Cutter and a Sash Tool.

No. 2. Nickel Plated, with 18 Cutters...price 12.50

Stanley's Adjustable Planes.

Wood Planes.

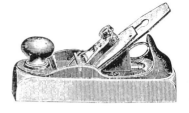

No. 122.

No. 135.

No.		Each.
122	Smooth, 8 inches in Length, 1¾ in. Cutter,	$
135	Handle Smooth, 10 inches in Length, 2⅛ in. Cutter,	

No. 127.

127	Jack,	15 inches in Length, 2⅛ in. Cutter,	$
129	Fore,	20 " " " 2⅜ " "	
132	Jointer,	26 " " " 2⅝ " "	

Steel Planes.

No. 104.

No. 105.

104	Smooth, 9 inches in Length, 2⅛ in. Cutter,	$
105	Jack, 14 " " " 2⅛ " "	

ONE IN A BOX.

Stanley's Adjustable Planes.

Iron Block Planes.

No. 110.

No.										EACH.
101	Block,	3½	inches in Length,	1	in. Cutter,				$	
102	"	5½	"	"	"	1⅜	"	"		
103	"	5½	"	"	"	1⅜	"	"	Adjustable,	
110	"	7½	"	"	"	1¾	"	"		
120	"	7½	"	"	"	1¾	"	"	Adjustable,	

Stanley's

Adjustable Circular Planes.

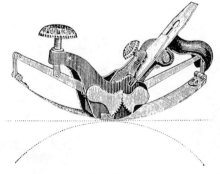

No. 113.

113   1¾ in. Cutter, $

ONE IN A BOX.

PLANES

Stanley Patent Universal Plane

This tool in the hands of an ordinary Carpenter, can be used for all lines of work covered by a full assortment of so-called Fancy Planes.

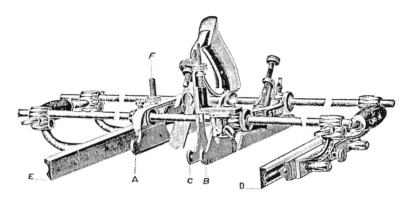

No. 55. Stanley's Universal Plane, with 52 Tools, Bits, etc...price 22.50

The Plane is Nickel Plated; the 52 Cutters are arranged in four separate cases, and the entire outfit is packed in a neat wooden box.

This Plane consists of:

A MAIN STOCK (A) with two sets of transverse sliding arms, a Depth Gauge (F) adjusted by screw, and a Slitting Cutter with stop.

A SLIDING SECTION (B) with a vertically adjustable bottom.

THE AUXILIARY CENTER BOTTOM (C) is to be placed in front of the Cutter, as an extra support, or stop, when needed. This bottom is adjustable both vertically and laterally.

FENCES (D) AND (E). Fence D has a lateral adjustment by means of a screw, for extra fine work. The fences can be used on either side of the Plane, and the Rosewood guides can be tilted to any desired angle, up to 45 degrees, by loosening screws on the face. Fence E can be reversed for center beading wide boards.

AN ADJUSTABLE STOP to be used in beading the edges of matched boards is inserted on left hand side of sliding section (B).

No. 55 Plane as a Moulding Plane

No. 55 Plane as a Chamfer

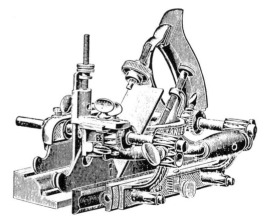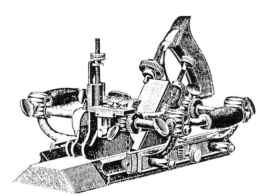

PLANES

ROUTER PLANES

Made by Stanley

No. 73. Baby Router. 3 inches long, ¼ inch Cutter. A handy tool for small work..................each **.75**

No. 71½. 7½ inches long, with ¼ and ½ inch Cutter and a diamond nose Smoothing Cutter........each **2.75**

No. 71. 7½ inches long, with 3 Cutters. Has attachment for closing the throat, for use on narrow surface ....each **3.25**

MATCH PLANES

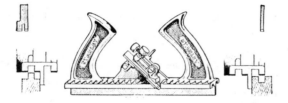 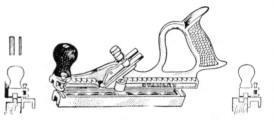

No. 48. Cuts ⁵⁄₁₆ inch Groove on Boards ¾ inch to 1¾ inch. Centers on ⅞ inch......................each **4.25**

No. 49. Cuts ⁵⁄₁₆ inch Groove on Boards ½ inch to ¾ inch. Centers on ½ inch......................each **4.25**

No. 147. Cuts ⁵⁄₁₆ inch Groove on Boards ½ inch to ¾ inch. Centers on ⅝ inch......................each **3.50**

No. 148. Cuts ¼ inch Groove on Boards ¾ inch to 1 inch. Centers on ⅞ inch......................each **3.75**

BAILEY'S ADJUSTABLE BELT PLANE

This tool is used by Belt Makers for chamfering down the laps of a Belt before fastening them together. It is equally well adapted to use in repairing Belts in all manufacturing establishments.

No. 11. Belt Makers' Plane, 2⅜ inch Cutter..each **3.50**

IRON PLANES

STANLEY BULL NOSE RABBET

Adjustable

Japanned iron frame and lever; polished bottom, tempered steel cutter. For working in close corners and other difficult places. Throat can be adjusted for coarse or fine work.

Length 4 inches, width cutter 1 1/16 inch.

Each
No. 75—Wt. each 5/8 lb.............$0.80

STANLEY SIDE RABBET

N°98
Right Hand.

N°99
Left Hand.

Nickel plated iron frame, tempered steel cutter, fitted with depth gage. Rosewood handle.

For side rabbeting in trimming dados, mouldings, and grooves of all kinds.

Reversible nose piece allows working in corners. Ground sides and bottoms.

Nos.	Each	Lgth. in.	Width of cutter, in.	Wt. per doz., lbs.
98	$2.30	4	1/2	1/2
99	2.30	4	1/2	1/2

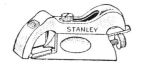

Right and left hand nickel plated frame, tempered steel cutters fitted with depth gage.

For side rabbeting in trimming dados, mouldings and grooves. Reversible nose allows working in close quarters.

Length 5 1/2 inches, cutter width 1/2 in.

Each
No. 79—Wt. each 1 lb.............$2.40

STANLEY CABINET MAKERS RABBET

Bull Nose Pattern

Nickel plated iron frame. Tempered steel cutter, throat adjustable for fine or coarse work. Cutters adjustable endwise, front can be removed to make a chisel plane, lies flat either side. For fine cabinet work. Length 4 inches, cutter width 1 inch.

Each
No. 90—Wt. each 1 1/8 lbs..........$4.50

All above, one in a box.

IRON PLANES

STANLEY BENCH RABBET

Regular Style

Japanned malleable iron frame, tempered steel cutters adjustable endwise and sidewise. Ground bottom and sides. Rosewood handle and knob.

Smooth and Jack.

Nos.	Each	Kind	Lgth. in.	Width cutter, in.	Wt. each lbs.
10 1/2	$6.00	Smooth	9 1/4	2 1/8	3 1/4
10	7.20	Jack	13	2 1/8	4 1/4

STANLEY RABBET

With Adjustable Depth Gage

Japanned iron frame, nickel plated trimmings. Tempered steel cutters. Fitted with spur and adjustable depth gage.

These planes will lie perfectly flat on either side and can be used with either right or left hand while planing into corners or up against perpendicular surfaces.

Nos.	Each	Lgth. in.	Width cutter, in.	Wt. each lbs.
190	$2.10	8	1 1/2	2 1/2
191	2.10	8	1 1/4	2 1/4
192	2.10	8	1	2

STANLEY DUPLEX, FILLETSTER AND RABBET

With Depth Gage and Adjustable Fence

Japanned iron frame, nickel plated trimmings. Tempered steel cutter. Fitted with spur and adjustable depth gage.

This plane has two seats for the cutter, one for regular work and the other where a bull-nose is required. The adjustable fence can be used on either side and slides under the bottom, regulating the width of the cut. To work same as a rabbet plane, remove fence and arms.

Length 8 1/2 inches, cutter width 1 1/2 inches.

Each
No. 78—Wt. each 3 lbs.............$2.60

All above, one in a box.

IRON PLANES

STANLEY IMPROVED RABBET AND FILLETSTER

With fence and adjustable depth gage.

Japanned iron frame, nickel plated trimmings, tempered steel cutter. Will lie perfectly flat on either side, fitted with two spurs, front part of plane can be detached for bull nose work. Cutter is adjustable endwise by means of a lever.

Length 6 3/4 inches, width cutter, 1 inch.

Each
No. 278—Wt. each 2 lbs...........$3.50

STANLEY IMPROVED DADO

With Adjustable Depth Gage

Japanned iron frame, nickel plated trimmings, tempered steel cutter. Cuts true even in the narrow cuts. Spurs assure smooth clean cuts.

Nos.	Each	Lgth. in.	Width cutter, in.	Wt. each lbs.
39 1/4	$3.20	8	1/4	1 3/4
39 3/8	3.20	8	3/8	1 3/4
39 1/2	3.20	8	1/2	1 7/8
39 5/8	3.20	8	5/8	1 7/8
39 3/4	3.20	8	3/4	2
39 7/8	3.60	8	7/8	2 3/8
391	4.00	8	1	2 1/2

STANLEY SCRUB

Rounded Cutter

Japanned iron frame, tempered steel cutter. Hardwood handle and knob.

Used for quickly planing down to rough dimensions boards that are not convenient to rip with a saw.

Length 9 1/2 inches, cutter width 1 1/4 inches.

Each
No. 40—Wt. each 2 1/8 lbs..........$2.20

STANLEY CORNER ROUNDING

Japanned iron frame tempered steel cutters. For rounding corners.

Nos.	Each	Curve in.	Lgth. in.	Wt. each, lbs.
144 1/4	$1.70	1/4	7 1/2	1 1/8
144 3/8	1.70	3/8	7 1/2	1 1/8
144 1/2	1.70	1/2	7 1/2	1 1/8

All above, one in a box.

IRON PLANES

STANLEY EDGE TRIMMING

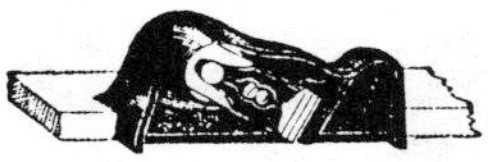

Japanned iron frame, tempered steel cutter works on a skew.

For trimming and squaring the edges of boards up to ⅞ inch for a square close fit. Wood blocks of various bevels may be attached enabling the user to make a slanting cut. Length 6 inches, cutter width ⅞ inch.

Each
No. 95—Wt. each 1¼ lbs..........$1.90

STANLEY BELT MAKERS

Adjustable Throat

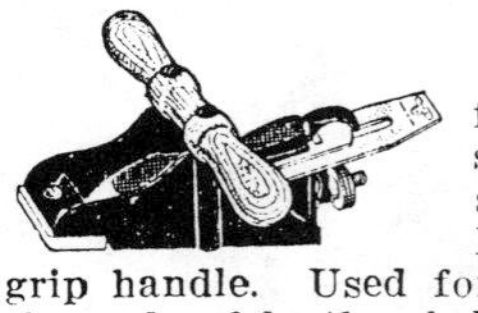

Japanned iron frame, tempered steel cutter can be adjusted endwise. Rosewood double grip handle. Used for chamfering down the ends of leather belts.

Length 5¾ inches, width cutter 2⅜ inches.

Each
No. 11—Wt. each 3½ lbs..........$5.00

STANLEY ADJUSTABLE CIRCULAR

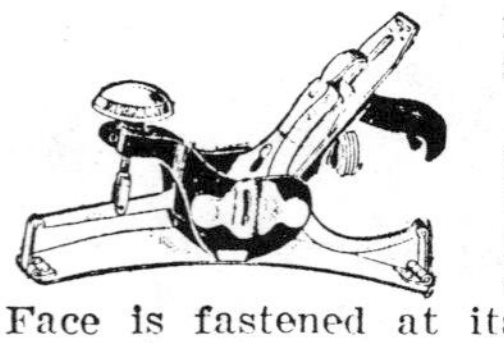

Japanned iron frame, tempered steel cutter.
The flexible steel bottoms can be adjusted to plane convex or concave surfaces. Face is fastened at its center to plane bottom and adjusted by means of screw and lever. Has graduated scale for setting face.

Length 10 inches, cutter width 1¾ in.

Each
No. 113—Wt. each 3¾ lbs.........$7.80

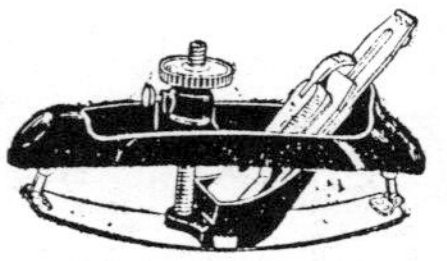

Japanned iron frame, tempered steel cutter. Flexible steel bottom can be adjusted to plane convex or concave surfaces.

Face is fastened at each end to plane body and adjusted by a screw at the center, frame provides a good hand hold. Length 10 inches, cutter width 1¾ inches.

Each
No. 20—Wt. each 4 lbs. $8.30

All above, one in a box.

IRON PLANES

STANLEY ROUTERS

Open Throat Three Cutters

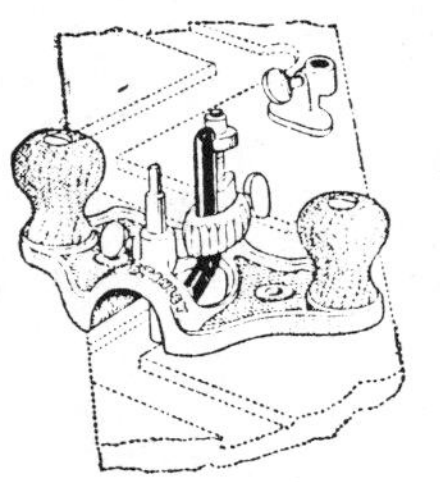

Cast iron frame nickel plated tempered steel cutters. Maple handles finished black.

For surfacing the bottom of grooves or other depressions. Wood bottoms can be attached. Cutters are adjustable and can be held in front for regular work or on back for bull nose work. Length 7½ inches, ¼ and ½ inch router cutters and V or smoothing cutter.

Each
No. 71—Wt. each 2⅝ lbs.........$4.10

Closed Throat

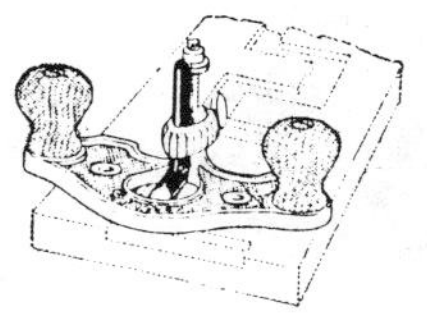

Cast iron frame nickel plated tempered steel cutters. Maple handles finished black. Used for surfacing bottom of grooves or other depressions. Wood bottom can be attached. Adjustable cutters can be held in front for regular work or held in back for bull nose work.

Length 7½ inches, ¼ and ½ inch router cutters and V or smoothing cutter.

Each
No. 71½—Wt. each 2⅛ lbs.........$3.30

Small Size

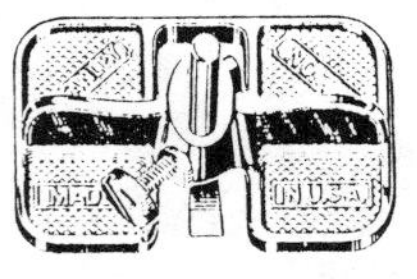

Cast iron nickel plated frame.

Used for very narrow cabinet work, inlay work cutting dados, applying lock plates, etc. Can be used for either regular or bull nose work, reversing cutter it can be used as depth gauge. Length 3 inches, cutter width ¼ inch.

Each
No. 271—Wt. each ⅜ lb. $0.90

STANLEY CORE BOX

With One Pair of Sections

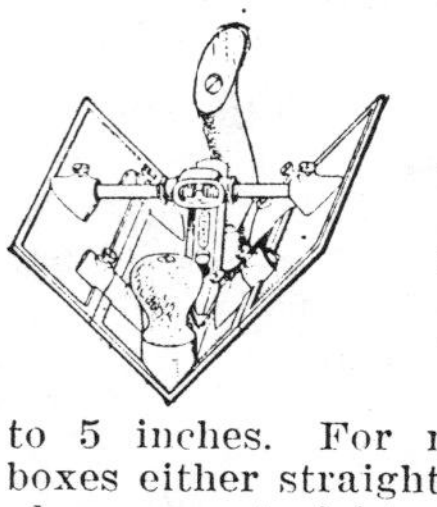

Cast iron frame nickel plated, rosewood handle and knob.

Furnished with one pair of sections to work semi-circles, 1 to 5 inches. For making circular core boxes either straight or tapered. Sides of plane are at right angles therefore point of plane will cut on the circumference of circle when sides rest on edges of cut. Length 10 inches, cutter width ⅞ inch.

Each
No. 57—Wt. each 5¾ lbs.........$12.00
Additional Sides ....Per pair 4.00

All above, one in a box.

IRON PLANES

STANLEY COMBINATION FORTY-FIVE

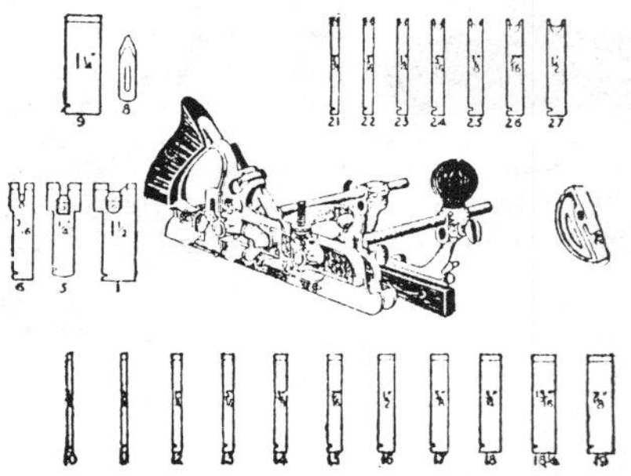

Equipped with 23 Cutters

Beading plane, plow, dado, rabbet and filletster, match plane, sash plane and slitting plane. Nickel plated iron frame; rosewood handle, knob and fence.

Each plane is regularly supplied with 11 plow and dado cutters, ⅛, 3/16, ¼, 5/16, ⅜, 7/16, ½, ⅝, ¾, 13/16 and ⅞ in.: seven beading tools, ⅛, 3/16, ¼, 5/16, ⅜, 7/16 and ½ in.; one 1½ in. sash tool, one each 3/16 and ¼ in. match tool; one 1¼ in. filletster and one slitting tool.

Each
No. 45—Length 11 in.; wt. each 9½ lbs. $15.90

COMBINATION FIFTY-FIVE

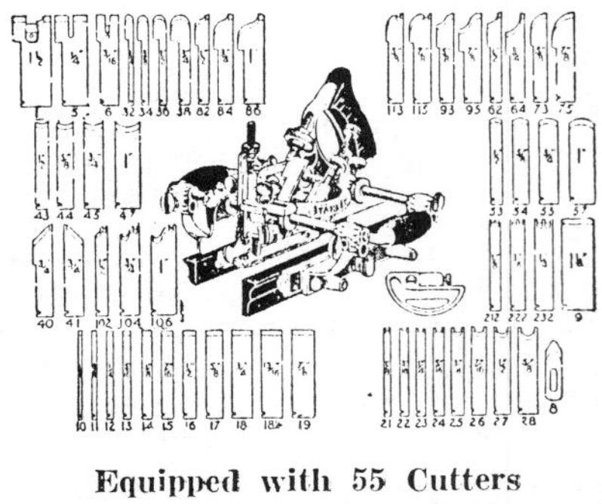

Equipped with 55 Cutters

This plane combines all the features of the Stanley Forty-five and in addition is also a Moulding Plane. Nickel plated iron frame, rosewood handle and fences.

Each plane has one 1½ in. sash tool; one each 3/16 and ¼ in. match tools; one slitting tool; one 1¼ in. filletster; 11 plow and dado tools, ⅛, 3/16, ¼, 5/16, ⅜, 7/16, ½, ⅝, ¾, 13/16 and ⅞ in.; eight beading tools, ⅛, 3/16, ¼, 5/16, ⅜, 7/16, ½ and ⅝ in.; four fluting tools, ¼, ⅜, ½ and ¾ in.; four hollows, ½, ⅝, ¾ and 1 in. four rounds, ½, ⅝, ¾ and 1 in.; two quarter hollows, ½ and ¾ in.; two quarter rounds, ⅝ and ⅞ in.; three reverse ogees, ½, ¾ and 1 in.; two Roman ogees, ⅝ and ⅞ in.; three Grecian ogees, ½, ¾ and 1 in.; two quarter rounds with bead, ⅝ and ⅞ in.; and three reeding tools, two beads, ⅛, 3/16 and ¼ in.; one each right and left hand chamfers, ¾ in.

Each
No. 55—Length 11 in.; wt. each 15 lbs. $31.26

All above, one in a box.

IRON PLANES
BAILEY BENCH, ADJUSTABLE

Smooth

Jack, Fore and Jointer

Japanned iron frame; polished face and sides; tempered steel cutter; adjustable endwise and sidewise; rosewood handle and knob.

With Flat Bottom

Nos.	Each	Style	Lth., in.	Cutter, in.	Wt. ea., lbs.
1	$3.70	Smooth	5½	1¼	1¼
2	3.80	Smooth	7	1⅝	2½
3	3.80	Smooth	8	1¾	3½
4	3.90	Smooth	9	2	3¾
4½	4.80	Smooth	10	2⅜	5
5	4.40	Jack	14	2	5
5¼	4.10	Jack	11½	1¾	3¾
5½	5.60	Jack	15	2⅜	6
6	6.20	Fore	18	2⅜	7
7	7.60	Jointer	22	2⅜	8
8	8.80	Jointer	24	2⅝	9½

One in a box.

Smooth

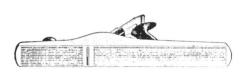

Jack, Fore and Jointer

Japanned iron frame, polished face and sides, tempered steel cutter, adjustable endwise and sidewise, rosewood handle and knob.

With Corrugated Bottom

Nos.	Each	Style	Lth., in.	Cutter, in.	Wt. ea., lbs.
3C	$4.00	Smooth	8	1⅝	3½
4C	4.10	Smooth	9	2	3¾
4½C	5.10	Smooth	10	2⅜	4⅞
5C	4.60	Jack	14	2	4¾
5½C	5.90	Jack	15	2⅜	3¾
6C	6.50	Fore	18	2⅜	6⅞
7C	7.90	Jointer	22	2⅜	7¾
8C	9.20	Jointer	24	2⅝	9¼

One in a box.

IRON PLANES
STANLEY "BED ROCK" BENCH ADJUSTABLE

Smooth

Jack, Fore and Jointer

The bottom of the frog is machined so as to make a tongue which fits into a groove formed in the bottom of the plane, this insures great solidity and perfect alignment between the frog and the bottom.

The movement of the frog in the groove for widening or opening the throat and the loosening or tightening of the frog to the base is governed by screw adjustment operated without moving cap or cutter. Rosewood handle and knob. Japanned iron frame.

With Flat Bottom

Nos.	Each	Style	Lth., in.	Cutter, in.	Wt. ea., lbs.
603	$4.00	Smooth	8	1¾	3½
604	4.10	Smooth	9	2	4
605	4.60	Jack	14	2	5
606	6.50	Fore	18	2⅜	7
607	7.90	Jointer	22	2⅜	8
608	9.20	Jointer	24	2⅝	10

One in a box.

ADJUSTABLE STEEL PLANES
STANLEY

Smooth

Jack

Similar in design to Bailey plane but with a pressed steel bottom and malleable iron frog and lever cap. Rosewood handle and knob.

With Flat Bottoms

Nos.	Each	Style	Lth., in.	Cutter, in.	Wt. ea., lbs.
S4	$5.30	Smooth	9	2	3⅛
S5	6.00	Jack	14	2	4

One in a box.

IRON PLANES
DEFIANCE BENCH, ADJUSTABLE

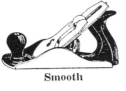

Smooth

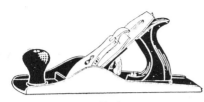

Jack

For household use.

Japanned iron frame, double plane iron tempered tool steel cutter, ground sides and bottoms. Red hardwood handle and knob.

With Flat Bottom

Nos.	Each	Style	Lth., in.	Cutter, in.	Wt. ea., lbs.
1203	$1.70	Smooth	8	1¾	3
1204	1.90	Smooth	9	2	3½
1205	2.20	Jack	14	2	4½

DEFIANCE BENCH, NON-ADJUSTABLE

Smooth

For household use. Japanned iron frame, single plane iron and screw down lever cap. Ground sides and bottom. Red hardwood handle and cap. Length 9 inches, cutter width 1¾ inches.

No. 1213—Wt. each 1¾ lbs.......$1.00

BLOCK PLANES
DEFIANCE NON-ADJUSTABLE

For household use. Japanned iron frame, tempered steel cutter, lever cap, sides polished. Black hardwood handle. Length 7 inches, cutter width 1¾ inches.

No. 1247—Wt. each 1⅜ lbs.......$0.60

DEFIANCE, ADJUSTABLE

For household use. Japanned iron frame. Adjustable endwise by means of steel screw, tool steel cutter, ground sides and bottom. Black hardwood handle. Length 7 in., cutter width 1⅝ in.

No. 1220—Wt. each 1½ lbs.......$1.10

All above, one in a box.

PLANES

STANLEY BAILEY, IRON BOTTOM BENCH

Japanned cast iron frame, polished bottoms, sides and caps; varnished rosewood knobs and handles. Tool steel cutters, tempered and polished; screw and lever adjustment.

SMOOTH, Plain Bottom.

Nos.	2	3	4	4½
Length, ins	7	8	9	10
Width cut, ins	1⅝	1¾	2	2⅜
Wt each, lbs	2½	3¼	2½	5
Each	$9 00	9 00	9 00	11 25

SMOOTH, Corrugated Bottom.

Nos.	2C	3C	4C	4½C
Length, ins	7	8	9	10
Width cut, ins	1⅝	1¾	2	2⅜
Wt each, lbs	2¼	3	3½	4
Each	$9 45	9 45	9 75	11 70

One in cardboard box.

STANLEY BAILEY, IRON BOTTOM BENCH

Japanned cast iron frame, polished bottoms, sides and caps; varnished rosewood knobs and handles. Tool steel cutters, tempered and polished; screw and lever adjustment.

Plain Bottom.

Style	Jack	Jack	Jack	Fore	Jointer	
Nos.	5¼	5	5½	6	7	8
Length, ins	11½	14	15	18	22	24
Width cut, ins	1¾	2	2¼	2⅜	2⅜	2⅝
Wt each, lbs	3¾	4¾	6	7	7½	9
Each	$9 75	10 20	13 50	14 70	18 00	20 25

Corrugated Bottom.

Style	Jack	Jack	Fore	Jointer	
Nos.	5C	5½C	6C	7C	8C
Length, ins	14	15	18	22	24
Width cut, ins	2	2¼	2⅜	2⅜	2⅝
Wt each, lbs	5	6	7	8	9
Each	$10 65	13 95	15 30	18 75	21 75

One in cardboard box.

STANLEY, SMOOTH IRON BOTTOM BENCH
"Bed Rock"

The cutter, frog and bottom are so designed that they are practically one solid piece of metal, thus preventing any chance of vibration. Frog may be adjusted either forward or backward without removing lever and cutter, while cutter is adjustable both end wise and side wise.

Plain Bottom.

Nos.	602	603	604
Length, ins	7	8	9
Size cutter, ins	1⅝	1¾	2
Wt each, lbs	2¾	3½	4
Each	$9 45	9 45	9 75

One in cardboard box.

PLANES

STANLEY, SMOOTH IRON BOTTOM BENCH
"Bed Rock"

The cutter, frog and bottom are so designed that they are practically one solid piece of metal, thus preventing any chance of vibration. Frogs may be adjusted either forward or backward without removing lever and cutter, while cutter is adjustable both end wise and side wise.

Plain Bottom, Jack.

No.	605
Length, ins	14
Size cutter, ins	2
Wt each, lbs	5½
Each	$10 80

One in cardboard box.

STANLEY BAILEY, IRON BLOCK

Cast iron frames, polished bottoms and sides, tool steel cutters, tempered and polished. True screw adjustment. Adjustable throat opening, lateral adjustment.

Adjustable, Without Handle.
Japanned Trimmings.

Nos.	9½	15
Length, ins	6	7
Width cutter, ins	1⅝	1⅝
Each	$4 65	5 25

One in cardboard box; wt 1½ lbs.

	Per Doz
No. 9½C—Extra cutters, 1¾ in; for No. 9½ plane	$12 00
No. 15C—Extra cutters, 1¾ in; for No. 15 plane	12 00

Half doz in cardboard box; wt doz 1½ lbs.

STANLEY, LOW ANGLE

This plane has the cutter set at a very low angle, which is of great advantage when working across the grain. Length 6 ins; width cutter 1½ ins.

	Each
No. 60—Nickeled trimmings	$6 00
No. 60½—Japanned trimmings	5 25

One in cardboard box; wt each 1¼ lbs.

STANLEY, KNUCKLE JOINT BLOCK

Fitted with a new and patented form of lever or cap. The knuckle joint permits of great leverage, consequently the lever can be placed in position or removed. When clamped in place, it will hold the cutter firmly to its seat. Length 7 ins; width cutter 1⅝ ins.

	Each
No. 65—Nickel plated trimmings	$7 20
No. 65½—Japanned trimmings	6 00

One in cardboard box; wt each 1½ lbs.

	Per Doz
No. 65C—Extra cutters, 1⅝ in; for No. 65 plane	$12 00
No. 65½C—Extra cutters, 1⅝ in; for No. 65½ plane	12 00

Half doz in cardboard box; wt doz 1½ lbs.

PLANES
KEYSTONE

These planes were designed and are intended for household and general use.

Strictly high grade quality. Blades are of polished steel; frames and caps cast iron, japanned, polished bottoms; polished sides; hardwood varnished knobs and handles.

KEYSTONE, SMOOTH
Non-Adjustable.

Single iron type.

No. 213K—Length 9 ins; 1¾ in. cutter_____ $2 25

One in cardboard box; wt each 1¾ lbs.

KEYSTONE, SMOOTH

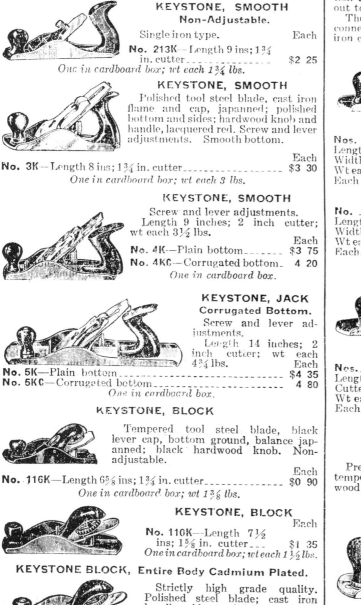

Polished tool steel blade, cast iron flame and cap, japanned; polished bottom and sides; hardwood knob and handle, lacquered red. Screw and lever adjustments. Smooth bottom.

Each

No. 3K—Length 8 ins; 1¾ in. cutter_____ $3 30

One in cardboard box; wt each 3 lbs.

KEYSTONE, SMOOTH

Screw and lever adjustments. Length 9 inches; 2 inch cutter; wt each 3½ lbs.

Each

No. 4K—Plain bottom_____ $3 75

No. 4KC—Corrugated bottom_ 4 20

One in cardboard box.

KEYSTONE, JACK
Corrugated Bottom.

Screw and lever adjustments.

Length 14 inches; 2 inch cutter; wt each 4¾ lbs.

Each

No. 5K—Plain bottom_____ $4 35

No. 5KC—Corrugated bottom_____ 4 80

One in cardboard box.

KEYSTONE, BLOCK

Tempered tool steel blade, black lever cap, bottom ground, balance japanned; black hardwood knob. Non-adjustable.

Each

No. 116K—Length 6⅝ ins; 1¾ in. cutter_____ $0 90

One in cardboard box; wt 1⅜ lbs.

KEYSTONE, BLOCK

Each

No. 110K—Length 7½ ins; 1⅝ in. cutter___ $1 35

One in cardboard box; wt each 1½ lbs.

KEYSTONE BLOCK, Entire Body Cadmium Plated.

Strictly high grade quality. Polished steel blade; cast iron handle, sides and bottom; hardwood knob. Body cadmium plated, rust-proof; handle, screw and knob black japanned.

Each

No. 110K-R—Length 7 ins; 1⅝ inch cutter_____ $1 59

One in cardboard box; wt each 1¼ lbs.

KEYSTONE, BLOCK
Adjustable.

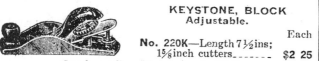

Each

No. 220K—Length 7½ ins; 1⅝ inch cutters_____ $2 25

One in cardboard box; wt each 1½ lbs.

PLANES
STANLEY GAGE, SELF-SETTING

Japanned smooth iron castings, polished face and sides, varnished rosewood handle and knob; brass screw adjustment; The self-setting feature lies in the fact that the plane iron if taken out to be sharpened goes back in exactly the same position as before removal. Likewise the plane cap when taken out to allow removal of cutter goes back in its same position.

The plane cap is so designed that by slight adjustment it connects the cutter to either single or double iron. The plane iron consists of three pieces; cutter, adjustment slide and binder plate, all being fastened by one screw. The adjustment slide is machined on its sides to accurately fit the groove machined in the frog and is permanently fixed both sideways and endwise.

SMOOTH, Plain Bottom.

Nos.	G3	G4
Length, ins	8¾	9
Width cutter, ins	1¾	2
Wt each, lbs	2¾	3
Each	$9 30	9 60

JACK, Plain Bottom.

No.	G5
Length, ins	14
Width cutter, ins	2
Wt each, lbs	4¼
Each	$10 80

One in cardboard box.

FORE AND JOINTER

Plain Bottom.

Nos.	Fore G6	Jointer G7
Length, ins	18	22
Cutter, ins	2¼	2½
Wt each, lbs	5¾	6½
Each	$15 00	18 60

One in cardboard box.

---- ✦ ----

STANLEY, BAILEY PATTERN

Pressed steel bottom, and adjustable front, tool steel cutter, tempered and polished; screw and lever adjustment. Rosewood handles and knobs.

JACK

Length 14 inches, width cut 2 inches.

Each

No. S5__ $14 25

One in cardboard box; wt each 4 lbs.

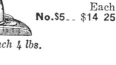

SMOOTH

Length 9 inches; width cut 2 inches.

Each

No. S4_____ $12 30

One in cardboard box; wt each 3¼ lbs.

55

PLANES
STANLEY BAILEY, IRON BLOCK

Cast iron frames, polished bottoms and sides, tool steel cutters, tempered and polished. True screw adjustment. Adjustable throat opening, lateral adjustment.

Knuckle Joint.

Has a patented form of lever or cap, which, being made entirely of steel. A great improvement in this plane is the great leverage of the knuckle joint, which, when clamped in place will hold the cutter firmly to its seat. Nickel plated cap, lever and screws.

Each
No. 18—Length 6 ins; 1⅝ in. cutter_____ $6 60
One in cardboard box; wt each 1½ lbs.
Per Doz
No. 18C—Extra cutters, 1⅝ in; for No. 18 plane_____ $12 00
Half doz in cardboard box; wt doz 1½ lbs.

STANLEY, IRON BLOCK

Japanned cast iron frames and caps; tool steel cutters, tempered and polished.

Toy Size. Not Adjustable.
Each
No. 101—Length 3½ ins; 1 in. cutter_____ $1 11
Half doz in cardboard box; wt each ¾ lb.

STANLEY, IRON BLOCK
Not Adjustable.
Each
No. 102—Length 5½ ins; 1⅜ in. cutter_____ $2 10
One in cardboard box; wt each 1 lb.
Per Doz
No. 102C—Extra cutters, 1⅜ in; for No. 102 plane_____ $7 20
Half doz in cardboard box; wt doz 1 lb.

STANLEY, IRON BLOCK
Adjustable.
Each
No. 103—Length 5½ ins; 1⅜ in. cutter_____ $2 40
One in cardboard box; wt each 1 lb.
Per Doz
No. 103C—Extra cutters, 1⅜ in; for No. 10 3plane_____ $9 90
Half doz in cardboard box; wt doz 1 lb.

STANLEY, IRON BLOCK
Hardwood Knob. Not Adjustable.
Each
No. 110—Length 7½ ins; 1⅝ in. cutter_____ $2 40
One in cardboard box; wt each 1½ lbs.
Per Doz
No. 110C—Extra cutters, 1⅝ in; for No. 110 plane_____ $9 90
Half doz in cardboard box; wt doz 1 lb.

PLANES

Japanned cast iron frame and caps, tool steel cutters, tempered and polished.

STANLEY, IRON BLOCK
Lever Adjustment.
Each
No. 120—Length 7 ins; 1⅝ in. cutter_____ $3 75
One in cardboard box; wt each 1½ lbs. Per Doz
No. 120C—Extra cutters, 1⅝ in; for No. 120 plane___ $12 00
Half doz in cardboard box; wt doz 1 lb.

STANLEY, IRON BLOCK
Rosewood Knob, Screw Adjustment.
Each
No. 220—Length 7 ins; 1⅝ in. cutter_____ $3 75
One in cardboard box; wt each 1½ lbs. Per Doz
No. 220C—Extra cutters, 1⅝ in; for No. 220 plane___ $12 00
Half doz in cardboard box; wt doz 1 lb.

STANLEY, IRON BLOCK
Rosewood Knob, Screw Adjustment.
Each
No. 203—Length 5½ ins; 1⅜ in. cutter_____ $3 75
One in cardboard box; wt each 1 lb. Per Doz
No. 203C—Extra cutters, 1⅜ in; for No. 203 plane___ $12 00
Half doz in cardboard box; wt doz 1 lb.

STANLEY, IRON BLOCK
Adjustable.
Low Angle.

Hardwood handle and knob. Fitted with patent adjustable throat, which enables the user to work equally well on hard or soft wood. Each
No. 62—Length 14 ins; 2 in. cutter_____ $14 10
One in cardboard box; wt each 4 lbs.

STANLEY, IRON BLOCK, Double End.
Easily used as a block plane or cutter; may be reversed for planing in close corners not eaisly reached with other planes.
Not Adjustable, Hardwood Knob. Each
No. 130—Length 8 ins; 1⅝ in. cutter_____ $4 20
One in cardboard box; wt each 1¾ lbs. Per Doz
No. 130C—Extra cutters, 1⅝ in; for No. 130 plane____ $9 90
Half doz in cardboard box; wt doz 1½ lbs.

STANLEY, IRON BLOCK
Adjustable Double End.
Hardwood knob; has two slots and movable cutter seat. When it is desired to use it as a bull nose plane the cap and cutter can be removed and the adjustable cutter seat reversed.
Each
No. 131—Length 8 ins; 1⅝ in. cutter_____ $7 05
One in cardboard box; wt each 1¾ lbs.

STANLEY, RABBET AND BLOCK
A detachable side will easily change this tool from a block plane to a rabbet plane or vice versa; the cutter is set on a skew. Each
No. 140—Length 7 ins; 1¾ in. cutter_____ $6 45
One in cardboard box; wt each 2 lbs. Per Doz
No. 140C—Extra cutters, 1⅝ ins; for No. 140 plane__ $16 20
Half doz in cardboard box; wt doz 1 lb.

PLANES

Japanned cast iron frame and caps, tool steel cutters, tempered and polished.

STANLEY, SIDE RABBET

For side-rabbeting and trimming dados, mouldings and grooves of all sorts. A reversible nose piece will give the tool a form by which it will work close up into corners when required.

Each

No. 98—Length 4 ins; ½ in. cutter _____ $6 00
One in cardboard box; wt each about ½ lbs.

STANLEY, BULL-NOSE RABBET

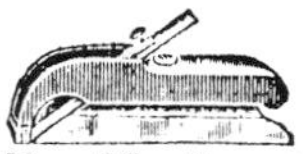

Non-adjustable, polished bottom, for general rabbeting and working into close corners.

Each

No. 75—Length 4 ins; 1 in. cutter _____ $2 10
One in cardboard box; wt about ¾ lb.

STANLEY, CARRIAGE MAKERS' RABBET

Varnished rosewood handle and knob; with screw and lever adjustments.

Each

No. 10½—Length 9 ins; 2⅛ in. cutter _____ $14 10
One in cardboard box; wt each about 9 lbs.

STANLEY, SCRUB

Japanned, cast iron frame; beech handle and knob. Designed for planing down to rough dimensions any board too wide to rip with saw. This is made possible by extra heavy cutter with rounded cutting edge.

Each

No. 40—Length 9½ ins; 1¼ in cutter _____ $5 10
One in cardboard box; wt each 2⅛ lbs.

STANLEY, IMPROVED RABBET

Japanned cast iron frame and handle. All fitted with detachable depth gauge. No. 190 with spur for working across grain. Length over all 8 inches.

Each

No. 192—1 inch cutter; wt each 2 lbs _____ $5 10
No. 191—1¼ in. cutter; wt each 2¼ lbs _____ 5 10
No. 190—1½ in. cutter; wt each 2½ lbs _____ 5 10
One in cardboard box.

STANLEY, DUPLEX RABBET AND FILLETSTER

Japanned cast iron frame and handle. Can be used as a bull nose rabbet. The arm to which the fence is secured can be screwed into either side of the stock, making a superior right or left hand filletster, with adjustable spur and depth gauge.

Each

No. 78—Length 8½ ins; 1½ in. cutter _____ $6 30
One in cardboard box; wt each about 3 lbs.

PLANES

STANLEY, RABBET AND FILLETSTER

Japanned cast iron frame, fence and handle. The arm to which the fence is secured can be screwed into either side of the stock, making a superior right or left hand filletster, with adjustable spur and depth gauge, allowing a groove to be cut any desired depth up to ½ inch. The screw at top of frame can be removed allowing the plane to be used as a bull nose rabbet. Plane is also equipped with spur for use in working across the grain.

Each

No. 278—Length 6¾ ins; 1 in. cutter _____ $8 55
One in cardboard box; wt each 2 lbs.

STANLEY, TONGUEING AND GROOVING

Nickel plated cast iron frame and handle; rosewood knob. Has two plow cutters of the same width, and one extra wide cutter. When the guide or fence is set both cutters work and a tongue can be made. Fence hung on a pivot, can be swung around end for end. This movement covers one of the cutters.

Each

No. 48—Length 10½ ins; cuts ⁵⁄₁₆ in. groove on boards ¾ to 1¼ ins; centers on ⅞ in _____ $12 30
One in cardboard box; wt each 3¾ lbs.

STANLEY, ADJUSTABLE CIRCULAR

Japanned cast iron frames, caps and handles; polished bottom. Can be adjusted to work on concave or convex surfaces; graduated scale on the gears, face can be set to work an arc of the same circle, both concave and convex.

Each

No. 113 —Length 10 ins; 1¾ in. cutter _____ $18 00
One in cardboard box; wt each about 4 lbs.

STANLEY, PLOW, DADO, FILLETSTER AND MATCHING

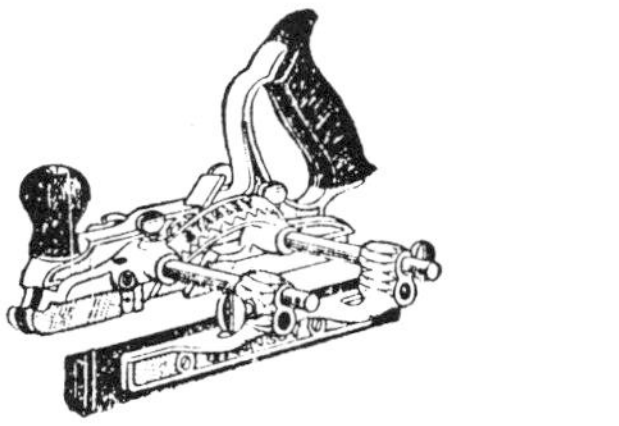

Nickel plated cast iron; rosewood handle and knob. Has 8 plow and dado bits, ³⁄₁₆ to 1¼ inch, one 1½ inch filletster cutter, 1 slitting blade, one ¼ inch tongueing tool. Is readily converted into a filletster, plow or matching plane. All the tools except the slitting blade are secured on the main stock.

Each

No. 46—With 11 cutters; length 10½ ins _____ $29 25
One in cardboard box; wt each 6 lbs.

STANLEY, ADJUSTABLE BEADING, RABBET AND MATCHING

Nickel plated cast iron; rosewood handle, knob and fence.

Fitted with an adjustable fence or guide and a depth gauge also with spurs for use when working across the grain. Has one 1½ inch sash tool, one ¼ inch match tool, one slitting tool, one 1¼ inch filletster, eleven plow and dado tools, ⅛ to ⅞ inch, seven beading tools, ⅛ to ½ inch.

Each

No. 45—With 22 cutters; length 11 ins _____ $36 00
One in cardboard box; wt each 9½ lbs.

PLANES

STANLEY, ADJUSTABLE. BEADING AND MATCHING

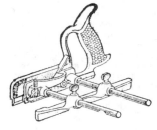

Nickel plated cast iron stock and frame. For ordinary center beading. By adjusting fence, center beading can be done up to 5 inches from the edge of a board. Except for working across the grain, the spurs need not be used. Each plane furnished with 1/8, 3/16, 1/4, 5/16, 3/8, 7/16 and 1/2 inch beading tools, 1/4, 5/16, 3/8, 7/16, 1/2, 5/8, and 7/8 inch plow and dado bits, and a pair of 1/4 inch, tongueing tools.

Each

No. 50—With 15 cutters; length 9 1/4 ins _____ $21 00
One in cardboard box; wt 3 1/2 lbs.

STANLEY, PATENT, UNIVERSAL

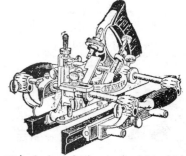

Consists of a main stock with two sets of transverse sliding arms, a depth gauge adjusted by a screw and a sliding arm, and a sliding cutter with stop. The bottom is adjustable both vertically and laterally.

Has one 1 1/2 inch sash tool, one 1 1/4 inch match tool, one slitting tool, one fillester, eleven plow and dado tools, 1/8 to 7/8 inch, nine beading tools, 1/8 to 3/4 inch, foul fluting tools, 1/4 to 3/4 inch, four hollow cutters, 1/2 to 1 inch, four round cutters, 1/2 to 1 inch, two quarter hollow cutters, 1/2 and 3/4 inch, two quarter round cutters, 5/8 and 7/8 inch, three reverse ogee cutters, 1/2 to 1 inch, two Roman ogee cutters, 5/8 and 7/8 inch, three Grecian ogee cutters, 1/2 to 1 inch, two 1/4 round cutters with bead, 5/8 and 7/8 inch, three reeding tools, two beads, 1/8 to 1/4 inch.

Each

No. 55—Nickel plated, cast iron frame; rosewood handles; complete with 53 tool steel cutters; tempered and polished, arranged in four separate cases _____ $72 00
One in cardboard box; wt complete about 15 1/4 lbs.

STANLEY, ADJUSTABLE SCRAPER

Japanned cast iron frame; rosewood handle and knob. The blade is adjustable endwise and for angle and can be firmly locked in any position desired.

This tool is used for scraping and finishing veneers, cabinet work or hard wood in any form. Can be used equally well as a tooth plane and scraping off old paint and glue.

Each

No. 112—Length 9 ins; 3 in. cutter _____ $11 25
One in cardboard box; wt each 4 lbs.

Per Doz

No. 12RB—Extra blades for 112 Planes, and Nos. 12 and 12 1/2 Scrapers _____ $18 00
One doz in cardboard box.

PLANES

STANLEY, WOOD WORKERS' HANDY ROUTER

Nickel plated cast iron; beechwood knobs; openthroat. Furnished with patented pointed cutters.

Perfectly adapted to smooth the bottom of grooves, panels or all depressions below the general surface of any wood work.

Bits can also be clamped to back side of upright post, and outside of stock. In this position will plane into corners, will router out mortises for sash frame pulleys, or will smooth surfaces not easily reached with any other tool.

Each

No. 71—With one cutter each, 1/4 and 1/2 in; length 7 1/2 ins _____ $9 75
One in cardboard box; wt each 2 5/8 lbs.

FIBRE BOARD CUTTERS
STANLEY

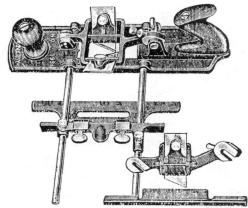

Japanned cast iron frame; rosewood handle and knob. Special tool steel cutters, correctly hardened and tempered to hold a keen cutting edge, and can be re-sharpened and honed in the same manner as regular plane iron. Cutters are held firmly and are easily and quickly adjusted for depth of cut. All parts are carefully machined and fitted and are replaceable. Especially designed as a combination tool for slitting, beveling, and grooving Masonite, Celotex, Insulite, Upson Board and any other fibre board.

Cutting off or slitting is easier, faster and leaves smooth edges. In addition, it can be used to bevel edges, cut beveled edge battens, cut grooves, make decorative designs such as squares, parallel lines, bricks and similar patterns.

Each

No. 193—Length 12 1/4 ins _____ $21 00
One in box complete with all attachments; wt each 6 lbs.

BEADERS
STANLEY UNIVERSAL

Nickel plated cast iron. For beading, reeding or fluting straight or irregular surfaces and light routering. Furnished with square gauge for straight work; oval gauge for curved work, eight superior cutters, embracing 6 ordinary sizes of beads 1/8 to 1/2 inch; 4 sets of reeds, 2 fluters, 3/16 and 1/4 inch and double router iron, 1/8 and 1/4 inch and a 5/8 inch blank.

Each

No. 66—Length over all 10 ins; width of cutters 1/8 to 1 in. assorted; wt each about 1 1/4 lbs _____ $5 40
One in cardboard box.

CARRIAGE MAKERS' RABBET PLANES

Adapted for mining, wagon making and other heavy work.

Flat Bottom.

Nos.	10½	10
Length, in.	9	13
Cutter, in.	2⅛	2⅛
W't, lbs.	3	4½
Each	$6.80	8.20

ONE IN A BOX

SIDE RABBET PLANES

Convenient tools for side-rabbeting and trimming dados, mouldings and grooves of all sorts. A reversible nose piece will give each tool a form by which it will work close up into corners.

No. 98—4 in., nickel plated, right hand, w't 8 oz. ....each $2.80

ONE IN A BOX

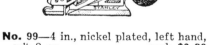

No. 99—4 in., nickel plated, left hand, w't 8 oz. ....each $2.80

ONE IN A BOX

UNIVERSAL HAND BEADERS

Very handy for beading, reeding or fluting straight or irregular surfaces and for light routering. The handles are curved to give ample room between the user's hands and the surface of the work.

No. 66—Width 11½ in., nickel plated stock, 7 steel cutters and 1 blank with 2 gauges for straight or curved work, w't 1¼ lbs, each $2.10

ONE IN A BOX

RABBET AND BLOCK PLANES

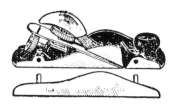

The detachable side will easily change this tool from block plane to a rabbet plane and vica versa. The cutter is adjustable end-wise and is set on askew.

No. 140—7 in., with detachable side, 1¾ in. cutter, w't 1¼ lbs.,

each $3.80

ONE IN A BOX

IMPROVED DADO

8 Inch, Iron Stock, with Depth Gauge and Two Adjustable Spurs.

Holds true in narrow widths where a wood plane will not. Has a skew cutter and adjustable depth gauge and spurs on each side of plane, thus allowing wear to be taken up and depth of the cut regulated.

Nos.	392	393	394
Cutter, in.	¼	⅜	½
Each	$3.70	3.95	4.20

Nos.	395	396	397
Cutter, in.	⅝	¾	⅞
Each	$4.40	4.60	4.80

ONE IN A BOX

CABINET MAKERS' RABBET PLANES

For fine cabinet or other work where extreme accuracy is required. The sides and bottom, being square with each other, the plane will lie perfectly flat on either side and can be worked either right or left hand. They have adjustable throats; this means that the width of the throat opening, or mouth, can be widened or narrowed as coarse or fine work may require. They are also fitted with the side groove or "Handy" grip feature. The cutters are adjustable end-wise.

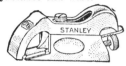

Nickel Plated, with Adjustable Throat.

No. 90—4 in., bull nose, adjustable, 1 in. cutter, w't 1 lb. ...each $5.10

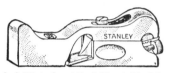

Nickel Plated, with Adjustable Throat.

Nos.	92	93	94
Length, in.	5½	6½	7½
Cutter, in.	¾	1	1¼
W't, lbs.	1½	1¾	2
Each	$5.10	6.10	7.10

ONE IN A BOX

CORNERING TOOLS

These tools are used by pattern makers and all wood workers for rounding sharp edges. They have a different size cutter at each end and their form is such that no depth gauge is required.

Nos.	28	29
Size, in.	5¾×⅝	5¾×⅞
Cutters, in.	1/16 & ⅛	¼ & ⅜
W't, lbs.	1¼	1½
Per dozen	$5.90	6.20

HALF DOZEN IN A BOX

CABINET SCRAPER BURNISHERS

This tool is used to put a smooth finishing edge to a cabinet scraper.

No. 01—Polished oval cast steel blade, wood handle with ferrule, entire length 8½ in., w't per doz. 1¼ lbs., per dozen $7.20

HALF DOZEN IN A BOX

"BAILEY" BLOCK PLANES

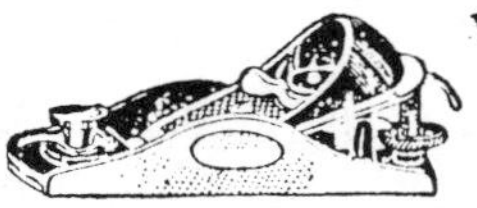

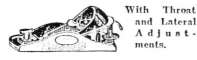

With Throat and Lateral Adjustments.

JAPANNED CAP

꞉os.	9½	15
Length, in.	6	7
Cutter, in.	1⅝	1⅝
W't each, lbs.	1½	1¾
Each	$2.90	3.10

NICKEL PLATED CAP

.	16	17
.gth, in.	6	7
.utter, in.	1⅝	1⅝
V't each, lbs.	1½	1¾
;ach	$3.30	3.60

ONE IN A BOX

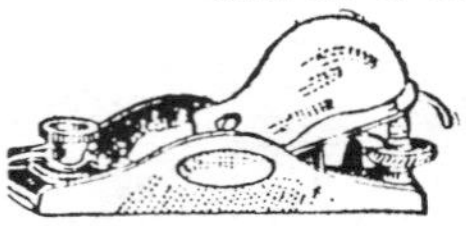

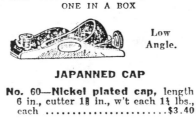

Knuckle joint with throat and lateral adjustment.

NICKEL PLATED CAP

The knuckle joint in the cap makes t a lever, too; and placing the cap in osition, will also clamp the cutter securely in its seat.

os.	18	19
ngth, in.	6	7
utter, in.	1⅝	1⅝
V't each, lbs.	1½	1½
;ach	$3.80	4.10

ONE IN A BOX

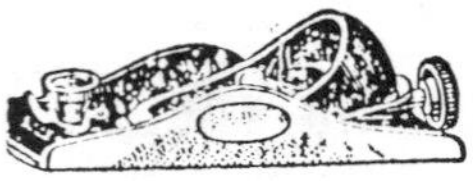

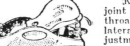

Low Angle.

JAPANNED CAP

No. 60—Nickel plated cap, length 6 in., cutter 1⅝ in., w't each 1½ lbs., each $3.40

Nos.	60½	65½
Length, in.	6	7
Cutter, in.	1⅝	1⅝
W't each, lbs.	1½	1½
Each	$3.10	3.30

No. 61—Nickel plated cap, length 6 in., cutter 1⅝ in., **rosewood knob,** w't 1½ lbs. ......each $2.90

ONE IN A BOX

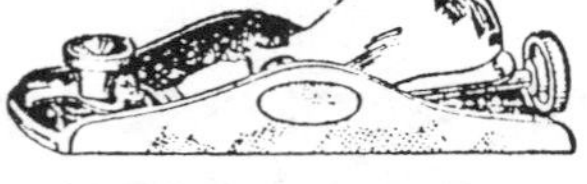

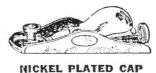

NICKEL PLATED CAP

No.	65
Length, in.	7
Cutter, in.	1⅝
W't each, lbs.	1½
Each	$4.00

ONE IN A BOX

BAILEY BLOCK PLANES

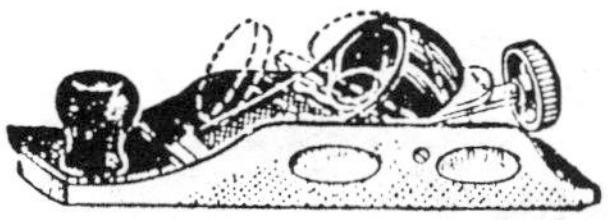

This plane has two slots and a movable cutter seat. When it is desirable to use it as a bull nose plane, the adjustable cutter seat can be reversed as indicated in cut.

No. 131—Double end, 8 in., 1⅝ in. cutter, w't 1½ lbs. ......each $3.60

ONE IN A BOX

STANLEY BLOCK PLANES

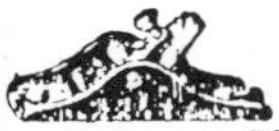

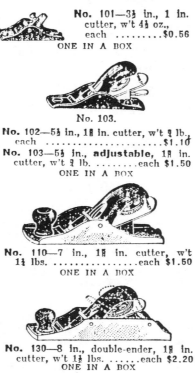

No. 101—3½ in., 1 in. cutter, w't 4½ oz., each $0.56

ONE IN A BOX

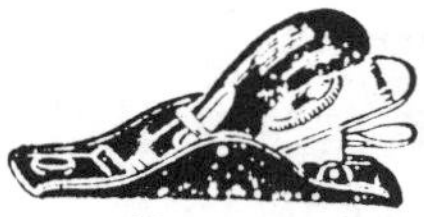

No. 103.

No. 102—5½ in., 1⅜ in. cutter, w't ¾ lb., each $1.10

No. 103—5½ in., **adjustable,** 1⅜ in. cutter, w't ⅞ lb. ....each $1.50

ONE IN A BOX

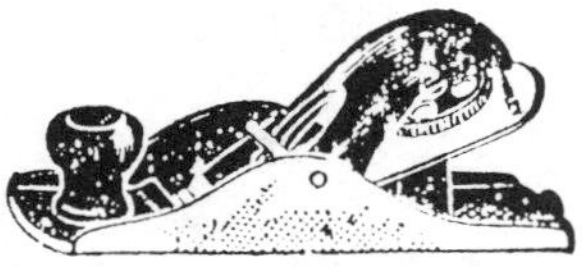

No. 110—7 in., 1⅝ in. cutter, w't 1¼ lbs. ....each $1.50

ONE IN A BOX

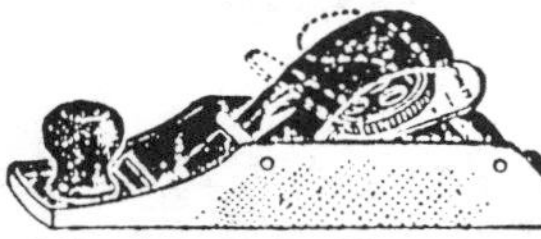

No. 130—8 in., double-ender, 1⅝ in. cutter, w't 1¼ lbs. ......each $2.20

ONE IN A BOX

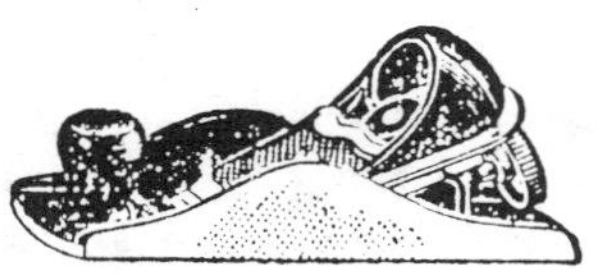

No. 220—7 in. adjustable, 1⅝ in. cutter, w't 1¼ lbs. ....each $2.20

ONE IN A BOX

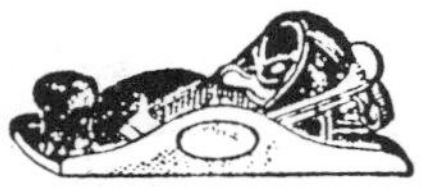

No. 203—Screw adjustment, rosewood knob, length 5½ in., 1⅜ in. cutter, w't ⅞ lb. ....each $1.90

ONE IN A BOX

CABINET MAKERS' EDGE PLANES

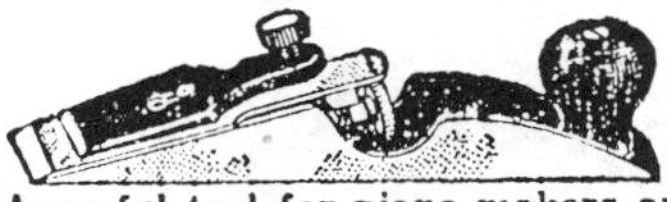

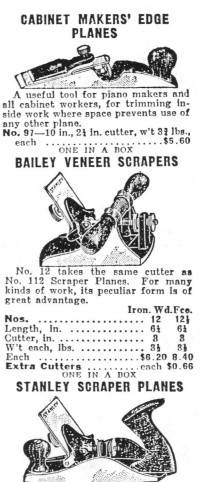

A useful tool for piano makers and all cabinet workers, for trimming inside work where space prevents use of any other plane.

No. 97—10 in., 2¼ in. cutter, w't 3¾ lbs., each $5.60

ONE IN A BOX

BAILEY VENEER SCRAPERS

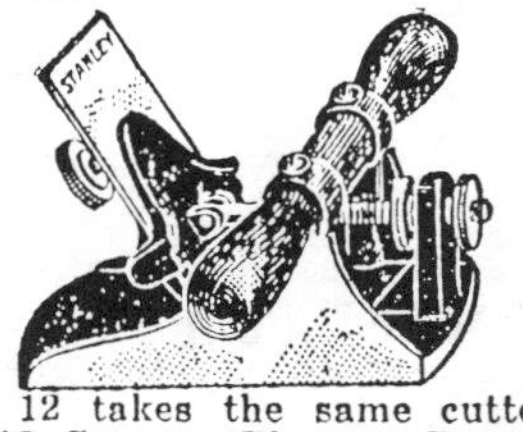

No. 12 takes the same cutter as No. 112 Scraper Planes. For many kinds of work, its peculiar form is of great advantage.

	Iron.	Wd.Fce.
Nos.	12	12½
Length, in.	6¼	6¼
Cutter, in.	3	3
W't each, lbs.	3½	3½
Each	$6.20	8.40
Extra Cutters ....each		$0.66

ONE IN A BOX

STANLEY SCRAPER PLANES

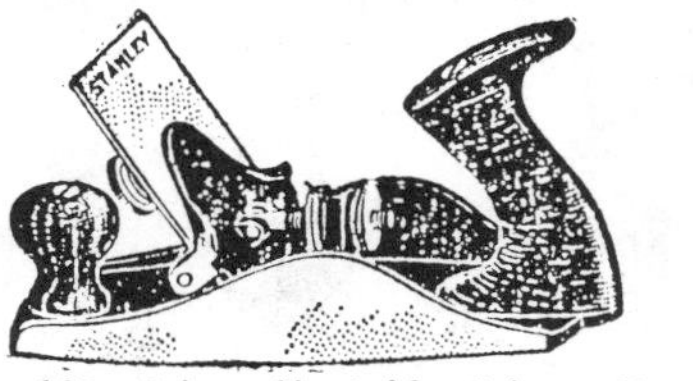

No. 112—9 in. adjustable, 3 in. cutter, with 1 scraper blade, w't 4 lbs., each $5.50

Extra Cutters, for scraping, each $0.66

Extra Cutters, for toothing, Nos. 22, 28, 32—22, 28 or 32 teeth each $0.90

ONE IN A BOX

BULL NOSE RABBET PLANES

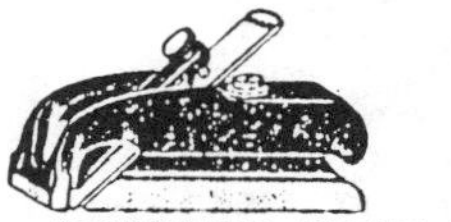

No. 75—4 in., iron stock, 1 in. cutter, w't 8 oz., each .$0.95

STANLEY EDGE TRIMMING PLANES

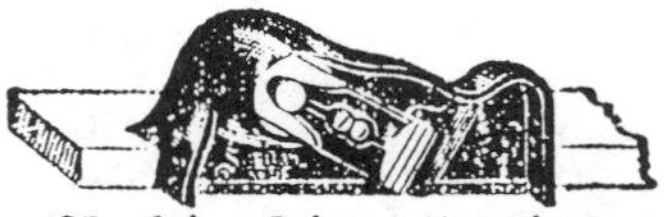

No. 95—6 in., ⅞ in. cutter, japanned, w't each 1¼ lbs. ....each $2.40

ONE IN A BOX

STANLEY ADJUSTABLE PLANES

TONGUING AND GROOVING

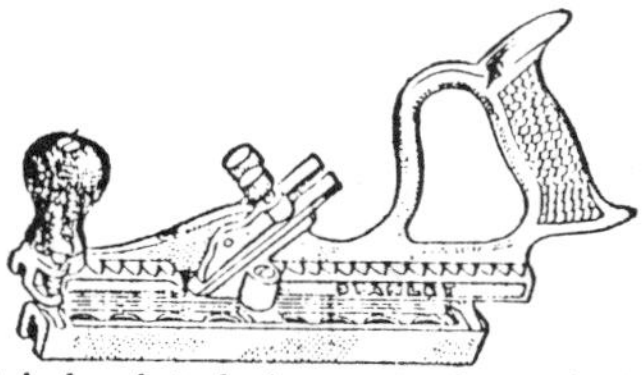

Nickel plated iron stock and face, including tonguing and grooving tools.

The fence is set in a center pivot and can be swung around and locked either way. Set one way it exposes two cutters for cutting the tongue and when reversed leaves only one exposed for making the groove.

No. 48—8¾ in., for ¾ to 1¼ in. boards, w't 3 lbs. ....each $6.80

No. 49—8 in., for ½ to ¾ in. boards, w't 2½ lbs. ....each $6.80

ONE IN A BOX

DOUBLE END MATCH

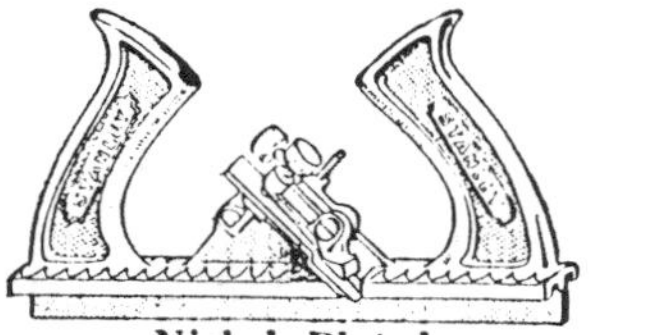

Nickel Plated.

Provided with both tongue and groove irons. With one side a tongue can be cut, and by reversing ends, the plane will cut a groove to fit.

No. 146—Matches ⅝ in. boards, cuts groove ⅛ in., w't 1½ lbs., each $5.10

No. 147—Matches ⅝ in. boards, cuts groove 3/16 in., w't 2 lbs., each $5.45

No. 148—Matches ⅞ in. boards, cuts groove ¼ in., w't 2¾ lbs., each $5.75

ONE IN A BOX

RABBET AND FILLISTER

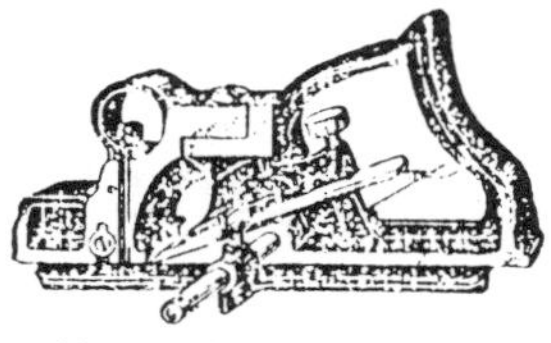

The sides and bottom being square with each other, the planes will lie perfectly flat on either side. Adjustable fence slides under bottom to regulate width of cut. Has one spur on each side and adjustable depth gauge. Is suitable for either right or left hand work. The front part of plane can be easily detached thus providing a bull nose plane.

No. 278—Japanned iron stock and fence, 6¾ in. long, 1 in. cutter, w't 2 lbs. ....each $4.10

ONE IN A BOX

IMPROVED RABBET

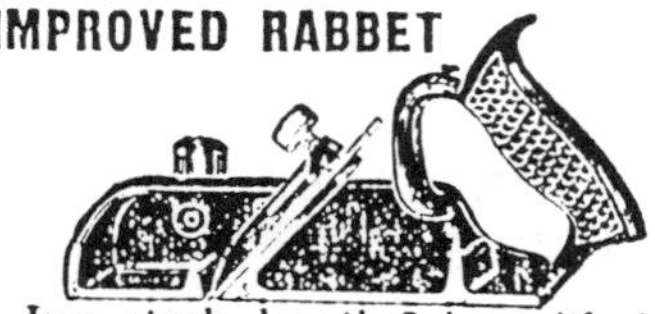

Iron stock, length 8 in., with depth gauge.

WITH SPUR

This plane will lie perfectly flat on either side, and can be used with right or left hand equally well, while planing into corners or up against perpendicular surfaces.

Nos.	190	191	192
Cutter, in.	1½	1¼	1
W't, lbs.	2½	2¼	2
Each	$3.80	3.55	3.30

ONE IN A BOX

DUPLEX RABBET AND FILLISTER

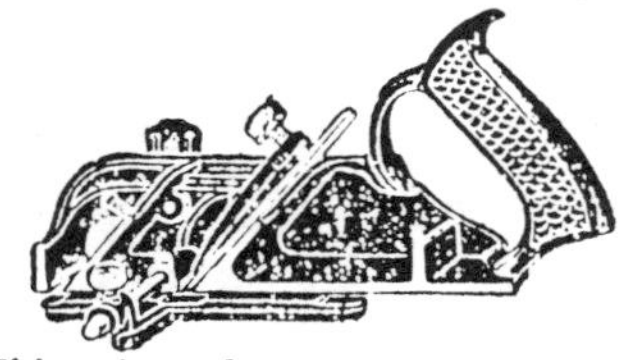

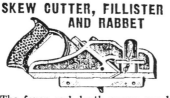

This plane has two seats for the cutter, one for regular work and the other where a bull nose is required. Has spur and removable depth gauge. Adjustable fence can be used on either side and slides under the bottom regulating width of cut. To use as rabbet plane, remove fence and arms.

No. 78—8½ in. iron stock and fence, 1½ in. cutter, w't 3 lbs., each $4.20

ONE IN A BOX

SKEW CUTTER, FILLISTER AND RABBET

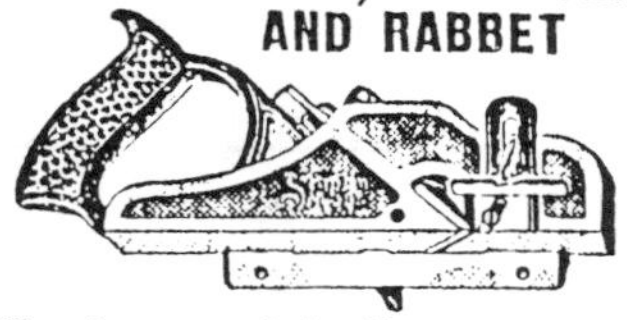

The fence and depth gauge can be attached to either side so that the plane can be used equally well for right or left hand work. The adjustable fence slides under the bottom, regulating the width of the cut. By removing arms and fence a skew cutter rabbet plane is obtained.

No. 289—8½ in., japanned, 1¾ in. cutter with fence and depth gauge and two adjustable spurs, one on each side, w't 4 lbs. ....each $4.90

ONE IN A BOX

WOODWORKERS' ROUTER

For surfacing the bottom of grooves and depressions parallel with the general surface of the work. The open throat design gives more freedom for chips and a better view of the work and cutter. The latter has an attachment for regulating the thickness of the chip and a second attachment for closing the throat for use on narrow surfaces.

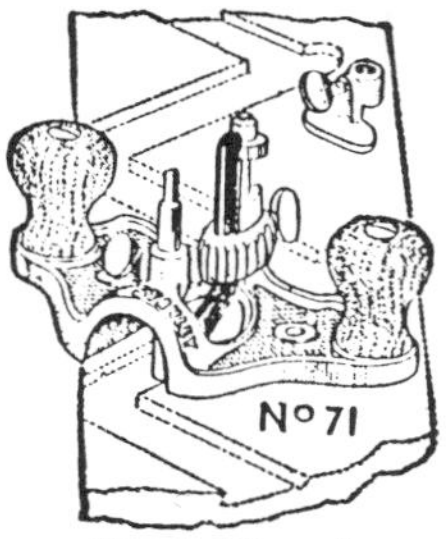

Open Throat.

No. 71—Nickel plated, width 7½ in., ¼ and ½ in. steel bits, with throat attachment, w't 2⅛ lbs., each $5.20

ONE IN A BOX

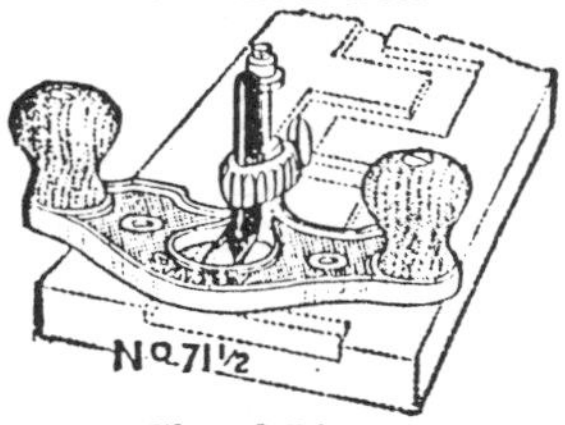

Closed Throat.

No. 71½—Nickel plated, width 7½ in., ¼ and ½ in. steel bits, w't 2¼ lbs., each $4.10

ONE IN A BOX

DOOR TRIM

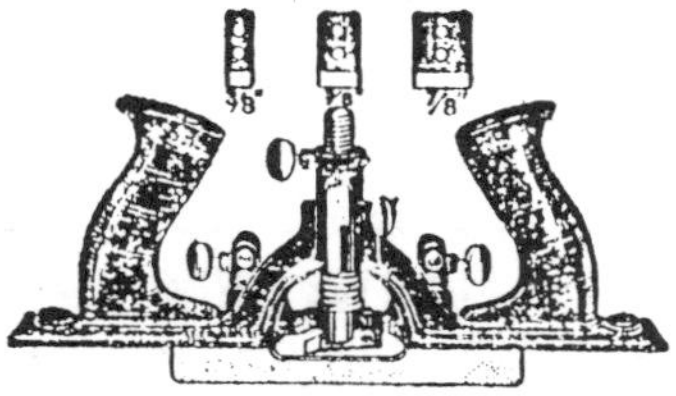

This new plane will make mortises for Butts, Face Plates, Strike Plates, Escutcheons, etc., without the use of a butt gauge or chisel. Cutter can be set to work from either end of the plane or across it. Spring prevents taking a heavier chip than can be easily carried.

No. 171—11 in., japanned, nickel plated trimmings, rosewood handles, 3 forged steel cutters, w't 3 lbs., each $7.50

ONE IN A BOX

STANLEY PLANES

BEADING, CENTER, PLOW, DADO, RABBET, FILLISTER, MATCH, SASH, SLITTING AND MOULDING

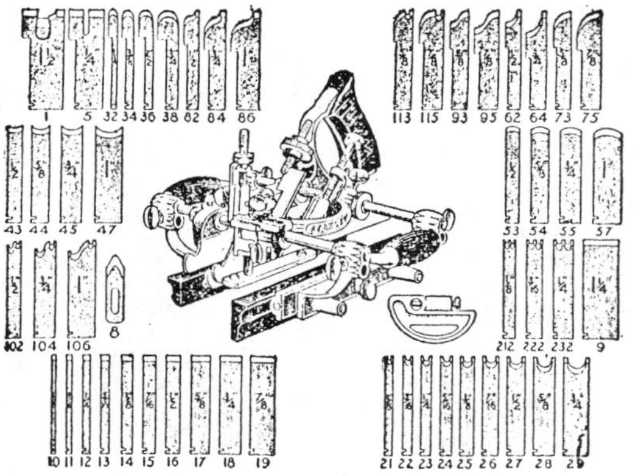

THE MOST COMPLETE STANLEY SET

Will accomodate cutters of almost any shape and size. All metal parts nickel plated, handle and fences of selected rosewood, all parts well finished.

No. 55—Length 10 in., w't 15¼ lbs., complete with 52 cutters, each $39.00

ONE IN A BOX

BEADING, CENTER BEADING, PLOW, DADO, RABBET, FILLISTER, MATCH PLANE, SASH AND SLITTING

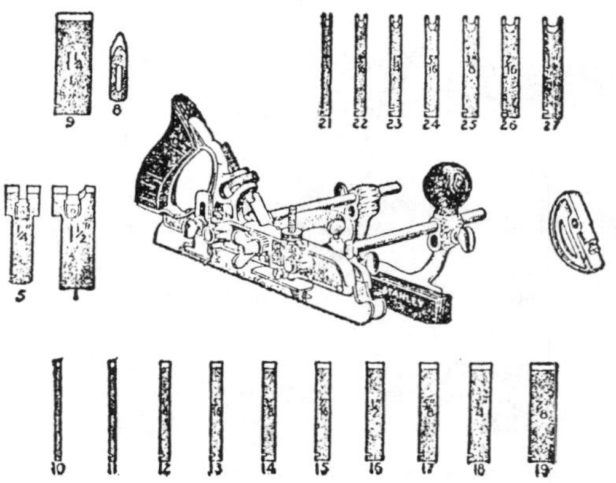

Seven beading tools, ⅛ in., 3/16 in., ¼ in., 5/16 in., ⅜ in., 7/16 in. and ½ in., ten plow and dado bits—⅛ in., 3/16 in., ¼ in., 5/16 in., ⅜ in., 7/16 in., ½ in., ⅝ in., ¾ in. and ⅞ in., a tonguing tool, a sash and a slitting cutter, are regularly furnished.

Each plane has an adjustable fence, a depth gauge, spurs for use across the grain, a cam leveling or steading rest and can be used either right or left hand.

No. 45—Nickel plated, with twenty tools .... each $19.80

Extra Bottoms and Cutters.

By substituting special bottoms for the sliding section, cutters as follows may be used. Special bottom required for each cutter. Prices of hollows and rounds include two cutters and two bottoms, of nosing tool, one cutter and one bottom.

No. 6—Hollow and round ½ in. cutters work ¾ in. circle,
per pair $3.00

No. 8—Hollow and round ⅝ in. cutters work 1 in. circle,
per pair 3.00

No. 10—Hollow and round ¾ in. cutters work 1¼ in. circle,
per pair 3.30

No. 12—Hollow and round 1 in. cutters work 1½ in. circle,
per pair 3.30

No. 5—Nosing tool, 1¼ in. cutters work 1½ in. circle...... each 2.40

Extra Cutters, 20 tool bits, etc. .... per set 10.00

Extra Screws .... per dozen .96

Extra Spurs .... per dozen .96

ONE IN A BOX

PLOW, BEADING AND MATCHING

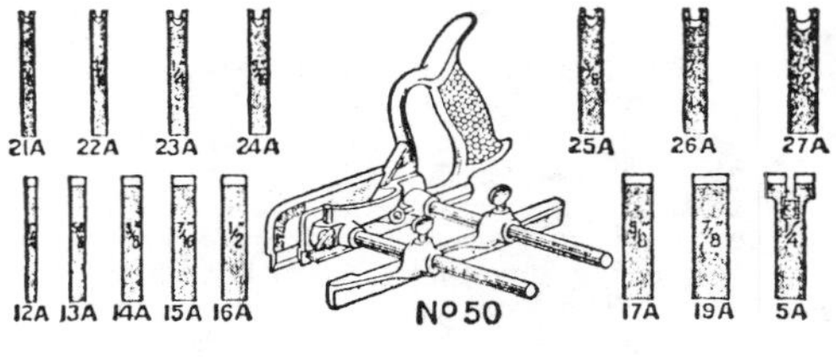

For light work, consists of a main stock with metal handle, carrying a spur and a depth gauge and forming a support for one side of cutter, a sliding section carrying a spur and forming a support for other side of cutter, a fence with a 5 inch adjustment.

The cutters comprise 7 plow and dado bits—¼, 5/16, ⅜, 7/16, ½, ⅝ and ⅞ inch, 7 beading tools, ⅛, 3/16, ¼, 5/16, ⅜, 7/16 and ½ inch, and a ¼ inch tonguing tool.

No. 50—Nickel plated, length 9½ inches, 15 cutters, w't 3½ lbs.,
each $10.90

ONE IN A BOX

PLOW, DADO, FILLISTER AND MATCHING

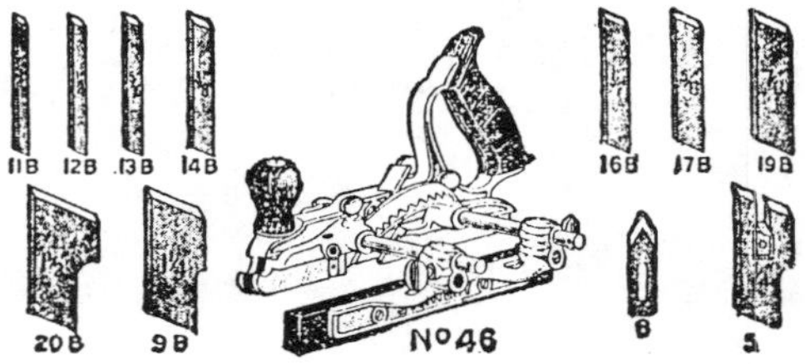

Skew cutters are the feature of this plane, main stock carries a spur, depth gauge, slitting cutter, sliding section carrying a spur forming an extra sole for the plane. Rosewood handle and knob.

Cutters comprise 8 plow and dado bits—3/16, ¼, 5/16, ⅜, ½, ⅝, ⅞, 1¼ in., 1½ in. fillister cutter, ¼ in. tonguing tool and slitting cutter.

No. 46—Nickel plated, length 10½ in., 11 cutters, w't 5¾ lbs., each $14.00

ONE IN A BOX

SIEGLEY AND STANLEY PLANES

SIEGLEY ADJUSTABLE IRON

SMOOTH

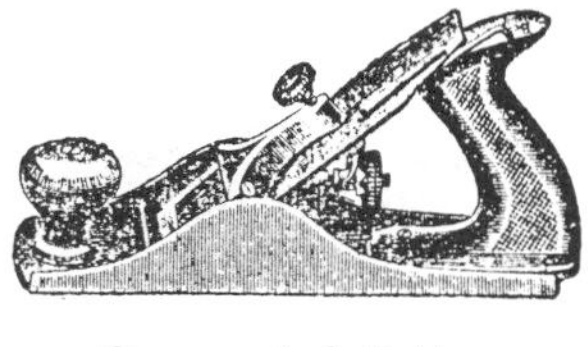

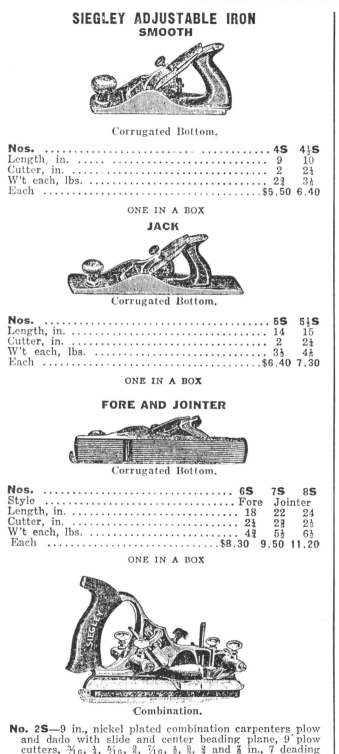

Corrugated Bottom.

Nos.	**4S**	**$4\frac{1}{2}$S**
Length, in.	9	10
Cutter, in.	2	$2\frac{1}{4}$
W't each, lbs.	$2\frac{3}{4}$	$3\frac{1}{8}$
Each	$5.50	6.40

ONE IN A BOX

JACK

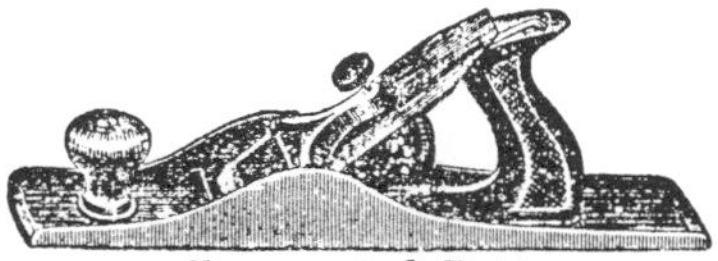

Corrugated Bottom.

Nos.	**5S**	**$5\frac{1}{2}$S**
Length, in.	14	15
Cutter, in.	2	$2\frac{1}{4}$
W't each, lbs.	$3\frac{1}{2}$	$4\frac{1}{8}$
Each	$6.40	7.30

ONE IN A BOX

FORE AND JOINTER

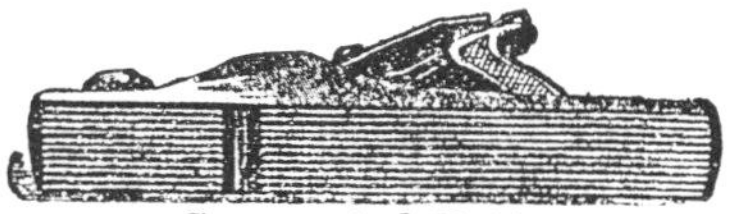

Corrugated Bottom.

Nos.	**6S**	**7S**	**8S**
Style	Fore	Jointer	
Length, in.	18	22	24
Cutter, in.	$2\frac{1}{4}$	$2\frac{3}{8}$	$2\frac{1}{2}$
W't each, lbs.	$4\frac{3}{4}$	$5\frac{1}{2}$	$6\frac{1}{2}$
Each	$8.30	9.50	11.20

ONE IN A BOX

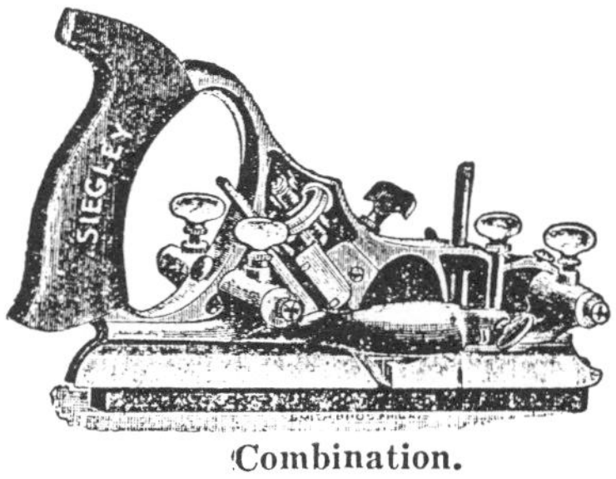

Combination.

No. 2S—9 in., nickel plated combination carpenters plow and dado with slide and center beading plane, 9 plow cutters, $\frac{3}{16}$, $\frac{1}{4}$, $\frac{5}{16}$, $\frac{3}{8}$, $\frac{7}{16}$, $\frac{1}{2}$, $\frac{5}{8}$, $\frac{3}{4}$ and $\frac{7}{8}$ in., 7 deading tool, $\frac{1}{8}$, $\frac{3}{16}$, $\frac{1}{4}$, $\frac{5}{16}$, $\frac{3}{8}$, $\frac{7}{16}$ and $\frac{1}{2}$, in., $\frac{7}{8}$ in. match cutter and sash tool, w't $7\frac{1}{2}$ lbs. ....each **$15.70**

ONE IN A BOX

STANLEY CIRCULAR

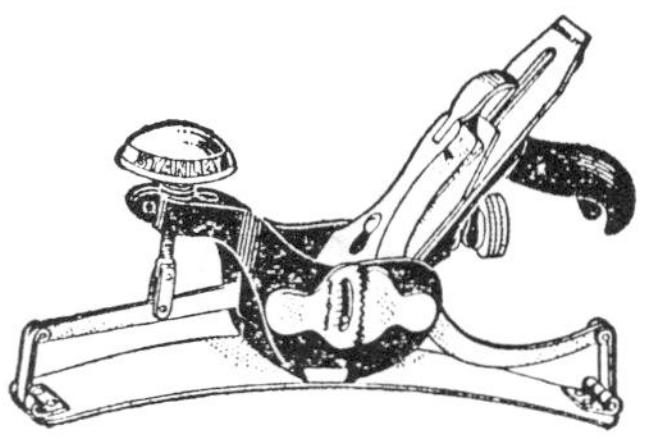

No. 113—10 in., adjustable, $1\frac{3}{4}$ in. cutter, w't $3\frac{1}{2}$ lbs., each ....$

ONE IN A BOX

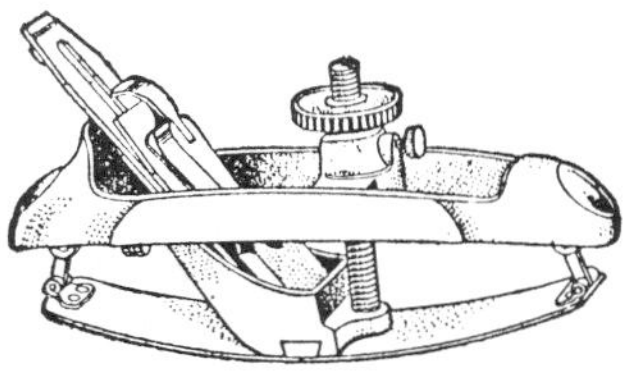

VICTOR, 10 in. adjustable, $1\frac{3}{4}$ in. cutter, w't each 4 lbs.

No. 20—**Japanned** ....each **$11.70**

ONE IN A BOX

STANLEY IMPROVED SCRUB

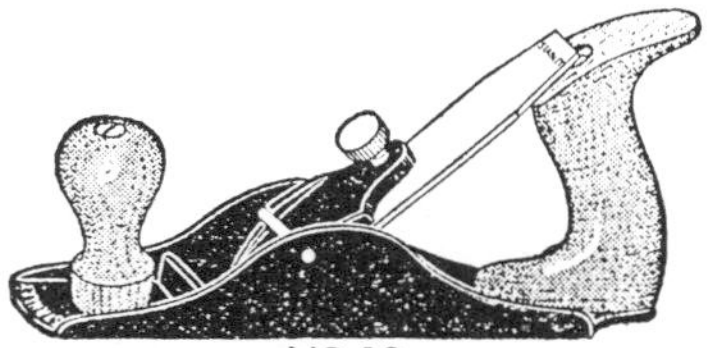

N°40

This tool has a single iron with cutting edge rounded, and is particularly adapted for roughing down work before using jack or other planes.

Nos.	**40**	**$40\frac{1}{2}$**
Length, in	$9\frac{1}{2}$	$10\frac{1}{2}$
Cutter, in.	$1\frac{1}{8}$	$1\frac{1}{2}$
Each	$3.10	4.20

ONE IN A BOX

STANLEY LOW ANGLE BLOCK

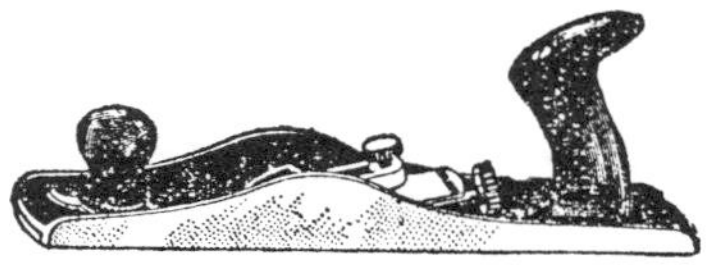

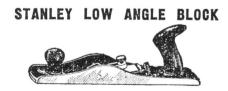

The construction of this plane is such that it is especially adapted for use in cutting across the grain on heavy work, where more power is required than can be obtained by use of the ordinary block plane. The plane is fitted with an adjustable throat, which enables the user to work equally well on hard or soft wood.

No. 62—14 in., 2 in. cutter, w't 4 lbs. ....each **$7.20**

ONE IN A BOX

STANLEY PLANES

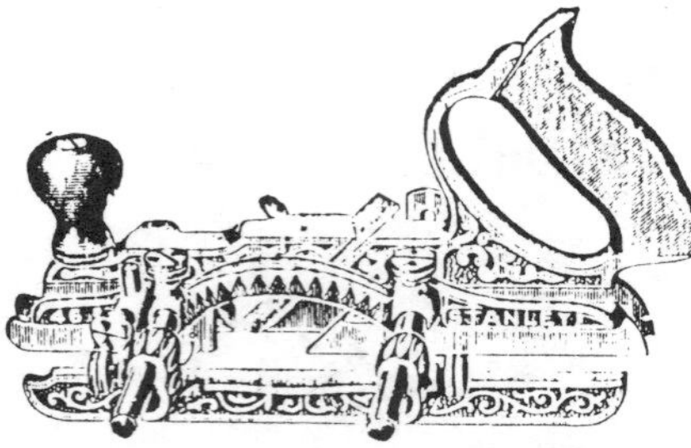

TRAUT'S ADJUSTABLE DADO, FILLETSTER, PLOW, ETC.

This Tool is Accompanied by Eight Plow and Dado Bits (1/16, 1/4, 3/16, 3/8, 1/2, 5/8, 7/8 and 1 1/4 Inch), a Fillester Cutter, a Slitting Blade and a Tonguing Tool All(Excepting the Slitting Blade) are Secured in the main stock on a skew.

No. 46 Nickel-plated Stock and Fence, 10 in. Long....Each, **$10.92**

STANLEY ADJUSTABLE BEADING, RABBET AND MATCHING PLANE

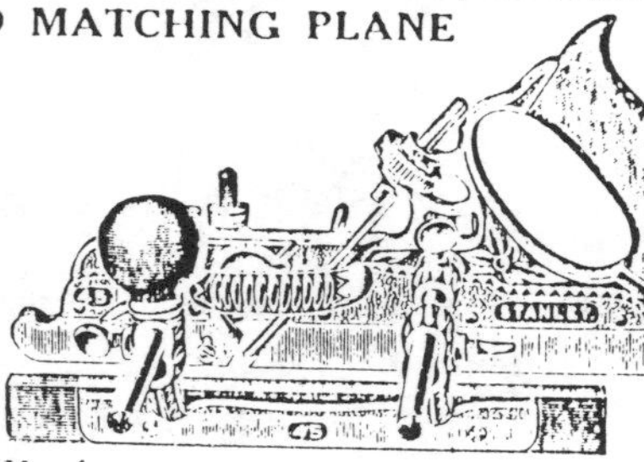

This Plane Combines a Main Stock and a Sliding Section so Arranged that Cutters of Different Widths Can be Used Each Plane is Fitted with an Adjustable Fence or Guide and a Depth Gauge, and also with Spurs for Use in Working Across the grain. This Plane can be Used Right or Left Hand.

This Plane Embraces Beading and Center Beading Plane; Rabbet and Fillester; Dado; Plow; Matching Plane; Sash Plane; and a Superior Slitting Plane.

Each Plane Has Seven Beading Tools (1/8, 3/16, 1/4, 5/16, 3/8, 7/16 and 1/2 Inch), Ten Plow and Dado Bits (1/8, 3/16, 1/4, 5/16, 3/8, 7/16, 1/2, 5/8, 3/4 and 7/8 inch), a Slitting Blade, a Tonguing Tool and a Sash Tool.

No. 45 Nickel-plated, with Twenty Tools, Bits, Etc....Each, **$12.00**

WOODWORKERS' ROUTER

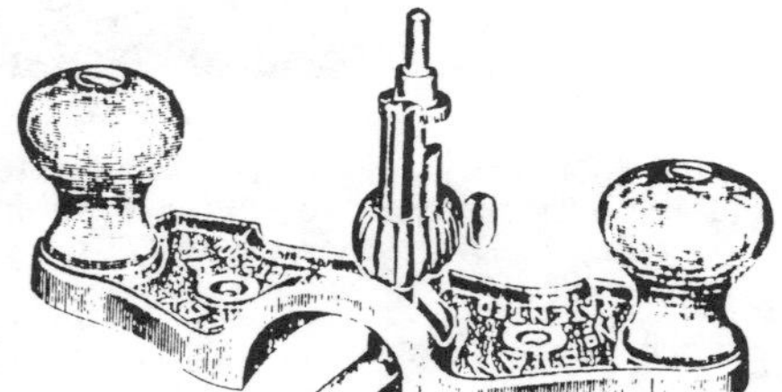

This Tool Should be Added to the Kit of Every Skilled Carpenter, Cabinet Maker, Stair Builder, Pattern Maker or Wheelwright. It is Perfectly Adapted to Smooth the Bottom of Grooves, Panels or All Depressions Below the General Surface of Any Woodwork.

The Bits Can also Be Clamped to the Back Side of the Upright Post and Outside the Stock. In this Position They will Plane into Corners, Will Router Out Mortises for Sash-frame Pulleys, or Will Smooth Surfaces Not Easily Reached with Any Other Tool

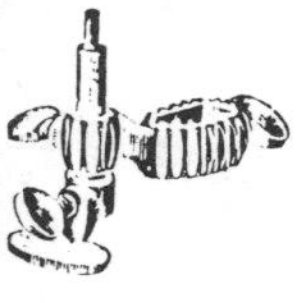

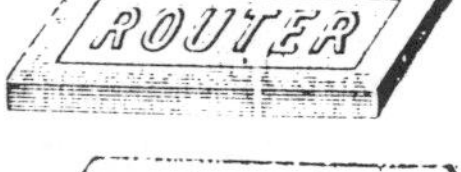

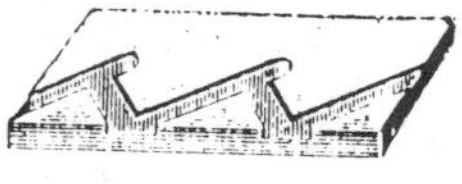

The Attachment Shown in Small Cut Is Furnished with Each Plane.

It Can Be Substituted for the Collar that Holds the Cutter When Work Requires a Plane with a Closed Throat.

No. 71 Nickel-plated Stock, with Steel Bits (1/4 and 1/2 in.).Each, **$2.80**

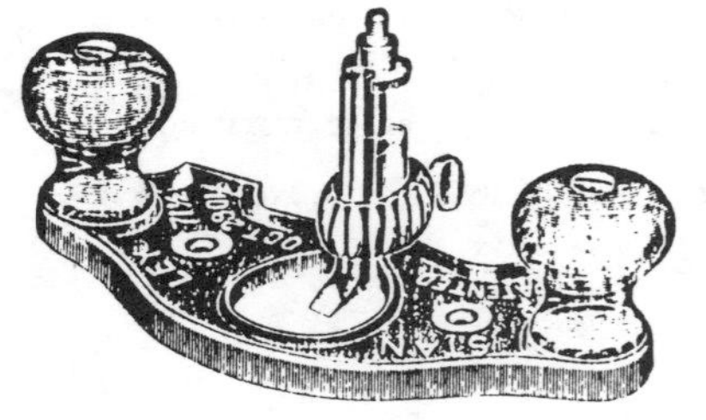

With Closed Throat

Nickel-plated Stock, with Steel Bits (1/4 and 1/2 Inch).

No. 71½..Each, **$2.20**

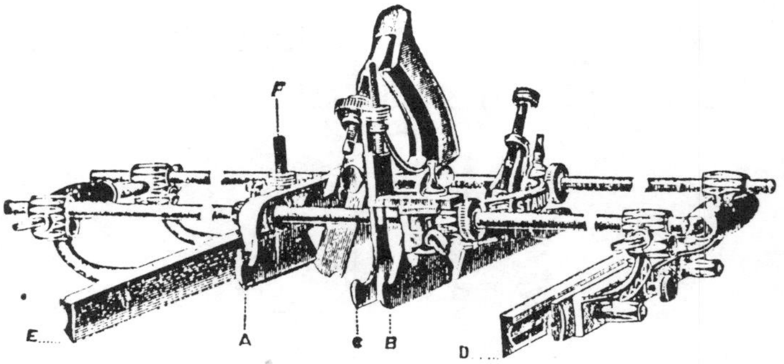

PATENT UNIVERSAL

No. 55 Stanley's Universal Plane, with 52 Tools, Etc...Each, **$23.86**

The Plane is Nickel-plated; the 52 Cutters are Arranged in four Separate Cases; and the Entire Outfit is Packed in a Neat Wooden Box.

This Plane Consists of:—

A Main Stock (A) with Two Sets of Transverse Sliding Arms, a Depth Gauge (F) adjusted by a Screw, and a Slitting Cutter with Stop.

A Sliding Section (B) with a Patent Vertically Adjustable Bottom.

The Auxiliary Bottom (C) is to be Placed in Front of the Cutter, as an Extra Support, or Stop, When Needed. This Bottom is Adjustable Both Vertically and Laterally.

Fences (D) and (E). Fence D Has a Lateral Adjustment by Means of a Screw, for Extra Fine Work. The Fences can be Used on Either Side of the Plane, and the Rosewood Guides Can be Tilted to any Desired Angle, up to 45°, by Loosening the Screws on the Face. Fence E Can be Reversed for Center Beading Wide Boards.

An Adjustable Stop to be Used in Beading the Edges of Matched Boards, is Inserted on the Left Hand Side of Sliding Section (B).

This Plane Takes the Place of a Full Assortment of So-called "Fancy Planes." The Same Assortment of "Fancy Planes" Would Cost Many Times as Much as No. 55 The Weight of this Plane and 52 Tools is 14 Pounds.

By Means of the Patent Adjustable Bottom and the Auxiliary Center Bottom it is Possible to Use a Cutter of Practically Any Shape with this Plane. This Design of Bottom is Not Used in any Other Plane Now Made. Special Cutters Will be Made to Order or Blanks from Which Workmen Can File up Any Form They May Require Will be Furnished as Ordered.

Directions

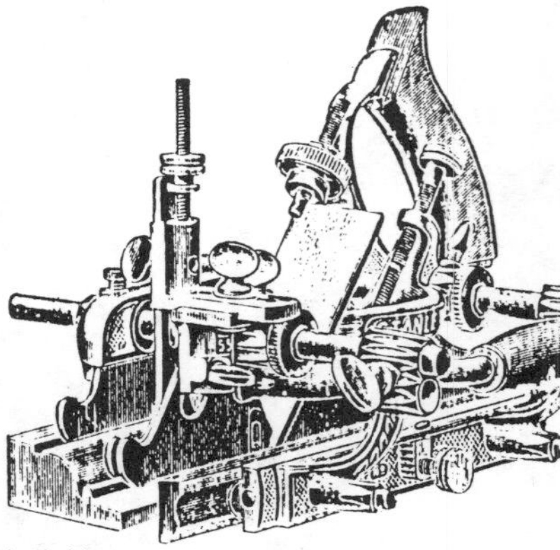

Moulding Plane.—Insert a Cutter, and Adjust Bottom of Sliding Section (B) to Conform to the Shape of the Cutter; then by Means of the Two Check-nuts on the Transverse Arms, fasten this Section Firmly—Before Tightening the Thumb-screws which Secure the Sliding Section to the Arms. When Needed, Adjust Auxiliary Center Bottom (C) for an Additional Support in Front of the Cutter.

By Tilting the Rosewood Guides on Fences D and E, Mouldings of Various Angles May be Formed.

Match, Sash, Beading, Reeding, Fluting, Hollow, Round, Plow, Rabbet, and Fillester Plane.—Use in Same Manner as for Mouldings. In Working Match and Sash Cutters, the Auxiliary Center Bottom (C) May be Used as a Stop.

Dado.—Remove the Fences (D and E) and Set the Spurs parallel with the Edges of Cutter. Insert Long Adjustable Stop on Left Hand Side of Sliding Section.

Slitting Plane.—Insert the Cutter and Stop on Right Hand Side of Main Stock, and Use Fence D or E for Guide.

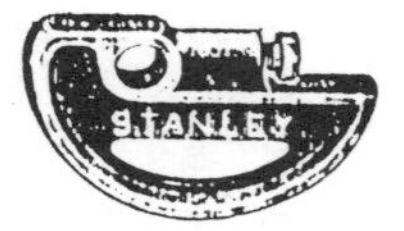

CAM REST

This Patented Rest is now Furnished with No. 55 and No. 45 Planes. It Can be Fastened to Either Arm Between Plane and Fence, When Set Wide Apart, and Helps to Keep the Plane Level.

All Above, One in a Box.

STANLEY PLANES

CIRCULAR

By Means of the Graduated Scale on the Gears, the Face can be Accurately Set to Work an Arc of the Same Circle, Both Concave and Convex, by Turning the Knob on the Front of the Plane.

No. 113 Adjustable Circular, 1¾ in. Cutter............Each, $4.30

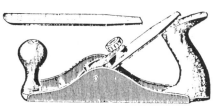

IMPROVED SCRUB PLANES

This Tool has a Single Iron, with the Cutting Edge Rounded. It is Particularly Adapted for Roughing Down Work Before Using a Jack or Other Plane.

No. 40 Iron Stock, 9½ in. in Length, 1¼ in. Cutter......Each, $1.54

BELT MAKERS

This Tool is Used by Belt Makers, for Chamfering Down the Laps of a Belt, Before Fastening Them Together. It is Equally Well Adapted to use in Repairing Belts in All Large Manufacturing Establishments.

No. 11 2⅜ in. Cutter..................................Each, $3.08

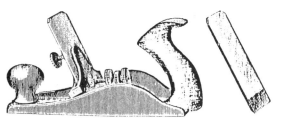

ADJUSTABLE SCRAPER PLANE

This Tool is Used for Scraping and Finishing Veneers or Cabinet Work. It can Also be Used as Tooth Plane.

No. 112 9 in. Long, 3 in. Cutter.....................Each, $2.94

ADJUSTABLE VENEER SCRAPER

This Tool Takes the Same Cutters as Scraper Plane No. 112, Described Above. For Many Kinds of Work its Peculiar Form is of Great Advantage.

No. 12 Adjustable Veneer Scraper, 3 in. Cutter............Each, $3.32
Cutters for Above Scraper.. Each .40

No. 12

CABINET-MAKERS' SCRAPER

The General Feature of These Scrapers is that When in Use the Cutter Rests Against the Front Edge of the Mouth Under a Slight Pressure.

In Working, the Cutter Springs Backward, Thereby Opening the Mouth and Allowing the Shaving to Pass Through it; but as Soon as Working Pressure is Released the Cutter Springs Back to Normal Position.

This Closes the Mouth and Prevents and Dust or Shaving Falling Through on the Finished Work.

These Scrapers are Made in Two Styles

First, a Rabbet Scraper with Handle and Knob Pivoted to Allow Tilting for Convenience in Working in Corners.

Cut Showing Pivoted Handle and Knob

Second, Without a Rabbet Mouth and with Stationary Handles.

No. 85 Rabbet Cabinet Scraper, Tilting Rosewood Handle and Knob, 2 in. Cutter. Length 8 in..........Each, $3.00
No. 87 Cabinet Scraper, Stationary Rosewood Handle and Knob, 2 in. Cutter, Length 8 in...............Each, 2.80

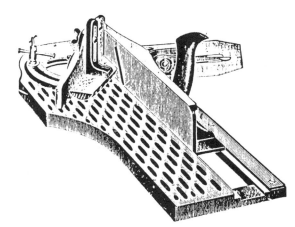

STANLEY CHUTE BOARD

This Tool, Sometimes Called a Jack Board, is a Very Important One for All Wood Workers, Especially Pattern Makers and Cabinet Makers. It is Also Useful for Amateurs.

The Board is Made of Cast Iron, of Ribbed Construction, and has an Adjustable Runway for the Plane.

The Swivel is Indexed for Cutting a Square and a Mitre, but can be Fastened with the Clamping Screw at any Desired Angle Between Zero and 90 Degrees.

The Plane Iron Being Fitted with a Lateral Adjustment, a Cut Giving any Ordinary Draft to a Pattern can be Made.

The Sliding Back will Support the Work Close to the Plane, Preventing it from Splintering.

The Sliding Back Clamp will Hold any Shaped Work in Position to be Planed.

The Plane is Specially Constructed to Fit the Board, and the Iron is Set on a Skew Making a Smooth, Keen Cut.

No. 52 Japanned, 22 in. Long, 9 in. Wide.............Each, $16.00

IRON BLOCK PLANES
STANLEY

Non-Adjustable

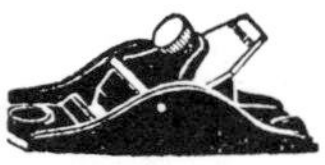

Japanned iron frame and trimmings, tempered steel cutters, boss inger rest on plate. Length 3½ inches, utter 1 inch.

Each
No. 101—Wt. each ¼ lb............$0.46

Adjustable

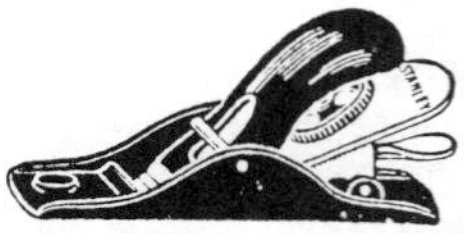

Japaned iron frame and trimmings. Cutter adjustable endwise by a lever. Bottom milled and ground, boss finger rest on plate. Tempered steel cutters. Length 5½ inches, cutter 1⅜ inch.

Each
No. 103—Wt. each ⅞ lb...........$1.00

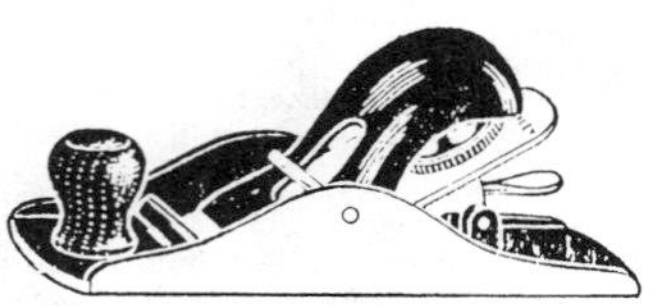

Adjustable

Japanned iron frame. Cutter adjusted endwise by lever. Bottom and sides milled and ground. Tempered steel cutters. Rosewood knob. Length 7 inches, cutter 1⅝ inches.

Each
No. 120—Wt. each 1⅜ lbs. $1.50

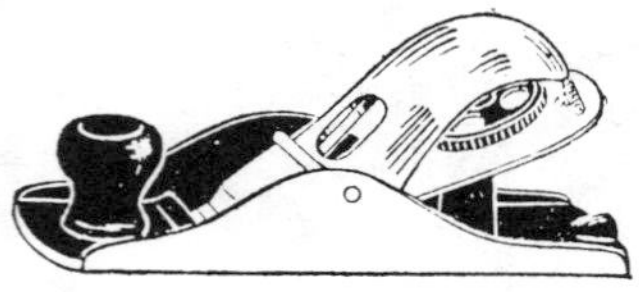

Non-Adjustable

Japanned iron frame. Bottom and sides are milled and ground. Tempered steel cutters. Nickel plated lever cap. Rosewood knob.

Length 7 inches, cutter width 1⅝ inches.

Each
No. 110—Wt. each 1⅜ lbs.........$1.00

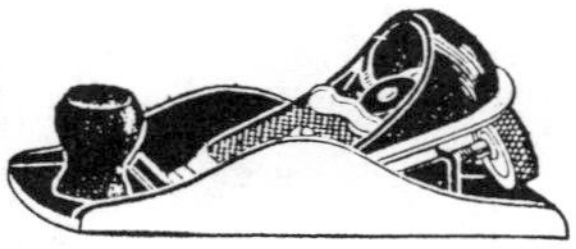

Adjustable

Japaned iron frame. Cutter adjusted endwise by lever. Bottom and sides milled and ground. Tempered steel cutter. Rosewood knob.

Length 7 inches, cutter width 1¼ inches.

Each
No. 220—Wt. each 1¼ lbs.........$1.50

All above, one in a box.

IRON BLOCK PLANES
STANLEY BAILEY PATTERN

Adjustable

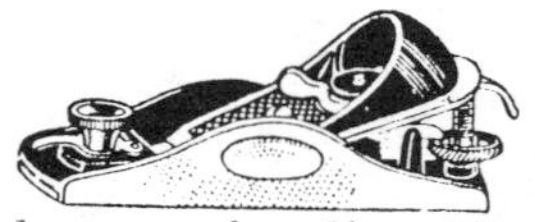

Japanned iron frame and trimmings; tempered steel cutter at 20 degree angle, adjustable endwise and sidewise; throat adjustable for coarse or fine work. Ground bottom and sides. Length 6 inches, cutter width 1⅝ in.

Each
No. 9½—Wt. each 1½ lbs.........$2.00

Adjustable

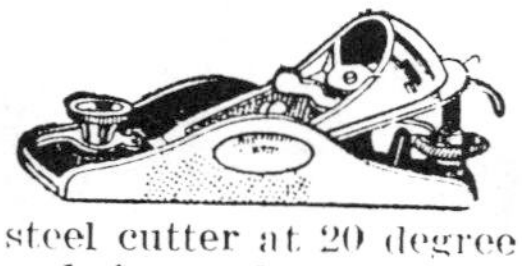

Japanned iron frame. Nickel plated trimmings; tempered steel cutter at 20 degree angle, adjustable endwise and sidewise; throat adjustable for coarse or fine work. Ground bottom and sides.

Nos.	Each	Length, inches	Width of cutter, inches	Wt. each, lbs.
16	$2.60	6	1⅝	1½
17	2.90	7	1⅝	1⅝

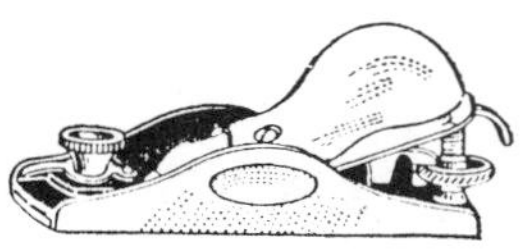

Adjustable Knuckle Joint

Japanned iron frame, nickel plated trimmings, tempered steel cutter. Knuckle joint in the cap makes it a lever, placing cap in position; clamps cutter securely to seat. Angle adjustable endwise and sidewise, ground bottom and sides.

Nos.	Each	Length, inches	Width of cutter, inches	Wt. each, lbs.
18	$2.70	6	1⅝	1½
19	3.00	7	1⅝	1⅝

STEEL BLOCK PLANES
STANLEY

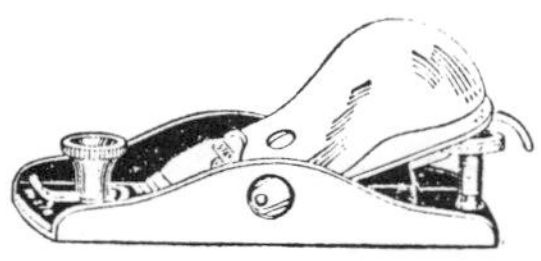

Adjustable, Knuckle Joint

Steel frame and front, tempered steel cutter. Knuckle joint in the cap makes it a lever, placing cap in position; clamps cutter securely to seat. Angle adjustable endwise and sidewise; ground bottom and sides.

Length 6 inches, cutter width 1⅝ inches.

Each
No. S18—Wt. each 1¼ lbs.........$3.70

All above, one in a box.

IRON BLOCK PLANES
STANLEY LOW ANGLE

Adjustable, Knuckle Joint

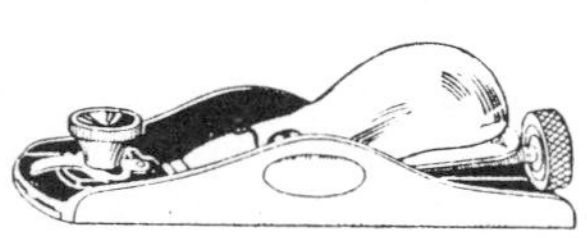

Japanned iron frame, nickel plated trimmings, tempered steel cutter at 12 degree angle. Knuckle joint in the cap makes it a lever cutter, adjusted endwise by means of adjusting screw; ground sides and bottom.

Length 7 inches, cutter width 1⅝ inches.

Each
No. 65—Wt. each 1⅜ lbs..........$3.00

STANLEY DOUBLE END

Adjustable

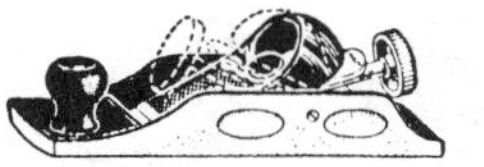

Japaned iron frame and trimmings. Tempered steel cutters adjustable endwise. Ground bottom and sides. Rosewood knob.

Two mouths and a reversible cutter seat. Converted into a bull nose plane by throwing over the adjusting screw, reversing cutter seat.

Length 8 in., cutter width ⅝ inch.

Each
No. 131—Wt. each 1¾ lbs.........$2.90

STANLEY BLOCK AND RABBET

Adjustable

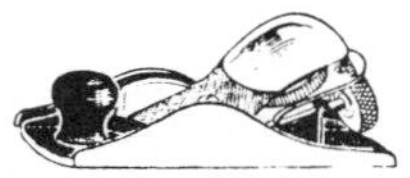

Japanned iron frame, nickel plated trimmings. A detachable side changes it from a block plane to a rabbet plane. Tempered steel skew cutter adjustable endwise, bottom and sides ground and milled. Rosewood handle. Length 7 inches, cutter width 1⅝ inches.

Each
No. 140—Wt. each 1⅝ lbs.........$2.60

STANLEY LOW ANGLE

Adjustable

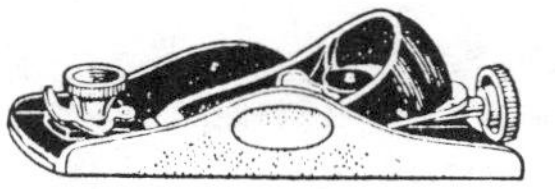

Japanned iron frame. Cutter at 12 degree angle and adjusted endwise by adjusting screw. Tempered steel cutter, ground bottom and sides.

Japanned Frame and Trimmings

Nos.	Each	Length, inches	Width, of cutter, inches	Wt. each, lbs.
60½	$2.20	6	1⅜	1⅛
65½	2.50	7	1⅝	1⅜

Japanned Frame, Nickel Plated Trimmings

No.	Each	Length, inches	Width of cutter, inches	Wt. each, lbs.
60	$2.50	6	1⅜	1⅛

All above, one in a box.

EXTRA PARTS FOR STANLEY PLANES

FOR BAILEY IRON PLANES

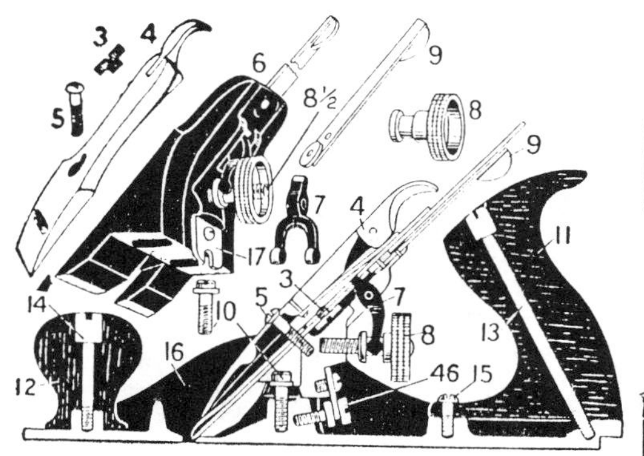

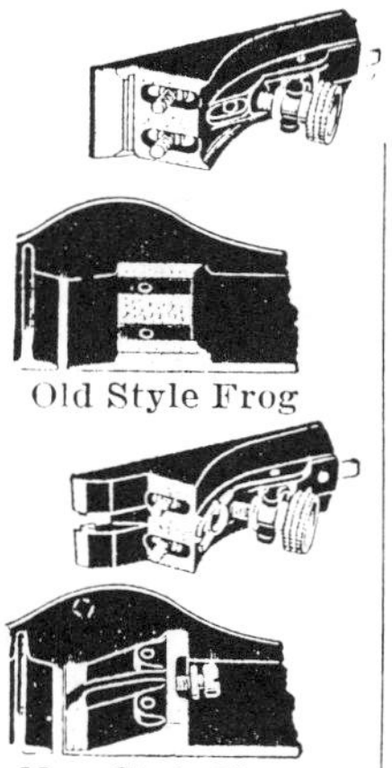

Old Style Frog

New Style Frog

FOR BED ROCK IRON PLANES

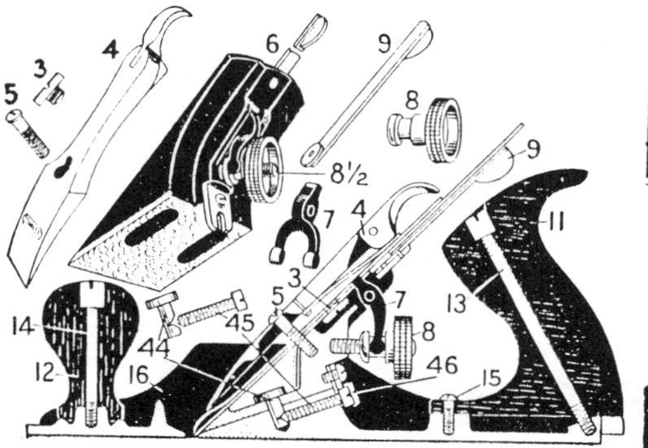

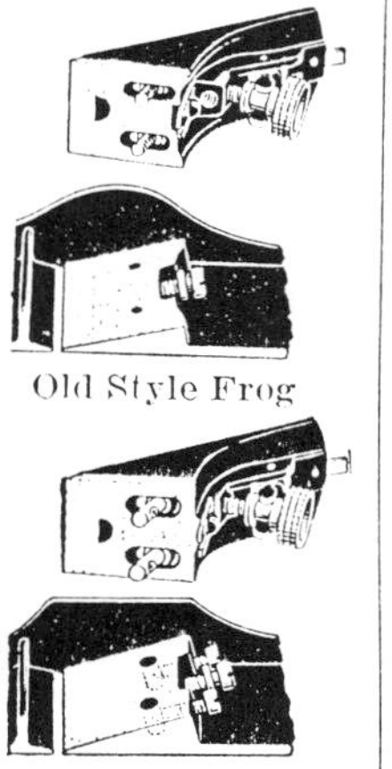

Old Style Frog

New Style Frog

FOR BAILEY WOOD PLANES

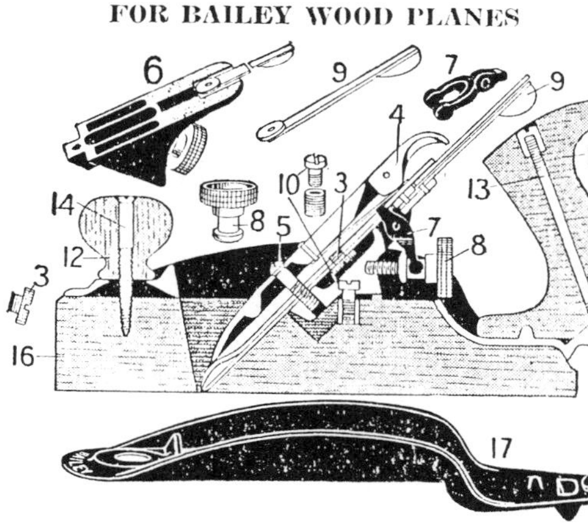

FOR STANLEY BAILEY AND STANLEY BLOCK PLANES

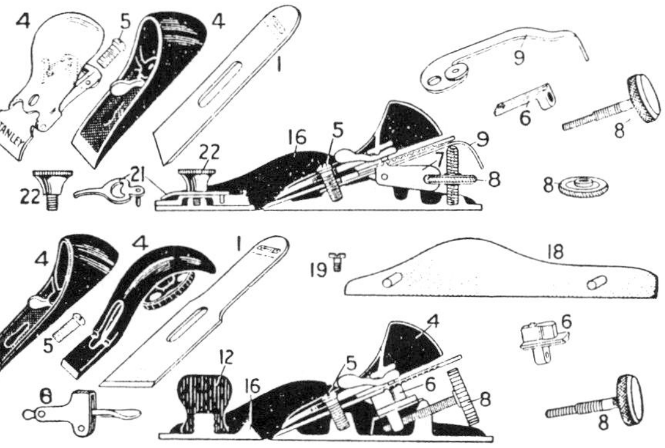

FOR BAILEY IRON PLANES

No.	Name of Part	Price for All Numbers	1 2 2C	3 3C	S4 A4 4 4C	4½ 4½C	S5 A5 5 5C	5¼ 5¼C	5½ 5½C	A6 6 6C	7 7C	8 8C
3	Cap Screw	$0.10										
4	Lever Cap	.50										
5	Lever Cap Screw	.10										
6	Frog Complete—specify new or old	.70										
7	"Y" Adjusting Lever	.10										
8	Adjusting Nut	.20										
9	Lateral Adjusting Lever	.20										
10	Frog Screw	.10										
11	Rosewood Plane Handle	.50										
3x 5x	Aluminum Plane Handles	.80										
	No. 3X Fits Planes 3, 4, 5¼											
	No. 5X Fits Planes 4½, 5, 5½, 6, 7, 8											
12	Plane Knob	.30										
13	Handle Bolt and Nut	.20										
14	Knob Bolt and Nut	.20										
15	Handle Toe Screw	.....				$0.10	$0.10	$0.10	$0.10	$0.10	$0.10	$0.10
16	Plane Bottom	.....	$1.70	$2.00	$2.00	2.40	2.40	2.40	2.40	3.30	4.70	5.70
17	Frog Clip and Screw	.20										
46	Frog Adjusting Screw	.10										

Add 10 per cent. for Corrugated Bottoms.
Add 30 per cent. for Bottoms and Frogs for Planes A4, A5, A6.
Add 10 per cent. for Bottoms and Frogs for Planes S4 and S5.
In ordering be sure to specify **number and name of Part** and **number of Plane**, thus: **No. 4 Lever Cap for No. 5 Plane.** It will also help us if you will include with your order a rough sketch or tracing of the part desired.

FOR BED ROCK IRON PLANES

No.	Name of Part / No. of Plane	602	603 603C	604 604C	604½ 604½C	605 605C 605¼	605½ 605½C	606 606C	607 607C	608 608C
3	Cap Screw	$.10	Price is the same for all numbers.							
4	Lever Cap	.50								
5	" " Screw	.10								
6	Frog Complete spe. new or old	1.00								
7	"Y" Adjusting Lever	.10								
8	Adjusting Nut	.20								
9	Lateral Adjusting Lever	.20								
11	Rosewood Plane Handle	.50								
	Aluminum Plane Handles	.80								
	No. 3X Fits 603-4-5¼									
	No. 5X Fits 605-6-7-8									
12	Rosewood Plane Knob	.30								
13	Handle Bolt and Nut	.20								
14	Knob " " "	.20								
15	Handle Toe Screw	......		......	$.10	$.10	$.10	$.10	$.10	$.10
16	Plane Bottom	2.20	$2.50	$2.50	3.00	3.00	3.20	4.10	6.20	7.00
44	Frog Pin	.20	.20	.20	.20	.20	.20	.20	.20	.20
45	" Clamping Screw	.10	.10	.10	.10	.10	.10	.10	.10	.10
46	" Adjusting "	.10	.10	.10	.10	10	.10	.10	.10	.10

Add 10 per cent. for Corrugated Bottoms.

In ordering be sure to specify **number and name of Part and number of Plane**, thus: No. 4 Lever Cap for No. 604 Plane. It will help us if you will include with your order a sketch or tracing of the part desired.

FOR BAILEY WOOD PLANES

No.	Name of Part / No. of Plane	22	24	35	26	27½	28	31	32	36
3	Cap Screw	$0.10	Price is the same for all numbers. Specify size of Plane for which part is wanted.							
4	Lever Cap	.40								
5	" " Screw	.10								
6	Frog Complete	.60								
7	"Y" Adjusting Lever	.10								
8	Adjusting Nut	.20								
9	Lateral Adjusting Lever	.20								
10	Frog Screw and Bushing	.20								
11	Plane Handle	...	$0.30	$0.30	$0.30	$0.30	$0.30	$0.30	$0.30	$0.30
12	" Knob	.20	.20	.20	.20	.20	.20	.20	.20	.20
13	Handle Bolt and Nut	...	.20	.20	.20	.20	.20	.20	.20	.20
14	Knob Screw	.10	.10	.10	.10	.10	.10	.10	.10	.10
16	Plane Bottom	.80	.80	.80	1.00	1.00	1.10	1.60	1.70	1.00
17	Top Casting	.40	.40	.40	.10	.10	.10	.40	.40	.40

FOR STANLEY BAILEY AND STANLEY BLOCK PLANES

No.	Name of Part / No. of Plane	9½	15	16 17	S18 A18 18 19	60 60½	62	61 63	65	65½	164
4	Lever	$0.25	$0.25	$0.35	$0.65	$0.35	$0.35	$0.35	$0.80	$0.25	$0.35
5	" Screw	.10	.10	.10	.10	.10	.10	.10	.10	.10	.10
6	Adjusting Slide	....	....	....	....	.20	.20	.20	.20	.20	.20
7	" Lever	.10	.10	.10	.10	....	....	....	....	....	....
8	" Nut	.20	.20	.20	.20	.20	.20	.20	.20	.20	.20
9	Lateral Adjusting Lever	.20	.20	.20	.20	....	....	....	....	....	....
11	Plane Handle	....	....	....	....	....	.60	....	....	....	.40
16	" Bottom	1.40	1.50	1.50	1.50	1.20	3.50	1.00	1.50	1.50	3.00
21	Eccentric Plate	.20	.20	.20	.20	.20	.20	....	.20	.20	.20
22	Finger Rest Knob	.20	.20	.20	.20	.20	.30	.20	.20	.20	.30

Add 30 per cent. for Bottom, for Plane A18.
Add 10 per cent for Bottom, for Plane S18.

No.	Name of Part / No. of Plane	100 101	102 *103	110	120	130	131	140	203	220
4	Lever	$0.10	$0.20	$0.20	$0.20	$0.20	$0.20	$0.30	$0.20	$0.20
5	" Screw	....	....	....	....	....	.10	.10	.10	.10
6	Adjusting Slide	....	*.30	....	.30	....	.30	.20	.20	.20
8	" Nut	....	....	....	....	....	.20	.20	.20	.20
12	Plane Knob	....	....	.20	.20	.20	.30	.30	.30	.30
16	" Bottom	.30	.40	.50	.60	.70	1.40	1.50	.50	.60
18	Detachable Side	....	....	....	....	....	....	.50	....	....
19	Side Screw (Pair)	....	....	....	....	....	....	.20	....	....

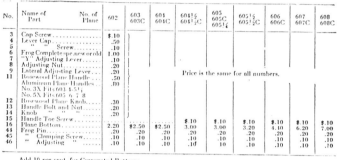

PLANES

BAILEY ADJUSTABLE WOOD PLANES

Screw Adjustment

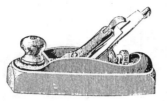

No. 22   Smooth, 8 in. Long, 1¾ in. Cutter............Each, $2.00
No. 23   Smooth, 9 in. Long, 1¾ in. Cutter............Each, 2.00
No. 24   Smooth, 9 in. Long, 2   in. Cutter............Each, 2.00

One in a Box.

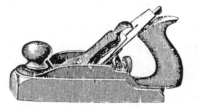

No. 35   Handle Smooth, 9 in. Long, 2   in. Cutter.....Each, $2.34
No. 36   Handle Smooth, 10 in. Long, 2⅜ in. Cutter.....Each, 2.78
No. 37   Jenny Smooth, 13 in. Long, 2⅝ in. Cuttetr.....Each, 2.94

One in a Box.

No. 26   Jack,   15 in. Long, 2   in. Cutter..........Each, $2.10
No. 27   Jack,   15 in. Long, 2⅛ in. Cutter..........Each, 2.46
No. 27½   Jack,   15 in. Long, 2¼ in. Cutter..........Each, 2.46
No. 28   Fore,   18 in. Long, 2⅜ in. Cutter..........Each, 2.78
No. 29   Fore,   20 in. Long, 2⅜ in. Cutter..........Each, 2.64
No. 30   Jointer, 22 in. Long, 2⅜ in. Cutter..........Each, 2.94
No. 31   Jointer, 24 in. Long, 2⅜ in. Cutter..........Each, 2.94
No. 32   Jointer, 26 in. Long, 2⅝ in. Cutter..........Each, 3.22
No. 33   Jointer, 28 in. Long, 2⅝ in. Cutter..........Each, 3.22

One in a Package.

STANLEY LOW ANGLE BLOCK PLANES

This Plane is Adapted for Use in Cutting Across the Grain on Heavy Work, and is Also Fitted with Patent Adjustable Throat Which Enables the User to Work on Hard or Soft Wood.

No. 62   Block, 14 in. Long, 2 in. Cutter.................Each, $4.00

One in a Box.

STANLEY ADJUSTABLE WOOD PLANES

Lever Adjustment

No. 122   Smooth, 8 in. Long, 1¾ in. Cutter..............Each, $1.54

One in a Box.

No. 127   Jack,   15 in. Long, 2⅛ in. Cutter...........Each, $2.00
No. 129   Fore,   20 in. Long, 2⅜ in. Cutter...........Each, 2.32
No. 132   Jointer, 26 in. Long, 2⅝ in. Cutter...........Each, 2.64

One in a Box.

WROUGHT STEEL PLANES

Especially Adapted for Working on Soft Woods.

No. 104   Smooth, 9 in. Long, 2⅛ in. Cutter..............Each, $2.78

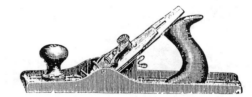

No. 105   Jack, 14 in. Long, 2⅛ in. Cutter...............Each, $3.56

One in a Box.

BAILEY LOW ANGLE BLOCK PLANES

These Planes Have the Cutters Set at a Very Low Angle, Which is of Great Advantage When Working Across the Grain.

No. 60½   Block, 6 in. Long, 1½ in. Cutter..............Each, $1.5
No. 65½   Block, 7 in. Long, 1¾ in. Cutter..............Each, 1.
No. 60   Block, Nickel Trimmings, 6 in. Long, 1½ in. Cut-
                 ter......................................Each,
No. 65   Block, Nickel Trimmings, 7 in. Long, 1¾ in. Cut-
                 ter ....Each, 1

One in a Box.

BAILEY ADJUSTABLE IRON PLANES

PLAIN BOTTOM				
No. 2	Smooth, 7 in. Long; 1⅝ in. Cutter	Each,	$2.78
No. 3	Smooth, 8 in. Long; 1¾ in. Cutter	Each,	2.80
No. 4	Smooth, 9 in. Long; 2 in. Cutter	Each,	3.06
No. 4½	Smooth, 10 in. Long; 2⅜ in. Cutter	Each,	3.70

CORRUGATED BOTTOM				
No. 2C	Smooth, 7 in. Long; 1⅝ in. Cutter	Each,	$2.78
No. 3C	Smooth, 8 in. Long; 1¾ in. Cutter	Each,	2.80
No. 4C	Smooth, 9 in. Long; 2 in. Cutter	Each,	3.06
No. 4½C	Smooth, 10 in. Long; 2⅜ in. Cutter	Each,	3.70

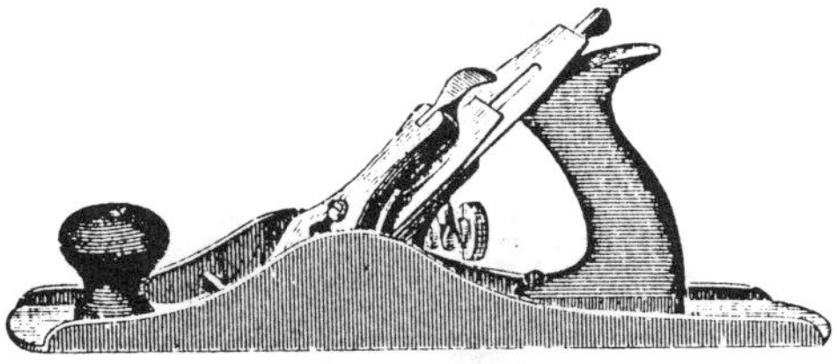

No. 5	Jack,	14 in. Long, 2 in. Cutter	Each,	$3.70
No. 5½	Jack,	15 in. Long, 2¼ in. Cutter	Each,	4.14
No. 6	Fore,	18 in. Long, 2⅜ in. Cutter	Each,	4.54
No. 7	Jointer,	22 in. Long, 2⅜ in. Cutter	Each,	5.14
No. 8	Jointer,	24 in. Long, 2⅝ in. Cutter	Each,	6.44

One in a Box.

No. 5C	Jack,	14 in. Long, 2 in. Cutter	Each,	$3.70
No. 5½C	Jack,	15 in. Long, 2¼ in. Cutter	Each,	4.14
No. 6C	Fore,	18 in. Long, 2⅜ in. Cutter	Each,	4.54
No. 7C	Jointer,	22 in. Long, 2⅜ in. Cutter	Each,	5.14
No. 8C	Jointer,	24 in. Long, 2⅝ in. Cutter	Each,	6.44

One in a Box.

"BED ROCK" PLANES

These Planes Combine the Utmost Solidity and Rigidity, with a Wider Range of Adjustments than Placed on any Iron Plane. Among the Novel Points in this Plane are:

A Frog with a Machined Face.

A Frog so Designed that the Entire Bottom of the Frog Rests Solidly on a Seat Formed in the Plane Body.

A Frog so Designed that its Sides Conform to Guides Formed in the Plane Body, which Guides Lend Accuracy of Adjustment to the Frog, as well as Prevent any Possibility of its Wobbling.

A Reliable Adjustment for Width of Throat Opening.

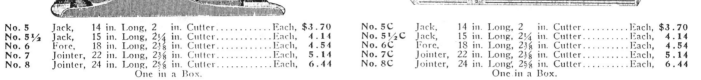

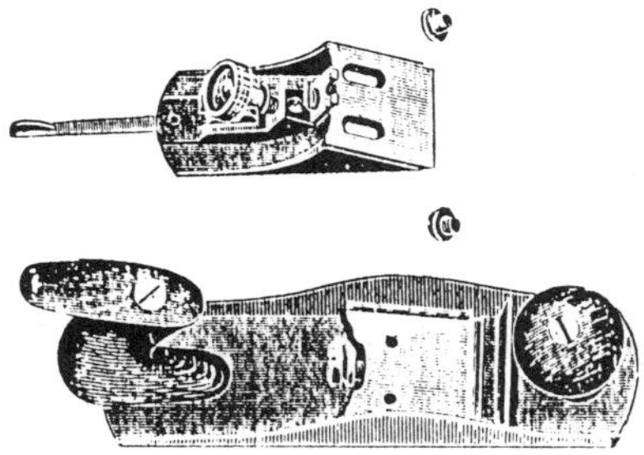

PLAIN BOTTOM				
No. 602	Smooth, 7 in. Long, 1⅝ in. Cutter	Each,	$3.16
No. 603	Smooth, 8 in. Long, 1¾ in. Cutter	Each,	3.30
No. 604	Smooth, 9 in. Long, 2 in. Cutter	Each,	3.58
No. 604½	Smooth, 10 in. Long, 2⅜ in. Cutter	Each,	4.20

CORRUGATED BOTTOM				
No. 602C	Smooth, 7 in. Long, 1⅝ in. Cutter	Each,	$3.16
No. 603C	Smooth, 8 in. Long, 1¾ in. Cutter	Each,	3.30
No. 604C	Smooth, 9 in. Long, 2 in. Cutter	Each,	3.58
No. 604½C	Smooth, 10 in. Long, 2⅜ in. Cutter	Each,	4.20

The Corrugated Bottom Lessens Friction and Makes an Easier Running Tool than the Smooth Bottom Plane.

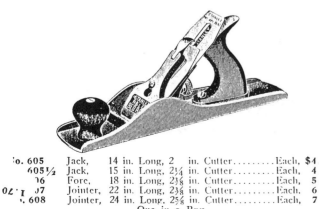

No. 605	Jack,	14 in. Long, 2 in. Cutter	Each,	$4.20
605½	Jack,	15 in. Long, 2¼ in. Cutter	Each,	4.58
606	Fore,	18 in. Long, 2⅜ in. Cutter	Each,	5.18
607	Jointer,	22 in. Long, 2⅜ in. Cutter	Each,	6.00
608	Jointer,	24 in. Long, 2⅝ in. Cutter	Each,	7.14

One in a Box.

No. 605C	Jack,	14 in. Long, 2 in. Cutter	Each,	$4.20
No. 605½C	Jack,	15 in. Long, 2¼ in. Cutter	Each,	4.58
No. 606C	Fore,	18 in. Long, 2⅜ in. Cutter	Each,	5.18
No. 607C	Jointer,	22 in. Long, 2⅜ in. Cutter	Each,	6.00
No. 608C	Jointer,	24 in. Long, 2⅝ in. Cutter	Each,	7.14

One in a Box.

PLANES

BAILEY ADJUSTABLE BLOCK PLANES

Each Plane has an Adjustable Throat Opening, a Lateral Adjustment and the "Handy Feature," Which Give the Workman a More Secure Grip on the Tool.

No. 9½ Block, 6 in. Long, 1¾ in. Cutter.............Each, $1.40

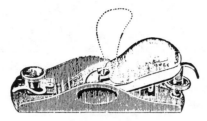

KNUCKLE JOINT

No. 18 Nickel Trimmings, 6 in. Long, 1¾ in. Cutter....Each, $1.68
No. 19 Nickel Trimmings, 7 in. Long, 1¾ in. Cutter....Each, 1.80

DOUBLE END BLOCK

This Plane has Two Slots and a Movable Cutter Seat. When it is to be Used as a Bull Nose Plane the Cap and Cutter can be Removed and the Adjustable Cutter Seat Reversed.

No. 131 Japanned, 8 in. Long, 1¾ in. Cutter.............Each, $1.70

STANLEY ADJUSTABLE RABBET PLANES

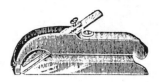

BULL NOSE RABBET

Japanned Top; Polished Bottom and Blade.
No. 75 4 in. Long, 1 in. Cutter.........................Each, $0.80

CABINET MAKERS' RABBET

This Plane is Designed for Fine Cabinet Work. The Sides and Bottom Being Square with Each Other, the Plane will Lie Perfectly Flat on Either Side, and can be Used Right or Left. Both the Cutter and Width of Throat Opening Are Adjustable. The Plane is Nickel-plated and Fitted with the "Handy" Feature.

No. 90 Bull Nose, 4 in. Long, 1 in. Cutter.............Each, $2.94

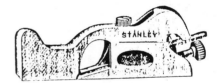

No. 93 Rabbet Plane, 6½ in. Long, 1 in. Cutter........Each, $3.52

STANLEY BLOCK PLANES

Japanned Cap and Sides; Ground Face

No. 101 Without Handle, 3½ in. Long; 1 in. Cut; Not Adjustable ....Each, $0.24

No. 100 With Handle, 3½ in. Long; 1 in. Cut; Not Adjustable..Each, $0.34

No. 110 Non-adjustable; 7½ in. Long; 1¾ in. Cut.................Each, $0.70

No. 220 Adjustable; 7½ in. Long; 1¾ in. Cut; with Screw Adjustment ....Each, $1.00
One in a Box.

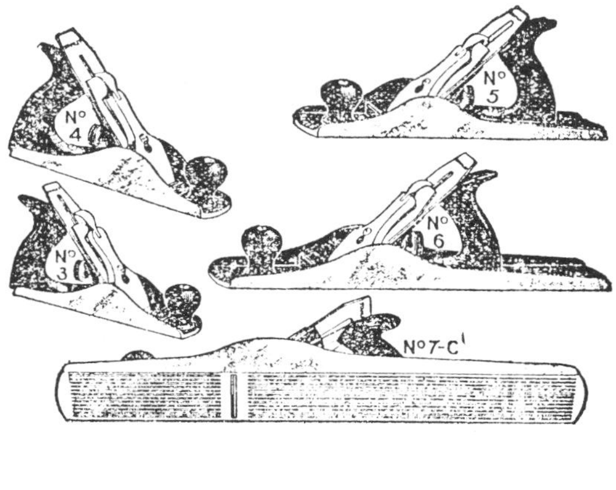

PLANES

"BAILEY" ADJUSTABLE IRON

The handle and knob are made of highly finished, thoroughly seasoned rosewood. The English steel cutter is tempered, ground and honed, ready for use, is adjustable both endwise and sidewise, and bedded to the heel of bevel. The width of mouth can be varied by changing the setting of the frog. Bottoms, either flat or corrugated—see cut 7C—as desired.

Flat Bottom	Corrugated Bottom	Type	Length	Cutter	W't	Each
No. 1		Smooth	5½ in.	1¼ in.	1¼ lbs.	$3.80
No. 2		Smooth	7 in.	1⅝ in.	2¼ lbs.	4.90
No. 3	No. 3 C	Smooth	8 in.	1¾ in.	3⅛ lbs.	5.40
No. 4	No. 4 C	Smooth	9 in.	2 in.	3¾ lbs.	5.90
No. 4½	No. 4½C	Smooth	10 in.	2⅜ in.	4¾ lbs.	6.75
No. 5¼	No. 5¼C	Jr.Jack	11½ in.	1¾ in.	4 lbs.	6.05
No. 5	No. 5 C	Jack	14 in.	2 in.	4¾ lbs.	6.75
No. 5½	No. 5½C	Jack	15 in.	2¼ in.	6¾ lbs.	7.60
No. 6	No. 6 C	Fore	18 in.	2⅜ in.	7¾ lbs.	8.70
No. 7	No. 7 C	Jointer	22 in.	2⅜ in.	8⅛ lbs.	9.90
No. 8	No. 8 C	Jointer	24 in.	2⅝ in.	9¾ lbs.	11.90

ONE IN A BOX

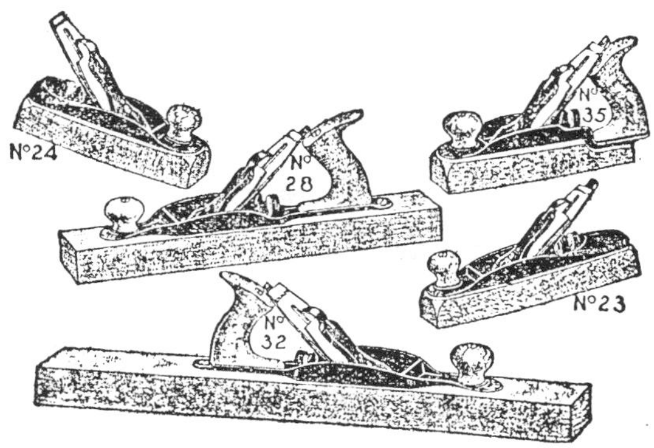

"BAILEY" WOOD

These planes are made for those wanting a wood bottom plane of superior quality. Made of specially selected, well seasoned Beech. The cutters are the celebrated Bailey cutters and are adjustable both endwise and sidewise.

	Type	Length	Cutter	W't	Each
No. 24	Smooth	9 in.	2 in.	2⅞ lbs.	$4.60
No. 26	Jack	15 in.	2 in.	3¾ lbs.	4.70
No. 27½	Jack	15 in.	2¼ in.	4¾ lbs.	5.50
No. 28	Fore	18 in.	2⅜ in.	5½ lbs.	6.00
No. 31	Jointer	24 in.	2⅜ in.	6½ lbs.	6.50
No. 32	Jointer	26 in.	2⅝ in.	7⅝ lbs.	6.90
No. 35	Handle Smooth	9 in.	2 in.	3¼ lbs.	5.30

ONE IN A BOX

STANLEY "BED ROCK"

For fine work on hard and knotty wood, this plane surpasses all others.

The cutter, frog and bottom are so machined and fitted that they are practically one solid piece of metal, thus preventing any chance of vibration.

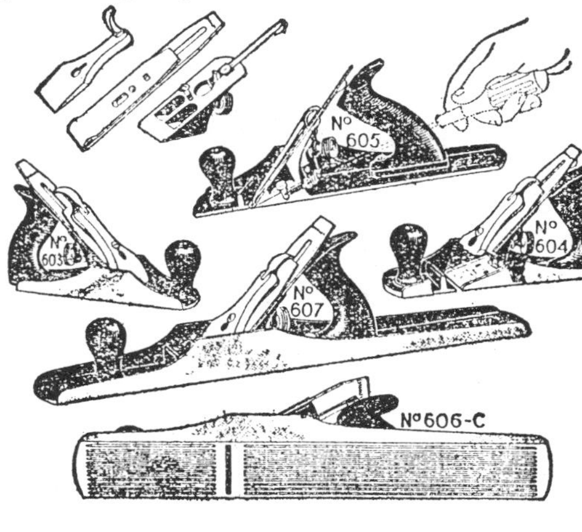

The frog travels in a groove, ensuring it being square with the mouth of the plane, and preventing shifting or "wobbling."

The width of the mouth can be regulated by use of a screw driver as shown in the cut, without removing the cutter and lever.

The cutters are made of the best English steel and are adjustable both endwise and sidewise.

The shape of the sides, a distinctive feature, adds greatly to the strength of the plane.

The handles and knobs are of rosewood and finely finished.

Bottoms either flat or corrugated (see No. 606C) as desired.

Flat Bottom	Corrugated Bottom	Type	Length	Cutter	W't	Each
No. 602		Smooth	7 in.	1⅝ in.	2¼ lbs.	$5.40
No. 603	No. 603 C	Smooth	8 in.	1¾ in.	3¼ lbs.	5.90
No. 604	No. 604 C	Smooth	9 in.	2 in.	3⅝ lbs.	6.50
No. 604½	No. 604½C	Smooth	10 in.	2⅜ in.	4¾ lbs.	7.45
No. 605	No. 605 C	Jack	14 in.	2 in.	4½ lbs.	7.40
No. 605½	No. 605½C	Jack	15 in.	2¼ in.	6½ lbs.	8.40
No. 606	No. 606 C	Fore	18 in.	2⅜ in.	7⅝ lbs.	9.50
No. 607	No. 607 C	Jointer	22 in.	2⅜ in.	8¾ lbs.	10.90
No. 608	No. 608 C	Jointer	24 in.	2⅝ in.	9¾ lbs.	13.00

ONE IN A BOX

WOOD SCRAPERS

HEATHER CABINET

No. 1080 With Raised Handles, Length 11 in. Blade 2¾ in.
....Each, $1.30

By Means of Thumb Screw, Blade can be Slightly Curved as Desired.
No. 01080 Extra Blades.....................Per Dozen, $3.60

STANLEY CABINET

The Blade of this Scraper May be Sprung to a Slight Curve by the Thumb-screw Shown at the Center of Cut, which will be Found a Great Advantage in Working with this Tool.
No. 80 Raised Handles, 11 in., 2¾ in. Blade...........Each, $1.30
No. 080 Cutters for Above Scrapers..............Per Dozen, 4.20

STANLEY IMPROVED WOOD

This Scraper can be Adjusted to any Desired Pitch, and May be Worked Toward or from the Person Using it. The Roller Acts as a Support to Relieve the Strain on the Wrists and Hands of the Workman. The Handle can be Detached for Working Into Corners.
No. 83 Wood Scraper, With Handles and Roller, 3 in. Blade
.....................................Each, $1.40

One in a Box.

STANLEY WOOD FACE CABINET

With Rosewood Face, which Goes Over a Surface Very Smoothly; Blade is Set at an Angle to Give Satisfactory Work at all Times.
No. 81 Raised Handles 11 in. Long, 2½ in. Blade........Each, $2.10

One in a Box.

ATKINS RAM'S HORN

Rams Horn, Maple Wood Stock, Two Handles, Hardened Steel Blade. The Blade can be Removed for Sharpening by Loosening the Screws. The Elastic Blade Seat Gives the Tool a Curved Scraping Surface and Prevents it from Jumping or Chattering. It is Operated by Pushing Instead of Pulling.
No. 95...Each, $2.00

One in a Box.

ATKINS PERFECTION

The Blade Measures 3 x 3 Inches and is 16 Gauge, Making it Very Stiff, and Preventing Springing. The Beveled Edge is for Cutting a Shaving off of Hardwood Floors. Scraping can be Done in Corners and Along the Casing Without Removing the Blade.
No. 085 Perfection ....Each, $1.20

Six in a Box.

STARRETT UNIVERSAL

The Edges of the Blade are Ground Perfectly Square. There are Eight Sharp Cutting Edges, and Any One of them can Almost Instantly be Brought Into Use by Means of the Handle with its Ball Joint Connection. The Head Grip can be Slipped off and on Instantly. Polished Steel Blade, Rosewood Handle and Grip.
No. 194 3 x 4¼ in. Blade.....................Each, $1.00 1.60
Extra Blades ....Each, .15   .24

One in a Box.

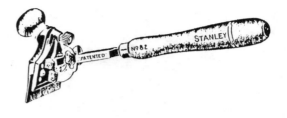

STANLEY

So Arranged the Blade can be Set at Any Angle.

Tool Steel Blade; Japanned Cast Iron Frame and Handle Shank; Polished Maple Handle and Knob; Steel Screws.
No. 32 14½ in. Long, 3 in. Blade...................Each, $1.40

One in a Box.

AXES, HATCHETS, ADZES, ETC.

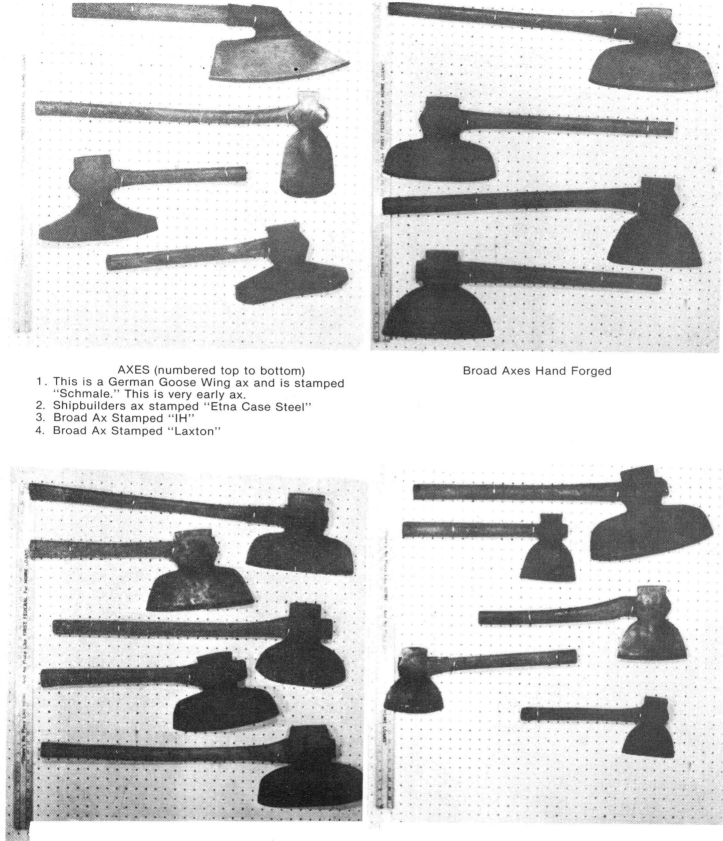

AXES (numbered top to bottom)
1. This is a German Goose Wing ax and is stamped "Schmale." This is very early ax.
2. Shipbuilders ax stamped "Etna Case Steel"
3. Broad Ax Stamped "IH"
4. Broad Ax Stamped "Laxton"

Broad Axes Hand Forged

BROAD AXES (numbered top to bottom)
2. Stamped "I Blood" Elston, NY
3. Stamped "Thomas Fleming"

Broad Axe and Hatchets (numbered top to bottom)
1. Stamped "Fe Hurd"
#2 thru 5 are Hatchets
3. Stamped "C. List"
#2 Stamped "E. Edgerton, Paineville, Ohio"

BROAD AXES (numbered top to bottom)
1. Stamped "J. S. Felton & Co."
2. Stamped "R. J. Frost"
3. "Reliable Co." Stamp
"Well Tool Co. Cleveland Ohio"
5. "Cast Steel"

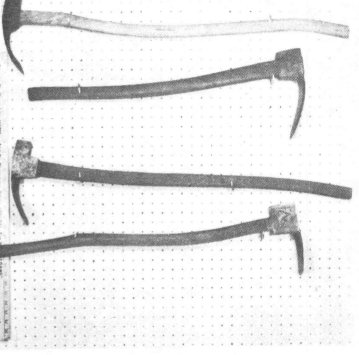

Foot Adze

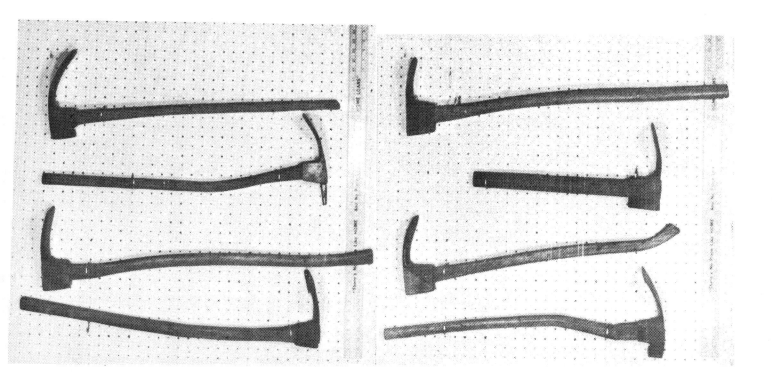

Foot Adze
Top, Stamped "W. Fletcher, Sheffield"
Second Top, Ship Builders Adze

Foot Adze

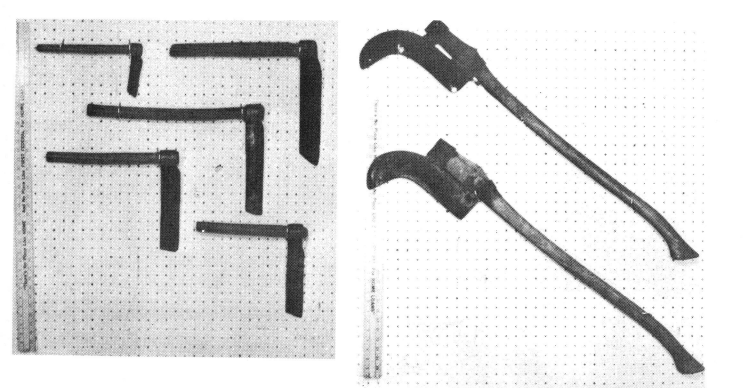

Wood Froe

Brush Axes

HANDLED SINGLE BIT AXES

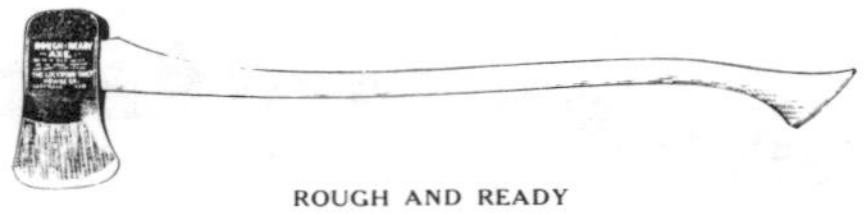

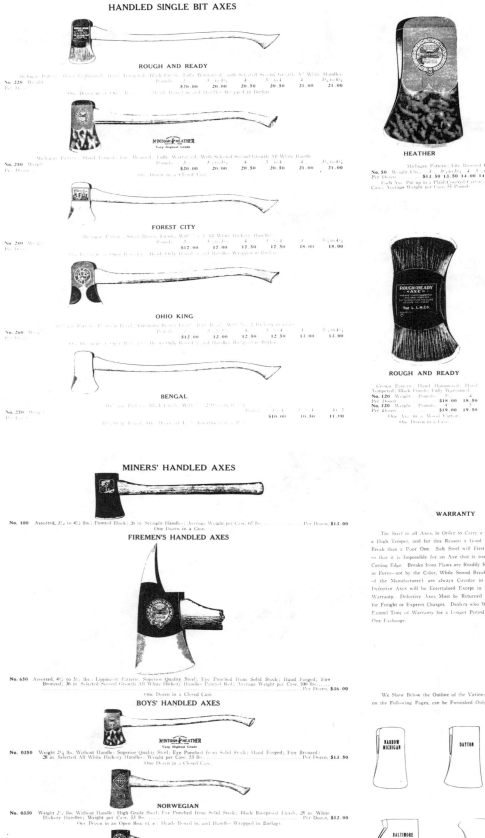

ROUGH AND READY

Michigan Pattern; Hand Hammered; Hand Tempered; Black Finish; Fully Warranted; with Selected Second Growth All White Handles.

No. 220 Weight	Pounds,	3½	3¼ to 3¾	4	3½ to 4½	4½	3¾ to 4¾
Per Dozen		$20.00	20.00	20.50	20.50	21.00	21.00

One Dozen in an Open Box (i. e.: Heads Boxed in and Handles Wrapped in Burlap).

McINTOSH HEATHER
Very Highest Grade

Michigan Pattern; Hand Forged; Fire Bronzed; Fully Warranted; With Selected Second Growth All White Handle.

No. 250 Weight	Pounds,	3½	3¼ to 3¾	4	3½ to 4½	4½	3¾ to 4¾
Per Dozen		$20.00	20.00	20.50	20.50	21.00	21.00

One Dozen in a Closed Case.

FOREST CITY

Michigan Pattern; Silver Bronze Finish; With No. 1 All White Hickory Handles.

No. 240 Weight	Pounds,	3½	3¼ to 3¾	4	3½ to 4½	4½	3¾ to 4¾
Per Dozen		$17.00	17.00	17.50	17.50	18.00	18.00

One Dozen in an Open Box (i. e.: Heads Only Boxed in and Handles Wrapped in Burlap).

OHIO KING

Michigan Pattern; Aluminum Bronze Finish; With No. 2 Hickory Handles.

No. 260 Weight	Pounds,	3½	3¼ to 3¾	4	3½ to 4½	4½	3¾ to 4¾
Per Dozen		$12.00	12.00	12.50	12.50	13.00	13.00

One Dozen in an Open Box (i. e.: Heads Only Boxed in and Handles Wrapped in Burlap).

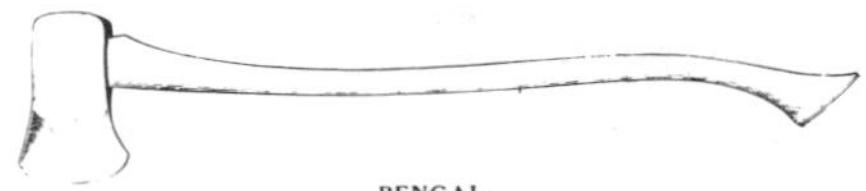

BENGAL

Michigan Pattern; Black Finish; With No. 2 Hickory Handles.

No. 270 Weight	Pounds,	3 to 4	3½ to 4½	4 to 5
Per Dozen		$10.00	10.50	11.00

Heads Only Boxed; One Dozen of Each Assortment in a Box.

MINERS' HANDLED AXES

No. 100 Assorted, 3½ to 4½ lbs.; Painted Black; 26 in. Straight Handles; Average Weight per Case, 65 lbs. .... Per Dozen, **$13.00**
One Dozen in a Case.

FIREMEN'S HANDLED AXES

No. 650 Assorted, 4½ to 5½ lbs.; Lippincott Pattern; Superior Quality Steel; Eye Punched from Solid Stock; Hand Forged; Fire Bronzed; 36 in. Selected Second Growth All White Hickory Handles Painted Red; Average Weight per Case, 100 lbs. .... Per Dozen, **$36.00**
One Dozen in a Closed Case.

BOYS' HANDLED AXES

McINTOSH HEATHER
Very Highest Grade

No. 0350 Weight 2¼ lbs. Without Handle; Superior Quality Steel; Eye Punched from Solid Stock; Hand Forged; Fire Bronzed; 28 in. Selected All White Hickory Handles; Weight per Case, 53 lbs. .... Per Dozen, **$13.50**
One Dozen in a Closed Case.

NORWEGIAN

No. 0330 Weight 2¼ lbs. Without Handle; High Grade Steel; Eye Punched from Solid Stock; Black Rustproof Finish; 28 in. White Hickory Handles; Weight per Case, 53 lbs. .... Per Dozen, **$12.00**
One Dozen in an Open Box (i. e.: Heads Boxed in, and Handles Wrapped in Burlap).

CLEVELAND

No. 0370 Weight 2 lbs. Without Handle; Cast Steel; Painted Red; Polished Bits; 26 in. No. 2 Hickory Handles; Weight per Case, 45 lbs. .... Per Dozen, **$9.00**
One Dozen in an Open Box (i. e.: Heads Boxed in, and Handles Wrapped in Burlap).

SINGLE BIT AXES

McINTOSH HEATHER
Very Highest Grade

The BEST AXE that Skill and Long Experience Can Produce.

Everything that Enters into the Manufacture of this Axe is Carefully Selected, and Best in the World.

THE EYE is Not Welded, but Punched Out of Solid Stock, and thus Cannot Expand or Split.

THE BIT or Cutting Edge is Made from Best Quality Crucible Cast Steel FULLY WARRANTED of Good Temper and Free from Flaws.

FOREST CITY

First Quality in Every Respect. Highest Grade Crucible Steel Bit, Hand Tempered and Ground. Each Axe is Carefully Inspected and Tested Before Leaving the Factory.

HEATHER

Michigan Pattern; Fire Bronzed Finish.

No. 50 Weight, Lbs.,	3½	3¼ to 3¾	4	3½ to 4½	4½	3¾ to 4¾
Per Dozen	$13.50	13.50	14.00	14.00	14.50	14.50

Each Axe Put up in a Plaid Covered Carton; One Dozen Axes in a Case; Average Weight per Case, 55 Pounds.

FOREST CITY

Michigan Pattern; Silver Bronze Finish.

No. 40 Weight, Lbs.,	3½	3¼ to 3¾	4	3½ to 4½	4½	3¾ to 4¾
Per Dozen	$12.00	12.00	12.50	12.50	13.00	13.00

Each Axe Wrapped in Paper; One Dozen Axes in a Case; Average Weight per Case, 55 Pounds.

DOUBLE BIT AXES

ROUGH AND READY

Crown Pattern; Hand Hammered; Hand Tempered; Black Finish; Fully Warranted.

No. 120 Weight Pounds,	3½	4
Per Dozen	$18.00	18.50
No. 120 Weight Pounds,	4½	5
Per Dozen	$19.00	19.50

One Axe in a Wood Carton;
One Dozen in a Case.

FOREST CITY

Crown Pattern; Silver Bronze Finish.

No. 140 Wt. lbs.,	3½	4	4½
Per Dozen	$17.00	17.50	18.00
No. 140 Wt. lbs.,		5	5½
Per Dozen		$18.50	19.00

One Axe in a Wood Carton;
One Dozen in a Case.

ROBERT MANN

Crown Pattern; Gold Bronze Finish.

No. 180 Weight Pounds,	3½ to 4½	4 to 5
Per Dozen	$13.00	13.50

One Dozen in a Case.

AXES

WARRANTY

The Steel in all Axes, in Order to Carry a Good Edge, Must be of a High Temper, and for this Reason a Good Axe is More Likely to Break than a Poor One. Soft Steel will First Bend and then Break, so that it is Impossible for an Axe that is too Soft to Hold a Good Cutting Edge. Breaks from Flaws are Readily Known by being Angular in Form—not by the Color, While Sound Breaks (which are no Fault of the Manufacturer) are always Circular in Form. No Claim for Defective Axes will be Entertained Except in Accordance with Above Warranty. Defective Axes Must be Returned Free of Expense to us for Freight or Express Charges. Dealers who Warrant Axes should not Extend Time of Warranty for a Longer Period than 30 Days, with but One Exchange.

VARIOUS PATTERNS OF AXES

We Show Below the Outline of the Various Patterns of Axes. Any of these Patterns which are not Included in Our Stock Line as Shown on the Following Pages, can be Furnished Only for Direct Shipment from Factory.

AXES.

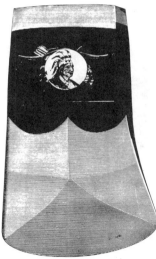

Cuyahoga Chief.

Graves, Bright & Co.'s Cuyahoga Chief Axe, Bronzed. $

    Weights, 3 to 4 lbs., 3¼ to 4¼ lbs., 3½ to 4½ lbs., 3¾ to 4¾ lbs., 4 to 5 lbs.

ONE DOZEN IN A BOX.

HANDLED AXES.

Hibbard, Spencer & Co.'s Handled Axe, $
Graves, Bright & Co.'s Cuyahoga Chief Handled Axe,
Jay Handled Axe,

AXES.

Western Pattern.

Per Dozen.

Hunt's Refined Cast-Steel Axe, Bronzed, $

  Weights, 3 to 4 lbs., 3¼ to 4¼ lbs., 3½ to 4½ lbs., 3¾ to 4¾ lbs., 4 to 5 lbs., 4½ to 5½ lbs.

Hunt's Refined Cast-Steel Beveled Axe, Bronzed, $

    Weights, 3½ to 4½ lbs., 4 to 5 lbs.

ONE DOZEN IN A BOX.

7

AXES.

Double Bitted.

Per Dozen.

Hibbard, Spencer & Co.'s Double Bitted Axe, Bronzed, $

    Weights, 3½ to 4½ lbs., 4 to 5 lbs., 4½ to 5½ lbs., 5 to 6 lbs.

ONE DOZEN IN A BOX.

BROAD AXES.

Per Dozen.

Blood's Refined Cast-Steel Broad Axe, Bronzed, $

    Weights, 6 to 8 lbs., 7 to 9 lbs., 8 to 10 lbs.

    Cut, 11 to 13 inches.

HALF DOZEN IN A BOX.

AXES.

Yankee Crown.

Per Dozen.

Hibbard, Spencer & Co.'s Yankee Crown Axe, Bronzed, $
Weights, 3 to 4 lbs., 3¼ to 4¼ lbs., 3½ to 4½ lbs., 3¾ to 4¾ lbs., 4 to 5 lbs., 4½ to 5½ lbs.

Hibbard, Spencer & Co.'s Yankee Crown Beveled Axe, Bronzed, $
Weights, 3½ to 4½ lbs., 4 to 5 lbs.

ONE DOZEN IN A BOX

AXES.

Wisconsin Pattern.

Per Dozen.

A. C. Bartlett's Wisconsin Pattern Axe, Bronzed, $
Weights, 3½ to 4½ lbs., 3¾ to 4¾ lbs., 4 to 5 lbs., 4½ to 5½ lbs.

A. C. Bartlett's Wisconsin Pattern Beveled Axe, Bronzed, $
Weights, 3½ to 4½ lbs., 4 to 5 lbs.

ONE DOZEN IN A BOX.

AXES.

Western Crown.

Per Dozen.

Hibbard, Spencer & Co.'s Western Crown Axe, Bronzed, $
Weights, 3 to 4 lbs., 3¼ to 4¼ lbs., 3½ to 4½ lbs., 3¾ to 4¾ lbs., 4 to 5 lbs., 4½ to 5½ lbs.

ONE DOZEN IN A BOX.

AXES.

Michigan Pattern.

Per Dozen.

A. C. Bartlett's Michigan Pattern Axe, Bronzed, $
Weights, 3½ to 4½ lbs., 3¾ to 4¾ lbs., 4 to 5 lbs., 4½ to 5½ lbs.

ONE DOZEN IN A BOX

78

WOOD CHOPPERS' WEDGES

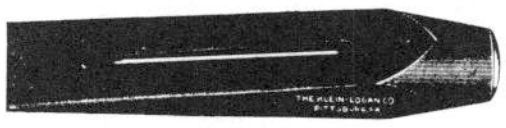

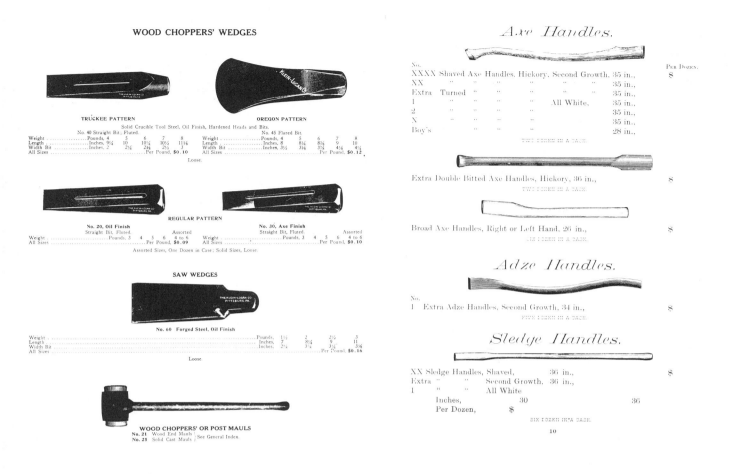

TRUCKEE PATTERN

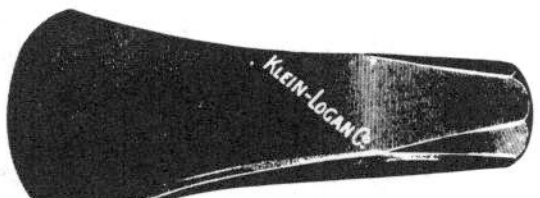

OREGON PATTERN

Solid Crucible Tool Steel, Oil Finish, Hardened Heads and Bits.

No. 40 Straight Bit; Fluted.

Weight .... Pounds,	4	5	6	7	8
Length .... Inches,	9¼	10	10¼	10½	11⅝
Width Bit .... Inches,	2	2¼	2⅜	2½	3
All Sizes .... Per Pound, $0.10					

No. 45 Flared Bit.

Weight .... Pounds,	4	5	6	7	8
Length .... Inches,	8	8¼	8⅞	9	10
Width Bit .... Inches,	3½	3⅝	3⅞	4⅛	4¼
All Sizes .... Per Pound, $0.12					

Loose.

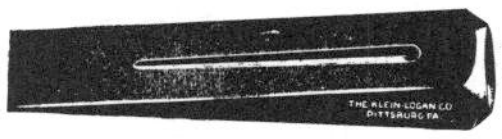

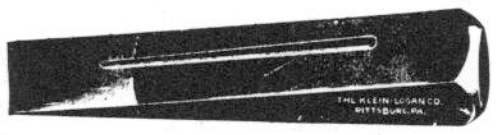

REGULAR PATTERN

No. 20, Oil Finish

Straight Bit, Fluted.

					Assorted
Weight .... Pounds,	3	4	5	6	4 to 6
All Sizes .... Per Pound, $0.09					

No. 30, Axe Finish

Straight Bit, Fluted.

					Assorted
Weight .... Pounds,	3	4	5	6	4 to 6
All Sizes .... Per Pound, $0.10					

Assorted Sizes, One Dozen in Case; Solid Sizes, Loose.

SAW WEDGES

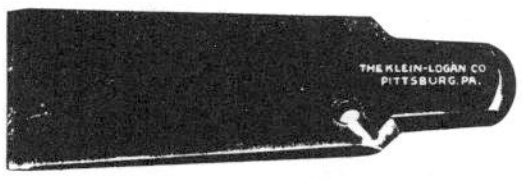

No. 60 Forged Steel, Oil Finish

Weight .... Pounds,	1½	2	2½	3
Length .... Inches,	7	8¼	9	11
Width Bit .... Inches,	2⅞	3⅛	3¼	3⅜
All Sizes .... Per Pound, $0.16				

Loose.

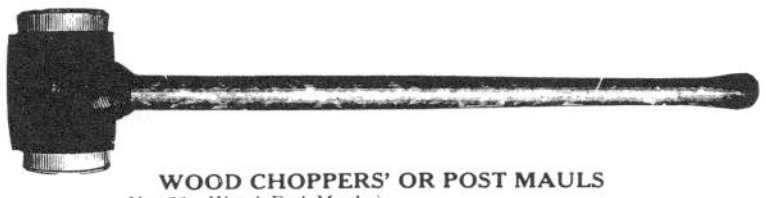

WOOD CHOPPERS' OR POST MAULS

No. 21 Wood End Mauls } See General Index.
No. 25 Solid Cast Mauls }

Axe Handles.

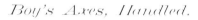

No.			PER DOZEN.
XXXX	Shaved Axe Handles, Hickory, Second Growth,	35 in.,	$
XX	" " " " " "	35 in.,	
Extra	Turned " " " " "	35 in.,	
1	" " " " All White,	35 in.,	
2	" " " "	35 in.,	
X	" " " "	35 in.,	
Boy's	" " "	28 in.,	

TWO DOZEN IN A CASE.

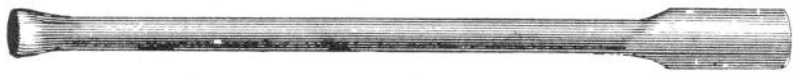

Extra Double Bitted Axe Handles, Hickory, 36 in., $

TWO DOZEN IN A CASE.

Broad Axe Handles, Right or Left Hand, 26 in., $

SIX DOZEN IN A CASE.

Adze Handles.

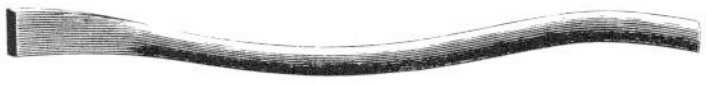

No.

1 Extra Adze Handles, Second Growth, 34 in., $

FIVE DOZEN IN A CASE.

Sledge Handles.

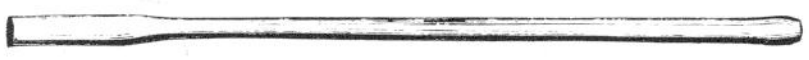

XX Sledge Handles, Shaved,	36 in.,		$
Extra " " Second Growth,	36 in.,		
1 " " All White			
Inches,	30	36	
Per Dozen,	$		

SIX DOZEN IN A CASE.

10

AXES.

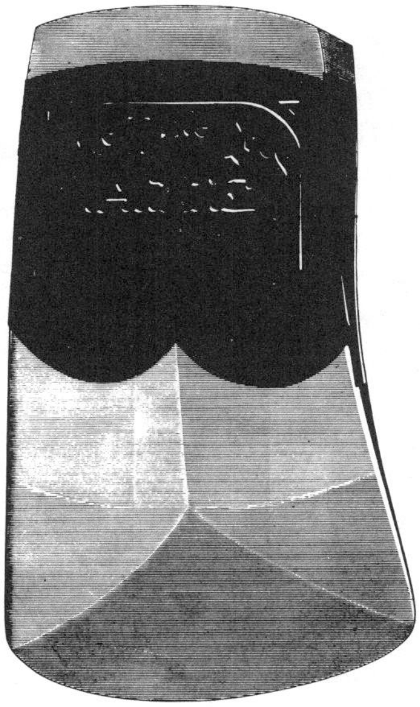

Pine Tree.

PER DOZEN.

Hibbard, Spencer & Co.'s Pine Tree Axe, Bronzed, $

Weights, 3 to 4 lbs., 3¼ to 4¼ lbs., 3½ to 4½ lbs., 3¾ to 4¾ lbs., 4 to 5 lbs.

ONE DOZEN IN A BOX.

Boy's Axes, Handled.

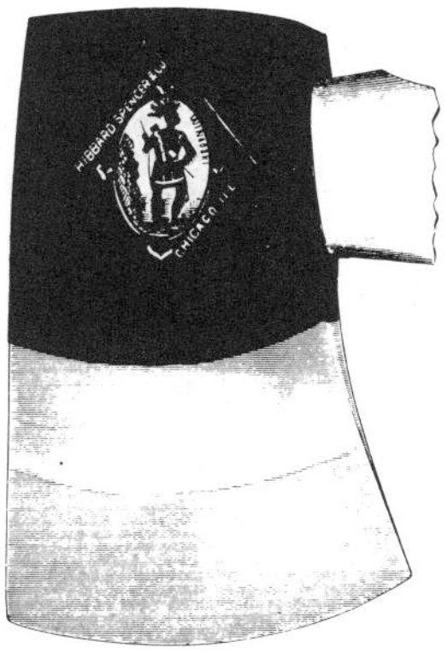

PER DOZEN.

Blood's Extra Cast-Steel, Bronzed, 2¾ lbs., 26 in. Handle, $
Hibbard, Spencer & Co.'s Winooski, Bronzed, 2½ " 26 in. "

Hunter's Hatchets.

(See Cut Above.)

Blood's Extra Cast-Steel, Bronzed, $
3 in. Cut, Length of Handle, 16 inches.

HALF DOZEN IN A PACKAGE.

CARPENTER'S ADZES

MINTOSH & HEATHER
Very Highest Grade

Superior Quality Steel, Oil Tempered, Hand Forged, Fire Bronzed, Polished Head and Bit, Highly Finished, Ground and Sharpened
No. 11 Extra Full Weight, Width Cut, 3 , 4, 4½ and 4 in.
Per Dozen, **$26.00**
Each Adze Packed in Plaid Covered Box.
One Half Dozen in Wood Case

OHIO KING

Cast Steel with Crucible Steel Bit; Aluminum Bronzed; Polished Head and Bit
No. 10 Extra Full Weight, Width Cut, 3 , 4, 4½, and 4 in.
Per Dozen, **$21.60**
One Half Dozen in a Box.

Specify Width of Cut When Ordering.

CLEVELAND

Cast Steel, Gold Bronzed, Polished Head and Bit
No. 12 Width Cut, 4 in Per Dozen, **$16.80**
One Half Dozen in a Box.

RAILROAD ADZES

No. 15
OHIO KING

Cast Steel with Crucible Steel Bit; Aluminum Bronzed; Polished Head and Bit.
No. 15 Width Cut, 5 to 6 in.
Per Dozen **$22.50**

CLEVELAND

Cast Steel, Gold Bronzed, Polished Head and Bit
No. 17 Width Cut, 5 to 6 in.
Per Dozen, **$19.00**
One Dozen in a Box.

SHIP CARPENTER'S ADZES

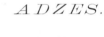

No. 20 PLAIN

No. 25 LIPPED

OHIO KING

Cast Steel with Inlaid Crucible Steel Bit; Aluminum Bronzed; Polished Head and Bit.
No. 20 Plain; Width of Cut, 4½ in .... Per Dozen, **$24.00**
No. 25 Lipped; Width of Cut, 5 in .... Per Dozen, **32.00**
One Half-Dozen in a Box.

Mattocks.

Adze Eye.

Long Cutter.

	Per Dozen.
Cast-Steel, Adze Eye, Axe Finish, Short Cutter,	$
" " " " Long "	

Cast-Steel, Axe Finish, Short Cutter, $
"   "   "   Long   "
Hunt's English Cast-Steel, Axe Finish, Short Cutter,
"   "   "   "   "   Long   "

Grub Hoes.

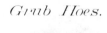

No.				Per Dozen.
1	Cast-Steel, Oval Eye, Axe Finish, 3 lbs..			$
2	" " " " 3½ "		
1	" " Round " 3 "		
2	" " " " " 3½ "		

TWO DOZEN IN A CASE.

ADZES.

Carpenter's Adze.

Blood's English Cast-Steel Carpenter's Adze, Bronzed,

Cut, 4½ inches.

Per Dozen.
$

ONE DOZEN IN A BOX.

ADZES.

Railroad Adze.

Blood's English Cast-Steel Railroad Adze, Bronzed,

Cut, 5 to 6 inches.

Per Dozen.
$

ONE DOZEN IN A BOX.

PICKS AND MATTOCKS

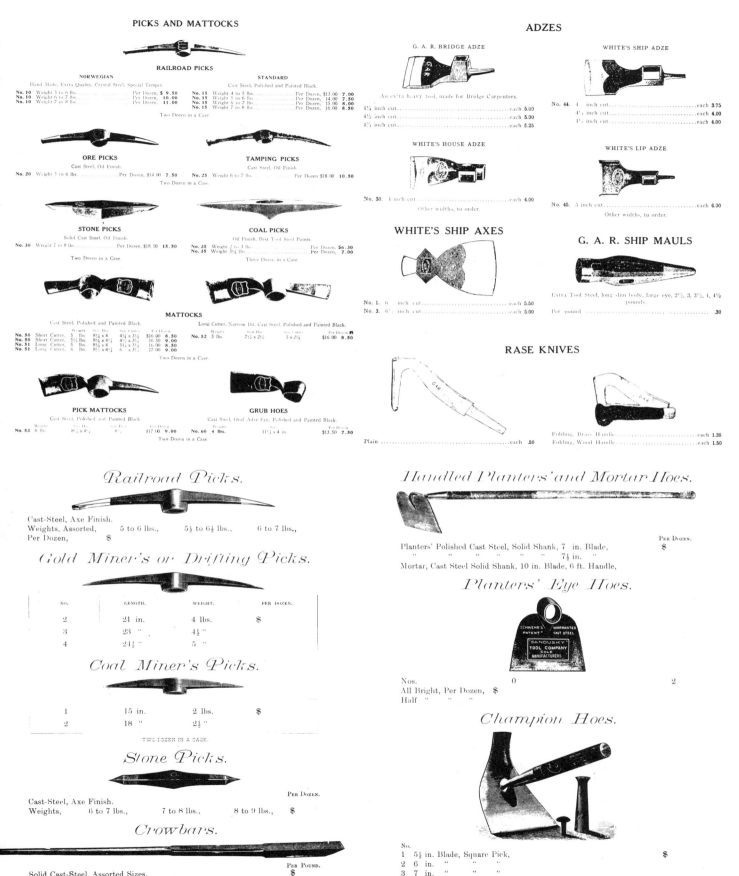

RAILROAD PICKS

NORWEGIAN

Hand Made, Extra Quality, Crystal Steel, Special Temper.

No. 10	Weight 5 to 6 lbs.	Per Dozen,	**$ 9.50**
No. 10	Weight 6 to 7 lbs.	Per Dozen,	**10.00**
No. 10	Weight 7 to 8 lbs.	Per Dozen,	**11.00**

STANDARD

Cast Steel, Polished and Painted Black.

No. 15	Weight 4 to 5 lbs.	Per Dozen,	$13.00	**7.00**
No. 15	Weight 5 to 6 lbs.	Per Dozen,	14.00	**7.50**
No. 15	Weight 6 to 7 lbs.	Per Dozen,	15.00	**8.00**
No. 15	Weight 7 to 8 lbs.	Per Dozen,	16.00	**8.50**

Two Dozen in a Case.

ORE PICKS

Cast Steel, Oil Finish.

No. 20 Weight 5 to 6 lbs. .... Per Dozen, $14.00 **7.50**

TAMPING PICKS

Cast Steel, Oil Finish.

No. 25 Weight 6 to 7 lbs. .... Per Dozen $18.00 **10.50**

Two Dozen in a Case.

STONE PICKS

Solid Cast Steel, Oil Finish.

No. 30 Weight 7 to 8 lbs. .... Per Dozen, $18.50 **15.50**

Two Dozen in a Case.

COAL PICKS

Oil Finish, Best Tool Steel Points.

No. 35	Weight 2 to 3 lbs.	Per Dozen,	**$6.30**
No. 35	Weight 3¼ lbs.	Per Dozen,	**7.00**

Three Dozen in a Case.

MATTOCKS

Cast Steel, Polished and Painted Black.

		Weight	Size Hoe	Size Cutter	Per Dozen	
No. 50	Short Cutter,	5 lbs.	8¼ x 4	4¼ x 3¼	$16.00	**8.50**
No. 50	Short Cutter,	5½ lbs.	8¼ x 4¼	4½ x 3½	16.50	**9.00**
No. 51	Long Cutter,	5 lbs.	8¼ x 4	5¼ x 3¼	16.00	**8.50**
No. 51	Long Cutter,	6 lbs.	8½ x 4¼	6 x 3½	17.00	**9.00**

Long Cutter, Narrow Bit, Cast Steel, Polished and Painted Black.

	Weight	Size Hoe	Size Cutter	Per Dozen	
No. 52	5 lbs.	7½ x 2½	5 x 2¼	$16.00	**8.50**

Two Dozen in a Case.

PICK MATTOCKS

Cast Steel, Polished and Painted Black.

	Weight	Size Hoe	Size Pick	Per Dozen	
No. 53	6 lbs.	8½ x 4¼	8½	$17.00	**9.00**

GRUB HOES

Cast Steel, Oval Adze Eye, Polished and Painted Black.

	Weight	Size	Per Dozen	
No. 60	**4 lbs.**	11¼ x 4 in.	$13.50	**7.50**

Two Dozen in a Case.

ADZES

G. A. R. BRIDGE ADZE

An extra heavy tool, made for Bridge Carpenters.

4¼ inch cut .... each **5.00**
4½ inch cut .... each **5.00**
4¾ inch cut .... each **5.25**

WHITE'S SHIP ADZE

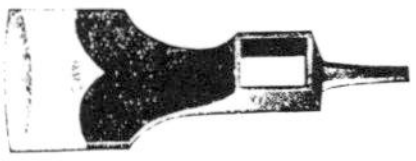

No. 44. 4 inch cut .... each **3.75**
4¼ inch cut .... each **4.00**
4½ inch cut .... each **4.00**

WHITE'S HOUSE ADZE

No. 30. 4 inch cut .... each **4.00**

Other widths, to order.

WHITE'S LIP ADZE

No. 45. 5 inch cut .... each **6.00**

Other widths, to order.

WHITE'S SHIP AXES

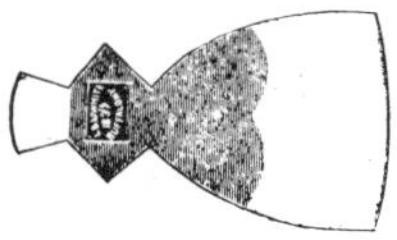

No. 1. 6 inch cut .... each **5.50**
No. 3. 6½ inch cut .... each **5.00**

G. A. R. SHIP MAULS

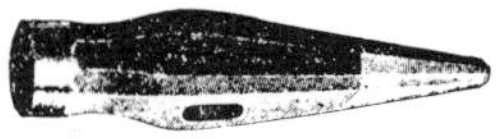

Extra Tool Steel, long slim body, large eye, 2½, 3, 3½, 4, 4½ pounds.

Per pound .... **.30**

RASE KNIVES

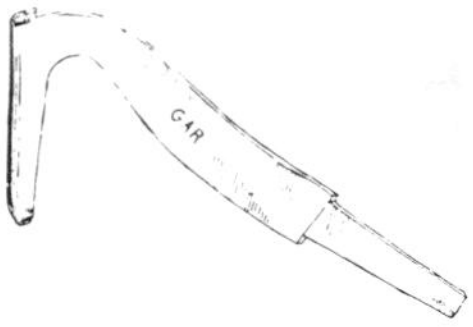

Plain .... each **.50**

Folding, Brass Handle .... each **1.35**
Folding, Wood Handle .... each **1.50**

Railroad Picks.

Cast-Steel, Axe Finish.
Weights, Assorted, 5 to 6 lbs., 5½ to 6½ lbs., 6 to 7 lbs.,
Per Dozen, $

Gold Miner's or Drifting Picks.

No.	Length.	Weight.	Per Dozen.
2	21 in.	4 lbs.	$
3	23 "	4½ "	
4	24½ "	5 "	

Coal Miner's Picks.

1	15 in.	2 lbs.	$
2	18 "	2½ "	

TWO DOZEN IN A CASE.

Stone Picks.

Per Dozen.

Cast-Steel, Axe Finish.
Weights, 6 to 7 lbs., 7 to 8 lbs., 8 to 9 lbs., $

Crowbars.

Per Pound.

Solid Cast-Steel, Assorted Sizes, $
Steel Point, " "

Handled Planters' and Mortar Hoes.

Per Dozen.

Planters' Polished Cast Steel, Solid Shank, 7 in. Blade, $
" " " " " " 7½ in. "
Mortar, Cast Steel Solid Shank, 10 in. Blade, 6 ft. Handle,

Planters' Eye Hoes.

Nos. 0 2
All Bright, Per Dozen, $
Half " " "

Champion Hoes.

No.		
1	5½ in. Blade, Square Pick,	$
2	6 in. " " "	
3	7 in. " " "	

ONE DOZEN IN A BUNDLE.

Mallets.

STONECUTTERS'.

5 to 5¾ inches, Hickory . . . .

SQUARE.
MORTISED HANDLES

No. 8, Hickory,　6　in. long x 2½ x 3½ in.

TINNERS'.

5 to 5¾ inches, Hickory . . . .

ROUND.
MORTISED HANDLES.

No. 2, Hickory,　5½ in. long x 3½ in. diam

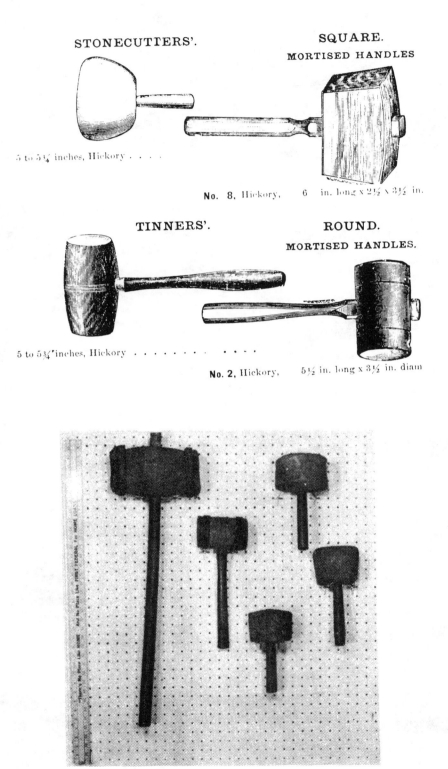

Wood Mallets

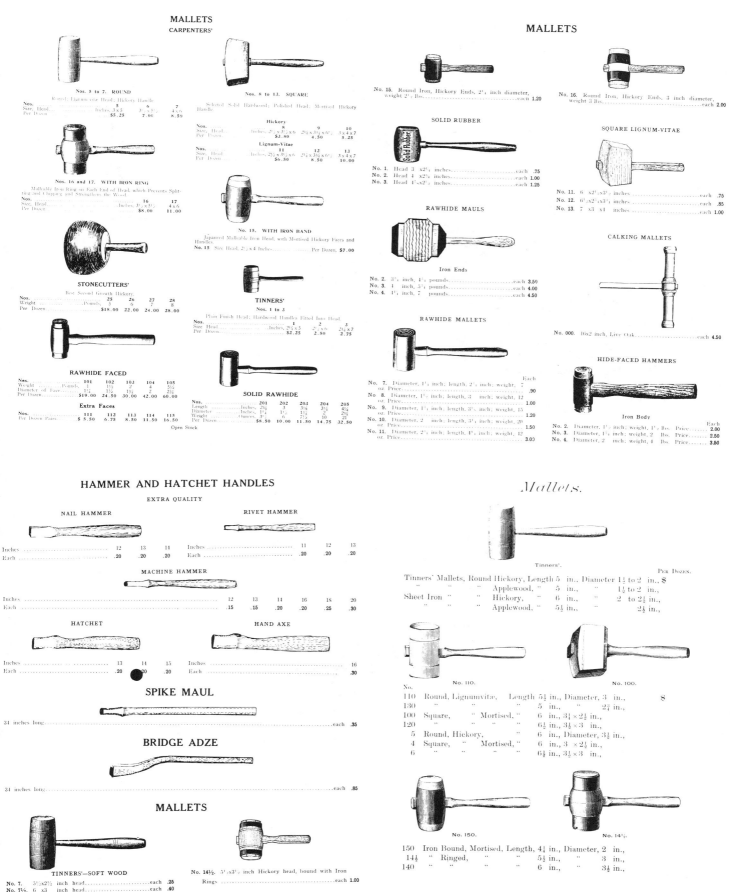

MALLETS
CARPENTERS'

Nos. 5 to 7. ROUND

Round; Lignum-vitae Head; Hickory Handle

Nos.	5	6	7
Size, Head	Inches, 3 x 5	3½ x 5½	4 x 6
Per Dozen	$5.25	7.00	8.50

Nos. 16 and 17. WITH IRON RING

Malleable Iron Ring on Each End of Head, which Prevents Splitting and Chipping and Strengthens the Wood

Nos.	16	17
Size, Head	Inches, 3½ x 5½	4 x 6
Per Dozen	$8.00	11.00

STONECUTTERS'

Best Second Growth Hickory

Nos.	25	26	27	28
Weight	Pounds, 5	6	7	8
Per Dozen	$18.00	22.00	24.00	28.00

RAWHIDE FACED

Nos.	101	102	103	104	105
Weight	Pounds, 1	1½	2	4	5½
Diameter of Face	Inches, 1¼	1½	1¾	2	2½
Per Dozen	$19.00	24.50	30.00	42.00	60.00

Extra Faces

Nos.	111	112	113	114	115
Per Dozen Pairs	$5.50	6.75	8.50	11.50	16.50

Open Stock

Nos. 8 to 13. SQUARE

Selected Solid Hardwood; Polished Head; Mortised Hickory Handle.

Hickory

Nos.	8	9	10
Size, Head	Inches, 2½ x 3½ x 6	2¾ x 3¾ x 6½	3 x 4 x 7
Per Dozen	$3.80	4.50	5.25

Lignum-Vitae

Nos.	11	12	13
Size, Head	Inches, 2½ x 3½ x 6	2¾ x 3¾ x 6½	3 x 4 x 7
Per Dozen	$6.50	8.50	10.00

No. 15. WITH IRON BAND

Japanned Malleable Iron Head, with Mortised Hickory Faces and Handles.

No. 15 Size Head, 2½ x 4 inches................Per Dozen, $7.00

TINNERS'
Nos. 1 to 3

Plain Finish Head; Hardwood Handles Fitted Into Head

	1	2	3
Size Head	Inches, 2½ x 5	2¾ x 6	2¾ x 7
Per Dozen	$2.25	2.50	2.75

SOLID RAWHIDE

Nos.	201	202	203	204	205
Length	Inches, 2¾	3	3¼	3½	4½
Diameter	Inches, 1¼	1½	1¾	2	2½
Weight	Ounces, 3½	6	7½	10	21
Per Dozen	$8.50	10.00	11.50	14.75	32.50

MALLETS

No. 15. Round Iron, Hickory Ends, 2½ inch diameter, weight 2½ lbs........................each 1.20

SOLID RUBBER

No. 1. Head 3 x2½ inches.......................each .75
No. 2. Head 4 x2¾ inches.......................each 1.00
No. 3. Head 4½x2½ inches.......................each 1.25

RAWHIDE MAULS

Iron Ends

No. 2. 3½ inch, 4½ pounds.....................each 3.50
No. 3. 4 inch, 5½ pounds.....................each 4.00
No. 4. 4½ inch, 7 pounds.....................each 4.50

RAWHIDE MALLETS

		Each
No. 7. Diameter, 1½ inch; length, 2½ inch; weight, 7 oz. Price		.90
No. 8. Diameter, 1¾ inch; length, 3 inch; weight, 12 oz. Price		1.00
No. 9. Diameter, 1¾ inch; length, 3¼ inch; weight, 15 oz. Price		1.20
No. 10. Diameter, 2 inch; length, 3¼ inch; weight, 20 oz. Price		1.50
No. 11. Diameter, 2¼ inch; length, 4¼ inch; weight, 12 oz. Price		3.00

No. 16. Round Iron, Hickory Ends, 3 inch diameter, weight 3 lbs.........................each 2.00

SQUARE LIGNUM-VITAE

No. 11. 6 x2½x3½ inches ....each .75
No. 12. 6½x2¾x3¾ inches ....each .85
No. 13. 7 x3 x4 inches ....each 1.00

CALKING MALLETS

No. 000. 16x2 inch, Live Oak...................each 4.50

HIDE-FACED HAMMERS

Iron Body

		Each
No. 2. Diameter, 1½ inch; weight, 1½ lbs Price		2.00
No. 3. Diameter, 1¾ inch; weight, 2 lbs Price		2.50
No. 4. Diameter, 2 inch; weight, 4 lbs Price		3.50

HAMMER AND HATCHET HANDLES
EXTRA QUALITY

NAIL HAMMER

Inches	12	13	14
Each	.20	.20	.20

RIVET HAMMER

Inches	11	12	13
Each	.20	.20	.20

MACHINE HAMMER

Inches	12	13	14	16	18	20
Each	.15	.15	.20	.20	.25	.30

HATCHET

Inches	13	14	15
Each	.20	.20	.20

HAND AXE

Inches	16
Each	.30

SPIKE MAUL

34 inches long..............................each .35

BRIDGE ADZE

34 inches long..............................each .85

MALLETS

TINNERS'—SOFT WOOD

No. 7. 5½x2½ inch head........................each .25
No. 7½. 6 x3 inch head.........................each .40
Special price in dozen lots.

No. 14½. 5½x3½ inch Hickory head, bound with Iron Rings ....each 1.00

Mallets.

Tinners'.

				Per Dozen.
Tinners' Mallets, Round Hickory, Length 5 in., Diameter 1½ to 2 in.,				$
" " " Applewood, " 5 in., " 1½ to 2 in.,				
Sheet Iron " " Hickory, " 6 in., " 2 to 2½ in.,				
" " " Applewood, " 5½ in., " 2½ in.,				

No. 110. **No. 100.**

No.					$
110	Round, Lignumvitae,	Length 5½ in., Diameter 3 in.,			
130	" "	" 5 in., " 2¾ in.,			
100	Square, " Mortised, "	6 in., 3¼ x 2½ in.,			
120	" " "	6½ in., 3½ x 3 in.,			
5	Round, Hickory, "	6 in., Diameter 3½ in.,			
4	Square, " Mortised, "	6 in., 3 x 2½ in.,			
6	" " "	6½ in., 3½ x 3 in.,			

No. 150. **No. 14½.**

150	Iron Bound, Mortised, Length, 4½ in., Diameter, 2 in.,
14½	" Ringed, " 5½ in., " 3 in.,
140	" " " 6 in., " 3½ in.,

MASONS' HAMMERS.

SINGLE FACE.

Solid Cast Steel, Axe Finish.

BUSH HAMMERS.

Solid Cast Steel, 4 to 12 pounds

WITH TEETH.

QUARRY PICKS.

Solid Cast Steel, Oil Finish.

MACADAMIZING HAMMERS.

Weight each.......................... 1 to 2 pounds

Mauls.

RAILROAD SPIKE.

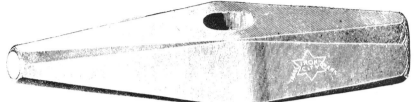

Solid Cast Steel

COAL.

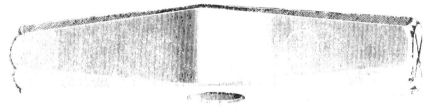

NAPPING HAMMERS.

Solid Cast Steel, Oil Finish, Polished Faces.

BRIDGE BUILDERS' RIVETING HAMMERS.

Solid Tool Steel, Octagon Pattern, Polished Ends.

Stonemasons' Hammers.
TOOTH AXES.

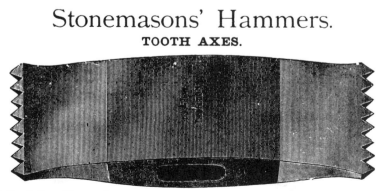

Solid Cast Steel, 5 to 10 pounds . . . .

Yerkes & Plumb's Cast-Steel Hammers.

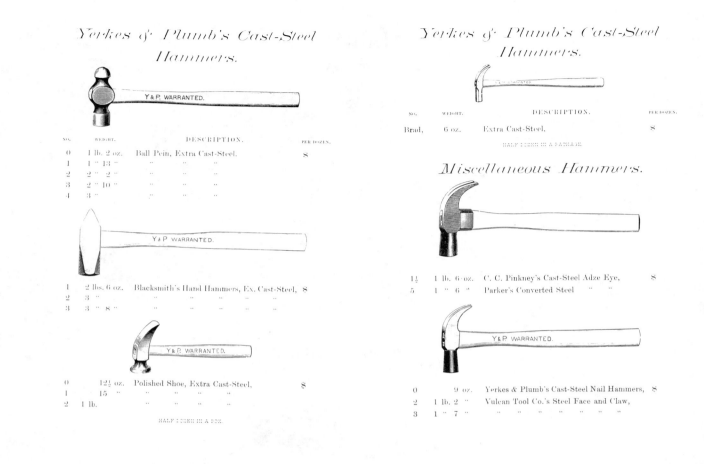

NO.	WEIGHT.	DESCRIPTION.	PER DOZEN.
0	1 lb. 2 oz.	Ball Pein, Extra Cast-Steel,	8
1	1 " 13 "	" " "	"
2	2 " 2 "	" " "	"
3	2 " 10 "	" " "	"
4	3 "	" " "	"

	2 lbs. 6 oz.	Blacksmith's Hand Hammers, Ex. Cast-Steel,	8
2	3 "	" " "	"
3	3 " 8 "	" " "	"

0	12½ oz.	Polished Shoe, Extra Cast-Steel,	8
1	15 "	" " "	"
2	1 lb.	" " "	"

HALF DOZEN IN A BOX.

Yerkes & Plumb's Cast-Steel Hammers.

NO.	WEIGHT.	DESCRIPTION.	PER DOZEN.
Brad,	6 oz.	Extra Cast-Steel,	8

HALF DOZEN IN A PACKAGE.

Miscellaneous Hammers.

1½	1 lb. 6 oz.	C. C. Pinkney's Cast-Steel Adze Eye,	8
5	1 " 6 "	Parker's Converted Steel " "	"

0	9 oz.	Yerkes & Plumb's Cast-Steel Nail Hammers,	8
2	1 lb. 2 "	Vulcan Tool Co.'s Steel Face and Claw,	"
3	1 " 7 "	" " " "	"

NAIL HAMMERS

BELL FACE

No. 50.	28 ounces	each 2.25
No. 51.	19 ounces	each 1.60
No. 51½.	16 ounces	each 1.50
No. 52.	12 ounces	each 1.40
No. 52½.	9 ounces	each 1.35
No. 53.	7 ounces	each 1.25
No. 54.	5 ounces	each 1.20

STRAIGHT CLAW

No. 51A.	19 ounces	each 1.75
No. 51½A.	16 ounces	each 1.60
No. 52A.	12 ounces	each 1.50

TRADESMAN'S SPECIAL

No. 999. A heavy hammer, weighing 28 ounces. Head like a machinist's hammer, with carpenter's claw. Just the tool for concrete form makers, plumbers, and for use on plugging chisels............each 2.00

OCTAGON HEAD

No. 31F.	19 ounces	each 1.75
No. 31½F.	16 ounces	each 1.65

BOX NAILERS
WITH CORRUGATED HEAD

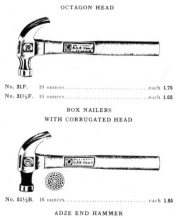

No. 51½B.	16 ounces	each 1.85

ADZE END HAMMER

No. 777. 24 ounces. Adze End, 2¼ inch wide. For Packers, Plumbers, Electricians...........each 1.50

STANDARD

Medium Quality

No. O11½.	16 ounces	each .85
No. O12.	12 ounces	each .75

Yerkes & Plumb's Cast-Steel Hammers.

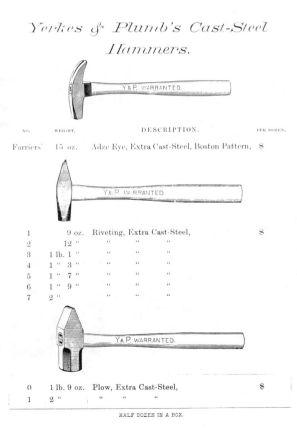

NO.	WEIGHT.	DESCRIPTION.	PER DOZEN.
Farriers'	15 oz.	Adze Eye, Extra Cast-Steel, Boston Pattern,	8

1	9 oz.	Riveting, Extra Cast-Steel,	8
2	12 "	" " "	"
3	1 lb. 1 "	" " "	"
4	1 " 3 "	" " "	"
5	1 " 7 "	" " "	"
6	1 " 9 "	" " "	"
7	2 "	" " "	"

0	1 lb. 9 oz.	Plow, Extra Cast-Steel,	8
1	2 "	" " "	

HALF DOZEN IN A BOX.

HAMMERS

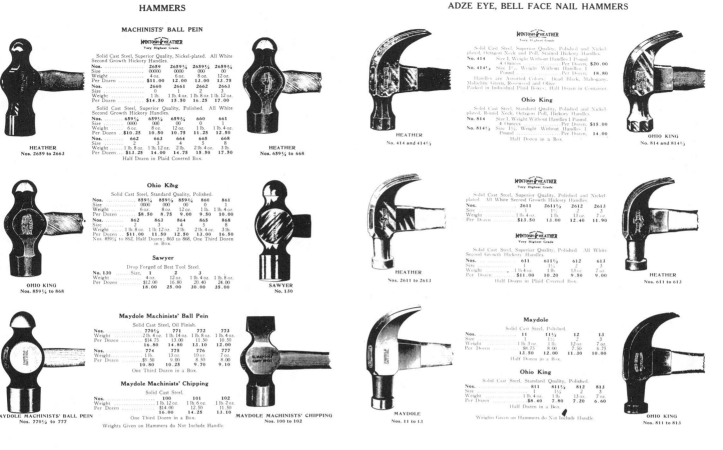

MACHINISTS' BALL PEIN

McINTOSH HEATHER
Very Highest Grade

Solid Cast Steel, Superior Quality, Nickel-plated. All White Second Growth Hickory Handles.

Nos.	2659	2659¼	2659¾	2659¾
Size	00000	0000	000	00
Weight	4 oz.	6 oz.	8 oz.	12 oz.
Per Dozen	$11.00	12.00	13.00	13.75
Nos.	2660	2661	2662	2663
Size	0	1	2	3
Weight	1 lb.	1 lb. 4 oz.	1 lb. 8 oz.	1 lb. 12 oz.
Per Dozen	$14.50	15.50	16.25	17.00

Solid Cast Steel, Superior Quality, Polished. All White Second Growth Hickory Handles.

Nos.	659¼	659½	659¾	660	661
Size	0000	000	00	0	1
Weight	6 oz.	8 oz.	12 oz.	1 lb.	1 lb. 4 oz.
Per Dozen	$8.50	10.50	10.75	11.25	12.50
Nos.	662	663	664	665	668
Size	2	3	4	5	8
Weight	1 lb. 8 oz.	1 lb. 12 oz.	2 lb.	2 lb. 4 oz.	3 lb.
Per Dozen	$13.25	14.00	14.75	15.50	17.50

Half Dozen in Plaid Covered Box.

HEATHER
Nos. 2659 to 2663

HEATHER
Nos. 659¼ to 668

Ohio King
Solid Cast Steel, Standard Quality, Polished.

Nos.	859¼	859½	859¾	860	861
Size	0000	000	00	0	1
Weight	6 oz.	8 oz.	12 oz.	1 lb.	1 lb. 4 oz.
Per Dozen	$8.50	8.75	9.00	9.50	10.00
Nos.	862	863	864	865	868
Size	2	3	4	5	8
Weight	1 lb. 8 oz.	1 lb. 12 oz.	2 lb.	2 lb. 4 oz.	3 lb.
Per Dozen	$11.00	11.50	12.50	13.00	16.50

Nos. 859¼ to 852, Half Dozen; 863 to 868, One Third Dozen in Box.

Sawyer
Drop Forged of Best Tool Steel.

No. 130	Size,	1	2	3
Weight	4 oz.	12 oz.	1 lb. 4 oz.	1 lb. 8 oz.
Per Dozen	$12.00	16.80	20.40	24.00
	18.00	25.00	30.00	35.00

OHIO KING
Nos. 859¼ to 868

SAWYER
No. 130

Maydole Machinists' Ball Pein
Solid Cast Steel, Oil Finish.

Nos.	770½	771	772	773
Weight	2 lb. 4 oz.	1 lb. 14 oz.	1 lb. 8 oz.	1 lb. 4 oz.
Per Dozen	$14.75	13.50	11.50	10.50
	16.80	14.80	13.10	12.00
Nos.	774	775	776	777
Weight	1 lb.	13 oz.	10 oz.	7 oz.
Per Dozen	$9.50	9.00	8.50	8.00
	10.80	10.25	9.70	9.10

One Third Dozen in a Box.

Maydole Machinists' Chipping
Solid Cast Steel.

Nos.	100	101	102
Weight	1 lb. 6 oz.	1 lb. 6 oz.	1 lb. 2 oz.
Per Dozen	$14.00	12.50	11.50
	16.00	14.25	13.10

One Third Dozen in a Box.

MAYDOLE MACHINISTS' BALL PEIN
Nos. 770½ to 777

MAYDOLE MACHINISTS' CHIPPING
Nos. 100 to 102

Weights Given on Hammers do Not Include Handle.

ADZE EYE, BELL FACE NAIL HAMMERS

McINTOSH HEATHER
Very Highest Grade

Solid Cast Steel, Superior Quality, Polished and Nickel-plated, Octagon Neck and Poll, Stained Hickory Handles.

No. 414   Size 1, Weight Without Handles 1 Pound
4 Ounces .... Per Dozen, $20.00
No. 414½   Size 1½, Weight Without Handles 1
Pound .... Per Dozen, 18.80
Handles are Assorted Colors: Dead Black, Mahogany, Malachite Green, Rosewood and Olive.
Packed in Individual Plaid Boxes. Half Dozen in Container.

Ohio King
Solid Cast Steel, Standard Quality, Polished and Nickel-plated, Round Neck, Octagon Poll, Hickory Handles.

No. 814   Size 1, Weight Without Handles 1 Pound
4 Ounces .... Per Dozen, $15.00
No. 814½   Size 1½, Weight Without Handles 1
Pound .... Per Dozen, 14.00
Half Dozen in a Box.

HEATHER
No. 414 and 414½

OHIO KING
No. 814 and 814½

McINTOSH HEATHER
Very Highest Grade

Solid Cast Steel, Superior Quality, Polished and Nickel-plated. All White Second Growth Hickory Handles.

Nos.	2611	2611½	2612	2613
Size	1	1½	2	3
Weight	1 lb. 4 oz.	1 lb.	12 oz.	7 oz.
Per Dozen	$13.50	13.00	12.40	11.90

McINTOSH HEATHER
Very Highest Grade

Solid Cast Steel, Superior Quality, Polished. All White Second Growth Hickory Handles.

Nos.	611	611½	612	613
Size	1	1½	2	3
Weight	1 lb. 4 oz.	1 lb.	13 oz.	9 oz.
Per Dozen	$11.00	10.20	9.80	9.00

Half Dozen in Plaid Covered Box.

HEATHER
Nos. 2611 to 2613

HEATHER
Nos. 611 to 613

Maydole
Solid Cast Steel, Polished.

Nos.	11	11½	12	13
Size	1	1½	2	3
Weight	1 lb. 3 oz.	1 lb.	12 oz.	7 oz.
Per Dozen	$8.75	8.00	7.50	6.75
	13.50	12.00	11.30	10.00

Half Dozen in a Box.

Ohio King
Solid Cast Steel, Standard Quality, Polished.

Nos.	811	811½	812	813
Size	1	1½	2	3
Weight	1 lb. 4 oz.	1 lb.	13 oz.	7 oz.
Per Dozen	$8.40	7.80	7.20	6.60

Half Dozen in a Box.

MAYDOLE
Nos. 11 to 13

OHIO KING
Nos. 811 to 813

Weights Given on Hammers do Not Include Handle.

D. Maydole & Co.'s Cast-Steel Hammers.

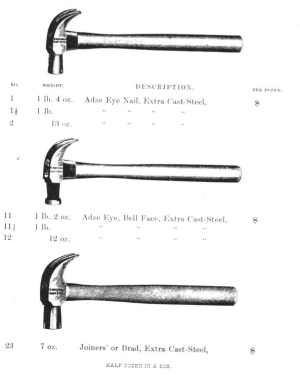

NO.	WEIGHT.	DESCRIPTION.	PER DOZEN.
1	1 lb. 4 oz.	Adze Eye Nail, Extra Cast-Steel,	$
1½	1 lb.	" " " "	
2	13 oz.	" " " "	
11	1 lb. 2 oz.	Adze Eye, Bell Face, Extra Cast-Steel,	$
11½	1 lb.	" " " " "	
12	12 oz.	" " " " "	
23	7 oz.	Joiners' or Brad, Extra Cast-Steel,	$

HALF DOZEN IN A BOX.

D. Maydole & Co.'s Cast-Steel Hammers.

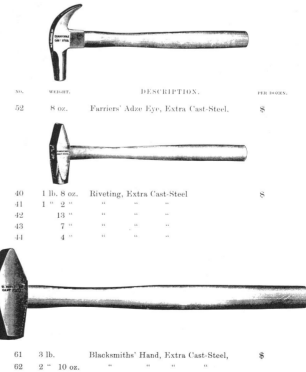

NO.	WEIGHT.	DESCRIPTION.	PER DOZEN.
52	8 oz.	Farriers' Adze Eye, Extra Cast-Steel.	$
40	1 lb. 8 oz.	Riveting, Extra Cast-Steel	$
41	1 " 2 "	" "	
42	13 "	" "	
43	7 "	" "	
44	4 "	" "	
61	3 lb.	Blacksmiths' Hand, Extra Cast-Steel,	$
62	2 " 10 oz.	" " " "	

HALF DOZEN IN A BOX.

FARRIERS' DRIVING HAMMERS

Solid Drop Forged Crucible Cast Steel, Perfectly Tempered; Second Growth Handles

No. 64 Heller Bros. Standard Pattern; Weights 14, 16 and 18 oz. ....Per Dozen, **$13.20**
Half Dozen in Box.

No. 51 Champion, Standard Pattern; Weights 15 and 16 oz. ....Per Dozen, **$12.00**
Half Dozen in Box.

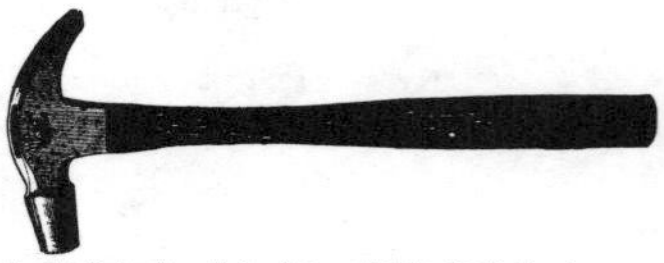

No. 65 Heller Bros. Heller Pattern; Weights 15, 16, 17 and 18 oz. ....Per Dozen, **$16.50**
Half Dozen in Box.

No. 50 Champion, Round Poll Pattern; Weights 15 and 16 oz. ....Per Dozen, **$15.00**
Half Dozen in Box.

No 69 Heller Bros. Scotch Pattern; Weights 15, 16, 17 and 18 oz. ....Per Dozen, **$16.50**
Half Dozen in Box.

No. 13 Champion, Scotch Pattern; Weights 16 and 18 oz. ....Per Dozen, **$15.00**
Half Dozen in Box.

FARRIERS' ROUNDING HAMMERS

No. 61 Heller Bros. Rounding Hammer; Weights 1 lb. 14 oz. to 2 lb. 8 oz. ....Per Dozen, **$31.68**
One Quarter Dozen in Box.

No. 4 Champion Maud S Rounding Hammer; Weights 2 lb. to 2½ lb. ....Per Dozen, **$28.80**
One Quarter Dozen in Box.

FARRIERS' FITTING HAMMERS

No. 62 Heller Bros Fitting Hammer; Weights 2, 2¼ and 2½ lb. ....Per Dozen, **$26.40**
One Quarter Dozen in Box.

No. 5 Champion Fitting Hammer; Weights 2, 2¼ and 2½ lb. ....Per Dozen, **$24.00**
One Quarter Dozen in Box.

HAMMERS

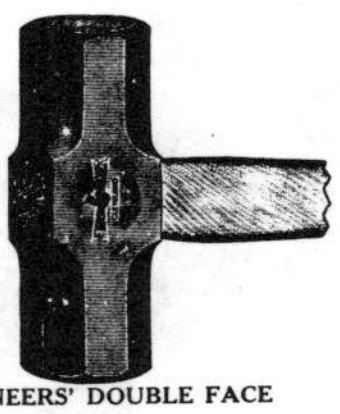

ENGINEERS' DOUBLE FACE

McINTOSH HEATHER
Very Highest Grade
Nos. 711 and 712

Solid Cast Steel, Superior Quality; All White Second Growth Hickory Handles.
No. 711 Weight 1 lb. 8 oz. ....Per Dozen, **$14.50**
No. 712 Weight 2 lb. 6 oz. ....Per Dozen, **16.50**
Half Dozen in Plaid Covered Box.

PAVING HAMMERS, HANDLED

Cast Steel, Hand Forged, Natural Finish, Hickory Handle.
No. 370 Weight 3 lb. ....Per Dozen, **48.00**

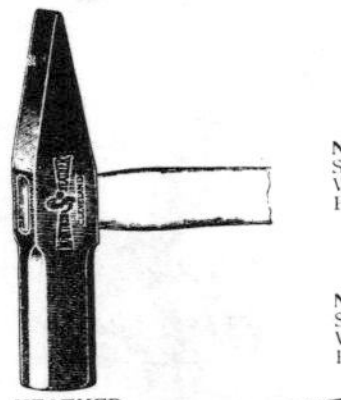

HEATHER
TINNER'S RIVETING
Nos. 671 to 674

McINTOSH HEATHER
Very Highest Grade

Tinners' Riveting

Solid Cast Steel, Superior Quality, Polished

Nos.	**671**	**672**	**673**	**674**
Size of Steel....Inches,	1⅛	1	⅞	¾
Weight	1 lb. 4 oz.	1 lb.	12 oz.	8 oz.
Per Dozen	**$13.00**	**10.50**	**9.25**	**7.25**

Tinners' Setting

Nos.	**681**	**682**	**683**	**684**
Size of Steel....Inches,	1⅛	1	⅞	¾
Weight	1 lb. 4 oz.	1 lb.	12 oz.	8 oz.
Per Dozen	**$13.00**	**10.50**	**9.25**	**7.25**

Half Dozen in Plaid Covered Box.

HEATHER
TINNER'S SETTING
Nos. 681 to 684

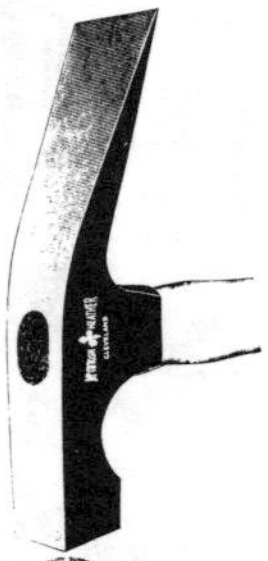

McINTOSH HEATHER
Very Highest Grade

BRICKLAYERS'

Solid Cast Steel, Superior Quality Hand Made; All White Second Growth Hickory Handles.
No. 773 Special Pattern; Weight 2 lb. ....Per Dozen, **$14.50**
One Quarter Dozen in Box.

SCOTCH BRICK HAMMERS

For Brick Sidewalk and Paving Use; for Cutting, Scraping a Sorting Brick and Leveling Bed and Tamping Sand.
No. 573 1⅛ in. Bits, Weight 2 lb. ....Per Dozen, **$19.**

Weights Given on Hammers Do Not Include Handle.

BLACKSMITHS' HAND HAMMERS

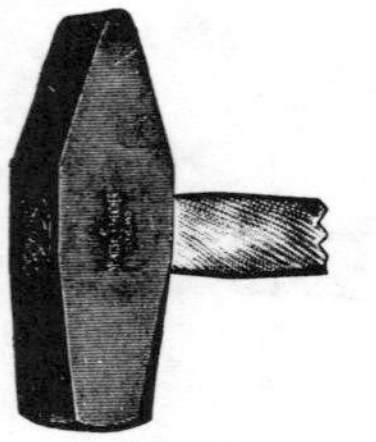

Nos. 721 to 723
HEATHER

McINTOSH HEATHER
Very Highest Grade

Solid Cast Steel, Superior Quality, Polished; All White Second Growth Hickory Handles.

Nos.	**721**	**722**	**723**
Weight	2 lb.	2 lb. 10 oz.	3 lb.
Per Dozen	**$14.00**	**15.00**	**16.00**

Half Dozen in Plaid Covered Box.

Ohio King

Solid Cast Steel, Standard Quality, Polished.

Nos.	**821**	**822**	**823**
Weight	2 lb.	2 lb. 10 oz.	3 lb.
Per Dozen	**$12.00**	**13.00**	**14.00**

Half Dozen in Box.

Maydole

Solid Cast Steel.
No. 61 Weight 3 lb. ....Per Dozen, $15.00 **17.00**
No. 62 Weight 2 lb. 10 oz. ....Per Dozen, 14.00 **16.00**
One Third Dozen in Box.

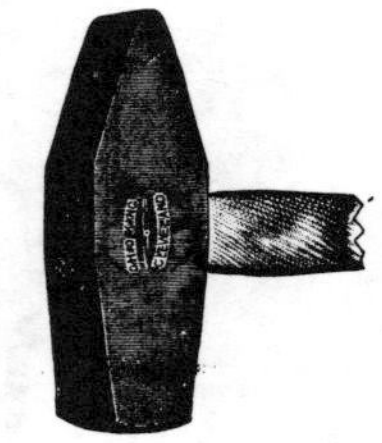

Nos. 821 to 823
OHIO KING

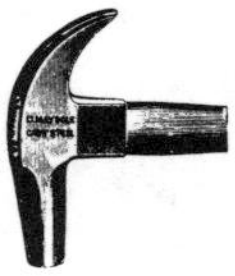

FARRIERS' HAMMERS

McINTOSH HEATHER
Very Highest Grade

Adze Eye, Solid Cast Steel, Superior Quality; All White Second Growth Hickory Handles.
No. 651 Weight 9 oz., Cincinnati Pattern ....Per Dozen, **$10.00**
No. 652 Weight 7 oz. ....Per Dozen, **$9.75**
Half Dozen in Plaid Covered Box.

MAYDOLE

Adze Eye, Cast Steel.
No. 253 Weight 8 oz.. Per Doz., $7.00 **9.25**
Half Dozen in a Box.

FARRIERS' SHARPENING HAMMERS

No. 67

No. 67 Heller Bros., Weight 2¼ lb. ....Per Dozen, **$31.68**
Quarter Dozen in a Box.

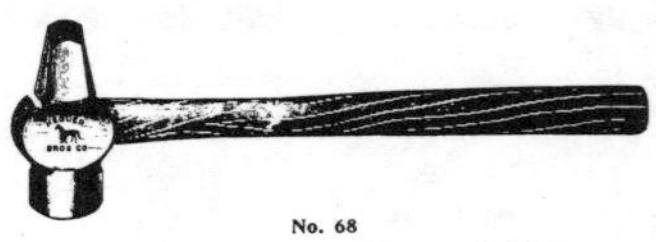

No. 68

No. 68 Heller Bros., with Corrugated Pein, Weight 2¼ lb. ....Per Dozen, **$31.68**

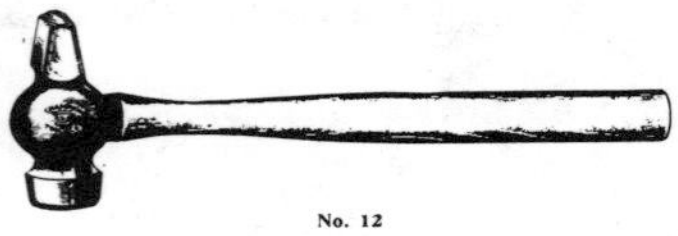

No. 12

No. 12 Champion, with Corrugated Pein, Weight 2¼ lb. ....Per Dozen, **$28.80**
Quarter Dozen in Box.
Weights Given on Hammers Do Not Include Handle.

HAMMERS

CAST IRON NAIL

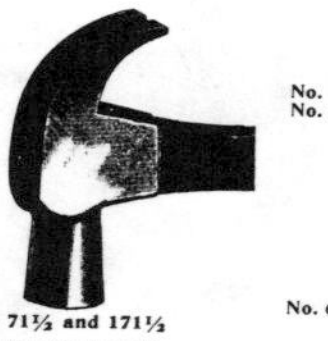

Nos. 71½ and 171½
CAST IRON NAIL

Adze Eye, Full Polished, Steel Finish, Varnished Handle.
No. 71½ Weight 1 lb. 4 oz. ....Per Dozen, **$2.00**
No. 171½ Same as Above, but Nickel-plated........Per Dozen, **3.00**
One Half Dozen in a Box.

McINTOSH HEATHER
Very Highest Grade

BRAD

Solid Cast Steel, Superior Quality, Polished.
No. 656 Weight 4 oz. ....Per Dozen, **$7.50**
Half Dozen in Plaid Covered Box.

No. 656
HEATHER BRAD

PLAIN EYE RIVETING

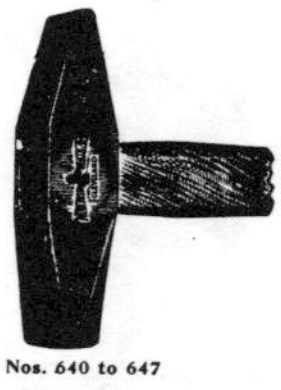

Nos. 640 to 647
HEATHER

McINTOSH HEATHER
Very Highest Grade

Solid Cast Steel, Superior Quality, Polished; All White Second Growth Hickory Handles.

Nos.	**640**	**641**	**642**	**643**	**644**	**645**	**646**	**647**
Size	0	1	2	3	4	5	6	7
Weight	4 oz.	7 oz.	9 oz.	12 oz.	15 oz.	1 lb. 2 oz.	1 lb. 6 oz.	1 lb. 10 oz.
Per Dozen	**$7.25**	**7.50**	**8.00**	**8.50**	**8.75**	**9.25**	**10.00**	**10.50**

Half Dozen in Plaid Covered Box.

OHIO KING

Solid Cast Steel, Standard Quality, Polished.

Nos.	**840**	**841**	**842**	**843**	**844**	**845**
Size	0	1	2	3	4	5
Weight	4 oz.	7 oz.	9 oz.	12 oz.	15 oz.	1 lb. 2 oz.
Per Dozen	**$6.50**	**6.60**	**6.90**	**7.25**	**7.50**	**8.00**

Half Dozen in a Box.

Nos. 840 to 847
OHIO KING

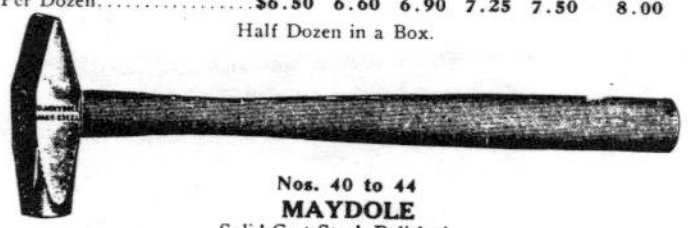

Nos. 40 to 44

MAYDOLE

Solid Cast Steel, Polished.

Nos.	**40**	**41**	**42**	**42½**	**43**	**44**
Weight	1 lb. 8 oz.	1 lb. 2 oz.	13 oz.	10 oz.	7 oz.	4 oz.
Per Dozen	$8.50	7.25	6.00	5.50	5.25	5.00
	11.00	**9.50**	**7.80**	**7.15**	**6.85**	**6.50**

Half Dozen in a Box.

ENGINEERS' RIVETING

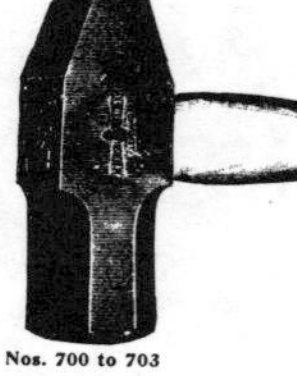

Nos. 700 to 703
HEATHER

McINTOSH HEATHER
Very Highest Grade

Solid Cast Steel, Superior Quality, Polished. All White Second Growth Hickory Handles.

Nos.	**700**	**701**	**702**	**703**
Size	0	1	2	3
Weight	1 lb. 2 oz.	1 lb. 10 oz.	2 lbs.	2 lb. 8 oz.
Per Dozen	**$12.00**	**13.00**	**14.00**	**15.00**

Half Dozen in Plaid Covered Box.

OHIO KING

Solid Cast Steel, Standard Quality. Polished.
No. 0802 Size 2, Weight 2 lb. ....Per Dozen, **$12.00**
No. 0803 Size 3, Weight 2 lb. 8 oz. ....Per Dozen, **13.00**
Half Dozen in a Box.

MAYDOLE

Solid Cast Steel. Polished.
No. 91 Weight 2 lb. 4 oz. ....Per Dozen, $13.00 **14.80**
No. 92 Weight 1 lb. 12 oz. ....Per Dozen, 12.00 **13.75**
One-third Dozen in a Box.
Weights Given on Hammers do Not Include Handle.

Nos. 0802 and 0803
OHIO KING

HAMMERS

UPHOLSTERERS AND TRIMMERS'

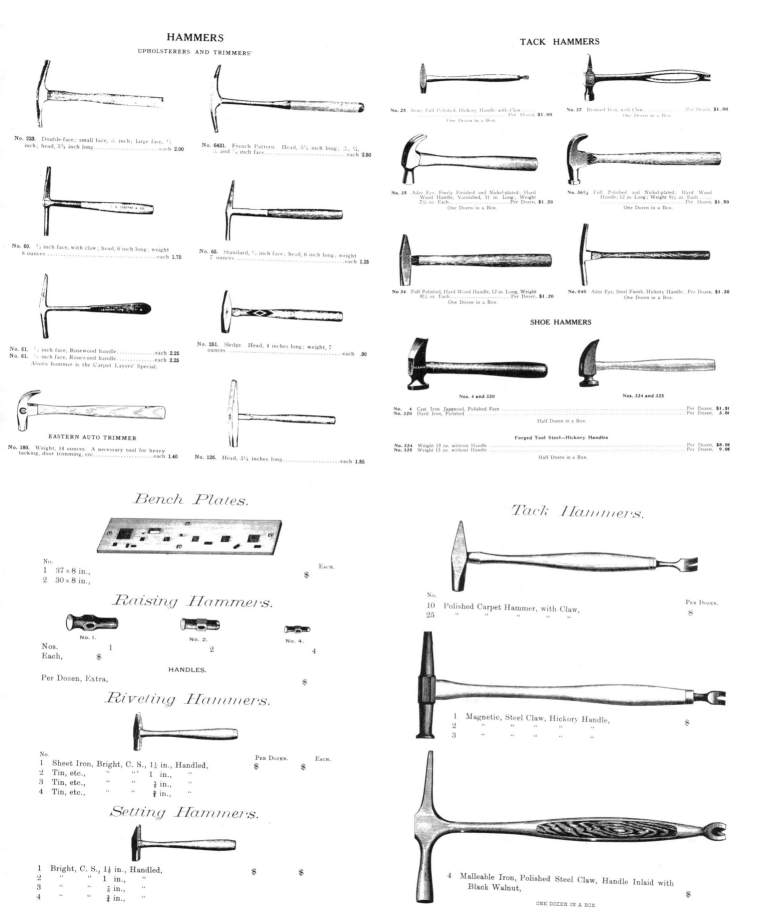

No. 223. Double-face; small face, ⅛ inch; large face, ½ inch; head, 5¾ inch long.....................each 2.00

No. 6431. French Pattern. Head, 5¾ inch long; ⅛, ¼, ⅜ and ⅝ inch face.....................each 2.50

No. 60. ½ inch face, with claw; head, 6 inch long; weight 8 ounces.....................each 1.75

No. 65. Standard, ½ inch face; head, 6 inch long; weight 7 ounces.....................each 1.25

No. 61. ½ inch face, Rosewood handle.....................each 2.25
No. 61. ⅝ inch face, Rosewood handle.....................each 2.25
Above hammer is the Carpet Layers' Special.

No. 251. Sledge. Head, 4 inches long; weight, 7 ounces.....................each .90

EASTERN AUTO TRIMMER

No. 180. Weight, 14 ounces. A necessary tool for heavy tacking, door trimming, etc.....................each 1.40

No. 126. Head, 5¼ inches long.....................each 1.85

TACK HAMMERS

No. 25 Iron; Full Polished, Hickory Handle with Claw.....Per Dozen, $1.00
One Dozen in a Box.

No. 37 Bronzed Iron, with Claw.....................Per Dozen, $1.00
One Dozen in a Box.

No. 35 Adze Eye, Finely Finished and Nickel-plated; Hard Wood Handle, Varnished, 11 in. Long; Weight 7½ oz. Each.....................Per Dozen, $1.20
One Dozen in a Box.

No. 36½ Full Polished and Nickel-plated; Hard Wood Handle, 12 in. Long; Weight 9½ oz. Each.....................Per Dozen, $1.50
One Dozen in a Box.

No 34 Full Polished, Hard Wood Handle, 12 in. Long, Weight 8½ oz. Each.....................Per Dozen, $1.20
One Dozen in a Box.

No. 040 Adze Eye, Steel Finish, Hickory Handle..Per Dozen, $1.20
One Dozen in a Box.

SHOE HAMMERS

Nos. 4 and 320

Nos. 324 and 325

No. 4 Cast Iron Japanned, Polished Face.....................Per Dozen, $1.50
No. 320 Hard Iron, Polished.....................Per Dozen, 3.00
Half Dozen in a Box.

Forged Tool Steel—Hickory Handles

No. 324 Weight 13 oz. without Handle.....................Per Dozen, $8.00
No. 325 Weight 15 oz. without Handle.....................Per Dozen, 9.00
Half Dozen in a Box.

Bench Plates.

No.		Each.
1	37 × 8 in.,	$
2	30 × 8 in.,	

Raising Hammers.

No. 1.   No. 2.   No. 4.

Nos.	1	2	4
Each,	$		

HANDLES.

Per Dozen, Extra, $

Riveting Hammers.

No.			Per Dozen.	Each.
1	Sheet Iron, Bright, C. S., 1⅛ in., Handled,		$	$
2	Tin, etc., " " 1 in., "			
3	Tin, etc., " " ⅞ in., "			
4	Tin, etc., " " ¾ in., "			

Setting Hammers.

1	Bright, C. S., 1⅛ in., Handled,	$	$
2	" " 1 in., "		
3	" " ⅞ in., "		
4	" " ¾ in., "		

Tack Hammers.

No.		Per Dozen.
10	Polished Carpet Hammer, with Claw,	
25	" " " "	$

1	Magnetic, Steel Claw, Hickory Handle,	
2	" " " "	
3	" " " "	$

4	Malleable Iron, Polished Steel Claw, Handle Inlaid with Black Walnut,	$

ONE DOZEN IN A BOX.

Stone Sledges.

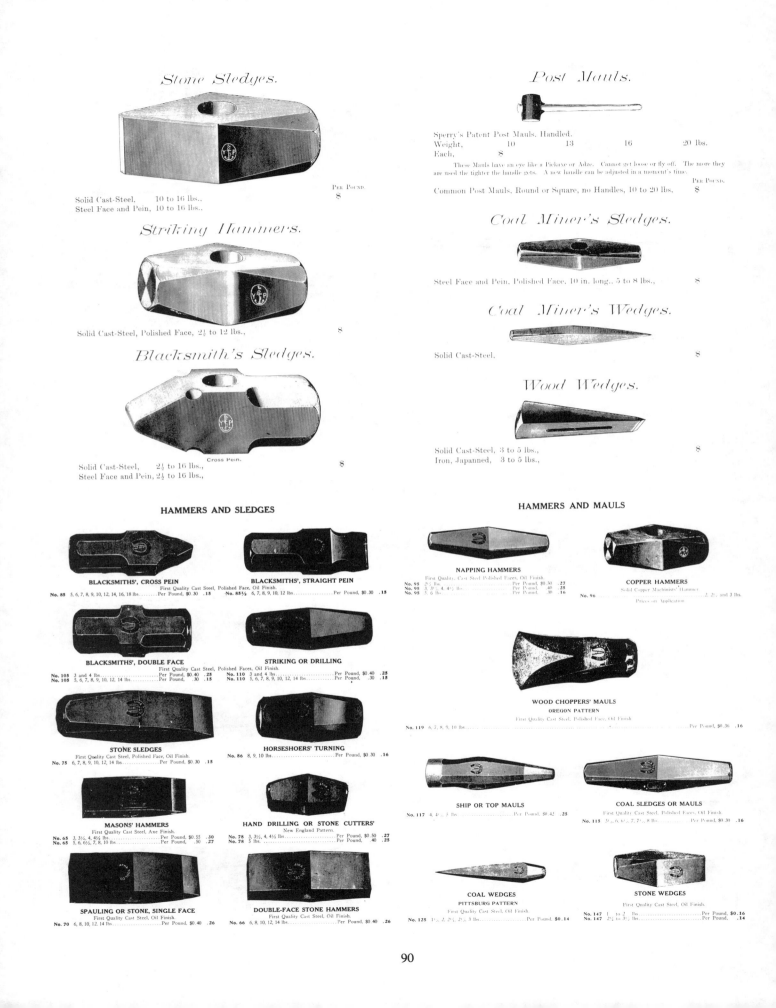

Solid Cast-Steel,   10 to 16 lbs.,
Steel Face and Pein, 10 to 16 lbs.,

Per Pound.
$

Striking Hammers.

Solid Cast-Steel, Polished Face, 2½ to 12 lbs., $

Blacksmith's Sledges.

Cross Pein.

Solid Cast-Steel,   2½ to 16 lbs.,
Steel Face and Pein, 2½ to 16 lbs., $

Post Mauls.

Sperry's Patent Post Mauls, Handled.

Weight,   10   13   16   20 lbs.
Each, $

These Mauls have an eye like a Pickaxe or Adze. Cannot get loose or fly off. The more they are used the tighter the handle gets. A new handle can be adjusted in a moment's time.

Common Post Mauls, Round or Square, no Handles, 10 to 20 lbs.,   Per Pound. $

Coal Miner's Sledges.

Steel Face and Pein, Polished Face, 10 in. long., 5 to 8 lbs., $

Coal Miner's Wedges.

Solid Cast-Steel, $

Wood Wedges.

Solid Cast-Steel, 3 to 5 lbs., $
Iron, Japanned,   3 to 5 lbs.,

HAMMERS AND SLEDGES

BLACKSMITHS', CROSS PEIN
First Quality Cast Steel, Polished Face, Oil Finish.
No. 85 5, 6, 7, 8, 9, 10, 12, 14, 16, 18 lbs....Per Pound, $0.30 .15

BLACKSMITHS', STRAIGHT PEIN
No. 85½ 6, 7, 8, 9, 10, 12 lbs..................Per Pound, $0.30 .15

BLACKSMITHS', DOUBLE FACE
First Quality Cast Steel, Polished Face, Oil Finish.
No. 105 3 and 4 lbs......................Per Pound, $0.40 .25
No. 105 5, 6, 7, 8, 9, 10, 12, 14 lbs..........Per Pound, .30 .15

STRIKING OR DRILLING
First Quality Cast Steel, Polished Faces, Oil Finish.
No. 110 3 and 4 lbs......................Per Pound, $0.40 .25
No. 110 5, 6, 7, 8, 9, 10, 12, 14 lbs...........Per Pound, .30 .18

STONE SLEDGES
First Quality Cast Steel, Polished Face, Oil Finish.
No. 75 6, 7, 8, 9, 10, 12, 14 lbs..............Per Pound, $0.30 .15

HORSESHOERS' TURNING
No. 86 8, 9, 10 lbs......................Per Pound, $0.30 .16

MASONS' HAMMERS
First Quality Cast Steel, Axe Finish.
No. 65 3, 3½, 4, 4½ lbs.................Per Pound, $0.55 .30
No. 65 5, 6, 6½, 7, 8, 10 lbs................Per Pound, .50 .27

HAND DRILLING OR STONE CUTTERS'
New England Pattern.
No. 78 3, 3½, 4, 4½ lbs.................Per Pound, $0.50 .27
No. 78 5 lbs.........................Per Pound, .40 .25

SPAULING OR STONE, SINGLE FACE
First Quality Cast Steel, Oil Finish.
No. 70 6, 8, 10, 12, 14 lbs..............Per Pound, $0.40 .26

DOUBLE-FACE STONE HAMMERS
First Quality Cast Steel, Oil Finish.
No. 66 6, 8, 10, 12, 14 lbs..............Per Pound, $0.40 .26

HAMMERS AND MAULS

NAPPING HAMMERS
First Quality, Cast Steel Polished Faces, Oil Finish.
No. 95 2½ lbs..........................Per Pound, $0.50 .27
No. 95 3, 3½, 4, 4½ lbs..................Per Pound, .40 .25
No. 95 5, 6 lbs........................Per Pound, .30 .16

COPPER HAMMERS
Solid Copper Machinists' Hammer.
No. 96 ....2, 2½, and 3 lbs.
Prices on Application

WOOD CHOPPERS' MAULS
OREGON PATTERN
First Quality Cast Steel, Polished Face, Oil Finish.
No. 119 6, 7, 8, 9, 10 lbs..............Per Pound, $0.36 .16

SHIP OR TOP MAULS
No. 117 4, 4½, 5 lbs..............Per Pound, $0.42 .25

COAL SLEDGES OR MAULS
First Quality Cast Steel, Polished Faces, Oil Finish.
No. 115 5½, 6, 6½, 7, 7½, 8 lbs......Per Pound, $0.30 .16

COAL WEDGES
PITTSBURG PATTERN
First Quality Cast Steel, Oil Finish.
No. 125 1½, 2, 2½, 2½, 3 lbs..........Per Pound, $0.14

STONE WEDGES
First Quality Cast Steel, Oil Finish.
No. 147 1 to 2 lbs..............Per Pound, $0.16
No. 147 2½ to 3½ lbs..............Per Pound, .14

HATCHETS

HALF

CLEVELAND

Solid Cast Steel; Gold Bronzed; Plain Eye; Octagon Poll; Plain Face; Polished Head and Bit.

Nos.	821	822
Size	1	2
Width Cut .... Inches	3½	3¼
Per Dozen	$7.20	7.50

MOHAWK

Cast Steel; Blue Finish; Plain Eye; Octagon Poll; Plain Face; Polished Head and Bit.

Nos.	921	922
Size	1	2
Width Cut .... Inches	3⅝	3¼
Per Dozen	$6.00	6.50

Half Dozen in a Box.

RIGGING

NORWEGIAN

Selected Solid Cast Steel; Black Rust-proof Finish; Plain Eye; Octagon Poll; Checkered Face; 19 Inch Knob End Handle.

No.	0523
Width Cut .... Inches	2¾
Face .... Inches	1⅝
Per Dozen	$12.00

OHIO KING

Hatchets are Forged from Crucible Cast Steel; Tempered Head and Bit; Ground and Sharpened; Second Growth Hickory Handles.

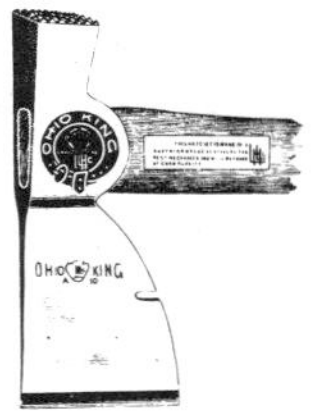

BARREL

McINTOSH & HEATHER
Very Highest Grade

Highest Grade Solid Forged Steel; Fire Bronzed; Plain Eye; Square Head; Checkered Face; Polished Head and Bit.

No.	190
Width Cut .... Inches	2½
Per Dozen	$11.00

Half Dozen in Plaid Covered Box.

OHIO KING

Extra Grade Cast Steel, Full Polished; Plain Eye; Square Head; Checkered Face.
No. 195 2½ in Cut ......Per Dozen, $9.50

CLEVELAND

Good Grade Cast Steel, Full Polished; Plain Eye; Square Head; Checkered Face.
No. 196 2¼ in Cut ......Per Dozen, $7.00

Half Dozen in a Box.

UNIVERSAL POCKET

McINTOSH & HEATHER
Very Highest Grade

Highest Grade Solid Forged Steel, Full Polished; Plain Eye; Octagon Pole, Plain Face.
No. 600 Size 0. Cut 2¼ Inches.
.... Per Dozen, $12.50

Half Dozen in Plaid Covered Box.

Hatchets.

Jim Nye Lath.

Jim Nye's Solid Cast-Steel Lath Hatchets, Full Polished, 2¼ in.,

PER DOZEN,
$

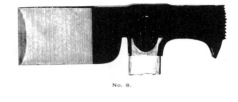

No. 8.

No.
8   Selsor & Co.'s Extra Cast-Steel Lath Hatchets, Bronzed, 2¼ in., $
12   "   "   "   "   "   "   "   2 "

HALF DOZEN IN A PACKAGE.

HATCHETS

G. A. R. SPECIAL

This hatchet is specially constructed for the mechanic who wants a heavy hatchet without much concave to sides of blade. Body is of Tough Norway Iron almost unbreakable. Head is faced with heavy plug of Best Tool Steel. A good flooring hatchet.

Each 2.00

GERMANTOWN
Half Hatchets

No. 320 Size 2. Polished steel, 3½ inch cut, very thin blade ....each 2.25

Bronzed Steel

No. 317½. Size 1. 3½ inch cut....................each 1.90
No. 318. Size 2. 3½ inch cut....................each 2.00

GERMANTOWN
Rustless Black Finish

Half   **Shingling**

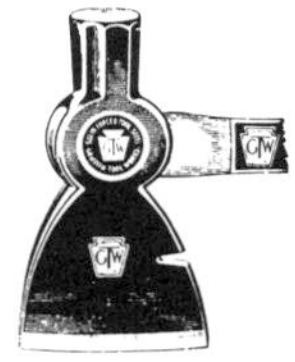

No. 5415.	Size 1.	3¾ inch cut ....each 1.65	No. 5410.	Size 1.	3¾ inch cut ....each 1.50
No. 5416.	Size 2.	3¾ inch cut ....each 1.75	No. 5411.	Size 2.	3¾ inch cut ....each 1.60
No. 5417.	Size 3.	3¾ inch cut ....each 2.00	No. 5412.	Size 3.	4¼ inch cut ....each 1.75

HATCHETS

GERMANTOWN

Lathing   **Lathing**

No. 5420. Size 1. 2 inch cut....................each 1.65
No. 5421. Size 2. 2½ inch cut....................each 1.75

No. 293. 9-row head, 2 inch cut....................each 2.5
No. 294. 10-row head, 2 inch cut....................each 2.7

ORANGE BOX   **DRY GOODS**    **BARREL**

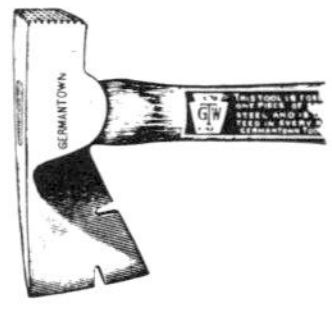

No. 282. 6½ inch long. Cut 2¼ inch. Often used for shingling.......each 2.50

No. 207½. Head 6½ inch long. Cut 3½ inch ....each 2.00

No. 132. Head 6 inch long. Cut 2½ inch ....each 2.25

SECOND QUALITY

Half   **Shingling**

No. 394. Size 2..........................each 1.25

No. 392. Size 2..........................each 1.25

91

CLAW HATCHETS

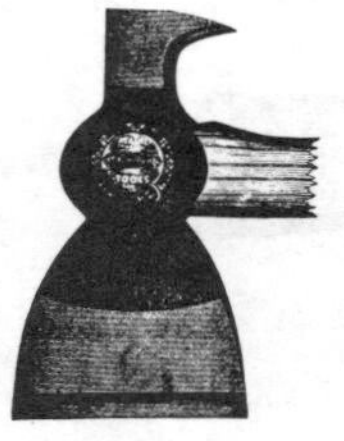
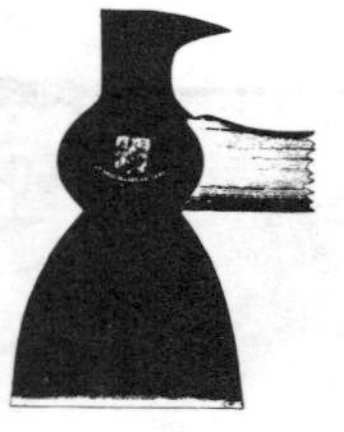
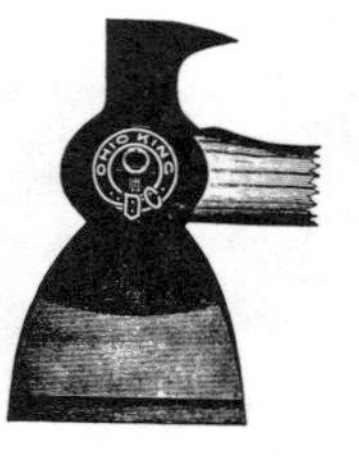

McINTOSH HEATHER
Very Highest Grade

Fire Bronzed; Plain Eye; Square Poll; Nickel-plated Head and Polished Bit.

Nos.	631	632	633
Size	1	2	3
Width Cut...Inches,	3½	3⅞	4⅛
Per Dozen	$11.00	11.75	12.50

Half Dozen in Plaid Covered Box.

NORWEGIAN

Solid Cast Steel, Black Rust-proof Finish; Plain Eye; Square Poll.

No.	532
Size	2
Width Cut...Inches,	3⅞
Per Dozen	$10.50

Half Dozen in Box.

OHIO KING

Green Bronzed; Plain Eye; Square Poll; Polished Head and Bit.

Nos.	731	732	733
Size	1	2	3
Width Cut...Inches,	3½	3⅞	4⅛
Per Dozen	$9.00	9.50	10.00

Half Dozen in Box.

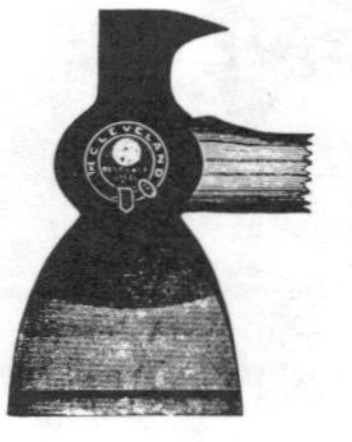
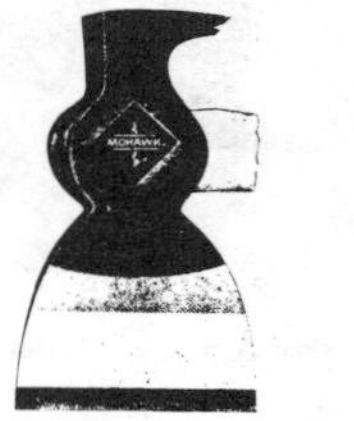
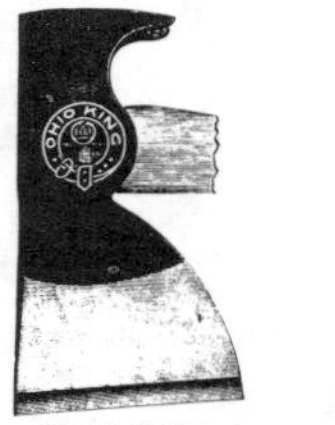

CLEVELAND

Solid Cast Steel, Gold Bronzed; Plain Eye; Square Poll; Polished Head and Bit.

No.	832
Size	2
Width Cut...Inches,	3⅞
Per Dozen	$8.00

MOHAWK

Cast Steel, Blue Finish; Plain Eye; Square Poll; Polished Head and Bit.

No.	932
Size	2
Width Cut...Inches,	3⅞
Per Dozen	$7.00

Half Dozen in Box.

CLAW HALF

OHIO KING

Green Bronzed; Plain Eye; Square Poll; Polished Head and Bit.

No.	732½
Size	2
Width Cut...Inches,	3⅛
Per Dozen	$9.50

HALF HATCHETS

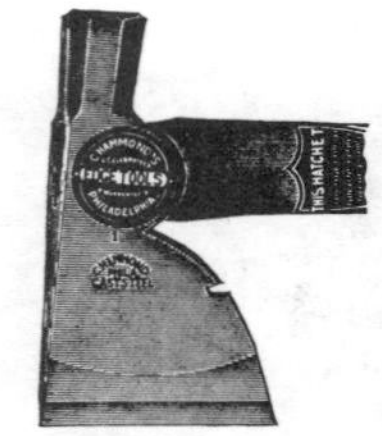
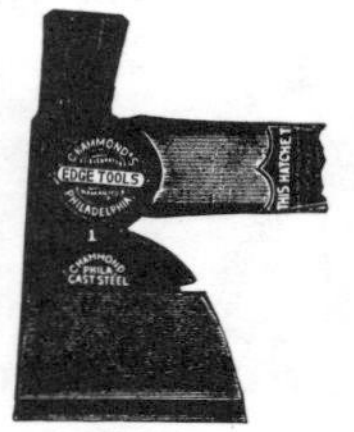
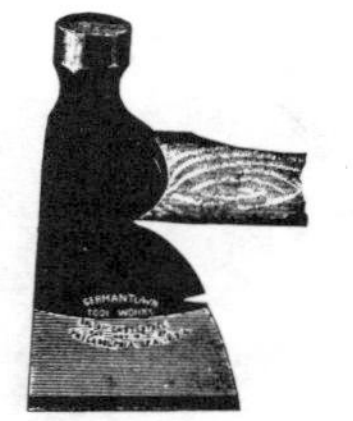

HAMMOND

All Steel, with Best Tool Steel on Head and Inserted for Cutting Edge; Plaid Eye; Octagon Poll; Full Polished.

Nos.	40	41
Size	1	2
Width Cut...Inches,	3¼	3½
Per Dozen	$13.50	14.00

HAMMOND

Forged from Swedish Iron with Best Tool Steel Inserted for Cutting Edge; Fire Bronzed; Plain Eye; Octagon Poll; Plain Face.

Nos.	30	31	32
Size	1	2	3
Width Cut...Inches,	3¼	3½	3¾
Per Dozen	$10.50	11.00	11.75

GERMANTOWN

Solid Cast Steel; Fire Bronzed; Plain Eye; Octagon Neck; Round Poll; Polished Head and Bit.

Nos.	317½	318	318½
Size	1	2	3
Width Cut...Inches,	3¼	3½	3¾
Per Dozen	$14.00	14.50	15.50

Half Dozen in a Box.

NORWEGIAN

Hatchets are Forged from Solid Steel; Head and Bit Tempered; Ground and Sharpened; Selected Second Browth Hickory Handles.

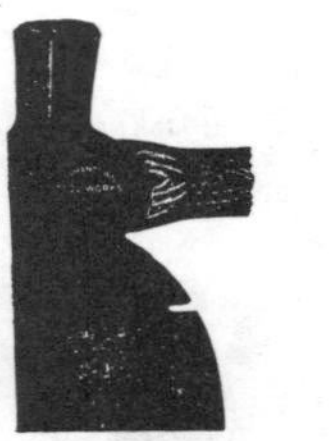
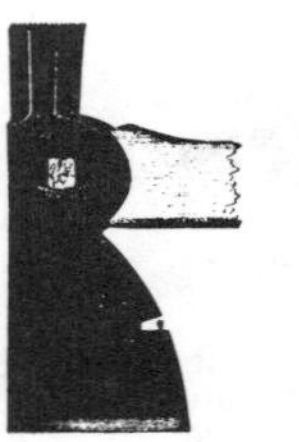
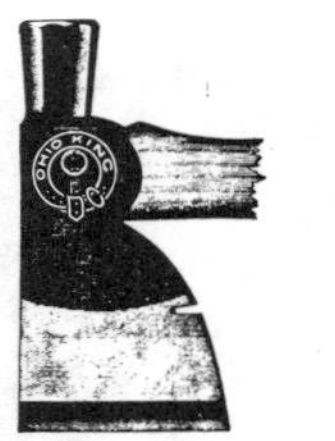

GERMANTOWN

Solid Cast Steel, Olive Bronzed; Plain Eye; Octagon Poll; Plain Face; Polished Head and Bit.

No.	338
Size	2
Width Cut...Inches,	3½
Per Dozen	$12.00

NORWEGIAN

Solid Cast Steel; Black Rustproof Finish; Plain Eye; Octagon Poll; Plain Face.

Nos.	521	522	523
Size	1	2	3
Width Cut...Inches,	3⅛	3⅜	3⅝
Per Dozen	$10.00	10.50	11.00

OHIO KING

Green Bronzed; Plain Eye; Octagon Poll; Plain Face; Polished Head and Bit.

Nos.	721	722	723
Size	1	2	3
Width Cut...Inches,	3⅛	3⅜	3⅝
Per Dozen	$8.40	8.80	9.30

Half Dozen in a Box.

SPORTSMAN'S HATCHETS

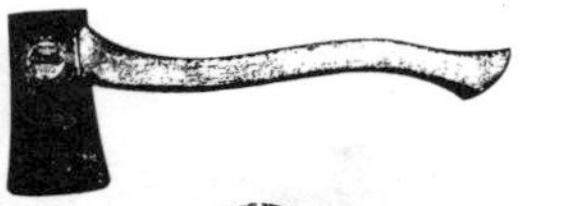

McINTOSH HEATHER
Very Highest Grade

Fire Bronzed; Polished Head and Bit; Superior Quality of Steel; Hand Forged; 14-in. Second Growth Hickory Axe Shape Handle.

No. 750 Width Cut, 2¾ in.; Weight, 14 oz. ...Per Dozen, **$10.50**
One Half Dozen in Plaid Covered Box.

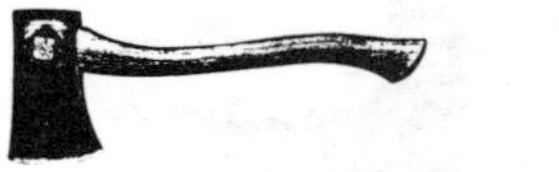

NORWEGIAN

Black Rustproof Finish; Tempered Head and Bit; Solid Crucible Steel; 14 Inch Second Growth Hickory Axe Shape Handles.

No. 730 Width Cut, 2¾ in.; Weight, 14 oz. ....Per Dozen, **$10.00**
One Half Dozen in a Box.

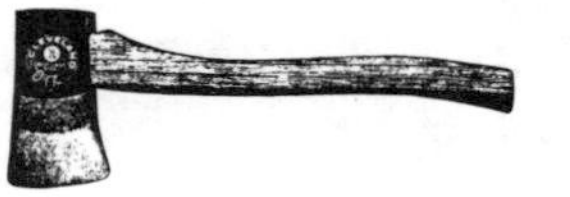

CLEVELAND

Solid Steel; Gold Bronzed; Polished Bit; 14 Inch Handle.

No. 770 Width Cut, 3 in.; Weight, 14 oz. ......Per Dozen, **$8.00**
One Half Dozen in a Box.

MARBLE'S SAFETY POCKET AXES

Large Enough to Fell a Tree and Small Enough to Carry in the Pocket. A Perfect Axe for "Blazing," Clearing a Trail, Setting a Tent, and as Necessary in the Woods as a Gun or Knife. The Nickel plated Spring Hinged Guard is Lined with Lead and Folds into the Handle. The Blade is Made of Tool Steel, Carefully Tempered and Sharpened. The Metal Handles Are Drop Forged and Will Never Break. Side Plates Are of Rubber. The Wood Handles Are of Selected Hickory and Have Nickel-plated Guard and Receiver.

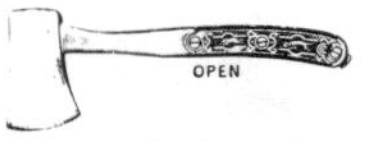

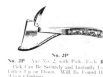

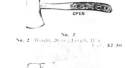

No. 2

No. 2 Weight, 20 oz.; Length, 11 in. ....Each, **$2.50**

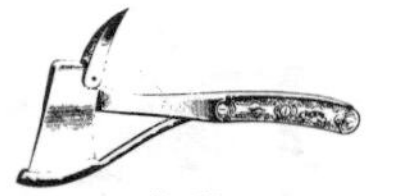

No. 2P

No. 2P Axe No. 2, with Pick. Each, **$4.00**
Pick Can Be Securely and Instantly Locked Either Up or Down. Will Be Found Handy When Climbing.

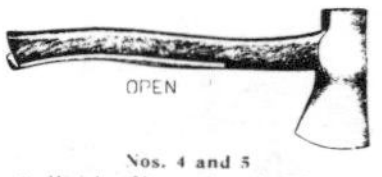

Nos. 4 and 5

No. 4 Weight, 24 oz.; Length, 12 in. ....Each, **$1.75**
No. 5 Weight 16 oz.; Length, 11 in. ....Each, **1.50**

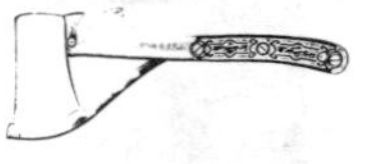

No. 2½

No. 2½ Axe No. 2, with Claw. Each, **$2.75**
Nail Claw Is Strong Enough to Pull a 10 Penny Nail from a Seasoned Hemlock Plank.

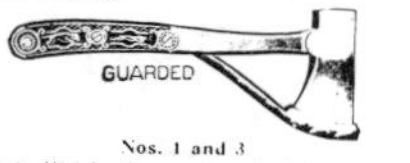

Nos. 1 and 3

No. 1 Weight, 16 oz.; Length, 10 in. ....Each, **$2.50**
No. 3 Weight, 27 oz.; Length, 12 in. ....Each, **3.00**

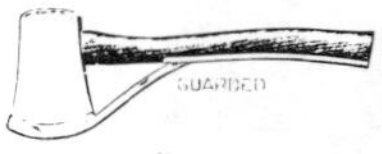

No. 6

No. 6 Weight, 20 oz.; Length, 12 in.; with Welded Steel Bit; Each, **$1.50**

All the Above Packed Two in Paper Box; Six Boxes in a Case.

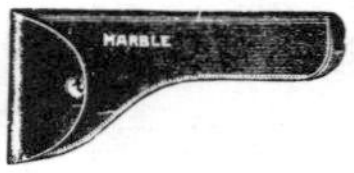

MARBLE'S LEATHER AXE SHEATHS

No. 19 Leather Sheath, Full Length ....Each, **$1.00**
No. 20 Leather Sheath, Half Length ....Each, **.75**

HALF HATCHETS

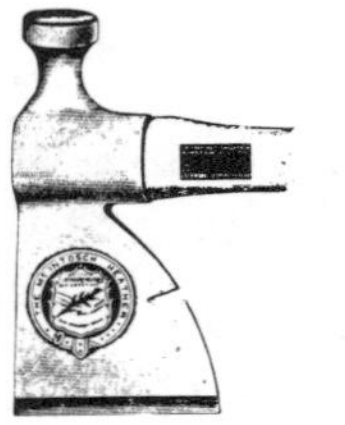
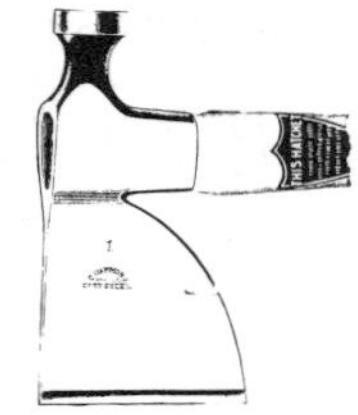
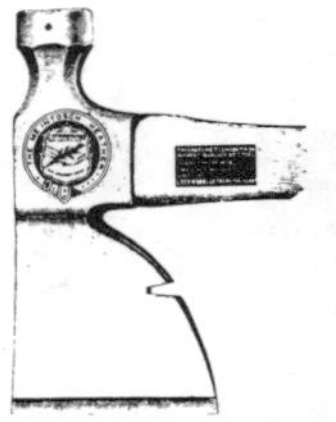

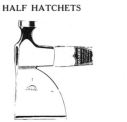

McINTOSH HEATHER
Very Highest Grade

Haines Pattern

Full Polished; Adze Eye; Round Poll; Bell Face.

Nos.	1421	1422
Size	1	2
Width Cut...Inches,	[illegible]	[illegible]
Per Dozen	$17.80	18.50

Half Dozen in Plaid Covered Box.

HAMMOND'S

Haines Pattern

Forged from the Best Grade of Crucible Steel; Full Polished; Adze Eye; Round Poll; Bell Face.

Nos.	45	46
Size	1	2
Width Cut...Inches,	[illegible]	[illegible]
Per Dozen	$15.50	16.00

Half Dozen in a Box.

McINTOSH HEATHER
Very Highest Grade

Polished and Etched; Adze Eye; Octagon Neck; Round Poll.

Nos.	1521	1522
Size	1	2
Width Cut...Inches,	[illegible]	[illegible]
Per Dozen	$13.50	14.00

Half Dozen in a Plaid Covered Box.

McINTOSH HEATHER
Very Highest Grade

Hatchets are Forged from Highest Grade Crucible Cast Steel Obtainable; Head and Bit Tempered ABSOLUTELY PERFECT; Ground and Sharpened and Fully Guaranteed; Handles Are Selected All White Second Growth Hickory.

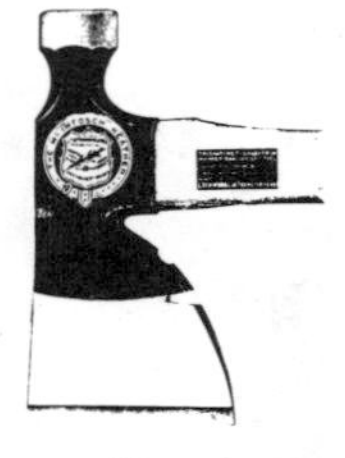
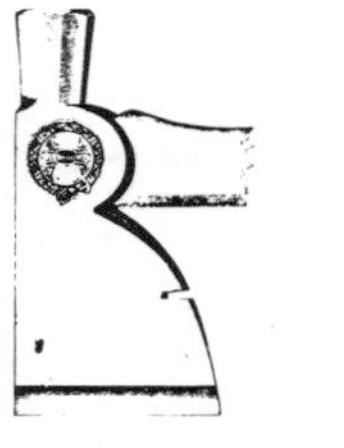
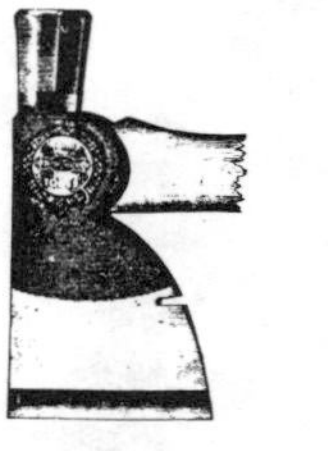

McINTOSH HEATHER
Very Highest Grade

Fire Bronzed; Adze Eye; Octagon Neck; Round Poll; Nickel-plated Head and Bit.

Nos.	1621	1622
Size	1	2
Width Cut...Inches,	[illegible]	[illegible]
Per Dozen	$12.00	13.00

McINTOSH HEATHER
Very Highest Grade

Full Polished and Etched; Plain Eye; Octagon Poll; Plain Face.

Nos.	421	422
Size	1	2
Width Cut...Inches,	[illegible]	[illegible]
Per Dozen	$11.50	12.00

Half Dozen in Plaid Covered Box.

McINTOSH HEATHER
Very Highest Grade

Fire Bronzed; Plain Eye; Octagon Poll; Plain Face; Nickel-plated Head and Polished Bit.

Nos.	621	622	623
Size	1	2	3
Width Cut...Inches,	[illegible]	[illegible]	[illegible]
Per Dozen	$10.00	10.80	11.5

LATHING HATCHETS

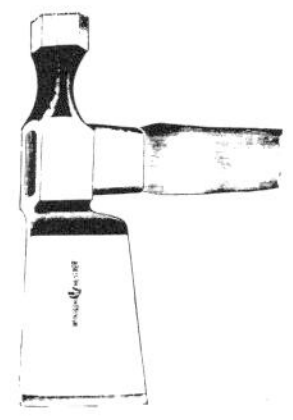

McINTOSH HEATHER
Very Highest Grade

NEW YORK PATTERN

Adze Eye; Solid Crucible Steel, Full Polished; Checkered Head, Weight 14 Ounces.

No. 1291 Cut 2¼ in. .... Per Dozen, **$17.50**

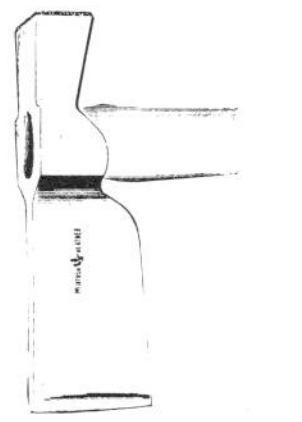

McINTOSH HEATHER
Very Highest Grade

NEW ENGLAND PATTERN

Solid Crucible Steel, Full Polished; Checkered Head; 9 Rows, 64 Points; Weight, 14 Ounces.

No. 1292 Cut 2⅜ in. .... Per Dozen, **$20.00**

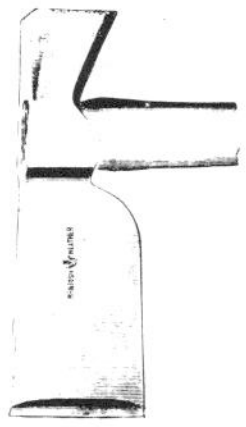

McINTOSH HEATHER
Very Highest Grade

CHICAGO PATTERN

Solid Crucible Steel, Full Polished; Checkered Head; 9 Rows, 81 Points; Weight, 16 Ounces.

No. 1293 Cut 2⅜ in. .... Per Dozen, **$22.00**

Half Dozen in Plaid Covered Box

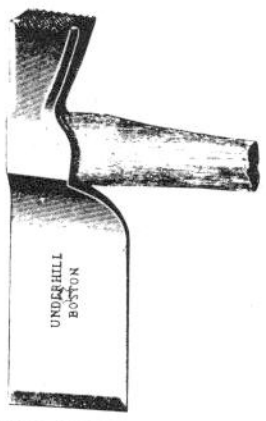

GENUINE UNDERHILL

Boston Pattern; Solid Crucible Steel, Full Polished; Extra Thin Blade; Checkered Head; 8 Rows, 64 Points; Weight, 14 Ounces.

No. 92 Cut 2 in. .... Per Dozen, **$30.00**

Half Dozen in a Box.

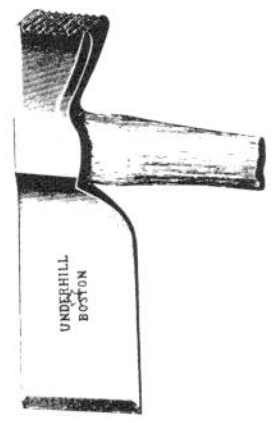

CHICAGO PATTERN

Solid Crucible Steel, Full Polished; Checkered Head; 9 Rows, 81 Points; Weight, 14 Ounces.

No. 93 Cut 2 in. .... Per Dozen, **$32.50**

Half Dozen in a Box.

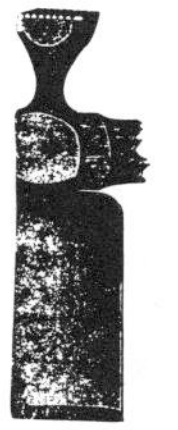

UNDERHILL PATTERN

Bell Face; Solid Crucible Steel, Full Polished; Checkered Head; 8 Rows, 64 Points; Weight 14 Ounces.

No. 97 Cut 2 in. .... Per Dozen, **$23.00**

Half Dozen in a Box.

All Above Hatchets Have Extra White Hickory Handles.

Weights Given on Hatchets do not Include Handle.

SHINGLING HATCHETS

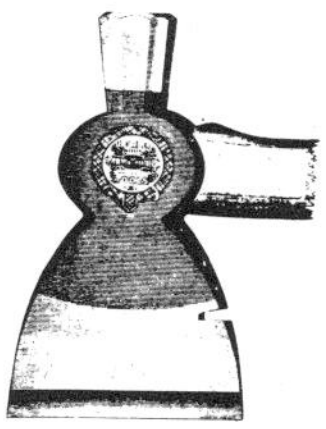

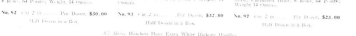

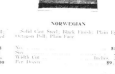

HEATHER

Fire Bronzed; Plain Eye; Octagon Poll; Plain Face; Nickelplated Head and Polished Bit.

Nos.	**611**	**612**	**613**
Size	1	2	3
Width Cut, Inches	3½	3⅞	4⅜
Per Dozen	**$10.00**	**10.50**	**11.00**

Half Dozen in Plaid Covered Box.

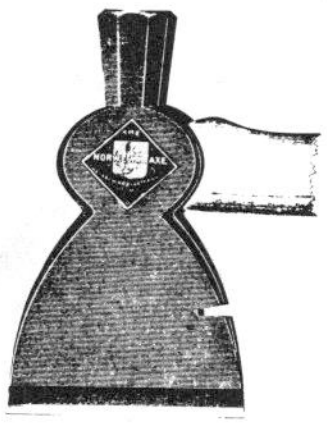

NORWEGIAN

Solid Cast Steel; Black Finish; Plain Eye; Octagon Poll; Plain Face.

No.	**512**
Size	2
Width Cut .... Inches,	3⅞
Per Dozen	**$9.75**

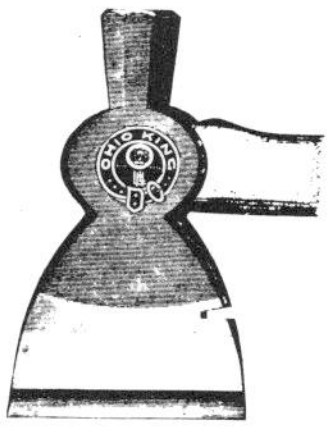

OHIO KING

Green Bronzed; Plain Eye; Octagon Poll; Plain Face; Polished Head and Bit.

Nos.	**711**	**712**	**713**
Size	1	2	3
Width Cut, Inches	3½	3⅞	4⅜
Per Dozen	**$8.00**	**8.50**	**9.25**

Half Dozen in Box.

CLEVELAND

Hatchets Are Medium Grade, Which Will Give Satisfactory Service, Though Not so Carefully Inspected or Finished as the Higher Grade Lines.

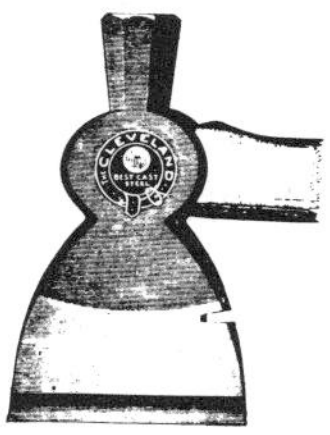

CLEVELAND

Solid Cast Steel; Gold Bronzed; Plain Eye; Octagon Poll; Plain Face; Polished Head and Bit.

No.	**812**
Size	2
Width Cut .... Inches,	3⅞
Per Dozen	**$7.25**

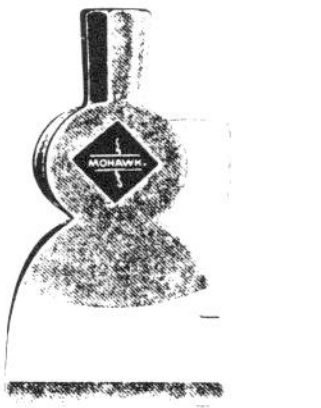

MOHAWK

Cast Steel; Blue Finish; Plain Eye; Octagon Poll; Plain Face; Polished Head and Bit.

No.	**912**
Size	2
Width Cut .... Inches,	3⅞
Per Dozen	**$6.00**

Half Dozen in Box.

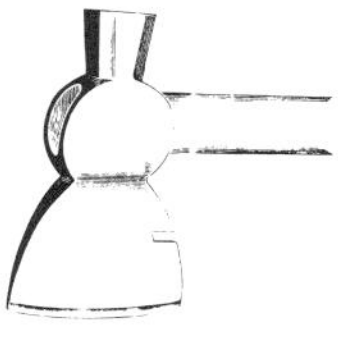

CAST IRON

Gold Bronzed; Plain Eye; Octagon Poll; Plain Face.

No.	**1012**
Size	2
Width Cut .... Inches,	3⅞
Per Dozen	**$2.50**

LATHING HATCHETS

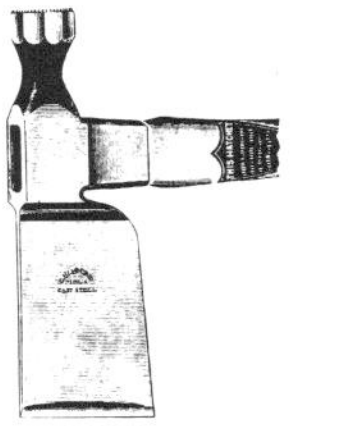

HAMMOND

New York Pattern; Adze Eye; Solid Crucible Steel, Full Polished; Checkered Head; Weight, 14 Ounces.

No. 85 Cut 2¼ in. .... Per Dozen, **$15.60**

Half Dozen in a Box.

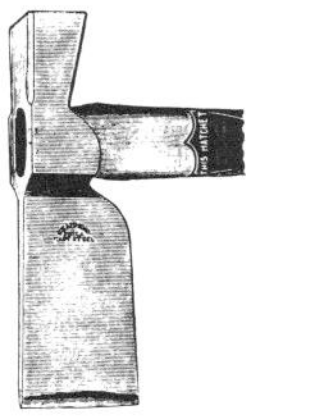

HAMMOND

New England Pattern; Solid Crucible Steel, Full Polished; Checkered Head; 8 Rows, 64 Points; Weight, 14 Ounces.

No. 95 Cut 2⅜ in. .... Per Dozen, **$15.60**

Half Dozen in a Box.

Weights Given on Hatchets do not Include Handle.

McINTOSH HEATHER
Very Highest Grade

Hatchets are Forged from Highest Grade Crucible Cast Steel Obtainable; Head and Bit Tempered Absolutely Perfect; Ground and Sharpened and Fully Guaranteed; Handles are Selected All White, Second Growth Hickory.

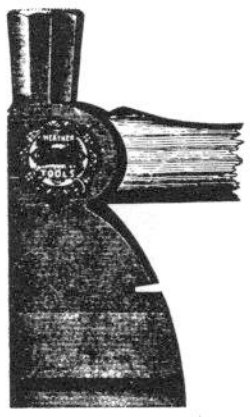

McINTOSH HEATHER
Very Highest Grade

Fire Bronzed; Plain Eye; Octagon Poll; Checkered Face; Nickel-plated Head and Polished Bit.

Nos.	**641**	**642**
Size	1	2
Width Cut .... Inches,	2½	2¾
Per Dozen	**$10.00**	**10.50**

Half Dozen in Plaid Covered Box.

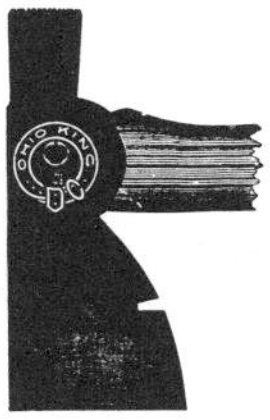

OHIO KING

Green Bronzed; Plain Eye; Octagon Poll; Checkered Face Polished Head and Bit.

Nos.	**741**	**742**
Size	1	2
Width Cut .... Inches,	2½	2¾
Per Dozen	**$8.00**	**8.50**

Half Dozen in Box.

HAND AXES

GERMANTOWN

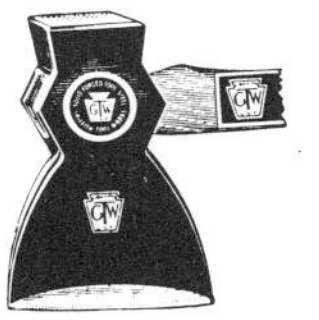

No. 562. 4½ inch cut .... each **2.25**
No. 563. 5 inch cut .... each **2.50**

WHITE'S

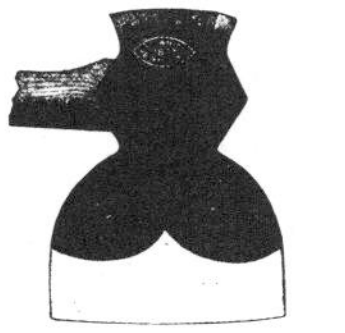

No. 7. 4½ inch cut .... each **2.50**
No. 6. 5 inch cut .... each **2.65**
No. 4. 6 inch cut .... each **2.85**
No. 2. 7 inch cut .... each **3.25**

HALF HAND AXES

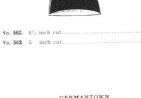

GERMANTOWN

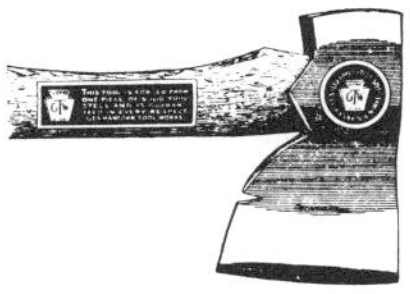

No. 462. Head 6¼ inch long, cut 4½ inch .... each **2.75**

WHITE'S

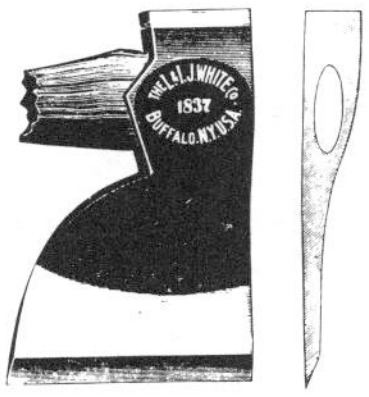

No. 27A-7. Head 6½ inch long, cut 3⅞ inch .... each **3.00**

HUNTERS' AXES

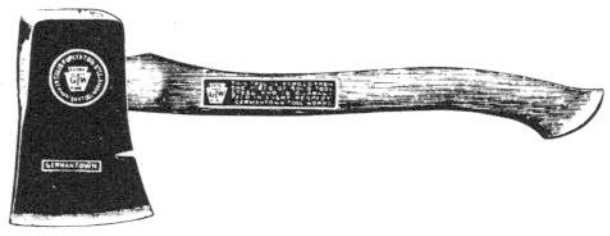

No. 375. Head 5½ inch long, cut 3¼ inch, handle 12 inch long .... each **1.75**

BROAD AXES

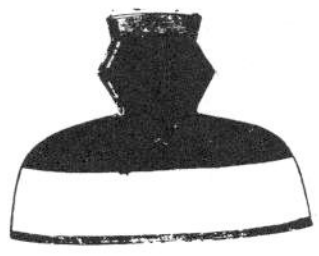

No. 12. 12 inch cut .... each **4.5**

BENCH OR BROAD HATCHETS

M'INTOSH & HEATHER
Very Highest Grade

Superior Quality Steel; Fire Bronzed; Plain Eye; Square Poll; Plain Face; Nickel-plated Head and Polished Bit.

Nos.	662	663	664	665
Sizes	2	3	4	5
Width Cut .... Inches,	4½	5	5½	6
Per Dozen	$13.00	14.50	16.50	18.50

One Third Dozen in Plaid Covered Box.

NORWEGIAN

Solid Cast Steel; Black Rustproof Finish; Plain Eye; Square Poll; Plain Face.

Nos.		562	563	564
Size		2	3	4
Width Cut .... Inches,		4½	5	5½
Per Dozen		$12.00	13.75	15.75

Half Dozen in Box.

OHIO KING

Solid Cast Steel; Green Bronzed; Plain Eye; Square Poll; Plain Face; Polished Head and Bit.

Nos.	762	763	764	765
Sizes	2	3	4	5
Width Cut .... Inches,	4½	5	5½	6
Per Dozen	$11.50	13.00	15.00	17.00

CLEVELAND

Cast Steel; Gold Bronzed; Plain Eye; Square Poll, Plain Face; Polished Head and Bit.

Nos.	962	963	964	965
Size	2	3	4	5
Width Cut .... Inches,	4½	5	5½	6
Per Dozen	$10.00	11.00	13.00	14.40

Half Dozen in Box.

Hatchets.

Blood's Extra Cast-Steel Broad Hatchets, Bronzed.

No.	3	4	5	6
Weight	2 lbs.	2½ lbs.	3 lbs.	3¾ lbs.
Width of Bit....	4¾ in.	5½ in.	6 in.	6¾ in.
Per Dozen........	$			

HALF DOZEN IN A PACKAGE.

Hatchets.

"Winooski."

Hibbard, Spencer & Co.'s Winooski Cast-Steel Claw Hatchets, Bronzed.

No.	1	2	3
Weight	1 lb. 10 oz.	2 lb.	2 lbs. 3 oz.
Width of Bit......	3¾ in.	4 in.	4¼ in.
Per Dozen........	$		

Tom Purdon's Cast-Steel Claw Hatchets, Black.

No.	1	2	3
Weight	1 lb. 10 oz.	2 lb.	2 lbs. 3 oz.
Width of Bit......	3½ in.	4 in.	4½ in.
Per Dozen........	$		

Blood's Extra Cast Steel Claw Hatchets, Bronzed.

No.	1	2	3
Weight	1 lb. 10 oz.	2 lb.	2 lbs. 3 oz.
Width of Bit.....	3½ oz.	3⅞ in.	4⅜ in.
Per Dozen........	$		

HALF DOZEN IN A PACKAGE.

Hatchets.

"Winooski."

Hibbard, Spencer & Co.'s Winooski Cast-Steel Shingling Hatchets, Bronzed.

No.	1	2	3
Weight	1 lb. 10 oz.	2 lbs.	2 lbs. 3 oz.
Width of Bit......	3¾ in.	4 in.	4¼ in.
Per Dozen........	$		

Tom Purdon's Cast-Steel Shingling Hatchets, Black.

No.	1	2	3
Weight	1 lb. 10 oz.	1 lb. 12 oz.	2 lbs. 3 oz.
Width of Bit......	3½ in.	4 in.	4½ in.
Per Dozen........	$		

Blood's Extra Cast-Steel Shingling Hatchets, Bronzed.

No.	1	2	3
Weight	1 lb. 10 oz.	2 lbs.	2 lbs. 3 oz.
Width of Bit.....	3½ in.	3⅞ in.	4⅜ in.
Per Dozen........	$		

HALF DOZEN IN A PACKAGE.

Cooper's Tools

Coopering or the making of wooden barrels is a very old trade. No doubt, barrels were made during the time of ancient Rome and Coopers have been high on the list of respected tradesmen. Cooper's tools are much harder to find than regular hand tools.

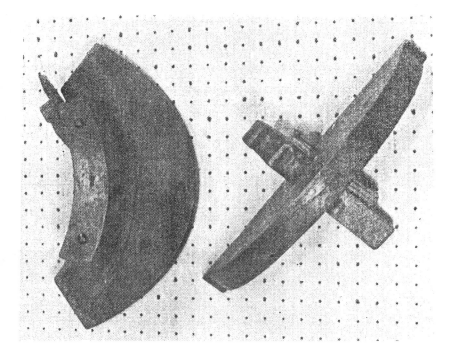

Left, Cooper's Croze
Right, Inside Groover

Cooper's Croze
Left, Metal
Right, Wood
Note — Used for making grooves and
bevels at top and bottom of barrels.

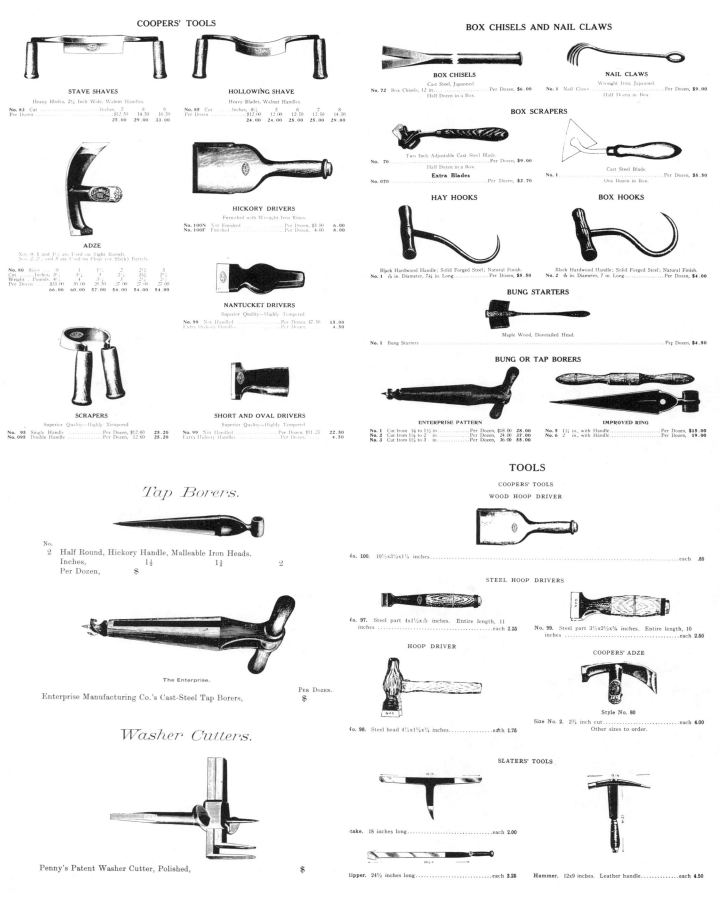

COOPERS' TOOLS

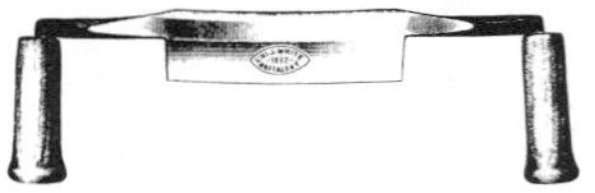

STAVE SHAVES

Heavy Blades, 2¼ Inch Wide, Walnut Handles.

No. 83 Cut .... Inches,	7	8	9
Per Dozen	$12.50	14.50	16.50
	25.00	**29.00**	**33.00**

HOLLOWING SHAVE

Heavy Blades, Walnut Handles.

No. 85 Cut .... Inches,	4½	5	6	7	8
Per Dozen	$12.00	12.00	12.50	12.50	14.50
	24.00	**24.00**	**25.00**	**25.00**	**29.00**

ADZE

Nos. 0, 1 and 1½ are Used on Tight Barrels.
Nos. 2, 2½ and 3 are Used on Flour (or Slack) Barrels.

No. 80 Sizes	0	1	1½	2	2½	3
Cut .... Inches,	3½	3¼	3	2¾	2¾	2½
Weight .. Pounds,	4½	4	3½	3	2¾	2½
Per Dozen	$33.00	30.00	28.50	27.00	27.00	27.00
	66.00	**60.00**	**57.00**	**54.00**	**54.00**	**54.00**

HICKORY DRIVERS

Furnished with Wrought Iron Rings.

No. 100N Not Finished .... Per Dozen, $3.00 **6.00**
No. 100F Finished .... Per Dozen, 4.00 **8.00**

NANTUCKET DRIVERS

Superior Quality—Highly Tempered

No. 98 Not Handled .... Per Dozen, $7.50 **15.00**
Extra Hickory Handles .... Per Dozen, ... **4.50**

SCRAPERS

Superior Quality—Highly Tempered

No. 95 Single Handle .... Per Dozen, $12.60 **25.20**
No. 095 Double Handle .... Per Dozen, 12.60 **25.20**

SHORT AND OVAL DRIVERS

Superior Quality—Highly Tempered

No. 99 Not Handled .... Per Dozen, $11.25 **22.50**
Extra Hickory Handles .... Per Dozen, ... **4.50**

BOX CHISELS AND NAIL CLAWS

BOX CHISELS

Cast Steel, Japanned.
No. 72 Box Chisels, 12 in. .... Per Dozen, **$6.00**
Half Dozen in a Box.

NAIL CLAWS

Wrought Iron, Japanned.
No. 1 Nail Claws .... Per Dozen, **$9.00**
Half Dozen in Box.

BOX SCRAPERS

Two Inch Adjustable Cast Steel Blade.
No. 70 .... Per Dozen, **$9.00**
Half Dozen in a Box.

Extra Blades
No. 070 .... Per Dozen, **$2.70**

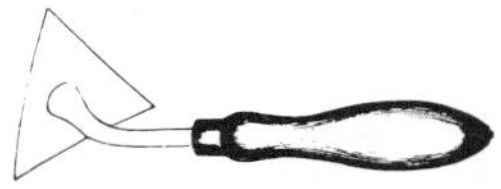

Cast Steel Blade.
No. 1 .... Per Dozen, **$5.50**
One Dozen in Box.

HAY HOOKS

Black Hardwood Handle; Solid Forged Steel; Natural Finish.
No. 1 $\frac{7}{16}$ in. Diameter, 7¾ in. Long .... Per Dozen, **$5.50**

BOX HOOKS

Black Hardwood Handle; Solid Forged Steel; Natural Finish.
No. 2 $\frac{7}{16}$ in. Diameter, 7 in. Long .... Per Dozen, **$4.00**

BUNG STARTERS

Maple Wood, Dovetailed Head.

No. 1 Bung Starters .... Per Dozen, **$4.50**

BUNG OR TAP BORERS

ENTERPRISE PATTERN

No. 1 Cut from ⅝ to 1½ in. .... Per Dozen, $18.00 **28.00**
No. 2 Cut from 1⅛ to 2 in. .... Per Dozen, 24.00 **37.00**
No. 3 Cut from 1½ to 3 in. .... Per Dozen, 36.00 **55.00**

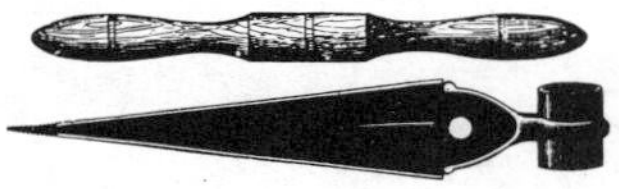

IMPROVED RING

No. 5 1¼ in., with Handle .... Per Dozen, **$15.00**
No. 6 2 in., with Handle .... Per Dozen, **19.00**

Tap Borers.

No.
2 Half Round, Hickory Handle, Malleable Iron Heads.
Inches, 1½ 1¾ 2
Per Dozen, $

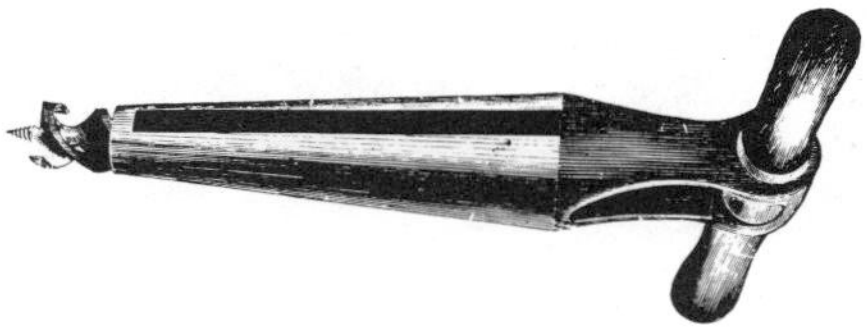

The Enterprise.

Enterprise Manufacturing Co.'s Cast-Steel Tap Borers, Per Dozen. $

Washer Cutters.

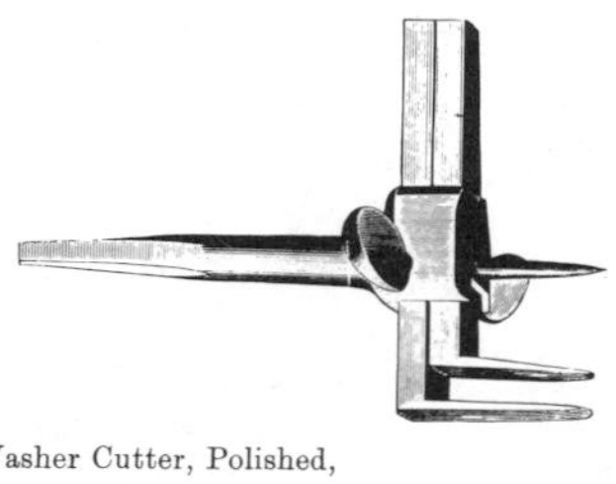

Penny's Patent Washer Cutter, Polished, $

TOOLS

COOPERS' TOOLS

WOOD HOOP DRIVER

No. 100. 10½x3½x1⅛ inches .... each **.85**

STEEL HOOP DRIVERS

No. 97. Steel part 4x1½x$\frac{5}{16}$ inches. Entire length, 11 inches .... each **2.25**

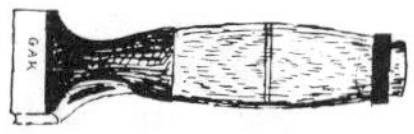

No. 99. Steel part 3½x2½x⅝ inches. Entire length, 10 inches .... each **2.50**

HOOP DRIVER

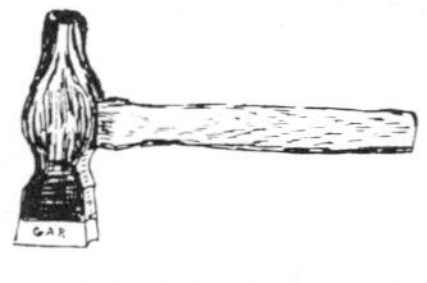

No. 98. Steel head 4½x1¼x¼ inches .... each **1.75**

COOPERS' ADZE

Style No. 80

Size No. 2. 2¾ inch cut .... each **4.00**
Other sizes to order.

SLATERS' TOOLS

Stake. 18 inches long .... each **2.00**

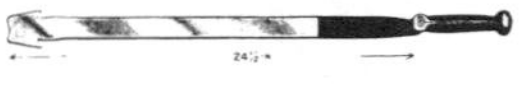

Ripper. 24½ inches long .... each **3.25**

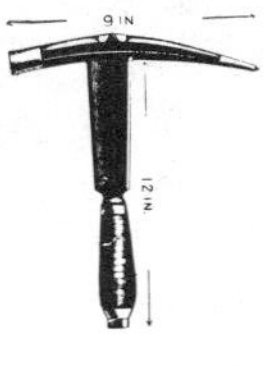

Hammer. 12x9 inches. Leather handle .... each **4.50**

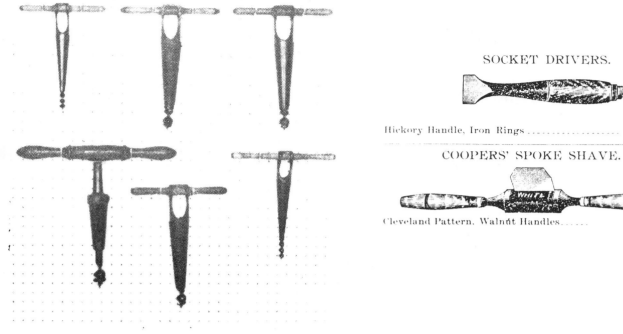

SOCKET DRIVERS.

Hickory Handle, Iron Rings ....

COOPERS' SPOKE SHAVE.

Cleveland Pattern, Walnut Handles.......

Bung Augers
Used in Barrel Making for Drilling Bung Holes

COOPERS' IRON SPOKE SHAVE.

Heavy Iron, 19 inch, 4 inch Cutter.....

BEER KEG CHAMPER KNIVES.

HICKORY DRIVERS

COOPERS' RIVET SETS.

No. 130.

HEAD FLOATS.

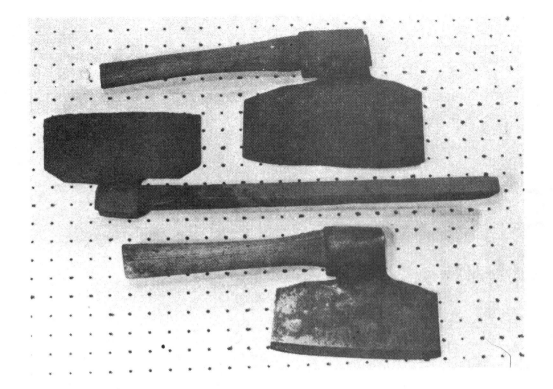

Cooper's Hatchets

Cooper's Hammers

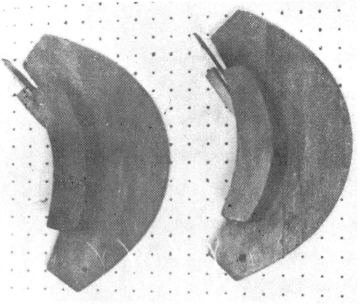

Cooper's Inside Planes

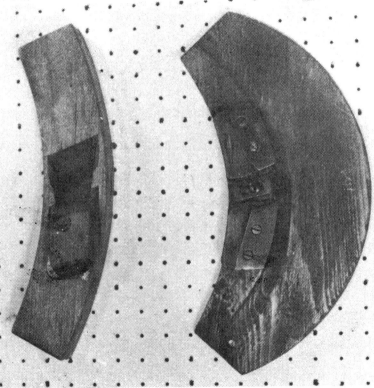

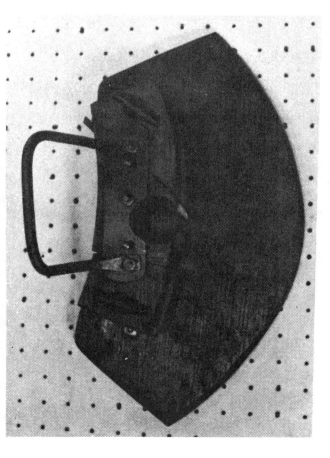

Cooper's Top and Bottom Groover

Left, Sunplane for leveling top
and bottom of Barrel
Right, Groove Plane

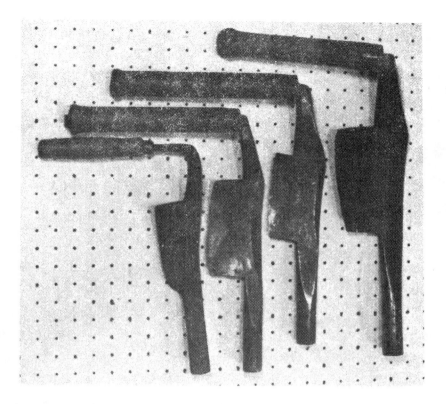

Cooper's Draw Knives

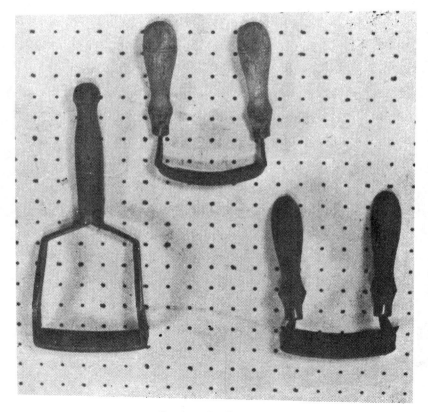

Cooper's Scrapers
For use inside Barrels

Blacksmith Tools

Since the founding of our nation, blacksmithing has been the most illustrated through books, poems, and songs. Truly, the Village Smithy was a mighty man.

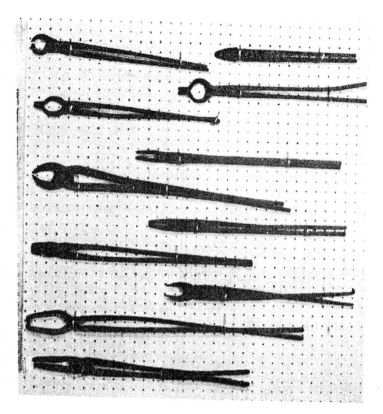

Blacksmith Tongs

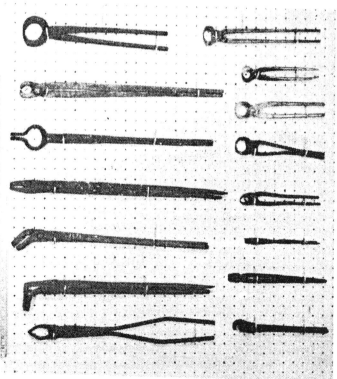

Blacksmith Tongs

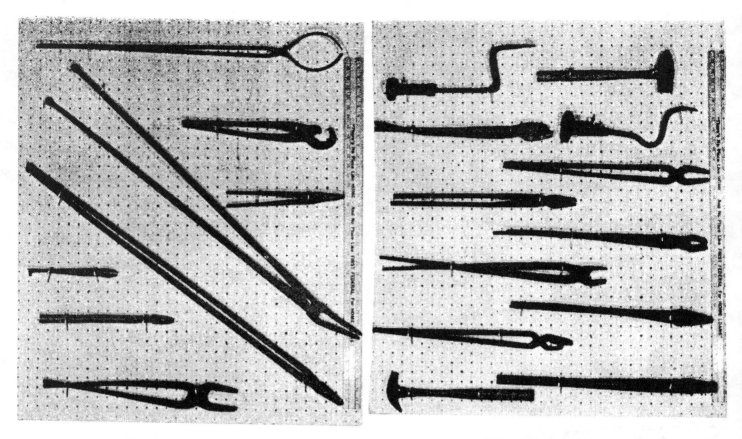

Blacksmith Tongs

Top Left, Buttress
Top Right and Bottom Left, Hammers
All Blacksmith Tongs
Second Top Right, Buttress

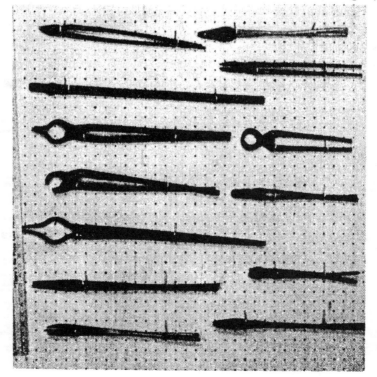

Blacksmith Tongs

Blacksmith's Anvil & Quenching Barrel

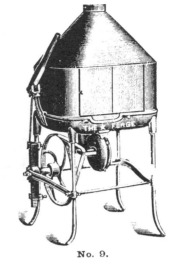

No. 9.

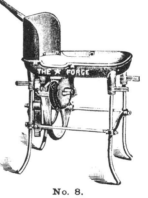

No. 8.

10-inch Fans, 24 x 30-inch Heaters, Fire-places 32 inches high.

BELLOWS.

BLACKSMITHS'.

28" X 42"

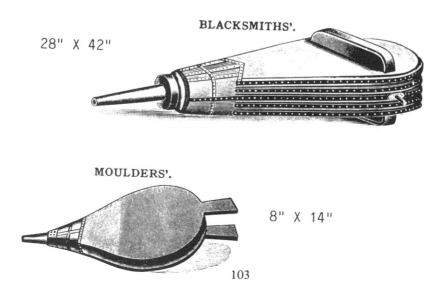

MOULDERS'.

8" X 14"

103

BLACKSMITHS' BLOWERS

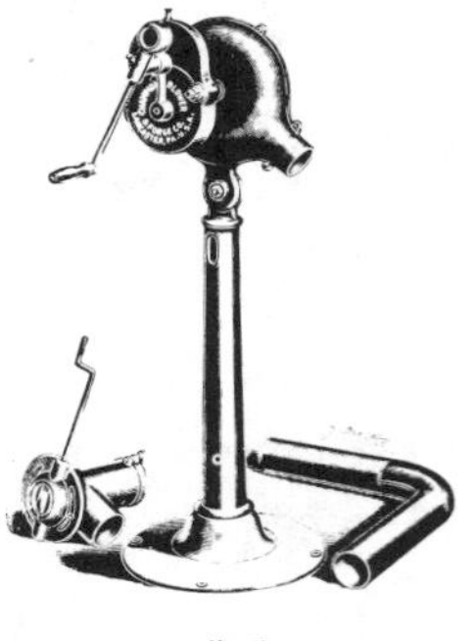

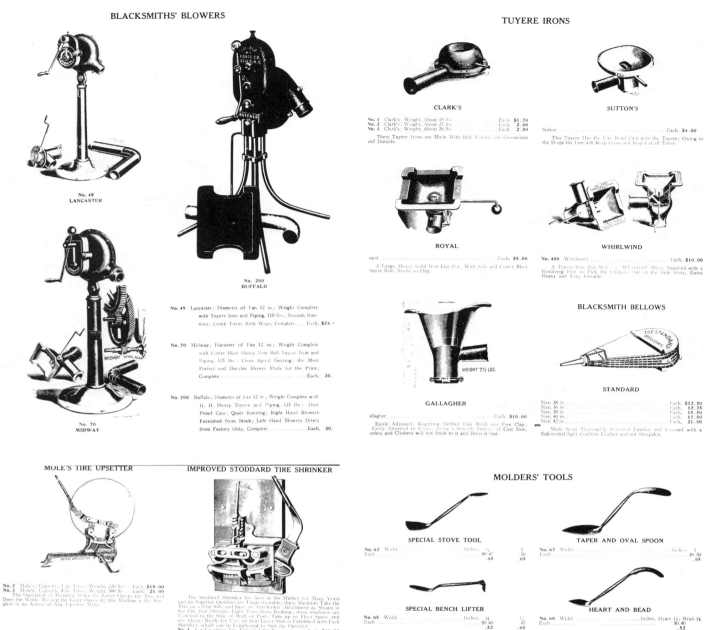

No. 49
LANCASTER

No. 200
BUFFALO

No. 70
MIDWAY

No. 49 Lancaster; Diameter of Fan 12 in.; Weight Complete with Tuyere Iron and Piping, 110 lbs.; Smooth Running; Crank Turns Both Ways, Complete .....Each, **$24.**

No. 70 Midway; Diameter of Fan 12 in.; Weight Complete with Center Blast Heavy Nest Ball Tuyere Iron and Piping, 125 lbs.; Cross Spiral Gearing; the Most Perfect and Durable Blower Made for the Price; Complete .....Each, **30.**

No. 200 Buffalo; Diameter of Fan 12 in.; Weight Complete with H. H. Heavy Tuyere and Piping, 125 lbs.; Dust Proof Case; Quiet Running; Right Hand Blowers Furnished from Stock; Left Hand Blowers Direct from Factory Only, Complete.....Each, **30.**

TUYERE IRONS

CLARK'S

No. 1 Clark's; Weight, About 18 lbs .....Each, **$1.70**
No. 2 Clark's; Weight, About 21 lbs .....Each, **2.00**
No. 3 Clark's; Weight, About 26 lbs .....Each, **2.50**

These Tuyere Irons are Made With Ball Valves; are Convenient and Durable.

SUTTON'S

Sutton .....Each, **$4.00**

This Tuyere Has the Fire Bowl Cast with the Tuyere; Owing to the Shape the Fire will Keep Clean and Bright at all Times.

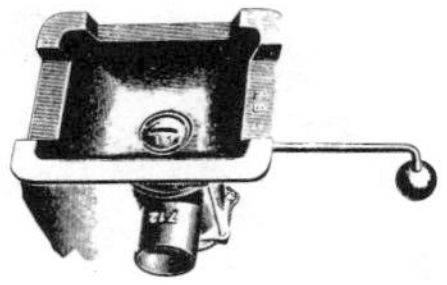

ROYAL

oyal .....Each, **$8.00**

A Large, Heavy Solid Iron Fire Pot; With Side and Center Blast 'uyere Ball; Needs no Clay.

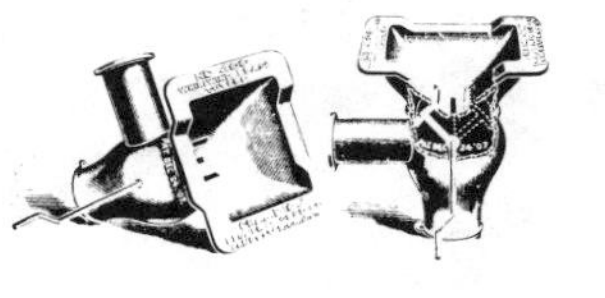

WHIRLWIND

No. 400 Whirlwind .....Each, **$10.00**

A Tuyere Iron that Makes a "Whirlwind" Blast; Supplied with a Revolving Pick to Pick the Clinkers Out of the Side Slots; Extra Heavy and Very Durable.

GALLAGHER

allagher .....Each, **$10.00**

Easily Adjusted; Requiring Neither Fire Brick nor Fire Clay; Easily Adjusted to Forge; Being a Smooth Surface of Cast Iron, inders and Clinkers will not Stick to it and Burn it Out.

BLACKSMITH BELLOWS

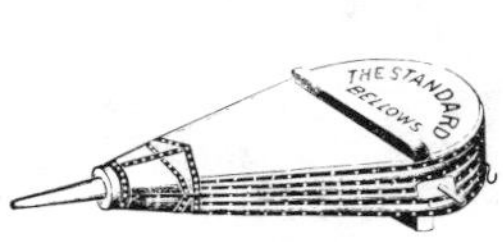

STANDARD

Size, 34 in .....Each, **$12.50**
Size, 36 in .....Each, **12.75**
Size, 38 in .....Each, **15.50**
Size, 40 in .....Each, **17.50**
Size, 42 in .....Each, **21.00**

Made from Thoroughly Seasoned Lumber and Covered with a Substantial Split Cowhide Leather and not Sheepskin.

MOLE'S TIRE UPSETTER

No. 2 Mole's; Capacity, 3 in. Tires; Weight, 220 lbs.....Each, **$19.00**
No. 3 Mole's; Capacity, 4 in. Tires; Weight, 300 lbs.....Each, **21.00**

The Operation of Bringing Down the Lever Grasps the Tire and Does the Work; Raising the Lever Opens it; this Machine is the Simplest in its Action of Any Upsetter Made

IMPROVED STODDARD TIRE SHRINKER

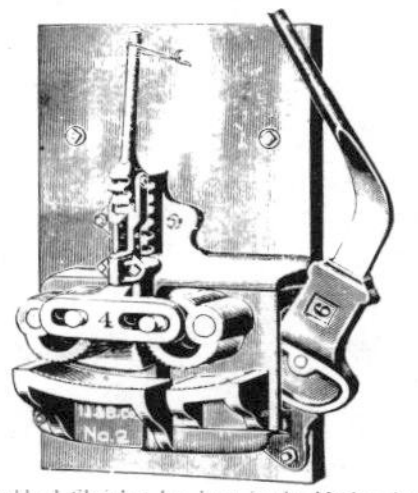

The Stoddard Shrinker has been in the Market for Many Years and its Superior Qualities are Unquestionable; these Machines Take the Tire on a Flat Side and have an Anti-kinker Attachment as Shown in the Cut, that Prevents Light Tires from Kinking; these machines are Fastened to the Side of Wall or Post; Take up no Floor Space, and are Always Ready for Use; an Iron Lever Stub is Furnished with Each Shrinker, which can be Lengthened to Suit the Operator.

No. 1 For Upsetting 2 in. Tires and Smaller .....Each, **$11.00**
No. 2 For Upsetting 4 in. Tires and Smaller .....Each, **19.50**
No. 3 *For Upsetting 4 in. Tires and Smaller; this is a Special Machine; Has Two Sets of Loose Jaws; can be Adjusted for Both Light and Heavy Tires; also for Upsetting Axles up to 1¼ in. Thick .....Each, **24.00**
No. 4 For Upsetting 6 in. Tires and Smaller .....Each, **32.00**

CHAMPION AMERICAN TIRE AND AXLE UPSETTER

No. 4 Champion American Upsetter .....Each, **$56.00**

All Parts Removable; can be Operated by One Man; Hammered Tool Steel Jaws; Capacity up to 4 x 1 Inch Round Edge Tire, and Axles up to 1¼ Inches; Weight, 325 Pounds; Best Medium Price Shrinker Made.

CHAMPION STAR TIRE AND AXLE UPSETTER

No. 1 Champion "Star" Shrinker Upsets or Welds Tire from ¼ to 5 x 1¼ in.; Upsets or Welds Axles, ¾ to 2½ in.; Upsets with One Revolution, 2 in.; Weight 900 lbs. .....Each, **$150.00**
No. 2 Champion "Star" Shrinker Upsets or Welds Tire from ¾ to 7 x 1½ in.; Upsets or Welds Axles, ¾ to 3½ in.; Upsets with One Revolution, 2 in.; Weight 1,200 lbs. .....Each, **180.00**
No. 3 Champion "Star" Shrinker Upsets or Welds Tire from ¾ to 8 x 1½ in.; Upsets or Welds Axles, ¾ to 3½ in.; Upsets with One Revolution, 2 in.; Weight 1,250 lbs. .....Each, **200.00**

MOLDERS' TOOLS

SPECIAL STOVE TOOL

No. 62 Width .....Inches, ¾ | 1
Each .....$0.45 | .50
.60 | **.65**

TAPER AND OVAL SPOON

No. 67 Width .....Inches, 1
Each $0.50
.65

SPECIAL BENCH LIFTER

No. 65 Width .....Inches, ⅜ | ½
Each .....$0.40 | .45
.52 | **.60**

HEART AND BEAD

No. 68 Width .....Inches, Heart ¼; Bead ⅜
Each $0.40
.52

TAPER AND ROUND SPOON

No. 66 Width .....Inches, 1
Each $0.50
.65

HEART AND FLUTE

No. 69 Width .....Inches, Heart 1; Flute ½
Each $0.50
.65

FLAT AND CIRCULAR FLANGE

No. 51 Width .....Inches, ½ | ⅝
Each .....$0.80 | .90
1.04 | **1.17**

CIRCULAR FLANGES

No. 50 Width .....Inches, ½ | ⅝
Each .....$0.80 | .90
1.04 | **1.17**

RAMMERS

No. 10 3½ x 15 in .....Per Dozen, **$8.00**

HAND BELLOWS

No. 8 8 in .....Per Dozen, **$10.00**

MOLDERS' BELLOWS

Very Highest Grade, Superior Quality Leather.

No. 10 10 in .....Per Dozen, **$22.00**
No. 12 12 in .....Per Dozen, **28.00**

Standard Grade.

No. 010 10 in .....Per Dozen, **$17.00**
No. 012 12 in .....Per Dozen, **22.00**

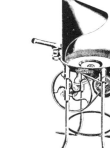

AGRICULTURAL

No. 150 With Shield; Diameter of Hearth, 18 in.; Fan, 8 in;
....Each, $11.50

Nos. 150 and 151 are General Purpose Agricultural Lever Forges;
Suitable for Farmers and Light Work

SPIRAL-GEARED RIVET
No. 78 With Shield

No. 78 Champion "Midway" Spiral-Geared Rivet Forge has Cast
Iron Hearth, and is Supplied with the "Midway" or Cross Spiral Gear-
ing; It is a Good, Strong and Durable Forge Suitable for Jewelers,
Bicycle Repairers, Tempering Tools, Tank Builders, Miners, Pros-
pectors, Boilermakers, Elevated Railroad Contractors, etc.
No. 78 Champion "Midway" Spiral-Geared Rivet Forge;
With Cast Iron Hearth 22 in. Diameter; Height,
33 in.; Fan, 10 in. Diameter; With Shield;
Weight, 140 lbs ....Each, $30.00
No. 78 With Cast steel Hearth, 18 in. Diameter; Fan, 10
in. ....Each, 30.00

MACHINISTS' HAND AND POWER
No. 10 With Power and Hand Combined

No. 10 Champion Machinists' Hand and Power Forge is Constructed for a Combination Lever Attachment and Power Combined,
can be Worked Either by Power or Hand, and is very Convenient
Where Power is not Ready for Use at all Times.
No. 10 ....*

No. 25 With Half Hood   Each, $48.00

No. 25 Champion Machinists' Power Forge is Used by Machinists
in Shops where Power is Used.
The Fan is Provided with Blast Gate, and also with Tight and
Loose Pulleys.
No. 25 ....Each, $45.00

LEVER RIVET
No. 85 Champion Imperial Lever Rivet Forge with Shield.

Hearth, 22 in. Diameter; Height, 33 in.;
Fan, 9½ in. Diameter; Weight, 100 lbs. ....Each, $18.00

No. 85 Champion Imperial Lever Rivet Forge with Shield has been
on the Market for 16 Years, and in the Hands of Thousands of Users
who pronounce it a First Class Forge. The Lever Motion on this Forge
is the Same as No. 81 and is Handsomely Finished. It is a Strong
and Light Forge for all Kinds of Light Portable Work, also is a
Very Desirable Forge for Junk Use, Such as Jewelers, Bicycle Repairers, Heating and Tempering Tools in Connection with the Use of
Tankbuilders, Miners and Prospectors, Making Repairs on Boilers,
Bridges, by Elevated Railroad Builders, Farmers, etc. It is Easily
Carried About the Country, Being Light, Strong and Compact.

AGRICULTURAL

No. 151 With Half Hood, Diameter of Hearth, 18 in.; Fan,
8 in ....Each, $12.50

TOOLMAKERS' LEVER
No. 86 Champion Imperial Toolmakers' Lever Forge
with Half Hood. Hearth, 22 in Diameter;
Height, 33 in.; Fan, 9½ in. Diameter; Weight,
105 lbs. ....Each, $20.50

No. 86 Champion Imperial Lever Toolmakers' Forge with Half
Hood is Precisely the Same in Lever Motion, Construction and Finish
as the No. 85. It is Adapted for Tempering Tools, for Elevated Railroads, Tank and Bridge Builders, Miners, Prospectors, Boiler Repairing, Farmers, etc.

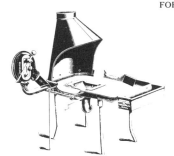

SPIRAL-GEARED MACHINISTS' PORTABLE
No. 73 With Half Hood

No. 73 Champion "Midway" Spiral-Geared Portable Forge with
Cast Iron Hearth. Hearth, 23 x 35 Inches; Fan, 10 Inches in Diameter;
with Half Hood; Weight, 190 Pounds
No. 73 ....Each, $40.00

SPIRAL-GEARED TOOLMAKERS'
No. 76 With Half Hood

No. 76 Champion "Midway" Spiral-Geared Forge; With Cast Iron
Hearth, 22 Inches in Diameter; Fan, 10 Inches in Diameter; With Half
Hood; Weight, 145 Pounds.
No. 76 ....Each, $33.00

FARRIERS' TOOL AND NAIL BOX

No. 200

No. 200
....Each, $3.50
Finely Finished and Thoroughly Made

TIRE MEASURING WHEELS

LITTLE GIANT

No. 1 Plain ....Each, $2.00
No. 2 Graduated ....Each, 2.50

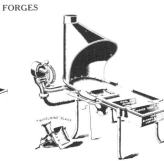

No. 433. With Half Hood

CHAMPION HORSE SHOER'S FOOT VISE

HUB BORERS

No. 2

The Best Machine for Light and Medium Work; it has Every
Adjustment Needed for the Most Perfect Work; Will Take Hubs up
to 10 Inches in Length
+No. 2 Special Little Giant ....Each, $45.00

No. 100

A Most Practical Foot Vise; has been on the Market a number
of Years and Over 10,000 Now in Use.
+No. 100 ....Each, $18.00

SPIRAL-GEARED BLACKSMITH

No. 71 "Midway" Spiral-Geared Blacksmith Forge.
With Cast Iron Hearth, 32 x 45 Inches, and Heavy Nest Tuyere Iron;
Height, 30 Inches; Fan, 12 Inches in Diameter; Without Water Tank;
Weight, 300 Pounds.
No. 71 Without Water Tank ....Each, $50.00
With Water Tank, Weight, 340 lbs. ....Each, 55.00

BALL-BEARING BLACKSMITH

No. 433 Champion Cast Iron Hearth Blacksmith Forge. Hearth,
32 x 45 Inches; Fan, 12 Inches in Diameter; With No. 400 Champion
"Whirlwind" Blast Anti-Clinker Heavy Nest Tuyere Iron and Blower;
Weight, 375 Pounds.
No. 433 ....Each, $55.00
With Water Tank, Weight, 400 Pounds ....Each, 60.00

LITTLE GIANT BOX PULLER

For Inserting or Removing Boxes in Hubs.
+No. 5 ....Each, $10.00

No. 3

The Latest Improved Machine for Light, Medium and Heavy
Work; the Adjustable Jaws Instantly and Perfectly Center Any Hub
from 2¾ to 9½ Inches Diameter; it Requires no Further Attention
for Hubs the Same Size; by Means of a New Device the Machine is
Adjustable to Any Length Hub, 6½ to 13 Inches Long; Quicker and
Easier in Operation than Any Other Machine
+No. 3 Special ....Each, $67.00

ROYAL (WESTERN CHIEF) BLACKSMITH
No. 100 With Half Hood

No. 100 Royal Western Chief; Cast Iron Hearth Blacksmith
Forge; Hearth, 31½ x 45½ Inches; Fan, 12 Inches Diameter; Height,
30 Inches; Made with Solid Fire Pot, With Tuyere and Royal Blower;
Weight, 295 Pounds.
No. 100 ....Each, $50.00
With Water Tank ....Each, 55.00

CHAMPION STEEL HORSESHOERS'
No. 408. With Half Hood

No. 408 Champion Steel Horseshoers' Forge, With Half Hood;
Hearth, 30 x 36 Inches; Height, 30 Inches; Fan, 12 Inches in Diameter;
With No. 400 Champion "Whirlwind" Blast Anti-Clinker Heavy Nest
Tuyere Iron; Weight, 295 Pounds.
No. 408 ....Each, $65.00
With Water Tank ....Each, 70.00

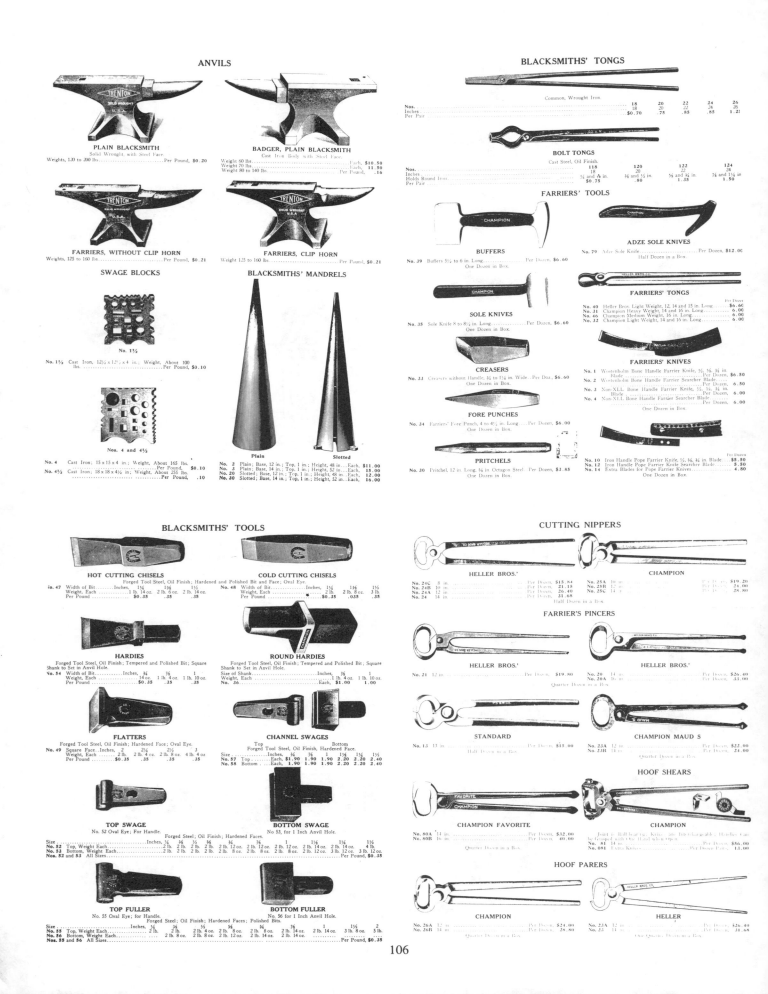

ANVILS

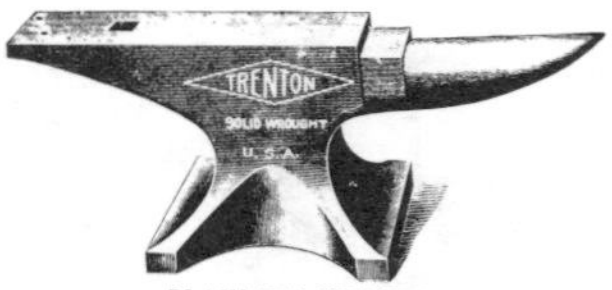

PLAIN BLACKSMITH

Solid Wrought, with Steel Face.

Weights, 120 to 200 lbs............................Per Pound, **$0.20**

BADGER, PLAIN BLACKSMITH

Cast Iron Body with Steel Face.

Weight 60 lbs............................Each, **$10.50**
Weight 70 lbs............................Each, **11.50**
Weight 80 to 140 lbs............................Per Pound, **.16**

FARRIERS, WITHOUT CLIP HORN

Weights, 125 to 160 lbs............................Per Pound, **$0.21**

FARRIERS, CLIP HORN

Weight 125 to 160 lbs............................Per Pound, **$0.21**

SWAGE BLOCKS

No. 1½

No. 1½ Cast Iron, 12½ x 12½ x 4 in.; Weight, About 100 lbs.............................Per Pound, **$0.10**

Nos. 4 and 4½

No. 4 Cast Iron; 15 x 15 x 4 in.; Weight, About 165 lbs.............................Per Pound, **$0.10**
No. 4½ Cast Iron; 18 x 18 x 4½ in; Weight, About 255 lbs.............................Per Pound, **.10**

BLACKSMITHS' MANDRELS

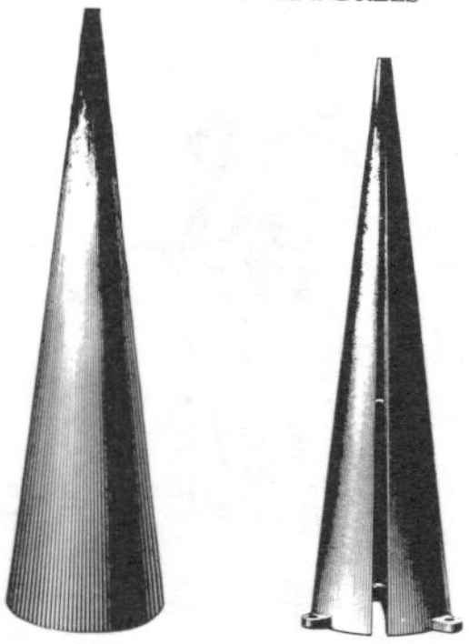

Plain **Slotted**

No. 2 Plain; Base, 12 in.; Top, 1 in.; Height, 48 in...Each, **$11.00**
No. 3 Plain; Base, 14 in.; Top, 1 in.; Height, 52 in...Each, **15.00**
No. 20 Slotted; Base, 12 in.; Top, 1 in.; Height, 48 in..Each, **12.00**
No. 30 Slotted; Base, 14 in.; Top, 1 in.; Height, 52 in..Each, **16.00**

BLACKSMITHS' TONGS

Common, Wrought Iron.

Nos.	**18**	**20**	**22**	**24**	**26**
Inches	18	20	22	24	26
Per Pair	**$0.70**	**.75**	**.85**	**.85**	**1.2!**

BOLT TONGS

Cast Steel, Oil Finish.

Nos.	**118**	**120**	**122**	**124**
Inches	18	20	22	24
Holds Round Iron	¼ and 5/16 in.	⅜ and ½ in.	⅝ and ¾ in.	⅞ and 1¼ in
Per Pair	**$0.75**	**.80**	**1.35**	**1.50**

FARRIERS' TOOLS

BUFFERS

No. 39 Buffers 5½ to 6 in. Long..................Per Dozen, **$6.60**
One Dozen in Box.

SOLE KNIVES

No. 35 Sole Knife 8 to 8½ in. Long...............Per Dozen, **$6.60**
One Dozen in Box.

CREASERS

No. 33 Creasers without Handle, ¾ to 1⅛ in. Wide..Per Doz., **$6.60**
One Dozen in Box.

FORE PUNCHES

No. 34 Farriers' Fore Punch, 4 to 4½ in. Long....Per Dozen, **$6.00**
One Dozen in Box.

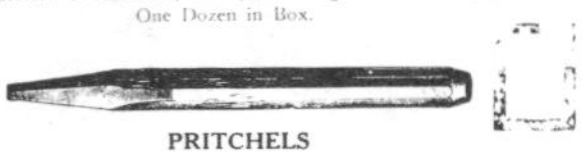

PRITCHELS

No. 30 Pritchel, 12 in. Long, ⅝ in. Octagon Steel..Per Dozen, **$3.85**
One Dozen in Box.

ADZE SOLE KNIVES

No. 79 Adze Sole Knife.........................Per Dozen, **$12.00**
Half Dozen in a Box.

FARRIERS' TONGS

Per Dozen

No. 40 Heller Bros. Light Weight, 12, 14 and 15 in. Long........**$6.60**
No. 31 Champion Heavy Weight, 14 and 16 in. Long............**6.00**
No. 46 Champion Medium Weight, 16 in. Long..................**6.00**
No. 32 Champion Light Weight, 14 and 16 in. Long.............**6.00**

FARRIERS' KNIVES

No. 1 Wostenholm Bone Handle Farrier Knife, ½, ⅝, ¾ in. Blade.............................Per Dozen, **$6.50**
No. 2 Wostenholm Bone Handle Farrier Searcher Blade..................................Per Dozen, **6.50**
No. 3 Non-XLL Bone Handle Farrier Knife, ½, ⅝, ¾ in. Blade.............................Per Dozen, **6.00**
No. 4 Non-XLL Bone Handle Farrier Searcher Blade..................................Per Dozen, **6.00**
One Dozen in Box.

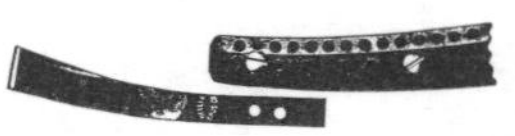

Per Dozen

No. 10 Iron Handle Pope Farrier Knife, ½, ⅝, ¾ in. Blade....**$5.50**
No. 12 Iron Handle Pope Farrier Knife Searcher Blade........**5.50**
No. 14 Extra Blades for Pope Farrier Knives..................**4.80**
One Dozen in Box.

BLACKSMITHS' TOOLS

HOT CUTTING CHISELS

COLD CUTTING CHISELS

Forged Tool Steel, Oil Finish; Hardened and Polished Bit and Face; Oval Eye.

No. 47	Width of Bit........Inches,	1¼	1⅜	1½
	Weight, Each	1 lb. 14 oz.	2 lb. 6 oz.	2 lb. 14 oz.
	Per Pound	**$0.35**	**.35**	**.35**

No. 48	Width of Bit........Inches,	1¼	1⅜	1½
	Weight, Each	2 lb.	2 lb. 8 oz.	3 lb.
	Per Pound	**$0.35**	**.035**	**.35**

HARDIES

Forged Tool Steel, Oil Finish; Tempered and Polished Bit; Square Shank to Set in Anvil Hole.

No. 54	Width of Bit........Inches,	¾	⅞	1
	Weight, Each	14 oz.	1 lb. 4 oz.	1 lb. 10 oz.
	Per Pound	**$0.35**	**.35**	**.35**

ROUND HARDIES

Forged Tool Steel, Oil Finish; Tempered and Polished Bit; Square Shank to Set in Anvil Hole.

Size of Shank........Inches,	⅞	1
Weight, Each	1 lb. 4 oz.	1 lb. 10 oz.
No. 36........Each,	**$1.00**	**1.00**

FLATTERS

Forged Tool Steel, Oil Finish; Hardened Face; Oval Eye.

No. 49	Square Face..Inches,	2	2¼	2½	3
	Weight, Each	2 lb.	2 lb. 4 oz.	2 lb. 8 oz.	4 lb. 4 oz
	Per Pound	**$0.35**	**.35**	**.35**	**.35**

CHANNEL SWAGES

Top Bottom

Forged Tool Steel, Oil Finish, Hardened Face.

Size........Inches,	¾	⅞	1	1⅛	1¼	1½
No. 57 Top........Each,	**$1.90**	**1.90**	**1.90**	**2.20**	**2.20**	**2.40**
No. 58 Bottom....Each,	**1.90**	**1.90**	**1.90**	**2.20**	**2.20**	**2.40**

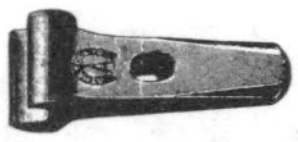

TOP SWAGE

No. 52 Oval Eye; For Handle.

BOTTOM SWAGE

No 53, for 1 Inch Anvil Hole.

Forged Steel; Oil Finish; Hardened Faces.

Size........Inches,	¼	⅜	½	⅝	¾	⅞	1	1⅛	1¼	1½
No. 52 Top, Weight Each	2 lb.	2 lb.	2 lb.	2 lb.	2 lb. 12 oz.	2 lb. 12 oz.	2 lb. 12 oz.	2 lb. 14 oz.	2 lb. 14 oz.	4 lb.
No. 53 Bottom, Weight Each	2 lb.	2 lb.	2 lb.	2 lb.	2 lb. 8 oz.	2 lb. 8 oz.	2 lb. 8 oz.	2 lb. 12 oz.	3 lb. 12 oz.	3 lb. 12 oz.

Nos. 52 and 53 All Sizes........................Per Pound, **$0.35**

TOP FULLER

No. 55 Oval Eye; for Handle.

BOTTOM FULLER

No. 56 for 1 Inch Anvil Hole.

Forged Steel; Oil Finish; Hardened Faces; Polished Bits.

Size........Inches,	¼	⅜	½	⅝	¾	⅞	1	1½	2
No. 55 Top, Weight Each	2 lb.	2 lb.	2 lb. 4 oz.	2 lb. 8 oz.	2 lb. 8 oz.	2 lb. 14 oz.	2 lb. 14 oz.	3 lb. 8 oz.	5 lb.
No. 56 Bottom, Weight Each	....	2 lb. 8 oz.	2 lb. 8 oz.	2 lb. 12 oz.	2 lb. 14 oz.	2 lb. 14 oz.	....	....	....

Nos. 55 and 56 All Sizes........................Per Pound, **$0.35**

CUTTING NIPPERS

HELLER BROS.'

No. 24C 8 in.........................Per Dozen, **$15.84**
No. 24B 10 in.........................Per Dozen, **21.15**
No. 24A 12 in.........................Per Dozen, **26.40**
No. 24 14 in.........................Per Dozen, **31.68**

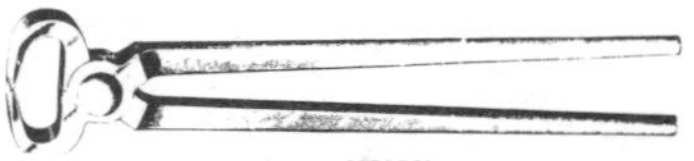

CHAMPION

No. 25A 10 in.........................Per Dozen, **$19.20**
No. 25B 12 in.........................Per Dozen, **24.00**
No. 25C 14 in.........................Per Dozen, **28.80**

Half Dozen in a Box.

FARRIER'S PINCERS

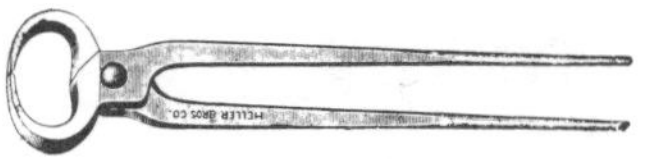

HELLER BROS.'

No. 21 12 in.........................Per Dozen, **$19.80**

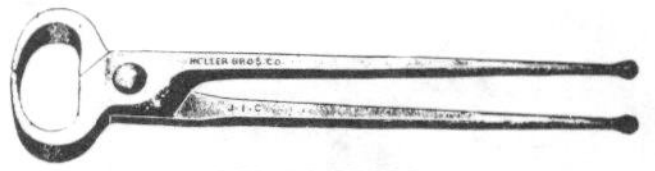

HELLER BROS.'

No. 20 14 in.........................Per Dozen, **$26.40**
No. 20A 16 in.........................Per Dozen, **33.00**

Quarter Dozen in a Box.

STANDARD

No. 13 13 in.........................Per Dozen, **$15.00**
Half Dozen in a Box.

CHAMPION MAUD S

No. 23A 12 in.........................Per Dozen, **$22.00**
No. 23B 14 in.........................Per Dozen, **24.00**
Quarter Dozen in a Box.

HOOF SHEARS

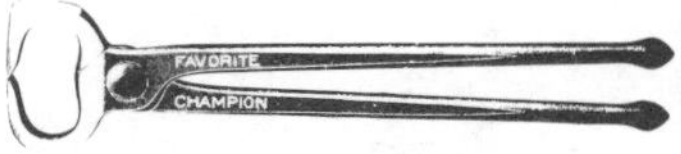

CHAMPION FAVORITE

No. 80A 14 in.........................Per Dozen, **$32.00**
No. 80B 16 in.........................Per Dozen, **40.00**
Quarter Dozen in a Box.

CHAMPION

Joint is Ball-bearing; Knives are Interchangeable; Handles Can be Grasped with One Hand when Open.

No. 81 14 in.........................Per Dozen, **$56.00**
No. 081 Extra Knives....................Per Dozen Pairs, **13.00**

HOOF PARERS

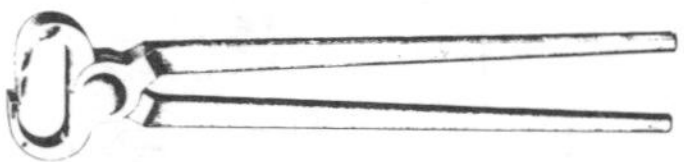

CHAMPION

No. 26A 12 in.........................Per Dozen, **$24.00**
No. 26B 14 in.........................Per Dozen, **28.80**
Quarter Dozen in a Box.

HELLER

No. 23A 12 in.........................Per Dozen, **$26.40**
No. 23 14 in.........................Per Dozen, **31.68**
One Quarter Dozen in a Box.

Braces, Bits, Hand Drills, Etc.

Drilling was important for fitting together early furniture, also in the construction of barns, houses, etc.

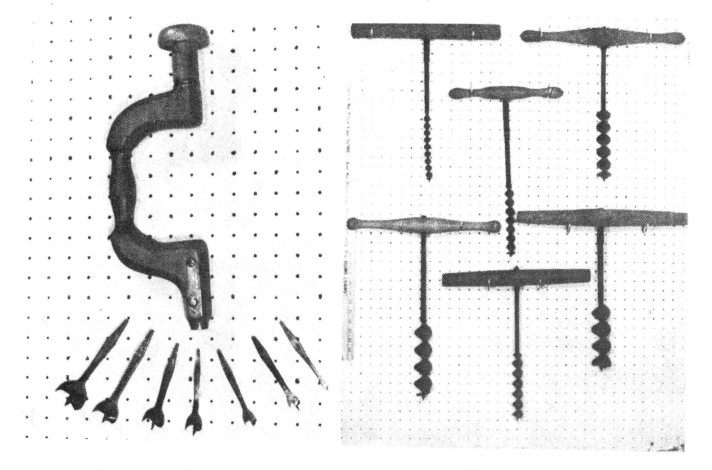

Early Brace & Bit Set   Hand Augers

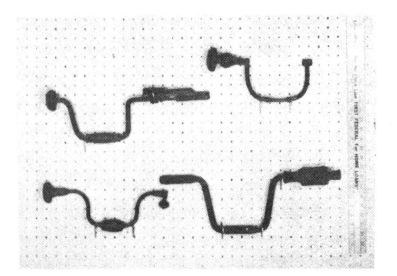

Early Braces

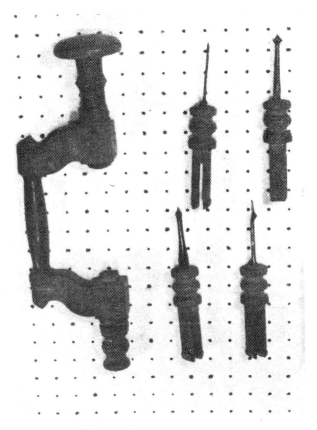

Very Early Homemade Brace and
Changeable Chucks, Probably one of kind

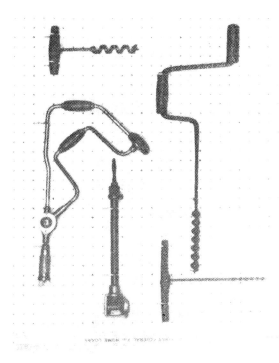

1. Top Left, Spiral Auger
2. Left, Corner Brace
3. Center, Corner Brace Attachment
4. Upper Right, Raft Auger 1-Piece Metal
5. Lower Right, Right Hand Auger

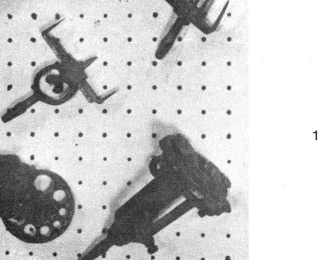

6. Top Left, Spoke Pointer
7. Top Right, Washer Cutter
8. Center, Washer Cutter
9. Bottom Left, Dowel Cutter
10. Bottom Right, Dowel Cutter

BIT BRACES
BARBER RATCHET

Nos. 30 to 33

		30	31	32	33
Sweep	Inches	14	12	10	
Per Doz.		$35.00	33.00	30.00	28.00

Nos. 60 to 63

		60	61	62	63
Sweep	Inches	14	12	10	
Per Doz.		$32.00	29.00	26.00	24.00

BARBER RATCHET

Nos. 121 to 123

		121	122	123
Sweep	Inches	12	10	
Per Doz.		$20.00	18.00	17.00

SPOFFORD

Nos. 107 to 112

		107	110	112
Sweep	Inches		10	
Per Doz.		$18.00	23.00	26.00

Nos. 3108 and 3110

		3108	3110
Sweep	Inches	8	10
Per Doz.		$14.50	15.50

Nos. 3008 and 3010

		3008	3010
Sweep	Inches	8	10
Per Doz.		$11.00	12.00

RATCHET BIT BRACES

STANLEY VICTOR

No. 921

		8	10	12
No. 921 Sweep	Inches			
Per Dozen		$33.00	36.00	38.40

One Sixth Dozen in a Box

Nos. 4208 to 4212

		4208	4210	4212
Sweep	Inches	8	10	12
Per Dozen		$23.50	27.50	30.50

One Half Dozen in a Box

Nos. 4108 to 4112

		4108	4110	4112
Sweep	Inches	8	10	12
Per Dozen		$22.00	24.00	26.00

One Half Dozen in a Box

Nos. 4008 to 4012

		4008	4010	4012
Sweep	Inches	8	10	12
Per Dozen		$18.50	19.50	23.00

Nos. 2108 and 2110

		2108	2110
Sweep	Inches	8	10
Per Dozen		$16.00	17.00

One Half Dozen in a Box

Nos. 2008 and 2010

		2008	2010
Sweep	Inches	8	10
Per Dozen		$14.00	15.00

BIT BRACES

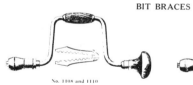

No. 1108 and 1110

		1108	1110
Sweep	Inches	8	10
Per Dozen		$9.00	

One Half Dozen in a Box

No. 1008 and 1010

		1008	1010
Sweep	Inches	8	10
Per Dozen		$6.50	7.50

No. 308 and 310

		308	310
Sweep	Inches	8	10
Per Dozen		$6.00	7.00

One Half Dozen in a Package

No. 25 8 Inch Sweep

No. 25 8 Inch Sweep .... Per Dozen	$3.00

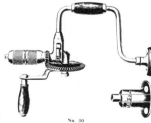

COMBINATION BRACE AND DRILL

No. 30

Nickel-plated Sweep and Chuck; Ball Bearing Cocobola Head and Handles; Forged Steel Alligator Jaws; Can be Used as a Brace or Breast Drill.

No. 30 10 Inch Sweep .... Per Dozen, **$65.00**

One Twelfth Dozen in a Box

CORNER BRACES

No. 100

No. 100 10 Inch Sweep .... Per Dozen, **$70.00**

One Twelfth Dozen in a Box

RATCHET BIT BRACES

BALL BEARING CHUCK AND HEAD

Nickel-plated Chuck, Head and Sleeves, Sweeps Are Straw Color, Tempered Finish, Cocobola Head and Handle

SECTIONAL VIEW

No. 4510 10 in. Sweep .... Per Dozen,	$30.00
No. 4512 12 in. Sweep .... Per Dozen,	36.00
No. 4514 14 in. Sweep .... Per Dozen,	44.00

The Chuck or Bit Holding Device, as per Illustration, Consists Principally of a Socket, Sleeve, Binder, Ball-retaining Ring and the Hardened Steel Jaws; the Ratchet is Formed at One End of the Socket, while the Outer End is Made Heavier than Usual to Resist the Extra Strain Caused by the Ball Bearing at the End of the Sleeve, which Enables the Operator to Exert Greater Power in Closing the Jaws on to a Bit or Drill; These Jaws are Specially Formed to Take Round Shank Drills from ¼ to About ½ Inch, as also Square Shank Bits.

At the End of the Sleeve is a Steel Washer, Next to which are Shown the Balls, which, with the Recessed Ring, Threaded to Prevent Any Possibility of Shifting Laterally, and Kept From Turning by a Small Screw, Forms the Ball Bearing Sleeve Device.

Should it Become Necessary at any Time to Renew the Jaws, First Remove the Socket from the Ratchet Frame; Then Take Out the Small Screw in the Recessed Ball Retaining Ring, which Then can be Unscrewed from the Socket, (Care Being Taken not to Lose the Balls Therein). This will Leave the Sleeve Free to be Taken from the Binder and Socket, When Both Jaws and Binder May be Removed.

It will be Noted that We Show a Wire Connection Between the Binder and Spring of the Jaws; While this is Not Essential, its Object is to Give a Positive Return Motion to the Jaws.

One Quarter Dozen in a Plaid Covered Box.

Nos. 4406 to 4414

Nickel-plated Sleeves, Sweeps Are Natural Straw Color Tempered Finish, Cocobola Head and Handles, Nickel-plated Ball Bearing Heads. The Jaws Are Bored from a Solid Bar. The Threads Are Cut on the Inside and Knurled on the Outside. The Socket is a Steel Forging. The Jaws Are Steel Forged and Hardened and Operate by Easy Springs. These Braces will Hold all Sizes of Square and Round Shank from ½ Inch and Smaller.

Nos.		4406	4408	4410	4412	4414
Sweep	Inches	6	8	10	12	14
Per Dozen		$32.00	32.00	35.00	39.00	43.00

One Quarter Dozen in a Plaid Covered Box.

HAND DRILLS

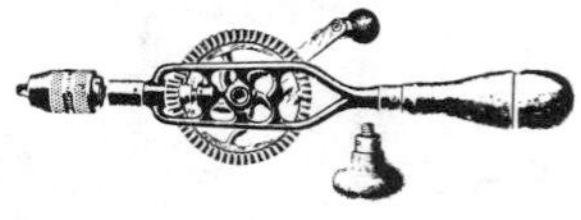

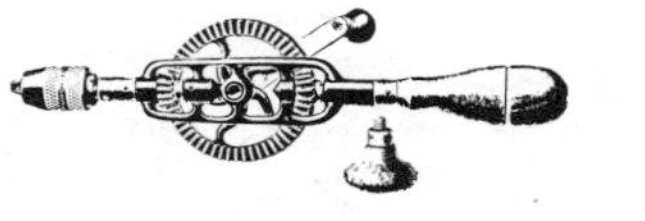

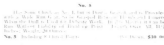

MILLERS FALLS

No. 1

These Drills Are Provided with Chucks Having Three Jaws, Resting in Solid Sockets. There Are No Springs to Get Out of Place or Out of Order. The Chucks Are Nickeled and the Handle [illegible] They Hold Drills from 0 to [illegible] Inch. A Side Handle, as Shown, [illegible] is Furnished with this Drill.

No. 1 Including 8 Fluted Points in Hollow Handle ... Per Dozen **$27.00**

No. 5

Has Same Chuck as No. 1, but is Double Geared, and is Provided with a Wide Rim Gear, to be Grasped Between Thumb and Fingers When the Drill is Used for Delicate Work. In This Manner it Can be Run Without Liability of Breaking Point. Length Over All, 11½ Inches; Weight, 20 Ounces.

No. 5 Including 8 Fluted Points ... Per Dozen, **$30.00**

One Twelfth Dozen in a Box

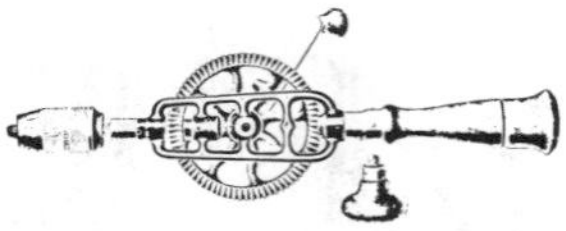

No. 2 Ball Bearing

Drill No. 2 is Same in General Finish as No. 1, Described Above. It Has Cut Gears and an Adjustable Friction Roll to Prevent Gears from Springing Out of Engagement.

No. 2 With 8 Fluted Points ... Per Dozen **$18.00**

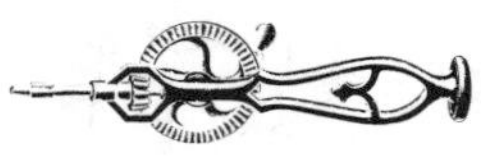

No. 4

No. 4 Drill is 8 Inches in Length and Weighs 8 Ounces. It is Made of Iron, with Rosewood Handle, and has Chuck for Holding the Drill Points. This Chuck is Made on a New Plan, and it Centers and Holds the Drill Perfectly. With each Drill Stock We Send a Box Containing Six Superior Drill Points of Various Sizes.

No. 4 With 6 Drills ... Per Dozen **$11.00**

One Twelfth Dozen in a Box

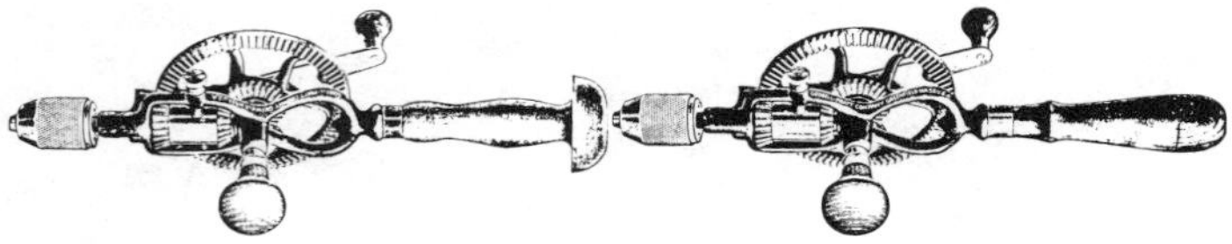

GOODELL'S

No. 5½B **No. 5½**

Japanned Malleable Iron Frame, Cut Gear Teeth, Bright Parts Nickel - plated, Polished Hardwood Handle

This Tool is Intended to Fill a Long-felt Want for a Combination Hand and Breast Drill, the Shape of the Handle Admitting of its Use the Latter Way. It Has Two Speeds, [illegible] size Drills, Double Gears, Two Speeds, [illegible] jawed, Capacity 0 to ⅜ Inch. It Has Knurled Nut, Nickel plated, Well Made and Accurate.

No. 5½B Without Drills ... Per Dozen, **$60.00**

This Drill Embraces Features Never Before Used Upon Tools of this Character, and is Unquestionably the Finest Ever Produced. It has Double Gears, Two Speeds, and a Chuck, with Capacity to ⅜ Inch, as Noted Below. Speeds—It Has Two Speeds, Changed by Turning the Nut on the Frame Marked "F" and "S". Chuck—Three-jawed; Capacity 0 to ⅜ Inch. It has Knurled Nut; Nickel plated, Well-made and Accurate.

No. 5½ Without Drills ... Per Dozen, **$60.00**

One Twelfth Dozen in a Box

HAND DRILLS

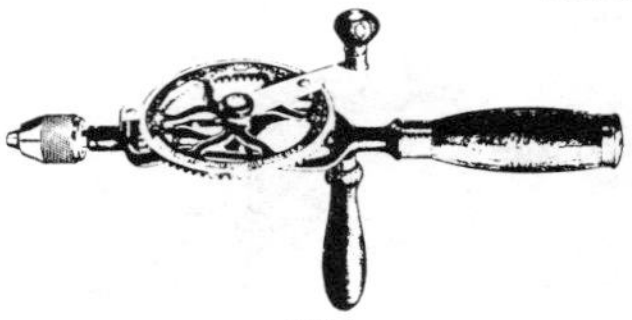

No. 015

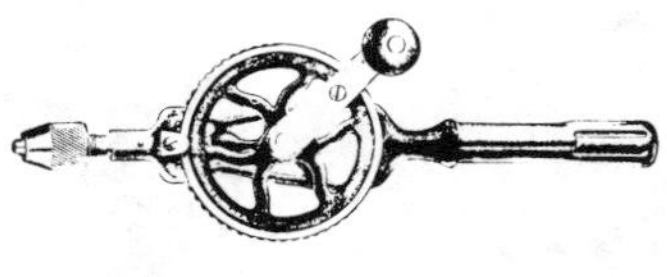

No. 19

GOODELL'S

[illegible]

No. 015 [illegible] ... **$15.00** No. 19 [illegible] ... **$20.00**

[illegible]

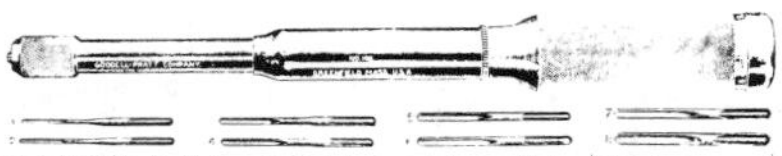

No. 108 Full Nickel [illegible] with 8 Drill Points [illegible] ... **$26.00**

One in a Box

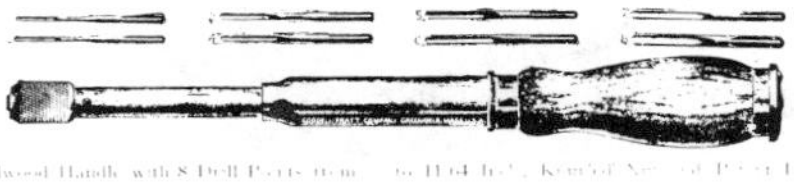

No. 3½ Nickel Plated, Hardwood Handle with 8 Drill Points from [illegible] to 11-64 Inch, Knurled Nut [illegible] Drill Holder, Length, 9½ Inches ... Per Dozen **$24.00**

One in a Box

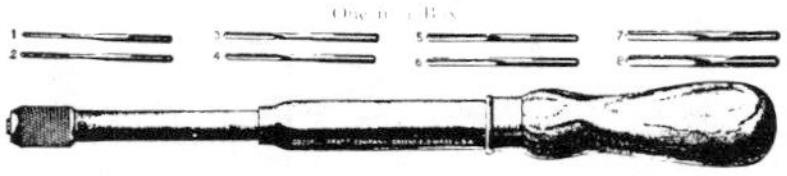

No. 2½ Nickel-plated, Cocobolo Handle, with 8 Drill Points from 1-64 to 11-64 Inch, Knurled Nut [illegible] Drill Holder, Length, 9½ Inches ... Per Dozen, **$16.00**

One in a Box

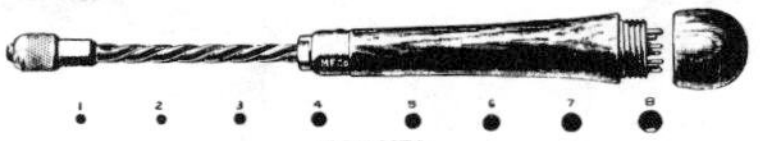

GRAVES

No. 2 Cocobolo Hollow Handle, with 8 Drill Points from [illegible] to 11-64 [illegible], Each Point in a Separate Cell in Handle, Length with Drill Point, 14½ Inches; One Metal Drill Gauge Furnished with Each Tool ... Per Dozen, **$16.50**

One in a Box

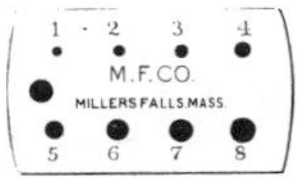

DRILL GAUGE

With Each No. 2 Drill a Steel Gauge is Furnished, by the Use of Which One May Determine the Size Drill Point to Use for Any Certain Sized Screw.

Directions—Get the Size of the Screw by Seeing Which Hole in the Gauge it Fits and Then Use the Next Smaller Size Drill Point.

BREAST DRILLS

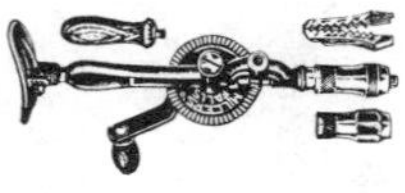

No. 112. Millers Falls

A low-priced Drill for those who use same only occasionally. Length, 15 inches. One speed only. Will hold only square-shank drills.

Each 3.00

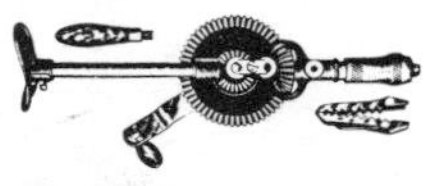

No. 19. Millers Falls

Length, 18 inches. Fast or slow speed adjusted by changing gear from one opening to the other. Has 2-jaw chuck for square-shank bit-brace drills.

Each 3.75

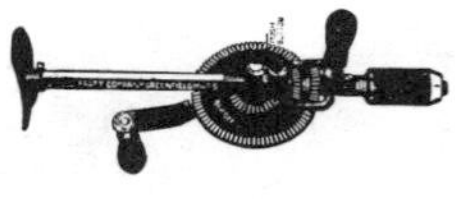

No. 219. Goodell

Length, 16½ inches. Fast or slow speed adjusted by changing gear from one opening to the other. 2-jaw chuck for square-shank bit-brace drills.

Each 3.75

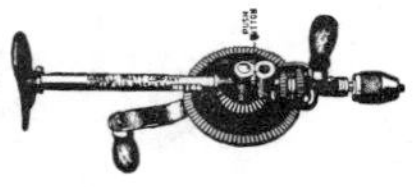

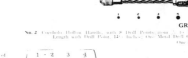

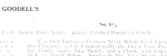

No. 477. Goodell

Length, 16½ inches. Fast or slow speed adjusted by changing gear from one opening to the other. 3-jaw chuck for round-shank drills.

Each 4.50

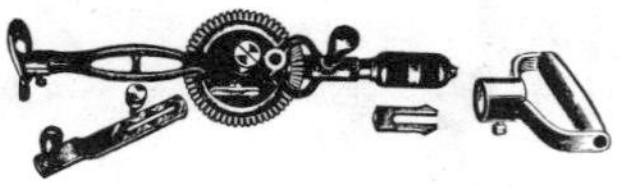

No. 12. Millers Falls

Length, 17½ inches. Fast or slow speed adjusted by changing gear from one opening to the other. 2-jaw chuck for square-shank bit-brace drills.

Each 4.75

This same stock, with spade handle instead of breast plate, is No. 15, at same price.

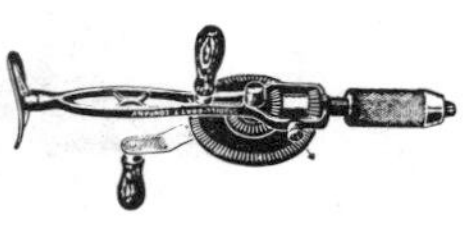

No. 07. Goodell

Length, 16½ inches. Fast or slow speed changed by turning shifter knob between pinions. 2-jaw chuck for square-shank bit-stock drills.

Each 4.75

HAND DRILLS

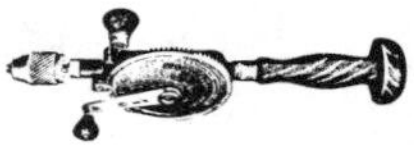

No. 1616. Goodell

Length, 11½ inches. Frame is of aluminum, being as strong as iron but very light. 3-jaw chuck. Capacity, 0 to ⅜ inch.

Each 3.75

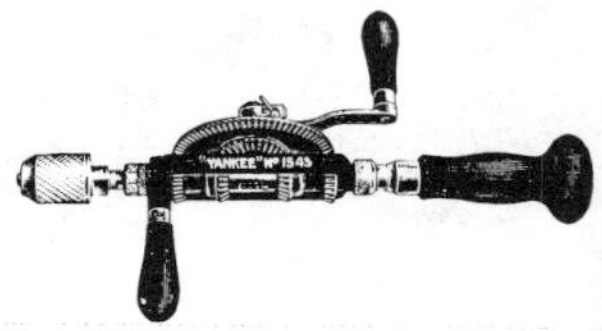

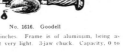

No. 1545. Yankee

Length, 16 inches. Double speed. Right or left hand ratchet. 3-jaw chuck. Capacity, 0 to ⅜ inch.

Each 8.50

GOODELL DRILL CHUCKS

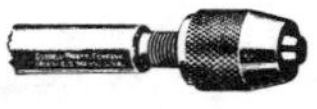

Accurately Turned ½-Inch Round Shanks

No. 14.	Capacity, 0 to $\frac{5}{32}$ inch	each 1.30
No. 15.	Capacity, 0 to ¼ inch	each 1.65
No. 15½.	Capacity, 0 to ⅜ inch	each 2.00
No. 16.	Capacity, 0 to ½ inch	each 2.75

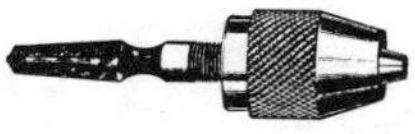

Square Bit Brace Shanks

No. 14B.	Capacity, 0 to $\frac{5}{32}$ inch	each 1.60
No. 15B.	Capacity, 0 to ¼ inch	each 2.10
No. 15½B.	Capacity, 0 to ⅜ inch	each 2.75
No. 16B.	Capacity, 0 to ½ inch	each 3.25

BENCH DRILLS

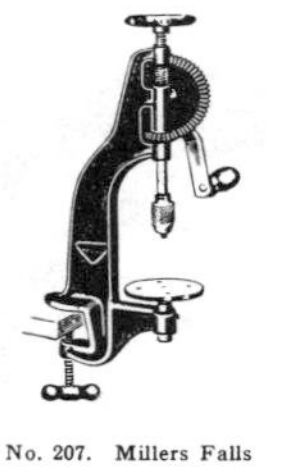

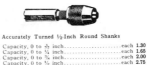

No. 207. Millers Falls

Height, 18 inches. Weight, 8½ lbs. Hand feed. 3-jaw chuck. Capacity, 0 to ¼ inch. A neat little drill for light work.

Each 7.50

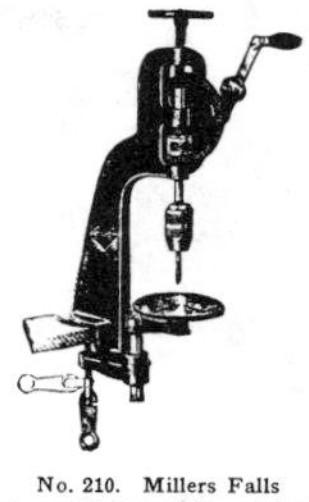

No. 210. Millers Falls

Height, 22 inches. Weight, 17 lbs. May be changed from fast to slow speed by means of knurled sleeve between pinions. 3-jaw chuck. Capacity, to ½ inch.

Each 12.75

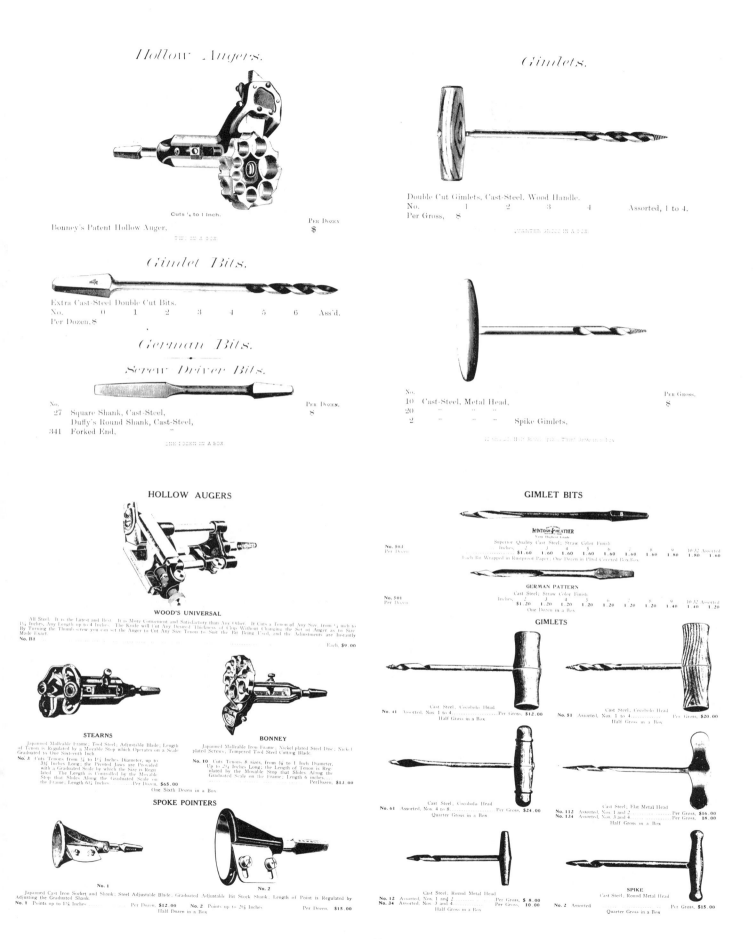

Hollow Augers.

Cuts ¼ to 1 Inch.

Bonney's Patent Hollow Auger,

PER DOZEN
$

TEN IN A BOX

Gimlet Bits.

Extra Cast-Steel Double Cut Bits.

No. 0 1 2 3 4 5 6 Ass'd.
Per Dozen, $

German Bits.

Screw Driver Bits.

No.		PER DOZEN
27	Square Shank, Cast-Steel,	$
	Duffy's Round Shank, Cast-Steel,	
341	Forked End,	

ONE DOZEN IN A BOX

Gimlets.

Double Cut Gimlets, Cast-Steel, Wood Handle.
No. 1 2 3 4 Assorted, 1 to 4.
Per Gross, $

QUARTER GROSS IN A BOX

No.			PER GROSS
10	Cast-Steel, Metal Head,		$
20	" " "		
2	" " "	Spike Gimlets,	

HOLLOW AUGERS

WOOD'S UNIVERSAL

All Steel. It is the Latest and Best. It is More Convenient and Satisfactory than Any Other. It Cuts a Tenon of Any Size, from ¼ inch to 1¼ Inches, Any Length up to 4 Inches. The Knife will Cut Any Desired Thickness of Chip Without Changing the Set of Auger as to Size. By Turning the Thumb-screw you can set the Auger to Cut Any Size Tenon to Suit the Bit Being Used, and the Adjustments are Instantly Made Exact.
No. B1

Each. $9.00

STEARNS

Japanned Malleable Frame; Tool Steel; Adjustable Blade; Length of Tenon is Regulated by a Movable Stop which Operates on a Scale Graduated to One Sixteenth Inch.
No. 3 Cuts Tenons from ¼ to 1¼ Inches Diameter, up to 3½ Inches Long, the Pivoted Jaws are Provided with a Graduated Scale by which the Size is Regulated. The Length is Controlled by the Movable Stop that Slides Along the Graduated Scale on the Frame, Length 6¼ Inches.
Per Dozen, $65.00
One Sixth Dozen in a Box

BONNEY

Japanned Malleable Iron Frame; Nickel plated Steel Disc; Nickel plated Screws; Tempered Tool Steel Cutting Blade.
No. 10 Cuts Tenons 8 sizes, from ⅜ to 1 Inch Diameter, Up to 2¼ Inches Long; the Length of Tenon is Regulated by the Movable Stop that Slides Along the Graduated Scale on the Frame; Length 6 inches.
Per Dozen, $13.00

SPOKE POINTERS

No. 1

No. 2

Japanned Cast Iron Socket and Shank; Steel Adjustable Blade; Graduated Adjustable Bit Stock Shank; Length of Point is Regulated by Adjusting the Graduated Shank.
No. 1 Points up to 1¼ Inches . . . . Per Dozen, $12.00   No. 2 Points up to 2¼ Inches . . . . . Per Dozen, $15.00
Half Dozen in a Box

GIMLET BITS

McINTOSH-HEATHER
Very Highest Grade
Superior Quality Cast Steel; Straw Color Finish
No. 503
Per Dozen
Inches, 2 3 4 5 6 7 8 9 10 32 Assorted
$1.60 1.60 1.60 1.60 1.60 1.60 1.60 1.80 1.80 1.60
Each Bit Wrapped in Rustproof Paper; One Dozen in Plaid Covered Box Box

GERMAN PATTERN
Cast Steel; Straw Color Finish
No. 501
Per Dozen
Inches, 2 3 4 5 6 7 8 9 10 32 Assorted
$1.20 1.20 1.20 1.20 1.20 1.20 1.20 1.40 1.40 1.20
One Dozen in a Box

GIMLETS

Cast Steel, Cocobolo Head
No. 41 Assorted, Nos. 1 to 4 . . . . Per Gross, $12.00
Half Gross in a Box

Cast Steel, Cocobolo Head
No. 51 Assorted, Nos. 1 to 4 . . . . Per Gross, $20.00
Half Gross in a Box

Cast Steel, Cocobolo Head
No. 61 Assorted, Nos. 4 to 8 . . . . Per Gross, $24.00
Quarter Gross in a Box

Cast Steel, Flat Metal Head
No. 112 Assorted, Nos. 1 and 2 . . . . Per Gross, $16.00
No. 134 Assorted, Nos. 3 and 4 . . . . Per Gross, 18.00
Half Gross in a Box

Cast Steel, Round Metal Head
No. 12 Assorted, Nos. 1 and 2 . . . . Per Gross, $ 8.00
No. 34 Assorted, Nos. 3 and 4 . . . . Per Gross, 10.00
Half Gross in a Box

SPIKE
Cast Steel, Round Metal Head
No. 2 Assorted . . . . Per Gross, $15.00
Quarter Gross in a Box

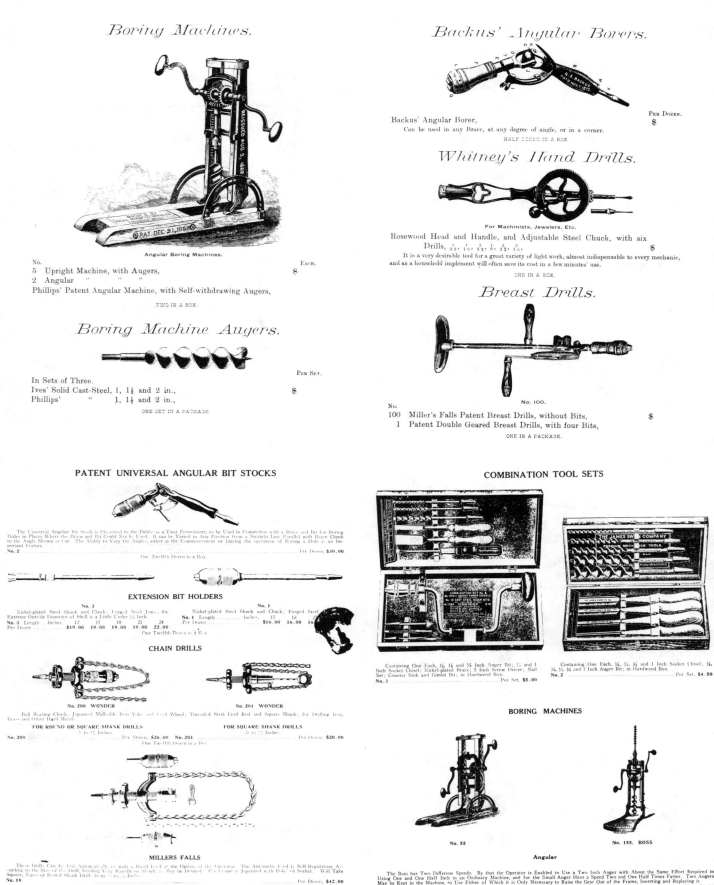

Boring Machines.

Angular Boring Machines.

No.   Each.
5 Upright Machine, with Augers, $
2 Angular   "   "   "
Phillips' Patent Angular Machine, with Self-withdrawing Augers,

TWO IN A BOX.

Boring Machine Augers.

Per Set.
In Sets of Three.
Ives' Solid Cast-Steel, 1, 1½ and 2 in., $
Phillips'   "   1, 1½ and 2 in.,

ONE SET IN A PACKAGE.

Backus' Angular Borers.

Per Dozen.
$
Backus' Angular Borer,
    Can be used in any Brace, at any degree of angle, or in a corner.
HALF DOZEN IN A BOX.

Whitney's Hand Drills.

For Machinists, Jewelers, Etc.
Rosewood Head and Handle, and Adjustable Steel Chuck, with six
    Drills, ¼, ³⁄₃₂, ⅛, ⁵⁄₃₂, ³⁄₁₆, $
    It is a very desirable tool for a great variety of light work, almost indispensable to every mechanic,
and as a household implement will often save its cost in a few minutes' use.

ONE IN A BOX.

Breast Drills.

No. 100.

No. $
100 Miller's Falls Patent Breast Drills, without Bits,
  1 Patent Double Geared Breast Drills, with four Bits,

ONE IN A PACKAGE.

PATENT UNIVERSAL ANGULAR BIT STOCKS

The Universal Angular Bit Stock is Presented to the Public as a Time Economizer, to be Used in Connection with a Brace and Bit for Boring Holes in Places Where the Brace and Bit Could Not be Used. It can be Varied in Any Position from a Straight Line Parallel with Brace Chuck to the Angle Shown in Cut. The Ability to Vary the Angles, either at the Commencement or During the operation of Boring a Hole is an Important Feature.
No. 2 .... Per Dozen, $30.00

One-Twelfth Dozen in a Box.

EXTENSION BIT HOLDERS

No. 3   No. 1
Nickel-plated Steel Shank and Chuck; Forged Steel Jaws, the   Nickel-plated Steel Shank and Chuck; Forged Steel
Extreme Outside Diameter of Shell is a Little Under ¾ Inch.
No. 3 Length ...Inches,   12   15   18   21   24   No. 1 Length .... Inches,   15   18   2
Per Dozen $19.00 19.00 19.00 19.00 22.00   Per Dozen $16.00 16.00 16

One Twelfth Dozen in a Box.

CHAIN DRILLS

No. 200 WONDER   No. 201 WONDER
Ball Bearing Chuck; Japanned Malleable Iron Yoke and Feed Wheel; Threaded Steel Feed Rod and Square Shank; for Drilling Iron,
Brass and Other Hard Metals.
FOR ROUND OR SQUARE SHANK DRILLS   FOR SQUARE SHANK DRILLS
No. 200 .... Per Dozen, $26.00 No. 201 .... Per Dozen, $20.00

One Twelfth Dozen in a Box.

MILLERS FALLS

These Drills Can Be Fed Automatically or with a Hand Feed at the Option of the Operator. The Automatic Feed is Self-Regulating, According to the Size of the Drill, Feeding Very Rapidly or Slowly as May be Desired. The Frame is Japanned with Polished Socket. Will Take Square, Taper or Round Shank Drill from ⅛ to ½ Inch.
No. 18 .... Per Dozen, $42.00

One Twelfth Dozen in a Box.

COMBINATION TOOL SETS

THE JAMES SWAN COMPANY

Containing One Each, ¼, ⅜ and ½ Inch Auger Bit; ½ and 1   Containing One Each, ¼, ½, ¾ and 1 Inch Socket Chisel; ¼,
Inch Socket Chisel; Nickel-plated Brace; 5 Inch Screw Driver; Nail   ⅜, ½, ¾ and 1 Inch Auger Bit; in Hardwood Box.
Set; Counter Sink and Gimlet Bit; in Hardwood Box.   No. 2 .... Per Set, $4.50
No. 3 .... Per Set, $5.00

BORING MACHINES

No. 55   No. 155. BOSS

Angular

The Boss has Two Different Speeds. By that the Operator is Enabled to Use a Two Inch Auger with About the Same Effort Required in Using One and One Half Inch in an Ordinary Machine, and for the Small Auger Have a Speed Two and One Half Times Faster. Two Augers May be Kept in the Machine, to Use Either of Which it is Only Necessary to Raise the Gear Out of the Frame, Inverting and Replacing it.
No. 55 Without Augers........................Each, $7.00   No. 155 Boss; Two Speed; Without Augers........Each, $9.50

112

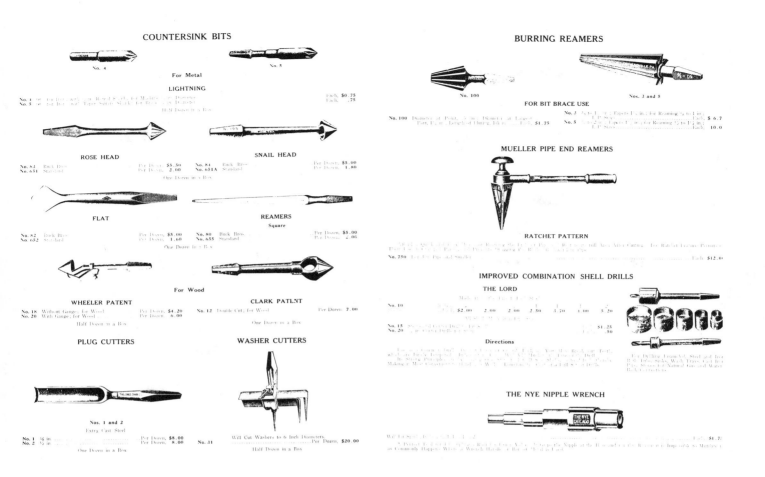

COUNTERSINK BITS

No. 4   No. 5

For Metal

LIGHTNING

No. 4 .... Round Shank, for Metal ...... Each, $0.75
No. 5 .... Taper Square Shank, for Brace ...... Each, .75

Half Dozen in a Box

ROSE HEAD   SNAIL HEAD

No. 83   Back Bros ...... Per Dozen, $3.50   No. 84   Back Bros ...... Per Dozen, $5.00
No. 651   Standard ...... Per Dozen, 2.00   No. 651A   Standard ...... Per Dozen, 1.80

One Dozen in a Box

FLAT   REAMERS

Square

No. 82   Back Bros ...... Per Dozen, $5.00   No. 80   Back Bros ...... Per Dozen, $5.00
No. 652   Standard ...... Per Dozen, 1.60   No. 655   Standard ...... Per Dozen, 2.00

One Dozen in a Box

For Wood

WHEELER PATENT   CLARK PATENT

No. 18   Without Gauge; for Wood ...... Per Dozen, $4.20   No. 12   Double Cut; for Wood ...... Per Dozen, 7.00
No. 20   With Gauge; for Wood ...... Per Dozen, 6.00

Half Dozen in a Box   One Dozen in a Box

PLUG CUTTERS   WASHER CUTTERS

Nos. 1 and 2

Extra Cast Steel

No. 1   ⅜ in ...... Per Dozen, $8.00   No. 31   Will Cut Washers to 6 Inch Diameters ...... Per Dozen, $20.00
No. 2   ½ in ...... Per Dozen, 8.00

One Dozen in a Box   Half Dozen in a Box

BURRING REAMERS

No. 100   Nos. 3 and 5

FOR BIT BRACE USE

No. 100   Diameter at Point, ⅛ inch, Diameter at Largest
Part, ½ in., Length of Cutting, 1½ in ...... Each, $1.75

No. 3   Tool Tapers ¾ in., for Reaming ⅜ to 1 in.;
E. P. Steel ...... Each, $6.75
No. 5   Tool ⅞ Tapers 1¾ in., for Reaming ½ to 1½ in.;
E. P. Steel ...... Each, 10.0

MUELLER PIPE END REAMERS

RATCHET PATTERN

No. 750   For Gas Pipe and Smaller ...... Each, $12.00

IMPROVED COMBINATION SHELL DRILLS

THE LORD

No. 10 ...... $2.00   2.00   2.00   2.30   3.70   4.00   5.20

No. 15 ...... $1.25
No. 20 ...... 1.50

Directions

THE NYE NIPPLE WRENCH

Angers and Auger Bits.

Hibbard, Spencer & Co.'s Winooski Angers.

Solid Cast Steel, Brass Nut, Full Polished Shank.

Inches,	⅜	½	⅝	¾	⅞	1
Per Dozen,	$5 00	5 00	6 00	7 50	8 00	8 50

Inches,	1¼	1½	1¾	2	2¼	2½
Per Dozen,	$10 00	12 00	14 00	17 00	20 00	25 00

Hibbard, Spencer & Co.'s Winooski Auger Bits.

Extra Cast-Steel, with Double Spurs and Lips.

Inches,	3/	4/	5/	6/	7/	8/	9/	10/	11/	12/	13/	14/	15/	16/16ths.
Per Dozen,	$3.50	3.00	3.00	3.25	3.25	3.50	3.50	4.00	4.25	4.50	4.75	5.00	5.50	6.00

Set of 24 quarters, assorted, { 4/ 5/ 6/ 7/ 8/ 9/ 10/ 11/ 12/16ths. } Per Set, $3.50
               { 1   1   2   1   2   1   2   1   1 }

Set of 32½ quarters, assorted, { 4/ 5/ 6/ 7/ 8/ 9/ 10/ 11/ 12/ 13/ 14/ 15/ 16/16ths. } Per Set, $4.50
               { 1   1   1   1   1   1   1   1   1   1   1   1 }

Separate Sizes, Half Dozen in a Box; Assorted, One Set in a Box.

Spoke Pointers.

No.
2   Stearns' Patent Spoke Pointer, Cast-Steel, Adjustable Knife,   Per Dozen. $

HALF DOZEN IN A BOX.

Hollow Augers.

Ives' New Patent Hollow Augers, with Two Cutters.

Inches,	½	⅝	¾	⅞	1
Per Dozen,	$				

Cuts ¼ to 1 Inch.

Stearns' Patent Expansive Hollow Augers, $

TWO IN A BOX.

Barber's Patent Bit Braces.

Lignumvitæ Head, Rosewood Handle, and Nickel Plated Cast-Steel Sweep, Socket, Jaws and Pin.

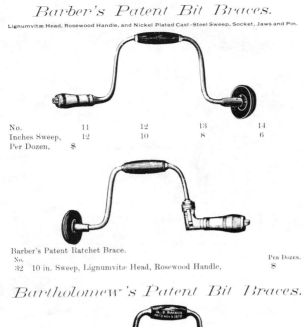

No.	11	12	13	14
Inches Sweep,	12	10	8	6
Per Dozen,	$			

Barber's Patent Ratchet Brace.

No.		Per Dozen.
32	10 in. Sweep, Lignumvitæ Head, Rosewood Handle,	$

Bartholomew's Patent Bit Braces.

117	8 in. Sweep, Wood Head and Handle,	$
118	9½ in. " " "	

HALF DOZEN IN A PACKAGE.

Bartholomew's Patent Bit Braces.

Patent Ratchet.

No.		Per Dozen.
129	10½ in. Sweep, Wood Head and Handle,	$

Spofford's Patent Bit Braces.

Rosewood Head, Revolving Handle.

107	7 in. Sweep, with Thumb Screw,	$
108	8 in. " " " "	
110	10 in. " " " "	

Barker's Improved Bit Braces.

With Black Walnut or Lignumvitæ Head and Handle.

No.	6	8	10	12
Per Dozen.	$			

HALF DOZEN IN A PACKAGE.

11

Bartholomew's Common Bit Braces.

No.		Per Dozen.
25	8¼ in. Sweep, Wood Head and Handle, Thumb Screw,	$
30	10½ in. " " " " "	

Common Bit Braces.

40	Malleable Iron, 8 in. Sweep, Thumb Screw,	$

Brace Wrenches.

Amidon's Patent Brace Wrench, $

A most convenient tool for Farmers, Car Builders, and all Mechanics using either a Brace or a Wrench.

HALF DOZEN IN A PACKAGE.

Backus' Patent Bit Braces.

Lignumvitæ Head, Rosewood Handle, Wrought Iron Sweep and Socket, Jaws and Pin of Hardened Steel.

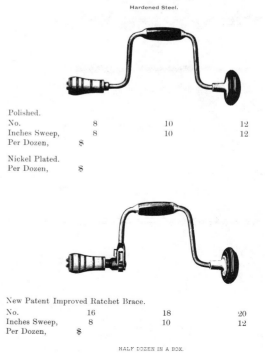

Polished.

No.	8	10	12
Inches Sweep,	8	10	12
Per Dozen,	$		

Nickel Plated.

Per Dozen,	$

New Patent Improved Ratchet Brace.

No.	16	18	20
Inches Sweep,	8	10	12
Per Dozen,	$		

HALF DOZEN IN A BOX.

RECIPROCATING DRILLS

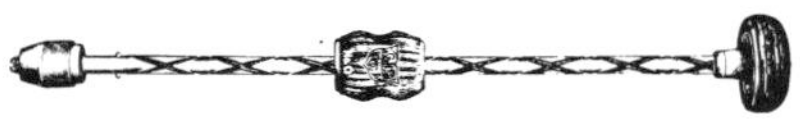

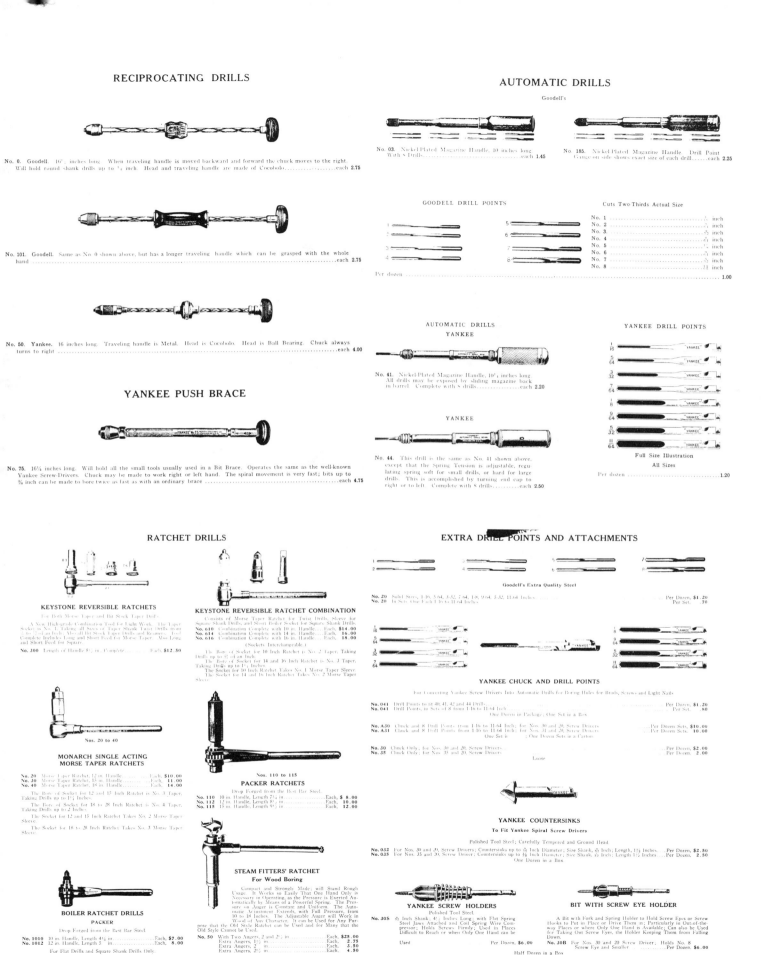

No. 0. Goodell. 16½ inches long. When traveling handle is moved backward and forward the chuck moves to the right. Will hold round shank drills up to ¼ inch. Head and traveling handle are made of Cocobolo.................. each **2.75**

No. 101. Goodell. Same as No. 0 shown above, but has a longer traveling handle which can be grasped with the whole hand .... each **2.75**

No. 50. Yankee. 16 inches long. Traveling handle is Metal. Head is Cocobolo. Head is Ball Bearing. Chuck always turns to right .... each **4.00**

YANKEE PUSH BRACE

No. 75. 16¼ inches long. Will hold all the small tools usually used in a Bit Brace. Operates the same as the well-known Yankee Screw-Drivers. Chuck may be made to work right or left hand. The spiral movement is very fast; bits up to ⅜ inch can be made to bore twice as fast as with an ordinary brace .... each **4.75**

AUTOMATIC DRILLS

Goodell's

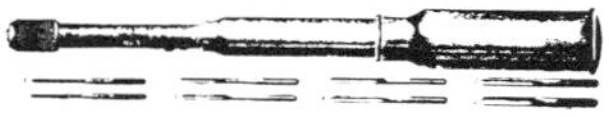

No. 03. Nickel-Plated Magazine Handle, 10 inches long. With 8 Drills... each **1.45**

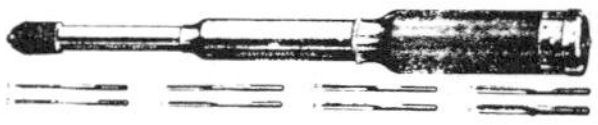

No. 185. Nickel-Plated Magazine Handle. Drill Point Gauge on side shows exact size of each drill...... each **2.25**

GOODELL DRILL POINTS

Cuts Two-Thirds Actual Size

No. 1 .... 1/16 inch
No. 2 .... 5/64 inch
No. 3 .... 3/32 inch
No. 4 .... 7/64 inch
No. 5 .... 1/8 inch
No. 6 .... 9/64 inch
No. 7 .... 5/32 inch
No. 8 .... 11/64 inch

Per dozen **1.00**

AUTOMATIC DRILLS
YANKEE

No. 41. Nickel-Plated Magazine Handle, 10¼ inches long. All drills may be exposed by sliding magazine back in barrel. Complete with 8 drills.................. each **2.20**

YANKEE

No. 44. This drill is the same as No. 41 shown above, except that the Spring Tension is adjustable, regulating spring soft for small drills, or hard for large drills. This is accomplished by turning end cap to right or to left. Complete with 8 drills.......... each **2.50**

YANKEE DRILL POINTS

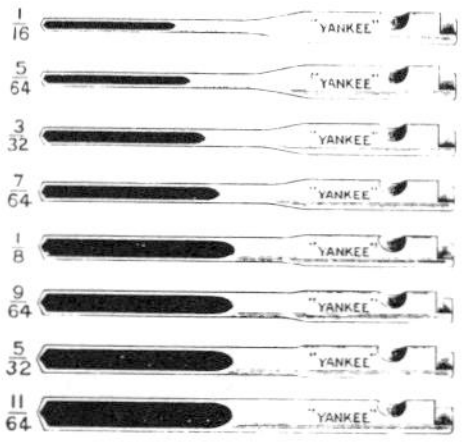

Full Size Illustration
All Sizes

Per dozen **1.20**

RATCHET DRILLS

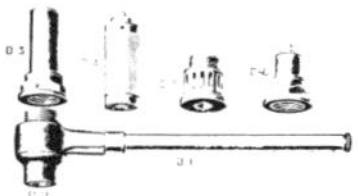

KEYSTONE REVERSIBLE RATCHETS

For Both Morse Taper and Bit Stock Taper Drills.

A New High-grade Combination Tool for Light Work. The Taper Socket is No. 1, Taking all Sizes of Taper Shank Twist Drills from ⅛ to ½ of an Inch; Also all Bit Stock Taper Drills and Reamers. Tool Complete Includes Long and Short Feed for Morse Taper. Also Long and Short Feed for Square.

No. 300 Length of Handle 8½ in., Complete........ Each, **$12.50**

KEYSTONE REVERSIBLE RATCHET COMBINATION

Consists of Morse Taper Ratchet for Twist Drills, Sleeve for Square Shank Drills, and Short Boiler Socket for Square Shank Drills.

No. 610 Combination Complete with 10 in. Handle.... Each, **$14.00**
No. 614 Combination Complete with 14 in. Handle.... Each, **16.00**
No. 616 Combination Complete with 16 in. Handle.... Each, **18.00**

(Sockets Interchangeable.)

The Bore of Socket for 10 Inch Ratchet is No. 2 Taper, Taking Drills up to ⅞ of an Inch.
The Bore of Socket for 14 and 16 Inch Ratchet is No. 3 Taper, Taking Drills up to 1¼ Inches.
The Socket for 10 Inch Ratchet Takes No. 1 Morse Taper Sleeve.
The Socket for 14 and 16 Inch Ratchet Takes No. 2 Morse Taper Sleeve.

Nos. 20 to 40

MONARCH SINGLE ACTING MORSE TAPER RATCHETS

No. 20 Morse Taper Ratchet, 12 in. Handle.............. Each, **$10.00**
No. 30 Morse Taper Ratchet, 15 in. Handle.............. Each, **11.00**
No. 40 Morse Taper Ratchet, 18 in. Handle.............. Each, **14.00**

The Bore of Socket for 12 and 15 Inch Ratchet is No. 3 Taper, Taking Drills up to 1¼ Inches.

The Bore of Socket for 18 to 28 Inch Ratchet is No. 4 Taper, Taking Drills up to 2 Inches.

The Socket for 12 and 15 Inch Ratchet Takes No. 2 Morse Taper Sleeve.

The Socket for 18 to 28 Inch Ratchet Takes No. 3 Morse Taper Sleeve.

Nos. 110 to 115

PACKER RATCHETS

Drop Forged from the Best Bar Steel.

No. 110 10 in. Handle, Length 7¾ in...................... Each, **$ 8.00**
No. 112 12 in. Handle, Length 8½ in...................... Each, **10.00**
No. 115 15 in. Handle, Length 9½ in...................... Each, **12.00**

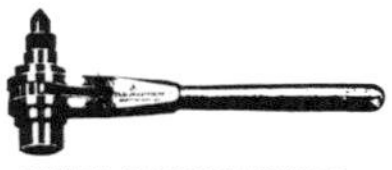

BOILER RATCHET DRILLS
PACKER

Drop Forged from the Best Bar Steel.

No. 1010 10 in. Handle, Length 4¾ in.................. Each, **$7.00**
No. 1012 12 in. Handle, Length 5 in.................. Each, **8.00**

For Flat Drills and Square Shank Drills Only.

STEAM FITTERS' RATCHET
For Wood Boring

Compact and Strongly Made; will Stand Rough Usage. It Works so Easily That One Hand Only is Necessary in Operating, as the Pressure is Exerted Automatically by Means of a Powerful Spring. The Pressure on Auger is Constant and Uniform. The Automatic Adjustment Extends, with Full Pressure, from 10 to 18 Inches. The Adjustable Auger will Work in Wood of Any Character. It can be Used for Any Purpose that the Old Style Ratchet can be Used and for Many that the Old Style Cannot be Used.

No. 50 With Two Augers, 2 and 2½ in................ Each, **$25.00**
Extra Augers, 1½ in................................ Each, **2.75**
Extra Augers, 2 in................................ Each, **3.50**
Extra Augers, 2½ in................................ Each, **4.50**

EXTRA DRILL POINTS AND ATTACHMENTS

Goodell's Extra Quality Steel

No. 20 Solid Sizes, 1-16, 5-64, 3-32, 7-64, 1-8, 9-64, 5-32, 11-64 Inches........ Per Dozen, **$1.20**
No. 20 In Sets. One Each 1-16 to 11-64 Inches........ Per Set. **.70**

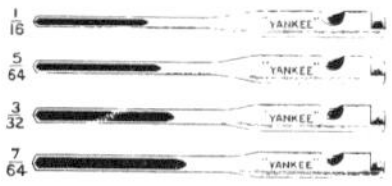

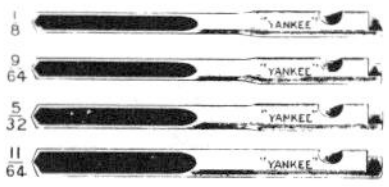

YANKEE CHUCK AND DRILL POINTS

For Converting Yankee Screw Drivers Into Automatic Drills for Boring Holes for Brads, Screws and Light Nails

No. 041 Drill Points to fit 40, 41, 42 and 44 Drills........ Per Dozen, **$1.20**
No. 041 Drill Points, in Sets of 8 from 1-16 to 11-64 Inch........ Per Set. **.80**

One Dozen in Package; One Set in a Box

No. A30 Chuck and 8 Drill Points from 1-16 to 11-64 Inch; for Nos. 30 and 20, Screw Drivers........ Per Dozen Sets, **$10.00**
No. A31 Chuck and 8 Drill Points from 1-16 to 11-64 Inch; for Nos. 31 and 20, Screw Drivers........ Per Dozen Sets. **10.00**

One Set in ; One Dozen Sets in a Carton

No. 30 Chuck Only; for Nos. 30 and 20, Screw Drivers........ Per Dozen, **$2.00**
No. 35 Chuck Only; for Nos. 35 and 20, Screw Drivers........ Per Dozen. **2.00**

Loose

YANKEE COUNTERSINKS

To Fit Yankee Spiral Screw Drivers

Polished Tool Steel; Carefully Tempered and Ground Head.

No. 032 For Nos. 30 and 20, Screw Drivers; Countersinks up to 7/16 Inch Diameter; Size Shank, 9/32 Inch; Length, 1⅞ Inches.... Per Dozen, **$2.50**
No. 035 For Nos. 35 and 20, Screw Driver; Countersinks up to ⅜ Inch Diameter; Size Shank, 7/32 Inch; Length 1½ Inches.... Per Dozen, **2.50**

One Dozen in a Box

YANKEE SCREW HOLDERS

Polished Tool Steel.

No. 30S 9/32 Inch Shank; 4½ Inches Long; with Flat Spring Steel Jaws Attached and Coil Spring Wire Compressor; Holds Screws Firmly; Used in Places Difficult to Reach or when Only One Hand can be Used........ Per Dozen, **$6.00**

BIT WITH SCREW EYE HOLDER

A Bit with Fork and Spring Holder to Hold Screw Eyes or Screw Hooks to Put in Place or Drive Them in; Particularly in Out-of-the-way Places or where Only One Hand is Available; Can also be Used for Taking Out Screw Eyes, the Holder Keeping Them from Falling Down.

No. 30B For Nos. 30 and 20 Screw Driver; Holds No. 8 Screw Eye and Smaller........ Per Dozen, **$6.00**

Half Dozen in a Box

Draw Knives, Spoke Shaves

Wheel makers and carpenters made much use of the early draw knives and shaves.

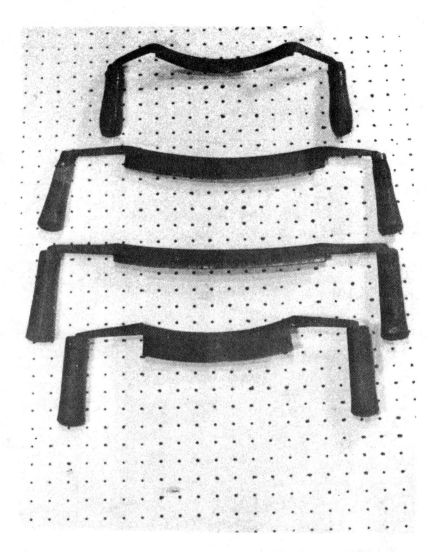

Draw Knives

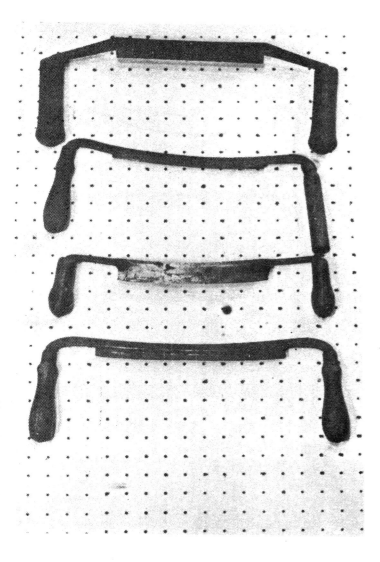

Draw Knives

DRAWING KNIVES.

Razor Blade Drawing Knives, drop forged from Best Quality Crucible Steel,

Wilkinsons' Folding and Adjustable Handle Drawing Knives

117

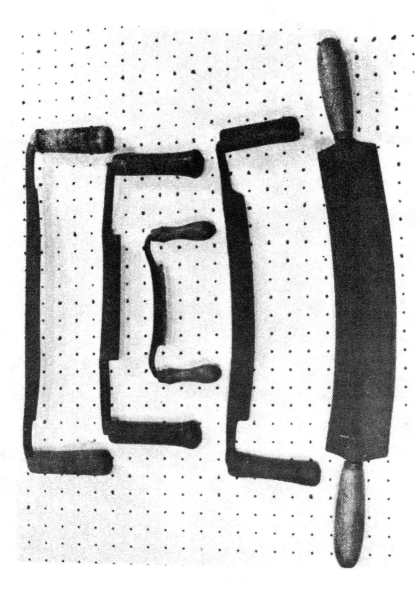

Draw Knives Left to Right
1.   2.   3.
   4.   5. Plinter Drawknife

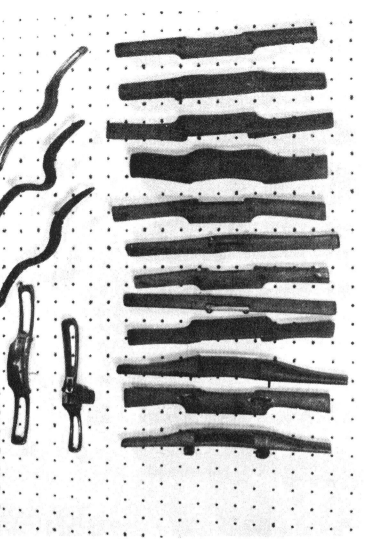

Spoke Shaves
5 on Left are Metal

Spoke Shaves All Wood

119

UNIVERSAL HAND BEADERS

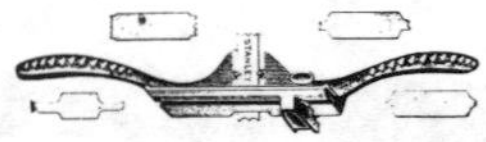

For Beading, Reeding or Fluting Straight or Irregular Surfaces, and for all Kinds of Light Routering. With Square Gauge for Straight, and an Oval Gauge for Curved Work.

Seven Superior Steel Cutters go with Each Tool. Both Ends are Sharpened, thus Embracing Six Ordinary Sizes of Beads, Four Sets of Reeds, Two Fluters and a Double Router Iron (1/8 and 1/4 inch).

No. 66 Nickel-plated Stock, with Seven Steel Cutters ....Per Dozen, **$16.40**

One Twelfth Dozen in Box.

CLAPBOARD MARKERS

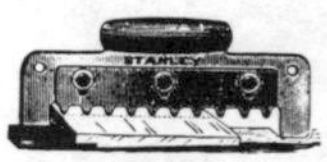

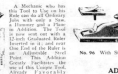

No. 88

This Ingenious Tool can be Used with One Hand, while the Other is Employed in Holding a Clapboard in Position. The Marking Blade is Easily Adjusted to any Thickness of Clapboard, or Siding. The Sharp Edges of the Teeth are just Parallel with the Legs when Placed Against the Corner-board or Window Casing. By Moving the Tool Half an Inch, it will Mark a Full line across the Clapboard, Exactly Over and Conformed to the Edge of the Corner-board. There is then no Difficulty in Sawing for a Perfectly Close Joint.

No. 88 Metal Stock; Wood Handle; Steel Blade..Per Dozen, **$9.00**

One Twelfth Dozen in Box.

STANLEY "ODD-JOBS"

(Ten Tools in One)

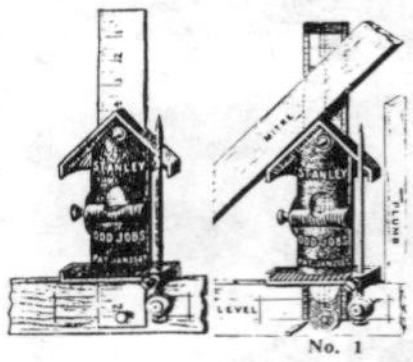

No. 1

A Mechanic who has this Tool to Use on his Rule can do all Ordinary Jobs with only a Saw, a Hammer and a Plane in Addition. The Tool is now sent out with a 12-inch Graduated Ruler Inserted in it; and near One End of the Ruler is an Adjustable Steel Point. This Addition Greatly Facilitates the use of this Unique Tool, Already Favorably Known to Mechanics, Amateurs and House-keepers.

No. 1 Odd Jobs; Nickel-plated; with Rule......Per Dozen, **$12.60**

One Twelfth Dozen in a Box.

AUGER BIT GAUGES

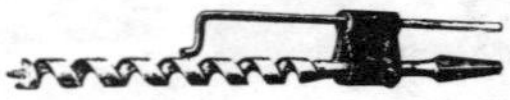

No. 1

This Shows the Gauge in all its Parts. One Bolt with Thumb Screw Tightens the Clamps on the Gauge Spindle and Auger Bit at the Same Time. It will Fit any Size Bit and Exactly Gauge the Depth of Hole to be Bored.

No. 1 Auger Bit Gauge........................Per Dozen, **$6.00**

Half Dozen in Box.

CORNERING TOOLS

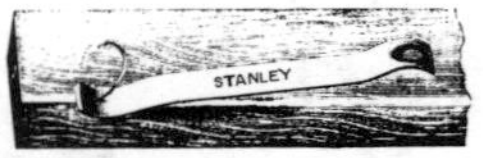

No. 28 and 29

For Pattern-Makers, and Used by all Wood-Workers, in Rounding Sharp Edges. The Tool is made in Two Numbers, with a Different Size Cutter at Each End; so Sharpened that Owners can Always Cut with the Grain Without Changing Position of the Work. It requires no Depth Gauge, as the Form of the Tool Allows it to Cut Only to a Certain Depth.

No. 28 3/16 and 1/8 in.; Flat Steel..................Per Dozen, **$4.40**
No. 29 1/4 and 3/8 in.; Flat Steel..................Per Dozen, **4.60**

One Half Dozen in Box.

CLAPBOARD GAUGES

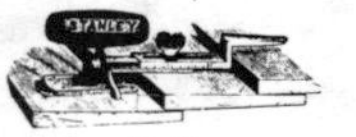

No. 89

Two Thin Steel Blades, which Form a Part of the Base of the Tool, will Slide Under the Last Clapboard Already Laid (see Broken Corner in Engraving). When the Bottom of the Gauge is Brought Firmly up to the Lower Edge of the Clapboard, Press the Handle Over Sidewise, and this will Force Another Thin Blade Down into the Next Lower Clapboard, Rendering the Tool Immovable. The Clapboard to be Laid can be held any Width to the Weather, by Means of the Graduated Scale on the Tool; and After the Tool is Released, the Mark Left is so Light that Painting Alone Will Fill it.

No. 89 Metal Stock; Wood Handle; Steel Blade..Per Dozen, **$9.00**

Quarter Dozen in a Box.

ADJUSTABLE CHISEL GAUGES

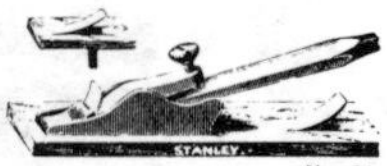

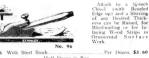

No. 96

Attach to a 1/4-inch Chisel (with Beveled Edge up) and a Shaving of any Desired Thickness can be Raised, for Blind-nailing or for Inlaying Wood Strips in Ornamental Surface Work.

No. 96 With Steel Stock........................Per Dozen, **$3.60**

Half Dozen in Box.

ADJUSTABLE BIT GAUGES

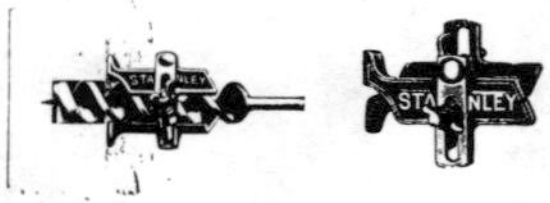

No. 49

Using this Tool the Workman is Able to Bore any Number of Holes to a Given Depth. A Stop Being Placed on Both Sides of the Bit, when the Proper Depth is Reached the Bit Remains Upright and Does not Bend or Break the Worm. Being Adjustable, the Gauge can be Attached to any Size Bit, up to One Inch in Diameter. By Loosening the Thumb Screws, the Shank of the Bit can be Inserted in the Gauge, and the Twist of the Bit Turned to the Required Depth.

No. 49 Adjustable Bit Gauge; Nickel-plated; 2½ in. Long. ....Per Dozen, **$10.50**

One Twelfth Dozen in Box.

SPOKE SHAVES

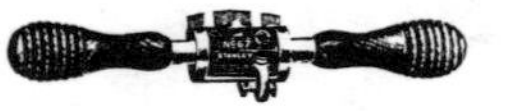

No. 67

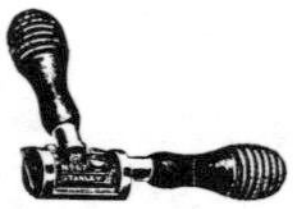

No. 67

UNIVERSAL

Both Handles are Detachable, and Either of them can be Screwed into a Socket on Top of the Stock, thus Enabling the Owner to Work into the Corners, or Panels, as no Other Spoke Shave can do.

No. 67 Nickel-plated; Rosewood Handle; Length, 9¼ Inches; Cutter 1¾ Inch........................Per Dozen, **$25.00**

One Twelfth Dozen in a Box.

RAZOR EDGE SPOKE SHAVES

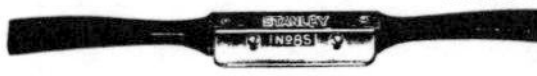

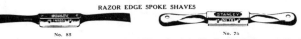

No. 85

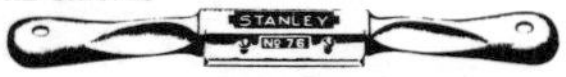

No. 76

So Called from the Shape of the Cutter, which is Hollow Ground, Giving a Keen Cutting Edge. The Adjustable Front can be Moved up or Down, Opening or Closing the Mouth, and with the Cutter Properly Adjusted a Coarse or Very Fine Shaving can be Cut.

No. 85 Boxwood; Length 12 in.; 2½ in. Cutter..Per Dozen, **$18.00**

No. 76 Nickel-plated; Length 11 in.; 2½ in. Cutter Per Dozen, **$17.00**

One Quarter Dozen in a Box.

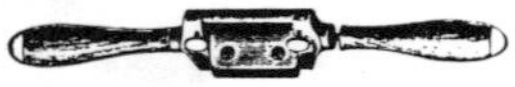

No. 200

MILLERS FALLS

The Circular Shape of this Tool Adapts it to Work in Small Circles. Either Handle can be Removed.

No. 200 Rosewood Handles; 10 In. 2 in. Cutter..Per Dozen, **$15.00**

One Half Dozen in a Box.

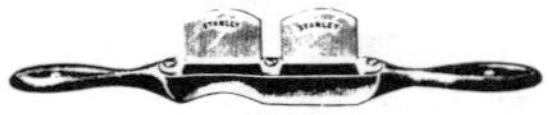

No. 60

No. 60 Double Cutter; Hollow and Straight; 10 in.; 1½ in. Cutter........................Per Dozen, **$6.00**

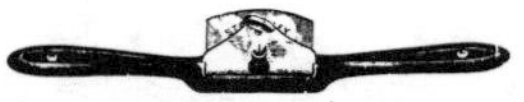

No. 52

No. 52 Double Iron; Straight Handle; 10 in.; 2⅛ in. Cutter........................Per Dozen, **$4.50**

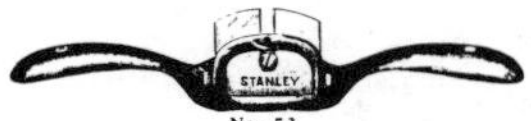

No. 53

No. 53 Adjustable, Raised Handle; 10 in.; 2⅛ in. Cutter........................Per Dozen, **$6.00**

One Half Dozen in a Box.

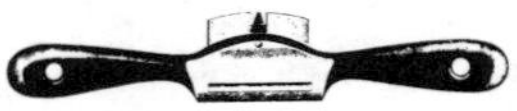

No. 63

No. 63 Convex Iron; Straight Handle; 9 in.; 1¾ in. Cutter........................Per Dozen, **$2.50**

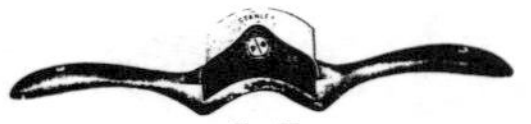

No. 55

No. 55 Model Double Iron; Hollow Face; 10 in.; 2⅛ in. Cutter........................Per Dozen, **$4.00**

One Half Dozen in a Box.

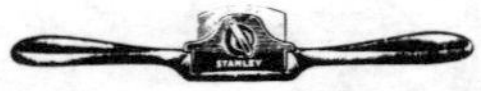

No. 64

No. 64 Straight Handle; 9 in.; 1¾ in. Cutter (with Thumb Screw)........................Per Dozen, **$2.50**

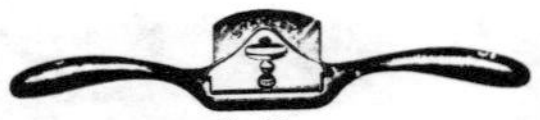

No. 51

No. 51 Double Iron; Raised Handle; 10 in.; 2⅛ in. Cutter........................Per Dozen, **$4.50**

One Half Dozen in a Box.

DRAWING KNIVES

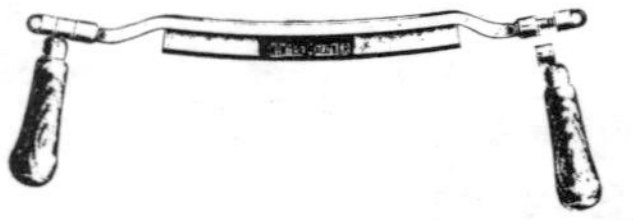

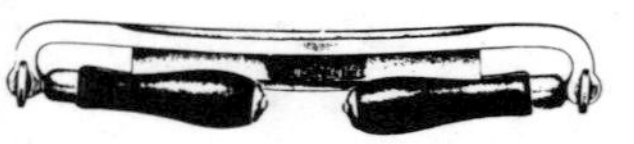

McINTOSH HEATHER
Very Highest Grade

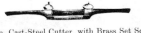

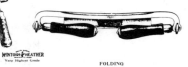

ADJUSTABLE

Razor Blade; Mirror Finish; Forged from Best Grade Tool Steel; Sharpened and Ground; Bog Oak Stained Adjustable Capped Handles.

No. 14	Length ....Inches,	8	9	10
Per Dozen	....	**$21.00**	**24.00**	**26.00**

One Quarter Dozen in Plaid Covered Box.

FOLDING

Razor Blade; Mirror Finish; Forged from Best Grade Tool Steel; Sharpened and Ground; Bog Oak Stained Folding Capped Handles.

No. 15	Length ....Inches,	8
Per Dozen	....	**$36.00**

One Twelfth Dozen in Plaid Covered Box.

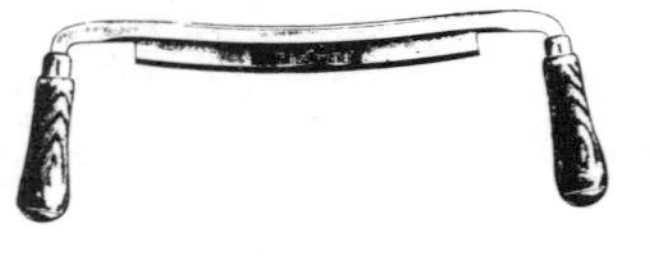

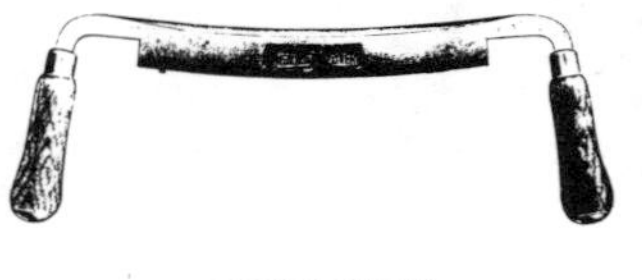

CARPENTERS'

CARRIAGE MAKERS'

Mirror Finished Blade; Forged from Best Grade Tool Steel; Sharpened and Ground; Bog Oak Stained Capped Handles.

Carpenter's Razor Blade

No. 1	Length ....Inches,	8	9	10
Per Dozen	....	**$15.00**	**16.00**	**17.50**

Carriage Makers'

No. 2	Length ....Inches,	8	9	10
Per Dozen	....	**$17.00**	**18.80**	**19.6[illegible]**

One Quarter Dozen in Plaid Covered Box.

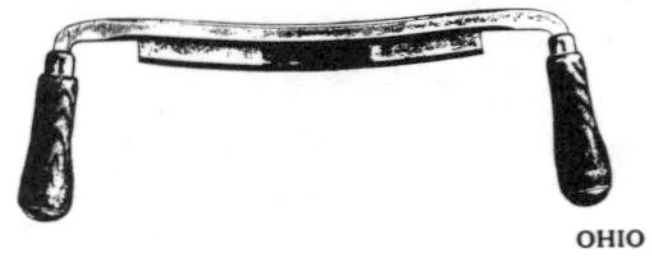

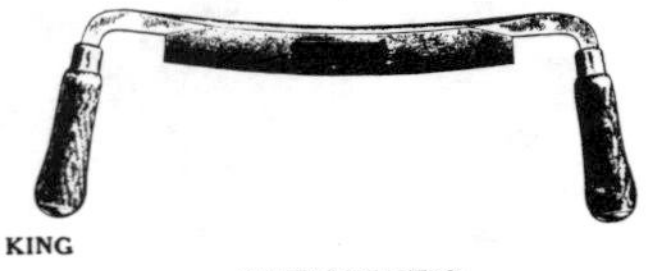

OHIO KING

CARPENTERS'

CARRIAGE MAKERS'

Polished Blade and Shank; Crucible Cast Steel; Hardwood Capped Handles.

Carpenter's Razor Blade

No. 01	Length ....Inches,	8	9	10
Per Dozen	....	$13.50	14.40	15.60
		13.50	**14.40**	**15.60**

Carriage Makers'

No. 02	Length ....Inches,	8	9	10
Per Dozen	....	$12.00	13.00	14.00
		16.80	**18.20**	**19.60**

Half Dozen in a Box.

Wood Spoke Shaves.

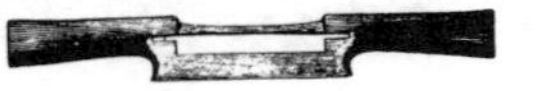

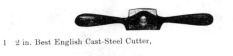

No.				Per Dozen.
4	Beechwood,	2½ in.	Cast-Steel Cutter,	$
5	"	3 in.	" "	
6	" Plated	2½ in.	" "	
7	" "	3 in.	" "	
10	Boxwood,	2½ in.	" "	
12	"	3 in.	" "	

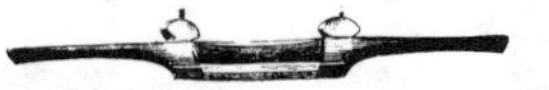

8	Beechwood, 2½ in. Cast-Steel Cutter, with Brass Set Screws,	$
9	" 3 in. " " " " "	

Iron Spoke Shaves.

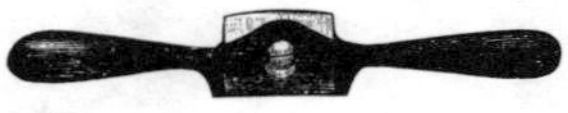

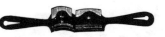

1	2 in. Best English Cast-Steel Cutter,	$

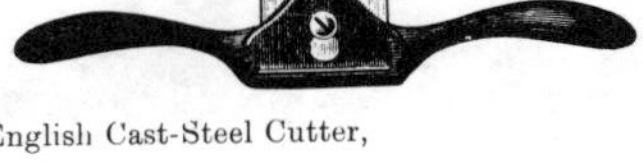

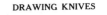

2	2¼ in. Best English Cast-Steel Cutter,	$

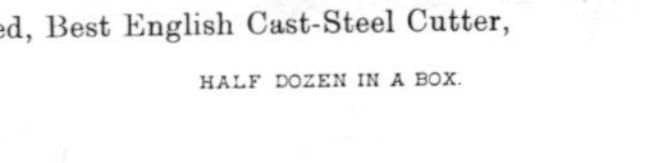

3	Double Bitted, Best English Cast-Steel Cutter,	$

HALF DOZEN IN A BOX.

Wrenches

Wrenches came into being early in the industrial revolution. The first ones were made by blacksmiths and later were manufactured in factories for use on new equipment then being invented.

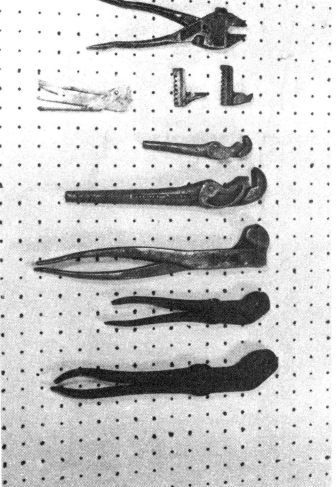

Top to Bottom
1. Eifol Flash Plier Wrench
Pat. 1916 (two Jaws below)
2. (left of Jaws) Comb. Adj. & Alligator
with Screwdriver
3-4 Stillston Type
5-6-7 Adj. Grip Pliers

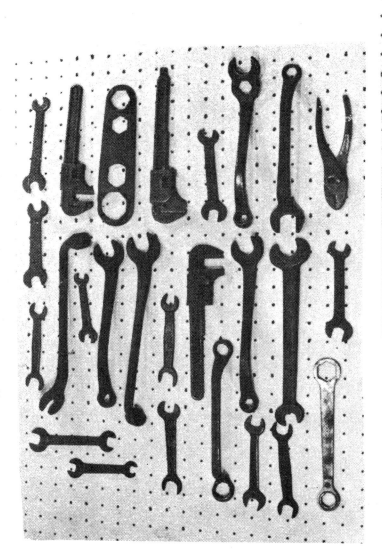

Ford Model "A" & "T" Wrenches & Pliers
All have Ford name and were original
equipment with car.
Wrenches   Pliers

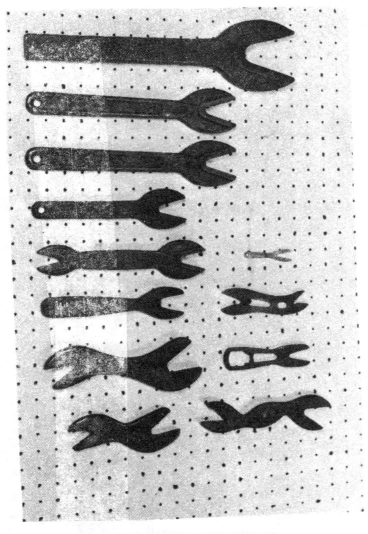

ALLIGATOR WRENCHES
Right Row, 3rd down has die built in handle

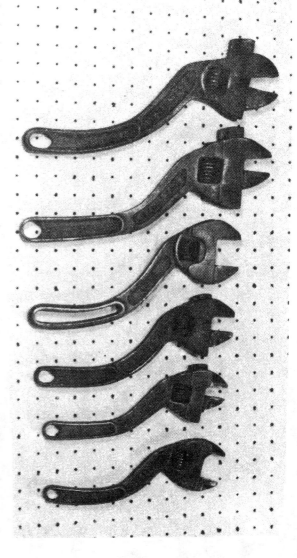

"S" Crescent Wrenches

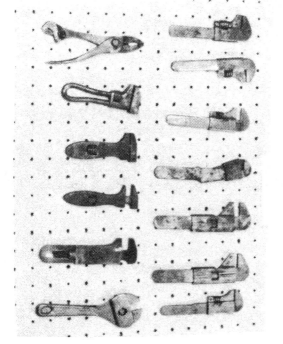

All on Right Bicycle Wrenches
All on Left Adj. Wrench except 4-in-1 Plier
Top

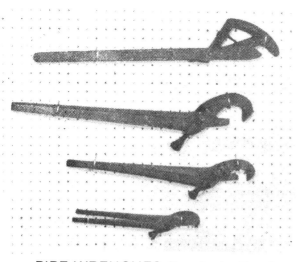

PIPE WRENCHES (top to bottom)
Hoe Corp. Poughkeepsie, NY
Ashcraft Tools 1886
Ashcraft Tools 1886
Ashcraft Tools 1886

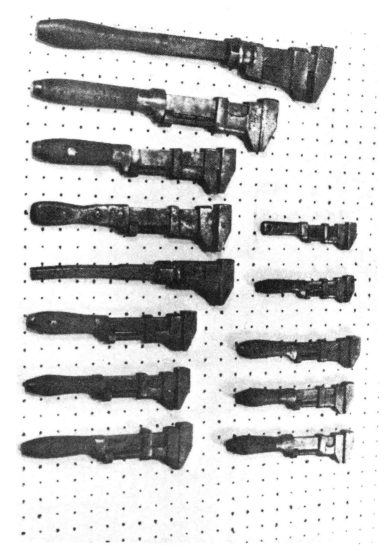

MONKEY WRENCHES

Steam Tractor Wrenches

123

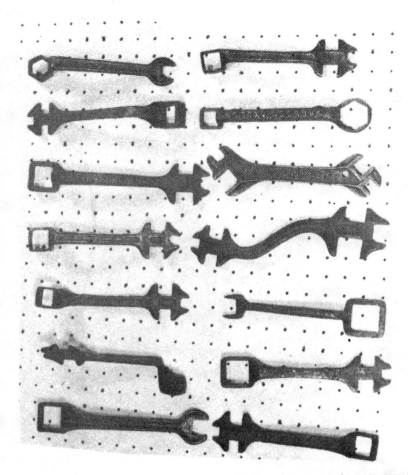

Buggy Wrenches

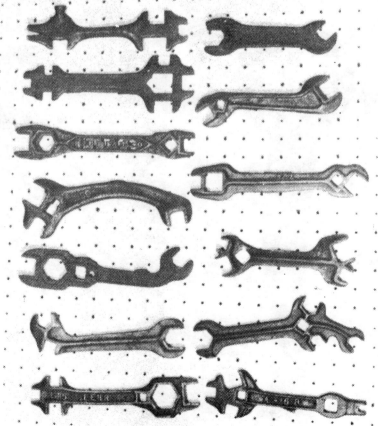

Farm Implement Wrenches

124

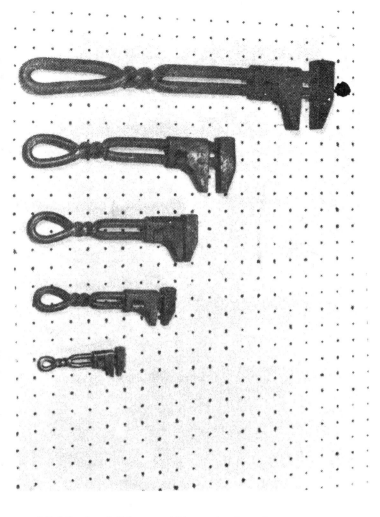

All Marked "Acme Wrench Co. Pat. 1883"

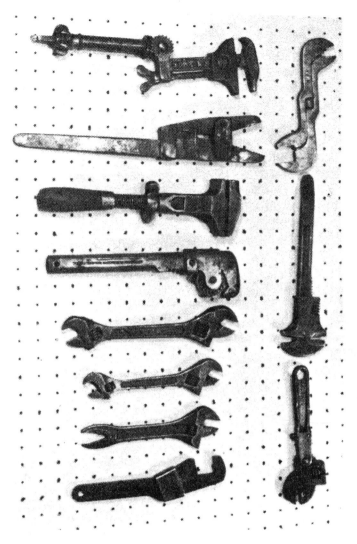

MISC. WRENCHES

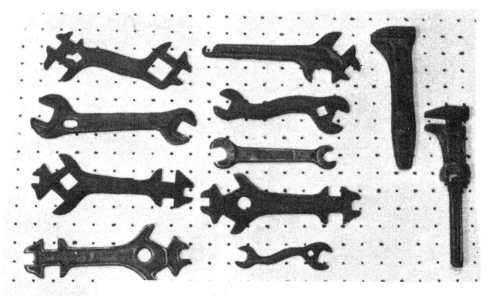

International Harvester Wrenches
Two Monkey Wrenches at Right

TRACK TOOLS

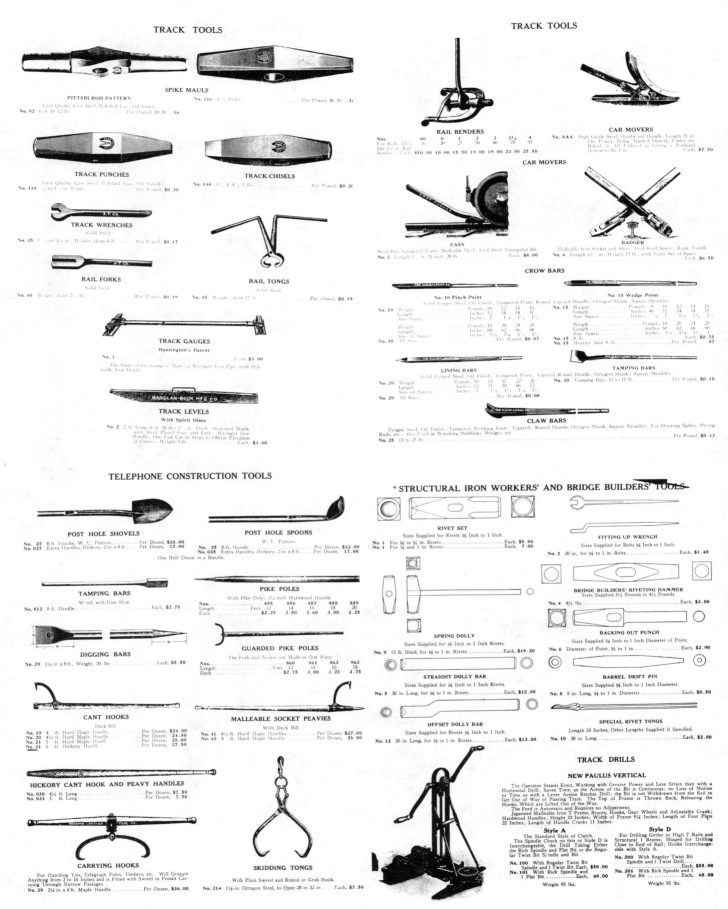

SPIKE MAULS

PITTSBURGH PATTERN

First Quality Cast Steel, Polished Face, Oil Finish

No. 92 6, 8, 10, 12 lbs. .... Per Pound, $0.30 .16

No. 116 8, 9, 10 lbs. .... Per Pound, $0.30 .16

TRACK PUNCHES

First Quality Cast Steel, Polished Face, Oil Finish.

No. 118 ¾ to 1½ in. Points .... Per Pound, **$0.30**

TRACK CHISELS

No. 148 3½, 4, 4½, 5 lbs. .... Per Pound, **$0.30**

TRACK WRENCHES

Solid Steel

No. 35 1⅛ and 1⅜ in.; Weight, about 4 lb. .... Per Pound, **$0.17**

RAIL FORKS

Solid Steel

No. 40 Weight, about 7½ lb. .... Per Pound, **$0.19**

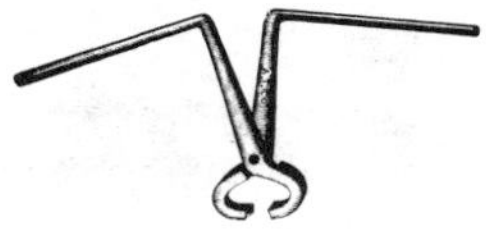

RAIL TONGS

Solid Steel

No. 45 Weight, about 17 lb. .... Per Pound, **$0.19**

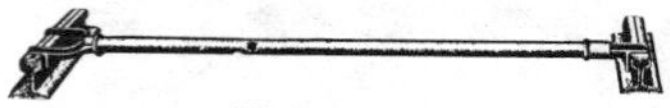

TRACK GAUGES

Huntington's Patent

No. 1 .... Each, **$3.00**

The Stem of this Gauge is Made of Wrought Iron Pipe, with Malleable Iron Heads.

TRACK LEVELS

With Spirit Glass

No. 2 7 ft. Long, 6 in. Wide; 1½ in. Thick; Seasoned Maple, with Steel Plated Face and Ends; Wrought Iron Handle; One End Cut in Steps to Obtain Elevation at Curves; Weight 9 lb. .... Each, **$3.00**

TRACK TOOLS

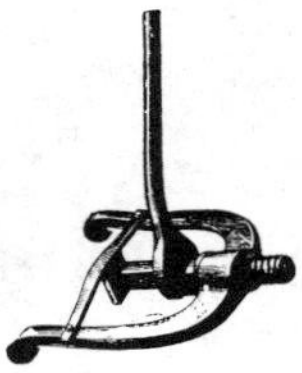

RAIL BENDERS

Nos.	00	0	1	2	3	3½	4
For Rails, Lbs.	16	20	25	50	60	70	95
Jim Crow Rail Bender ... Each,	$10.00	10.00	15.50	19.00	19.00	23.00	25.50

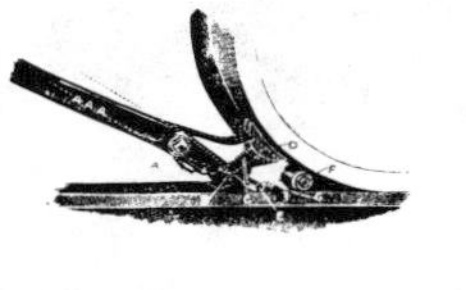

CAR MOVERS

No. AAA High Grade Steel, Hardwood Handle, Length 51 in. The Power, Being Applied Directly Under the Wheel, is All Utilized in Giving a Forward Motion to the Car .... Each, **$7.50**

CAR MOVERS

EASY

Steel Bar, Tempered Point; Malleable Heel; Tool Steel, Triangular Bit.

No. 3 Length 5½ ft. Weight 20 lb. .... Each, **$8.00**

BADGER

Malleable Iron Socket and Shoe; Tool Steel Spurs; Maple Handle.

No. 4 Length 62½ in., Weight 15 lb.; with Extra Set of Spurs .... Each, **$6.50**

CROW BARS

No. 10 Pinch Point

No. 15 Wedge Point

Solid Forged Steel, Oil Finish; Tempered Point, Round Tapered Handle; Octagon Shank; Square Shoulder

No. 10 Weight	Pounds, 10	12	14	16	
Length	Inches, 52	54	54	57	
Size Square	Inches, 1	1⅛	1¼	1¼	
Weight	Pounds, 18	20	24	28	
Length	Inches, 60	62	66	68	
Size of Square	Inches, 1⅜	1⅜	1½	1½	

No. 10 All Sizes .... Per Pound, **$0.07**

No. 15 Weight	Pounds, 8	10	12	14	16
Length	Inches, 48	52	54	54	57
Size Square	Inches, ⅞	1	1⅛	1¼	1¼
Weight	Pounds, 18	20	24	28	
Length	Inches, 60	62	66	68	
Size Square	Inches, 1⅜	1⅜	1½	1½	

No. 15 8 lb. .... Each, **$0.75**

No. 15 Heavier than 8 lb. .... Per Pound, **.07**

LINING BARS

Solid Forged Steel, Oil Finish; Tempered Point; Tapered Round Handle, Octagon Shank; Square Shoulder

No. 20 Weight	Pounds, 10	13	17	22	26
Length	Inches, 52	55	58	66	72
Size of Square	Inches, 1	1⅛	1¼	1⅜	1½

No. 20 All Sizes .... Per Pound, **$0.08**

TAMPING BARS

No. 30 Tamping Bars, 12 to 15 lb. .... Per Pound, **$0.10**

CLAW BARS

Forged Steel, Oil Finish; Tempered Working Ends; Tapered; Round Handle, Octagon Shank, Square Shoulder; For Drawing Spikes, Prying Rails, etc.; Also Used in Wrecking Buildings, Bridges, etc.

No. 25 15 to 25 lb. .... Per Pound, **$0.12**

TELEPHONE CONSTRUCTION TOOLS

POST HOLE SHOVELS

No. 27 8-ft. Handle, W. U. Pattern .... Per Dozen, **$33.00**

No. 027 Extra Handles, Hickory, 2 in. x 8 ft. .... Per Dozen, **17.00**

POST HOLE SPOONS

W. U. Pattern.

No. 25 8-ft. Handle .... Per Dozen, **$33.00**

No. 025 Extra Handles, Hickory, 2 in. x 8 ft. .... Per Dozen, **17.00**

One Half Dozen in a Bundle.

TAMPING BARS

Wood, with Iron Shoe.

No. 812 8-ft. Handle .... Each, **$2.75**

PIKE POLES

With Pike Only; 2½-inch Hardwood Handle.

Nos.	855	856	857	858	859
Length ... Feet,	12	14	16	18	20
Each	$2.25	2.50	2.60	3.00	3.25

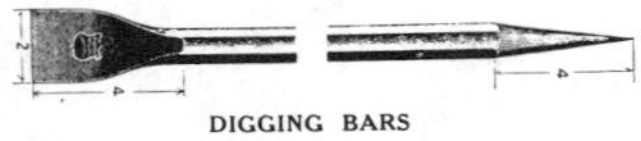

DIGGING BARS

No. 29 1⅛ in. x 8 ft., Weight, 30 lbs. .... Each, **$5.50**

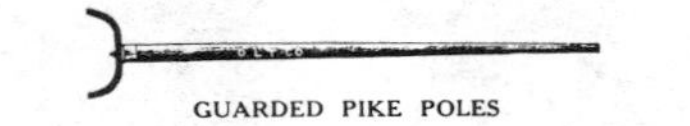

GUARDED PIKE POLES

The Fork and Socket are Made in One Piece.

Nos.	860	861	862	863
Length ... Feet,	12	14	16	18
Each	$2.75	3.00	3.25	3.75

CANT HOOKS

Duck Bill

No. 19 4 -ft. Hard Maple Handle .... Per Dozen, **$24.00**

No. 20 4½-ft. Hard Maple Handle .... Per Dozen, **24.50**

No. 21 5 -ft. Hard Maple Handl .... Per Dozen, **25.00**

No. 31 5 -ft. Hickory Handle .... Per Dozen, **27.50**

MALLEABLE SOCKET PEAVIES

With Duck Bill.

No. 41 4½-ft. Hard Maple Handles .... Per Dozen, **$27.00**

No. 42 4 -ft. Hard Maple Handle .... Per Dozen, **26.00**

HICKORY CANT HOOK AND PEAVY HANDLES

No. 030 4½ ft. Long .... Per Dozen, **$7.50**

No. 031 5 ft. Long .... Per Dozen, **7.50**

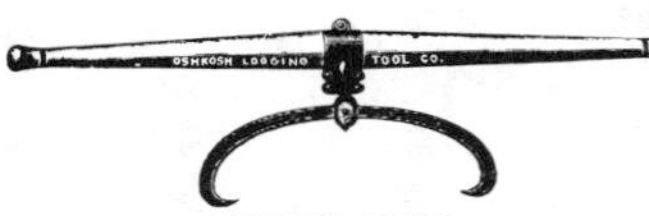

CARRYING HOOKS

For Handling Ties, Telegraph Poles, Timbers, etc. Will Grapple Anything from 3 to 16 Inches and is Fitted with Swivel to Permit Carrying Through Narrow Passages.

No. 29 2½ in. x 4 ft. Maple Handle .... Per Dozen, **$36.00**

SKIDDING TONGS

With Plain Swivel and Round or Grab Hook.

No. 314 1⅛-in. Octagon Steel, to Open 28 to 32 in. .... Each, **$7.50**

+ STRUCTURAL IRON WORKERS' AND BRIDGE BUILDERS' TOOLS

RIVET SET

Sizes Supplied for Rivets ⅜ Inch to 1 Inch.

No. 1 For ⅜ to ¾ in. Rivets .... Each, **$5.00**

No. 1 For ⅞ and 1 in. Rivets .... Each, **7.00**

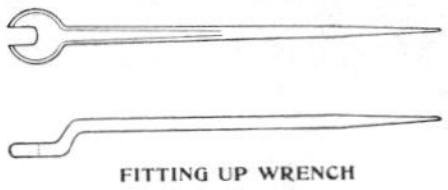

FITTING UP WRENCH

Sizes Supplied for Bolts ⅜ Inch to 1 Inch.

No. 2 20 in., for ⅜ to 1 in. Bolts .... Each, **$1.40**

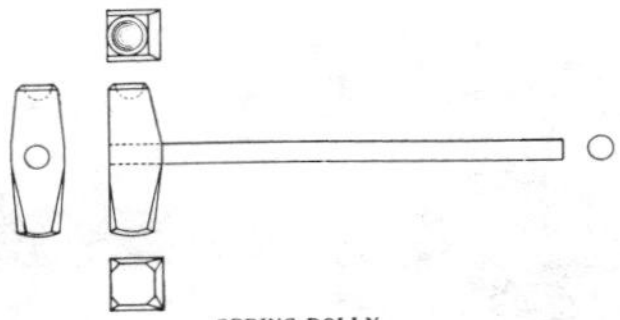

SPRING DOLLY

Sizes Supplied for ⅜ Inch to 1 Inch Rivets.

No. 9 15 lb. Head, for ⅜ to 1 in. Rivets .... Each, **$19.20**

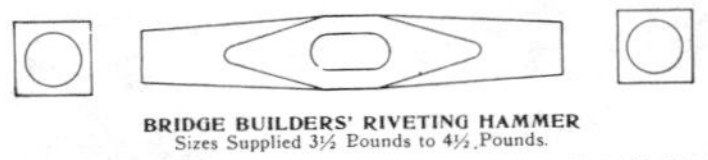

BRIDGE BUILDERS' RIVETING HAMMER

Sizes Supplied 3½ Bounds to 4½ Pounds.

No. 4 4½ lbs. .... Each, **$3.00**

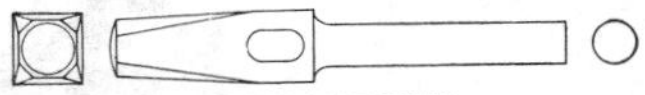

BACKING OUT PUNCH

Sizes Supplied ⅜ Inch to 1 Inch Diameter of Point.

No. 6 Diameter of Point, ⅜ to 1 in. .... Each, **$2.00**

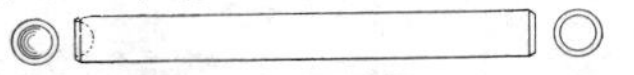

STRAIGHT DOLLY BAR

Sizes Supplied for ⅜ Inch to 1 Inch Rivets.

No. 5 30 in. Long, for ⅜ to 1 in. Rivets .... Each, **$12.00**

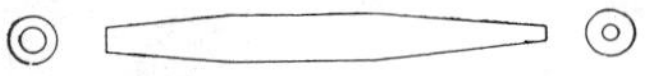

BARREL DRIFT PIN

Sizes Supplied ⅜ Inch to 1 Inch Diameter.

No. 8 9 in. Long, ⅜ to 1 in. Diameter .... Each, **$0.50**

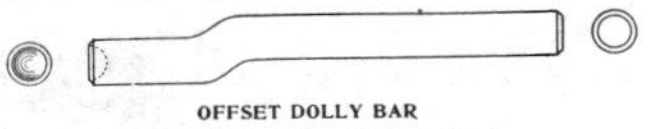

OFFSET DOLLY BAR

Sizes Supplied for Rivets ⅜ Inch to 1 Inch.

No. 12 30 in. Long, for ⅜ to 1 in. Rivets .... Each, **$12.00**

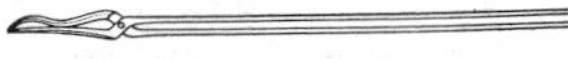

SPECIAL RIVET TONGS

Length 30 Inches, Other Lengths Supplied if Specified.

No. 10 30 in. Long .... Each, **$2.00**

TRACK DRILLS

NEW PAULUS VERTICAL

The Operator Stands Erect, Working with Greater Power and Less Strain than with a Horizontal Drill; Saves Time, as the Action of the Bit is Continuous; no Loss of Motion or Time as with a Lever Action Ratchet Drill; the Bit is not Withdrawn from the Rail to Get Out of Way of Passing Train. The Top of Frame is Thrown Back, Releasing the Hooks, Which are Lifted Out of the Way.

The Feed is Automatic and Requires no Adjustment.

Japanned Malleable Iron T Frame, Braces, Hooks, Gear Wheels and Adjustable Crank; Hardwood Handles; Height 33 Inches; Width of Frame 9¾ Inches; Length of Foot Plate 22 Inches; Length of Handle Cranks 11 Inches.

Style A

The Standard Style of Clutch.

The Spindle Chuck on this or Style D is Interchangeable, the Drill Taking Either the Rich Spindle and Flat Bit or the Regular Twist Bit Spindle and Bit.

No. 100 With Regular Twist Bit Spindle and 1 Twist Bit. Each, **$50.00**

No. 101 With Rich Spindle and 1 Flat Bit .... Each, **60.00**

Weight 95 lbs.

Style D

For Drilling Girder or High T Rails and Structural I Beams; Shaped for Drilling Close to End of Rail; Hooks Interchangeable with Style A.

No. 200 With Regular Twist Bit Spindle and 1 Twist Drill .... Each, **$55.00**

No. 201 With Rich Spindle and 1 Flat Bit .... Each, **65.00**

Weight 95 lbs.

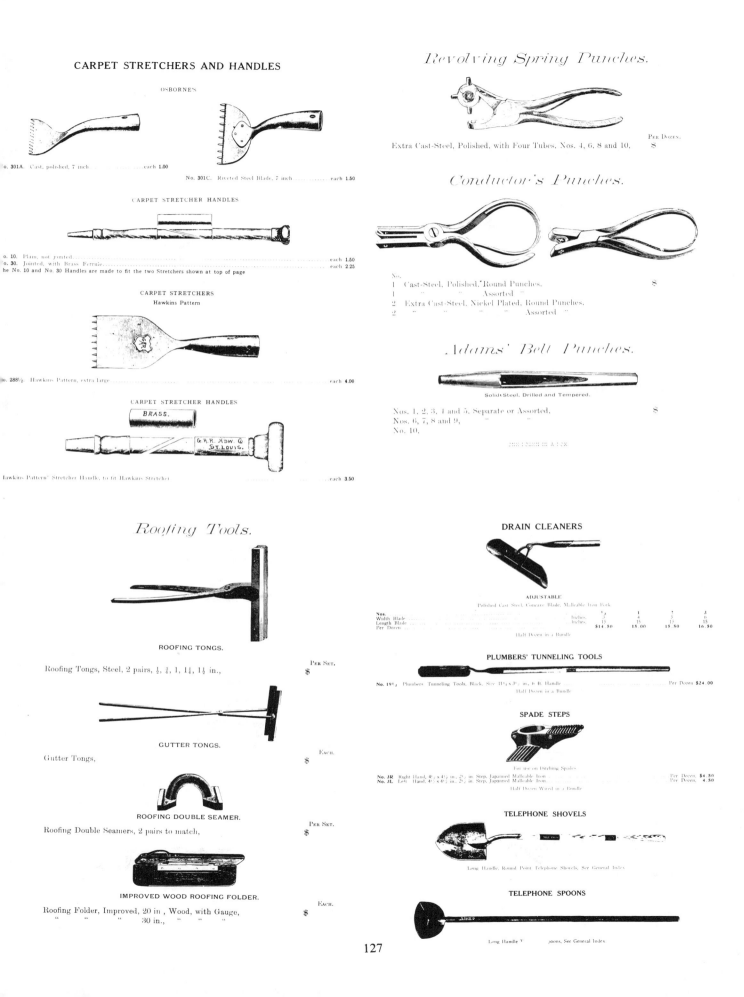

CARPET STRETCHERS AND HANDLES

OSBORNE'S

No. 301A. Cast, polished, 7 inch ....each 1.00

No. 301C. Riveted Steel Blade, 7 inch ....each 1.50

CARPET STRETCHER HANDLES

No. 10. Plain, not jointed ....each 1.50
No. 30. Jointed, with Brass Ferrule ....each 2.25
The No. 10 and No. 30 Handles are made to fit the two Stretchers shown at top of page

CARPET STRETCHERS

Hawkins Pattern

No. 288½. Hawkins Pattern, extra large ....each 4.00

CARPET STRETCHER HANDLES

BRASS.

G. H. H. Hdw. Co.
St. Louis.

"Hawkins Pattern" Stretcher Handle, to fit Hawkins Stretcher ....each 3.50

Revolving Spring Punches.

Extra Cast-Steel, Polished, with Four Tubes, Nos. 4, 6, 8 and 10,

Per Dozen.
$

Conductor's Punches.

No.		Per Dozen
1	Cast-Steel, Polished, Round Punches.	$
1	" " Assorted "	
2	Extra Cast-Steel, Nickel Plated, Round Punches.	
2	" " " Assorted "	

Adams' Belt Punches.

Solid Steel, Drilled and Tempered.

Nos. 1, 2, 3, 4 and 5, Separate or Assorted, $
Nos. 6, 7, 8 and 9,   "
No. 10,

Roofing Tools.

ROOFING TONGS.

Roofing Tongs, Steel, 2 pairs, ½, ¾, 1, 1¼, 1½ in.,   Per Set.
$

GUTTER TONGS.

Gutter Tongs,   Each.
$

ROOFING DOUBLE SEAMER.

Roofing Double Seamers, 2 pairs to match,   Per Set.
$

IMPROVED WOOD ROOFING FOLDER.

Roofing Folder, Improved, 20 in., Wood, with Gauge,   Each.
"   "   "   30 in., $

DRAIN CLEANERS

ADJUSTABLE

Polished Cast Steel, Concave Blade, Malleable Iron Fork.

Nos.				
Width Blade .... Inches.	3	4	5	6
Length Blade .... Inches.	13	15	15	15
Per Dozen	$14.50	15.00	15.50	16.50

Half Dozen in a Bundle

PLUMBERS' TUNNELING TOOLS

No. 19½. Plumbers' Tunneling Tools, Black, Size 11¼ x 3½ in., 6 ft. Handle ....Per Dozen $24.00
Half Dozen in a Bundle

SPADE STEPS

For use on Ditching Spades.

No. 3R. Right Hand, 4½ x 4½ in., 2½ in. Step, Japanned Malleable Iron ....Per Dozen $4.50
No. 3L. Left Hand, 4½ x 4½ in., 2½ in. Step, Japanned Malleable Iron ....Per Dozen 4.50
Half Dozen Wired in a Bundle

TELEPHONE SHOVELS

Long Handle, Round Point Telephone Shovels, See General Index

TELEPHONE SPOONS

Long Handle Telephone Spoons, See General Index

127

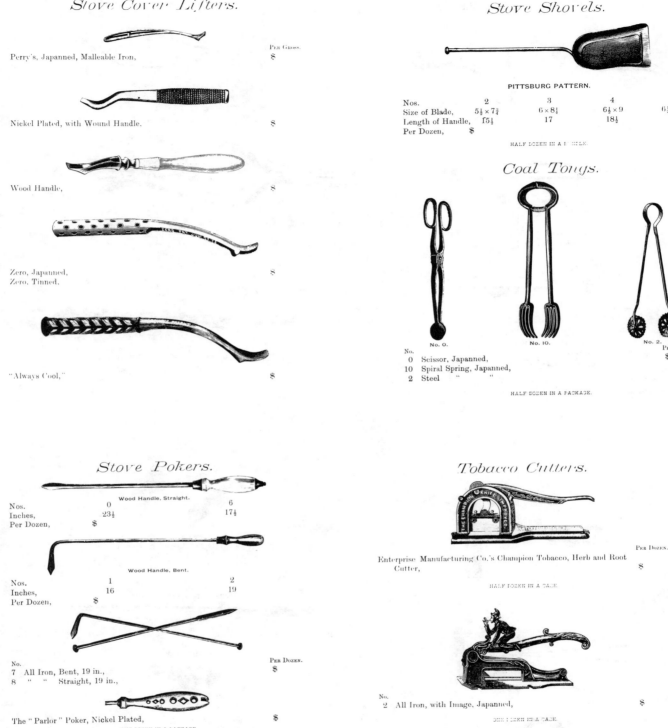

Stove Cover Lifters.

Perry's, Japanned, Malleable Iron,

Nickel Plated, with Wound Handle.

Wood Handle,

Zero, Japanned,
Zero, Tinned.

"Always Cool,"

Per Gross.
$

Stove Shovels.

PITTSBURG PATTERN.

Nos.	2	3	4	5
Size of Blade,	5½ × 7¾	6 × 8¼	6½ × 9	6½ × 9 in.
Length of Handle,	15½	17	18½	24 in.
Per Dozen,	$			

HALF DOZEN IN A BUNDLE.

Coal Tongs.

No. 0.   No. 10.   No. 2.   Per Dozen.
$

No.		
0	Scissor, Japanned,	
10	Spiral Spring, Japanned,	
2	Steel	"

HALF DOZEN IN A PACKAGE.

Stove Pokers.

Wood Handle, Straight.

Nos.	0	6
Inches,	23½	17½
Per Dozen,	$	

Wood Handle, Bent.

Nos.	1	2
Inches,	16	19
Per Dozen,	$	

No.		Per Dozen.
7	All Iron, Bent, 19 in.,	$
8	" " Straight, 19 in.,	

The "Parlor" Poker, Nickel Plated,
$

ONE DOZEN IN A PACKAGE.

Japanned, Iron Head Fire Irons.

Nos.	7	8	9
Inches,	20	22	26
With Pokers, Per Dozen, $			
Without "			

QUARTER DOZEN SETS IN A PACKAGE.

Tobacco Cutters.

Per Dozen.

Enterprise Manufacturing Co.'s Champion Tobacco, Herb and Root
Cutter,
$

HALF DOZEN IN A CASE.

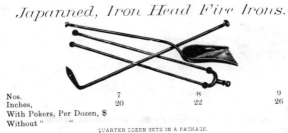

No.		
2	All Iron, with Image, Japanned,	$

ONE DOZEN IN A CASE.

Butter and Cheese Tryers.

4½ in., Nickel Plated,
5 in., Polished,
21 in., "
24 in., "
24 in., Nickel Plated,

$

128

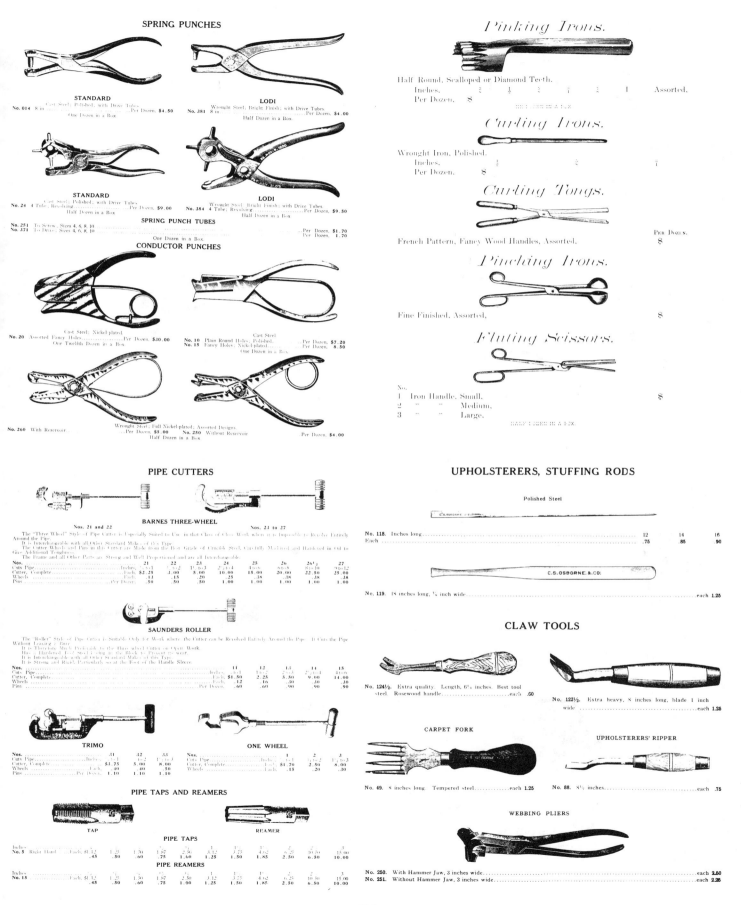

SPRING PUNCHES

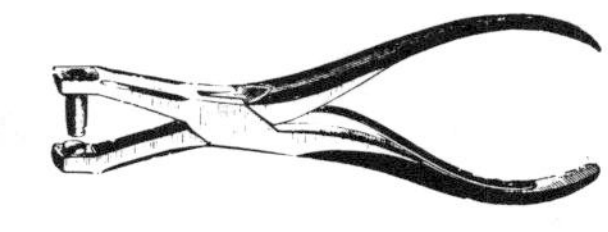

STANDARD

No. 014 Cast Steel; Polished; with Drive Tubes. 8 in. ....Per Dozen, **$4.50**
One Dozen in a Box

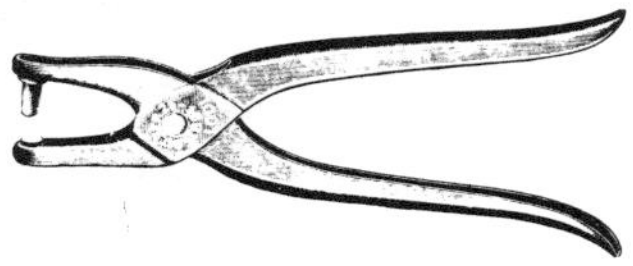

LODI

No. 381 Wrought Steel, Bright Finish; with Drive Tubes. 8 in. ....Per Dozen, **$4.00**
Half Dozen in a Box.

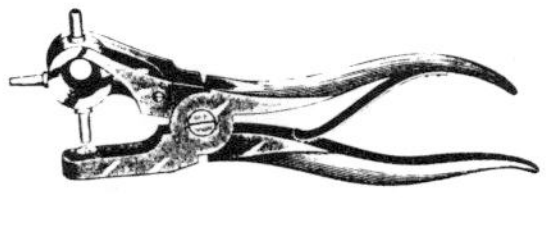

STANDARD

No. 24 Cast Steel; Polished; with Drive Tubes. 4 Tube; Revolving....Per Dozen, **$9.00**
Half Dozen in a Box

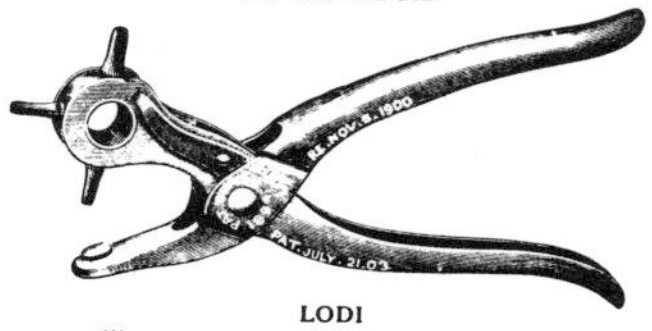

LODI

No. 384 Wrought Steel; Bright Finish; with Drive Tubes. 4 Tube; Revolving....Per Dozen, **$9.50**
Half Dozen in a Box

SPRING PUNCH TUBES

No. 251 To Screw, Sizes 4, 6, 8, 10 ....Per Dozen, **$1.70**
No. 371 To Drive; Sizes 4, 6, 8, 10 ....Per Dozen, **1.70**
One Dozen in a Box.

CONDUCTOR PUNCHES

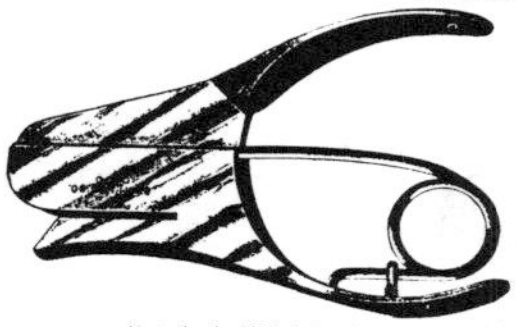

Cast Steel; Nickel-plated.
No. 20 Assorted Fancy Holes....Per Dozen, **$30.00**
One Twelfth Dozen in a Box.

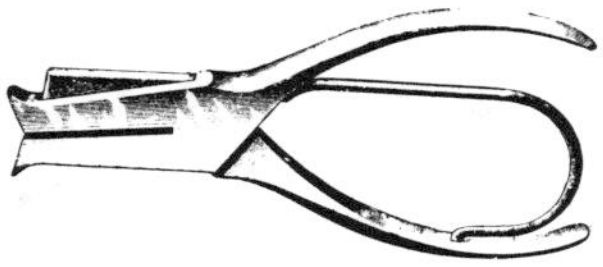

Cast Steel
No. 10 Plain Round Holes; Polished....Per Dozen, **$7.20**
No. 15 Fancy Holes; Nickel-plated....Per Dozen, **8.50**
One Dozen in a Box.

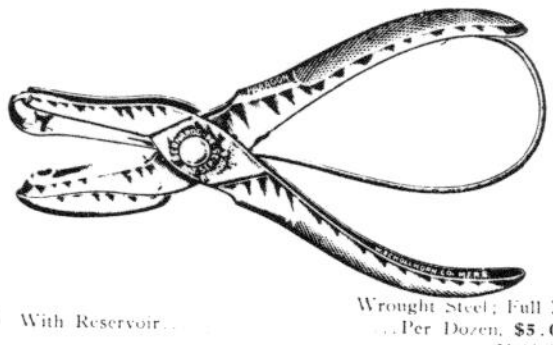

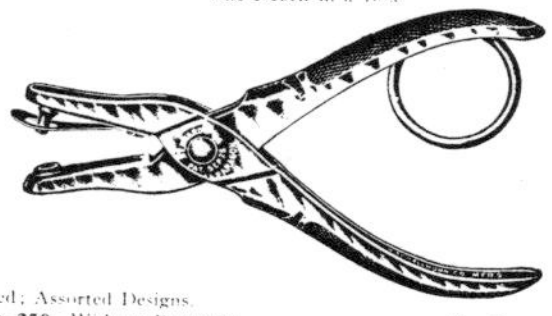

Wrought Steel; Full Nickel-plated; Assorted Designs.
No. 260 With Reservoir....Per Dozen, **$5.00** **No. 250** Without Reservoir ....Per Dozen, **$4.00**
Half Dozen in a Box.

Pinking Irons.

Half Round, Scalloped or Diamond Teeth.
Inches, [illegible] 1/4 [illegible] [illegible] [illegible] 1 Assorted,
Per Dozen, $

[illegible] IN A BOX

Curling Irons.

Wrought Iron, Polished.
Inches, 1/4 [illegible] [illegible]
Per Dozen, $

Curling Tongs.

	Per Dozen.
French Pattern, Fancy Wood Handles, Assorted,	$

Pinching Irons.

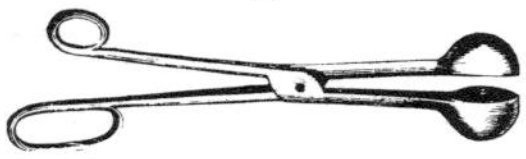

Fine Finished, Assorted, $

Fluting Scissors.

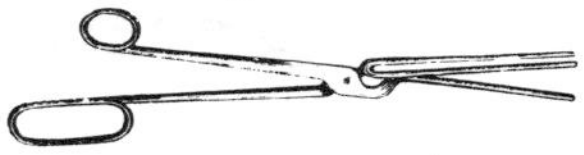

No.		
1	Iron Handle, Small,	$
2	" " Medium,	
3	" " Large,	

HALF DOZEN IN A BOX.

PIPE CUTTERS

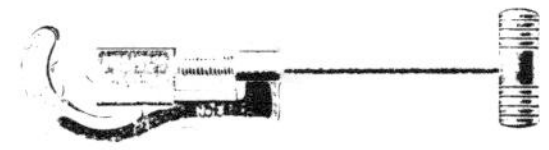

BARNES THREE-WHEEL

Nos. 21 and 22 — **Nos. 23 to 27**

The "Three Wheel" Style of Pipe Cutter is Especially Suited to Use in that Class of Close Work where it is Impossible to Revolve Entirely Around the Pipe.
It is Interchangeable with all Other Standard Makes of this Type.
The Cutter Wheels and Pins in this Cutter are Made from the Best Grade of Crucible Steel, Carefully Machined and Hardened in Oil to Give Additional Toughness.
The Frame and all Other Parts are Strong and Well Proportioned and are all Interchangeable.

Nos.	**21**	**22**	**23**	**24**	**25**	**26**	**26½**	**27**
Cuts Pipe....Inches,	1/8 to 1	1 to 2	1½ to 3	2½ to 4	4 to 6	6 to 8	8 to 10	9 to 12
Cutter, Complete....Each,	**$2.25**	**3.00**	**5.00**	**10.00**	**15.00**	**20.00**	**22.50**	**25.00**
Wheels....Each,	**.13**	**.15**	**.20**	**.25**	**.38**	**.38**	**.38**	**.38**
Pins....Per Dozen,	**.50**	**.50**	**.50**	**1.00**	**1.00**	**1.00**	**1.00**	**1.00**

SAUNDERS ROLLER

The "Roller" Style of Pipe Cutter is Suitable Only for Work where the Cutter can be Revolved Entirely Around the Pipe. It Cuts the Pipe Without Leaving a Burr.
It is Therefore Much Preferable to the Three-wheel Cutter on Open Work.
Has a Hardened Tool Steel Lining in the Block to Prevent its wear.
It is Interchangeable with all Other Standard Makes of this Type.
It is Strong and Rigid, Particularly so at the Foot of the Handle Sleeve.

Nos.	**11**	**12**	**13**	**14**	**15**
Cuts Pipe....Inches,	1/8 to 1	1 to 2	2 to 3	2½ to 4	4 to 6
Cutter, Complete....Each,	**$1.50**	**2.25**	**5.50**	**9.00**	**14.00**
Wheels....Each,	**.12**	**.16**	**.30**	**.30**	**.30**
Pins....Per Dozen,	**.60**	**.60**	**.90**	**.90**	**.90**

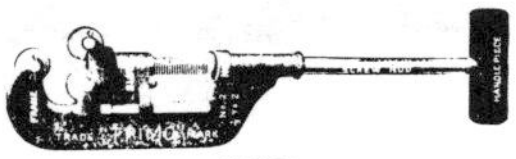

TRIMO

Nos.	**31**	**32**	**33**
Cuts Pipe....Inches,	1/8 to 1	[illegible] to 2	1¼ to 3
Cutter, Complete....	**$3.75**	**5.00**	**8.00**
Wheels....Each,	**.40**	**.40**	**.50**
Pins....Per Dozen,	**1.10**	**1.10**	**1.10**

ONE WHEEL

Nos.	**1**	**2**	**3**
Cuts Pipe....Inches,	1/8 to 1	1/4 to 2	1¼ to 3
Cutter, Complete....Each,	**$1.70**	**2.50**	**8.00**
Wheels....Each,	**.15**	**.20**	**.30**

PIPE TAPS AND REAMERS

TAP

REAMER

PIPE TAPS

Inches....	1/8	1/4	3/8	1/2	3/4	1	1¼	1½	2	2½	3
No. 5 Right Hand....Each,	$1.12	1.25	1.50	1.87	2.50	3.12	3.75	4.62	6.25	10.50	15.00
	.45	**.50**	**.60**	**.75**	**1.00**	**1.25**	**1.50**	**1.85**	**2.50**	**6.50**	**10.00**

PIPE REAMERS

Inches....	1/8	1/4	3/8	1/2	3/4	1	1¼	1½	2	2½	3
No. 15....Each,	$1.12	1.25	1.50	1.87	2.50	3.12	3.75	4.62	6.25	10.50	15.00
	.45	**.50**	**.60**	**.75**	**1.00**	**1.25**	**1.50**	**1.85**	**2.50**	**6.50**	**10.00**

UPHOLSTERERS, STUFFING RODS

Polished Steel

No. 118. Inches long....	12	14	16
Each....	.75	.85	.90

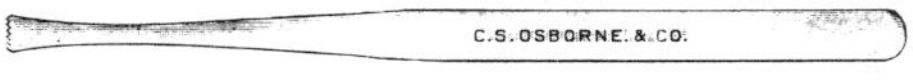

No. 119. 18 inches long, 7/8 inch wide....each **1.25**

CLAW TOOLS

No. 124½. Extra quality. Length, 6¼ inches. Best tool steel. Rosewood handle....each **.60**

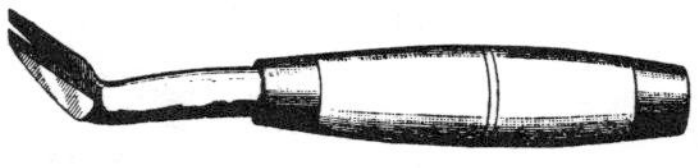

No. 122½. Extra heavy, 8 inches long, blade 1 inch wide....each **1.25**

CARPET FORK

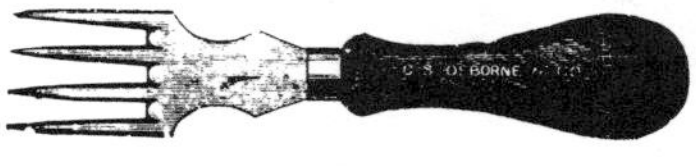

No. 49. 8 inches long. Tempered steel....each **1.25**

UPHOLSTERERS' RIPPER

No. 88. 8½ inches....each **.75**

WEBBING PLIERS

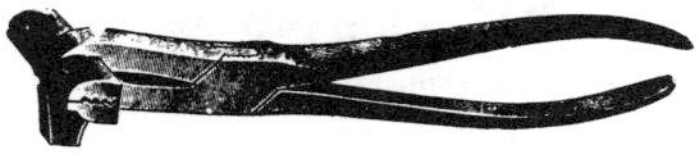

No. 250. With Hammer Jaw, 3 inches wide....each **2.50**
No. 251. Without Hammer Jaw, 3 inches wide....each **2.25**

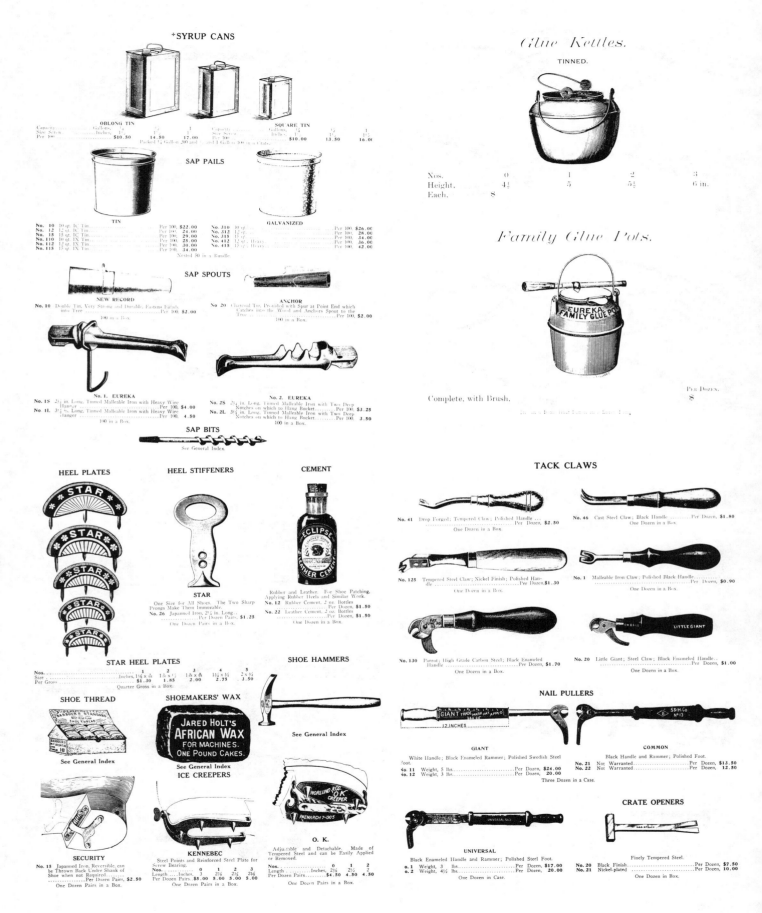

+SYRUP CANS

OBLONG TIN

Capacity .... Gallons,	¼	½	1
Size Screw .... Inches,	1½	1½	1½
Per 100	**$10.50**	**14.50**	**17.00**

SQUARE TIN

Capacity .... Gallons,	¼	½	1
Size Screw .... Inches,	1½	1½	1½
Per 100	**$10.00**	**13.50**	**16.0**

Packed ¼ Gallon 200 and ½ and 1 Gallon 100 in a Crate.

SAP PAILS

TIN

No. 10 10 qt. IC Tin........ Per 100, **$22.00**
No. 12 12 qt. IC Tin........ Per 100, **24.00**
No. 15 15 qt. IC Tin........ Per 100, **29.00**
No. 110 10 qt. IX Tin........ Per 100, **25.00**
No. 112 12 qt. IX Tin........ Per 100, **30.00**
No. 115 15 qt. IX Tin........ Per 100, **34.00**

GALVANIZED

No. 310 10 qt........ Per 100, **$26.00**
No. 312 12 qt........ Per 100, **28.00**
No. 315 15 qt........ Per 100, **34.00**
No. 412 12 qt., Heavy........ Per 100, **36.00**
No. 415 15 qt., Heavy........ Per 100, **42.00**

Nested 50 in a Bundle.

SAP SPOUTS

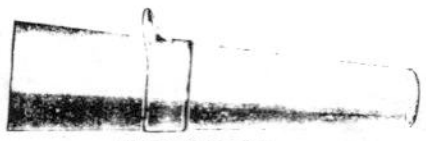

NEW RECORD

No. 10 Double Tin, Very Strong and Durable, Fastens Firmly into Tree .... Per 100, **$2.00**

100 in a Box.

ANCHOR

No 20 Charcoal Tin, Provided with Spur at Point End which Catches into the Wood and Anchors Spout to the Tree .... Per 100, **$2.00**

100 in a Box.

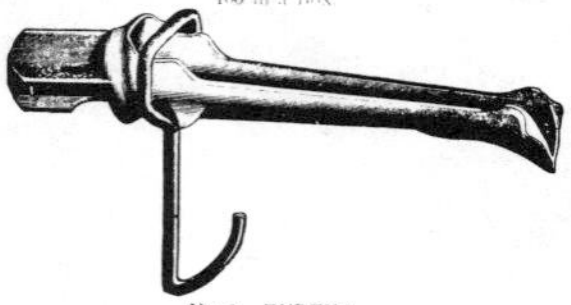

No. 1. EUREKA

No. 1S 2¾ in. Long, Tinned Malleable Iron with Heavy Wire Hanger .... Per 100, **$4.00**
No. 1L 3¼ in. Long, Tinned Malleable Iron with Heavy Wire Hanger .... Per 100, **4.50**

100 in a Box.

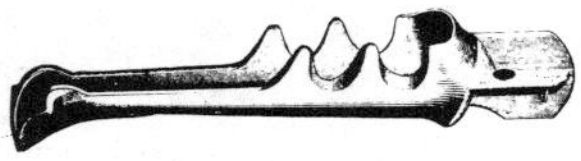

No. 2. EUREKA

No. 2S 2¾ in. Long, Tinned Malleable Iron with Two Deep Notches on which to Hang Bucket........ Per 100, **$3.25**
No. 2L 3¼ in. Long, Tinned Malleable Iron with Two Deep Notches on which to Hang Bucket........ Per 100, **3.50**

100 in a Box.

SAP BITS

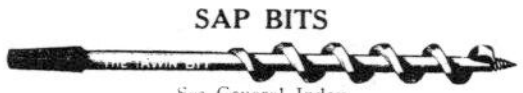

See General Index.

Glue Kettles.

TINNED.

Nos.	0	1	2	3
Height,	4½	5	5½	6 in.
Each,	$			

Family Glue Pots.

EUREKA
FAMILY GLUE POT

Complete, with Brush, Per Dozen. $

HEEL PLATES

STAR
STAR
STAR
STAR
STAR

HEEL STIFFENERS

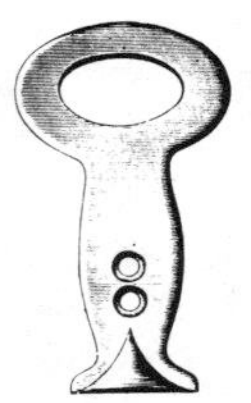

STAR

One Size for All Shoes. The Two Sharp Prongs Make Them Immovable.

No. 26 Japanned Iron, 2¼ in. Long........ Per Dozen Pairs, **$1.25**

One Dozen Pairs in a Box.

CEMENT

ECLIPSE
LEATHER CEMENT

Rubber and Leather. For Shoe Patching, Applying Rubber Heels and Similar Work.

No. 12 Rubber Cement, 2 oz. Bottles .... Per Dozen, **$1.50**
No. 22 Leather Cement, 2 oz. Bottles .... Per Dozen, **$1.50**

One Dozen in a Box.

STAR HEEL PLATES

Nos.	1	2	3	4	5
Size .... Inches,	1⅛ x 7/16	1 5/16 x ½	1 7/16 x 9/16	1¾ x ¾	2 x ¾
Per Gross	**$1.30**	**1.85**	**2.00**	**2.75**	**3.50**

Quarter Gross in a Box.

SHOE HAMMERS

See General Index

SHOE THREAD

BARBOUR'S STANDARD
SHOE THREAD

See General Index

SHOEMAKERS' WAX

JARED HOLT'S
AFRICAN WAX
FOR MACHINES.
ONE POUND CAKES.

See General Index

ICE CREEPERS

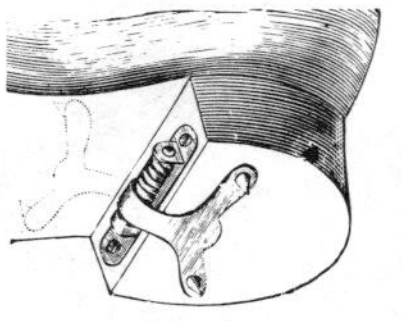

SECURITY

No. 15 Japanned Iron, Reversible, can be Thrown Back Under Shank of Shoe when not Required........ Per Dozen Pairs, **$2.50**

One Dozen Pairs in a Box.

KENNEBEC

Steel Points and Reinforced Steel Plate for Screw Bearing.

Nos.	0	1	2	3
Length ....Inches,	3	2⅞	2¾	2⅝
Per Dozen Pairs..	**$5.00**	**5.00**	**5.00**	**5.00**

One Dozen Pairs in a Box.

NORLUND & CO.
O.K.
CREEPER
PAT.MARCH 7-1905

O. K.

Adjustable and Detachable. Made of Tempered Steel and can be Easily Applied or Removed.

Nos.	0	1	2
Length .... Inches,	2⅞	2½	2
Per Dozen Pairs........	**$4.50**	**4.50**	**4.50**

One Dozen Pairs in a Box.

TACK CLAWS

No. 41 Drop Forged; Tempered Claw; Polished Handle .... Per Dozen, **$2.50**

One Dozen in a Box.

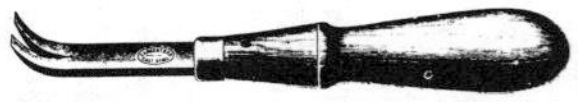

No. 46 Cast Steel Claw; Black Handle .... Per Dozen, **$1.80**

One Dozen in a Box.

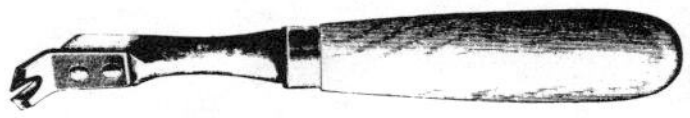

No. 125 Tempered Steel Claw; Nickel Finish; Polished Handle .... Per Dozen, **$1.30**

One Dozen in a Box.

No. 1 Malleable Iron Claw; Polished Black Handle........ Per Dozen, **$0.90**

One Dozen in a Box.

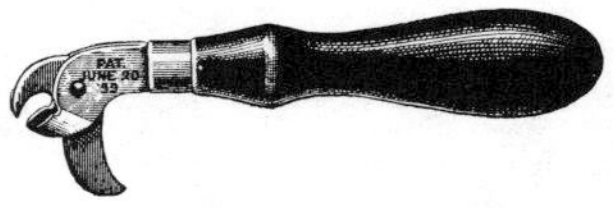
PAT.
JUNE 20
'33

No. 130 Parrot; High Grade Carbon Steel; Black Enameled Handle .... Per Dozen, **$1.70**

One Dozen in a Box.

LITTLE GIANT

No. 20 Little Giant; Steel Claw; Black Enameled Handle........ Per Dozen, **$1.00**

One Dozen in a Box.

NAIL PULLERS

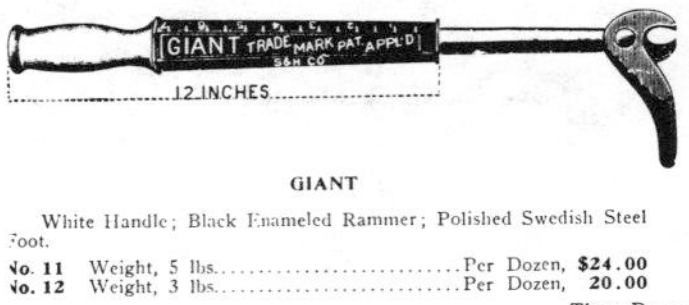
GIANT TRADE MARK PAT. APPL'D
S&H CO
12 INCHES

GIANT

White Handle; Black Enameled Rammer; Polished Swedish Steel Foot.

No. 11 Weight, 5 lbs........ Per Dozen, **$24.00**
No. 12 Weight, 3 lbs........ Per Dozen, **20.00**

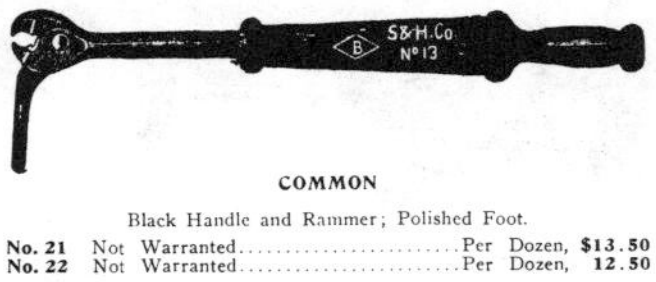
S&H.Co
B
Nº 13

COMMON

Black Handle and Rammer; Polished Foot.

No. 21 Not Warranted........ Per Dozen, **$13.50**
No. 22 Not Warranted........ Per Dozen, **12.50**

Three Dozen in a Case.

UNIVERSAL NO 2

UNIVERSAL

Black Enameled Handle and Rammer; Polished Steel Foot.

No. 1 Weight, 3 lbs........ Per Dozen, **$17.00**
No. 2 Weight, 4½ lbs........ Per Dozen, **20.00**

One Dozen in Case.

CRATE OPENERS

Finely Tempered Steel.

No. 20 Black Finish........ Per Dozen, **$7.50**
No. 21 Nickel-plated .... Per Dozen, **10.00**

One Dozen in Box.

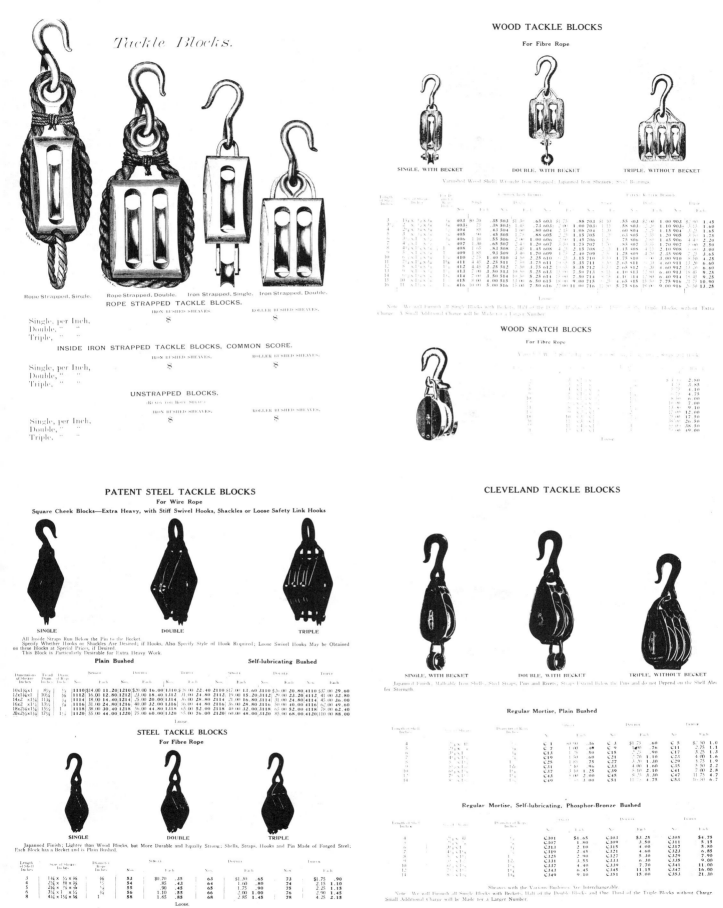

Tackle Blocks.

Rope Strapped, Single.   Rope Strapped, Double.   Iron Strapped, Single.   Iron Strapped, Double.

ROPE STRAPPED TACKLE BLOCKS.

	IRON BUSHED SHEAVES.	ROLLER BUSHED SHEAVES.
Single, per Inch,	$	$
Double, " "		
Triple, " "		

INSIDE IRON STRAPPED TACKLE BLOCKS, COMMON SCORE.

	IRON BUSHED SHEAVES.	ROLLER BUSHED SHEAVES.
Single, per Inch,	$	$
Double, " "		
Triple, " "		

UNSTRAPPED BLOCKS.

(READY FOR ROPE STRAP.)

	IRON BUSHED SHEAVES.	ROLLER BUSHED SHEAVES.
Single, per Inch,	$	$
Double, " "		
Triple, " "		

WOOD TACKLE BLOCKS

For Fibre Rope

SINGLE, WITH BECKET   DOUBLE, WITH BECKET   TRIPLE, WITHOUT BECKET

Varnished Wood Shells; Wrought Iron Strapped; Japanned Iron Sheaves; Steel Bearings.

Note—We will Furnish all Single Blocks with Beckets, Half of the Double Blocks and One Third of the Triple Blocks without Extra Charge. A Small Additional Charge will be Made for a Larger Number.

WOOD SNATCH BLOCKS

For Fibre Rope

PATENT STEEL TACKLE BLOCKS

For Wire Rope

Square Cheek Blocks—Extra Heavy, with Stiff Swivel Hooks, Shackles or Loose Safety Link Hooks

SINGLE   DOUBLE   TRIPLE

All Inside Straps Run Below the Pin to the Becket.
Specify Whether Hooks or Shackles Are Desired; if Hooks, Also Specify Style of Hook Required; Loose Swivel Hooks May be Obtained on these Blocks at Special Prices, if Desired.
This Block is Particularly Desirable for Extra Heavy Work.

Plain Bushed

Self-lubricating Bushed

STEEL TACKLE BLOCKS

For Fibre Rope

SINGLE   DOUBLE   TRIPLE

Japanned Finish; Lighter than Wood Blocks, but More Durable and Equally Strong; Shells, Straps, Hooks and Pin Made of Forged Steel; Each Block has a Becket and is Plain Bushed.

CLEVELAND TACKLE BLOCKS

SINGLE, WITH BECKET   DOUBLE, WITH BECKET   TRIPLE, WITHOUT BECKET

Japanned Finish; Malleable Iron Shells, Steel Straps, Pins and Rivets; Straps Extend Below the Pins and do not Depend on the Shell Alone for Strength.

Regular Mortise, Plain Bushed

Regular Mortise, Self-lubricating, Phosphor-Bronze Bushed

Sheaves with the Various Bushings Are Interchangeable.
Note—We will Furnish all Single Blocks with Beckets, Half of the Double Blocks and One Third of the Triple Blocks without Charge. A Small Additional Charge will be Made for a Larger Number.

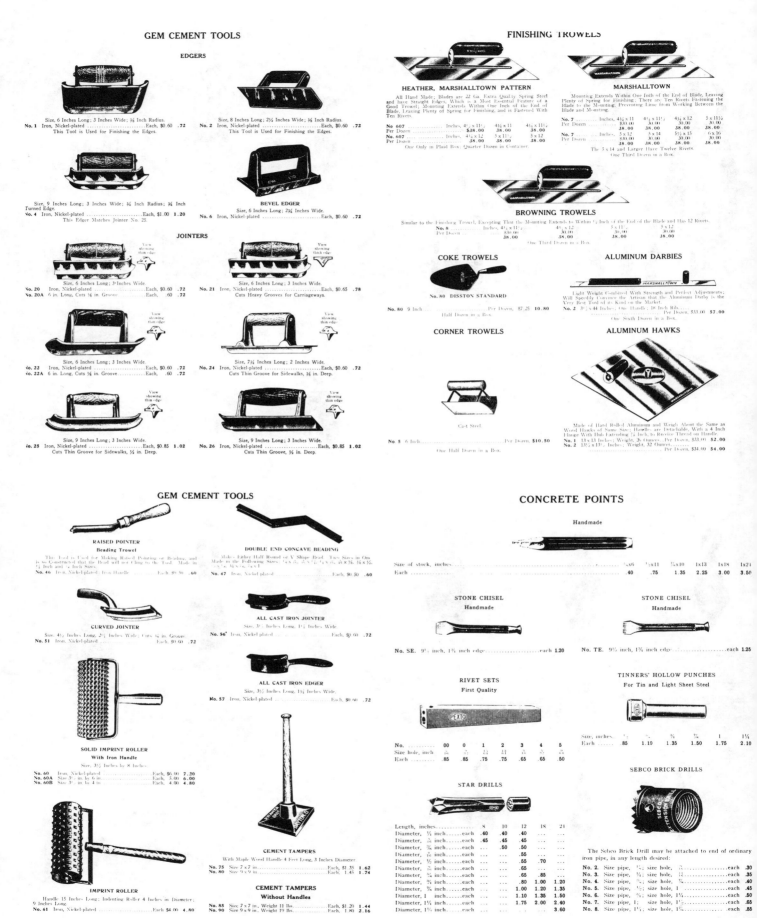

GEM CEMENT TOOLS

EDGERS

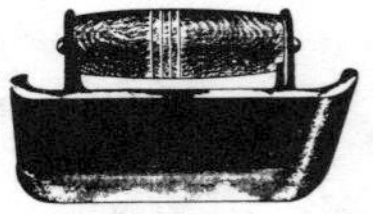

Size, 6 Inches Long; 3 Inches Wide; ⅜ Inch Radius.
No. 1 Iron, Nickel-plated ....Each, $0.60 **.72**
This Tool is Used for Finishing the Edges.

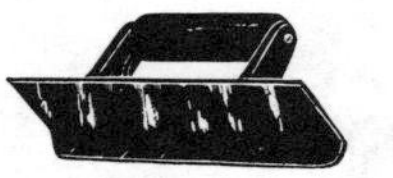

Size, 8 Inches Long; 2½ Inches Wide; ⅜ Inch Radius.
No. 2 Iron, Nickel-plated ....Each, $0.60 **.72**
This Tool is Used for Finishing the Edges.

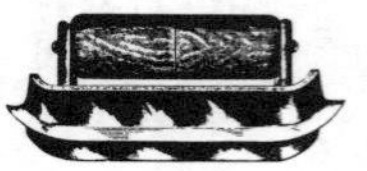

Size, 9 Inches Long; 3 Inches Wide; ¾ Inch Radius; ¾ Inch Turned Edge.
No. 4 Iron, Nickel-plated ....Each, $1.00 **1.20**
This Edger Matches Jointer No. 25.

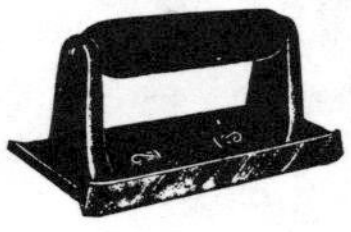

BEVEL EDGER
Size, 6 Inches Long; 2¾ Inches Wide.
No. 6 Iron, Nickel-plated ....Each, $0.60 **.72**

JOINTERS

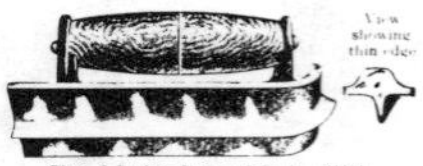
View showing thin edge

Size, 6 Inches Long; 3 Inches Wide.
No. 20 Iron, Nickel-plated ....Each, $0.60 **.72**
No. 20A 6 in. Long, Cuts ⅛ in. Groove........Each, .60 **.72**

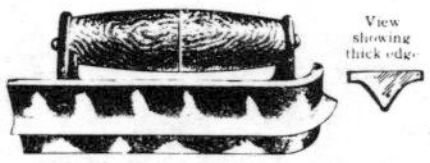
View showing thick edge

Size, 6 Inches Long; 3 Inches Wide.
No. 21 Iron, Nickel-plated ....Each, $0.65 **.78**
Cuts Heavy Grooves for Carriageways.

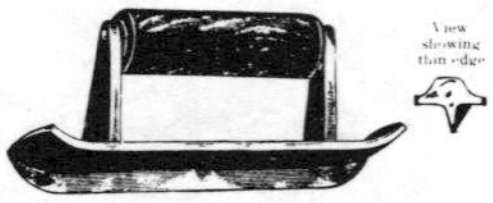
View showing thin edge

Size, 6 Inches Long; 3 Inches Wide.
No. 22 Iron, Nickel-plated ....Each, $0.60 **.72**
No. 22A 6 in. Long, Cuts ⅜ in. Groove........Each, .60 **.72**

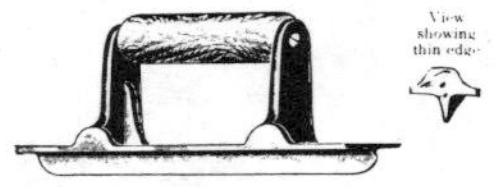
View showing thin edge

Size, 7¾ Inches Long; 2 Inches Wide.
No. 24 Iron, Nickel-plated ....Each, $0.60 **.72**
Cuts Thin Groove for Sidewalks, ⅜ in. Deep.

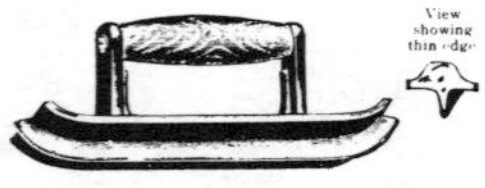
View showing thin edge

Size, 9 Inches Long; 3 Inches Wide.
No. 25 Iron, Nickel-plated ....Each, $0.85 **1.02**
Cuts Thin Groove for Sidewalks, ½ in. Deep.

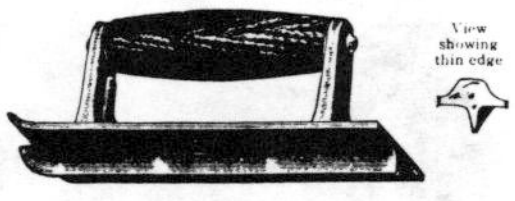
View showing thin edge

Size, 9 Inches Long; 3 Inches Wide.
No. 26 Iron, Nickel-plated ....Each, $0.85 **1.02**
Cuts Thin Groove, ½ in. Deep.

FINISHING TROWELS

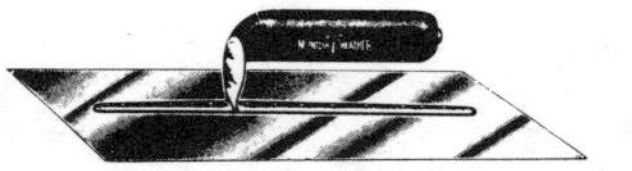

HEATHER, MARSHALLTOWN PATTERN

All Hand Made; Blades are 22 Ga. Extra Quality Spring Steel and have Straight Edges, Which is a Most Essential Feature of a Good Trowel; Mounting Extends Within One Inch of the End of Blade, Leaving Plenty of Spring for Finishing, and is Fastened With Ten Rivets.

No. 607 .... Inches,	4½ x 11½	4¾ x 11	4¾ x 11½
Per Dozen	**$38.00**	**38.00**	**38.00**
No. 607 .... Inches,	4¾ x 12	5 x 11½	5 x 12
Per Dozen	**38.00**	**38.00**	**38.00**

One Only in Plaid Box; Quarter Dozen in Container.

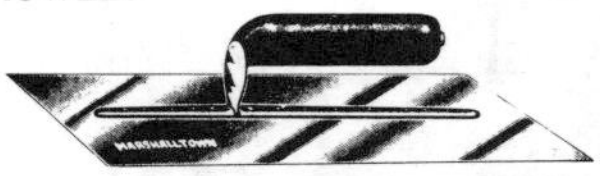

MARSHALLTOWN

Mounting Extends Within One Inch of the End of Blade, Leaving Plenty of Spring for Finishing; There are Ten Rivets Fastening the Blade to the Mounting, Preventing Lime from Working Between the Blade and Mounting.

No. 7 .... Inches,	4¾ x 11	4¾ x 11½	4¾ x 12	5 x 11½
Per Dozen	$30.00	30.00	30.00	30.00
	38.00	**38.00**	**38.00**	**38.00**
No. 7 .... Inches,	5 x 12	5 x 14	5½ x 15	6 x 16
Per Dozen	$30.00	30.00	30.00	30.00
	38.00	**38.00**	**38.00**	**38.00**

The 5 x 14 and Larger Have Twelve Rivets.
One Third Dozen in a Box.

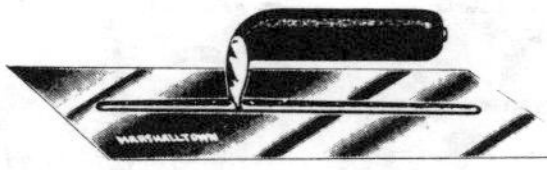

BROWNING TROWELS

Similar to the Finishing Trowel, Excepting That the Mounting Extends to Within ½ Inch of the End of the Blade and Has 12 Rivets.

No. 8 .... Inches,	4¾ x 11½	4¾ x 12	5 x 11½	5 x 12
Per Dozen	$30.00	30.00	30.00	30.00
	38.00	**38.00**	**38.00**	**38.00**

One Third Dozen in a Box.

COKE TROWELS

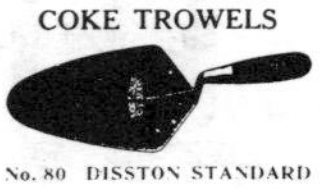

No. 80 DISSTON STANDARD

No. 80 9 Inch........................Per Dozen, $7.25 **10.80**
Half Dozen in a Box.

ALUMINUM DARBIES

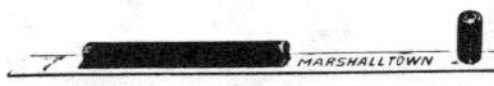
MARSHALLTOWN

Light Weight Combined With Strength and Perfect Adjustments; Will Speedily Convince the Artisan that the Aluminum Darby is the Very Best Tool of its Kind on the Market.
No. 2 3½ x 44 Inches; One Handle; 18 Inch Rib..... ....Per Dozen, $33.00 **57.00**
One Sixth Dozen in a Box.

CORNER TROWELS

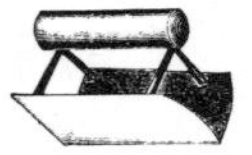

Cast Steel.

No. 5 6 Inch........................Per Dozen, **$10.50**
One Half Dozen in a Box.

ALUMINUM HAWKS

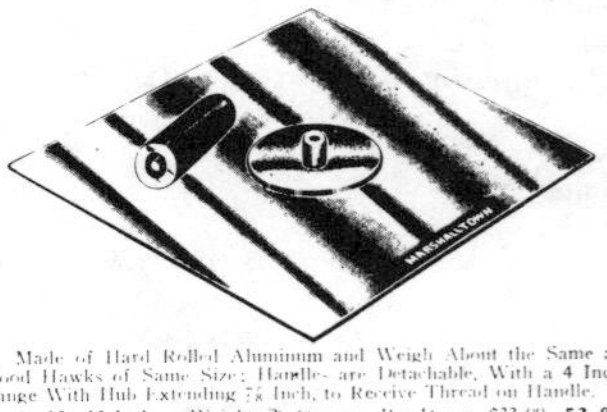
MARSHALLTOWN

Made of Hard Rolled Aluminum and Weigh About the Same as Wood Hawks of Same Size; Handles are Detachable, With a 4 Inch Flange With Hub Extending ⅞ Inch, to Receive Thread on Handle.
No. 1 13 x 13 Inches; Weight, 26 Ounces..Per Dozen, $33.00 **52.00**
No. 2 13½ x 13½ Inches; Weight, 32 Ounces........ ....Per Dozen, $34.00 **54.00**

GEM CEMENT TOOLS

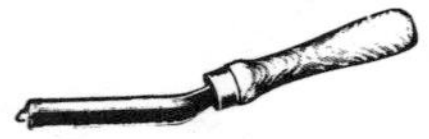

RAISED POINTER
Beading Trowel

This Tool is Used for Making Raised Pointing or Beading, and is so Constructed that the Bead will not Cling to the Tool. Made in ¼ Inch and ⅜ Inch Sizes.
No. 46 Iron, Nickel-plated; Iron Handle ....Each, $0.50 **.60**

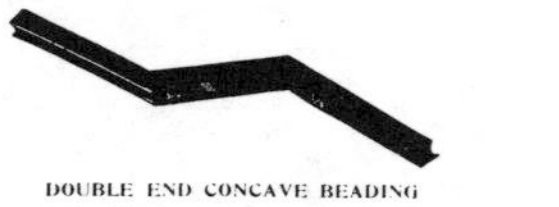

DOUBLE END CONCAVE BEADING

Makes Either Half Round or V Shape Bead. Two Sizes in One Made in the Following Sizes: ⅛ x 3/16, 3/16 x ¼, ¼ x 5/16, ⅜ x ⅝, ⅜ x ½, ½ x ⅝, ¾ x ⅞, ⅞ x 1.
No. 47 Iron, Nickel plated ....Each, $0.50 **.60**

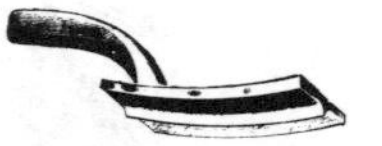

CURVED JOINTER

Size, 4½ Inches Long, 2¼ Inches Wide; Cuts ⅝ in. Groove.
No. 51 Iron, Nickel-plated ....Each, $0.60 **.72**

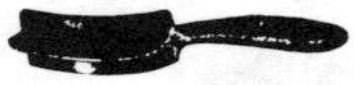

ALL CAST IRON JOINTER

Size, 3½ Inches Long, 1¼ Inches Wide.
No. 56' Iron, Nickel plated ....Each, $0.60 **.72**

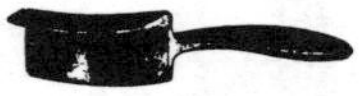

ALL CAST IRON EDGER

Size, 3½ Inches Long, 1¾ Inches Wide.
No. 57 Iron, Nickel-plated ....Each, $0.60 **.72**

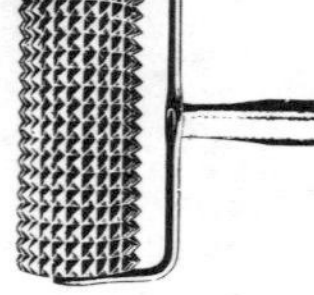

SOLID IMPRINT ROLLER
With Iron Handle

Size, 3½ Inches by 8 Inches.

No. 60 Iron, Nickel-plated ....Each, $6.00 **7.20**
No. 60A Size 3½ in. by 6 in....................Each, 5.00 **6.00**
No. 60B Size 3½ in. by 4 in....................Each, 4.00 **4.80**

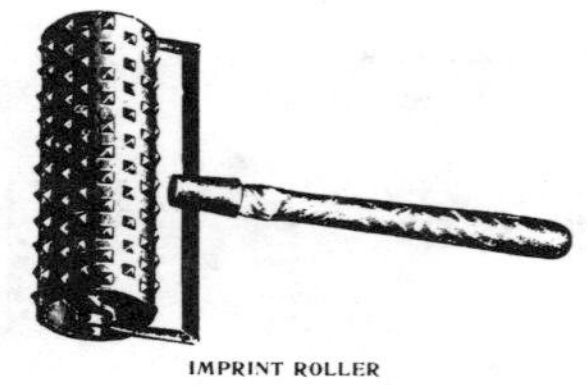

IMPRINT ROLLER

Handle 15 Inches Long; Indenting Roller 4 Inches in Diameter; 9 Inches Long.
No. 61 Iron, Nickel-plated ....Each $4.00 **4.80**

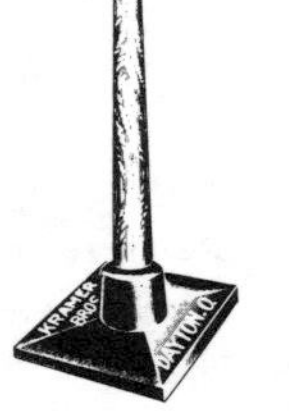
KRAMER BROS
DAYTON, O.

CEMENT TAMPERS

With Maple Wood Handle 4 Feet Long, 3 Inches Diameter.

No. 75 Size 7 x 7 in........................Each, $1.35 **1.62**
No. 80 Size 9 x 9 in........................Each, 1.45 **1.74**

CEMENT TAMPERS
Without Handles

No. 85 Size 7 x 7 in., Weight 11 lbs.............Each, $1.20 **1.44**
No. 90 Size 9 x 9 in., Weight 19 lbs.............Each, 1.80 **2.16**

CONCRETE POINTS

Handmade

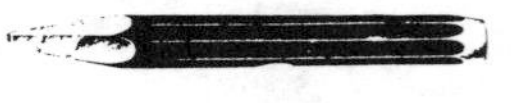

Size of stock, inches........	⅜x6	½x11	⅞x10	1x13	1x18	1x21
Each	**.40**	**.75**	**1.35**	**2.25**	**3.00**	**3.50**

STONE CHISEL
Handmade

No. SE. 9½ inch, 1¾ inch edge....................each **1.20**

STONE CHISEL
Handmade

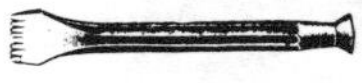

No. TE. 9½ inch, 1¾ inch edge....................each **1.25**

RIVET SETS
First Quality

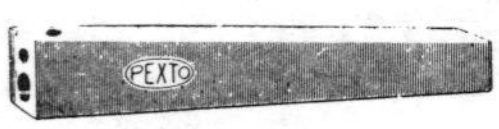
PEXTO

No.	**00**	**0**	**1**	**2**	**3**	**4**	**5**
Size hole, inch	5/16	9/32	17/64	15/64	3/16	5/32	9/64
Each	**.85**	**.85**	**.75**	**.75**	**.65**	**.65**	**.50**

TINNERS' HOLLOW PUNCHES
For Tin and Light Sheet Steel

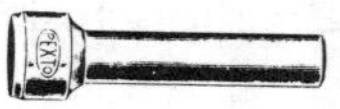
PEXTO

Size, inches........	½	⅝	¾	⅞	1	1¼
Each	**.85**	**1.10**	**1.35**	**1.50**	**1.75**	**2.10**

STAR DRILLS

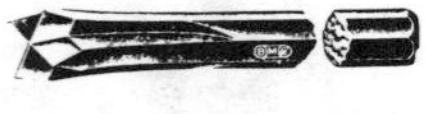

Length, inches........	8	10	12	18	21
Diameter, ¼ inch......each	**.40**	**.40**	**.40**	...	...
Diameter, 5/16 inch......each	**.45**	**.45**	**.45**	...	...
Diameter, ⅜ inch......each	...	**.50**	**.50**	...	...
Diameter, 7/16 inch......each	...	...	**.55**	...	...
Diameter, ½ inch......each	...	...	**.55**	**.70**	...
Diameter, 9/16 inch......each	...	...	**.65**	...	...
Diameter, ⅝ inch......each	...	...	**.65**	**.85**	...
Diameter, ¾ inch......each	...	...	**.80**	**1.00**	**1.20**
Diameter, ⅞ inch......each	...	...	**1.00**	**1.20**	**1.35**
Diameter, 1 inch......each	...	...	**1.10**	**1.35**	**1.50**
Diameter, 1¼ inch......each	...	...	**1.75**	**2.00**	**2.40**
Diameter, 1½ inch......each	...	...	...	...	**3.60**

SEBCO BRICK DRILLS

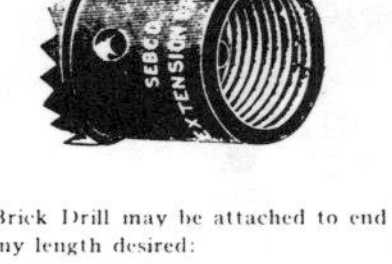
SEBCO
EXTENSION DRILL

The Sebco Brick Drill may be attached to end of ordinary iron pipe, in any length desired:

No. 2. Size pipe, ⅛; size hole, 9/16....................each **.30**
No. 3. Size pipe, ¼; size hole, 11/16....................each **.35**
No. 4. Size pipe, ⅜; size hole, ⅞....................each **.40**
No. 5. Size pipe, ½; size hole, 1 ....each **.45**
No. 6. Size pipe, ¾; size hole, 1¼....................each **.50**
No. 7. Size pipe, 1; size hole, 1½....................each **.65**
No. 8. Size pipe, 1¼; size hole, 1⅞....................each **.85**

Pointing Trowels.

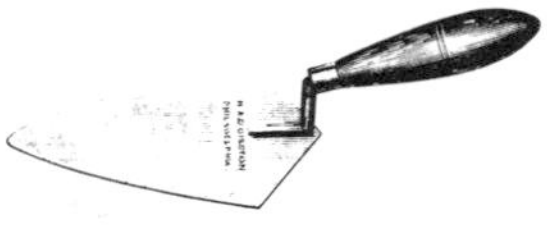

Lothrop's Pointing Trowels.			
Inches,	4	4½	5
Per Dozen,	$		

Corner Trowels.

	Per Dozen.
6 in. Lothrop's Corner Trowels.	$

HALF DOZEN IN A BOX.

Garden Trowels.

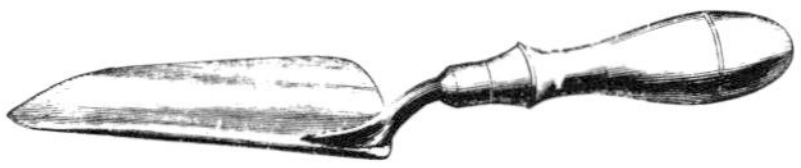

Cast-Steel.

Inches,	6	7	8
Per Dozen,	$		

ONE DOZEN IN A BOX.

GEM CEMENT TOOLS

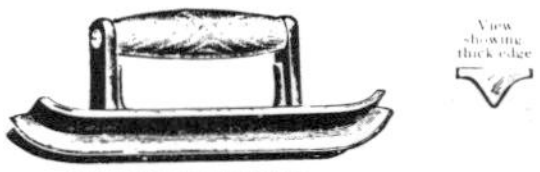

DRIVEWAY GROOVER

Size, 9 Inches Long, 3 Inches Wide; Cuts Heavy Groove ¾ Inch Deep.
No. 27 Iron, Nickel-plated ....Each, $0.85 **1.02**

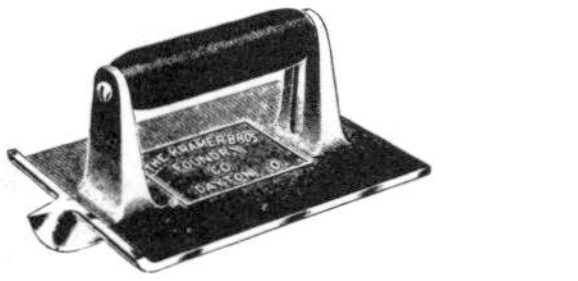

JOINTER

Size, 6 Inches Long, 4¾ Inches Wide; Cuts Thin Groove, ⅝ Inch Deep.
No. 28 Iron, Nickel-plated ....Each, $0.75 **.90**

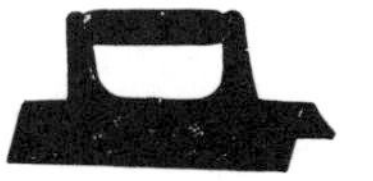

INSIDE SQUARE ANGLE

Size, 8 Inches Long, 2¼ Inch Sides.
No. 30 Iron, Nickel-plated ....Each, $1.00 **1.20**
No. 30½ 6 in. Long............................Each, .60 **.72**

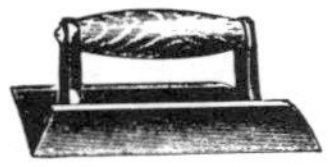

OUTSIDE SQUARE ANGLE

Size, 8 Inches Long, 2¼ Inches Wide.
No. 31 Iron, Nickel-plated ....Each, $1.00 **1.20**
No. 31½ 6 in. Long............................Each, .60 **.72**

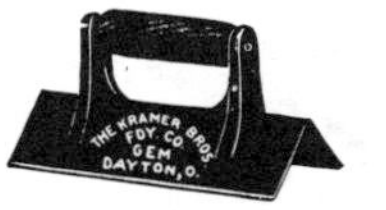

INSIDE ROUND ANGLE TOOL

Size, 8 Inches Long, 2¼ Inch Sides; Radius ¾ Inch.
No. 32 Iron, Nickel-plated ....Each, $1.00 **1.20**

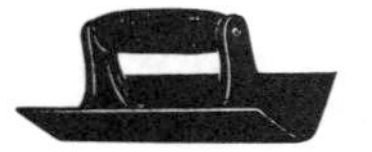

OUTSIDE ROUND ANGLE

Size 8 Inches Long, 2¼ Inch Sides; Radius ¾ Inch.
No. 33 Iron, Nickel-plated ....Each, $1.00 **1.20**

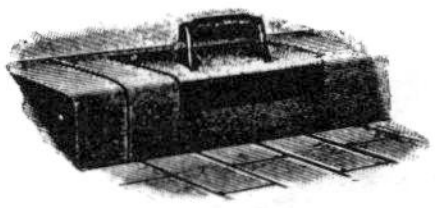

CURB TOOL

Size, 10 Inches Long, 5½ Inches Wide, 2 Inch Side; 1 Inch Radius.
No. 36 Iron, Nickel-plated ....Each, $2.00 **2.40**

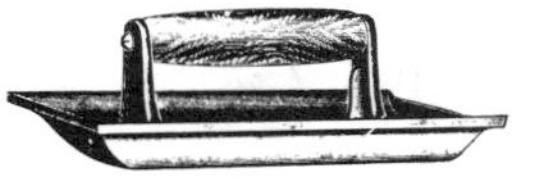

GUTTER TOOL

Size, 9 Inches Long, 6 Inches Wide, 1 Inch Deep.
No. 40 Iron, Nickel-plated ....Each, $1.50 **1.80**

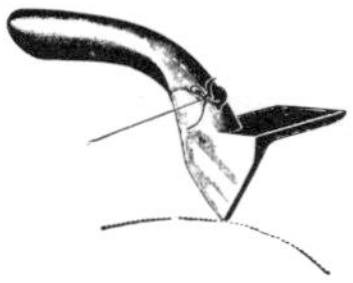

RADIUS TOOL

No. 42½ Iron, Nickel-plated ....Each, $0.50 **.60**

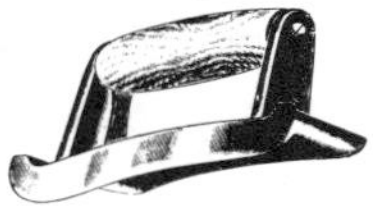

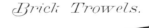

OUT-CURVE EDGER

Size, 5 Inches Long, 2 Inches Wide; ⅝ Inch Turned Edge with a Radius of ¼ Inch.
No. 43 Iron, Nickel-plated ....Each, $0.50 **.60**

BRICK TROWELS

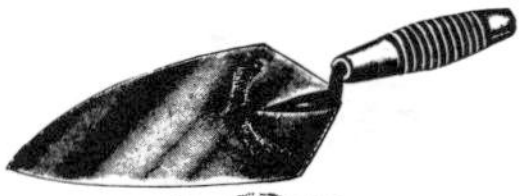

McINTOSH HEATHER
Very Highest Grade

Superior Quality Tool Steel; Hardened and Tempered; Leather Handles, with Bog Oak Wood Tips; Fully Guaranteed. These Trowels are Extra Heavy, Being Used Especially on Vitrified and Paving Brick.

No. 30 ....Inches,	10½	11	11½
Width ....Inches,	6	6¼	6⅜
Per Dozen....	**$26.00**	**26.00**	**27.00**

One Only in Plaid Box, Quarter Dozen in Container.

BRADE'S
London Pattern

Spring Steel Blade; Tempered; Ground and Polished; Natural Finish Shank; Hickory Handle; Polished Ferrule.

No. 35 ....Inches,	10½	11	11½	12	12½
Width ....Inches,	4½	4¾	4⅞	5	5⅛
Per Dozen....	$11.50	12.00	12.50	13.00	13.50
	20.70	**21.60**	**22.50**	**23.40**	**24.30**

Half Dozen in a Box.

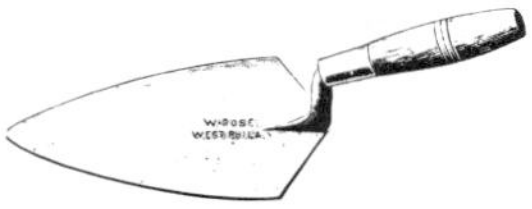

ROSE
Philadelphia Pattern

Extra Quality Steel Blade; Tempered; Ground and Polished; Steel Ferrule.

No. 40 ...Inches,	10	10½	11	11½	12	12½	13
Width ....Inches,	4⅞	5⅛	5⅜	5½	5½	5⅝	5¾
Per Dozen........	$13.25	13.75	14.25	14.75	15.25	15.75	16.25
	22.50	**23.35**	**24.20**	**25.05**	**25.90**	**26.75**	**27.60**

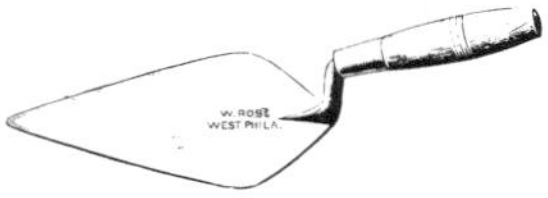

ROSE
London Pattern

Solid Steel Blue Lacquered Shank; Gum Wood Handle; Long Polished

No. 41 .....Inches,	10	10½	11	11½	12	12½
Width ....Inches,	4¼	4½	4¾	4⅞	5⅛	5¼
Per Dozen..........	$13.25	13.75	14.25	14.75	15.25	15.75
	22.50	**23.35**	**24.20**	**25.05**	**25.90**	**26.75**

Half Dozen in a Box.

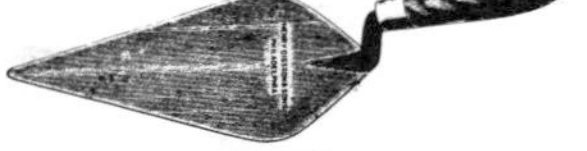

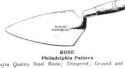

DISSTON
London Pattern

Polished Cast Steel Blade; Solid, Polished Steel Shank; Polished Beech Handle.

No. 25 ...Inches,	10	10½	11	11½	12	12½	13
Width ....Inches,	4⅜	4½	4⅝	4¾	5	5¼	5⅜
Per Dozen........	$10.00	10.50	11.00	11.50	12.00	12.75	13.50
	14.25	**15.00**	**15.75**	**16.50**	**17.10**	**18.25**	**19.25**

OHIO KING
London Pattern

Cast Steel Blade; Solid Steel Shank; Beech Handle.

No. 20 ....Inches,	10	10½	11	11½	12
Width ....Inches,	4⅜	4½	4¾	4⅞	5⅛
Per Dozen....	$7.25	7.50	7.75	8.00	8.25
	11.60	**12.00**	**12.40**	**12.80**	**13.20**

Half Dozen in a Box.

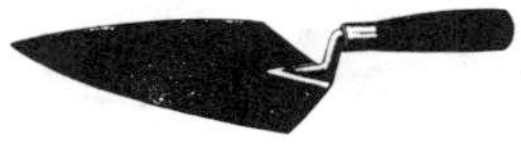

HANDY

No. 45 10 in.; Cast Steel Blade; Malleable Iron Shank, Riveted to Blade; Beech Handle......Per Dozen, **$4.00**

One Dozen in a Box.

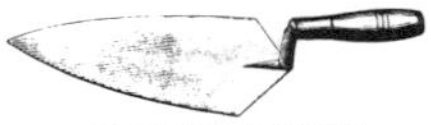

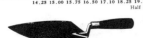

POINTING TROWELS
OHIO KING

Cast Steel Blade; Beech Handle; Brass Ferrule.

No. 10 Standard ....Inches,	4½	5	5½	6
Width ....Inches,	2¼	2⅜	2½	2¾
Per Dozen....	**$4.70**	**4.80**	**5.00**	**5.30**

No. 55 Handy; 5 in. Blade; Riveted Shank.......Per Dozen, **$2.00**

One Dozen in a Box.

Brick Trowels.

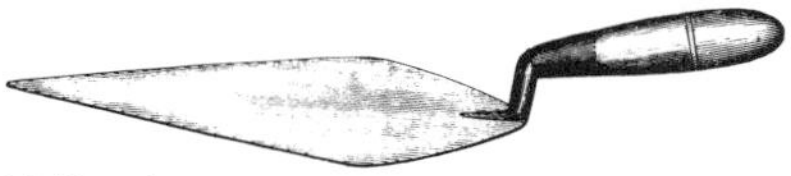

Lothrop's Brick Trowels.				
Inches,	9	10	11	12
Per Dozen,	$			

Rose's Brick Trowels.				
Inches,	10	11	12	13
Per Dozen,	$			

Brade's Brick Trowels.						
Inches,	10	10½	11	11½	12	13	14
Per Dozen, $							

HALF DOZEN IN A PACKAGE.

Plastering Trowels.

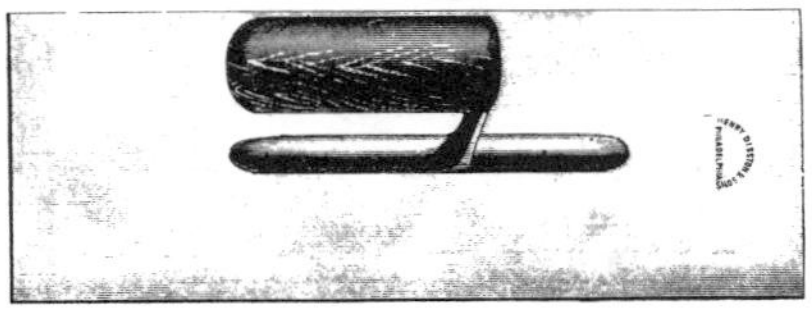

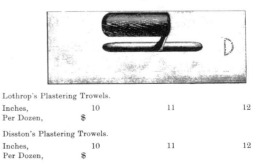

Lothrop's Plastering Trowels.			
Inches,	10	11	12
Per Dozen,	$		

Disston's Plastering Trowels.			
Inches,	10	11	12
Per Dozen,	$		

HALF DOZEN IN A BOX.

Round Nose Plyers.

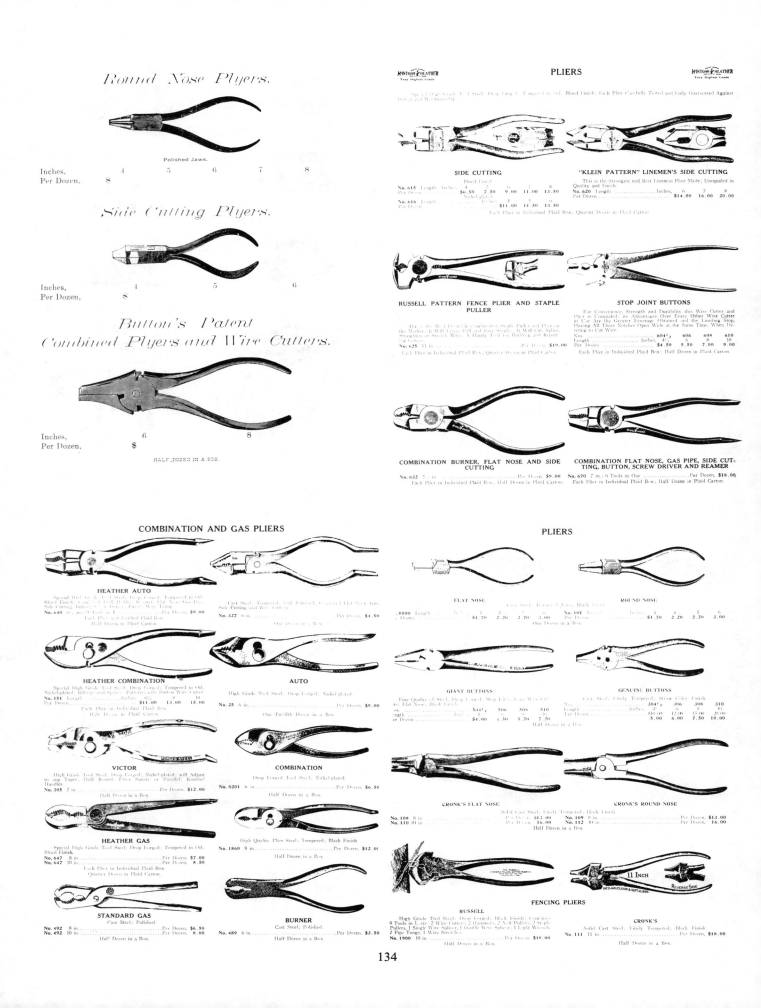

Polished Jaws.

Inches,	4	5	6	7	8
Per Dozen,	$				

Side Cutting Plyers.

Inches,	4	5	6
Per Dozen,	$		

Button's Patent Combined Plyers and Wire Cutters.

Inches,	6	8
Per Dozen,	$	

HALF DOZEN IN A BOX.

SIDE CUTTING

Blued Finish
No. 615 Length, Inches.
No. 616 Length

"KLEIN PATTERN" LINEMEN'S SIDE CUTTING

This is the Strongest and Best Lineman Plier Made; Unequaled in Quality and Finish.
No. 620 Length .... Inches, 6 7 8
Per Dozen $14.00 16.00 20.00

Each Plier in Individual Plaid Box; Quarter Dozen in Plaid Carton.

RUSSELL PATTERN FENCE PLIER AND STAPLE PULLER

No. 625 .... Per Dozen, $19.00
Each Plier in Individual Plaid Box; Quarter Dozen in Plaid Carton.

STOP JOINT BUTTONS

For Convenience, Strength and Durability this Wire Cutter and Plier is Unequaled; its Advantages Over Every Other Wire Cutter in Use Are the Greater Leverage Obtained and the Limiting Stop, Having All Three Notches Open Wide at the Same Time, When Desiring to Cut Wire.
No. 604½ 606 608 610
Length .... Inches, 6 8 10
Per Dozen $4.50 5.50 7.00 9.00
Each Plier in Individual Plaid Box; Half Dozen in Plaid Carton.

COMBINATION BURNER, FLAT NOSE AND SIDE CUTTING

No. 632 5 in .... Per Dozen, $9.00
Each Plier in Individual Plaid Box; Half Dozen in Plaid Carton.

COMBINATION FLAT NOSE, GAS PIPE, SIDE CUTTING, BUTTON, SCREW DRIVER AND REAMER

No. 670 7 in.; 6 Tools in One .... Per Dozen, $18.00
Each Plier in Individual Plaid Box; Half Dozen in Plaid Carton.

COMBINATION AND GAS PLIERS

HEATHER AUTO

Special High Grade Tool Steel; Drop Forged; Tempered in Oil; Blued Finish; Combined Drill Holder, Reamer, Flat Nose Gas Plier, Side Cutting, Button, Screw Driver, Pipe and Wire Tying.
No. 640 6 in.; 9 Tools in 1 .... Per Dozen, $9.00
Each Plier in Individual Plaid Box
Half Dozen in Plaid Carton.

Cast Steel; Tempered; Dull Polished; Combined Flat Nose, Gas, Side Cutting and Wire Cutting
No. 327 5 in .... Per Dozen, $4.50
One Dozen in a Box.

HEATHER COMBINATION

Special High Grade Tool Steel; Drop Forged; Tempered in Oil; Nickel-plated; Babbitt and Spence Pattern, with Button Wire Cutter.
No. 151 Length .... Inches, 6½ 8 10
Per Dozen $11.00 13.00 15.00
Each Plier in Individual Plaid Box
Half Dozen in Plaid Carton.

AUTO

High Grade Tool Steel; Drop Forged; Nickel plated.
No. 25 6 in .... Per Dozen, $9.00
One Twelfth Dozen in a Box.

VICTOR

High Grade Tool Steel; Drop Forged; Nickel-plated; will Adjust to any Taper; Half Round, Three Square or Parallel; Knurled Handles.
No. 305 7 in .... Per Dozen, $12.00
Half Dozen in a Box.

COMBINATION

Drop Forged Tool Steel; Nickel-plated.
No. 0201 6 in .... Per Dozen, $6.50
Half Dozen in a Box.

HEATHER GAS

Special High Grade Tool Steel; Tempered in Oil; Blued Finish.
No. 647 8 in .... Per Dozen, $7.00
No. 647 10 in .... Per Dozen, 8.50
Each Plier in Individual Plaid Box.
Quarter Dozen in Plaid Carton.

High Quality Plier Steel; Tempered; Black Finish.
No. 1860 9 in .... Per Dozen, $12.00
Half Dozen in a Box.

STANDARD GAS

Cast Steel; Polished.
No. 492 8 in .... Per Dozen, $6.50
No. 492 10 in .... Per Dozen, 8.00
Half Dozen in a Box.

BURNER

Cast Steel; Polished.
No. 489 6 in .... Per Dozen, $3.50
Half Dozen in a Box.

PLIERS

FLAT NOSE

Cast Steel; Tempered Jaws; Black Finish
No. 0100 Length .. Inches, 3 4 5 6
Dozen $1.70 2.20 2.70 3.00
One Dozen in a Box

ROUND NOSE

No. 101 .... Inches, 3 4 5 6
Per Dozen $1.70 2.20 2.70 3.00

GIANT BUTTONS

Fine Quality of Steel; Drop Forged; Stop Joint; Long Wire Cutters; Flat Nose; Black Finish.
No. 504½ 506 508 510
Length 4½
Per Dozen $4.00 4.30 5.70 7.20

GENUINE BUTTONS

Cast Steel; Finely Tempered; Straw Color Finish.
No. 304½ 306 308 310
Length .... Inches, 4½
Per Dozen $10.00 12.00 15.00 20.00
Per Dozen 5.00 6.00 7.50 10.00
Half Dozen in a Box.

CRONK'S FLAT NOSE

Solid Cast Steel; Finely Tempered; Black Finish
No. 108 8 in .... Per Dozen, $13.00
No. 110 10 in .... Per Dozen, 16.00
Half Dozen in a Box.

CRONK'S ROUND NOSE

No. 109 8 in .... Per Dozen, $13.00
No. 112 10 in .... Per Dozen, 16.00
Half Dozen in a Box.

FENCING PLIERS

RUSSELL

High Grade Tool Steel; Drop Forged; Black Finish; Combines 9 Tools in 1, viz; 2 Wire Cutters, 2 Hammers, 2 Nail Pullers, 2 Staple Pullers, 1 Single Wire Splicer, 1 Double Wire Splicer, 1 Light Wrench, 2 Pipe Tongs, 1 Wire Stretcher.
No. 1900 10 in .... Per Dozen, $18.00
Half Dozen in a Box.

11 INCH
REVERSE SIDE

CRONK'S

Solid Cast Steel; Finely Tempered; Black Finish.
No. 111 11 in .... Per Dozen, $18.00
Half Dozen in a Box.

PUNCHES, COLD CHISELS, ETC.

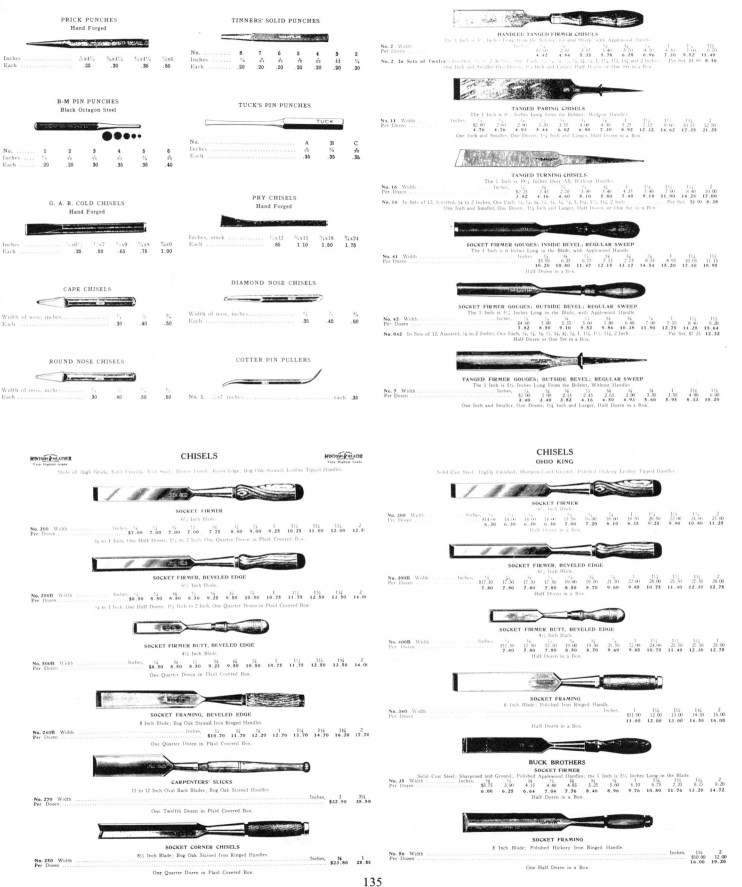

PRICK PUNCHES
Hand Forged

Inches	5/16x4½	3/8x4½	1/2x4½	1/2x6
Each	.25	.30	.35	.50

TINNERS' SOLID PUNCHES

No.	8	7	6	5	4	3	2
Inches	1/8	9/64	5/32	3/16	7/32	11/64	1/4
Each	.20	.20	.20	.20	.20	.20	.20

B-M PIN PUNCHES
Black Octagon Steel

No.	1	2	3	4	5	6
Inches	1/8	5/32	3/16	7/32	1/4	9/32
Each	.20	.25	.30	.35	.35	.40

TUCK'S PIN PUNCHES

No.	A	B	C
Inches	3/32	1/8	5/32
Each	.35	.35	.35

G. A. R. COLD CHISELS
Hand Forged

Inches	3/8x6½	1/2x7	5/8x9	3/4x8	7/8x9
Each	.35	.50	.65	.75	1.00

PRY CHISELS
Hand Forged

Inches, stock	1/2x12	5/8x15	3/4x18	3/4x24
Each	.85	1.10	1.50	1.75

CAPE CHISELS

Width of nose, inches	1/4	5/16	3/8
Each	.30	.40	.50

DIAMOND NOSE CHISELS

Width of nose, inches	1/4	5/16	3/8
Each	.35	.45	.60

ROUND NOSE CHISELS

Width of nose, inches	1/4	5/16	3/8	1/2
Each	.30	.40	.50	.60

COTTER PIN PULLERS

No. 1. [illegible]x7 inches .... each .35

BUCK BROS. CHISELS AND GOUGES

HANDLED TANGED FIRMER CHISELS
The 1 Inch is 5½ Inches Long from the Bolster; Ground Sharp; with Applewood Handle.

No. 2 Width ... Inches	1/4	3/8	1/2	5/8	3/4	7/8	1	1¼	1½
Per Dozen	$2.60	2.85	3.15	3.40	3.70	4.10	4.30	5.60	6.70
	4.42	4.84	5.35	5.78	6.28	6.96	7.30	9.52	11.40

No. 2 In Sets of Twelve—Assorted, 1/8 to 2 Inches, One Each, 1/8, 1/4, 3/8, 1/2, 5/8, 3/4, 7/8, 1, 1¼, 1½, 1¾ and 2 Inches .... Per Set, $4.80 **8.16**

One Inch and Smaller One Dozen; 1¼ Inch and Larger, Half Dozen, or One Set in a Box.

TANGED PARING CHISELS
The 1 Inch is 8½ Inches Long from the Bolster; Without Handles.

No. 11 Width ... Inches,	1/8	1/4	3/8	1/2	5/8	3/4	7/8	1	1¼	1½	1¾	2
Per Dozen	$2.80	2.80	2.90	3.20	3.55	4.00	4.30	5.25	7.15	8.60	10.15	12.50
	4.76	4.76	4.93	5.44	6.02	6.80	7.30	8.92	12.32	14.62	17.25	21.25

One Inch and Smaller, One Dozen; 1¼ Inch and Larger, Half Dozen in a Box.

TANGED TURNING CHISELS
The 1 Inch is 10¼ Inches Over All, Without Handles.

No. 16 Width ... Inches,	1/4	3/8	1/2	5/8	3/4	1	1¼	1½	1¾	2
Per Dozen	$2.25	2.45	2.70	3.00	3.40	4.35	5.40	7.00	8.40	10.00
	3.82	4.16	4.60	5.10	5.80	7.40	9.18	11.90	14.28	17.00

No. 16 In Sets of 12, Assorted, 1/8 to 2 Inches, One Each, 1/8, 1/4, 3/8, 1/2, 5/8, 3/4, 7/8, 1, 1¼, 1½, 1¾, 2 Inch .... Per Set, $4.90 **8.38**

One Inch and Smaller, One Dozen; 1¼ Inch and Larger, Half Dozen, or One Set in a Box.

SOCKET FIRMER GOUGES; INSIDE BEVEL; REGULAR SWEEP
The 1 Inch is 6 Inches Long in the Blade, with Applewood Handle.

No. 41 Width ... Inches	1/4	3/8	1/2	5/8	3/4	7/8	1	1¼	1½
Per Dozen	$5.95	6.35	6.75	7.15	7.75	8.55	8.95	10.05	11.15
	10.20	10.80	11.47	12.15	13.17	14.54	15.20	17.10	18.95

Half Dozen in a Box.

SOCKET FIRMER GOUGES; OUTSIDE BEVEL; REGULAR SWEEP
The 1 Inch is 5½ Inches Long in the Blade, with Applewood Handle.

No. 42 Width ... Inches,	1/8	1/4	3/8	1/2	5/8	3/4	7/8	1	1¼	1½
Per Dozen	$4.60	5.00	5.35	5.60	5.80	6.40	7.00	7.50	8.40	9.20
	7.82	8.50	9.10	9.52	9.86	10.38	11.90	12.75	14.28	15.64

No. 042 In Sets of 12, Assorted, 1/8 to 2 Inches, One Each, 1/8, 1/4, 3/8, 1/2, 5/8, 3/4, 7/8, 1, 1¼, 1½, 1¾, 2 Inch .... Per Set, $7.25 **12.32**

Half Dozen or One Set in a Box.

TANGED FIRMER GOUGES; OUTSIDE BEVEL; REGULAR SWEEP
The 1 Inch is 5½ Inches Long From the Bolster, Without Handles.

No. 7 Width ... Inches,	1/8	1/4	3/8	1/2	5/8	3/4	7/8	1	1¼	1½
Per Dozen	$2.00	2.00	2.15	2.45	2.65	2.90	3.30	3.50	4.90	6.00
	3.40	3.40	3.82	4.16	4.50	4.93	5.60	5.95	8.33	10.20

One Inch and Smaller, One Dozen; 1¼ Inch and Larger, Half Dozen in a Box.

CHISELS

McINTOSH-HEATHER — Very Highest Grade

Made of High Grade, Solid Crucible Tool Steel; Mirror Finish, Razor Edge; Bog Oak Stained, Leather Tipped Handles.

SOCKET FIRMER
6½ Inch Blade.

No. 200 Width ... Inches,	1/8	1/4	3/8	1/2	5/8	3/4	7/8	1	1¼	1½	1¾	2
Per Dozen	$7.00	7.00	7.00	7.00	7.75	8.00	9.00	9.25	10.25	11.00	12.00	12.50

1/8 to 1 Inch, One Half Dozen; 1¼ to 2 Inch, One Quarter Dozen in Plaid Covered Box.

SOCKET FIRMER, BEVELED EDGE
6½ Inch Blade.

No. 200B Width ... Inches,	1/8	1/4	3/8	1/2	5/8	3/4	7/8	1	1¼	1½	1¾	2
Per Dozen	$8.50	8.50	8.50	8.50	9.25	9.50	10.50	10.75	11.75	12.50	13.50	14.00

1/8 to 1 Inch, One Half Dozen; 1¼ Inch to 2 Inch, One Quarter Dozen in Plaid Covered Box.

SOCKET FIRMER BUTT, BEVELED EDGE
4½ Inch Blade.

No. 500B Width ... Inches,	1/4	3/8	1/2	5/8	3/4	7/8	1	1¼	1½	1¾	2
Per Dozen	$8.50	8.50	8.50	9.25	9.50	10.50	10.75	11.75	12.50	13.50	14.00

One Quarter Dozen in Plaid Covered Box.

SOCKET FRAMING, BEVELED EDGE
8 Inch Blade; Bog Oak Stained Iron Ringed Handles.

No. 240B Width ... Inches,	1/2	3/4	7/8	1	1¼	1½	1¾	2
Per Dozen	$10.70	11.70	12.20	12.70	13.70	14.70	16.20	17.70

One Quarter Dozen in Plaid Covered Box.

CARPENTERS' SLICKS
11 to 12 Inch Oval Back Blades; Bog Oak Stained Handles.

No. 270 Width ... Inches,	3	3½
Per Dozen	$32.90	38.50

One Twelfth Dozen in Plaid Covered Box.

SOCKET CORNER CHISELS
8½ Inch Blade; Bog Oak Stained Iron Ringed Handles.

No. 250 Width ... Inches,	3/4	1
Per Dozen	$23.80	25.50

One Quarter Dozen in Plaid Covered Box.

CHISELS
OHIO KING

Solid Cast Steel, Highly Finished; Sharpened and Ground, Polished Hickory Leather Tipped Handles.

SOCKET FIRMER
6½ Inch Blade.

No. 300 Width ... Inches,	1/8	1/4	3/8	1/2	5/8	3/4	7/8	1	1¼	1½	1¾	2
Per Dozen	$14.00	14.00	14.00	14.00	15.50	16.00	18.00	18.50	20.50	22.00	24.00	25.00
	6.30	6.30	6.30	6.30	7.00	7.20	8.10	8.35	9.25	9.90	10.80	11.25

Half Dozen in a Box.

SOCKET FIRMER, BEVELED EDGE
6½ Inch Blade.

No. 300B Width ... Inches,	1/8	1/4	3/8	1/2	5/8	3/4	7/8	1	1¼	1½	1¾	2
Per Dozen	$17.50	17.50	17.50	17.50	19.00	19.50	21.50	22.00	24.00	25.50	27.50	28.00
	7.80	7.80	7.80	7.80	8.50	8.70	9.60	9.85	10.75	11.40	12.30	12.75

Half Dozen in a Box.

SOCKET FIRMER BUTT, BEVELED EDGE
4½ Inch Blade.

No. 400B Width ... Inches,	1/4	3/8	1/2	5/8	3/4	7/8	1	1¼	1½	1¾	1
Per Dozen	$17.50	17.50	17.50	19.00	19.50	21.50	22.00	24.00	25.50	27.50	28.00
	7.80	7.80	7.80	8.50	8.70	9.60	9.85	10.75	11.40	12.30	12.75

Half Dozen in a Box.

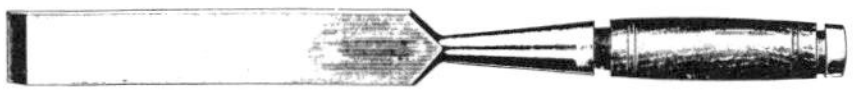

SOCKET FRAMING
8 Inch Blade; Polished Iron Ringed Handle.

No. 340 Width ... Inches,	1	1¼	1½	1¾	2
Per Dozen	$11.00	12.00	13.00	14.50	16.00
	11.00	12.00	13.00	14.50	16.00

Half Dozen in a Box.

BUCK BROTHERS
SOCKET FIRMER
Solid Cast Steel; Sharpened and Ground; Polished Applewood Handles; the 1 Inch is 5½ Inches Long in the Blade.

No. 35 Width ... Inches,	1/8	1/4	3/8	1/2	5/8	3/4	7/8	1	1¼	1½	1¾	2
Per Dozen	$3.75	3.90	4.15	4.40	4.85	5.25	5.60	6.10	6.75	7.35	8.25	9.20
	6.00	6.25	6.64	7.04	7.76	8.40	8.96	9.76	10.80	11.76	13.20	14.72

Half Dozen in a Box.

SOCKET FRAMING
8 Inch Blade; Polished Hickory Iron Ringed Handle.

No. 56 Width ... Inches,	1½	2
Per Dozen	$10.00	12.00
	16.00	19.20

One Half Dozen in a Box.

Punches.

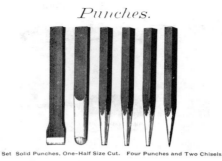

Set Solid Punches, One-Half Size Cut. Four Punches and Two Chisels.

SOLID.

Square, Cast Steel, Nos. 0, 1, 2, 3, 4, 5, 6, 7, and Prick, each, $
Set Solid Punches, Nos. 1, 4, 6 and Prick Punches, ¾ in. Wire, and
    Lantern Chisels, per set, $

HOLLOW.

All sizes, to and including 1¾ in. diameter, round, per inch, $
All sizes above 1¾ in. diameter, per inch,
Set of Hollow Punches, 1 each, ½, ¾, 1, 1½, 1¾, per set,

Cast Steel Chisels.

LANTERN.

                                       Each.

Common Size, $

WIRE.

Inches,	⅛	¼	½	⅝	¾	⅞	1	1⅛	1¼	1½
Each, $										

COLD.

Inches,	⅛	⅜	½	⅝	¾	⅞	1
Per Pound, $							

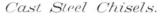

NAIL SETS

SYRACUSE
Light Round Pattern

No.	91	92	93	94
Points, inch	1/32	2/32	3/32	¼
Each	.15	.15	.15	.15

SYRACUSE
Heavy Round Pattern

No.	112	123	124	125
Points, inch	1/32	2/32	¼	3/32
Each	.25	.25	.25	.25

SYRACUSE
Light Square Pattern

No.	91N	92N	93N	94N
Points, inch	1/32	2/32	3/32	¼
Each	.20	.20	.20	.20

O. K. PATTERN
Square Head

No.	451	452	453	454
Points, inch	1/32	2/32	3/32	¼
Each	.20	.20	.20	.20

SURE GRIP
Very Heavy, 7/32 Inch Wide

No.	4	3	2	1
Points, inch	1/32	⅛	3/32	1/16
Each	.30	.30	.30	.30

CAR BUILDERS'
Hand Forged

Inches	4¼x⅝x⅞	7x⅝x⅞
Each	.65	1.00

PARKS BRAD PUSHER

No Nail Set Required.
Push Brad in Instead of Hammering.

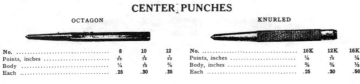

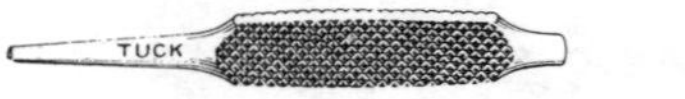

Price, each .75

The barrel of this tool is made of brass. The center ram is magnetized steel. If one hand is engaged in holding a piece in place, grasp barrel of set between first and second fingers, and pull until magnetic ram is exposed, when it will readily pick up brad.

CENTER PUNCHES

OCTAGON

No.	8	10	12
Points, inches	1/32	1/16	⅛
Body	¼	5/16	⅜
Each	.25	.30	.35

KNURLED

No.	10K	12K	16K
Points, inches	⅛	7/32	¼
Body, inches	⅜	7/16	½
Each	.25	.30	.50

Box Chisels.

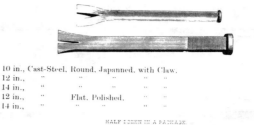

                                           Per Dozen.

10 in., Cast-Steel, Round, Japanned, with Claw. $
12 in.,   "   "   "   "   "
14 in.,   "   "   "   "   "
12 in.,   "   Flat, Polished.
14 in.,   "   "   "

HALF DOZEN IN A PACKAGE.

Capewell's Giant Nail Pullers.

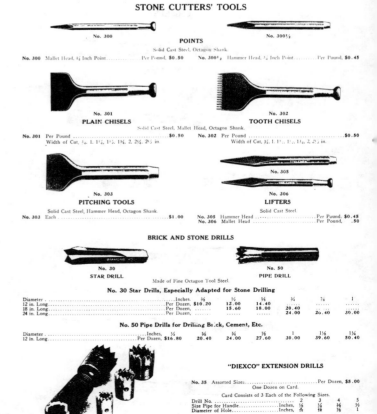

No.			Each.
1	Large Size, for general use,		$
2	Small "		

STONE CUTTERS' TOOLS

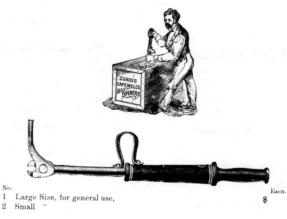

No. 300   **No. 300½**

POINTS
Solid Cast Steel, Octagon Shank.

No. 300 Mallet Head, ½ Inch Point.........Per Pound, $0.50   No. 300½ Hammer Head, ½ Inch Point.........Per Pound, $0.45

No. 301   **No. 302**

PLAIN CHISELS
Solid Cast Steel, Mallet Head, Octagon Shank.

TOOTH CHISELS

No. 301 Per Pound........................$0.50   No. 302 Per Pound........................$0.50
    Width of Cut, ¾, 1, 1¼, 1½, 1¾, 2, 2¼, 2½ in.   Width of Cut, ¾, 1, 1¼, 1½, 1¾, 2, 2½ in.

No. 305

No. 303   **No. 306**

PITCHING TOOLS
Solid Cast Steel, Hammer Head, Octagon Shank.

LIFTERS
Solid Cast Steel.

No. 303 Each......................$1.00   No. 305 Hammer Head....................Per Pound, $0.45
                                   No. 306 Mallet Head....................Per Pound, .50

BRICK AND STONE DRILLS

No. 30   **No. 50**
STAR DRILL   **PIPE DRILL**

Made of Fine Octagon Tool Steel.

No. 30 Star Drills, Especially Adapted for Stone Drilling

Diameter	Inches.	⅜	½	⅝	¾	⅞	1
12 in. Long	Per Dozen, $10.20	12.00	14.40				
18 in. Long		15.60	18.00	20.40			
24 in. Long			24.00	26.40	30.00		

No. 50 Pipe Drills for Drilling Brick, Cement, Etc.

	Inches.	½	⅝	¾	⅞	1	1⅛	1¼
12 in. Long	Per Dozen, $16.80	20.40	24.00	27.60	30.00	39.60	50.40

"DIEXCO" EXTENSION DRILLS

No. 35 Assorted Sizes....................Per Dozen, $8.00
One Dozen on Card.
Card Consists of 3 Each of the Following Sizes.

Drill No.		2	3	4	5
Size Pipe for Handle	Inches,	⅛	⅛	¼	¼
Diameter of Hole	Inches,	5/16	3/16	⅜	½

136

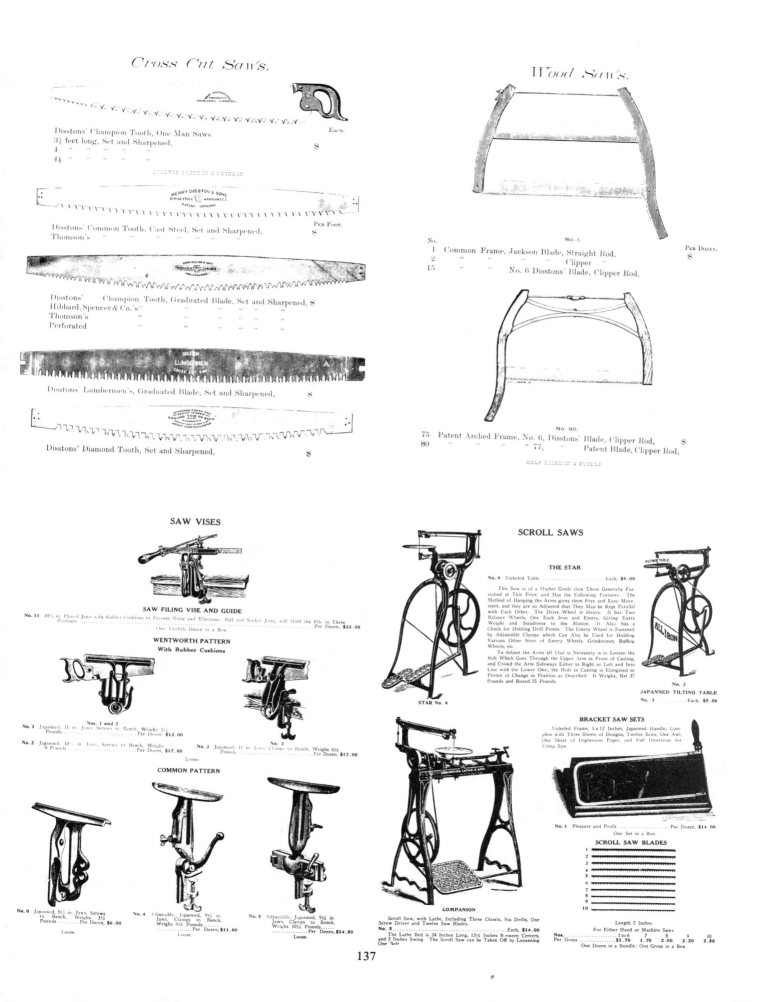

Cross Cut Saws.

Disstons' Champion Tooth, One Man Saws.
3½ feet long, Set and Sharpened,   Each.
4   "   " $
4½ "   "

ONE TOOTH BOXED IN A PACKAGE

Disstons' Common Tooth, Cast Steel, Set and Sharpened,   Per Foot.
Thomson's $

Disstons'   Champion Tooth, Graduated Blade, Set and Sharpened, $
Hibbard, Spencer & Co.'s"   "   "   "
Thomson's   "   "   "
Perforated   "   "   "

Disstons' Lumbermen's, Graduated Blade, Set and Sharpened, $

Disstons' Diamond Tooth, Set and Sharpened, $

Wood Saws.

No.			Per Dozen.
1	Common Frame, Jackson Blade, Straight Rod,		$
2	" " " Clipper "		
15	" " No. 6 Disstons' Blade, Clipper Rod,		

NO. 80.

75	Patent Arched Frame, No. 6, Disstons' Blade, Clipper Rod,	$
80	" " " 77, Patent Blade, Clipper Rod,	

HALF DOZEN IN A BUNDLE.

SAW VISES

SAW FILING VISE AND GUIDE
No. 11 10½ in. Planed Jaws with Rubber Cushions to Prevent Noise and Vibration; Ball and Socket Joint, will Hold the File in Three Positions ....Per Dozen, $33.00
One Twelfth Dozen in a Box.

WENTWORTH PATTERN
With Rubber Cushions

Nos. 1 and 2
No. 1 Japanned, 11 in. Jaws, Screws to Bench, Weighs 5½ Pounds ....Per Dozen, $13.00
No. 2 Japanned, 14½ in. Jaws, Screws to Bench, Weighs 9 Pounds ....Per Dozen, $17.00
Loose.

No. 3
No. 3 Japanned, 11 in. Jaws, Clamps to Bench, Weighs 6½ Pounds ....Per Dozen, $17.00
Loose.

COMMON PATTERN

No. 0 Japanned, 9½ in. Jaws, Screws to Bench, Weighs 3½ Pounds ....Per Dozen, $6.00
Loose.

No. 4 Adjustable, Japanned, 9½ in. Jaws, Clamps to Bench, Weighs 6½ Pounds ....Per Dozen, $11.00
Loose.

No. 5 Adjustable, Japanned, 9½ in. Jaws, Clamps to Bench, Weighs 10½ Pounds ....Per Dozen, $14.50
Loose.

SCROLL SAWS

THE STAR
No. 8 Nickeled Table ....Each, $9.00

This Saw is of a Higher Grade than Those Generally Furnished at This Price, and Has the Following Features: The Method of Hanging the Arms gives them Free and Easy Movement, and they are so Adjusted that They May be Kept Parallel with Each Other. The Drive Wheel is Heavy. It has Two Balance Wheels, One Each Iron and Emery, Giving Extra Weight and Steadiness to the Motion. It Also has a Chuck for Holding Drill Points. The Emery Wheel is Fastened by Adjustable Clamps which Can Also be Used for Holding Various Other Sizes of Emery Wheels, Grindstones, Buffing Wheels, etc.
To Adjust the Arms all That is Necessary is to Loosen the Bolt Which Goes Through the Upper Arm in Front of Casting, and Crowd the Arm Sideways Either to Right or Left and Into Line with the Lower One; the Hole in Casting is Elongated to Permit of Change in Position as Described. It Weighs, Net 37 Pounds and Boxed 55 Pounds.

STAR No. 8

JAPANNED TILTING TABLE
No. 3 ....Each, $5.00

BRACKET SAW SETS
Nickeled Frame, 5 x 12 Inches, Japanned Handle, Complete with Three Sheets of Designs, Twelve Saws, One Awl, One Sheet of Impression Paper, and Full Directions for Using Saw

No. 1 Pleasure and Profit ....Per Dozen, $14.00
One Set in a Box.

COMPANION
Scroll Saw, with Lathe, Including Three Chisels, Six Drills, One Screw Driver and Twelve Saw Blades.
No. 5 ....Each, $14.00
The Lathe Bed is 24 Inches Long, 13½ Inches Between Centers, and 5 Inches Swing. The Scroll Saw can be Taken Off by Loosening One Bolt.

SCROLL SAW BLADES
Length 5 Inches.
For Either Hand or Machine Saws

Nos.	1 to 6	7	8	9	10
Per Gross	$1.70	1.70	2.00	2.20	2.50

One Dozen in a Bundle; One Gross in a Box.

Back Saws.

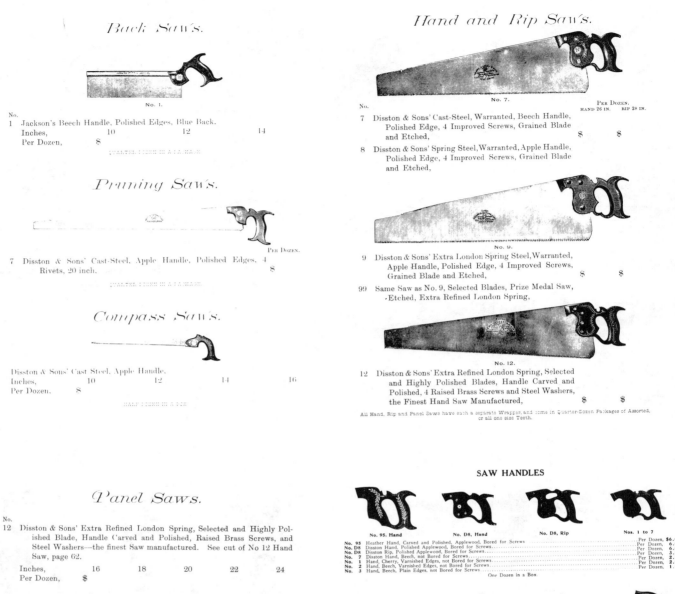

No.
1   Jackson's Beech Handle, Polished Edges, Blue Back.

Inches,	10	12	14
Per Dozen,	$		

QUARTER DOZEN IN A PACKAGE.

Pruning Saws.

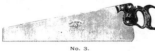

PER DOZEN.

7   Disston & Sons' Cast-Steel, Apple Handle, Polished Edges, 4 Rivets, 20 inch. $

QUARTER DOZEN IN A PACKAGE.

Compass Saws.

Disston & Sons' Cast Steel, Apple Handle.

Inches,	10	12	14	16
Per Dozen,	$			

HALF DOZEN IN A BOX.

Panel Saws.

No.
12   Disston & Sons' Extra Refined London Spring, Selected and Highly Polished Blade, Handle Carved and Polished, Raised Brass Screws, and Steel Washers—the finest Saw manufactured.   See cut of No 12 Hand Saw, page 62.

Inches,	16	18	20	22	24
Per Dozen,	$				

3   Brown, Beech Handle, Polished Edge, 3 Rivets, Grained Blade, Etched.

Inches,	16	18	20	22
Per Dozen,	$			

No. 3

All Hand, Rip and Panel Saws have each a separate Wrapper, and come in Quarter-Dozen Packages of Assorted, or all one size Teeth.

Back Saws.

No. 4

4   Disston & Sons' Apple Handle, Polished Edges, Blue Back.

Inches,	10	12	14	16
Per Dozen,	$			

7   Disston & Sons', same as No. 4, with Polished Steel Back.

Inches,	10	12	14	16
Per Dozen,	$			

QUARTER DOZEN IN A PACKAGE.

5

Hand and Rip Saws.

No. 7.

No.   PER DOZEN.
                                              HAND 26 IN.   RIP 28 IN.
7   Disston & Sons' Cast-Steel, Warranted, Beech Handle, Polished Edge, 4 Improved Screws, Grained Blade and Etched, $ $

8   Disston & Sons' Spring Steel, Warranted, Apple Handle, Polished Edge, 4 Improved Screws, Grained Blade and Etched,

No. 9.

9   Disston & Sons' Extra London Spring Steel, Warranted, Apple Handle, Polished Edge, 4 Improved Screws, Grained Blade and Etched, $ $

99   Same Saw as No. 9, Selected Blades, Prize Medal Saw, Etched, Extra Refined London Spring,

No. 12.

12   Disston & Sons' Extra Refined London Spring, Selected and Highly Polished Blades, Handle Carved and Polished, 4 Raised Brass Screws and Steel Washers, the Finest Hand Saw Manufactured, $ $

All Hand, Rip and Panel Saws have each a separate Wrapper, and come in Quarter-Dozen Packages of Assorted, or all one size Teeth.

SAW HANDLES

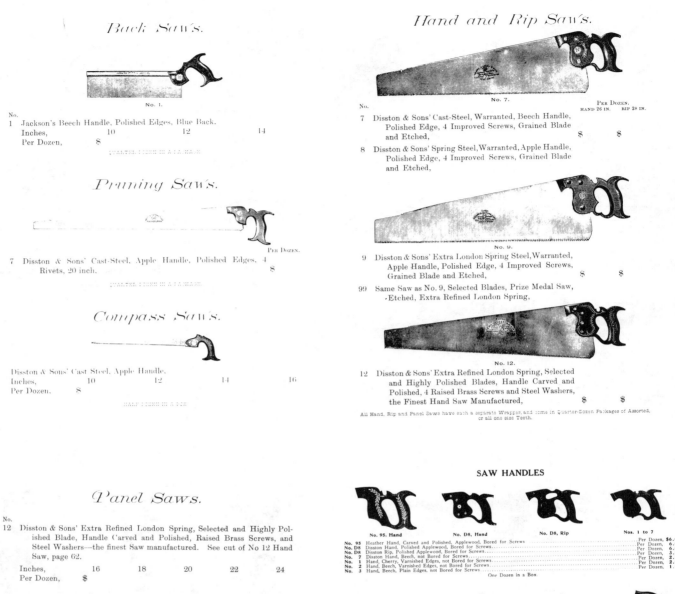

No. 95, Hand   No. D8, Hand   No. D8, Rip   Nos. 1 to 7

		Per Dozen,
No. 95	Heather Hand, Carved and Polished, Applewood, Bored for Screws	$6.00
No. D8	Disston Hand, Polished Applewood, Bored for Screws	6.00
No. D8	Disston Rip, Polished Applewood, Bored for Screws	6.80
No. 7	Disston Hand, Beech, not Bored for Screws	3.80
No. 1	Hand, Cherry, Varnished Edges, not Bored for Screws	2.80
No. 2	Hand, Beech, Varnished Edges, not Bored for Screws	2.00
No. 3	Hand, Beech, Plain Edges, not Bored for Screws	1.90

One Dozen in a Box.

No. 4, Panel   No. 7, Back   No. 5, Butcher   No. 6, Compass

		Per Dozen,
No. 4	Panel, Beech, Polished Edges, not Bored for Screws	$2.00
No. 7	Back, Beech, Varnished Edges, not Bored for Screws	2.70
No. 5	Butcher, Beech, Varnished Edges, not Bored for Screws	2.70
No. 6	Compass, Beech, Varnished Edges, Bored for Screws	2.00

One Dozen in a Box.

SAW SETS

HAMMER
Made Entirely of Tool Steel for Cross Cut Saws.

No. 25	Genuine Whiting	Per Dozen, $12.00
No. 125	Whiting's Pattern	Per Dozen, 10.00

Half Dozen in a Box.

AIKEN'S
Solid Cast Steel

No. 01	Genuine Aiken's	Per Dozen, $13.00
No. 5	Aiken's Pattern	Per Dozen, 9.00

Half Dozen in a Box.

STILLMAN PATTERN
Wood Handle Lever, for Hand Saws

No. 40		Per Dozen, $3.00

Half Dozen in a Box.

SMITH'S

No. 10	Smith's Improved	Per Dozen, $12.00

Half Dozen in a Box.

Butchers' Bow Back Saws.

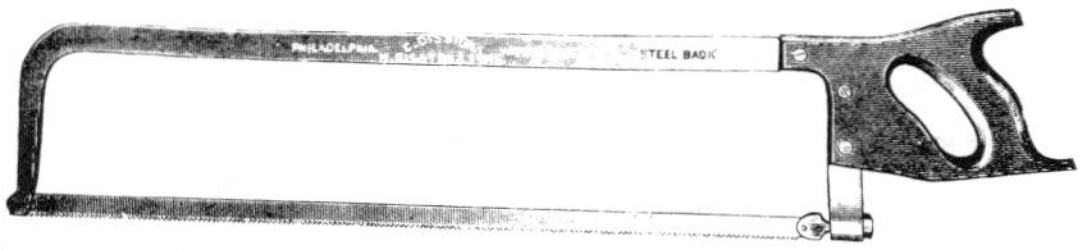

No.
7   Flat Steel Back.
Inches,   24   26   28
Per Dozen, $

QUARTER DOZEN IN A PACKAGE.

Kitchen Saws.

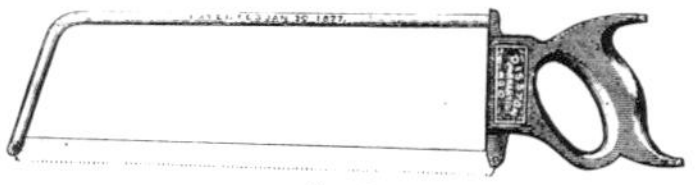

No. O.

0   Oval Back.
Inches,   12   14
Per Dozen, $

HALF DOZEN IN A BOX

Hack Saws.

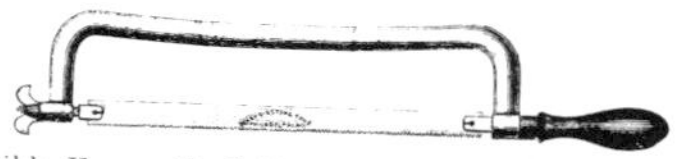

Disstons' Reversible Frame Hack Saw.
Inches,   8   10   12
Per Dozen, $

QUARTER DOZEN IN A PACKAGE.

Bracket Saws.

Bracket Saw Frames,   Per Dozen.
                                           $
    "   Blades.   Per Gross.
                                           $

Butchers' Bow Back Saws.

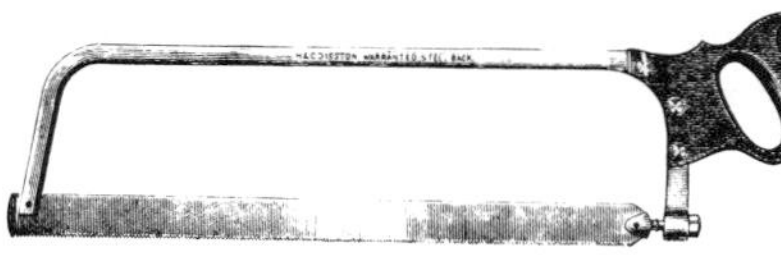

No.
1   Oval Back.
Inches,   20   22   24   26
Per Dozen, $

2   Flat Back.
Inches,   16   18   20   22   24
Per Dozen, $

QUARTER DOZEN IN A PACKAGE.

Key Hole Saws.

Disstons' Key-Hole Saw, with Iron Pad.

This is a cheap and convenient combination of a Key-hole Saw, Saw   Per Dozen.
Pad and Screw Driver, $

ONE DOZEN IN A BOX

Saw Pads.

Cut Wood Saw Pad.

German Saw Pads, $

Cast-Steel Key-hole Saws, Extra Ground, Set, and Sharpened, $

Nest of Saws.

COMBINING ONE EACH KEY-HOLE, COMPASS, AND TABLE OR PRUNING SAW.

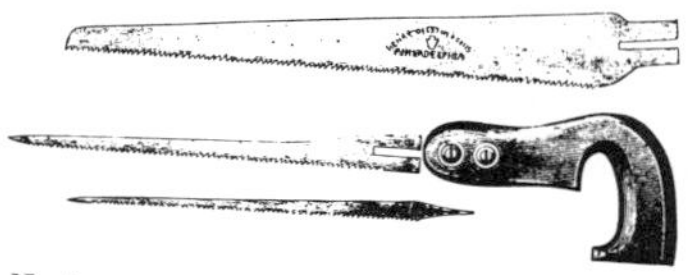

Price, per Dozen Nests, $

QUARTER DOZEN NESTS IN A PACKAGE.

Saw Bucks.

Patent Folding Saw Buck,   Per Dozen.
                                           $

HALF DOZEN IN A BUNDLE

Saw Rods.

Common Saw Rod, Lever Nut, $

Clipper Saw Rod, Patent Loop, $

ONE DOZEN IN A PACKAGE

Saw Sets.

Lever Saw Sets, Wood Handle, $

ONE DOZEN IN A BOX

139

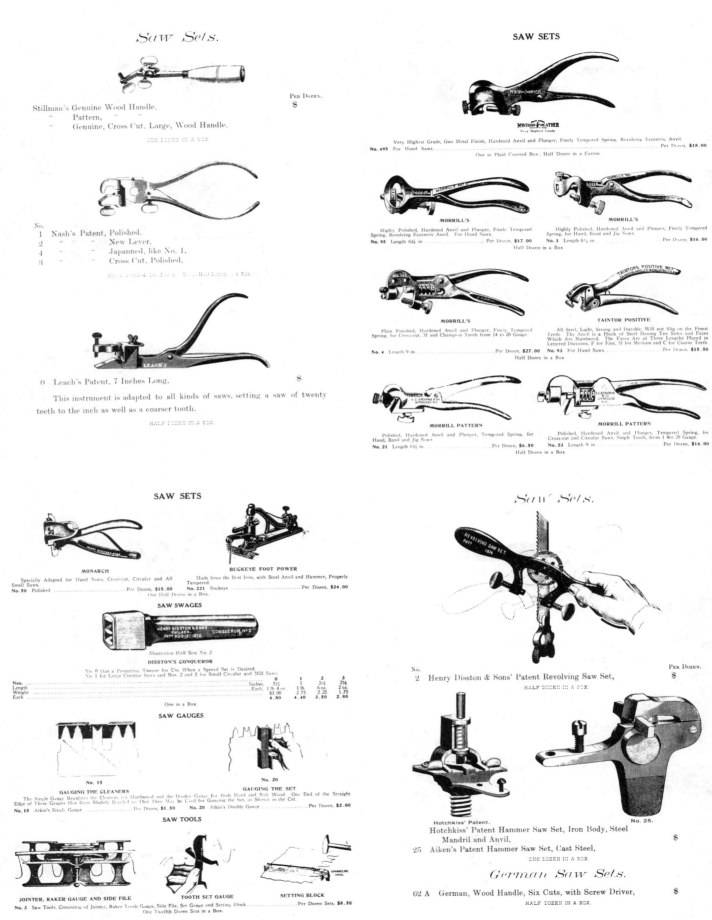

Saw Sets.

Stillman's Genuine Wood Handle.
" Pattern,
" Genuine, Cross Cut, Large, Wood Handle.

ONE DOZEN IN A BOX

PER DOZEN.
$

No.
1 Nash's Patent, Polished.
2 " " New Lever.
4 " " Japanned, like No. 1.
3 " " Cross Cut. Polished.

Nos. 1, 2, 3 and 4, One Doz. in a Box. Half Dozen in a Box.

0 Leach's Patent, 7 Inches Long, $

This instrument is adapted to all kinds of saws, setting a saw of twenty teeth to the inch as well as a coarser tooth.

HALF DOZEN IN A BOX.

SAW SETS

MINTOSH & HEATHER
Very Highest Grade

Very Highest Grade, Gun Metal Finish, Hardened Anvil and Plunger, Finely Tempered Spring, Revolving Eccentric Anvil.
No. 495 For Hand Saws................................Per Dozen, $18.00
One in Plaid Covered Box; Half Dozen in a Carton.

MORRILL'S
Highly Polished, Hardened Anvil and Plunger, Finely Tempered Spring, Revolving Eccentric Anvil. For Hand Saws.
No. 95 Length 6¾ in ....Per Dozen, $17.00

MORRILL'S
Highly Polished, Hardened Anvil and Plunger, Finely Tempered Spring, for Hand, Band and Jig Saws.
No. 1 Length 6¼ in............Per Dozen, $16.00
Half Dozen in a Box.

MORRILL'S
Plain Finished, Hardened Anvil and Plunger, Finely Tempered Spring, for Cross-cut, M and Champion Tooth from 14 to 20 Gauge.
No. 4 Length 9 in............Per Dozen, $27.00

TAINTOR POSITIVE
All Steel, Light, Strong and Durable. Will not Slip on the Finest Teeth. The Anvil is a Block of Steel Having Ten Sides and Faces Which Are Numbered. The Faces Are of Three Lengths Placed in Lettered Divisions, F for Fine, M for Medium and C for Coarse Teeth.
No. 93 For Hand Saws............Per Dozen, $15.50
Half Dozen in a Box.

MORRILL PATTERN
Polished, Hardened Anvil and Plunger, Tempered Spring, for Hand, Band and Jig Saws.
No. 21 Length 6¼ in............Per Dozen, $6.50

MORRILL PATTERN
Polished, Hardened Anvil and Plunger, Tempered Spring, for Cross-cut and Circular Saws, Single Tooth, from 1 to 20 Gauge.
No. 23 Length 9 in............Per Dozen, $16.00
Half Dozen in a Box.

SAW SETS

MONARCH
Specially Adapted for Hand Saws, Cross-cut, Circular and All Small Saws.
No. 50 Polished ....Per Dozen, $15.00
One Half Dozen in a Box.

BUCKEYE FOOT POWER
Made from the Best Iron, with Steel Anvil and Hammer, Properly Tempered.
No. 221 Buckeye ....Per Dozen, $24.00

SAW SWAGES

DISSTON'S CONQUEROR
Illustration Half Size No. 2

No. 0 Has a Protecting Tongue for Use When a Spread Set is Desired.
No. 1 for Large Circular Saws and Nos. 2 and 3 for Small Circular and Mill Saws.

Nos.	0	1	2	3
Length ....Inches,	5½	5	3½	2¾
Weight ....Each, 1 lb. 4 oz.	1 lb.	6 oz.	2 oz.	
Each	$3.00	2.75	2.25	1.75
	4.80	4.40	3.80	2.80

One in a Box.

SAW GAUGES

No. 15   No. 20

GAUGING THE CLEANERS   **GAUGING THE SET**

The Single Gauge Regulates the Cleaners for Hardwood and the Double Gauge for Both Hard and Soft Wood. One End of the Straight Edge of These Gauges Has Been Slightly Beveled so That They May be Used for Gauging the Set, as Shown in the Cut.
No. 15 Atkin's Single Gauge ....Per Dozen, $1.50   No. 20 Atkin's Double Gauge ....Per Dozen, $2.00

SAW TOOLS

JOINTER, RAKER GAUGE AND SIDE FILE   **TOOTH SET GAUGE**   **SETTING BLOCK**

No. 3 Saw Tools, Consisting of Jointer, Raker Tooth Gauge, Side File, Set Gauge and Setting Block............Per Dozen Sets, $8.50
One Twelfth Dozen Sets in a Box.

Saw Sets.

REVOLVING SAW SET PATT 1874

No.   PER DOZEN.
2 Henry Disston & Sons' Patent Revolving Saw Set, $
HALF DOZEN IN A BOX.

Hotchkiss' Patent.   No. 25

Hotchkiss' Patent Hammer Saw Set, Iron Body, Steel Mandril and Anvil, $
25 Aiken's Patent Hammer Saw Set, Cast Steel,
ONE DOZEN IN A BOX.

German Saw Sets.

62 A German, Wood Handle, Six Cuts, with Screw Driver, $
HALF DOZEN IN A BOX.

140

Bench Shears and Sheet Iron Cutters.

Nos.   1   2   3
Each, $

Nos. 1 and 2.   No. 3.

No. 1 Machine is designed to cut Sheet Iron any width and any thickness up to ⅛ inch, and Copper, Brass, Steel and other metals in proportion, and is intended particularly for use upon the work bench. The power employed is simple, and the machine durable. It is manufactured in the most thorough manner, and is fully warranted. Weighs 11 pounds.

No. 2 Machine is of the same design, and for the same purpose as the No. 1, but for heavier work. It will cut Sheet Iron up to 3/32 inch in thickness. Weighs 27 pounds.

No. 3 Machine is similar to Nos. 1 and 2, and is for the same purpose. To this size is applied the Compound Lever, by which the power is greatly increased. By means of the slotted Connecting Bar, the Lever Handle can be operated in any position desired. This machine will cut Sheet Iron up to 3/16 inch in thickness. Weighs 55 pounds.

Buttle's Fire Pots.

Each.
$

Buttle's Patent,

In offering this Improved Fire Pot to the trade, we believe that we have secured and combined all the necessary improvements to make a perfect article for heating Soldering Irons—economy, durability and convenience being considered.

Soldering Coppers.

EXTRA FINISH.

												Per Pound.
With Square Points for common use; with Flat Points, for Bottoms, &c.,												$
Nos.	1½	2	3	4	5	6	7	8	9	10	12	
Weight, Per Pair,	1½	2	3	4	5	6	7	8	9	10	12 lbs.	

Per Dozen.

Soldering Copper Handles, $

Cast Iron Tinners' Stakes.

Hollow Mandrel.

Double Seaming, with Four Heads.

Mandrel.   No. 1 Conductor's.

Round Head.

Each.
$

Hollow Mandrel, 3 ft. 4 in., entire length,
Double Seaming, with Four Heads,
Extra Heads, for Double Seaming,
No. 0, Mandrel, 3 ft. 4 in. long to the Standard,
No. 1, Mandrel, 2 ft. 10 in. long to the Standard,
No. 1, Conductor, Turned, Large End, 15 in., Small End, 11½ in. long,
Round Head,

Wrought Iron Tinners' Stakes.
WITH STEEL FACES.

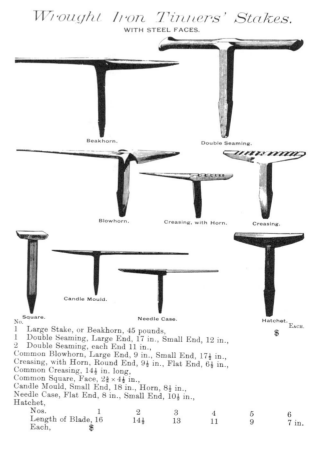

Beakhorn.   Double Seaming.

Blowhorn.   Creasing, with Horn.   Creasing.

Candle Mould.

Square.   Needle Case.   Hatchet.

Each.
$

No.
1   Large Stake, or Beakhorn, 45 pounds,
1   Double Seaming, Large End, 17 in., Small End, 12 in.,
2   Double Seaming, each End 11 in.
Common Blowhorn, Large End, 9 in., Small End, 17½ in.,
Creasing, with Horn, Round End, 9½ in., Flat End, 6½ in.,
Common Creasing, 14½ in. long,
Common Square, Face, 2⅝ × 4½ in.,
Candle Mould, Small End, 18 in., Horn, 8½ in.,
Needle Case, Flat End, 8 in., Small End, 10½ in.,
Hatchet,

Nos.	1	2	3	4	5	6
Length of Blade,	16	14½	13	11	9	7 in.
Each,	$					

Grooving Machines.

ENCASED.

No.		Each.
1	For Heavy Work, 20 in., with Rotary Standard,	$
	Extra Standards,	
	Extra Rollers,	

BRASS MOUNTED.

1	For Heavy Work, 20 in., with Standard,	$
	Extra Standards,	
	Extra Rollers,	

Crown Fluting Machines.

		Each.
6 in., No. 15 or 18 Rolls,		$
8 in., No. 15 or 18 Rolls,		

The Crown Fluting Machine has all the valuable features of the best machines in the market, and, in addition, possesses qualities of importance not to be found in other makes. The Spring is so placed that it will not be strained by the separation of the Rolls. The lower Roll projects free over the base plate, giving opportunity to do work which a post under the end of the Roll would interfere with. The machines are finished in a superior manner, with Swivel Clamp attachment, to fasten them either to the side or end of the table.

	Per Set.
Extra Fluter Heaters,	$

TINNERS' TOOLS AND MACHINES.

Tin Folding Machines.

O. W. STOW'S PATENT ADJUSTABLE BAR FOLDER.

Will turn Locks from 1-16 to 7-8 of an inch in width.

FOR TIN.

No.		Each.
0	20 in.,	$

This simple and admirable machine is decidedly the best in use. It forms a square joint, turns a narrow or wide lock, turns a round edge for wiring, and forms locks on very heavy plate with ease.

All the parts are now made by machinery, and are interchangeable, like a Waltham Watch or Springfield Rifle; that is, any part of one machine is exactly like the same part in another.

A graduated scale is connected with the Gauge, whereby the operator can determine at a glance the width of the lock the machine will form as adjusted.

Square Pan Swedges.

	Each.
Square Pan Swedge,	$

Square Pan Turners.

No.		
1	Steel, 20 in.,	$

Articles included in a Set of Tinners' Tools.

One Large Stake (or Beakhorn), No. 1,	$
One Blowhorn Stake,	
One Creasing Stake,	
One Square Stake,	
One Candle Mould Stake,	
One Needle Case Stake,	
One Set Hollow Punches, One each, $\frac{1}{2}$, $\frac{3}{4}$, 1, $1\frac{1}{2}$, $1\frac{3}{4}$ in.,	
One Set Solid Punches, Four Punches and Two Chisels,	
One Pair Shears, No. 4,	
One Raising Hammer, each No. 1 and No. 4, Handled,	
One Setting Hammer, each No. 2 and No. 3, Handled,	
One Riveting Hammer, No. 5,	
The Above Comprise a Full Set,	$

54

Stow's Encased Turning Machines

WITH EXTRA FACES, ADJUSTABLE BOXES, AND DUPLICATE PARTS.

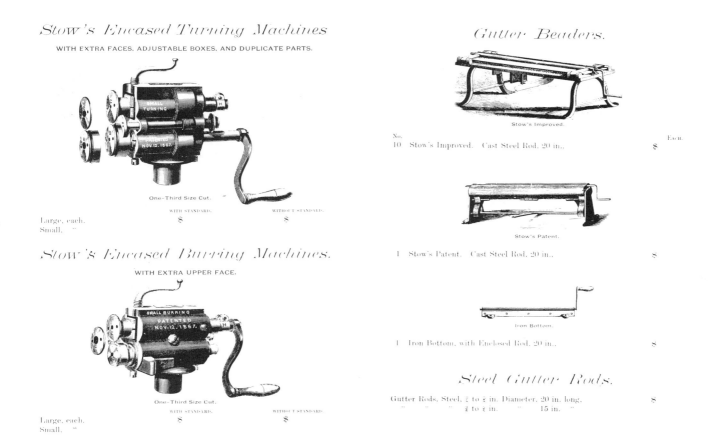

One-Third Size Cut.

	WITH STANDARD.	WITHOUT STANDARD.
Large, each.	$	$
Small, "		

Stow's Encased Burring Machines.

WITH EXTRA UPPER FACE.

One-Third Size Cut.

	WITH STANDARD.	WITHOUT STANDARD
Large, each.	$	$
Small, "		

Gutter Beaders.

Stow's Improved.

No.		EACH.
10	Stow's Improved. Cast Steel Rod, 20 in.,	$

Stow's Patent.

1	Stow's Patent. Cast Steel Rod, 20 in.,	$

Iron Bottom.

1	Iron Bottom, with Enclosed Rod, 20 in.,	$

Steel Gutter Rods.

Gutter Rods, Steel, ⅜ to ⅝ in. Diameter, 20 in. long,	$
" ⅜ to ⅝ in. " 15 in. "	

Sheet Iron Folding Machines.

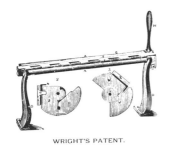

WRIGHT'S PATENT.

No.		EACH.
1	Wright's Patent Sheet Iron Folder, 30 in.,	$

WOOD BOTTOM.

1	Wood Bottom Sheet Iron Folder, 30 in.,	$

Burton's
Patent Double Seaming Machines.

NINE DISCS.

One-Sixth Size Cut.

	EACH.
Burton's Double Seamer, Complete,	$
Extra Discs,	

A Deflector for Stiffening Bottoms, and full sets of Discs for straight or flaring work accompany each Machine.

It is especially adapted for Pans.

Trammel Points.

Brass, with Cast-Steel Points.

No.		Per Dozen Pairs.
2	To fit Bar ¼ × ⅞ inches,	8

Bench Hooks.

Hotchkiss' Patent.

Reversible, Double Faced, Cast-Steel Hooks.

Per Dozen.
8

ONE DOZEN IN A BOX.

TRAMMEL POINTS

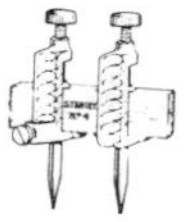

No. 4. Cast iron, steel points. For bars up to 1¼ inches wide....each 1.10
Cast brass, steel points. 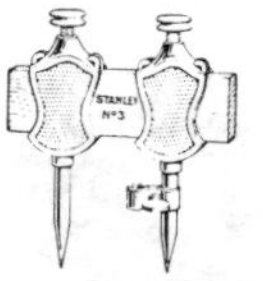

No. 1. For ⅝ inch bar.......each 1.40
No. 2. For 1 inch bar.......each 1.90
No. 3. For 1¼ inch bar.......each 2.35

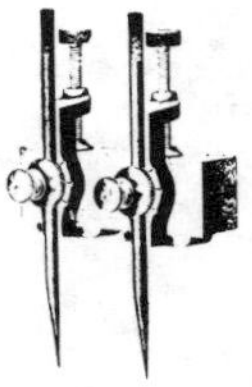

No. 59A. Will fit any bar from ¾ to 1⅛ inches wide................each 2.40

No. 50A. With 3 inch points, and spring point adjuster ....each 3.25
No. 50B. Same as above, without adjuster..........each 2.25

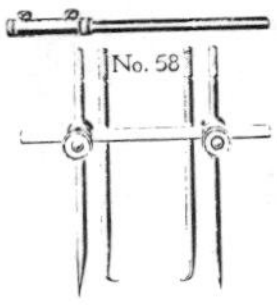

The beam of this tool is made of ⅜ inch round steel, with one side slightly flattened.
No. 58A. With 11 inch beam........................each 2.50
Extra 11 inch sections, with coupler................each .60

No. 5. Complete with one pair each long and short points ....each 3.00

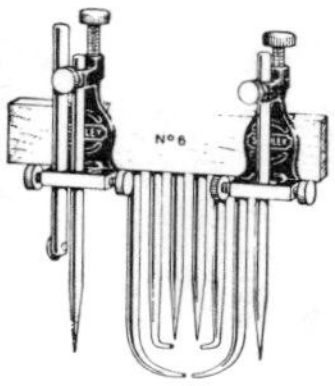

No. 6. Same as No. 5, with the addition of 4 curved points and a roller marker...................each 4.50

RULE TOOLS

Shows Tool Applied to Rule

Works on Carpenters' Ordinary Two Foot Rule (1 Inch Folded), and is Applied or Detached in an Instant; Gives a True Miter Line Gauge, Square and Depth Gauge ; Saves a Great Deal of Time and Vexatious Work ; is Very Light and Easily Carried in Vest, Trousers or Apron Pocket.
No. 10 Aluminum with Cast Brass Eccentric Lever Rule Fastener; Size 3 x 2¾ x 2⅝ in., ¼ in. Wide. Per Dozen, $4.50
One Dozen in an Easel Back Display Box.

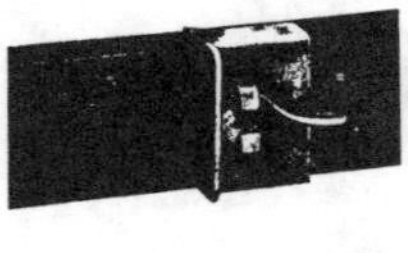

No. 100
RULE GAUGES

Clamps on any Standard Two Foot Rule, and can be Adjusted or Removed Instantly.
No. 100 Handy Rule Gauge.................Per Dozen, $1.75
One Dozen in a Box.

No. 92
BUTT GAUGES

This Gauge has Two Brass Bars, One Movable Within the Other. The Two Steel Blades or Markers at the Extreme End of the Inner Bar can be Moved to any Position by Means of Thumb Screw at Opposite End of Gauge.
No. 92 Rosewood Heads, Brass Plates..........Per Dozen, $21.00
One Twelfth Dozen in a Box.

No. 95
IMPROVED BUTT GAUGES

Has One Bar with Two Steel Cutters Fixed Upon it. When the Cutter at the Outer End of this Bar is Set for Gauging on the Edge of the Door, the Cutter at the Inner End of the Bar is Already Set for Gauging from the Back of the Jamb. The Other Bar has a Steel Cutter to Accurately Gauge for the Thickness of the Butt.
No. 95 Nickel-plated................:.......Per Dozen, $12.60
One Twelfth Dozen in a Box.

No. 94
With Two Bars; One for Gauging for Doors with Rabbeted Jambs and for Gauging from Moulded or Flat Casing; the Other for Gauging Thickness of Butts. Also Used as a Try Square.
No. 94 Nickel-plated Head and Bars..........Per Dozen, $17.00
One Twelfth Dozen in a Box.

No. 184
PANEL GAUGES

No. 184 Panel Gauge, Beechwood, Boxwood Thumb Screw, Oval Bar, Steel Points, 18 in. Long..Per Dozen, $5.30
Quarter Dozen in a Package

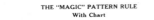

No. 186
SLITTING GAUGES

No. 186 Handled Slitting Gauge, With Roller, 17 in. Bar, Marked................................Per Dozen, $9.60
Quarter Dozen in a Package

LUMBER GAUGES

No. 00
Made of Aluminum, for Measuring Thickness of Lumber.
No. 00 ⅛, ¼, ⅜, ½, ¾, 1, 1¼, 1½, 1¾, 2 in.
One Twelfth Dozen in Box.
Per Dozen, $9.50

TINNERS' STEEL CIRCUMFERENCE RULES

One Side is a Circumference Rule. The Opposite Side Shows a Table of Measurements as Follows : Liquid Measure, Flaring ½ Pint to 5 Gallons; Dry Measure, Flaring, ¼ to 2 Bushels; Dry Measure, Straight, 1 Quart to 3 Bushels; Cans, Pitched Top, 1 to 10 Gallons; Cans, Flat Top, 1 to 200 Gallons.
No. 95 36 x 1¼ in., 16 Gauge, Plain....................................Each, $4.50

THE "MAGIC" PATTERN RULE
With Chart

For Laying Out Sheet Metal Elbow Patterns up to 14 Inches in Diameter and at Any Angle Desired. Consists of a ⅝ Inch Square Steel Bar, Marked Circumference Inches One Side, and Inches and 8ths Other Side. Fitted with Brass Sliding Trammel Heads with Set Screws, and Steel Points, All Nickel-plated. The Chart is 19 x 23 Inches in Size, Mounted on Linen and Very Durable, and Contains, Besides the Elbow Diagram, Rules for Cutting All Kinds of Flaring, Oval, Cylindrical, Cone-shaped Vessels, etc., with the Aid of the Magic. Besides all this, the Magic Can be Used for a Straight Edge, Rule, Circumference Rule and Trammel. Put up in Neat Hinged, Wooden Box and is Provided with Three Steel Ribbons of Different Gauges, Which May be Used According to Size of Elbow Wanted.
Magic Pattern Rule and Chart, Complete in Hinged Wooden Case............................Each, $8.50

TRAMMEL POINTS

BRONZE METAL
Polished Steel Points; with Pencil Holder, Attachable to Either Leg.

Nos.	1	2	3
Size	Small	Medium	Large
Length Points ....In.	1⅜	1¾	2
Length Over All..In.	3¾	4½	5¼
Per Dozen	$18.00	24.00	36.00

One Set in a Box.

IRON
Nickel-plated; Steel Points, Polished; the Socket will Take an Ordinary Pencil or Regular Carpenters Pencil.
No. 4 1⅜ in. Points; 3¾ in. Over All ....Per Dozen, $12.00
One Set in a Box.

BRASS
Polished Brass Trammel Heads and Pencil Socket; Tempered Steel Adjustable Points. Adapted for Use on Carpenter's Rule or Folding Rule of Ordinary Width; on Many Kinds of Work They Will Take the Place of Calipers and Dividers.
No. 99 Points ⅝ in. Long; Heads 1¾ in. Long; ⅞ in. Diameter......Per Dozen, $10.00
One Set in a Box.

144

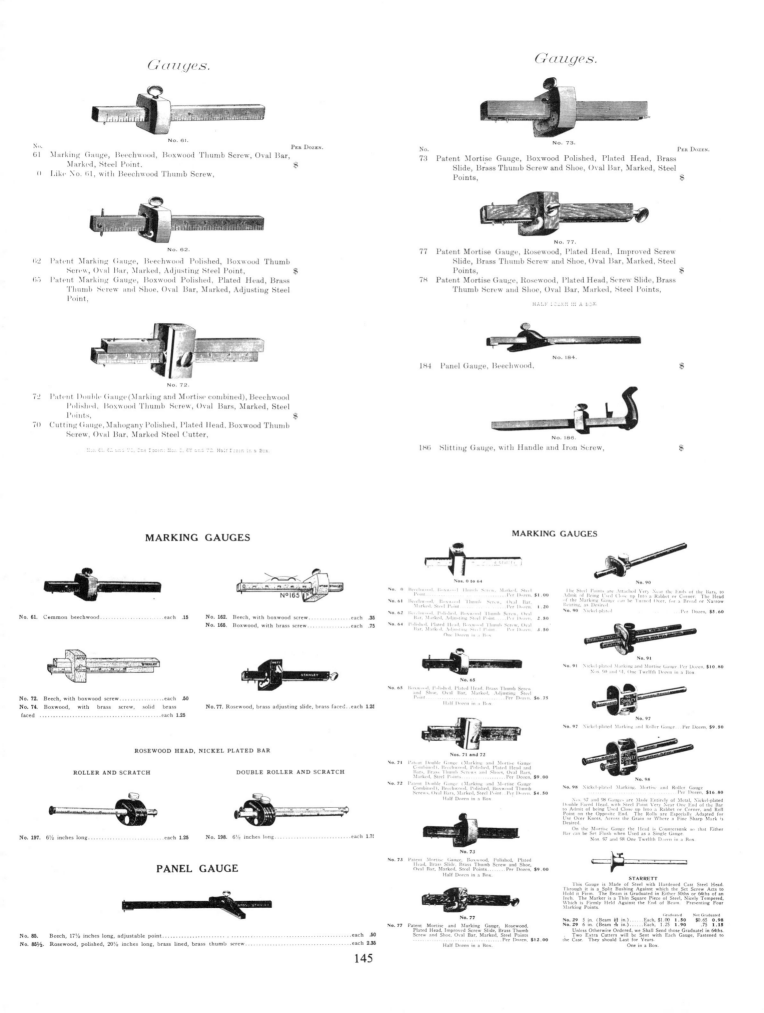

No. 61.

No.		PER DOZEN.
61	Marking Gauge, Beechwood, Boxwood Thumb Screw, Oval Bar, Marked, Steel Point.	$
0	Like No. 61, with Beechwood Thumb Screw,	

No. 62.

| 62 | Patent Marking Gauge, Beechwood Polished, Boxwood Thumb Screw, Oval Bar, Marked, Adjusting Steel Point, | $ |
| 65 | Patent Marking Gauge, Boxwood Polished, Plated Head, Brass Thumb Screw and Shoe, Oval Bar, Marked, Adjusting Steel Point, | |

No. 72.

| 72 | Patent Double Gauge (Marking and Mortise combined), Beechwood Polished, Boxwood Thumb Screw, Oval Bars, Marked, Steel Points, | $ |
| 70 | Cutting Gauge, Mahogany Polished, Plated Head, Boxwood Thumb Screw, Oval Bar, Marked Steel Cutter, | |

Nos. 61, 62 and 70, One Dozen; Nos. 0, 65 and 72, Half Dozen in a Box.

No. 73.

No.		PER DOZEN.
73	Patent Mortise Gauge, Boxwood Polished, Plated Head, Brass Slide, Brass Thumb Screw and Shoe, Oval Bar, Marked, Steel Points,	$

No. 77.

| 77 | Patent Mortise Gauge, Rosewood, Plated Head, Improved Screw Slide, Brass Thumb Screw and Shoe, Oval Bar, Marked, Steel Points, | $ |
| 78 | Patent Mortise Gauge, Rosewood, Plated Head, Screw Slide, Brass Thumb Screw and Shoe, Oval Bar, Marked, Steel Points, | |

HALF DOZEN IN A BOX.

No. 184.

| 184 | Panel Gauge, Beechwood, | $ |

No. 186.

| 186 | Slitting Gauge, with Handle and Iron Screw, | $ |

MARKING GAUGES

No. 61. Common beechwood.....................each .15

No. 162. Beech, with boxwood screw..............each .35
No. 165. Boxwood, with brass screw...............each .75

No. 72. Beech, with boxwood screw...............each .50
No. 74. Boxwood, with brass screw, solid brass faced ....each 1.25

No. 77. Rosewood, brass adjusting slide, brass faced..each 1.25

ROSEWOOD HEAD, NICKEL PLATED BAR

ROLLER AND SCRATCH

No. 197. 6½ inches long.......................each 1.25

DOUBLE ROLLER AND SCRATCH

No. 198. 6½ inches long.......................each 1.75

PANEL GAUGE

No. 85. Beech, 17½ inches long, adjustable point..each .50
No. 85½. Rosewood, polished, 20½ inches long, brass lined, brass thumb screw............................each 2.35

MARKING GAUGES

Nos. 0 to 64.

No. 0 Beechwood, Boxwood Thumb Screw, Marked, Steel Point...................................Per Dozen, $1.00
No. 61 Beechwood, Boxwood Thumb Screw, Oval Bar, Marked, Steel Point........................Per Dozen, 1.20
No. 62 Beechwood, Polished, Boxwood Thumb Screw, Oval Bar, Marked, Adjusting Steel Point......Per Dozen, 2.50
No. 64 Polished, Plated Head, Boxwood Thumb Screw, Oval Bar, Marked, Adjusting Steel Point......Per Dozen, 4.50
One Dozen in a Box.

No. 65.

No. 65 Boxwood, Polished, Plated Head, Brass Thumb Screw and Shoe, Oval Bar, Marked, Adjusting Steel Point.......................Per Dozen, $6.75
Half Dozen in a Box.

Nos. 71 and 72.

No. 71 Patent Double Gauge (Marking and Mortise Gauge Combined), Beechwood, Polished, Plated Head and Bars, Brass Thumb Screws and Shoes, Oval Bars, Marked, Steel Points.......................Per Dozen, $9.00
No. 72 Patent Double Gauge (Marking and Mortise Gauge Combined), Beechwood, Polished, Boxwood Thumb Screws, Oval Bars, Marked, Steel Point..Per Dozen, $4.50
Half Dozen in a Box.

No. 73.

No. 73 Patent Mortise Gauge, Boxwood, Polished, Plated Head, Brass Slide, Brass Thumb Screw and Shoe, Oval Bar, Marked, Steel Points.......Per Dozen, $9.00
Half Dozen in a Box.

No. 77.

No. 77 Patent Mortise and Marking Gauge, Rosewood, Plated Head, Improved Screw Slide, Brass Thumb Screw and Shoe, Oval Bar, Marked, Steel Points.......................Per Dozen, $12.00
Half Dozen in a Box.

No. 90.

The Steel Points are Attached Very Near the Ends of the Bars, to Admit of Being Used Close up Into a Rabbet or Corner, and The Head of the Marking Gauge can be Turned Over, for a Broad or Narrow Bearing, as Desired.
No. 90 Nickel-plated.........................Per Dozen, $5.60

No. 91.

No. 91 Nickel-plated Marking and Mortise Gauge..Per Dozen, $10.80
Nos. 90 and 91, One Twelfth Dozen in a Box.

No. 97.

No. 97 Nickel-plated Marking and Roller Gauge....Per Dozen, $9.50

No. 98.

No. 98 Nickel-plated Marking, Mortise and Roller Gauge.......................Per Dozen, $16.80

Nos. 97 and 98 Gauges are Made Entirely of Metal, Nickel-plated Double Faced Head, with Steel Point Very Near One End of the Bar to Admit of being Used Close up Into a Rabbet or Corner, and Roll Point on the Opposite End. The Rolls are Especially Adapted for Use Over Knots, Across the Grain or Where a Fine Sharp Mark is Desired.
On the Mortise Gauge the Head is Countersunk so that Either Bar can be Set Flush when Used as a Single Gauge.
Nos. 97 and 98 One Twelfth Dozen in a Box.

STARRETT

This Gauge is Made of Steel with Hardened Cast Steel Head. Through it is a Split Bushing Against which the Set Screw Acts to Hold it Firm. The Beam is Graduated in Either 50ths or 64ths of an Inch. The Marker is a Thin Square Piece of Steel, Nicely Tempered, Which is Firmly Held Against the End of Beam. Presenting Four Marking Points.

		Graduated		Not Graduated
No. 29	5 in. (Beam 11/16 in.).....Each, $1.00	1.50	$0.65	0.98
No. 29	6 in. (Beam 13/16 in.)....Each, 1.25	1.90	.75	1.15

Unless Otherwise Ordered, we Shall Send those Graduated in 64ths. Two Extra Cutters will be Sent with Each Gauge, Fastened to the Case. They should Last for Years.
One in a Box.

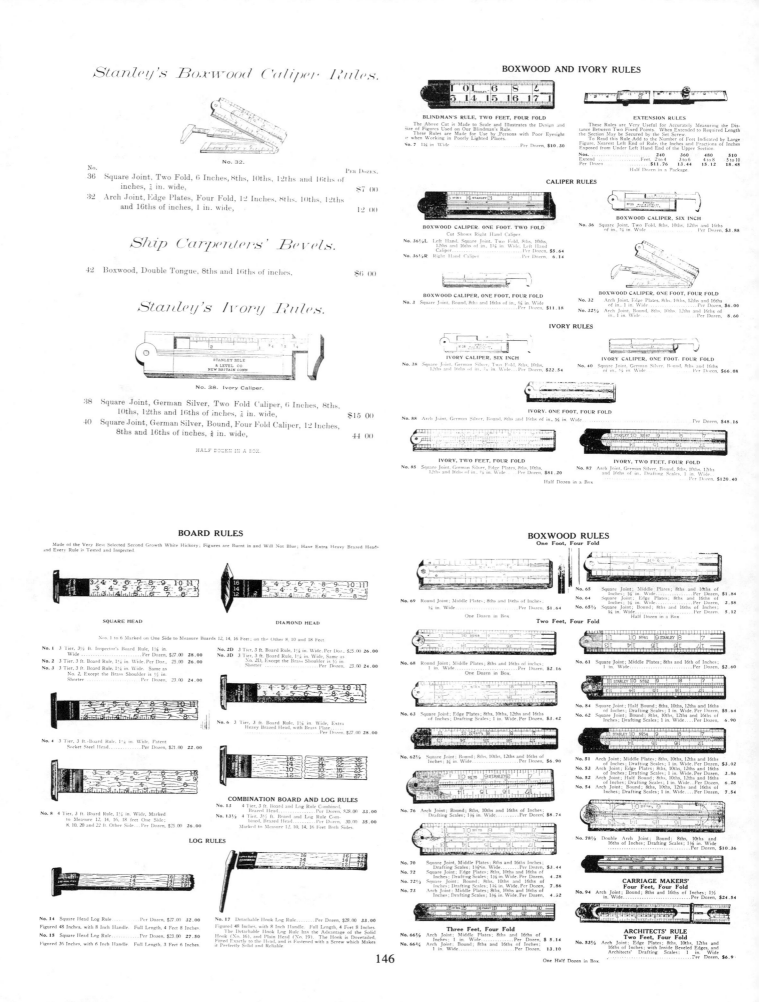

Stanley's Boxwood Caliper Rules.

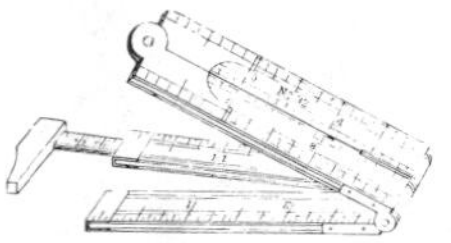

No. 32.

No.		Per Dozen.
36	Square Joint, Two Fold, 6 Inches, 8ths, 10ths, 12ths and 16ths of inches, ⅞ in. wide,	$7 00
32	Arch Joint, Edge Plates, Four Fold, 12 Inches, 8ths, 10ths, 12ths and 16ths of inches, 1 in. wide,	12 00

Ship Carpenters' Bevels.

42	Boxwood, Double Tongue, 8ths and 16ths of inches,	$6 00

Stanley's Ivory Rules.

No. 38. Ivory Caliper.

38	Square Joint, German Silver, Two Fold Caliper, 6 Inches, 8ths, 10ths, 12ths and 16ths of inches, ⅞ in. wide,	$15 00
40	Square Joint, German Silver, Bound, Four Fold Caliper, 12 Inches, 8ths and 16ths of inches, ⅝ in. wide,	44 00

HALF DOZEN IN A BOX.

BOXWOOD AND IVORY RULES

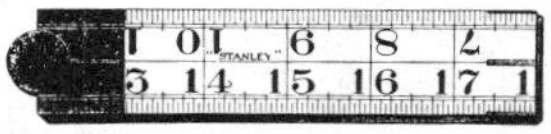

BLINDMAN'S RULE, TWO FEET, FOUR FOLD

The Above Cut is Made to Scale and Illustrates the Design and Size of Figures Used on Our Blindman's Rule.
These Rules are Made for Use by Persons with Poor Eyesight or when Working in Poorly Lighted Places.

No. 7 1⅜ in. Wide .... Per Dozen, $10.30

EXTENSION RULES

These Rules are Very Useful for Accurately Measuring the Distance Between Two Fixed Points. When Extended to Required Length the Section May be Secured by the Set Screw.
To Read this Rule Add to the Number of Feet Indicated by Large Figure, Nearest Left End of Rule, the Inches and Fractions of Inches Exposed from Under Left Hand End of the Upper Section.

Nos.	240	360	480	510
Extend .... Feet,	2 to 4	3 to 6	4 to 8	5 to 10
Per Dozen	$11.76	13.44	15.12	18.48

Half Dozen in a Package.

CALIPER RULES

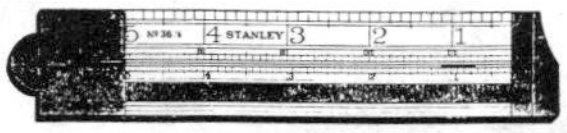

BOXWOOD CALIPER, ONE FOOT, TWO FOLD

Cut Shows Right Hand Caliper.

No. 36½L Left Hand, Square Joint, Two Fold, 8ths, 10ths, 12ths and 16ths of in., 1⅜ in. Wide, Left Hand Caliper .... Per Dozen, $5.64

No. 36½R Right Hand Caliper .... Per Dozen, 6.14

BOXWOOD CALIPER, SIX INCH

No. 36 Square Joint, Two Fold, 8ths, 10ths, 12ths and 16ths of in., ⅞ in. Wide .... Per Dozen, $3.88

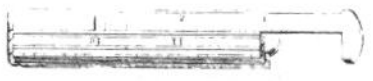

BOXWOOD CALIPER, ONE FOOT, FOUR FOLD

No. 3 Square Joint, Bound, 8ths and 16ths of in., ⅝ in. Wide .... Per Dozen, $11.18

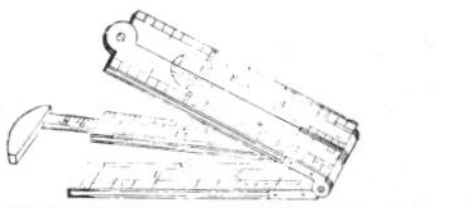

BOXWOOD CALIPER, ONE FOOT, FOUR FOLD

No. 32 Arch Joint, Edge Plates, 8ths, 10ths, 12ths and 16ths of in., 1 in. Wide .... Per Dozen, $6.00

No. 32½ Arch Joint, Bound, 8ths, 10ths, 12ths and 16ths of in., 1 in. Wide .... Per Dozen, 8.60

IVORY RULES

IVORY CALIPER, SIX INCH

No. 38 Square Joint, German Silver, Two Fold, 8ths, 10ths, 12ths and 16ths of in., ⅞ in. Wide ... Per Dozen, $22.54

IVORY CALIPER, ONE FOOT, FOUR FOLD

No. 40 Square Joint, German Silver, Bound, 8ths and 16ths of in., ⅝ in. Wide .... Per Dozen, $66.08

IVORY, ONE FOOT, FOUR FOLD

No. 88 Arch Joint, German Silver, Bound, 8ths and 16ths of in., ⅝ in. Wide .... Per Dozen, $48.16

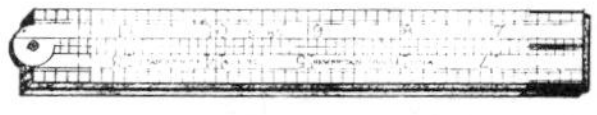

IVORY, TWO FEET, FOUR FOLD

No. 85 Square Joint, German Silver, Edge Plates, 8ths, 10ths, 12ths and 16ths of in., ⅞ in. Wide ... Per Dozen, $81.20

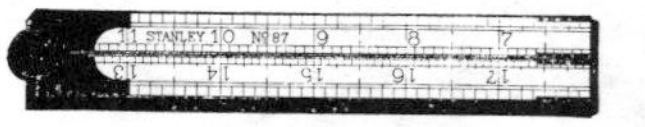

IVORY, TWO FEET, FOUR FOLD

No. 87 Arch Joint, German Silver, Bound, 8ths, 10ths, 12ths and 16ths of in., Drafting Scales, 1 in. Wide .... Per Dozen, $120.40

Half Dozen in a Box.

BOARD RULES

Made of the Very Best Selected Second Growth White Hickory; Figures are Burnt in and Will Not Blur; Have Extra Heavy Brazed Heads and Every Rule is Tested and Inspected.

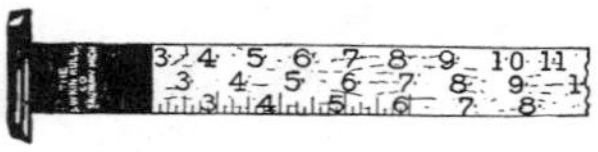

SQUARE HEAD

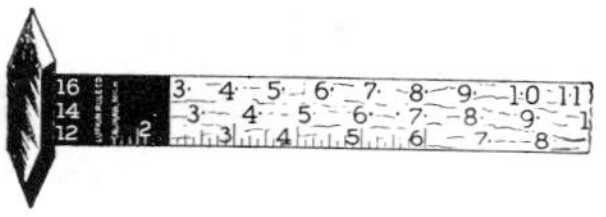

DIAMOND HEAD

Nos. 1 to 6 Marked on One Side to Measure Boards 12, 14, 16 Feet; on the Other 8, 10 and 18 Feet.

No. 1 3 Tier, 3½ ft. Inspector's Board Rule, 1⅛ in. Wide .... Per Dozen, $27.00 28.00

No. 2 3 Tier, 3 ft. Board Rule, 1⅛ in. Wide. Per Doz., 25.00 26.00

No. 3 3 Tier, 3 ft. Board Rule, 1⅛ in. Wide. Same as No. 2, Except the Brass Shoulder is ½ in. Shorter .... Per Dozen, 23.00 24.00

No. 2D 3 Tier, 3 ft. Board Rule, 1⅛ in. Wide. Per Doz., $25.00 26.00

No. 3D 3 Tier, 3 ft. Board Rule, 1⅛ in. Wide, Same as No. 2D, Except the Brass Shoulder is ½ in. Shorter .... Per Dozen, 23.00 24.00

No. 4 3 Tier, 3 ft. Board Rule, 1⅛ in. Wide, Patent Socket Steel Head .... Per Dozen, $21.00 22.00

No. 6 3 Tier, 3 ft. Board Rule, 1⅛ in. Wide, Extra Heavy Brazed Head, with Brass Plate .... Per Dozen, $27.00 28.00

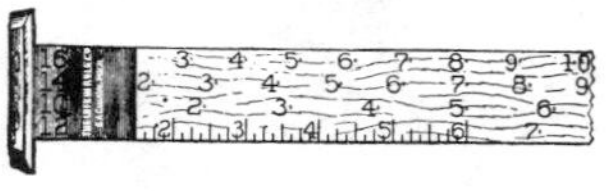

No. 8 4 Tier, 3 ft. Board Rule, 1½ in. Wide, Marked to Measure 12, 14, 16, 18 feet One Side; 8, 10, 20 and 22 ft. Other Side ... Per Dozen, $25.00 26.00

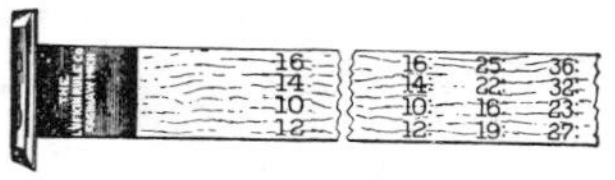

COMBINATION BOARD AND LOG RULES

No. 13 4 Tier, 3 ft. Board and Log Rule Combined, Brazed Head .... Per Dozen, $28.00 33.00

No. 13½ 4 Tier, 3½ ft. Board and Log Rule Combined, Brazed Head .... Per Dozen, 30.00 35.00

Marked to Measure 12, 10, 14, 16 Feet Both Sides.

LOG RULES

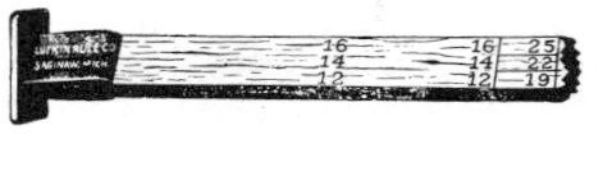

No. 14 Square Head Log Rule .... Per Dozen, $27.00 32.00

Figured 48 Inches, with 8 Inch Handle. Full Length, 4 Feet 8 Inches.

No. 15 Square Head Log Rule .... Per Dozen, $23.00 27.50

Figured 36 Inches, with 6 Inch Handle. Full Length, 3 Feet 6 Inches.

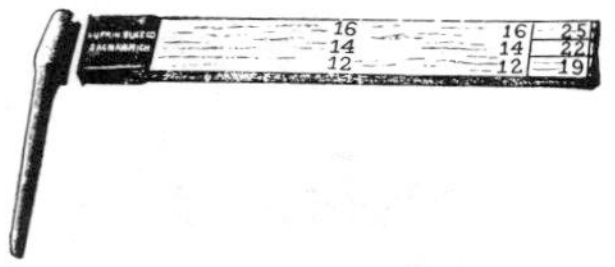

No. 17 Detachable Hook Log Rule .... Per Dozen, $28.00 33.00

Figured 48 Inches, with 8 Inch Handle. Full Length, 4 Feet 8 Inches.
The Detachable Hook Log Rule has the Advantage of the Solid Hook (No. 16), and Plain Head (No. 19). The Hook is Dovetailed, Fitted Exactly to the Head, and is Fastened with a Screw which Makes it Perfectly Solid and Reliable.

BOXWOOD RULES

One Foot, Four Fold

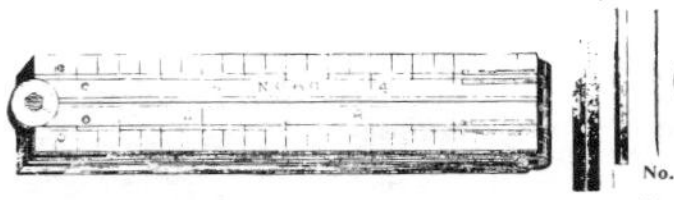

No. 69 Round Joint; Middle Plates; 8ths and 16ths of Inches, ⅝ in. Wide .... Per Dozen, $1.64

One Dozen in Box.

No. 65 Square Joint; Middle Plates; 8ths and 16ths of Inches; ⅝ in. Wide .... Per Dozen, $1.84

No. 64 Square Joint; Edge Plates; 8ths and 16ths of Inches; ⅝ in. Wide .... Per Dozen, 2.58

No. 65½ Square Joint; Bound; 8ths and 16ths of Inches; ⅝ in. Wide .... Per Dozen, 5.12

Half Dozen in a Box.

Two Feet, Four Fold

No. 68 Round Joint; Middle Plates; 8ths and 16ths of inches; 1 in. Wide .... Per Dozen, $2.16

One Dozen in Box.

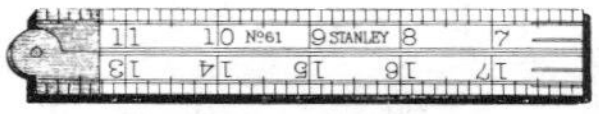

No. 61 Square Joint; Middle Plates; 8ths and 16th of Inches; 1 in. Wide .... Per Dozen, $2.60

No. 63 Square Joint; Edge Plates; 8ths, 10ths, 12ths and 16ths of Inches; Drafting Scales; 1 in. Wide. Per Dozen, $3.42

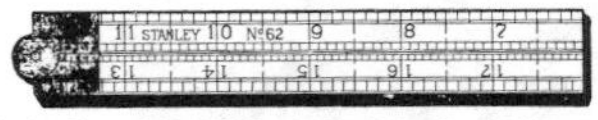

No. 84 Square Joint; Half Bound; 8ths, 10ths, 12ths and 16ths of Inches; Drafting Scales; 1 in. Wide. Per Dozen, $5.64

No. 62 Square Joint; Bound; 8ths, 10ths, 12ths and 16ths of Inches; Drafting Scales; 1 in. Wide ... Per Dozen, 6.90

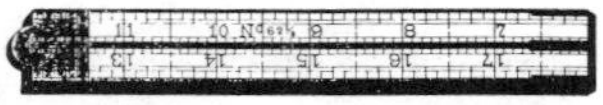

No. 62½ Square Joint; Bound; 8ths, 10ths, 12ths and 16ths of Inches; ¾ in. Wide .... Per Dozen, $6.90

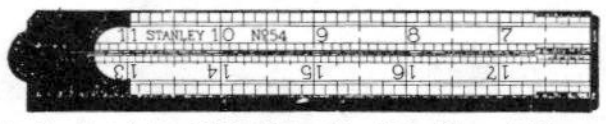

No. 51 Arch Joint; Middle Plates; 8ths, 10ths, 12ths and 16ths of Inches; Drafting Scales; 1 in. Wide. Per Dozen, $3.02

No. 53 Arch Joint; Edge Plates; 8ths, 10ths, 12ths and 16ths of Inches; Drafting Scales; 1 in. Wide. Per Dozen, 3.86

No. 52 Arch Joint; Half Bound; 8ths, 10ths, 12ths and 16ths of Inches; Drafting Scales; 1 in. Wide ... Per Dozen, 6.28

No. 54 Arch Joint; Bound; 8ths, 10ths, 12ths and 16ths of Inches; Drafting Scales; 1 in. Wide ... Per Dozen, 7.54

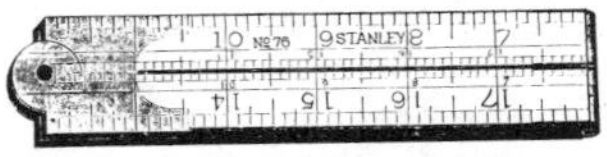

No. 76 Arch Joint; Bound; 8ths, 10ths and 16ths of Inches; Drafting Scales; 1⅜ in. Wide .... Per Dozen, $8.74

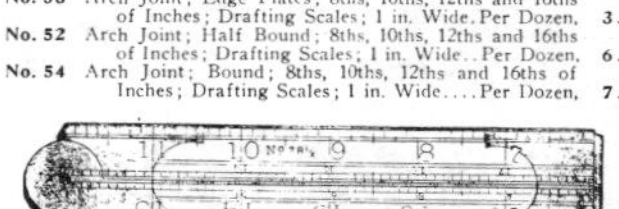

No. 78½ Double Arch Joint; Bound; 8ths, 10ths and 16ths of Inches; Drafting Scales; 1⅜ in. Wide .... Per Dozen, $10.36

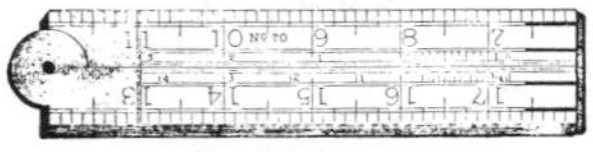

No. 70 Square Joint, Middle Plates; 8ths and 16ths Inches; Drafting Scales; 1⅜ in. Wide .... Per Dozen, $3.44

No. 72 Square Joint; Edge Plates; 8ths, 10ths and 16ths of Inches; Drafting Scales; 1⅜ in. Wide. Per Dozen, 4.28

No. 72½ Square Joint; Bound; 8ths, 10ths and 16ths of Inches; Drafting Scales; 1⅜ in. Wide. Per Dozen, 7.86

No. 73 Arch Joint; Middle Plates; 8ths, 10ths and 16ths of Inches; Drafting Scales; 1⅜ in. Wide. Per Dozen, 4.52

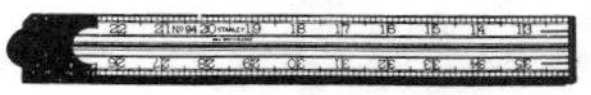

CARRIAGE MAKERS' Four Feet, Four Fold

No. 94 Arch Joint; Bound; 8ths and 16ths of Inches; 1½ in. Wide .... Per Dozen, $24.54

Three Feet, Four Fold

No. 66½ Arch Joint; Middle Plates; 8ths and 16ths of Inches; 1 in. Wide .... Per Dozen, $5.14

No. 66¾ Arch Joint; Bound; 8ths and 16ths of Inches; 1 in. Wide .... Per Dozen, 13.10

One Half Dozen in Box.

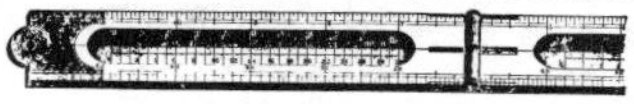

ARCHITECTS' RULE Two Feet, Four Fold

No. 53½ Arch Joint; Edge Plates; 8ths, 10ths, 12ths and 16ths of Inches; with Inside Beveled Edges, and Architects' Drafting Scales; 1 in. Wide .... Per Dozen, $6.9

Stanley's One Foot Boxwood Rules.

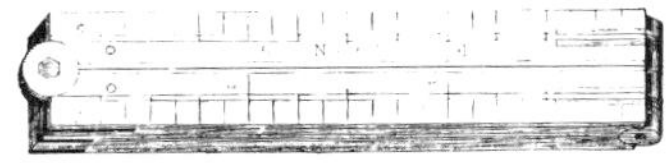

No. 69.

No.		PER DOZEN.
69	Round Joint, Middle Plates, 8ths and 16ths of inches, ⅝ in. wide,	$3 00

No. 65.

65	Square Joint, Middle Plates, 8ths and 16ths of inches, ⅝ in. wide,	$3 50
65½	" " Bound. " " " " ⅝ in. "	11 00

No. 57.

55	Arch Joint, Middle Plates, 8ths and 16ths of inches, ⅝ in. wide,	$4 00
56	" " Edge " " " " ⅝ in. "	6 00
57	" " Bound, " " " " ⅝ in. "	12 00

Stanley's Two Feet, Four Fold, Narrow Rules.

No. 68.

68	Round Joint, Middle Plate, 8ths and 16ths of inches. 1 in. wide,	$4 00
61	Square " " " " " 1 in. "	5 00

HALF DOZEN IN A BOX.

Stanley's Two Feet, Four Fold, Broad Rules.

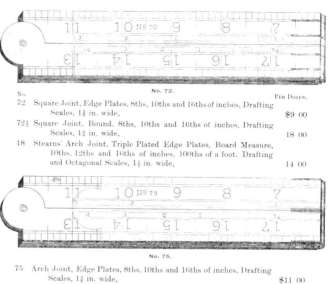

No. 72.

No.		PER DOZEN.
72	Square Joint, Edge Plates, 8ths, 10ths and 16ths of inches, Drafting Scales, 1⅜ in. wide,	$9 00
72½	Square Joint, Bound, 8ths, 10ths and 16ths of inches, Drafting Scales, 1⅜ in. wide,	18 00
18	Stearns' Arch Joint, Triple Plated Edge Plates, Board Measure, 10ths, 12ths and 16ths of inches, 100ths of a foot, Drafting and Octagonal Scales, 1½ in. wide,	14 00

No. 75.

75	Arch Joint, Edge Plates, 8ths. 10ths and 16ths of inches, Drafting Scales, 1⅜ in. wide,	$11 00
76	Arch Joint, Bound, 8ths, 10ths and 16ths of inches, Drafting Scales, 1⅜ in. wide.	20 00

Stanley's Two Feet Board Measures

81	Four Fold, Arch Joint, Edge Plates, 12th and 16ths of inches, Drafting Scales, 1⅜ in. wide,	$13 00

HALF DOZEN IN A BOX.

Stanley's Two Feet, Four Fold, Narrow Rules.

No. 63.

No.		PER DOZEN.
63	Square Joint, Edge Plates, 8ths, 10ths, 12ths and 16ths of inches, Drafting Scales, 1 in. wide,	$7 00
84	Square Joint, Half Bound, 8ths, 10ths, 12ths and 16ths of inches, Drafting Scales, 1 in. wide,	12 00
62	Square Joint, Bound, 8ths, 10ths, 12ths and 16ths of inches, Drafting Scales, 1 in. wide,	15 00
51	Arch Joint, Middle Plates, 8ths, 10ths, 12ths and 16ths of inches, Drafting Scales, 1 in. wide,	6 00
53	Arch Joint, Edge Plates, 8ths, 10ths, 12ths and 16ths of inches, Drafting Scales, 1 in. wide,	8 00

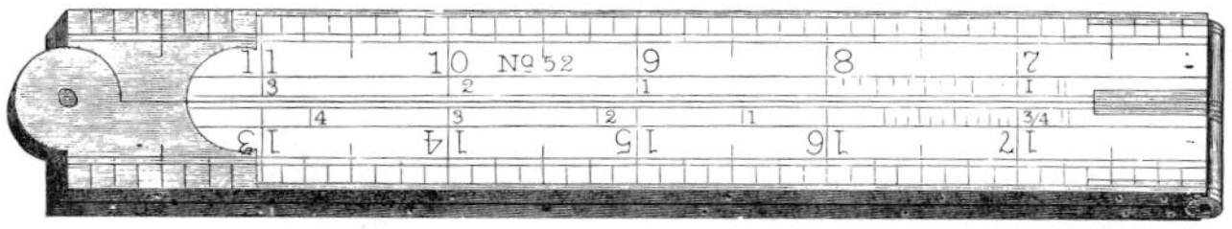

No. 52.

52	Arch Joint, Half Bound, 8ths, 10ths, 12ths and 16ths of inches, Drafting Scales, 1 in. wide,	$13 00
54	Arch Joint, Bound, 8ths, 10ths, 12ths and 16ths of inches, Drafting Scales, 1 in. wide,	16 00
59	Double Arch Joint, Bitted, 8ths, 10ths, 12ths and 16ths of inches, Drafting Scales. 1 in. wide,	9 00

HALF DOZEN IN A BOX.

Stanley's Ivory One Foot Four Fold Rules.

No.		PER DOZEN.
90	Round Joint, Brass Middle Plates, 8ths and 16ths of inches, ⅝ in. wide,	$10 00
92½	Square Joint, German Silver Middle Plates, 8ths and 16ths of inches, ⅝ in. wide,	14 00
91	Square Joint, German Silver Edge Plates, 8ths, 10ths, 12ths and 16ths of inches, ¾ in. wide,	23 00

HALF DOZEN IN A BOX.

Stanley's Board, Log and Wood Measures.

No. 43½.

No. 49.

43½	Board Stick, Flat, Hickory, Cast-Brass Head and Tip, 6 lines, 12 to 22 feet. 3 feet long,	$12 00
49	Board Stick, Flat, Hickory, Steel Head, Brazed, Extra Strong, 6 lines, 12 to 22 feet, 3 feet long,	26 00

Yard Sticks.

41	Brass Tipped, Polished,	$3 50
50	Hickory, Brass Capped Ends, Polished,	4 50

147

Measuring Tapes.

Plated.

Plastic.

No.		Per Dozen.
	Patent Spring, Nickel Plated Cases.	
24	3 feet, with Patent Stop, Linen Tape, ¼ in. wide.	$
25	5 " " " " " ¼ in. "	
	Patent Spring, Plastic Cases.	
26	3 feet, with Patent Stop, Linen Tape, ¼ in. wide,	
27	5 " " " " " ¼ in. "	

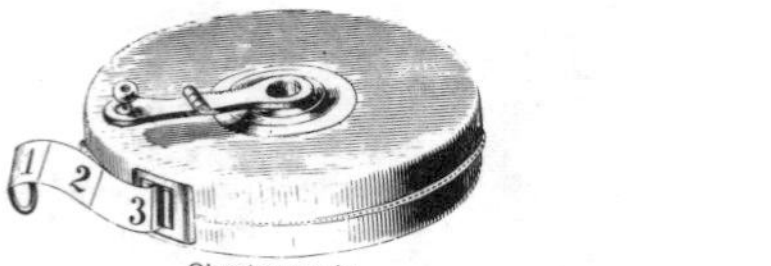
Chesterman's.

34 L Metallic Tape, Patent Leather Case, with Folding Handle.

Feet,	50	66	75	100
Price, each,	$			

Asses' Skin.

Patent Leather.

Asses' Skin, Brass Bound Case, with Folding Handle, Cotton Tapes, ½ in. wide.

No.	30	31	32	33	34	35	36	37
Feet,	25	30	40	50	66	75	80	100
Per Dozen, $								

Patent Leather Case, with Folding Handle, Best Cotton Tapes, ½ in. wide.

No.	40	41	42	43	45	46	47	48
Feet,	25	30	40	50	66	75	80	100
Per Dozen, $								

HALF DOZEN IN A BOX.

+K. & E. STEEL TAPES

Prices Given are Manufacturers' Lists. Net Prices Quoted on Application.

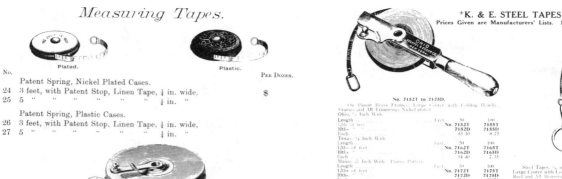

No. 7152T to 7175D.

On Patent Brass Frames; Large Center with Folding Handle, Frames and All Trimmings Nickel-plated.

Ohio, ½ Inch Wide

Length .... Feet,	50	100
12th of feet	No. 7152T	7155T
10ths " "	7152D	7155D
Each	$5.10	8.75

Texas, ⅜ Inch Wide

Length .... Feet,	50	100
12ths of feet	No. 7162T	7165T
10ths " "	7162D	7165D
Each	$4.40	7.55

Maine, ⅝ Inch Wide; Fames Pattern

Length .... Feet,	50	100
12ths of feet	No. 7172T	7175T
10ths " "	7172D	7175D
Each	$5.10	$8.75

One in a Box

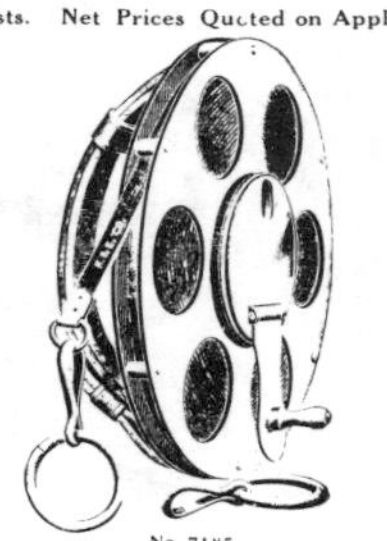

No. 7185

BERKELEY

Steel Tapes, ¼ in. Wide, Metal Reel with Leather Strap Handle. Large Center with Long Folding Handle; Two Handles for Tape Line, Reel and All Mountings Nickel-plated; Graduations Begin on the Line.

10th of Feet	No. 7182D	No. 7185D
Length .... Feet,	50	100
Each	$7.00	$12.00

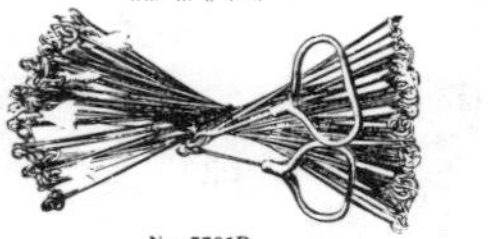

No. 7781B

+MEASURING CHAINS

Steel, U. S. Standard

		Each.
No. 7780A	Steel, W. G. 12, Brass Handles, Oval Rings, 50 Feet	$4.50
No. 7780B	Steel, W. G. 12, Brass Handles, Oval Rings, 100 Feet	8.00
No. 7780C	Steel, W. G. 12, Brass Handles, Oval Rings, 33 Feet (50 Links)	3.50
No. 7780D	Steel, W. G. 12, Brass Handles, Oval Rings, 66 Feet (100 Links)	6.50
No. 7181A	Steel, W. G. 12, Brass Handles, Brazed Links and Rings, 50 feet	6.00
No. 7781B	Steel, W. G. 12, Brass Handles, Brazed Links and Rings, 100 Feet	11.00
No. 7781C	Steel, W. G. 12, Brass Handles, Brazed Links and Rings, 33 Feet (50 Links)	5.50
No. 7781D	Steel, W. G. 12, Brass Handles, Brazed Links and Rings, 66 Feet (100 Links)	10.00

Chain No. 7781B has a Spring-hook (Snap) at 50 Feet, so that it can be Separated There and the Handle Attached for Using it as a 50 Foot Chain.

Iron, U. S. Standard

No. 7786A	Iron, W. G. 8, Brass Handles, 2 Round Rings, 50 Feet	$2.50
No. 7786B	Iron, W. G. 8, Brass Handles, 2 Round Rings, 100 Feet	3.50
No. 7786C	Iron, W. G. 8, Brass Handles, 2 Round Rings, 33 Feet (50 Links)	2.00
No. 7786D	Iron, W. G. 8, Brass Handles, 2 Round Rings, 66 Feet (100 Links)	3.20
No. 7787A	Iron, W. G. 8, Brass Handles, 3 Sawed Oval Rings, 50 Feet	3.50
No. 7787B	Iron, W. G. 8, Brass Handles, 3 Sawed Oval Rings, 100 Feet	5.50
No. 7787C	Iron, W. G. 8, Brass Handles, 3 Sawed Oval Rings, 33 Feet (50 Links)	2.70
No. 7787D	Iron, W. G. 8, Brass Handles, 3 Sawed Oval Rings, 66 Feet (100 Links)	4.25

+EXCELSIOR BAND CHAINS

The Excelsior Band Chains are of Heavy Blued Steel Ribbon ¼ Inch Wide, (Except No. 7668). They are Graduated and Marked by Rivets at Every Foot or Link and Numbered at Every 5 Feet or 5 Links on Brass Plates Riveted to the Tape, with Additional Number Marks at Every 10 Feet or Links. The Number Plates Have Rounded Edges so That They Will Not Catch, and They Are Notched to Insure Correct Locating of the Plumbing Cord.

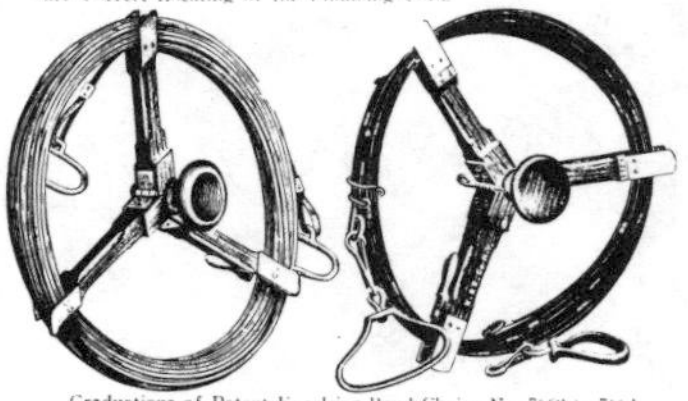
Graduations of Patent Excelsior Band Chains No. 7660 to 7663

No. 7660	Excelsior Band Chains; ¼ in. Wide; 50 Feet; Graduated Every Foot, End-feet to 10ths..Each,	$4.00
No. 7660B	Excelsior Band Chains; ¼ in. Wide; 100 Feet; Graduated Every Foot, End-feet to 10ths..Each,	5.00
No. 7660C	Excelsior Band Chains; ¼ in. Wide; 200 Feet; Graduated Every Foot, End-feet to 10ths..Each,	7.50
No. 7660D	Excelsior Band Chains; ¼ in. wide; 300 Feet; Graduated Every Foot, End-feet to 10ths..Each,	10.00

+EXCELSIOR RAILROAD BAND CHAIN

Graduations of Excelsior Band Chains No. 7668.

No. 7668 Excelsior Band Chain, Extra Heavy, for Railroad Work, Etc.; ⅛ in. Wide; 100 Feet, Graduated Every Foot on Brass Sleeves, End-feet to 10ths; Very Substantial Band Chain for Rough Work.. Handles Attached by Strong Spring Hooks and Solid Rings; Best Quality of Workmanship Throughout; Reel Similar to 7660; a Correct and Very Substantial Band Chain for Rough Work.. ....Each, $10.00

KEUFFEL AND ESSER TAPES

POPULAR LINEN

Bend Leather Case; Nickel-plated Trimmings; Flat Folding Handles; Center Adjustable for Wear; Stout Linen Tape; End Reinforced with Leather; Marked in Feet, Inches and 12ths on One Side Only.

Width of Tape ⅝ Inch.

Nos.	**7512T**	**7514T**	**7515T**
Length .... Feet,	50	75	100
Per Dozen	$19.00	23.75	28.50
Per Dozen	**32.30**	**40.36**	**48.44**

DARTMOUTH METALLIC

Bend Leather Case; Nickel-plated Trimmings; Long Folding Handle; Center Adjustable for Wear; Tape Interwoven with Metal and Leather; Reinforced Ends; Marked in Feet; Inches and 12ths on One side only.

Width of Tape, ⅝ Inch.

Nos.	**7440T**	**7442T**	**7444T**	**7445T**
Length ....Feet,	25	50	75	100
Per Dozen	$19.80	29.25	36.25	45.60
Per Dozen	**33.66**	**49.72**	**61.62**	**79.72**

No. 7442D 50 ft.; Marked in 10ths ..... Per Dozen, $29.25 **49.72**

One Half Dozen in Box.

HOME STEEL

Bend Leather Case; Nickel-plated Trimmings; Large Center, Long Folding Handle; Center Adjustable for Wear; Flexible Steel Tape; Marked in Feet, Inches and 12ths on One Side Only.

Width of Tape, ⅜ Inch.

Nos.	**7350T**	**7352T**	**7354T**	**7355T**
Length ....Feet,	25	50	75	100
Each	$3.20	3.90	5.10	6.60
Each	**5.76**	**7.00**	**9.18**	**11.88**

One in a Box

LILIPUT STEEL

Bend Leather Case; Nickel-plated Trimmings, Patent Center; Adjustable for Wear; Long Swiveling Flush Folding Handle Opened by Pushing Handle Pin from Opposite Side of Case; Marked on One Side Only.

Width of Tape, ¼ Inch.

No. 7272T 50 ft.; Steel; Marked in Feet, Inches and 12ths. ....Each, $4.45 **8.00**

No. 7272D 50 ft.; Steel; Marked in 10ths ....Each, $4.45 **8.00**

One in a Box.

CHESTERMAN TAPES

Russet Leather Case; Brass Trimmings and Folding Handle.

No. 34L 50 ft. Linen Metallic Tape; ⅝ in. Wide; Marked in Feet, Inches and 12ths........ ....Per Dozen, $31.20 **56.16**

No. 38L 50 ft.; ⅜ in. Steel Tape; Marked in Feet, Inches and 12ths........Per Dozen, $86.40 **155.50**

One Quarter Dozen in Box.

STARRETT STEEL TAPE

Nickel-plated Steel Case; Folding Flush Handles; Marked in Feet, Inches and 12ths on One Side Only.

Width of Tape, ⅜ Inch.

No. 1505				
Length ....Feet,	25	50	75	100
Each	$2.75	3.40	4.50	5.75
	4.96	**6.12**	**8.10**	**10.36**

One in a Box.

POCKET TAPES

Nickel-plated Case, Spring Wind, Center Stop; Good Quality ¼ Inch Cotton Tape, Marked in Inches and 8ths on One Side; Length 5 Feet.

No. 165 Universal ....Per Dozen, **$2.00**

One Dozen in Display Box.

Nickel-plated Case, Spring Wind, Center Stop; ¼ Inch Flexible Steel Tape; Marked in Inches and 16ths.

No. 3143 3 Feet........Per Dozen, **$4.50**

One Dozen in Display Box.

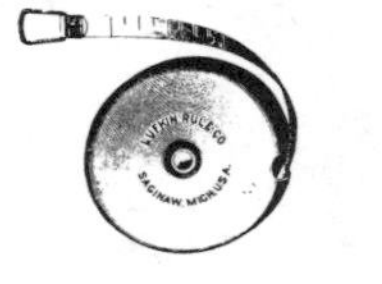

Nickel-plated Brass Case, Spring Wind, Center Stop; ¼ Inch Enameled Linen Tape, Marked on One Side in Inches and 8ths.

No. 173 3 Feet..........Per Dozen, **$6.00**

No. 175 5 Feet..........Per Dozen, **7.00**

One Dozen in Box.

POCKET STEEL TAPES

Round Edge Nickel-plated Brass Case, Spring Wind, Center Stop; Marked Inches and 16ths One Side Only; Width of Tape ¼ Inch.

Nos.	**143**	**145**	**146**	**148**
Length .....Feet,	3	5	6	8
Per Dozen	$7.00	9.00	10.00	14.00
	10.50	**13.50**	**15.00**	**21.00**

One Half Dozen in Box.

German Silver Case, Spring Wind, Center Stop, Marked Inches and 16ths, One Side Only; Width of Tape ¼ Inch.

Nos.	**153**	**155**	**156**	**158**	**1510**
Length, Ft.,	3	5	6	8	10
Per Dozen	$8.50	11.00	12.00	18.00	25.00
	13.00	**16.50**	**18.00**	**27.00**	**37.00**

One Half Dozen in Box.

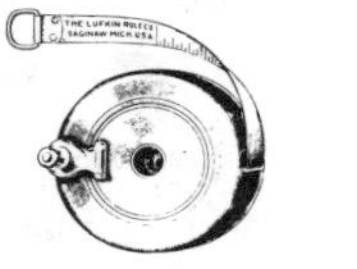

Nickel-plated Case; Marked in Feet, Inches and 16ths, One Side Only; Width of Tape ⅜ Inch.

Nos.	**108**	**112**	**115**	**120**
Length ....Feet,	8	12	15	20
Per Dozen	$15.00	18.00	21.00	24.00
	22.50	**27.00**	**31.50**	**36.00**

One Half Dozen in Box.

MEASURING TAPES

Nickel-plated Case, Flush Winding Device; Closely Woven Cotton Tape Marked on One Side Only. Width of Tape ½ Inch.

No. 53 Brilliant, Length 50 ft....................Per Dozen, **$5.00**

One Dozen in Display Box.

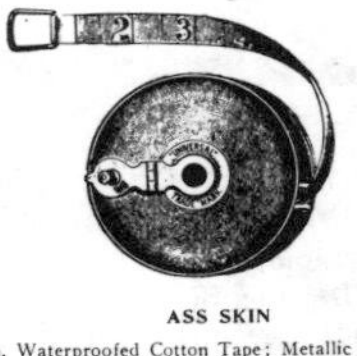

ASS SKIN

½ Inch, Waterproofed Cotton Tape; Metallic Case, Cream Enameled Side, Brass Bound; Brass Folding Handle; Brass Ring and Trimmings. Marked on One Side Only, in Feet, Inches and ½ Inch.

Nos.	**710**	**712**	**713**	**714**	**715**	**716**
Length ....Feet,	25	40	50	66	75	100
Per Dozen	$3.75	4.50	5.00	6.00	7.50	9.00
	5.00	**6.00**	**6.60**	**8.00**	**10.00**	**12.00**

One Half Dozen in Box.

SLIDING T BEVELS

EUREKA

Nickel-plated Cast Iron Handle; Steel Blade; with Thumb to Turn Blade at any Angle.

No. 18 Length ... Inches,	6	8	10
Per Dozen	**$8.75**	**11.25**	**12.25**

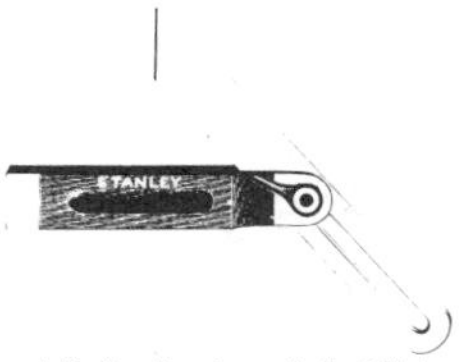

Rosewood Handles; Brass Lever; the Bevel Blade can be Made Fast or Loose by Moving the Lever with the Thumb of the Hand which Grasps the Handle.

No. 25 Length ... Inches,	6	8	10	12
Per Dozen	**$4.50**	**5.00**	**5.25**	**6.00**

One Half Dozen in Box.

ANGLE DIVIDERS

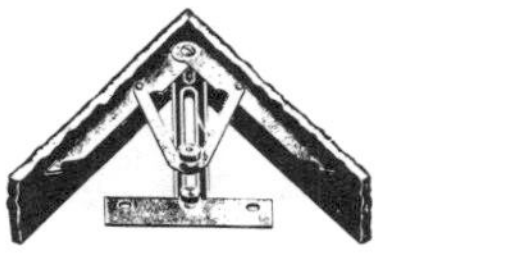

Nickel-plated; Steel Blades; with this Tool Any Angle can be Found and Bisected. Fitting Any Wood Work to Odd Angles can be Done Easily. It is Graduated for Parts of Circles and can be Used as a Try or T Square.

No. 30 Angle Divider .... Per Dozen, **$27.00**

One Twelfth Dozen in Box

LEVEL SIGHTS

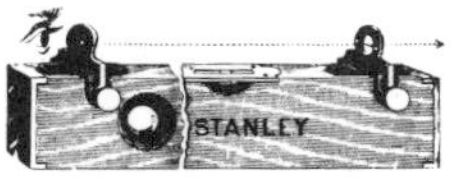

No. 1 For Wood .... Per Dozen Pair, **$13.00**

One Twelfth Dozen Pairs in Box.

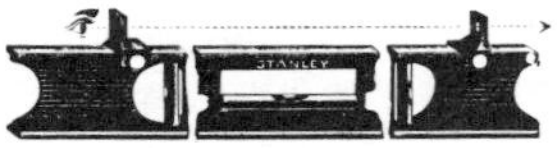

No. 2 For Iron .... Per Dozen Pair, **$13.00**

One Twelfth Dozen Pairs in Box.

PROVED LEVEL GLASSES

Extra Thick Tubing; Marked by Two Indelible Lines so that the Glass can be Accurately Set in a Level.

Length ... Inches,	1½	1¾	2	2½	3
Per Dozen	**$1.10**	**1.16**	**1.20**	**1.30**	**1.36**
Length ... Inches,	3½	4	Assorted		
Per Dozen	**$1.40**	**1.50**	**1.40**		

One Dozen in Box.

LEVELING STANDS

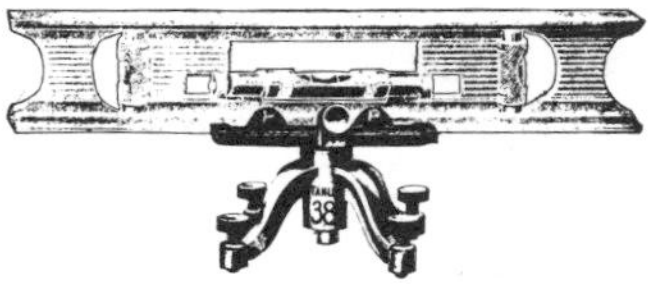

Cast Iron; Nickel-plated; with Set Screws in Base of Legs to Obtain a Level Position on an Inclined or Uneven Surface.

No. 38 .... Per Dozen, **$24.00**

One Twelfth Dozen in Box.

BIT AND SQUARE LEVELS

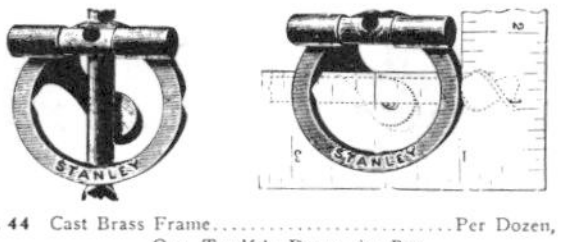

No. 44 Cast Brass Frame .... Per Dozen, **5.50**

One Twelfth Dozen in Box.

PLUMB BOBS

STARRETT'S MERCURY

Made from Solid Steel, Bored and Filled with Mercury, giving them a very Great Weight in Proportion to their Size. Hardened and Ground Points; Patent Device for Fastening End of Line; Complete with Line.

No. 87 Nickel plated; Weight ... Ounces	3½	6	12	16
Length ... Inches,	4	5	5½	6
Diameter ... Inches,	½	⅝	⅞	1
Each	$1.00	1.50	2.00	2.50
Each	**1.70**	**2.55**	**3.40**	**4.25**

One in a Box.

BROWN & SHARPE'S MERCURY

Made from Solid Steel, Bored and Filled with Mercury, giving them a Very Great Weight in Proportion to their Size. Hardened and Ground Points. Complete with Silk Line. Nickel-plated.

Nos.	**793**	**794**	**795**	**796**
Weight ... Ounces,	3½	6	12	16
Length ... Inches,	4	4½	5⅜	6
Diameter ... Inches,	½	⅝	⅞	1
Each	$1.00	1.50	2.00	2.50
Each	**1.80**	**2.70**	**3.60**	**4.50**

One in a Box.

HOLD FAST

Solid Steel; Hexagon Body; Nickel-plated; Complete with Cord

No. 1 Weight 8 oz. .... Per Dozen, **$5.00**

One Half Dozen in a Box.

No. 02

STANLEY ADJUSTABLE

Bronze Body; Steel Point; Fitted with Reel on Which the Line is Held. A Steel Spring Holds the Line at Any Point. Complete with Line.

No. 02 Weight 12 oz. .... Per Dozen, **$30.00**

One Twelfth Dozen in a Box.

No. 5

SCREW TOP, CAST BRASS

Polished Cast Brass; Steel Point.

No. 5 Weight 6½ oz. .... Per Dozen, **$8.00**

Half Dozen in a Box.

No. 2 to 0

JAPANNED CAST IRON

Adjusted Top ... Nos.	**2**	**00**	**0**
Weight	9½ oz.	1 lb. 2 oz.	2 lb. 10 oz.
Per Dozen	**$1.60**	**2.70**	**4.70**

No. 2, One Dozen; 00 and 0, Half Dozen in a Box.

No. 21

NICKEL-PLATED CAST IRON

No. 21 Weight 6 oz., with Adjusted Top .... Per Dozen, **$2.80**

One Dozen in a Box.

Plumb Bobs.

No. 1.

No. 2.

No. 4.

No.		$
1	Iron, Japanned, Weight, 9½ oz.,	
2	Brass, Steel Point, " 6 "	
4	Lead, " " " 13 "	

HALF DOZEN IN A BOX.

Oil Stones.

	Per Pound. $
Arkansas Oil Stones, Assorted, ¾ to 1½ lbs.,	
Washita " " Extra, Assorted ½ to 1½ lbs.,	
" " " No. 1, " ½ to 1½ lbs.,	
" " " No. 2, " ½ to 1½ lbs.,	
Washita Slips, Assorted,	
Hindostan Oil or Water Stones, Assorted, ½ to 1½ lbs.,	
Hindostan Axe " " ¼ to ¾ lbs.,	
Hindostan Slips, "	
Diamond "	
Sand Stones,	

PLUMB BOBS

CAST IRON

Japanned

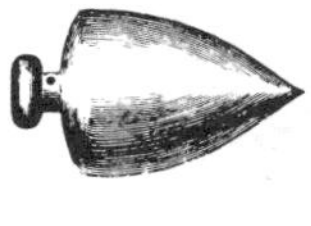

No. 1. Weight 9 ounces ...... each **.15**
No. 1¼. Weight 18 ounces ...... each **.20**
No. 1½. Weight 24 ounces ...... each **.30**
No. 5. Weight 44 ounces ...... each **.50**

SLIM JIM

Cast Brass—Steel Point

8 ounce .... each **1.50**
12 ounce .... each **2.00**
16 ounce .... each **2.75**
24 ounce .... each **3.75**

CAST BRASS

With Steel Points

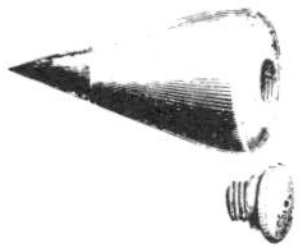

No. 15. Weight 6 ounces ...... each **.75**
No. 16. Weight 10 ounces ...... each **.90**
No. 18. Weight 16 ounces ...... each **1.25**

MERCURY BOBS

Turned Hollow Steel; Mercury Filled.

No. 874. 4 x½ inches, 3½ ounces .... each **1.65**
No. 875. 5 x⅝ inches, 6 ounces .... each **2.15**
No. 875½. 5½x⅞ inches, 12 ounces .... each **2.75**
No. 876. 6 x 1 inches, 16 ounces .... each **3.25**

CAN'T ROLL

Octagon Steel—Nickel Plated

No. 10. ⅞x3½ inches, weight 8 ounces .... each **.65**
No. 20. 1⅛x3¾ inches, weight 14 ounces .... each **.90**

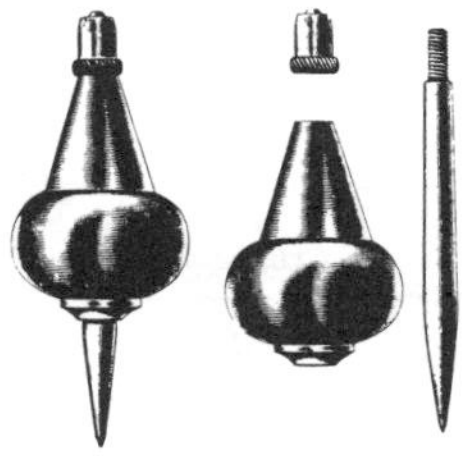

COMMON SENSE PLUMB BOBS

Solid Bronze. Removable Point. Not Reversible.

No. 0. Diameter, 1¾ inches, weight, 1 pound .... each **3.00**
No. 1. Diameter, 2⅜ inches; weight, 2 pounds .... each **4.00**
No. 3. Diameter, 2⅝ inches; weight, 2¾ pounds .... each **5.50**
No. 4. Diameter, 2¾ inches; weight, 3¼ pounds .... each **6.00**
No. 5. Diameter, 2⅞ inches; weight, 3½ pounds .... each **6.50**

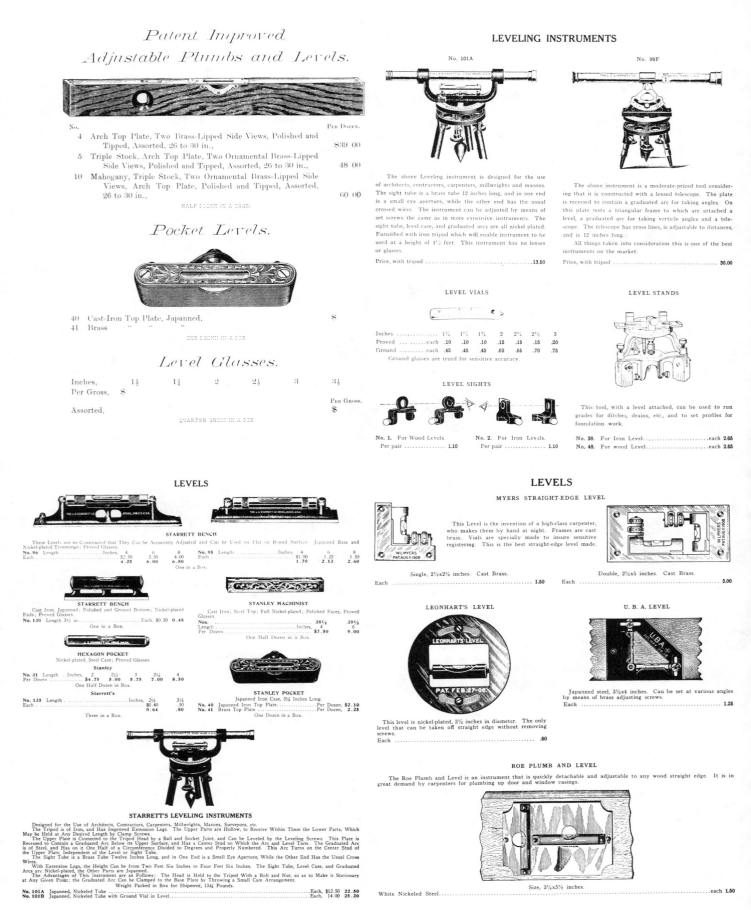

Patent Improved Adjustable Plumbs and Levels.

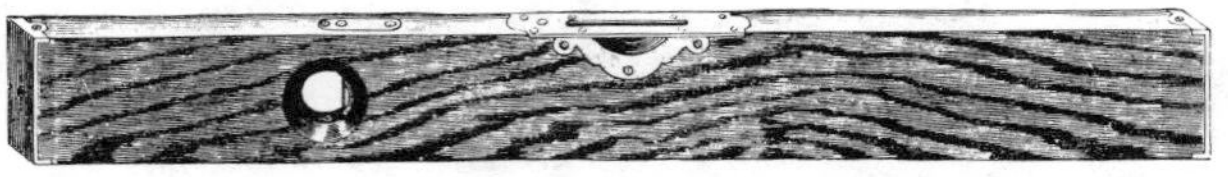

No.		Per Dozen.
4	Arch Top Plate, Two Brass-Lipped Side Views, Polished and Tipped, Assorted, 26 to 30 in.,	$39 00
5	Triple Stock, Arch Top Plate, Two Ornamental Brass-Lipped Side Views, Polished and Tipped, Assorted, 26 to 30 in.,	48 00
10	Mahogany, Triple Stock, Two Ornamental Brass-Lipped Side Views, Arch Top Plate, Polished and Tipped, Assorted, 26 to 30 in.,	60 00

HALF DOZEN IN A CASE.

Pocket Levels.

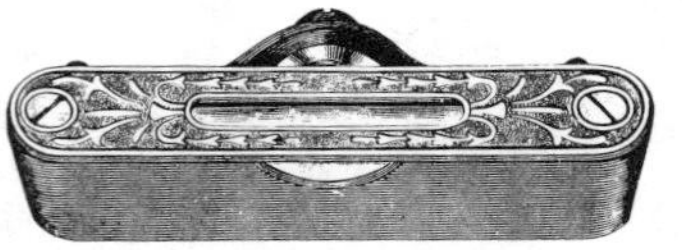

40	Cast-Iron Top Plate, Japanned,	$
41	Brass " " "	

ONE DOZEN IN A BOX.

Level Glasses.

Inches,	$1\frac{1}{2}$	$1\frac{3}{4}$	2	$2\frac{1}{2}$	3	$3\frac{1}{2}$
Per Gross,	$					

Per Gross.

Assorted, $

QUARTER GROSS IN A BOX.

LEVELING INSTRUMENTS

No. 101A

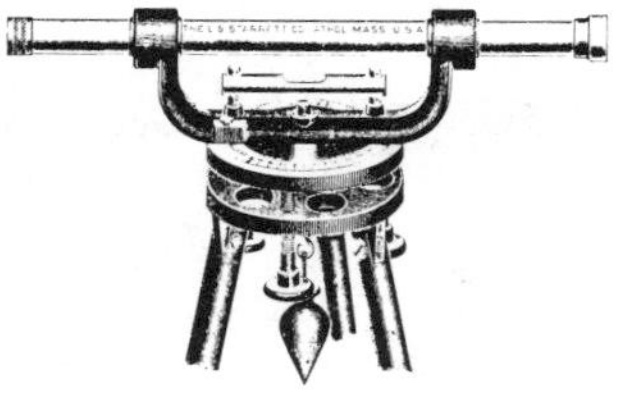

The above Leveling instrument is designed for the use of architects, contractors, carpenters, millwrights and masons. The sight tube is a brass tube 12 inches long, and in one end is a small eye aperture, while the other end has the usual crossed wires. The instrument can be adjusted by means of set screws the same as in more expensive instruments. The sight tube, level case, and graduated arcs are all nickel plated. Furnished with iron tripod which will enable instrument to be used at a height of 4½ feet. This instrument has no lenses or glasses.

Price, with tripod 13.50

No. 99F

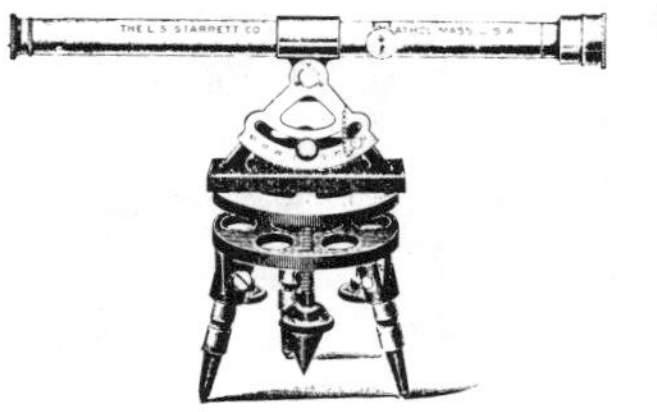

The above instrument is a moderate-priced tool considering that it is constructed with a lensed telescope. The plate is recessed to contain a graduated arc for taking angles. On this plate rests a triangular frame to which are attached a level, a graduated arc for taking verticle angles and a telescope. The telescope has cross lines, is adjustable to distances, and is 12 inches long.

All things taken into consideration this is one of the best instruments on the market.

Price, with tripod 36.00

LEVEL VIALS

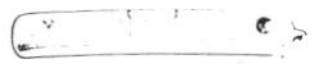

Inches	1¼	1½	1¾	2	2¼	2½	3
Proved ... .each	.10	.10	.10	.15	.15	.15	.20
Ground ....each	.45	.45	.45	.60	.65	.70	.75

Ground glasses are trued for sensitive accuracy.

LEVEL SIGHTS

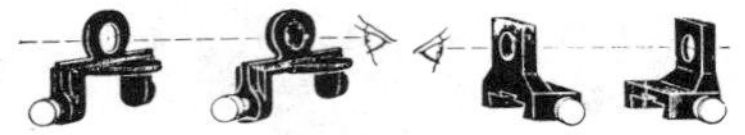

No. 1. For Wood Levels. Per pair 1.10

No. 2. For Iron Levels. Per pair 1.10

LEVEL STANDS

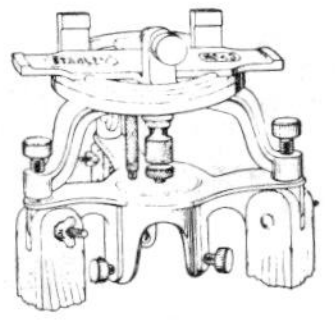

This tool, with a level attached, can be used to run grades for ditches, drains, etc., and to set profiles for foundation work.

No. 38. For Iron Level........................each 2.65

No. 48. For wood Level.......................each 2.65

LEVELS

STARRETT BENCH

These Levels are so Constructed that They Can be Accurately Adjusted and Can be Used on Flat or Round Surface. Japanned Base and Nickel-plated Trimmings; Proved Glasses.

No. 96 Length ....Inches,	4	6	8
Each	$2.50	3.50	4.00
	4.25	**6.00**	**6.80**

No. 95 Length ....Inches,	4	6	8
Each	$1.00	1.25	1.50
	1.70	**2.13**	**2.60**

One in a Box.

STARRETT BENCH

Cast Iron, Japanned; Polished and Ground Bottom; Nickel-plated Ends; Proved Glasses.

No. 130 Length 3½ in..........................Each, $0.30 **0.48**

One in a Box.

HEXAGON POCKET

Nickel-plated, Steel Case; Proved Glasses.

Stanley

No. 31 Length ..Inches,	2	2½	3	3½	4
Per Dozen	**$4.75**	**5.00**	**5.75**	**7.00**	**8.50**

One Half Dozen in Box.

Starrett's

No. 135 Length ....Inches,	2½	3½
Each	$0.40	.50
	0.64	**.80**

Three in a Box.

STANLEY MACHINIST

Cast Iron; Steel Top; Full Nickel-plated; Polished Faces, Proved Glasses.

Nos.	**38½**	**39½**
Length ....Inches,	4	6
Per Dozen	**$7.50**	**9.00**

One Half Dozen in a Box.

STANLEY POCKET

Japanned Iron Case, 3¼ Inches Long.

No. 40 Japanned Iron Top Plate.................Per Dozen, **$2.10**
No. 41 Brass Top Plate ....Per Dozen, **2.25**

One Dozen in a Box.

STARRETT'S LEVELING INSTRUMENTS

Designed for the Use of Architects, Contractors, Carpenters, Millwrights, Masons, Surveyors, etc.

The Tripod is of Iron, and Has Improved Extension Legs. The Upper Parts are Hollow, to Receive Within Them the Lower Parts, Which May be Held at Any Desired Length by Clamp Screws.

The Upper Plate is Connected to the Tripod Head by a Ball and Socket Joint, and Can be Leveled by the Leveling Screws. This Plate is Recessed to Contain a Graduated Arc Below its Upper Surface, and Has a Center Stud on Which the Arc and Level Turn. The Graduated Arc is of Steel, and Has on it One Half of a Circumference Divided to Degrees and Properly Numbered. This Arc Turns on the Center Stud of the Upper Plate, Independent of the Level or Sight Tube.

The Sight Tube is a Brass Tube Twelve Inches Long, and in One End is a Small Eye Aperture, While the Other End Has the Usual Cross Wires.

With Extension Legs, the Height Can be from Two Feet Six Inches to Four Feet Six Inches. The Sight Tube, Level Case, and Graduated Arcs are Nickel-plated, the Other Parts are Japanned.

The Advantages of This Instrument are as Follows: The Head is Held to the Tripod With a Bolt and Nut, so as to Make it Stationary at Any Given Point; the Graduated Arc Can be Clamped to the Base Plate by Throwing a Small Cam Arrangement.

Weight Packed in Box for Shipment, 13¼ Pounds.

No. 101A Japanned, Nickeled Tube ....Each, $12.50 **22.50**
No. 101B Japanned, Nickeled Tube with Ground Vial in Level..........Each, 14.00 **25.20**

LEVELS

MYERS STRAIGHT-EDGE LEVEL

This Level is the invention of a high-class carpenter, who makes them by hand at night. Frames are cast brass. Vials are specially made to insure sensitive registering. This is the best straight-edge level made.

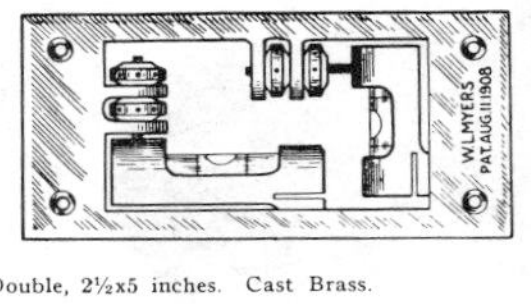

Single, 2½x2½ inches. Cast Brass.

Each 1.50

Double, 2½x5 inches. Cast Brass.

Each 3.00

LEONHART'S LEVEL

This level is nickel-plated, 3½ inches in diameter. The only level that can be taken off straight edge without removing screws.

Each .... .60

U. B. A. LEVEL

Japanned steel, 3½x4 inches. Can be set at various angles by means of brass adjusting screws.

Each 1.25

ROE PLUMB AND LEVEL

The Roe Plumb and Level is an instrument that is quickly detachable and adjustable to any wood straight edge. It is in great demand by carpenters for plumbing up door and window casings.

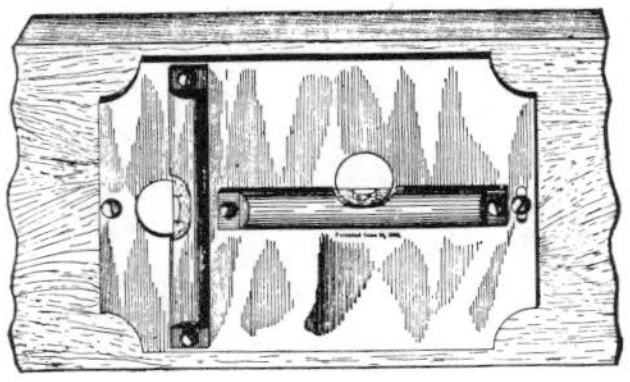

Size, 3¼x5½ inches.

White Nickeled Steel...each 1.50

Plumbs and Levels.

No.		Per Dozen.
102	Levels, Arch Top Plate, Two Side Views, Polished, Assorted, 10 to 16 in.,	$9 00
103	Levels, Arch Top Plate, Two Side Views, Polished, Assorted, 18 to 24 in.,	12 00

| 00 | Plumb and Level, Arch Top Plate, Two Side Views, Polished, Assorted, 18 to 24 in., | $16 00 |
| 0 | Plumb and Level, Arch Top Plate, Two Side Views, Polished, Assorted, 24 to 30 in., | 18 00 |

Patent Improved Adjustable Plumbs and Levels.

| 1 | Mahogany, Arch Top Plate, Two Side Views, Polished, Assorted, 26 to 30 in., | $27 00 |
| 2 | Polished, Arch Top Plate, Two Brass-Lipped Side Views, Assorted, 26 to 30 in., | 27 00 |

| 3 | Arch Top Plate, Two Side Views, Polished and Tipped, Assorted, 26 to 30 in., | $32 00 |

HALF DOZEN IN A CASE.

PLUMBS AND LEVELS

The Vials or Level Glasses in all these Levels can be Easily Placed in any Position and Securely Fastened by Two Small Screws and will Never Slip or Get Out of Order.

Hardwood; Cherry Finished; Brass Tipped; Brass Side View Plates.

No. 53 Three Piece; Two Holes; Assorted, 24 to 30 inch...Per Dozen, **$34.00**
No. 51 One Piece; Three Hole; Assorted, 24 to 30 in....Per Dozen, **$29.00**
No. 50 One Piece; Two Holes; Assorted, 24 to 30 in....Per Dozen, **25.00**
No. 55 Mason; One Piece, Two Plumbs and One Level, 42 in. Long...Per Dozen, **34.00**

One Twelfth Dozen in Box.

MASONS' LEVELS

Hardwood; Cherry Finish; Arch Top Plate; Two Plumbs, Two Side Views.
No. 7½ 36 Inches Long...Per Dozen, **$27.00**

Cherry Wood; Mahogany Finish; Brass Top Plate; Two Brass Lipped Side Views; Two Plumbs; Proved Glasses.
No. 45 48 Inches Long...Per Dozen, **$52.00**

Cherry Wood; Mahogany Finish; Brass Top Plate; Beveled Side and Plumb Views.
No. 35 42 Inches Long...Per Dozen, **$28.00**

Cherry Wood; Mahogany Finish; Brass Top Plate; Two Plumb Views.
No. 45½ 48 Inches Long...Per Dozen, **$46.00**

One Half Dozen in Box.

STANLEY IRON LEVELS

Style of 6 and 9 inch.   Style of 12 to 24 Inch.

Japanned Frame; Nickel-plated Trimmings; Two Plumbs and Proved Glasses.

No. 36	Length	Inches,	9	12	18	24
Per Dozen			$25.00	29.00	35.00	40.00

One Twelfth Dozen in a Box.

Style of 6 and 9 inch.   Style of 12 to 24 Inch.

Nickel-plated Frame and Trimmings; Two Plumbs; Ground Glasses Protected by Eclipse Cases.

No. 37	Length	Inches,	9	12	18	24
Per Dozen			$38.00	43.00	52.00	63.00

One Twelfth Dozen in a Box.

STARRETT'S IRON LEVELS

Style of 4 to 9 inch.   Style of 12 to 24 Inch.

Japanned Frame; Nickel-plated Trimmings; Two Plumbs; Can be Used on Round or Flat Surface; Ground Glasses.

No. 132	Length	Inches,	4	6	9	12	18	24
Each			$1.35	1.50	1.65	1.75	2.00	2.25
			2.16	2.40	2.64	2.80	3.20	3.40

One in a Box.

LEVELS

No. 44E—TORPEDO

Size, 9x1½x¾ inches.
Rosewood, brass top plate...each **1.00**

No. 2312—MIDGET

Size, 12x2½ inches.
Mahogany finished wood
Each...**1.25**

No. 39E—UTILITY

White pine stock, 2½x1½ inches. Red finish.

Inches long	18	21
Each	1.20	1.35

No. 47E—EMPIRE

Walnut stock, 2½x1½ inches. Polished.

Inches long	21	24	26	28
Each	2.00	2.25	2.50	2.75

Vials on above levels are covered with round protecting glass, held in place by an aluminum ring.

No. 4500—NARROW STRATTON

Genuine Mahogany. Stock 2x1 inches.
Brass Bound all around

Length, inches	12	18	24	28
Each	4.00	4.25	4.50	5.00

No. 25—STANLEY
Adjustable

Genuine Mahogany. Stock 3½x1½ inches.
Brass Tipped, Brass Side Trims

Length, inches	24	26	28	30
Each	3.25	3.25	3.45	3.65

EMPIRE MASON LEVEL

No. 3348 48 inch. White Pine, Weather Proof Red Finish...each **3.25**

STANLEY IRON LEVELS

No. 36G. Stock 2½x¾ inches. Fitted with Proved Glass. Bottom is grooved.

6 inch	each 1.85
9 inch	each 2.10
12 inch	each 2.35
18 inch	each 2.75
24 inch	each 3.00

No. 37G. Stock 2½x¾ inches. Fitted with Ground Glasses. Bottom is grooved.

6 inch	each 2.35
9 inch	each 2.75
12 inch	each 3.00
18 inch	each 3.50
24 inch	each 4.25

LEVELS

No. 237—STANLEY ALUMINUM

Length, inches	12	18	24
Each	3.25	4.00	4.75

No. 200—VOGEL ALUMINUM

This Level has Aluminum Top and Bottom, Thin Steel Center

Length, inches	18	24	28
Each	4.75	5.50	6.50

EMPIRE ALUMINUM

The 28-inch size has Double Plumb Glasses in each end.

Length, inches	18	24	28
Each	4.00	5.25	6.50

STEVENS LINE LEVEL

For leveling two points a great distance apart. Hang on an ordinary chalk line.
Each...**.65**

No. 34G—STANLEY

Grooved Bottom, Ground Glasses.

Length, inches	4	6	8	10
Each	1.70	1.85	2.50	2.75

No. 98—STARRETT

Grooved Bottom

Ground, Graduated Vials. 12-inch size has Plumb Glass.

Length, inches	6	8	12
Each	3.85	4.50	6.30

STANLEY VICTOR

Nickeled Iron.
No. 38½ 4 inches long...each **.80**
No. 39½ 6 inches long...each **1.00**

No. 31—STANLEY

Nickel-Plated Octagan Case.

Length, inches	2	2½	3	3½
Each	.60	.75	.80	.85

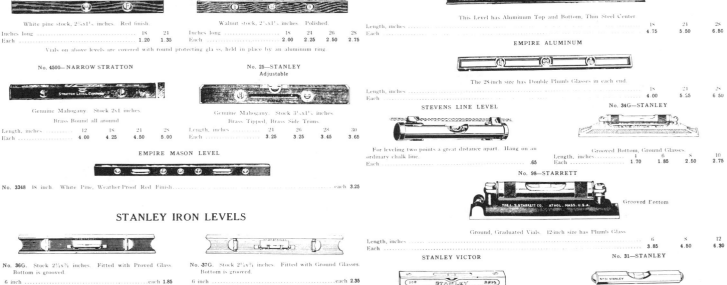

VISES

COMBINATION PIPE

Swivel-Base

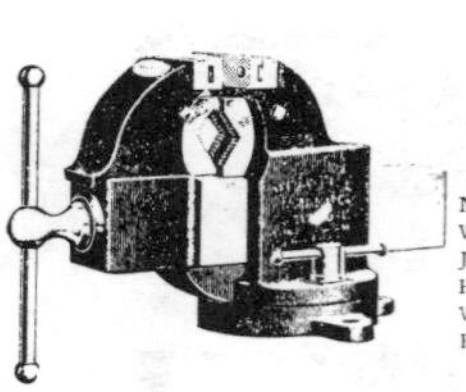

No.	324	324½
Width of Jaw, inches	4	4½
Jaws open, inches	5½	6
Holds Pipe, inches	⅛ to 2½	⅛ to 3½
Weight each, pounds	54	76
Each	16.00	20.00

PEERLESS PIPE GRIP

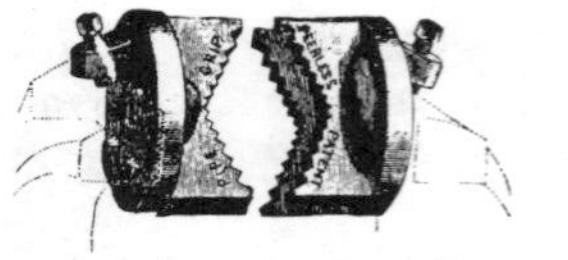

No. 1. Fits any 3 to 4½ inch Vise. Holds Pipe ¼ to 2½ inch ....per pair **3.00**

HAND VISES

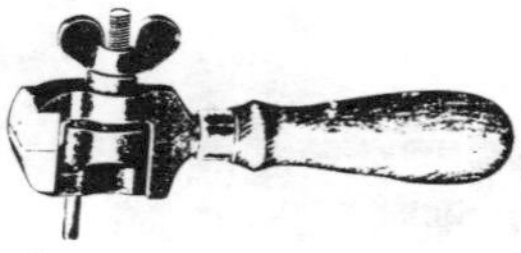

No. 40. 6½ inch. 1¼ inch Jaw........................ **1.40**

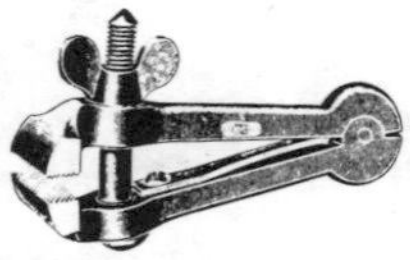

No. 660

Length, inches	4½	5½
Each	1.20	.165

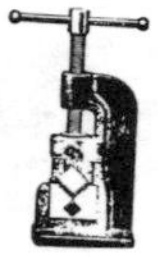

No. 200

Small size; takes up to 1 inch pipe ....each **2.35**

KEY FILERS' VISE

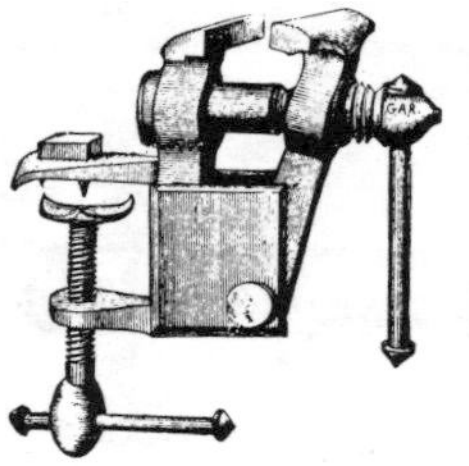

Wrought Iron—Steel Jaws

No. 171. 2½ inch Jaw................................each **2.50**
No. 171. 3 inch Jaw................................each **3.00**
No. 171. 3½ inch Jaw................................each **3.50**

PIPE VISES

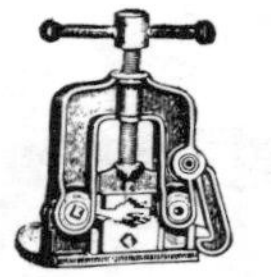

No. 0. ⅛ to 2 inch pipe......each **3.00**
No. 1. ⅛ to 2½ inch pipe......each **4.00**
No. 2. ⅛ to 3½ inch pipe......each **5.50**

VISES

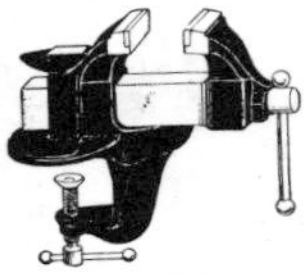

CLAMP BASE—IRON JAW

No.	741	742	743
Width of jaw, inches	1½	1¾	2
Weight each, lbs.	3	3¼	3½
Each	1.35	1.65	1.90

CLAMP BASE—STEEL FACED JAWS

No.	762	763	765	766
Width of jaw, inches	1¾	2	2½	3
Weight each, lbs.	3¼	3½	4	5
Each	2.00	2.25	2.85	4.25

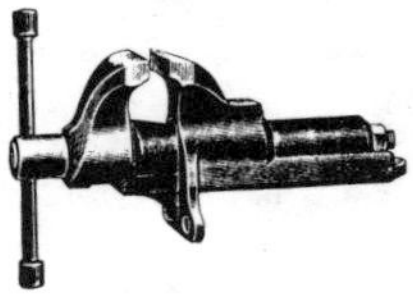

No.	5212
Width of Jaw, inches	2
Weight each, lbs.	7
Each	2.75

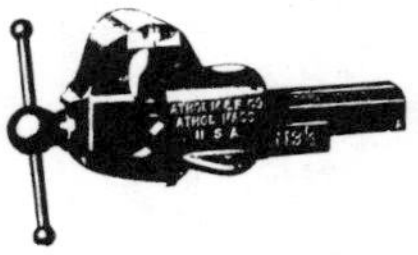

No.	112½	113	113½	114
Width of Jaw, inches	2½	3	3½	4
Weight each, lbs.	14	21	29	37
Each	4.50	5.25	6.50	7.50

MACHINISTS' STATIONARY BASE

No.	Width of Jaws	Jaws Open	Weight	Price
612½	2½ inches	3½ inches	12 lbs.	6.75
613	3 inches	4¼ inches	22½ lbs.	8.50
613½	3½ inches	5 inches	30 lbs.	9.50
614	4 inches	6 inches	42 lbs.	10.75
614½	4½ inches	6½ inches	58 lbs.	13.00

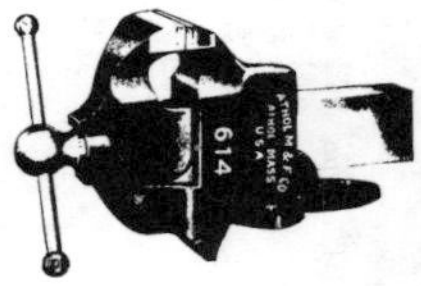

MACHINISTS' SWIVEL BASE

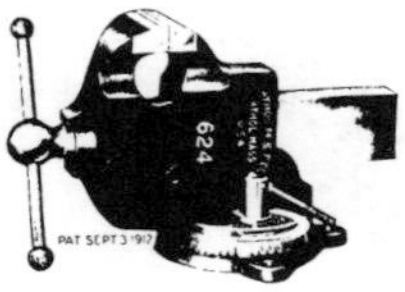

No.	Width of Jaws	Jaws Open	Weight	Price
622½	2½ inches	3½ inches	16 lbs.	8.50
623	3 inches	4¼ inches	27 lbs.	11.00
623½	3½ inches	5 inches	34 lbs.	12.75
624	4 inches	6 inches	50 lbs.	14.00
624½	4½ inches	6½ inches	70 lbs.	17.00

VISES

R.-W. WOOD WORKING VISES

Quick Acting

Built around a cam-operating Vise Nut composed of only two pieces, which form a working combination particularly powerful and simple. It is absolutely reliable in action and will not get out of order, as there are no springs nor small parts to wear out.

Reverse movement of handle disengages Vise Nut and permits instant adjustment of jaw to any desired width. Forward movement of handle immediately engages Vise Nut, and may be operated continuously until jaws close tight.

Vise Nut made of phosphor bronze—nut sleeve of grey iron.

Screw and guides made of cold rolled steel.

Jaws are of best grey iron with working surfaces ground and finished. Special design of ribs on jaws secures minimum deflection or spring under pressure as well as minimum weight.

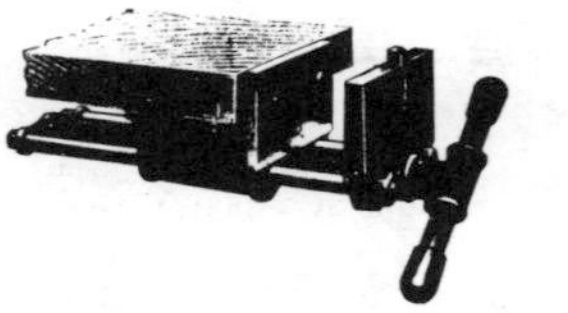

No. 430S-1. Width of jaw, 7 inches; depth of jaw, 4 inches; open, 10 inches............................each **8.00**

No. 430S-2. Width of jaw, 10 inches; depth of jaw, 5 inches; open, 12 inches............................each **9.00**

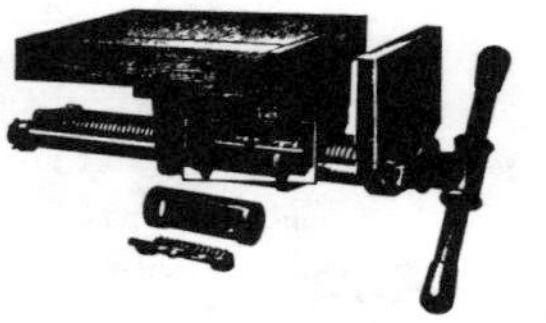

No. 430-1. Width of jaw, 7 inches; depth of jaw, 4 inches; open, 10 inches................................ **7.25**

No. 430-2. Width of jaw, 10 inches; depth of jaw, 5 inches; open, 12 inches................................ **8.25**

PLAIN SCREW

Wood Working Vise

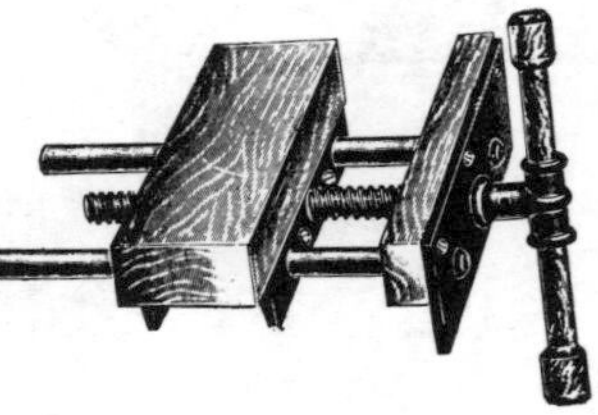

No. 0. Jaw, 10 inches wide, 2½ inches deep; opens 9 inches ....each **4.50**

CHAMPION

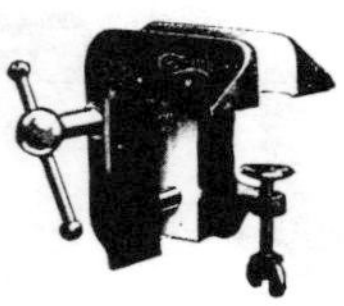

Carpenters' Vise

Illustration One-Fifth Actual Size.

A practical Woodworkers' Vise. Weighing only four pounds, it can be carried in the carpenter's kit. It will fasten to anything from ⅞ to 2¼ inches thick....each **3.00**

Vises.

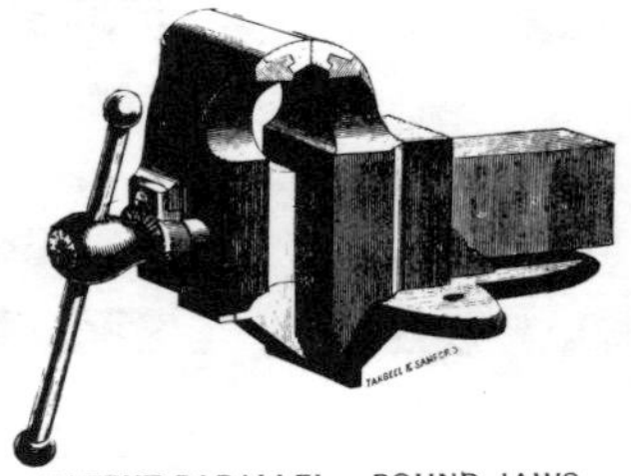

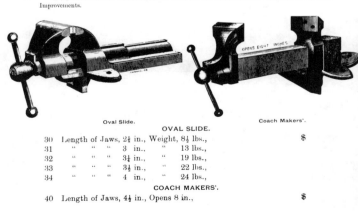

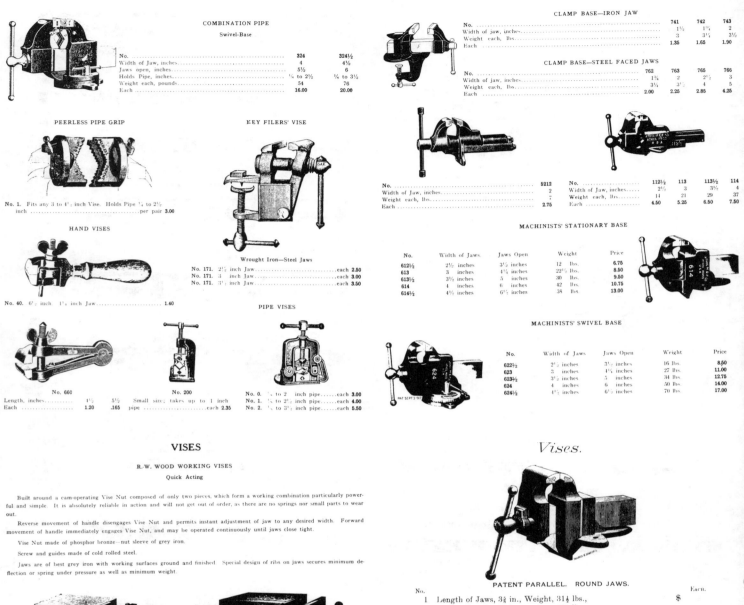

PATENT PARALLEL. ROUND JAWS.

No.		Each.
1	Length of Jaws, 3⅝ in., Weight, 31½ lbs.,	$
2	" " " 4¼ in., " 41½ lbs.,	
3	" " " 4¾ in., " 59½ lbs.,	
100	" " " 3⅝ in., " 31½ lbs.,	

No. 100 is the same as No. 1, without the Wrought Iron Strengtheners, or any of Parker's Patented Improvements.

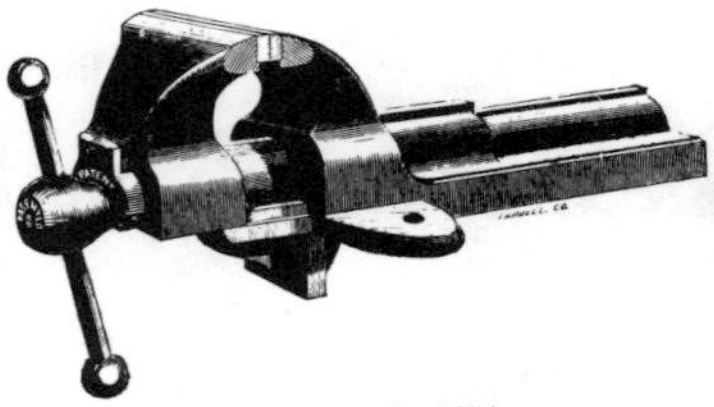

Oval Slide.

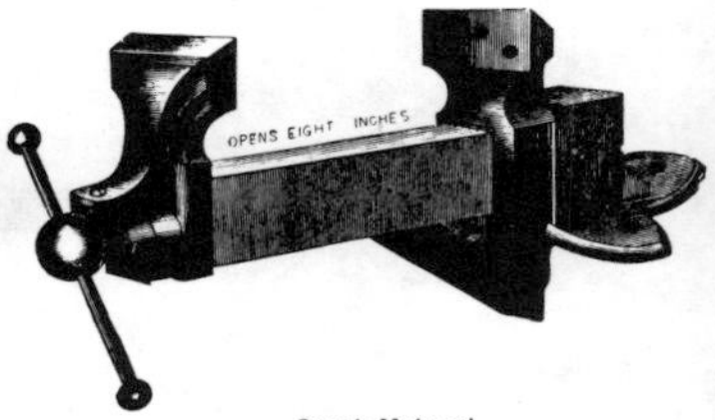

Coach Makers'.

OVAL SLIDE.

30	Length of Jaws, 2⅝ in., Weight, 8½ lbs.,	$
31	" " " 3 in., " 13 lbs.,	
32	" " " 3¼ in., " 19 lbs.,	
33	" " " 3½ in., " 22 lbs.,	
34	" " " 4 in., " 24 lbs.,	

COACH MAKERS'.

40	Length of Jaws, 4½ in., Opens 8 in.,	$

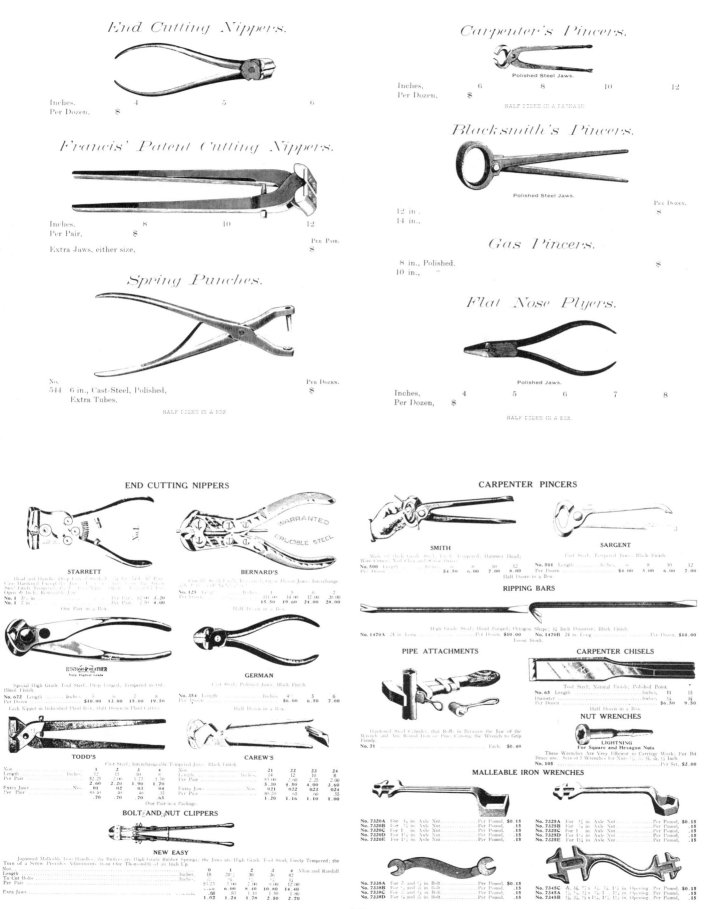

End Cutting Nippers.

Inches.	4	5	6
Per Dozen,	$		

Francis' Patent Cutting Nippers.

Inches,	8	10	12
Per Pair,	$		PER PAIR.

Extra Jaws, either size, $

Spring Punches.

No.
544   6 in., Cast-Steel, Polished,   PER DOZEN.
Extra Tubes, $

HALF DOZEN IN A BOX

Carpenter's Pincers.

Polished Steel Jaws.

Inches,	6	8	10	12
Per Dozen,	$			

HALF DOZEN IN A PACKAGE

Blacksmith's Pincers.

Polished Steel Jaws.

12 in.
14 in.,   PER DOZEN. $

Gas Pincers.

8 in., Polished.
10 in., " $

Flat Nose Plyers.

Polished Jaws.

Inches,	4	5	6	7	8
Per Dozen,	$				

HALF DOZEN IN A BOX

END CUTTING NIPPERS

STARRETT

No. 1.

Head and Handle, Drop Forged Steel, Fully Up-Set; All Parts Case Hardened Except the Jaws; Jaws of Best Quality Tool Steel Finely Tempered; 5½ or 7 Inch Nipper; Open 4 Inch; Removable Jaws.

Open ⅝ Inch, Removable Jaws.		
No. 1 5½ in.	Per Pair, $2.50	4.20
No. 1 7 in.	Per Pair, 2.50	4.00

One Pair in a Box.

BERNARD'S

WARRANTED CRUCIBLE STEEL

Crucible Steel Jaws; Forged Edges; Round Jaws; Interchangeable Parts; All New Stock.

No. 125 Length ...... Inches,	6	5	6	7
Per Dozen,	$11.00	14.00	17.00	23.00
	15.50	19.60	24.00	28.00

Half Dozen in a Box.

Very Highest Grade

Special High Grade Tool Steel, Drop Forged, Tempered in Oil, Blued Finish.

No. 672 Length ...... Inches,	6	5	6	7
Per Dozen	$10.00	13.00	15.00	19.50

Each Nipper in Individual Plaid Box, Half Dozen in Plaid Carton.

GERMAN

Cast Steel; Polished Jaws, Black Finish.

No. 354 Length ...... Inches,	4	5	6
Per Dozen	$6.00	6.50	7.00

Half Dozen in a Box.

TODD'S

Cast Steel; Interchangeable Tempered Jaws, Black Finish.

Nos.	1	2	3	4
Length ...... Inches,	12	11	10	8
Per Pair	$2.25	2.00	1.75	1.50
	2.60	2.20	1.90	1.70
Extra Jaws ...... No.	01	02	03	04
	.30	.30	.30	.35
Per Pair	.70	.70	.70	.65

CAREW'S

Nos.	21	22	23	24
Length ...... Inches,	14	12	10	8
Per Pair	$5.00	2.60	2.25	
	5.30	4.50	4.00	3.60
Extra Jaws ...... Nos.	.021	.022	.023	.024
Per Pair	$0.70	.65	.60	.55
	1.20	1.16	1.10	1.00

One Pair in a Package.

BOLT AND NUT CLIPPERS

NEW EASY

Japanned Malleable Iron Handles; the Butlers are High Grade Rubber Springs; the Jaws are High Grade Tool Steel, Finely Tempered; the Turn of a Screw Provides Adjustments from One Thousandth of an Inch Up.

Allan and Randall

	0	1	2	3	4
Length ...... Inches,	18	24½	30	36	42
To Cut Bolts ...... Inches,	¼	⅜	½	⅝	¾
Per Pair	$3.75	5.00	7.00	7.00	10.00
	4.20	6.00	8.40	10.80	14.40
Extra Jaws	.68	.83	1.18	1.50	1.80
	1.02	1.24	1.78	2.50	2.70

CARPENTER PINCERS

SMITH

Made of High Grade Steel, Finely Tempered; Hammer Head; Wire Cutter, Nail Claw and Screw Driver.

No. 500 Length ...... Inches,	6	8	10	12
Per Dozen	$4.50	6.00	7.00	8.00

Half Dozen in a Box.

SARGENT

Cast Steel; Tempered Jaws, Black Finish.

No. 501 Length ...... Inches,	6	8	10	12
Per Dozen	$4.00	5.00	6.00	7.00

RIPPING BARS

High Grade Steel; Hand Forged; Octagon Shape; ¾ Inch Diameter; Black Finish.

No. 1470A 24 in. Long	Per Dozen, $10.00	No. 1470B 24 in. Long	Per Dozen, $10.00

Loose Stock.

PIPE ATTACHMENTS

Hardened Steel Cylinder, that Rolls in Between the Jaw of the Wrench and Any Round Iron or Pipe, Causing the Wrench to Grip Firmly.

No. 71	Each, $0.40

CARPENTER CHISELS

Tool Steel; Natural Finish; Polished Point.

No. 65 Length ...... Inches,	11	15
Diameter ...... Inches,	⅝	¾
Per Dozen	$6.50	9.50

Half Dozen in a Box.

NUT WRENCHES

LIGHTNING
For Square and Hexagon Nuts

These Wrenches Are Very Efficient in Carriage Work; For Bit Brace use. Sets of 5 Wrenches for Nuts ¼, ⅜, ½, ⅝, ½ Inch.

No. 105	Per Set, $2.00

MALLEABLE IRON WRENCHES

No. 7320A	For ¾ in. Axle Nut	Per Pound, $0.15
No. 7320B	For ⅞ in. Axle Nut	Per Pound, .15
No. 7320C	For 1 in. Axle Nut	Per Pound, .15
No. 7320D	For 1¼ in. Axle Nut	Per Pound, .15
No. 7320E	For 1½ in. Axle Nut	Per Pound, .15

No. 7325A	For ¾ in. Axle Nut	Per Pound, $0.15
No. 7325B	For ⅞ in. Axle Nut	Per Pound, .15
No. 7325C	For 1 in. Axle Nut	Per Pound, .15
No. 7325D	For 1¼ in. Axle Nut	Per Pound, .15
No. 7325E	For 1½ in. Axle Nut	Per Pound, .15

No. 7338A	For ⅜ and ½ in. Bolt	Per Pound, $0.15
No. 7338B	For ½ and ⅝ in. Bolt	Per Pound, .15
No. 7338C	For ⅝ and ¾ in. Bolt	Per Pound, .15
No. 7338D	For ¾ and ⅞ in. Bolt	Per Pound, .15

No. 7345C	⅞, ⅞ x 1½, 1¾ in. Opening, Per Pound, $0.15
No. 7345A	⅞, ¾, ⅞ x 1¼, 1½ in. Opening, Per Pound, .15
No. 7345B	⅞, ¾, ⅞ x 1¼, 1¾ in. Opening, Per Pound, .15

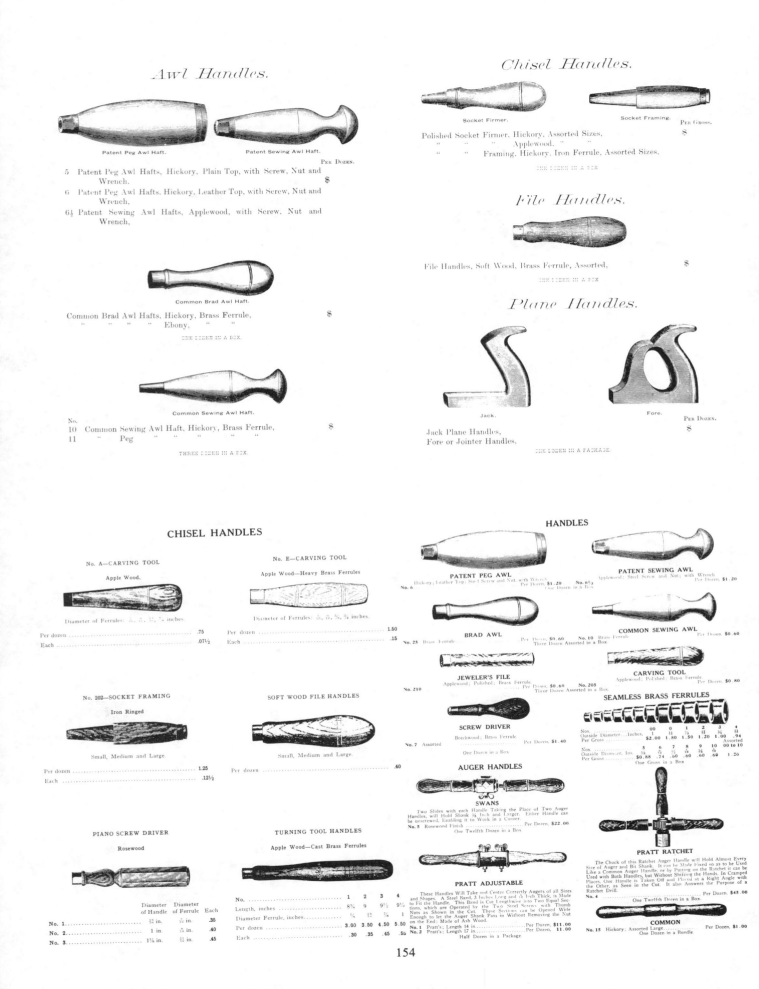

Awl Handles.

Patent Peg Awl Haft.

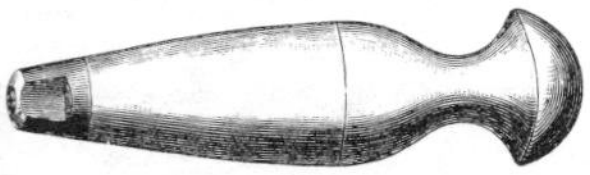

Patent Sewing Awl Haft.

PER DOZEN.

5 Patent Peg Awl Hafts, Hickory, Plain Top, with Screw, Nut and Wrench, $

6 Patent Peg Awl Hafts, Hickory, Leather Top, with Screw, Nut and Wrench,

6½ Patent Sewing Awl Hafts, Applewood, with Screw, Nut and Wrench,

Common Brad Awl Haft.

Common Brad Awl Hafts, Hickory, Brass Ferrule, $
" " " " Ebony,

ONE DOZEN IN A BOX.

Common Sewing Awl Haft.

No.
10 Common Sewing Awl Haft, Hickory, Brass Ferrule, $
11 " Peg " " " " "

THREE DOZEN IN A BOX.

Chisel Handles.

Socket Firmer.

Socket Framing.

PER GROSS.

Polished Socket Firmer, Hickory, Assorted Sizes, $
" " " Applewood, " "
" " Framing, Hickory, Iron Ferrule, Assorted Sizes,

ONE DOZEN IN A BOX.

File Handles.

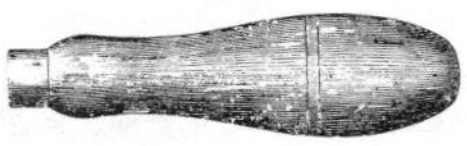

File Handles, Soft Wood, Brass Ferrule, Assorted, $

ONE DOZEN IN A BOX.

Plane Handles.

Jack.

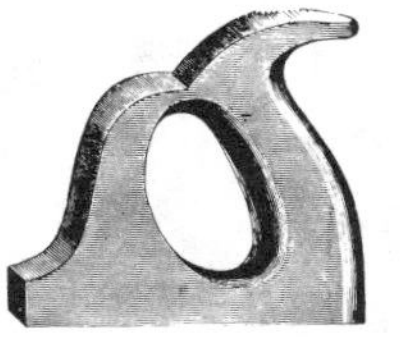

Fore.

PER DOZEN.

Jack Plane Handles, $
Fore or Jointer Handles,

ONE DOZEN IN A PACKAGE.

CHISEL HANDLES

No. A—CARVING TOOL

Apple Wood.

Diameter of Ferrules: 7/16, 9/16, 11/16, 7/8 inches.

Per dozen .... .75
Each .... .07½

No. E—CARVING TOOL

Apple Wood—Heavy Brass Ferrules

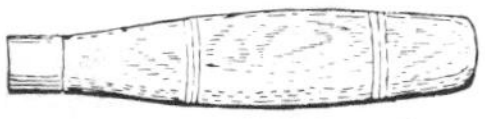

Diameter of Ferrules: 7/16, 9/16, 5/8, 3/4 inches.

Per dozen 1.50
Each .... .15

No. 202—SOCKET FRAMING

Iron Ringed

Small, Medium and Large.

Per dozen 1.25
Each .... .12½

SOFT WOOD FILE HANDLES

Small, Medium and Large.

Per dozen .... .40

PIANO SCREW DRIVER

Rosewood

	Diameter of Handle	Diameter of Ferrule	Each
No. 1	13/16 in.	7/16 in.	.35
No. 2	1 in.	9/16 in.	.40
No. 3	1⅛ in.	11/16 in.	.45

TURNING TOOL HANDLES

Apple Wood—Cast Brass Ferrules

No.	1	2	3	4
Length, inches	8⅜	9	9½	9½
Diameter Ferrule, inches	⅝	13/16	⅞	1
Per dozen	3.00	3.50	4.50	5.50
Each	.30	.35	.45	.55

HANDLES

PATENT PEG AWL

No. 6 Hickory; Leather Top; Steel Screw and Nut, with Wrench ... Per Dozen, **$1.20**

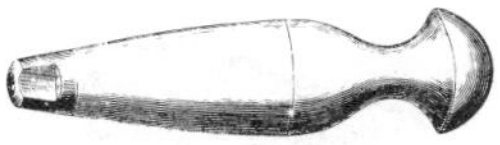

PATENT SEWING AWL

No. 6½ Applewood; Steel Screw and Nut; with Wrench ... Per Dozen, **$1.20**

One Dozen in a Box

BRAD AWL

No. 25 Brass Ferrule ... Per Dozen, **$0.60**

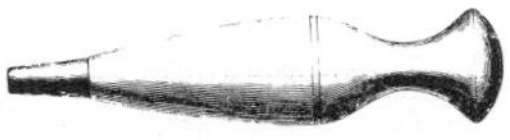

COMMON SEWING AWL

No. 10 Brass Ferrule ... Per Dozen, **$0.60**

Three Dozen Assorted in a Box.

JEWELER'S FILE

No. 210 Applewood; Polished; Brass Ferrule. ... Per Dozen, **$0.60**

CARVING TOOL

No. 205 Applewood; Polished; Brass Ferrule. ... Per Dozen, **$0.80**

Three Dozen Assorted in a Box.

SCREW DRIVER

Beechwood; Brass Ferrule

No. 7 Assorted ... Per Dozen, **$1.40**

One Dozen in a Box

SEAMLESS BRASS FERRULES

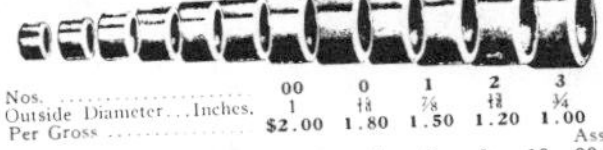

Nos.	00	0	1	2	3	4
Outside Diameter...Inches.	1	15/16	⅞	13/16	¾	11/16
Per Gross	$2.00	1.80	1.50	1.20	1.00	.94

Nos.	5	6	7	8	9	10	Assorted 00 to 10
Outside Diameter, Ins.	⅝	9/16	½	7/16	⅜	5/16	
Per Gross	$0.88	.74	.60	.60	.60	.60	1.20

One Gross in a Box

AUGER HANDLES

SWANS

Two Slides with each Handle Taking the Place of Two Auger Handles, will Hold Shank ⅜ Inch and Larger. Either Handle can be unscrewed, Enabling it to Work in a Corner.

No. 5 Rosewood Finish .... Per Dozen, **$22.00**

One Twelfth Dozen in a Box

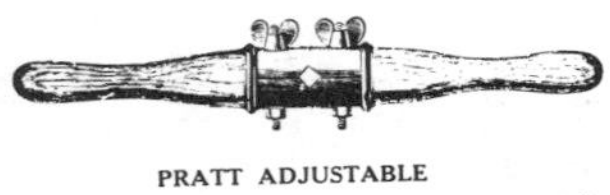

PRATT ADJUSTABLE

These Handles Will Take and Center Correctly Augers of all Sizes and Shapes. A Steel Band, 3 Inches Long and 3/16 Inch Thick, is Made to Fit the Handle. This Band is Cut Lengthwise into Two Equal Sections, which are Operated by the Two Steel Screws with Thumb Nuts as Shown in the Cut. These Sections can be Opened Wide Enough to let the Auger Shank Pass in Without Removing the Nut on the End; Made of Ash Wood.

No. 1 Pratt's; Length 14 in.................... Per Dozen, **$11.00**
No. 2 Pratt's; Length 17 in.................... Per Dozen, **11.00**

Half Dozen in a Package.

PRATT RATCHET

The Chuck of this Ratchet Auger Handle will Hold Almost Every Size of Auger and Bit Shank. It can be Made Fixed so as to be Used Like a Common Auger Handle, or by Putting on the Ratchet it can be Used with Both Handles, but Without Shifting the Hands. In Cramped Places, One Handle is Taken Off and Placed at a Right Angle with the Other, as Seen in the Cut. It also Answers the Purpose of a Ratchet Drill.

No. 4 .... Per Dozen, **$45.00**

One Twelfth Dozen in a Box.

COMMON

No. 15 Hickory; Assorted Large.................... Per Dozen, **$1.00**

One Dozen in a Bundle.

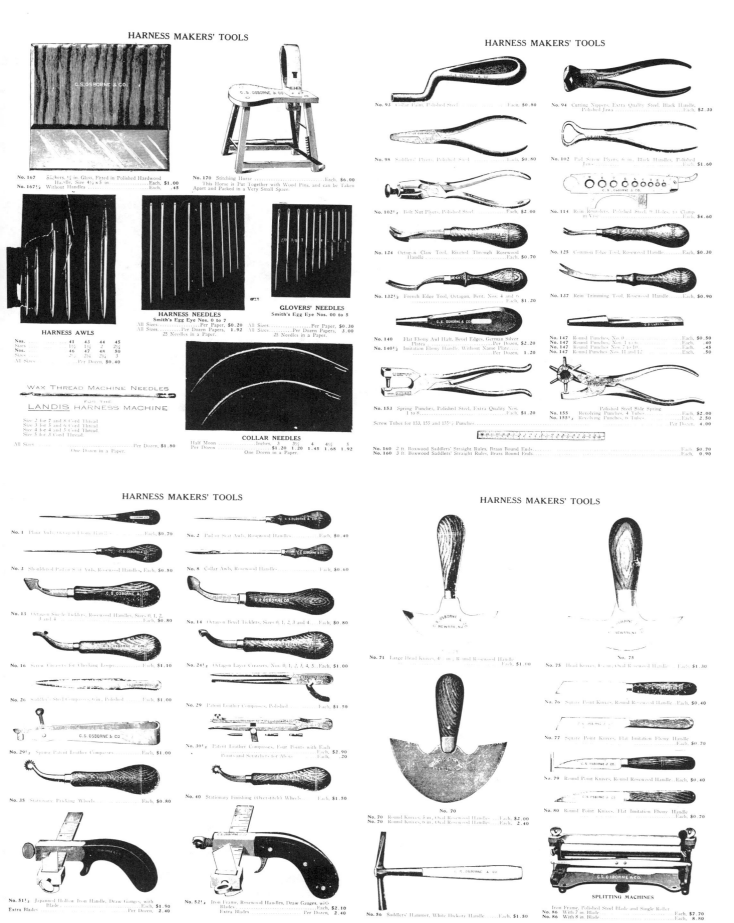

HARNESS MAKERS' TOOLS

No. 167 Slickers, ½ in. Glass, Fitted in Polished Hardwood Handle, Size 4½ x 5 in............Each, $1.00
No. 167½ Without Handles........................Each, .45

No. 170 Stitching Horse ....Each, $6.00
This Horse is Put Together with Wood Pins, and can be Taken Apart and Packed in a Very Small Space.

HARNESS AWLS

Nos.	41	43	44	45
Sizes	1½	1¾	2	2¼
Nos.	46	47	48	50
Sizes	2½	2¾	2¾	3
All Sizes			Per Dozen, $0.40	

WAX THREAD MACHINE NEEDLES
FOR THE
LANDIS HARNESS MACHINE

Size 2 for 7 and 8 Cord Thread.
Size 3 for 5 and 6 Cord Thread.
Size 4 for 4 and 5 Cord Thread.
Size 5 for 3 Cord Thread.

All Sizes ....Per Dozen, $1.80
One Dozen in a Paper.

HARNESS NEEDLES
Smith's Egg Eye Nos. 0 to 7
All Sizes....................Per Paper, $0.20
All Sizes....Per Dozen Papers, 1.92
25 Needles in a Paper.

GLOVERS' NEEDLES
Smith's Egg Eye Nos. 00 to 5
All Sizes....................Per Paper, $0.30
All Sizes....Per Dozen Papers, 3.00
25 Needles in a Paper.

COLLAR NEEDLES
Half Moon	Inches,	3	3½	4	4½	5
Per Dozen		$1.20	1.20	1.45	1.68	1.92
One Dozen in a Paper.

HARNESS MAKERS' TOOLS

No. 93 Collar Palm, Polished Steel........................Each, $0.80
No. 94 Cutting Nippers, Extra Quality Steel, Black Handle, Polished Jaws........................Each, $2.30

No. 98 Saddlers' Pliers, Polished Steel........................Each, $0.80
No. 102 Pad Screw Plyers, 6 in., Black Handle, Polished Jaws........................Each, $1.60

No. 102½ Bolt Nut Plyers, Polished Steel........................Each, $2.00
No. 114 Rein Rounders, Polished Steel, 9 Holes, to Clamp in Vice........................Each, $4.60

No. 124 Octagon Claw Tool, Riveted Through Rosewood Handle........................Each, $0.70
No. 125 Common Edge Tool, Rosewood Handle........Each, $0.30

No. 132½ French Edge Tool, Octagon, Bent, Nos. 4 and 6........................Each, $1.20
No. 137 Rein Trimming Tool, Rosewood Handle........Each, $0.90

No. 140 Flat Ebony Awl Haft, Bevel Edges, German Silver Plates........................Each, $2.20
No. 140½ Imitation Ebony Handle, Without Name Plate........Per Dozen, 1.20

No. 147 Round Punches, No. 0........................Each, $0.50
No. 147 Round Punches, Nos. 1 to 6........................Each, .40
No. 147 Round Punches, Nos. 7 to 10........................Each, .45
No. 147 Round Punches, Nos. 11 and 12........................Each, .50

No. 153 Spring Punches, Polished Steel, Extra Quality Nos. 1 to 8........................Each, $1.20
Screw Tubes for 153, 155 and 155½ Punches........................Per Dozen, 4.00

No. 155 Revolving Punches, 4 Tubes........................Each, $2.00
No. 155½ Revolving Punches, 6 Tubes........................Each, 2.50

No. 160 2 ft. Boxwood Saddlers' Straight Rules, Brass Bound Ends........................Each, $0.70
No. 160 3 ft. Boxwood Saddlers' Straight Rules, Brass Bound Ends........................Each, 0.90

HARNESS MAKERS' TOOLS

No. 1 Plain Awls, Octagon Ebony Handle........................Each, $0.70
No. 2 Pad or Seat Awls, Rosewood Handles........................Each, $0.40

No. 3 Shouldered Pad or Seat Awls, Rosewood Handles, Each, $0.50
No. 8 Collar Awls, Rosewood Handles........................Each, $0.60

No. 13 Octagon Single Ticklers, Rosewood Handles, Sizes 0, 1, 2, 3 and 4........................Each, $0.80
No. 14 Octagon Bevel Ticklers, Sizes 0, 1, 2, 3 and 4..Each, $0.80

No. 16 Screw Creasers for Checking Loops........................Each, $1.10
No. 24½ Octagon Layer Creasers, Nos. 0, 1, 2, 3, 4, 5..Each, $1.00

No. 26 Saddlers' Steel Compasses, 6 in., Polished........Each, $1.00
No. 29 Patent Leather Compasses, Polished........Each, $1.50

No. 29½ Spring Patent Leather Compasses........Each, $1.00
No. 30½ Patent Leather Compasses, Four Points with Each, $2.90
Points and Scratchers for Above........Each, .20

No. 35 Stationary Pricking Wheels........................Each, $0.80
No. 40 Stationary Finishing (Over-stitch) Wheels........Each, $1.50

No. 51½ Japanned Hollow Iron Handle, Draw Gauges, with Blade........................Each, $1.90
Extra Blades........................Per Dozen, 2.40

No. 52½ Iron Frame, Rosewood Handles, Draw Gauges, with Blades........................Each, $2.10
Extra Blades........................Per Dozen, 2.40

HARNESS MAKERS' TOOLS

No. 71 Large Head Knives, 4½ in., Round Rosewood Handle........................Each, $1.00
No. 75
No. 75 Head Knives, Large, Oval Rosewood Handle........Each, $1.30

No. 76 Square Point Knives, Round Rosewood Handle..Each, $0.40

No. 77 Square Point Knives, Flat Imitation Ebony Handle........................Each, $0.70

No. 79 Round Point Knives, Round Rosewood Handle...Each, $0.40

No. 80 Round Point Knives, Flat Imitation Ebony Handle........................Each, $0.70

No. 70
No. 70 Round Knives, 5 in., Oval Rosewood Handles....Each, $2.00
No. 70 Round Knives, 6 in., Oval Rosewood Handles....Each, 2.40

No. 56 Saddlers' Hammer, White Hickory Handle........Each, $1.50

SPLITTING MACHINES
Iron Frame, Polished Steel Blade and Single Roller
No. 86 With 7 in. Blade........................Each, $7.70
No. 86 With 8 in. Blade........................Each, 8.80

OILERS

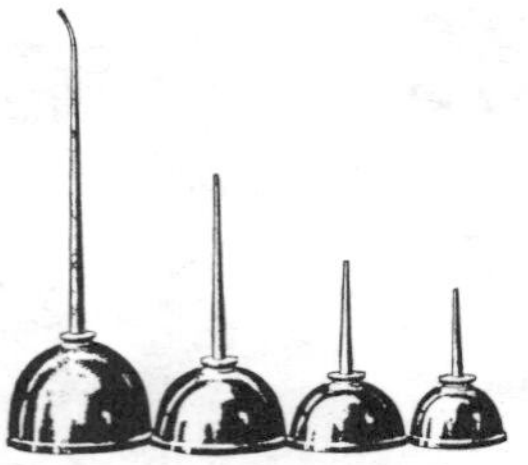

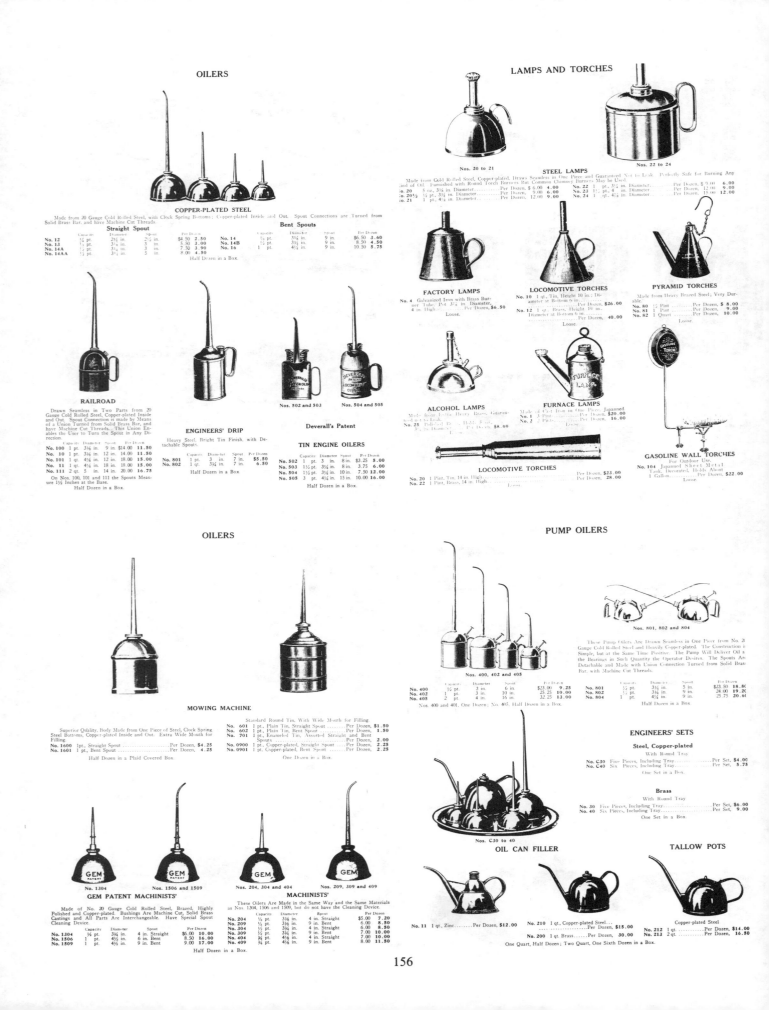

COPPER-PLATED STEEL

Made from 20 Gauge Cold Rolled Steel, with Clock Spring Bottoms; Copper-plated Inside and Out. Spout Connections are Turned from Solid Brass Bar, and have Machine Cut Threads.

Straight Spout

	Capacity	Diameter	Spout	Per Dozen	
No. 12	¼ pt.	2¾ in.	2½ in.	$4.50	**2.50**
No. 13	⅓ pt.	3⅛ in.	3 in.	5.50	**3.00**
No. 14A	½ pt.	3¼ in.	3 in.	7.50	**3.90**
No. 14AA	½ pt.	3¼ in.	5 in.	8.00	**4.50**

Bent Spouts

	Capacity	Diameter	Spout	Per Dozen	
No. 14	⅓ pt.	3⅛ in.	9 in.	$6.50	**3.60**
No. 14B	½ pt.	3¼ in.	9 in.	8.50	**4.50**
No. 16	1 pt.	4¼ in.	9 in.	10.50	**5.75**

Half Dozen in a Box.

RAILROAD

Drawn Seamless in Two Parts from 20 Gauge Cold Rolled Steel, Copper-plated Inside and Out. Spout Connection is made by Means of a Union Turned from Solid Brass Bar, and have Machine Cut Threads. This Union Enables the User to Turn the Spout in Any Direction.

	Capacity	Diameter	Spout	Per Dozen	
No. 100	1 pt.	3⅜ in.	9 in.	$14.00	**11.50**
No. 10	1 pt.	3⅜ in.	12 in.	14.00	**11.50**
No. 101	1 qt.	4⅛ in.	12 in.	18.00	**15.00**
No. 11	1 qt.	4⅛ in.	18 in.	18.00	**15.00**
No. 111	2 qt.	5 in.	14 in.	20.00	**16.75**

On Nos. 100, 101 and 111 the Spouts Measure 1½ Inches at the Base.

Half Dozen in a Box.

ENGINEERS' DRIP

Heavy Steel, Bright Tin Finish, with Detachable Spouts.

	Capacity	Diameter	Spout	Per Dozen
No. 801	1 pt.	3 in.	7 in.	**$5.50**
No. 802	1 qt.	3¼ in.	7 in.	**6.50**

Half Dozen in a Box.

Nos. 502 and 503

Nos. 504 and 505

Deverall's Patent

TIN ENGINE OILERS

	Capacity	Diameter	Spout	Per Dozen	
No. 502	1 pt.	3 in.	8 in.	$3.25	**5.00**
No. 503	1½ pt.	3¼ in.	8 in.	3.75	**6.00**
No. 504	1½ pt.	3¼ in.	10 in.	7.50	**12.00**
No. 505	3 pt.	4¼ in.	15 in.	10.00	**16.00**

Half Dozen in a Box.

LAMPS AND TORCHES

Nos. 20 to 21

Nos. 22 to 24

STEEL LAMPS

Made from Cold Rolled Steel, Copper-plated, Draws Seamless in One Piece and Guaranteed Not to Leak. Perfectly Safe for Burning Any Kind of Oil. Furnished with Round Torch Burners But Common Chimney Burners May be Used.

No. 20	5 oz., 3⅜ in. Diameter............Per Dozen,	$ 6.00	**4.00**
No. 20½	½ pt., 3¾ in. Diameter..........Per Dozen,	9.00	**6.00**
No. 21	1 pt., 4⅛ in. Diameter..........Per Dozen,	12.00	**9.00**
No. 22	1 pt., 3¼ in. Diameter..........Per Dozen,	$ 9.00	**6.00**
No. 23	1½ pt., 4 in. Diameter..........Per Dozen,	12.00	**9.00**
No. 24	1 qt., 4⅞ in. Diameter..........Per Dozen,	15.00	**12.00**

FACTORY LAMPS

No. 4 Galvanized Iron with Brass Burner Tube, Pot 3⅞ in. Diameter, 4 in. High............Per Dozen, **$6.50**

Loose.

LOCOMOTIVE TORCHES

No. 10 1 qt., Tin, Height 10 in.; Diameter at Bottom 6 in.........................Per Dozen, **$26.00**

No. 12 1 qt., Brass, Height 10 in., Diameter at Bottom 6 in.........................Per Dozen, **40.00**

Loose.

PYRAMID TORCHES

Made from Heavy Brazed Steel; Very Durable.

No. 80 ½ Pint ....Per Dozen, **$ 8.00**
No. 81 1 Pint ....Per Dozen, **9.00**
No. 82 1 Quart ....Per Dozen, **10.00**

Loose.

ALCOHOL LAMPS

Made from Extra Heavy Brass, Guaranteed not to Leak.

No. 25 Polished Brass, Holds 5 oz., 3¾ in. Diameter........Per Dozen, **$8.00**

Loose.

FURNACE LAMPS

Made of Cast Iron in One Piece, Japanned.

No. 1 3 Pints..............Per Dozen, **$20.00**
No. 2 2 Pints..............Per Dozen, **16.00**

Loose.

LOCOMOTIVE TORCHES

No. 20 1 Pint, Tin, 14 in. High..............................Per Dozen, **$23.00**
No. 22 1 Pint, Brass, 14 in. High..............................Per Dozen, **28.00**

Loose.

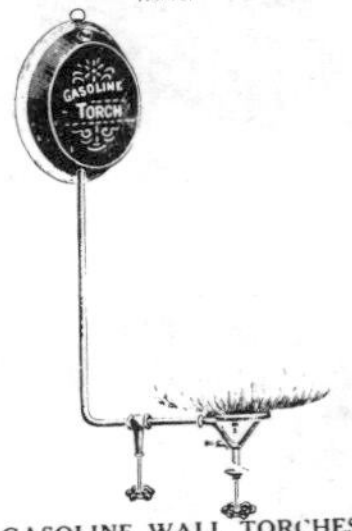

GASOLINE WALL TORCHES

For Outdoor Use.

No. 104 Japanned Sheet Metal Tank, Decorated, Holds About 1 Gallon............Per Dozen, **$22.00**

Loose.

OILERS

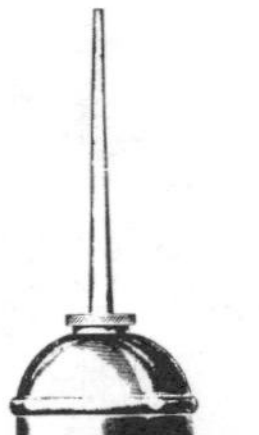

MOWING MACHINE

Superior Quality, Body Made from One Piece of Steel, Clock Spring Steel Bottoms, Copper-plated Inside and Out. Extra Wide Mouth for Filling.

No. 1600 1pt., Straight Spout ....Per Dozen, **$4.25**
No. 1601 1 pt., Bent Spout ....Per Dozen, **4.25**

Half Dozen in a Plaid Covered Box.

Standard Round Tin, With Wide Mouth for Filling.

No. 601 1 pt., Plain Tin, Straight Spout ....Per Dozen, **$1.50**
No. 602 1 pt., Plain Tin, Bent Spout ....Per Dozen, **1.50**
No. 701 1 pt., Enameled Tin, Assorted Straight and Bent Spouts ....Per Dozen, **2.00**
No. 0900 1 pt., Copper-plated, Straight Spout ....Per Dozen, **2.25**
No. 0901 1 pt., Copper-plated, Bent Spout ....Per Dozen, **2.25**

One Dozen in a Box.

No. 1304

Nos. 1506 and 1509

GEM PATENT MACHINISTS'

Made of No. 20 Gauge Cold Rolled Steel, Brazed, Highly Polished and Copper-plated. Bushings Are Machine Cut, Solid Brass Castings and All Parts Are Interchangeable. Have Special Spout Cleaning Device.

	Capacity	Diameter	Spout	Per Dozen	
No. 1304	½ pt.	3¼ in.	4 in. Straight	$6.00	**10.00**
No. 1506	1 pt.	4½ in.	6 in. Bent	8.50	**16.00**
No. 1509	1 pt.	4½ in.	9 in. Bent	9.00	**17.00**

Nos. 204, 304 and 404

Nos. 209, 309 and 409

MACHINISTS'

These Oilers Are Made in the Same Way and the Same Materials as Nos. 1304, 1506 and 1509, but do not have the Cleaning Device.

	Capacity	Diameter	Spout	Per Dozen	
No. 204	⅓ pt.	3⅛ in.	4 in. Straight	$5.00	**7.20**
No. 209	⅓ pt.	3⅛ in.	9 in. Bent	6.00	**8.50**
No. 304	½ pt.	3¼ in.	4 in. Straight	6.00	**8.50**
No. 309	½ pt.	3¼ in.	9 in. Bent	7.00	**10.00**
No. 404	¾ pt.	4⅛ in.	4 in. Straight	7.00	**10.00**
No. 409	¾ pt.	4⅛ in.	9 in. Bent	8.00	**11.50**

Half Dozen in a Box.

PUMP OILERS

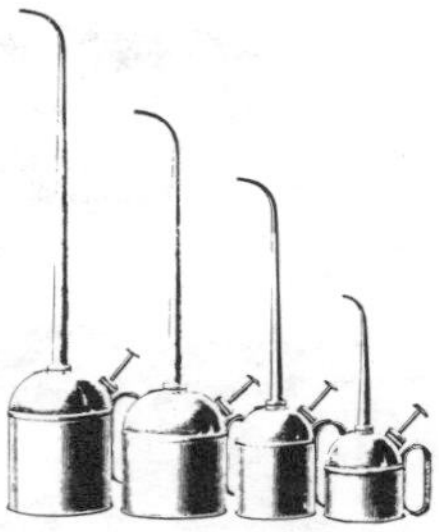

Nos. 400, 402 and 405

	Capacity	Diameter	Spout	Per Dozen	
No. 400	½ pt.	3 in.	6 in.	$23.00	**9.25**
No. 402	1 pt.	3 in.	10 in.	25.25	**10.00**
No. 405	2 pt.	4 in.	16 in.	32.25	**13.00**

Nos. 400 and 401, One Dozen; No. 405, Half Dozen in a Box.

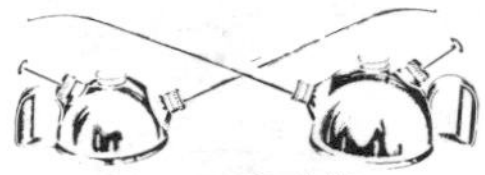

Nos. 801, 802 and 804

These Pump Oilers Are Drawn Seamless in One Piece from No. 2(Gauge Cold Rolled Steel and Heavily Copper-plated. The Construction i: Simple, but at the Same Time Positive. The Pump Will Deliver Oil a the Bearings in Such Quantity the Operator Desires. The Spouts Ar(Detachable and Made with Union Connection Turned from Solid Bras: Bar, with Machine Cut Threads.

	Capacity	Diameter	Spout	Per Dozen	
No. 801	½ pt.	3¼ in.	5 in.	$23.50	**18.8(**
No. 802	½ pt.	3¼ in.	9 in.	24.00	**19.2(**
No. 804	1 pt.	4¼ in.	9 in.	25.75	**20.6(**

Half Dozen in a Box.

Nos. C30 to 40

ENGINEERS' SETS

Steel, Copper-plated

With Round Tray

No. C30 Five Pieces, Including Tray........................Per Set, **$4.00**
No. C40 Six Pieces, Including Tray........................Per Set, **5.75**

One Set in a Box.

Brass

With Round Tray

No. 30 Five Pieces, Including Tray........................Per Set, **$6.00**
No. 40 Six Pieces, Including Tray........................Per Set, **9.00**

One Set in a Box.

OIL CAN FILLER

No. 11 1 qt., Zinc........Per Dozen, **$12.00**

No. 210 1 qt., Copper-plated Steel.........................Per Dozen, **$15.00**

No. 200 1 qt. Brass......Per Dozen, **30.00**

TALLOW POTS

Copper-plated Steel

No. 212 1 qt. ....Per Dozen, **$14.00**
No. 213 2 qt. ....Per Dozen, **16.50**

One Quart, Half Dozen; Two Quart, One Sixth Dozen in a Box.

Jacket Kerosene Oil Cans.

	PER DOZEN.
One Gallon,	$
Two "	

The materials are superior, and every Can warranted tight. The Ash Wood Case (Jacket) is nicely finished in Oil and Varnish, the Bail furnished with a Wood Roll, while our New Patent Top is complete, closing Nozzle, Spout and Vent perfectly, so there is no possibility of loss of Oil if the Can is upset.

HALF DOZEN IN A CASE

"Little Will" Oil Cans.

With Jacket.

"Little Will" Oil Can, with Standard, 5 Gallons, $

This complete Family and Shipping Oil Can is made of the best grades of Charcoal Tin Plates, double seamed and soldered. Warranted tight.

The Wood Veneer Case is nicely finished and varnished. The frame is made from one piece of No. 6 Wire, bent in such shape as to form a very strong and handsome support, is nicely painted, and is readily attached and detached. Handle and Trunions of Japanned Iron, strongly fastened with Clout Nails.

Patent Galvanized Oil Cans.

Gallons,	1	2
Per Dozen,	$	

These Oil Cans are made of Galvanized Iron, and have a painted Wood Bottom, fitted into the pail beneath the Iron Bottom, and is put on so that dampness cannot come in contact with the metal bottom, should the can be put in a wet place.

Wilson's Patent Lamp Filler.

Gallons,	1	2
Per Dozen,	$	

The Sides and Bottom of this superior Kerosene Can, are composed of Galvanized Iron, while the breast, which is least exposed to action of the Oil, is of Tin. The bottom is set up and the sides turn inward, forming a bead upon which the can rests. We feel warranted in saying that this Can, with ordinary care, will last a lifetime.

The distinguishing feature of this Can, however, is the arrangement of the Spout, Vent and Nozzle in such a manner that all are closed by a single Stopper, and the use of Caps for the Spouts entirely dispensed with.

HALF DOZEN IN A CASE

OILERS

CHACE'S

Zinc Body, Tin Bottom

Nos.	**0**	**1**	**1½**	**2**	**3**	**4**	**5**	**6**
Diam. of Bottom, in.	2⅛	2⅝	2⅞	3¼	3¾	4⅛	4½	4⅞
Per Dozen	$1.25	1.50	1.75	2.00	2.25	2.75	3.50	4.50
	.75	**.90**	**1.05**	**1.20**	**1.35**	**1.65**	**2.10**	**2.70**

Half Dozen in a Box.

EXTRA SPOUTS

Nos.	**1**	**2**	**3**	**4**
Per Dozen	$0.75	.80	.90	1.00

PARAGON

Zinc Body, Tin Bottom

No. 30 Diameter of Bottom 3¾ in. ....Per Dozen, $3.25 **2.75**
No. 40 Diameter of Bottom 4 in. ....Per Dozen, 3.75 **3.50**

Brass

No. 030 Diameter of Bottom 3¾ in. ....Per Dozen, $5.25 **6.50**
No. 040 Diameter of Bottom 4 in. ....Per Dozen, 6.00 **7.00**

Half Dozen in a Box.

Automatic Zinc

Nos.	**100**	**200**
Diameter at Top ....Inches,	2⅞	3¼
Per Dozen	$3.50	4.00
	4.75	**5.50**

Half Dozen in a Box.

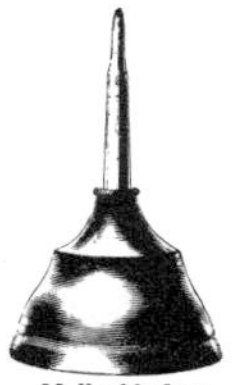

Malleable Iron

Nos.	**01**	**02**	**03**
Diameter of Bottom ....Inches,	3¼	3⅝	3⅞
Per Dozen	**$3.60**	**4.00**	**4.40**

Extra Spouts, 3 in. Long ....Per Dozen, **$1.50**

Oilers One Dozen in a Box.

SEWING MACHINE

Japanned

No. 665 2⅝ in. Diameter ....Per Dozen, **$1.25**

One Dozen in a Box.

BICYCLE

See General Index.

OIL CANS

No. 5D

DELPHOS NON-OVERFLOW

Heavy Galvanized Steel Body; Top is Made of Best Tin, Supported by Galvanized Iron Braces; Hinge Cover Conceals the Pump and Keeps out the Dirt; has a Neat Spun Edge, an Enameled Knob to Raise it and a Spring Catch to Hold it in Place; Wire Bail, Black Enameled Wood Handle; Double Tube Tin Pump; Impossible to Overfill Lamp or Vessel, for as Soon as Oil is Level with Pump Tubes, it is Syphoned Back into the Can Through One Tube as Fast as it Flows in Through the Other; Weight Per Dozen, 100 Pounds.

No. 5D Five Gallon......Per Dozen **$27.00**

No. 45

Made of Extra Heavy Galvanized Iron; Steam Tested, Guaranteed not to Leak; an Extraordinary High Grade Can; Wire Bail, Black Enameled Wood Grip; Solid Brass Lever Faucet, Highly Polished; Weight Per Dozen, 84 Pounds.

No. 45 Five Gallon.....Per Dozen, **$20.00**

No. 35

Made of 28 Gauge Galvanized Iron; Hand Soldered; Handsomely Striped with Red Enamel; Tee Faucet; a Strictly High Grade Can Throughout; Weight Per Dozen, 75 Pounds.

No. 35 Five Gallon.....Per Dozen, **$12.50**

Quarter Dozen in a Crate.

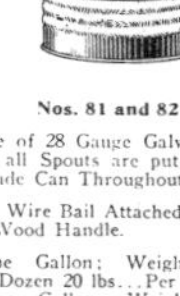

Nos. 81 and 82

Nos. 83 and 85

Made of 28 Gauge Galvanized Iron; Hand Soldered; Handsomely Striped with Red Enamel; all Spouts are put on from the Inside, Making them Firm and Strong; a Strictly High Grade Can Throughout.

Tin Top; Wire Bail Attached to Top; Black Enameled Wood Handle.

No. 81 One Gallon; Weight Per Dozen 20 lbs...Per Dozen, **$4.00**
No. 82 Two Gallon; Weight Per Dozen 38 lbs...Per Dozen, **6.50**

No. 81 One Dozen, No. 82 Half Dozen in a Crate.

Galvanized Top; Wire Bail Attached to Body; Black Enameled Wood Handle.

No. 83 Three Gallon; Weight Per Dozen 63 lbs...Per Dozen, **$9.00**
No. 85 Five Gallon; Weight Per Dozen 75 lbs...Per Dozen, **11.00**

Quarter Dozen in a Crate.

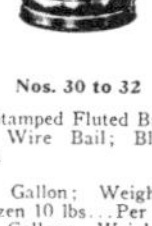

Nos. 30 to 32

Plain Tin; Stamped Fluted Breast; Soldered Bent Spout; Wire Bail; Black Enameled Wood Handle.

No. 30 Half Gallon; Weight Per Dozen 10 lbs...Per Dozen, **$3.40**
No. 31 One Gallon; Weight Per Dozen 15 lbs...Per Dozen, **4.50**
No. 32 Two Gallon; Weight Per Dozen 25 lbs...Per Dozen, **7.50**

Nos. 30 and 31 One Dozen, No. 32 Half Dozen in a Crate.

CLAMPS, ETC.

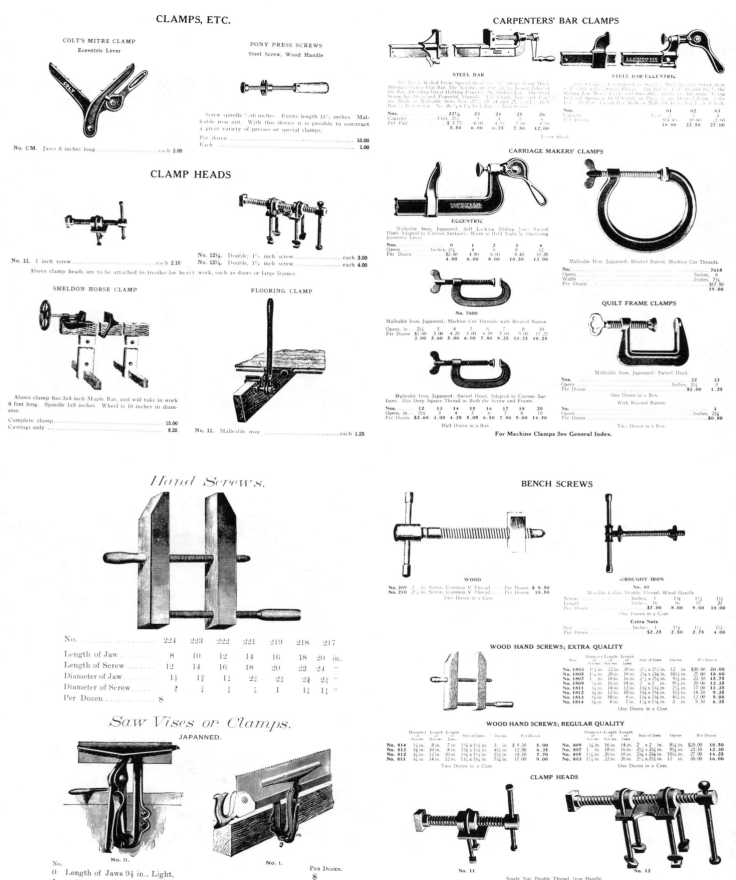

COLT'S MITRE CLAMP

Eccentric Lever

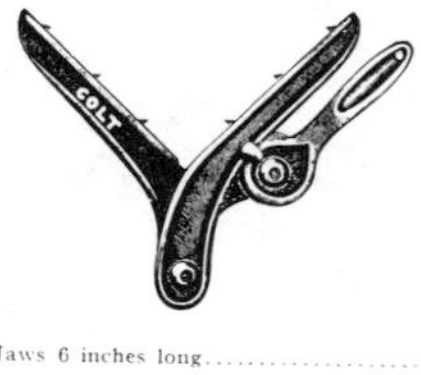

No. CM. Jaws 6 inches long........................each 2.00

PONY PRESS SCREWS

Steel Screw, Wood Handle

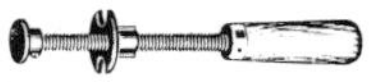

Screw spindle ½x6 inches. Entire length 11½ inches. Malleable iron nut. With this device it is possible to construct a great variety of presses or special clamps.

Per dozen 10.00
Each 1.00

CLAMP HEADS

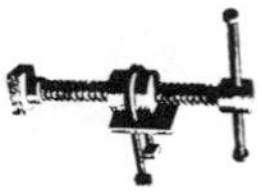

No. 11. 1 inch screw................................each 2.10

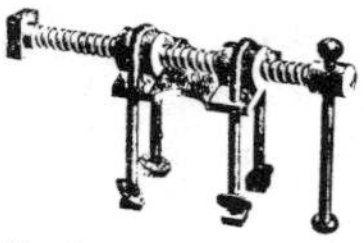

No. 12⅛. Double, 1⅛ inch screw..................each 3.00
No. 12¼. Double, 1¼ inch screw..................each 4.00

Above clamp heads are to be attached to trestles for heavy work, such as doors or large frames.

SHELDON HORSE CLAMP

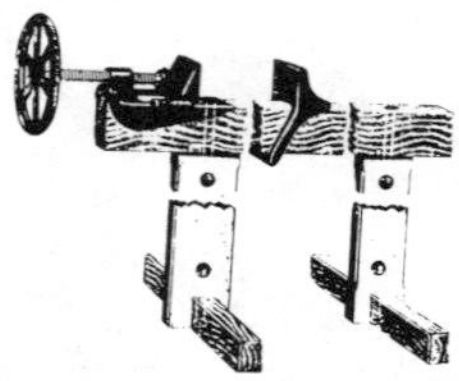

Above clamp has 3x4 inch Maple Bar, and will take in work 6 feet long. Spindle 1x9 inches. Wheel is 10 inches in diameter.

Complete clamp.. 15.00
Castings only 8.25

FLOORING CLAMP

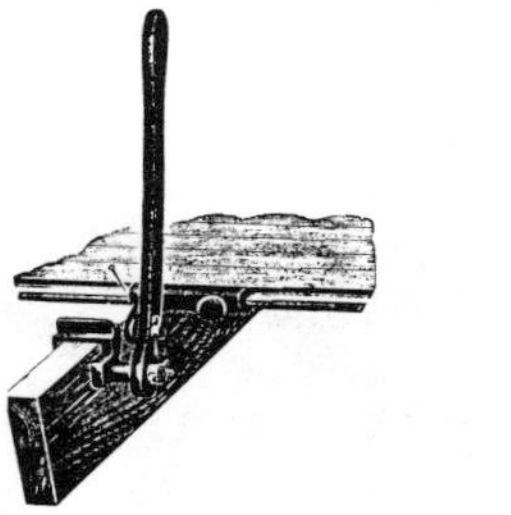

No. 11. Malleable iron ....each 1.25

CARPENTERS' BAR CLAMPS

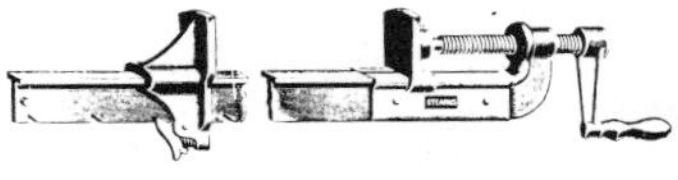

STEEL BAR

The Bar is Rolled From Special Steel, the "I" Shape Being Much Stronger than a Flat Bar. The Notches are Cut on the Lower Edge of the Bar, Affording Great Holding Power to the Sliding Jaw. The Steel Screw has Deep and Powerful Threads. The Crank, Jaws and Pawl are Made of Malleable Iron. Nos. 22½, 23, 24 and 25, ⅝ x 1¼ Inch Bar, ⅝ Inch Screw. No. 26, ¾ x 1¾ Inch Bar, ¾ Inch Screw.

Nos.	22½	23	24	25	26
Capacity ....Feet,	2½	3	4	5	6
Per Pair	$ 3.75	4.00	4.50	5.00	8.50
	5.50	**6.00**	**6.75**	**7.50**	**12.00**

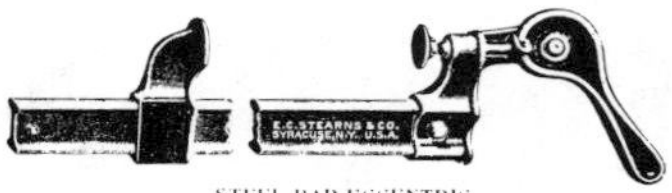

STEEL BAR ECCENTRIC

This Clamp is Constructed to Stand a Much Greater Strain than is Possible with a Single Flange. The Bar is of "I" Shaped Steel, the Sliding Jaw Moves Easily and Smoothly, and by an Automatic Acting Inclosed Spring is Held Firmly in Place at any Desired Point of the Bar. All Parts Except Bar Made of Malleable Iron. Bar 1⅛ x ⅜ Inch.

Nos.	01	02	03
Capacity ....Feet,	2	3	4
Per Dozen	$14.40	18.00	21.60
	18.00	**22.50**	**27.00**

Loose Stock

CARRIAGE MAKERS' CLAMPS

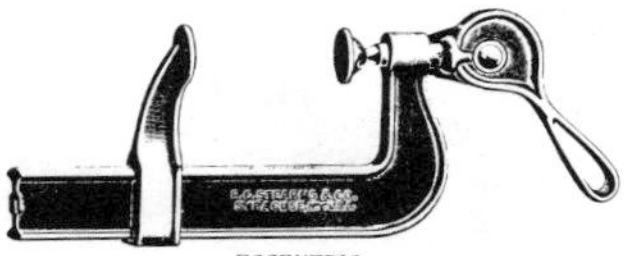

ECCENTRIC

Malleable Iron, Japanned; Self Locking Sliding Jaw; Swivel Head Adapted to Uneven Surfaces; Work is Held Tight by Operating Eccentric Lever.

Nos.	0	1	2	3	4
Opens ....Inches,	2¼	4	6	8	12
Per Dozen	$3.60	4.80	6.60	8.40	10.20
	4.00	**6.00**	**8.00**	**10.50**	**13.00**

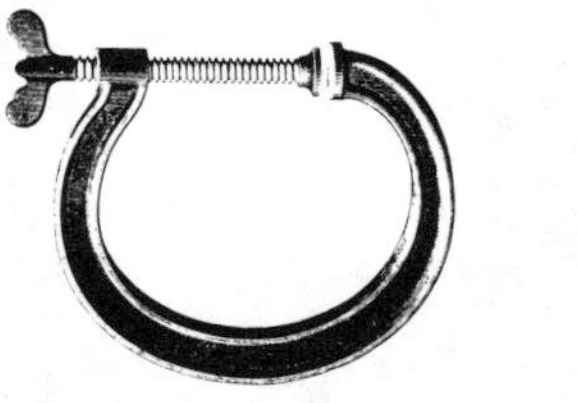

Malleable Iron, Japanned; Riveted Button, Machine Cut Threads.

No. 7618
Opens ....Inches, 6
Width ....Inches, 7½
Per Dozen $17.50
19.00

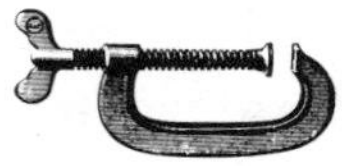

No. 7600

Malleable Iron, Japanned; Machine Cut Threads, with Riveted Button.

Opens, in...	2½	3	4	5	6	7	8	10
Per Dozen	$2.60	3.00	4.20	5.00	6.50	7.80	9.00	15.25
	3.00	**3.60**	**5.00**	**6.00**	**7.80**	**9.25**	**10.75**	**18.25**

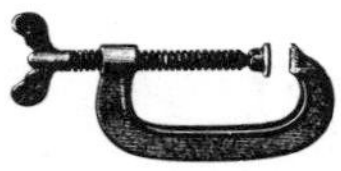

Malleable Iron, Japanned; Swivel Head, Adapted to Uneven Surfaces. Has Deep Square Thread in Both the Screw and Frame.

Nos.	12	13	14	15	16	17	18	20
Opens, in...	2½	3	4	5	6	7	8	10
Per Dozen	**$2.60**	**3.00**	**4.20**	**5.00**	**6.50**	**7.80**	**9.00**	**14.50**

Half Dozen in a Box.

QUILT FRAME CLAMPS

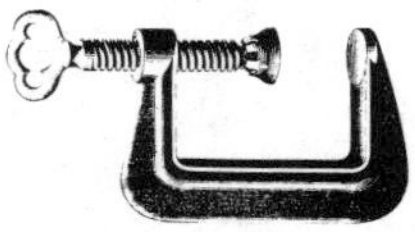

Malleable Iron, Japanned; Swivel Head.

Nos.	32	33
Opens ....Inches,	2¼	3
Per Dozen	**$1.00**	**1.25**

One Dozen in a Box.

With Riveted Button.

No. 1
Opens ....Inches, 2¼
Per Dozen **$0.80**

Two Dozen in a Box.

For Machine Clamps See General Index.

Hand Screws.

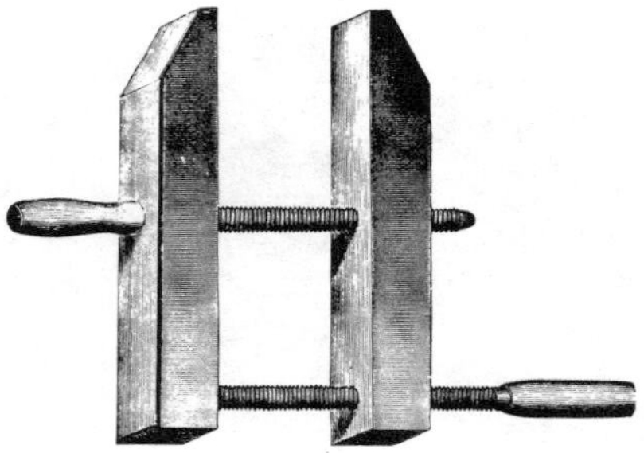

No.	224	223	222	221	219	218	217	
Length of Jaw..........	8	10	12	14	16	18	20	in.
Length of Screw	12	14	16	18	20	22	24	"
Diameter of Jaw........	1½	1¾	1⅞	2⅜	2⅜	2⅝	2⅝	"
Diameter of Screw	⅝	¾	¾	⅞	1	1⅛	1¼	"
Per Dozen .... $								

Saw Vises or Clamps.

JAPANNED.

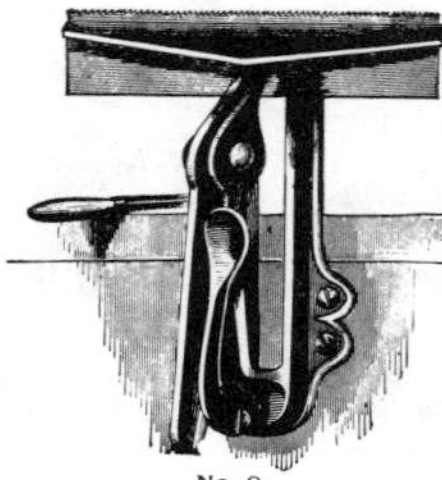

No. 0.

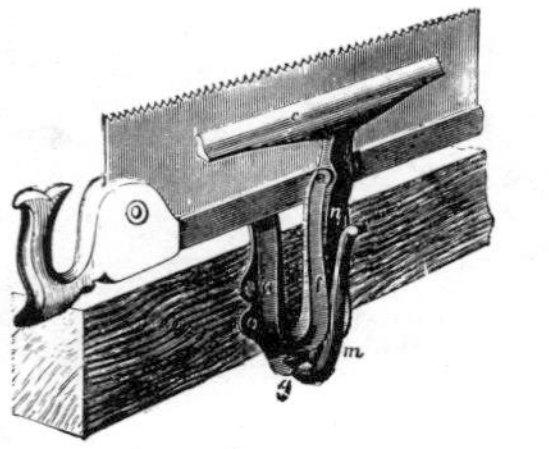

No. 1.

No.		Per Dozen.
0	Length of Jaws 9½ in., Light,	$
1	" " 9½ in., Heavy,	

BENCH SCREWS

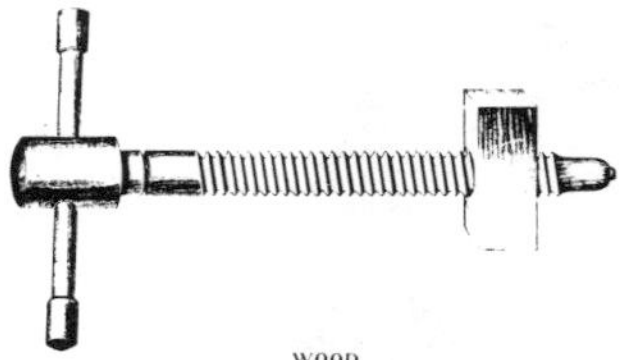

WOOD

No. 209 2 in. Screw, Common V Thread......Per Dozen, **$ 9.50**
No. 210 2½ in. Screw, Common V Thread......Per Dozen, **10.50**

Two Dozen in a Case.

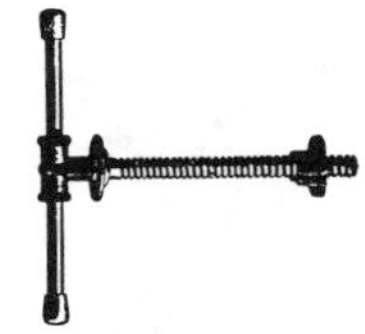

WROUGHT IRON

No. 40

Movable Collar, Double Thread, Wood Handle.

Screw ....Inches,	1	1⅛	1¼	1½
Length ....Inches,	16	16	17	20
Per Dozen	**$7.00**	**8.00**	**9.00**	**10.00**

One Dozen in a Case.

Extra Nuts

Size ....Inches,	1	1⅛	1¼	1½
Per Dozen	**$2.25**	**2.50**	**2.75**	**4.00**

WOOD HAND SCREWS; EXTRA QUALITY

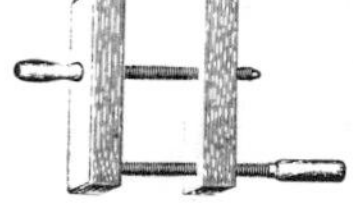

Nos.	Diameter of Screws	Length of Screws	Length of Jaws	Size of Jaws	Opens	Per Dozen	
No. 1803	1¼ in.	22 in.	20 in.	2½ x 2½ in.	12 in.	$30.00	**20.00**
No. 1805	1⅛ in.	20 in.	18 in.	2⅜ x 2⅜ in.	10½ in.	27.00	**18.00**
No. 1807	1 in.	18 in.	16 in.	2¼ x 2¼ in.	9¼ in.	23.50	**15.75**
No. 1809	⅞ in.	16 in.	14 in.	2 x 2 in.	8¼ in.	20.00	**13.35**
No. 1811	¾ in.	14 in.	12 in.	1¾ x 1¾ in.	7¼ in.	17.00	**11.35**
No. 1812	¾ in.	12 in.	10 in.	1⅝ x 1⅝ in.	5½ in.	14.50	**9.35**
No. 1813	⅝ in.	10 in.	8 in.	1⅜ x 1⅜ in.	4½ in.	12.00	**9.00**
No. 1814	⅝ in.	8 in.	7 in.	1⅛ x 1⅛ in.	3 in.	9.50	**6.35**

One Dozen in a Case.

WOOD HAND SCREWS; REGULAR QUALITY

	Diameter of Screws	Length of Screws	Length of Jaws	Size of Jaws	Opens	Per Dozen	
No. 814	⅝ in.	8 in.	7 in.	1⅛ x 1⅛ in.	3 in.	$ 9.50	**5.00**
No. 813	⅝ in.	10 in.	8 in.	1⅜ x 1⅜ in.	4½ in.	12.00	**6.35**
No. 812	¾ in.	12 in.	10 in.	1⅝ x 1⅝ in.	5½ in.	14.50	**7.70**
No. 811	¾ in.	14 in.	12 in.	1¾ x 1¾ in.	7¼ in.	17.00	**9.00**

Two Dozen in a Case.

	Diameter of Screws	Length of Screws	Length of Jaws	Size of Jaws	Opens	Per Dozen	
No. 809	⅞ in.	16 in.	14 in.	2 x 2 in.	8¼ in.	$20.00	**10.50**
No. 807	1 in.	18 in.	16 in.	2¼ x 2¼ in.	9¼ in.	23.50	**12.30**
No. 805	1⅛ in.	20 in.	18 in.	2⅜ x 2⅜ in.	10½ in.	27.00	**14.25**
No. 803	1¼ in.	22 in.	20 in.	2½ x 2½ in.	12 in.	30.00	**16.00**

One Dozen in a Case.

CLAMP HEADS

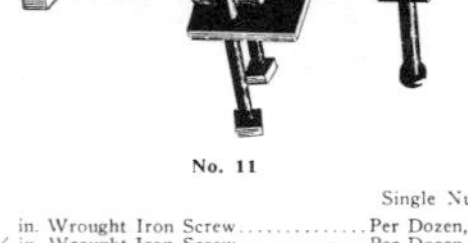

No. 11

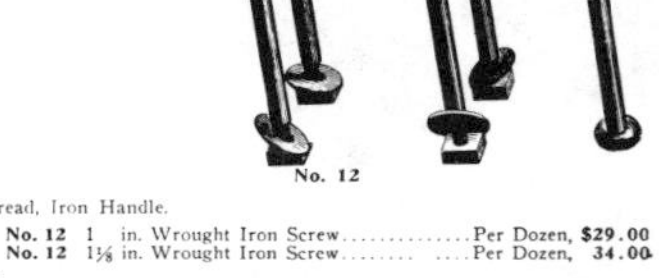

No. 12

Single Nut, Double Thread, Iron Handle.

No. 11 1 in. Wrought Iron Screw..............Per Dozen, **$21.50**
No. 11 1⅛ in. Wrought Iron Screw..............Per Dozen, **30.00**
No. 12 1 in. Wrought Iron Screw..............Per Dozen, **$29.00**
No. 12 1⅛ in. Wrought Iron Screw..............Per Dozen, **34.00**

Loose.

BOYS' TOOL CHESTS

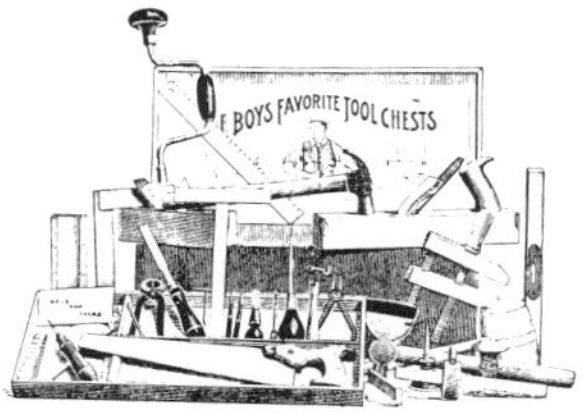

No. 5000 Size 20 x 11 x 8

Chestnut Box, Locked Corners; with Movable Tray; Hinged Lid, Beaded Mouldings, Bronzed Handles and Well Varnished; Containing 35 Tools; Including Polished Hammer and Hatchet ....Per Dozen, **$90.00**

No. 4500 Size 20 x 11 x 8

Chestnut Box; Locked Corners; with Movable Tray; Hinged Lid, Beaded Mouldings, Bronzed Handles and Well Varnished; Containing 32 Tools; Including Bracketsaw and Polished Hammer ....Per Dozen, **$80.00**

No. 3900 Size 19 x 10½ x 7

Chestnut Box; Locked Corners; with Movable Tray; Hinged Lid; Beaded Mouldings, Bronzed Handles and Well Varnished; Containing 30 Tools; Including Spirit Level and Polished Hammer ....Per Dozen, **$56.00**

Half Dozen in a Crate.

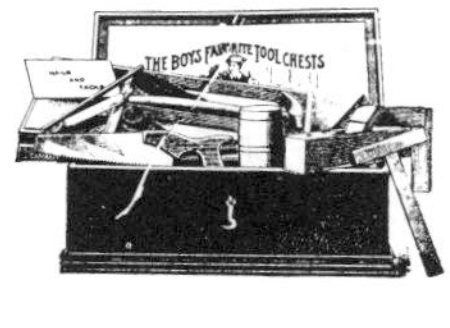

No. 3700 Size 16½ x 8¾ x 6

Chestnut Box; Locked Corners; with Movable Tray; Hinged Lid; Beaded Mouldings and Well Varnished; Containing 19 Tools; Including Hatchet........Per Dozen, **$25.00**

One Dozen in a Crate.

No. 3600 Size 15½ x 8 x 5½

Chestnut Box; Locked Corners; with Movable Tray; Hinged Lid; Beaded Mouldings and Well Varnished; Containing 16 Tools........................Per Dozen, **$20.00**

One Dozen in a Crate.

No. 380 Size 14½ x 7 x 5½

Chestnut Box; Locked Corners; with Movable Tray; Hinged Lid; Beaded Mouldings and Well Varnished; Containing 14 Tools........................Per Dozen, **$16.00**

Two Dozen in a Crate.

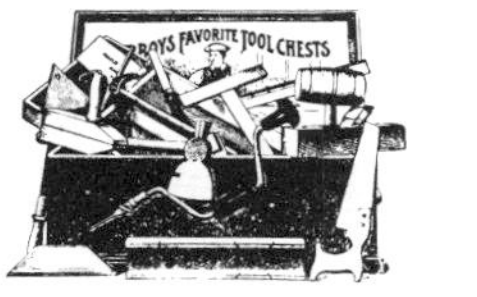

No. 3800 Size 19 x 10½ x 7

Chestnut Box, Lock Corners With Movable Tray; Hinged Lid; Beaded Mouldings; Bronzed Handles and Well Varnished; Containing 28 Tools; Including Brace and Bit ....Per Dozen, **$45.00**

No. 3725 Size 18 x 9¼ x 6½

Chestnut Box; Locked Corners; with Movable Tray; Hinged Lid; Beaded Mouldings; Bronzed Handles and Well Varnished; Containing 23 Tools; Including Brace and Bit ....Per Dozen, **$28.00**

One Dozen in a Crate.

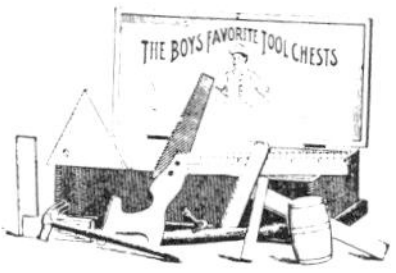

No. 360 Size 12½ x 6 x 4

Chestnut Box; Locked Corners; with Till; Hinged Lid; Beaded Mouldings and Well Varnished; Containing 10 Tools ....Per Dozen, **$12.00**

Four Dozen in a Crate.

No. 355 Size 11½ x 5½ x 3½

Chestnut Box; Locked Corners, Hinged Lid; Beaded Mouldings and Well Varnished; Containing 11 Tools ....Per Doz, **$8.00**

Six Dozen in a Crate.

No. 345 Size 10¾ x 5 x 3

Chestnut Box; Locked Corners, Hinged Lid; Beaded Mouldings and Well Varnished; Containing 10 Tools........................Per Dozen, **$5.00**

Six Dozen in a Crate.

CARPENTERS' TOOL CHESTS

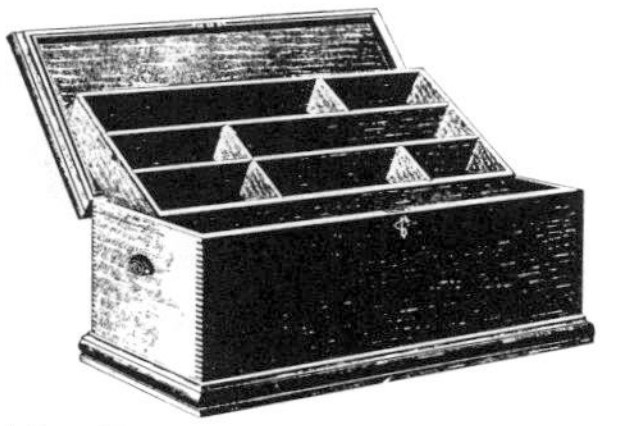

Made of Selected Ash, Varnished, Bronzed Handles, with Tray and Lock; 26 Inches Long, 12 Inches High and 15 Inches Wide.
No. 500 ....Each, **$9.00**

One in a Crate.

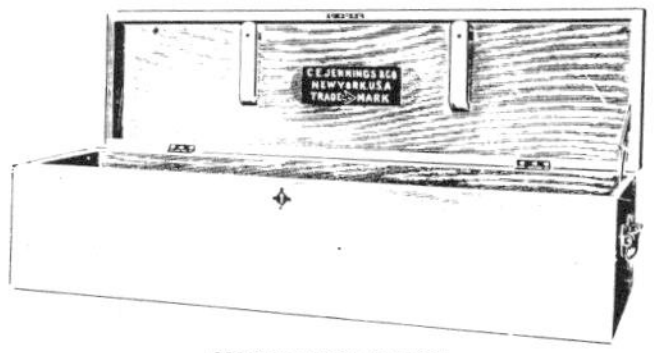

SHOULDER CHEST

This is a Portable Tool Chest, and can be Conveniently Carried on the Shoulder. It is Made of Chestnut, with Locked Corners; Has Lock, Elbow to Support Lid when Open, Drop Handles and a Rack for Holding Saws. Will Hold a 28 Inch Rip saw.
No. 20 Inside Dimensions, 33 Inches Long by 8 Inches Wide by 8 Inches Deep ....Each, **$6.00**

Six in a Crate.

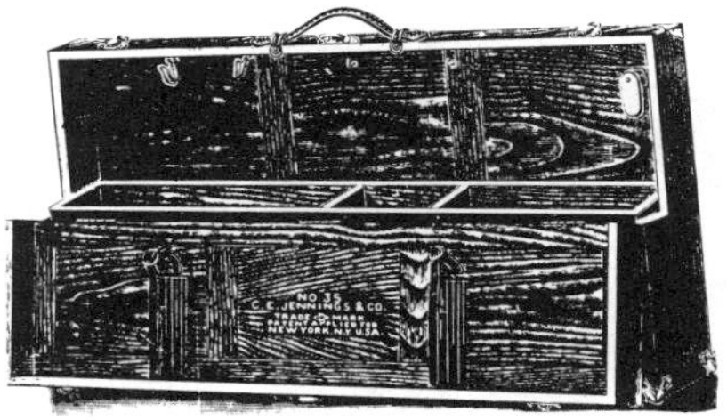

HAND CHESTS

Made of Selected Hard Wood Handsomely Finished and with Paneled Sides. Furnished with Brass Lock, Leather Handle with Rings for Strap Over Shoulder, Metal Clasps, Metal Corners, Saw Rack for Holding Four Saws, Including a 28 Inch Rip-saw, Hooks for Brace and Coping Saw, Wood Button for Try Square, Partitioned Tray for Bits, Chisels and Small Tools, Space in Bottom to Hold Planes, Levels, etc., and will Take a Steel Square with an 18 Inch Tongue.

Outside Dimensions, Length 34½ Inches, Height 17 Inches, Width 6 Inches.

Inside Dimensions, Length 33 Inches, Height 15¾ Inches, Width 5 Inches.

Inside Dimensions of Removable Tray, Length 32½ Inches, Height 1¾ Inches, Width 4½ Inches.

No. 35 ....Each, **$15.00**

Six in a Crate.

MACHINISTS' TOOL CHESTS

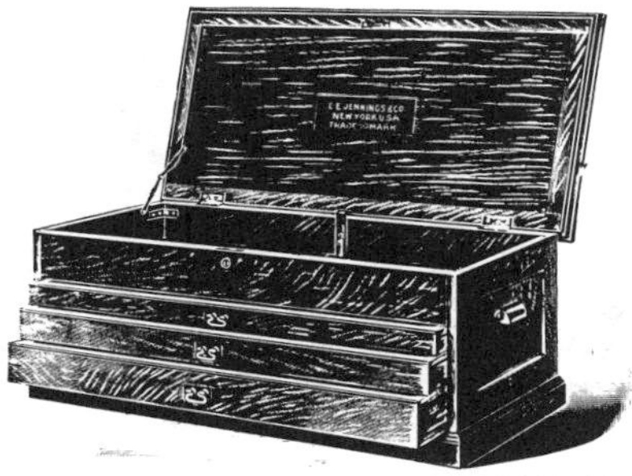

These Chests are Made of Selected Oak and Furnished With Brass Cylinder Locks and Nickel-plated Drawer Pulls. Each Chest is Provided With a Metal Elbow to Support Lid, a Patent Device for Locking All the Drawers at Once Automatically, by Closing of the Lid; Outside Dimensions, 29½ Inches Long, 14½ Inches Wide by 12 Inches High.

Receptacle Under Lid, 27 Inches Long by 11⅝ Inches Wide by 3⅛ Inches Deep.
First Drawer, 25⅞ Inches Long by 10½ Inches Wide by 1⅛ Inches Deep.
Second Drawer, 25⅞ Inches Long by 10½ Inches Wide by 1⅝ Inches Deep.
Third Drawer, 25⅞ Inches Long by 10½ Inches Wide by 2½ Inches Deep.

No. 23 With Three Drawers; Made of Quartered Oak; Antique Finish ....Each, **$17.00**

One in a Case.

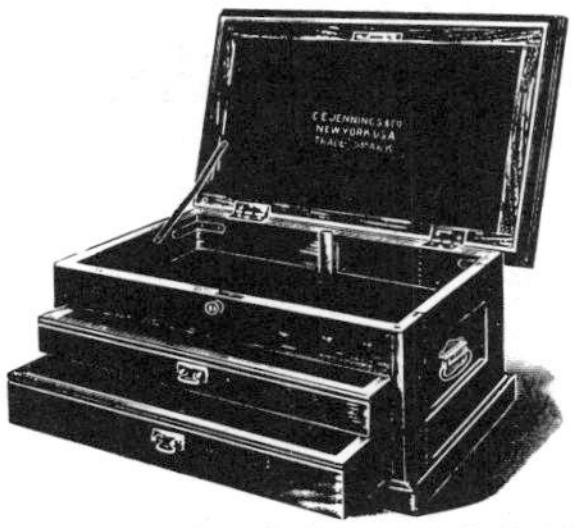

No. 21 Made of Selected Hardwood and are Furnished With a Brass Cylinder Lock, Nickel-plated Drawer Pulls, Drop Handles and an Automatic Locking Device. It is Made of Chestnut with Chestnut Panels and Mouldings.

Outside Dimensions, 20⅝ Inches Long by 13 Inches Wide by 10⅝ Inches High.

Inside Dimensions are as Follows:

Receptacle Under Lid, 18 Inches Long by 10¼ Inches Wide by 3⅛ Inches Deep.

First Drawer, 16⅞ inches Long by 9 Inches Wide by 1⅝ Inches Deep.

Second Drawer, 16⅞ Inches Long by 9 Inches Wide by 2½ Inches Deep.

Space Under Second Drawer, 1 Inch Deep.

No. 21 With Two Drawers ....Each, **$12.00**

One in a Case.

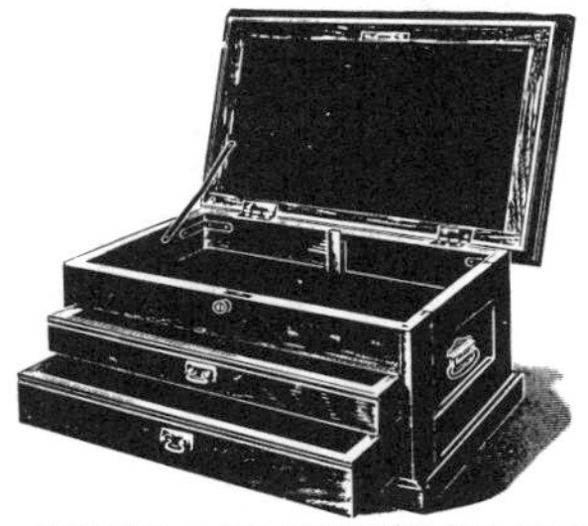

No. 25 Chests are Made of Selected Hard Woods, and are Furnished with Brass Cylinder Lock and Nickel-plated Drawer Pulls. Each Chest is Provided with a Metal Elbow to Support Lid and a Patent Device for Locking All the Drawers at Once Automatically, by the Closing of the Lid.

Outside Dimensions, 20⅝ Inches Long by 13 Inches Wide by 10⅝ Inches High.

Inside Dimensions are as Follows:

Receptacle Under Lid, 18 Inches Long by 10¼ Inches Wide by 3⅛ Inches Deep.

First Drawer, 16⅞ Inches Long by 9 Inches Wide by 1⅝ Inches Deep.

Second Drawer, 16⅞ Inches Long by 9 Inches Wide by 2½ Inches Deep.

Space Under Second Drawer, 1 Inch Deep.

No. 25 With Two Drawers, Made of Chestnut, With Black Walnut Panels ....Each, **$13.50**

Boy's Tool Chests.

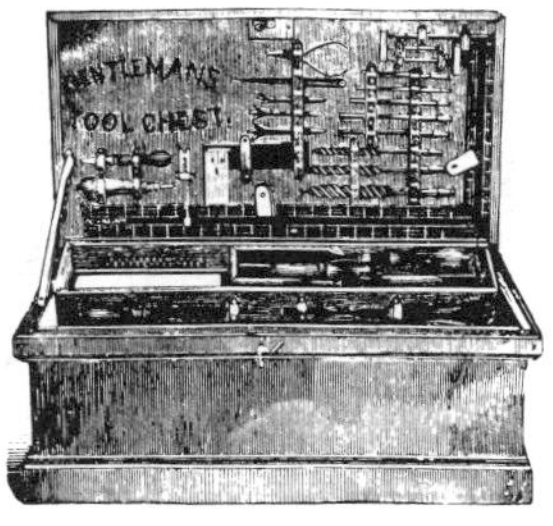

No.		Each.
1	Ten Tools,	$

Contents: Saw, Hammer, Chisel, Rule, Screw Driver, Brad Awl, Pencil, Gimlet, Gauge, Plane.

No.		Each.
2	Fifteen Tools,	$

Contents: Saw, Hammer, Plane, Hatchet, Gimlet, Chisel, File, Gauge, Pencil, Brad Awl, Brace, Brace Bit, Screw Driver, Mallet, Rule.

No.		Each.
3	Twenty Tools,	$

Contents: Saw, Hammer, Plane, Brace, Hatchet, Clamp, Screw Driver, Chisel, File, Gauge, Brace Bit, Rule, Pliers, Gimlet, Pencil, Brad Awl, Pocket Knife, Mallet, Nail Set, Try Square.

Youth's Tool Chests.

4 Twenty-five Tools, $

Contents: Saw, Hammer, Plane, Hatchet, Brace, 2 Brace Bits, 2 Chisels, Rule, File, Gauge, Screw Driver, Pliers, 2 Gimlets, Pencil, Try Square, Brad Awl, Mallet, Nail Set, Pocket Knife, Oil Stone, Scratch Awl, Oil Can.

5 Forty Tools, $

Contents: Saw, Hammer, Hatchet, 2 Planes, Brace, 4 Brace Bits, Try Square, Pocket Level, 2 Chisels, 2 Files, 3 Gimlets, Oil Stone, Oil Can, Rule, Chalk Line Reel, Clamp, Pliers, Gauge, Mallet, Screw Driver, Scratch Awl, 2 Brad Awls, Pencil, Compasses, Draw Knife, Nail Set, Tape Line, Pocket Knife, Bench Screw, Wrench.

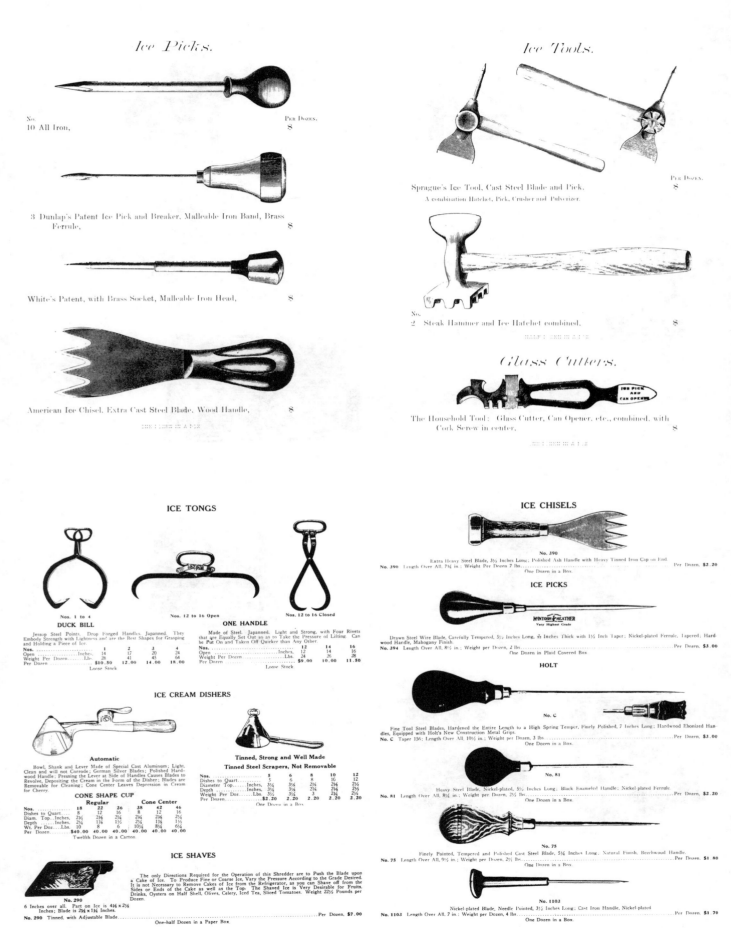

Ice Picks.

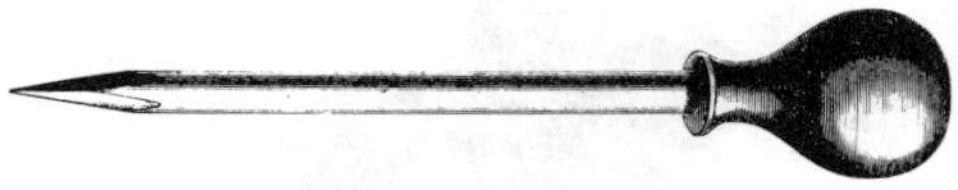

No.		Per Dozen.
10	All Iron,	$

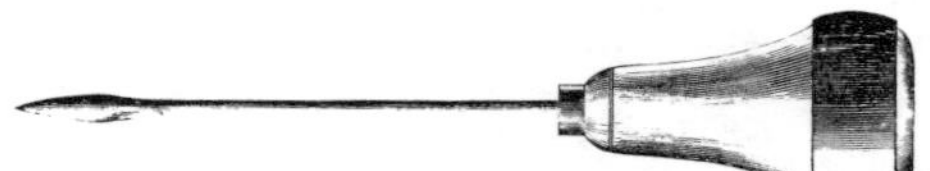

3 Dunlap's Patent Ice Pick and Breaker, Malleable Iron Band, Brass Ferrule, $

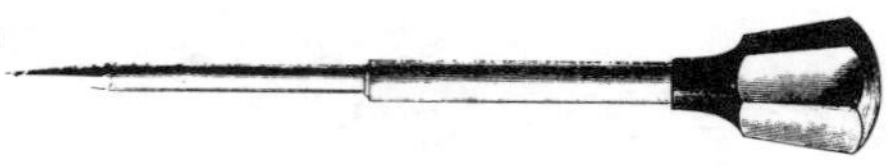

White's Patent, with Brass Socket, Malleable Iron Head, $

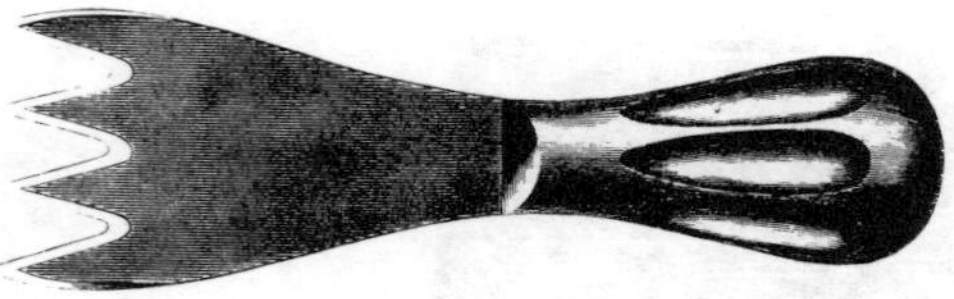

American Ice Chisel, Extra Cast Steel Blade, Wood Handle, $

Ice Tools.

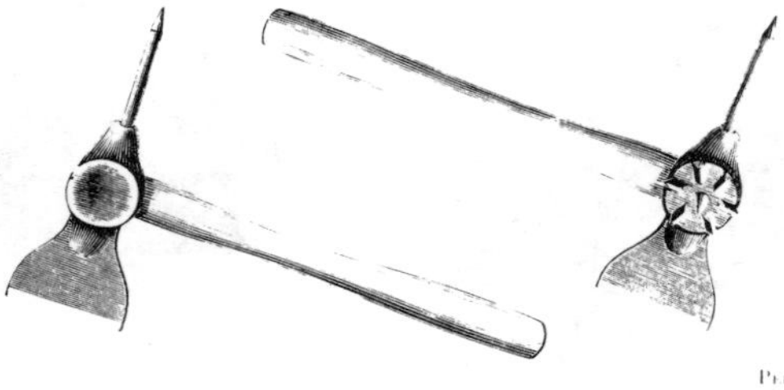

Sprague's Ice Tool, Cast Steel Blade and Pick, Per Dozen. $

A combination Hatchet, Pick, Crusher and Pulverizer.

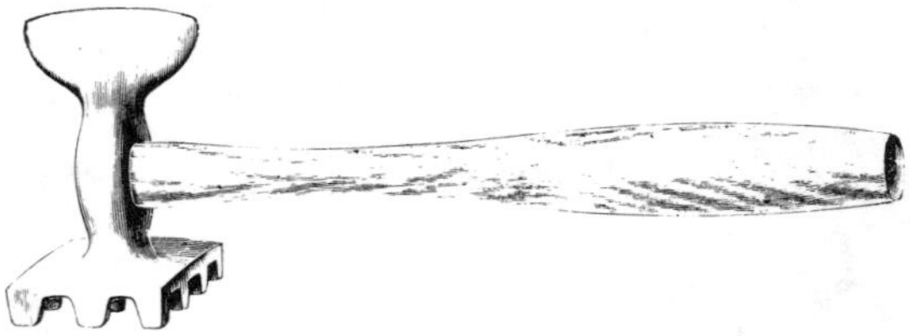

No.
2 Steak Hammer and Ice Hatchet combined, $

Glass Cutters.

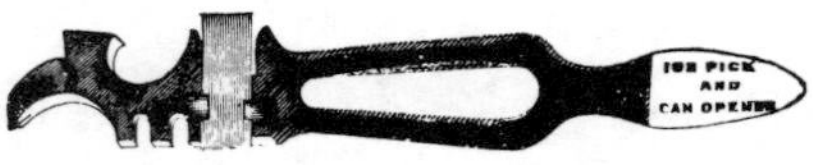

The Household Tool: Glass Cutter, Can Opener, etc., combined, with Cork Screw in center, $

ICE TONGS

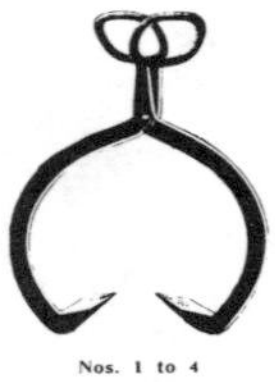

Nos. 1 to 4

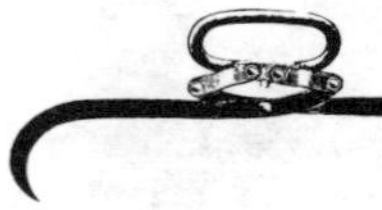

Nos. 12 to 16 Open

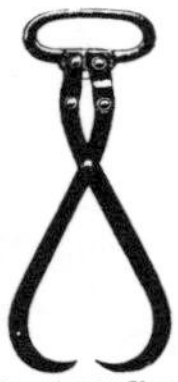

Nos. 12 to 16 Closed

DUCK BILL

Jessop Steel Points. Drop Forged Handles. Japanned. They Embody Strength with Lightness and are the Best Shapes for Grasping and Holding a Piece of Ice.

Nos.	1	2	3	4
Open ....Inches.	14	17	20	24
Weight Per Dozen....Lbs.	28	41	45	64
Per Dozen	$10.50	12.00	14.00	18.00

Loose Stock

ONE HANDLE

Made of Steel. Japanned. Light and Strong, with Four Rivets that are Equally Set Out so as to Take the Pressure of Lifting. Can be Put On and Taken Off Quicker than Any Other.

Nos.	12	14	16
Open ....Inches.	12	14	16
Weight Per Dozen....Lbs.	24	26	28
Per Dozen	$9.00	10.00	11.50

Loose Stock.

ICE CREAM DISHERS

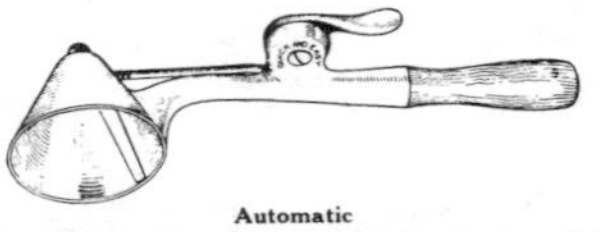

Automatic

Bowl, Shank and Lever Made of Special Cast Aluminum; Light, Clean and will not Corrode; German Silver Blades; Polished Hardwood Handle; Pressing the Lever at Side of Handles Causes Blades to Revolve, Depositing the Cream in the Form of the Disher; Blades are Removable for Cleaning; Cone Center Leaves Depression in Cream for Cherry.

CONE SHAPE CUP

	Regular			Cone Center		
Nos.	18	22	26	38	42	46
Dishes to Quart....	8	12	16	8	12	16
Diam. Top..Inches,	2¼	2⅜	2¼	2¾	2⅜	2¼
Depth ......Inches,	2¼	1⅞	1½	2¼	1⅞	1½
Wt. Per Doz....Lbs.	10	8	6	10¼	8¼	6¼
Per Dozen	$40.00	40.00	40.00	40.00	40.00	40.00

Twelfth Dozen in a Carton.

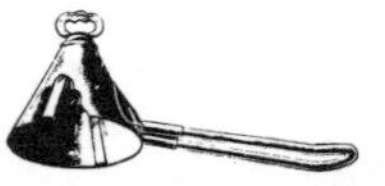

Tinned, Strong and Well Made

Tinned Steel Scrapers, Not Removable

Nos.	5	6	8	10	12
Dishes to Quart..........	5	6	8	16	12
Diameter Top......Inches,	3¼	3⅛	2⅞	2⅝	2½
Depth ....Inches,	3¼	3⅛	2⅞	2⅝	2½
Weight Per Doz......Lbs.	3½	3¼	3	2¾	2½
Per Dozen	$2.20	2.20	2.20	2.20	2.20

One Dozen in a Box.

ICE SHAVES

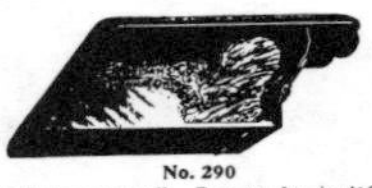

No. 290

6 Inches over all. Part on Ice is 4⅛ x 2⅛ Inches; Blade is 2⅝ x 1¾ Inches.

The only Directions Required for the Operation of this Shredder are to Push the Blade upon a Cake of Ice. To Produce Fine or Coarse Ice, Vary the Pressure According to the Grade Desired. It is not Necessary to Remove Cakes of Ice from the Refrigerator, as you can Shave off from the Sides or Ends of the Cake as well as the Top. The Shaved Ice is Very Desirable for Fruits, Drinks, Oysters on Half Shell, Olives, Celery, Iced Tea, Sliced Tomatoes. Weight 22½ Pounds per Dozen.

No. 290 Tinned, with Adjustable Blade........Per Dozen, **$7.00**

One-half Dozen in a Paper Box.

ICE CHISELS

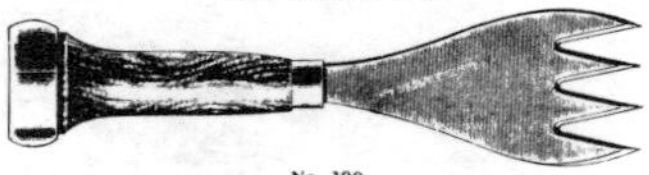

No. 390

Extra Heavy Steel Blade, 3½ Inches Long; Polished Ash Handle with Heavy Tinned Iron Cap on End.

No. 390 Length Over All, 7¾ in.; Weight Per Dozen 7 lbs........Per Dozen, **$2.20**

One Dozen in a Box.

ICE PICKS

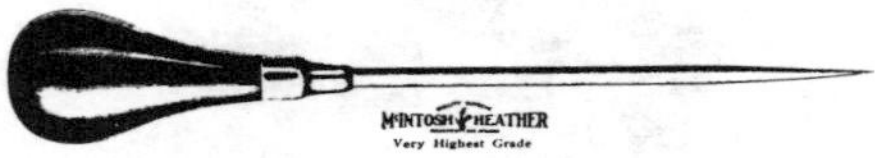

Drawn Steel Wire Blade, Carefully Tempered, 5½ Inches Long, 7/32 Inches Thick with 1½ Inch Taper; Nickel-plated Ferrule, Tapered; Hardwood Handle, Mahogany Finish.

No. 394 Length Over All, 8½ in.; Weight per Dozen, 2 lbs........Per Dozen, **$3.00**

One Dozen in Plaid Covered Box.

HOLT

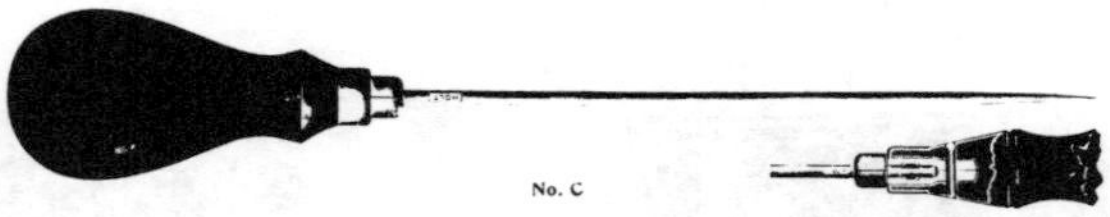

No. C

Fine Tool Steel Blades, Hardened the Entire Length to a High Spring Temper, Finely Polished, 7 Inches Long; Hardwood Ebonized Handles, Equipped with Holt's New Construction Metal Grips.

No. C Taper 156; Length Over All, 10½ in.; Weight per Dozen, 3 lbs........Per Dozen, **$3.00**

One Dozen in a Box.

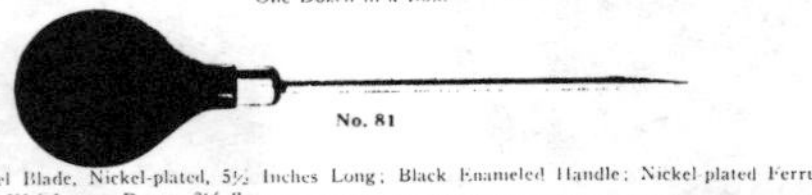

No. 81

Heavy Steel Blade, Nickel-plated, 5½ Inches Long; Black Enameled Handle; Nickel-plated Ferrule.

No. 81 Length Over All, 8¼ in.; Weight per Dozen, 2½ lbs........Per Dozen, **$2.20**

One Dozen in a Box.

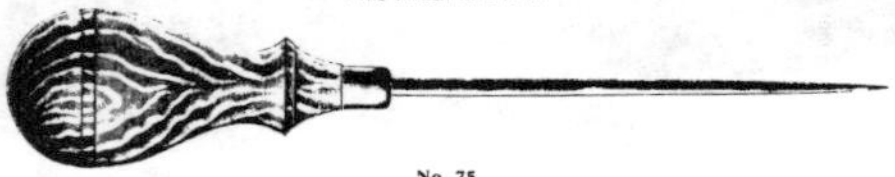

No. 75

Finely Pointed, Tempered and Polished Cast Steel Blade, 5¼ Inches Long. Natural Finish, Beechwood Handle.

No. 75 Length Over All, 9½ in.; Weight per Dozen, 2¼ lbs........Per Dozen, **$1.80**

One Dozen in a Box.

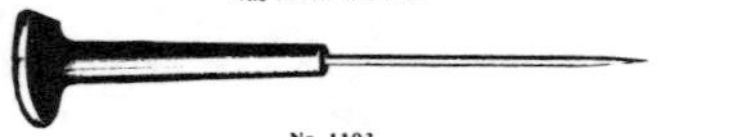

No. 1103

Nickel-plated Blade, Needle Pointed, 3½ Inches Long; Cast Iron Handle, Nickel-plated

No. 1103 Length Over All, 7 in.; Weight per Dozen, 4 lbs........Per Dozen, **$1.70**

One Dozen in a Box.

Try Squares.

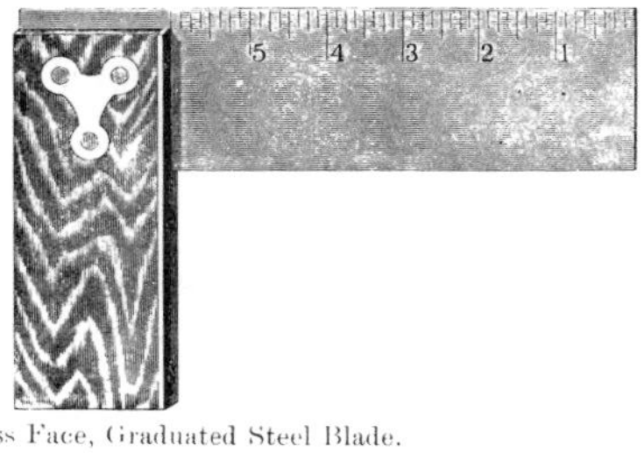

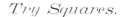

Rosewood, Brass Face, Graduated Steel Blade.

Inches	3	$4\frac{1}{2}$	6	$7\frac{1}{2}$	9	10
Per Dozen	$3 00	3 75	5 00	5 75	6 50	8 50

Winterbottom's Patent Try and Mitre Squares.

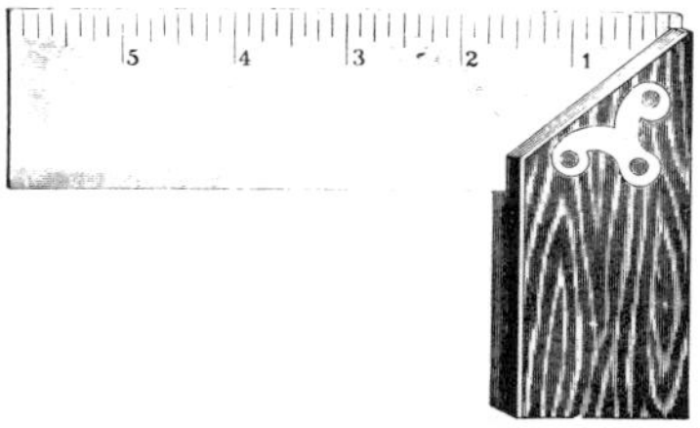

Inches	6	$7\frac{1}{2}$	9
Per Dozen	$5 00	6 00	7 00

This Tool can be used with equal convenience and accuracy as a Try Square or Mitre Square. By simply changing the position of the handle, and bringing the mitred face at the top of the handle against one edge of the work in hand, a perfect mitre, or angle of forty-five degrees, can be struck from either edge of the blade.

HALF DOZEN IN A BOX.

Improved Mitre Squares.

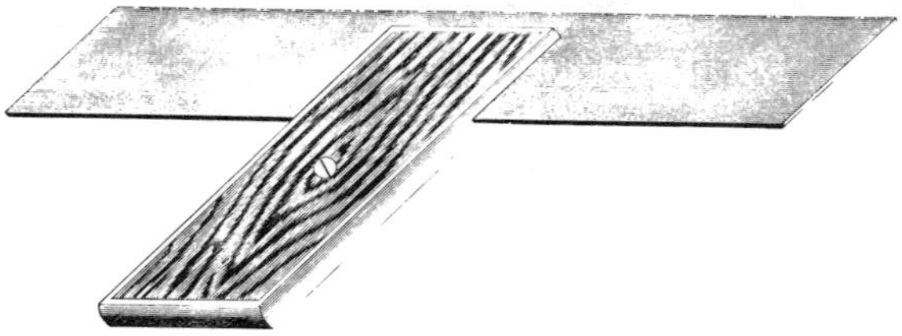

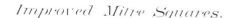

	Per Dozen
8 in. Iron Frame Handle, with Black Walnut Inlaid Sides,	$
10 " " " " " " " "	

Patent Sliding T Bevels.

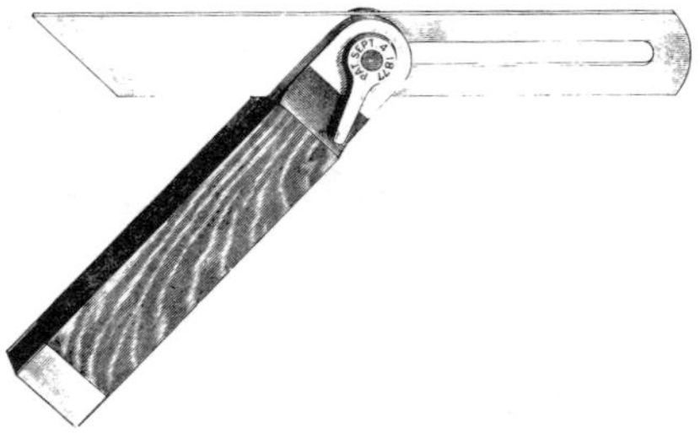

Rosewood, with Brass Thumb-Screw.

Inches	6	8	10	12	14
Per Dozen	$5 50	6 00	6 50	7 00	7 50

HALF DOZEN IN A BOX.

TRY SQUARES

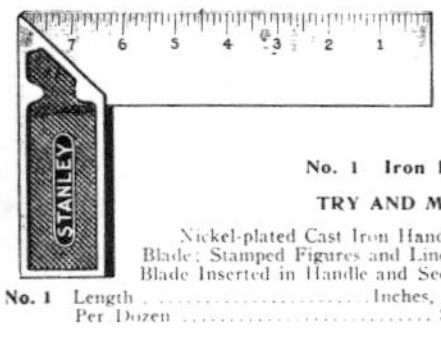

No. 1 Iron Handle

TRY AND MITER

Nickel-plated Cast Iron Handle; Polished Rolled Steel Blade; Stamped Figures and Lines, Graduated to 1/8 Inch; Blade Inserted in Handle and Secured with 3 Iron Rivets.

No. 1 Length	Inches, 4	6	8	
Per Dozen	**$6.75**	**8.25**	**10.00**	

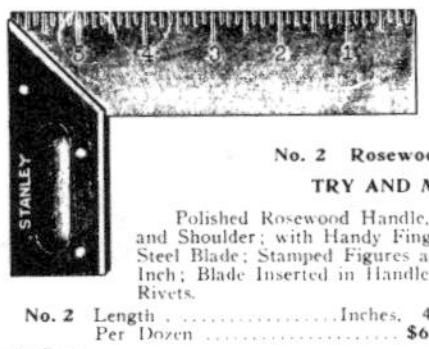

No. 2 Rosewood Handle

TRY AND MITER

Polished Rosewood Handle, Brass Faced Inner Edge and Shoulder; with Handy Finger Grooves; Blued Rolled Steel Blade; Stamped Figures and Lines, Graduated to 1/8 Inch; Blade Inserted in Handle and Secured with 3 Iron Rivets.

No. 2 Length	Inches, 4½	6	7½	9
Per Dozen	**$6.00**	**6.75**	**7.75**	**9.25**

Half Dozen in Box.

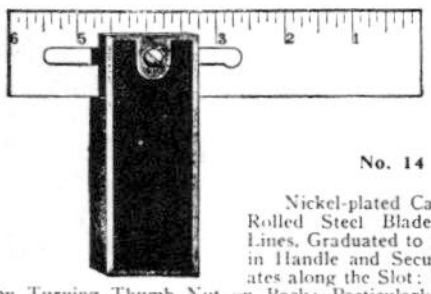

No. 14 Adjustable

Nickel-plated Cast Iron Handle; Polished Rolled Steel Blade; Stamped Figures and Lines, Graduated to 1/8 Inch; Blade is Inserted in Handle and Secured by Bolt, which Operates along the Slot; Held Rigidly at Any Point by Turning Thumb Nut on Back; Particularly Adapted for Measuring and Marking Depth of Butts, Locks, etc., on Doors and Windows.

No. 14 Length	Inches, 4	6
Per Dozen	**$5.50**	**6.75**

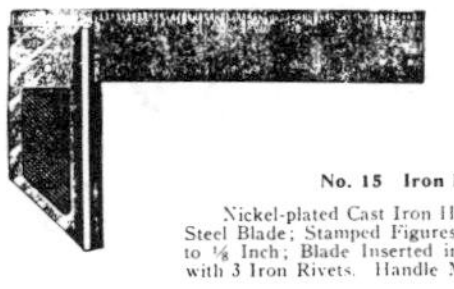

No. 15 Iron Handle

Nickel-plated Cast Iron Handle; Polished Rolled Steel Blade; Stamped Figures and Lines, Graduated to 1/8 Inch; Blade Inserted in Handle and Secured with 3 Iron Rivets. Handle Mitered on Lower End.

No. 15 Length	Inches, 7½
Per Dozen	**$12.00**

Half Dozen in Box.

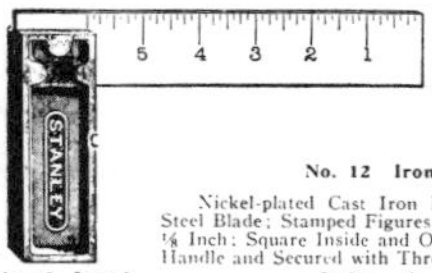

No. 12 Iron Handle

Nickel-plated Cast Iron Handle; Polished Rolled Steel Blade; Stamped Figures and Lines; Graduated to 1/8 Inch; Square Inside and Outside; Blade Inserted in Handle and Secured with Three Iron Rivets.

No. 12 Length	Inches, 4	6	8	10
Per Dozen	**$4.25**	**4.80**	**6.25**	**8.00**

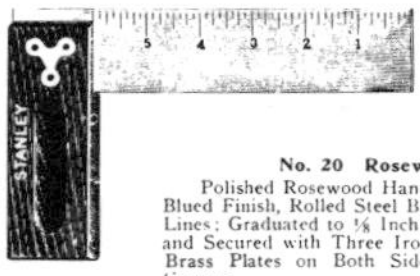

No. 20 Rosewood Handle

Polished Rosewood Handle, with Brass Face Edge; Blued Finish, Rolled Steel Blade; Stamped Figures and Lines; Graduated to 1/8 Inch; Blade Inserted in Handle and Secured with Three Iron Rivets, Passing Through Brass Plates on Both Sides; with "Handy" Finger Grooves.

No. 20 Length	Inches, 4½	6	7½	9	10	12
Per Dozen	**$4.00**	**5.00**	**5.50**	**7.00**	**7.80**	**9.25**

Half Dozen in Box.

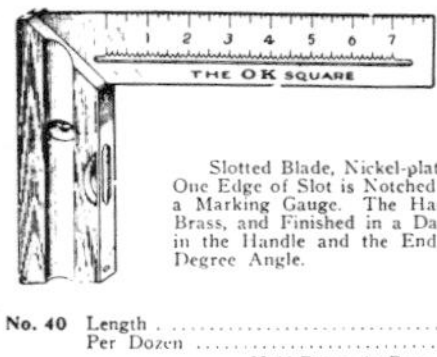

Slotted Blade, Nickel-plated; Graduated in 1/8 Inch. One Edge of Slot is Notched in 1/8 Inch to be Used for a Marking Gauge. The Handle is Birch Faced with Brass, and Finished in a Dark Color. It has a Level in the Handle and the End of Handle is Cut to 45 Degree Angle.

No. 40 Length	Inches, 8
Per Dozen	**$10.00**

Half Dozen in Box.

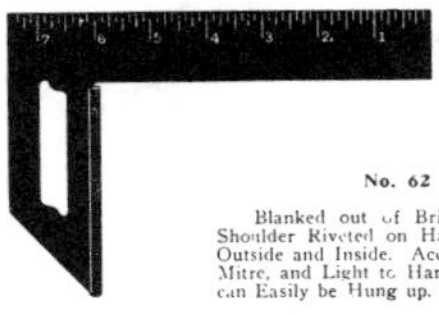

No. 62 Utility

Blanked out of Bright Sheet Steel. Steel Shoulder Riveted on Handle. Perfectly Square Outside and Inside. Accurately Graduated, True Mitre, and Light to Handle. When Not in Use can Easily be Hung up.

No. 62 Length	Inches, 7½
Per Dozen	**$3.00**

One Dozen in a Box.

Cold Chisels.

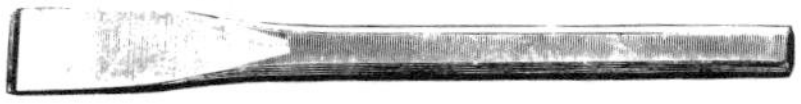

Per Pound.

Octagon, Half Polished, Cast-Steel.

Inches,	$\frac{1}{4}$	$\frac{3}{8}$	$\frac{1}{2}$	$\frac{5}{8}$	$\frac{3}{4}$	$\frac{7}{8}$	1	$
Weight, Per Dozen,	$2\frac{1}{2}$	4	$4\frac{1}{2}$	7	11	18	23 lbs.	

Squares.

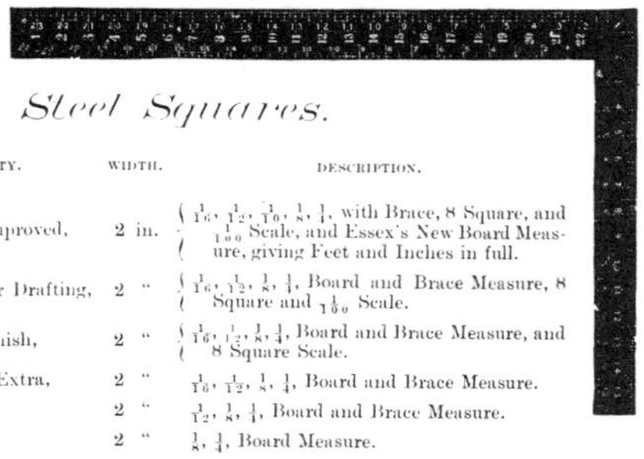

Steel Squares.

NO.	PER DOZ.	QUALITY.	WIDTH.	DESCRIPTION.
100	$66 00	Cast-Steel, Improved,	2 in.	$\frac{1}{16}$, $\frac{1}{12}$, $\frac{1}{10}$, $\frac{1}{8}$, $\frac{1}{4}$, with Brace, 8 Square, and $\frac{1}{100}$ Scale, and Essex's New Board Measure, giving Feet and Inches in full.
1	48 00	Cast-Steel, for Drafting,	2 "	$\frac{1}{16}$, $\frac{1}{12}$, $\frac{1}{8}$, $\frac{1}{4}$, Board and Brace Measure, 8 Square and $\frac{1}{100}$ Scale.
2	44 00	Cast-Steel Finish,	2 "	$\frac{1}{16}$, $\frac{1}{12}$, $\frac{1}{8}$, $\frac{1}{4}$, Board and Brace Measure, and 8 Square Scale.
3	35 00	Super Super Extra,	2 "	$\frac{1}{16}$, $\frac{1}{12}$, $\frac{1}{8}$, $\frac{1}{4}$, Board and Brace Measure.
5	32 50	Extra,	2 "	$\frac{1}{12}$, $\frac{1}{8}$, $\frac{1}{4}$, Board and Brace Measure.
7	30 00	. . . B,	2 "	$\frac{1}{8}$, $\frac{1}{4}$, Board Measure.
10	22 50	Extra, 1 Foot,	$1\frac{1}{2}$ "	$\frac{1}{12}$, $\frac{1}{8}$, $\frac{1}{4}$.
14	25 50	. . . B,	2 "	$\frac{1}{8}$, $\frac{1}{4}$, Board Measure.
3	42 00	Super Super Extra,	2 "	Nickel Plated.

QUARTER DOZEN IN A BOX.

Iron Squares.

NO.	PER DOZEN.	QUALITY.	WIDTH.	DESCRIPTION.
1	$6 00	Iron Squares,	$1\frac{1}{2}$ in.	$\frac{1}{8}$, $\frac{1}{4}$, Marked on One Side.
2	10 00	" "	$1\frac{1}{2}$ "	$\frac{1}{8}$, $\frac{1}{4}$, " Both "
4	14 00	" "	2 "	$\frac{1}{8}$, $\frac{1}{4}$, " " "

HALF DOZEN IN A PACKAGE.

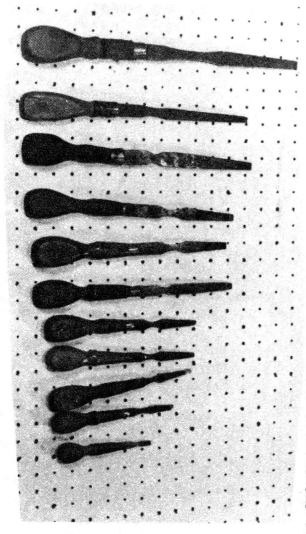

PIANO SCREW DRIVERS

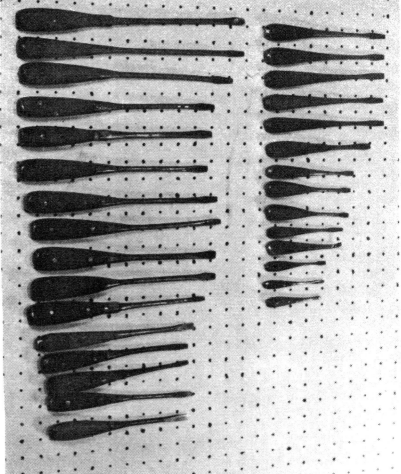

IRON HANDLED SCREWDRIVERS

162

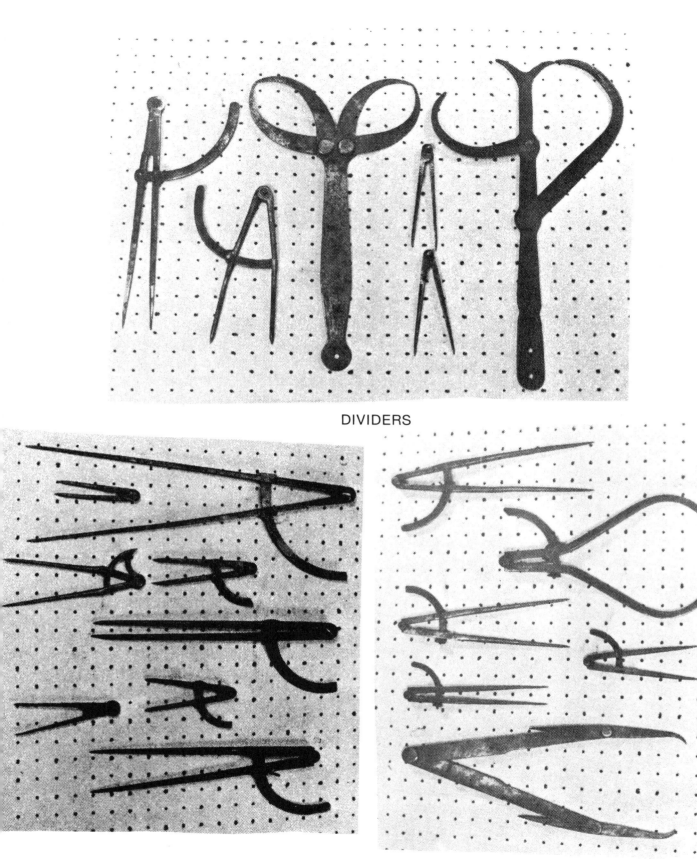

DIVIDERS

DIVIDERS

163

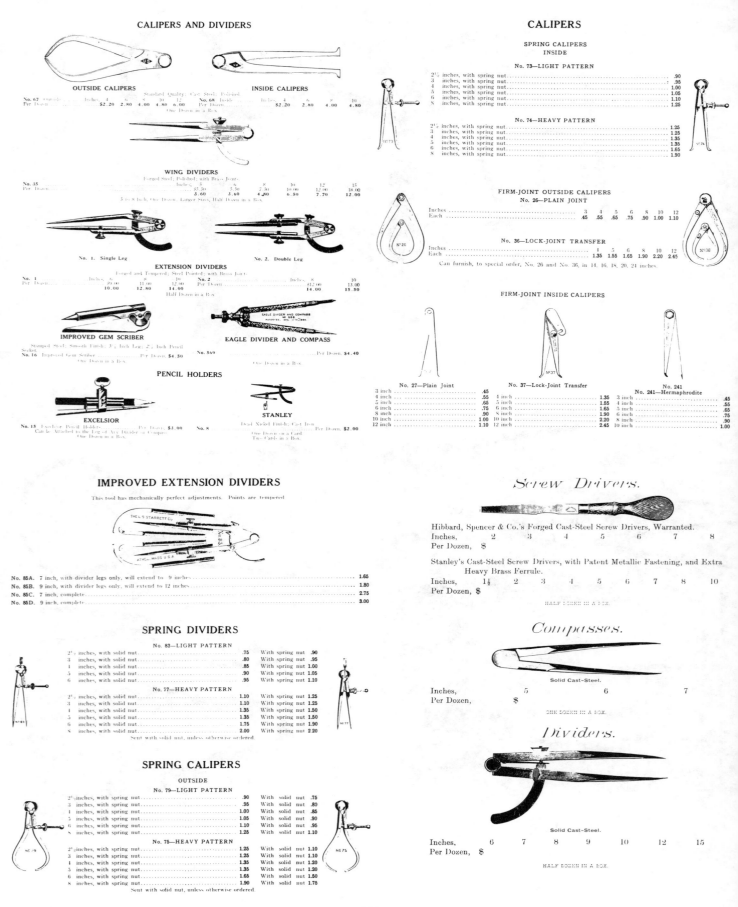

CALIPERS AND DIVIDERS

OUTSIDE CALIPERS   **INSIDE CALIPERS**

Standard Quality; Cast Steel; Polished

No. 67 Outside	Inches,	4	6	8	10	12	No. 68 Inside	Inches,	4	6	8	10
Per Dozen		$2.20	2.80	4.00	4.80	6.00	Per Dozen		$2.20	2.80	4.00	4.80

One Dozen in a Box.

WING DIVIDERS

Forged Steel; Polished; with Brass Joint

No. 35	Inches,	3	5	6	8	10	12	15
Per Dozen		$5.50	5.50	7.50	10.00	12.00	18.00	
		3.60			6.50	7.70	12.00	

3 to 8 inch, One Dozen. Larger Sizes, Half Dozen in a Box.

No. 1. Single Leg   **No. 2. Double Leg**

EXTENSION DIVIDERS

Forged and Tempered; Steel Pointed; with Brass Joint

No. 1	Inches,	6	8	10	No. 2	Inches,	8	10
Per Dozen		$9.00	11.00	12.00	Per Dozen		$12.00	13.00
		10.00	12.80	14.00			14.00	15.50

Half Dozen in a Box.

IMPROVED GEM SCRIBER   **EAGLE DIVIDER AND COMPASS**

Stamped Steel; Smooth Finish; 3½ inch Legs; 2½ inch Pencil Socket.

No. 16 Improved Gem Scriber ... Per Dozen, $4.50

One Dozen in a Box.

No. 869 ... Per Dozen, $4.40

One Dozen in a Box.

PENCIL HOLDERS

EXCELSIOR   **STANLEY**

No. 15 Excelsior Pencil Holders ... Per Dozen, $1.00

Can be Attached to the Leg of Any Divider or Compass.

One Dozen in a Box.

No. 8   Dead Nickel Finish; Cast Iron ... Per Dozen, $2.00

One Dozen on a Card.
Two Cards in a Box.

CALIPERS

SPRING CALIPERS
INSIDE

No. 73—LIGHT PATTERN

2½	inches, with spring nut	.90
3	inches, with spring nut	.95
4	inches, with spring nut	1.00
5	inches, with spring nut	1.05
6	inches, with spring nut	1.10
8	inches, with spring nut	1.25

No. 74—HEAVY PATTERN

2½	inches, with spring nut	1.25
3	inches, with spring nut	1.25
4	inches, with spring nut	1.35
5	inches, with spring nut	1.35
6	inches, with spring nut	1.65
8	inches, with spring nut	1.90

FIRM-JOINT OUTSIDE CALIPERS
No. 26—PLAIN JOINT

Inches	3	4	5	6	8	10	12
Each	.45	.55	.65	.75	.90	1.00	1.10

No. 36—LOCK-JOINT TRANSFER

Inches	4	5	6	8	10	12
Each	1.35	1.55	1.65	1.90	2.20	2.45

Can furnish, to special order, No. 26 and No. 36, in 14, 16, 18, 20, 24 inches.

FIRM-JOINT INSIDE CALIPERS

No. 27—Plain Joint   **No. 37—Lock-Joint Transfer**   **No. 241—Hermaphrodite**

3 inch	.45	4 inch	1.35	3 inch	.45
4 inch	.55	5 inch	1.55	4 inch	.55
5 inch	.65	6 inch	1.65	5 inch	.65
6 inch	.75	8 inch	1.90	6 inch	.75
8 inch	.90	10 inch	2.20	8 inch	.90
10 inch	1.00	12 inch	2.45	10 inch	1.00
12 inch	1.10				

IMPROVED EXTENSION DIVIDERS

This tool has mechanically perfect adjustments. Points are tempered

No. 85A.	7 inch, with divider legs only, will extend to 9 inches	1.65
No. 85B.	9 inch, with divider legs only, will extend to 12 inches	1.80
No. 85C.	7 inch, complete	2.75
No. 85D.	9 inch, complete	3.00

SPRING DIVIDERS

No. 83—LIGHT PATTERN

2½	inches, with solid nut	.75	With spring nut	.90
3	inches, with solid nut	.80	With spring nut	.95
4	inches, with solid nut	.85	With spring nut	1.00
5	inches, with solid nut	.90	With spring nut	1.05
6	inches, with solid nut	.95	With spring nut	1.10

No. 77—HEAVY PATTERN

2½	inches, with solid nut	1.10	With spring nut	1.25
3	inches, with solid nut	1.10	With spring nut	1.25
4	inches, with solid nut	1.35	With spring nut	1.50
5	inches, with solid nut	1.35	With spring nut	1.50
6	inches, with solid nut	1.75	With spring nut	1.90
8	inches, with solid nut	2.00	With spring nut	2.20

Sent with solid nut, unless otherwise ordered.

SPRING CALIPERS

OUTSIDE
No. 79—LIGHT PATTERN

2½	inches, with spring nut	.90	With solid nut	.75
3	inches, with spring nut	.95	With solid nut	.80
4	inches, with spring nut	1.00	With solid nut	.85
5	inches, with spring nut	1.05	With solid nut	.90
6	inches, with spring nut	1.10	With solid nut	.95
8	inches, with spring nut	1.25	With solid nut	1.10

No. 75—HEAVY PATTERN

2½	inches, with spring nut	1.25	With solid nut	1.10
3	inches, with spring nut	1.25	With solid nut	1.10
4	inches, with spring nut	1.35	With solid nut	1.20
5	inches, with spring nut	1.35	With solid nut	1.20
6	inches, with spring nut	1.65	With solid nut	1.50
8	inches, with spring nut	1.90	With solid nut	1.75

Sent with solid nut, unless otherwise ordered.

Screw Drivers.

Hibbard, Spencer & Co.'s Forged Cast-Steel Screw Drivers, Warranted.

Inches,	2	3	4	5	6	7	8
Per Dozen, $							

Stanley's Cast-Steel Screw Drivers, with Patent Metallic Fastening, and Extra Heavy Brass Ferrule.

Inches,	1½	2	3	4	5	6	7	8	10
Per Dozen, $									

HALF DOZEN IN A BOX.

Compasses.

Solid Cast-Steel.

Inches,	5	6	7
Per Dozen,	$		

ONE DOZEN IN A BOX.

Dividers.

Solid Cast-Steel.

Inches,	6	7	8	9	10	12	15
Per Dozen, $							

HALF DOZEN IN A BOX.

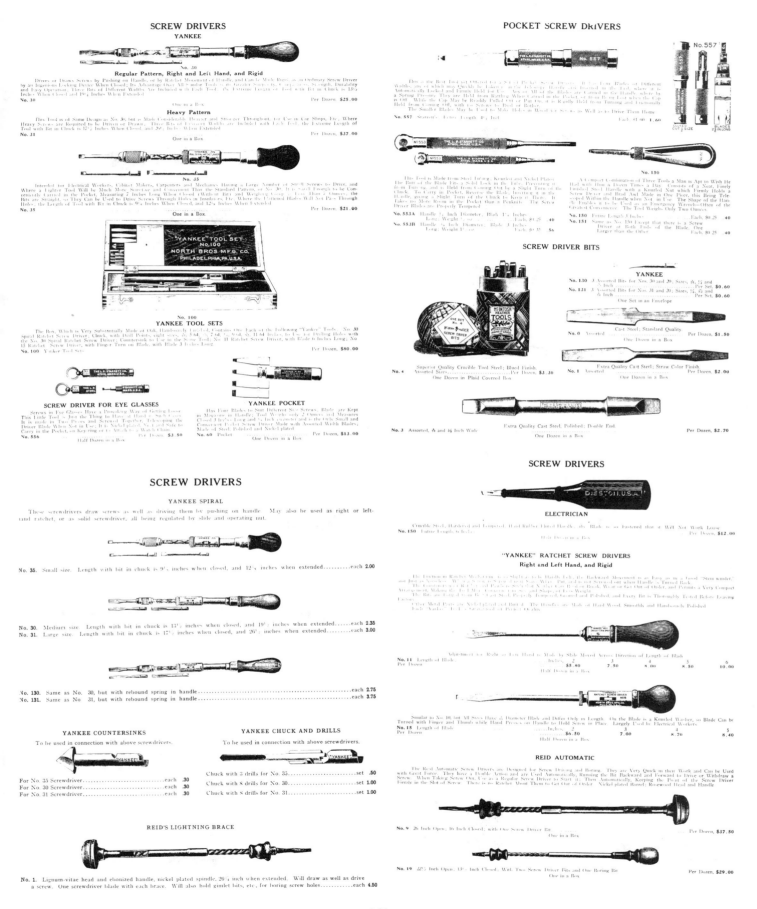

SCREW DRIVERS

YANKEE

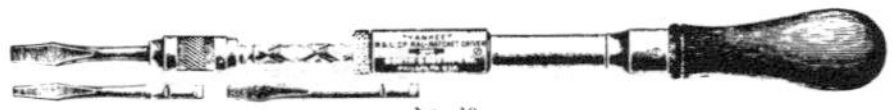

No. 30

Regular Pattern, Right and Left Hand, and Rigid

Drives or Draws Screws by Pushing on Handle, or by Ratchet Movement of Handle, and Can be Made Rigid, as an Ordinary Screw Driver by an Ingenious Locking Device When Closed; Its Advantage Over All Similar Tools is its Greater Simplicity, Compactness, Strength, Durability and Easy Operation; Three Bits of Different Widths Are Included with Each Tool; the Extreme Length of Tool with Bit in Chuck is 13½ Inches When Closed and 19¼ Inches When Extended

No. 30 Per Dozen, **$25.00**

One in a Box

Heavy Pattern

This Tool is of Same Design as No. 30, but is Made Considerably Heavier and Stronger Throughout, for Use in Car Shops, Etc., Where Heavy Screws are Required to be Driven or Drawn. Three Bits of Different Widths are Included with Each Tool, the Extreme Length of Tool with Bit in Chuck is 17½ Inches When Closed, and 26¼ Inches When Extended

No. 31 Per Dozen, **$37.00**

One in a Box

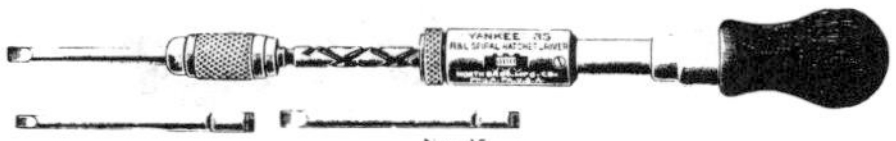

No. 35

Intended for Electrical Workers, Cabinet Makers, Carpenters and Mechanics Having a Large Number of Small Screws to Drive, and Where a Lighter Tool Will be Much More Sensitive and Convenient Than the Standard Pattern, or No. 30. It is Small Enough to be Conveniently Carried in the Pocket, Measuring 7 Inches Long When Closed (Without Bit) and Weighing Complete Less Than 7 Ounces; the Bits are Straight, so They Can be Used to Drive Screws Through Holes in Insulators, Etc., Where the Flattened Blades Will Not Pass Through Holes; the Length of Tool with Bit in Chuck is 9⅛ Inches When Closed, and 12⅝ Inches When Extended

No. 35 Per Dozen, **$21.00**

One in a Box

No. 100

YANKEE TOOL SETS

The Box, Which is Very Substantially Made of Oak, Handsomely Finished, Contains One Each of the Following "Yankee" Tools: No. 30 Spiral Ratchet Screw Driver; Chuck, with Drill Points, eight sizes, 1/16, 5/64, 3/32, 7/64, 1/8, 9/64, 5/32, 11/64 Inches, to Use for Drilling Holes with the No. 30 Spiral Ratchet Screw Driver; Countersink to Use in the Same Tool; No. 11 Ratchet Screw Driver, with Blade 6 Inches Long; No. 15 Ratchet Screw Driver, with Finger Turn on Blade, with Blade 3 Inches Long

No. 100 Yankee Tool Sets Per Dozen, **$80.00**

SCREW DRIVER FOR EYE GLASSES

Screws in Eye Glasses Have a Provoking Way of Getting Loose. This Little Tool is Just the Thing to Have at Hand in Such Cases. It is made in Two Pieces and Screwed Together, Telescoping the Driver Blade When Not in Use; It is Nickel-plated, Neat and Safe to Carry in the Pocket, on Key-ring or to Attach to a Watch Chain.

No. 556 Per Dozen, **$3.50**

Half Dozen in a Box

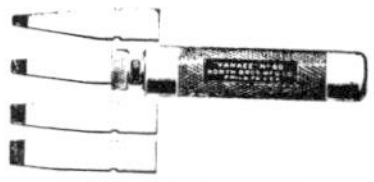

YANKEE POCKET

Has Four Blades to Suit Different Size Screws, Blades are Kept in Magazine in Handle; Tool Weighs only 2 Ounces and Measures Closed 3 Inches Long and ⅝ Inch Diameter and is the Only Small and Convenient Pocket Screw Driver Made with Assorted Width Blades; Made of Steel, Polished and Nickel-plated

No. 60 Pocket Per Dozen, **$13.00**

One Dozen in a Box

POCKET SCREW DRIVERS

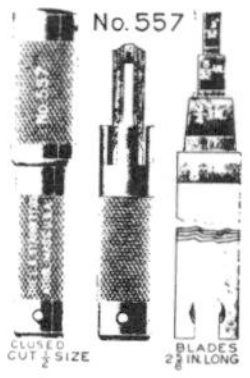

This is the Best Tool yet Offered for a Set of Pocket Screw Drivers. It Has Four Blades of Different Widths, any of which may Quickly be Taken from the Telescope Handle and Inserted in the End, where it is Automatically Locked and Firmly Held for Use. Any or All of the Blades are Carried in the Handle, where by a Spring Pressure They are Held from Rattling When Carried in the Pocket, or from Being Lost when the Cap is Off. While the Cap May be Readily Pulled Off or Put On, it is Rigidly Held from Turning and Frictionally Held from Coming Off, with no Screws to Bind or Bother.

The Smaller Blades May be Used to Make Holes in Wood for Screws as Well as to Drive Them Home

No. 557 Starrett's. Entire Length 4¼ Inch Each, $1.00 **1.60**

This Tool is Made from Steel Tubing, Knurled and Nickel Plated. The Butt of the Blade Fits a Solid Lock in the Tube, Preventing it from Turning, and is Held from Coming Out by a Slight Turn of the Chuck. To Carry in Pocket, Reverse the Blade, Inserting it in the Handle, giving a Slight Turn of the Chuck to Keep it There. It Takes no More Room in the Pocket than a Penknife. The Screw Driver Blades are Properly Tempered

No. 553A Handle ¼ Inch Diameter, Blade 1⅞ Inches Long; Weight ½ oz. Each, $0.25 **.40**

No. 553B Handle ⅜ Inch Diameter; Blade 3 Inches Long; Weight 1½ oz. Each, $0.35 **.56**

No. 150

A Compact Combination of Three Tools a Man is Apt to Wish He Had with Him a Dozen Times a Day. Consists of a Neat, Finely Finished Steel Handle with a Knurled Nut which Firmly Holds a Screw Driver and Brad Awl Made in One Piece, this Being Telescoped Within the Handle when Not in Use. The Shape of the Handle Enables it to be Used as an Emergency Wrench—Often of the Greatest Convenience. The Tool Weighs Only Two Ounces.

No. 150 Entire Length 3 Inches Each, $0.25 **.40**

No. 151 Same as No. 150 Except that there is a Screw Driver at Both Ends of the Blade, One Larger than the Other Each, $0.25 **.40**

SCREW DRIVER BITS

YANKEE

No. 130 3 Assorted Bits for Nos. 30 and 20; Sizes, 3/16, ¼ and 5/16 Inch Per Set, **$0.60**

No. 131 3 Assorted Bits for Nos. 31 and 20; Sizes, ¼, 9/32 and 5/16 Inch Per Set, **$0.60**

One Set in an Envelope

Superior Quality Crucible Tool Steel; Blued Finish.

No. 4 Assorted Sizes Per Dozen, **$3.30**

One Dozen in Plaid Covered Box

Cast Steel; Standard Quality.

No. 0 Assorted Per Dozen, **$1.50**

One Dozen in a Box

Extra Quality Cast Steel; Straw Color Finish.

No. 1 Assorted Per Dozen, **$2.00**

One Dozen in a Box

Extra Quality Cast Steel, Polished; Double End.

No. 3 Assorted, 3/16 and ⅛ Inch Wide Per Dozen, **$2.70**

One Dozen in a Box

SCREW DRIVERS

YANKEE SPIRAL

These screwdrivers draw screws as well as driving them by pushing on handle. May also be used as right or left-hand ratchet, or as solid screwdriver, all being regulated by slide and operating nut.

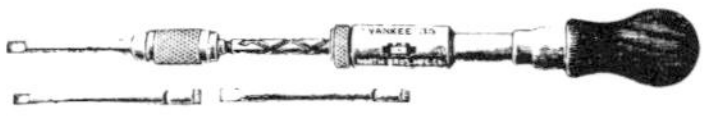

No. 35. Small size. Length with bit in chuck is 9⅛ inches when closed, and 12⅝ inches when extended..........each **2.00**

No. 30. Medium size. Length with bit in chuck is 13½ inches when closed, and 19¼ inches when extended......each **2.35**

No. 31. Large size. Length with bit in chuck is 17½ inches when closed, and 26¼ inches when extended.........each **3.00**

No. 130. Same as No. 30, but with rebound spring in handle..........each **2.75**

No. 131. Same as No. 31, but with rebound spring in handle..........each **3.75**

YANKEE COUNTERSINKS

To be used in connection with above screwdrivers.

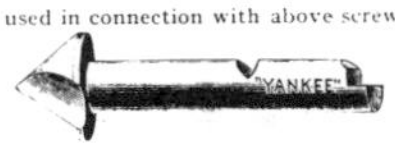

For No. 35 Screwdriver..........each **.30**

For No. 30 Screwdriver..........each **.30**

For No. 31 Screwdriver..........each **.30**

YANKEE CHUCK AND DRILLS

To be used in connection with above screwdrivers.

Chuck with 3 drills for No. 35..........set **.50**

Chuck with 8 drills for No. 30..........set **1.00**

Chuck with 8 drills for No. 31..........set **1.00**

REID'S LIGHTNING BRACE

No. 1. Lignum-vitae head and ebonized handle, nickel plated spindle, 26¼ inch when extended. Will draw as well as drive a screw. One screwdriver blade with each brace. Will also hold gimlet bits, etc., for boring screw holes..........each **4.50**

SCREW DRIVERS

ELECTRICIAN

Crucible Steel, Hardened and Tempered, Hard Rubber Fluted Handle, the Blade is so Fastened that it Will Not Work Loose

No. 150 Entire Length, 6 Inches Per Dozen, **$12.00**

Half Dozen in a Box

"YANKEE" RATCHET SCREW DRIVERS

Right and Left Hand, and Rigid

The Friction in Ratchet Mechanism is so Slight as to be Hardly Felt, the Backward Movement is as Easy as in a Good "Stem winder," and Just as Noiseless. When a Screw is Screwed in it Stays Where Put, and is not Screwed out when Handle is Turned Back.

The Construction of Ratchet and Pawls is Such that Neither Can Bind or Break, Wear or Get Out of Order, and Permits a Very Compact Arrangement, Making the Tool More Convenient in Size and Shape, of Less Weight.

The Bits are Forged from Best Cast Steel, Properly Tempered, Ground and Polished, and Every Bit is Thoroughly Tested Before Leaving Factory.

Other Metal Parts are Nickel-plated and Buffed. The Handles are Made of Hard Wood, Smoothly and Handsomely Polished.

Each "Yankee" Tool is Guaranteed of Perfect Quality.

Adjustment for Right or Left Hand is Made by Slide Moved Across Direction of Length of Blade

No. 11 Length of Blade, Inches	2	3	4	5	6
Per Dozen	**$5.80**	**7.50**	**8.00**	**8.50**	**10.00**

Half Dozen in a Box

Similar to No. 10, but All Sizes Have 3/16 Diameter Blade and Differ Only in Length. On the Blade is a Knurled Washer, so Blade Can be Turned with Finger and Thumb while Hand Presses on Handle to Hold Screw in Place. Largely Used by Electrical Workers

No. 15 Length of Blade, Inches	2	3	4	5
Per Dozen	**$6.50**	**7.00**	**8.70**	**8.40**

Half Dozen in a Box

REID AUTOMATIC

The Reid Automatic Screw Drivers are Designed for Screw Driving and Boring. They are Very Quick in their Work and Can be Used with Great Force. They have a Double Action and are Used Automatically, Running the Bit Backward and Forward to Drive or Withdraw a Screw. When Taking Screw Out, Use as a Regular Screw Driver to Start it; Then Automatically, Keeping the Point of the Screw Driver Firmly in the Slot of Screw. There is no Ratchet About Them to Get Out of Order. Nickel-plated Barrel; Rosewood Head and Handle

No. 9 26 Inch Open; 16 Inch Closed; with One Screw Driver Bit Per Dozen, **$37.50**

One in a Box

No. 19 22½ Inch Open; 13½ Inch Closed; With Two Screw Driver Bits and One Boring Bit Per Dozen, **$29.00**

One in a Box

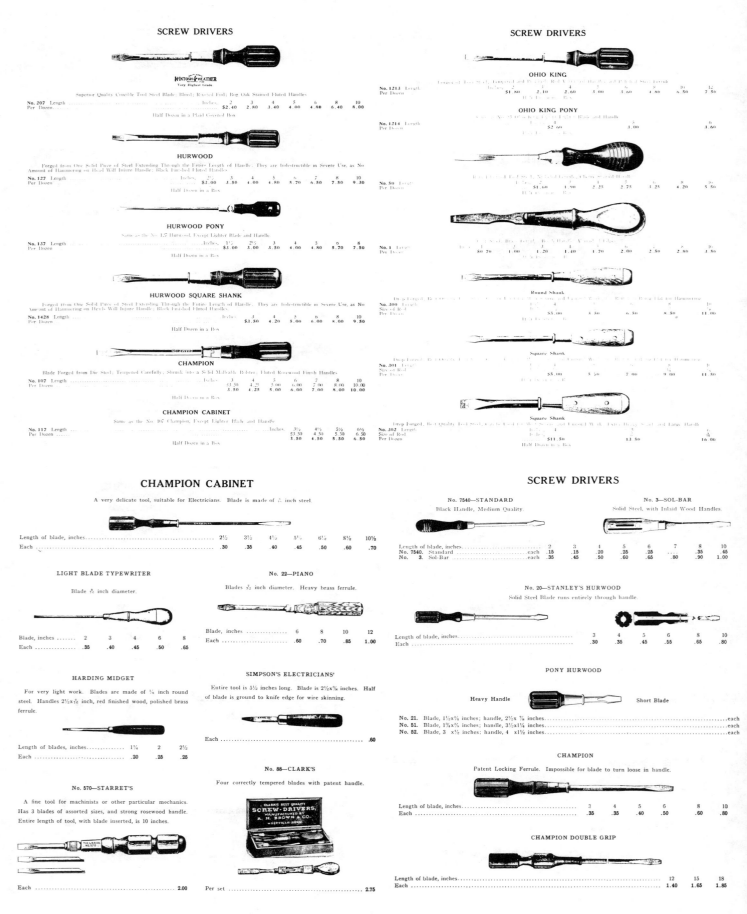

SCREW DRIVERS

McINTOSH HEATHER
Very Highest Grade

Superior Quality Crucible Tool Steel Blade; Blued; Riveted End; Bog Oak Stained Fluted Handles

No. 207 Length, Inches	2	3	4	5	6	8	10
Per Dozen	$2.40	2.80	3.40	4.00	4.80	6.40	8.00

Half Dozen in a Plaid Covered Box

HURWOOD

Forged from One Solid Piece of Steel Extending Through the Entire Length of Handle; They are Indestructible in Severe Use, as No Amount of Hammering on Heads Will Injure Handle; Black Finished Fluted Handles

No. 127 Length, Inches	2½	3	4	5	6	7	8	10
Per Dozen	$3.00	3.50	4.00	4.80	5.70	6.50	7.50	9.30

Half Dozen in a Box

HURWOOD PONY

Same as the No. 127 Hurwood, Except Lighter Blade and Handle

No. 137 Length, Inches	1½	2½	3	4	5	6	8
Per Dozen	$3.00	3.00	3.50	4.00	4.80	5.70	7.50

Half Dozen in a Box

HURWOOD SQUARE SHANK

Forged from One Solid Piece of Steel Extending Through the Entire Length of Handle; They are Indestructible in Severe Use, as No Amount of Hammering on Heels Will Injure Handle; Black Finished Fluted Handles

No. 1428 Length, Inches	3	4	5	6	8	10
Per Dozen	$3.50	4.20	5.00	6.00	8.00	9.50

Half Dozen in a Box

CHAMPION

Blade Forged from Die Steel; Tempered Carefully; Shrunk into a Solid Malleable Bolster; Fluted Rosewood Finish Handles

No. 107 Length, Inches	3	4	5	6	7	8	10
Per Dozen	$3.50	4.25	5.00	6.00	7.00	8.00	10.00
	3.80	4.25	5.00	6.00	7.00	8.00	10.00

Half Dozen in a Box

CHAMPION CABINET

Same as the No. 107 Champion, Except Lighter Blade and Handle

No. 117 Length, Inches	3½	4½	5½	6½
Per Dozen	$3.50	4.50	5.50	6.50
	3.50	4.50	5.50	6.50

Half Dozen in a Box

SCREW DRIVERS

OHIO KING

Forged of Tool Steel, Tempered and Polished; Red Varnished Hardwood Polished Steel Ferrule

No. 1213 Length, inches	2	3	4	5	6	8	10	12
Per Dozen	$1.80	2.10	2.60	3.00	3.60	4.80	6.50	7.50

OHIO KING PONY

No. 1214 Length	4	5	6
Per Dozen	$2.60	3.00	3.60

No. 50 Length						
	$1.60	1.90	2.25	2.75	3.25	4.20	5.50

No. 1 Length								
	$0.70	1.00	1.20	1.40	1.70	2.00	2.50	2.80	3.50

Round Shank

No. 300 Length	4	5	6	8	10
Size of Rod	$5.00	5.50	6.50	8.50	11.00

Square Shank

No. 301 Length				
Size of Rod	$5.00	5.50	7.00	9.00	11.50

Square Shank

No. 402 Length			
Size of Rod	$11.50	13.50	16.00

Half Dozen in a Box

CHAMPION CABINET

A very delicate tool, suitable for Electricians. Blade is made of ⅛ inch steel.

Length of blade, inches	2½	3½	4½	5½	6½	8½	10½
Each	.30	.35	.40	.45	.50	.60	.70

LIGHT BLADE TYPEWRITER

Blade ⅛ inch diameter.

Blade, inches	2	3	4	6	8
Each	.35	.40	.45	.50	.65

No. 22—PIANO

Blades ¼ inch diameter. Heavy brass ferrule.

Blade, inches	6	8	10	12
Each	.60	.70	.85	1.00

HARDING MIDGET

For very light work. Blades are made of ⅛ inch round steel. Handles 2½x1⅛ inch, red finished wood, polished brass ferrule.

Length of blades, inches	1¼	2	2½
Each	.20	.25	.25

SIMPSON'S ELECTRICIANS'

Entire tool is 5½ inches long. Blade is 2½x¾ inches. Half of blade is ground to knife edge for wire skinning.

Each ... .60

No. 88—CLARK'S

Four correctly tempered blades with patent handle.

Per set ... 2.75

No. 570—STARRET'S

A fine tool for machinists or other particular mechanics. Has 3 blades of assorted sizes, and strong rosewood handle. Entire length of tool, with blade inserted, is 10 inches.

Each ... 2.00

SCREW DRIVERS

No. 7540—STANDARD
Black Handle, Medium Quality.

No. 3—SOL-BAR
Solid Steel, with Inlaid Wood Handles.

Length of blade, inches	2	3	4	5	6	7	8	10
No. 7540. Standard, each	.15	.15	.20	.25	.25	....	.35	.45
No. 3. Sol-Bar, each	.35	.45	.50	.60	.65	.80	.90	1.00

No. 20—STANLEY'S HURWOOD

Solid Steel Blade runs entirely through handle.

Length of blade, inches	3	4	5	6	8	10
Each	.30	.35	.45	.55	.65	.80

PONY HURWOOD

Heavy Handle   Short Blade

No. 21. Blade, 1½x¼ inches; handle, 2½ x ⅞ inches ... each
No. 51. Blade, 1¾x⅜ inches; handle, 3½x1¼ inches ... each
No. 52. Blade, 3 x½ inches; handle, 4 x1¼ inches ... each

CHAMPION

Patent Locking Ferrule. Impossible for blade to turn loose in handle.

Length of blade, inches	3	4	5	6	8	10
Each	.35	.35	.40	.50	.60	.80

CHAMPION DOUBLE GRIP

Length of blade, inches	12	15	18
Each	1.40	1.65	1.85

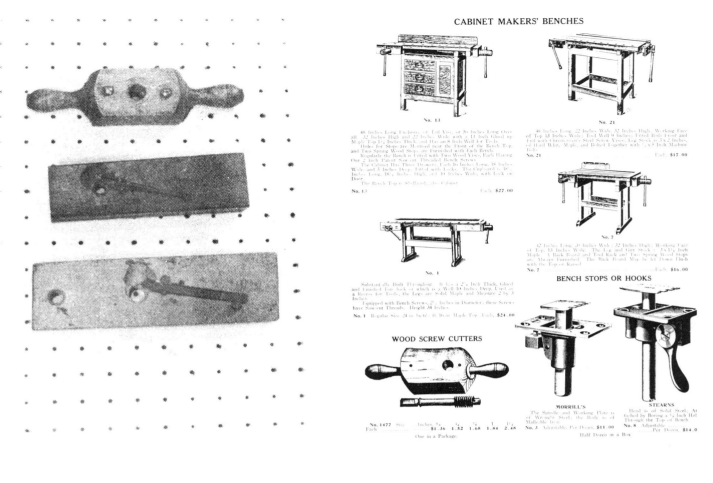

CABINET MAKERS' BENCHES

No. 13

48 Inches Long Exclusive of Tail Vise, or 56 Inches Long Over-all. 32 Inches High and 22 Inches Wide, with a 13 Inch Glued-up Maple Top 1¾ Inches Thick, and Has an 8 Inch Well for Tools. Holes for Stops are Mortised near the Front of the Bench Top, and Two Spring Wood Stops are Furnished with Each Bench.

Regularly the Bench is Fitted with Two Wood Vises, Each Having One 2 Inch Patent Saw-cut Threaded Bench Screws.

The Cabinet Has Three Drawers, Lock In Inches Long, 18 Inches Wide, and 5 Inches Deep, fitted with Locks. The Cupboard is 18 Inches Long, 18½ Inches High, and 10 Inches Wide, with Lock on Door.

The Bench Top is Shellaced, also Cabinet.

No. 13   Each, **$27.00**

No. 21

48 Inches Long, 22 Inches Wide, 32 Inches High, Working Face of Top 13 Inches Wide; Tool Well 9 Inches; Fitted Body Front and End with Christensen's Steel Screw Vises; Leg Stock is 3 x 2 Inches, of Hard White Maple, and Bolted Together with ⅜ x 5 Inch Machine Bolts.

No. 21   Each, **$17.00**

No. 7

42 Inches Long, 30 Inches Wide, 32 Inches High; Working Face of Top, 13 Inches Wide. The Leg and Girt Stock is 3 x 1½ Inch Maple. A Back Board and Tool Rack and Two Spring Wood Stops are Always Furnished. The Back Board May be let Down Flush with the Top or Raised.

No. 7   Each **$16.00**

No. 1

Substantially Built Throughout. It has a 2⅜ Inch Thick, Glued and Finished Top Stock to which is a Well 10 Inches Deep, Used as a Recess for Tools, the Legs are Solid Maple and Measure 2 by 3 Inches.

Equipped with Bench Screws, 2½ Inches in Diameter, these Screws have Saw-cut Threads. Height 34 Inches.

No. 1   Regular Size 24 in. by 60 in. Iron Maple Top, Each, **$24.00**

WOOD SCREW CUTTERS

No. 1477	Size	Inches	⅜	½	⅝	1	1¼
Each			$1.36	1.52	1.68	1.84	2.48

One in a Package.

BENCH STOPS OR HOOKS

MORRILL'S
The Spindle and Working Plate is of Wrought Steel, the Body is of Malleable Iron.
No. 3 Adjustable, Per Dozen, **$11.00**
Half Dozen in a Box

STEARNS
Head is of Solid Steel, Attached by Boring a ¾ Inch Hole Through the Top of Bench.
No. 8 Adjustable Per Dozen, **$14.0**

WOOD THREAD DIES

ROUTERS

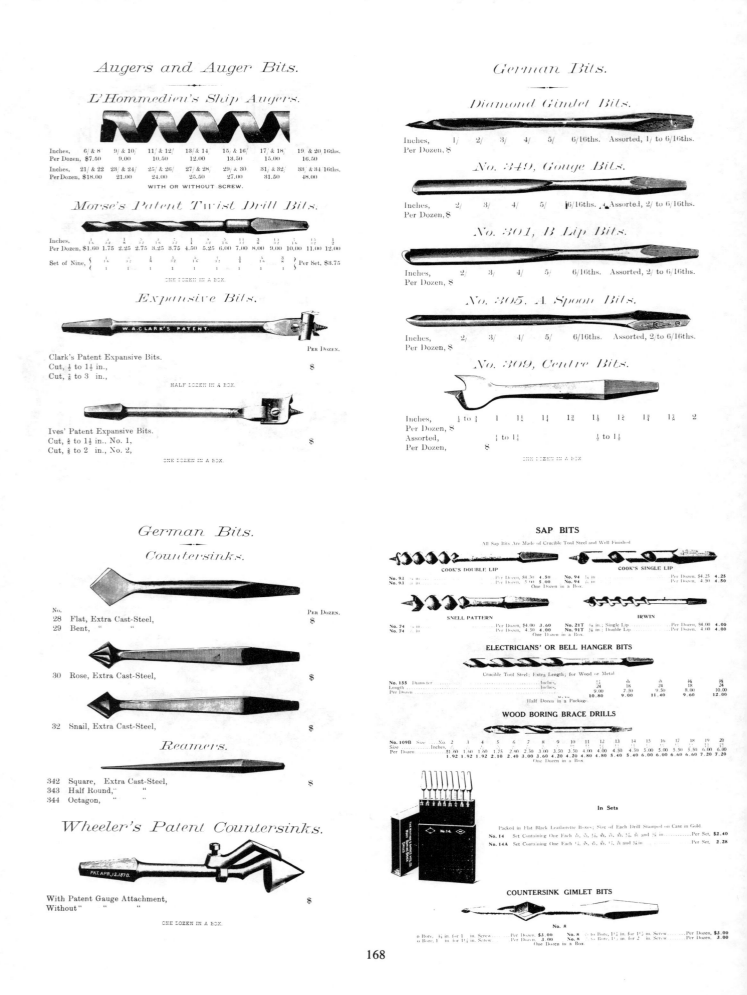

Augers and Auger Bits.

L'Hommedieu's Ship Augers.

Inches,	6/ & 8/	9/ & 10/	11/ & 12/	13/ & 14/	15/ & 16/	17/ & 18/	19/ & 20/ 16ths.
Per Dozen,	$7.50	9.00	10.50	12.00	13.50	15.00	16.50
Inches,	21/ & 22	23/ & 24/	25/ & 26/	27/ & 28/	29/ & 30	31/ & 32/	33/ & 34 16ths.
Per Dozen,	$18.00	21.00	24.00	25.50	27.00	31.50	48.00

WITH OR WITHOUT SCREW.

Morse's Patent Twist Drill Bits.

Inches,	$\frac{1}{16}$	$\frac{3}{32}$	$\frac{1}{8}$	$\frac{5}{32}$	$\frac{3}{16}$	$\frac{7}{32}$	$\frac{1}{4}$	$\frac{9}{32}$	$\frac{5}{16}$	$\frac{11}{32}$	$\frac{3}{8}$	$\frac{13}{32}$	$\frac{7}{16}$	$\frac{15}{32}$	$\frac{1}{2}$
Per Dozen,	$1.60	1.75	2.25	2.75	3.25	3.75	4.50	5.25	6.00	7.00	8.00	9.00	10.00	11.00	12.00

Set of Nine,	$\frac{1}{16}$	$\frac{3}{32}$	$\frac{1}{8}$	$\frac{5}{32}$	$\frac{3}{16}$	$\frac{7}{32}$	$\frac{1}{4}$	$\frac{5}{16}$	$\frac{3}{8}$	Per Set, $3.75
	1	1	1	1	1	1	1	1	1	

ONE DOZEN IN A BOX.

Expansive Bits.

	PER DOZEN.
Clark's Patent Expansive Bits.	
Cut, $\frac{1}{2}$ to $1\frac{1}{2}$ in.,	$
Cut, $\frac{7}{8}$ to 3 in.,	

HALF DOZEN IN A BOX.

Ives' Patent Expansive Bits.	
Cut, $\frac{5}{8}$ to $1\frac{1}{2}$ in., No. 1,	$
Cut, $\frac{5}{8}$ to 2 in., No. 2,	

ONE DOZEN IN A BOX.

German Bits.

Diamond Gimlet Bits.

Inches, 1/ 2/ 3/ 4/ 5/ 6/16ths. Assorted, 1/ to 6/16ths.
Per Dozen, $

No. 349, Gouge Bits.

Inches, 2/ 3/ 4/ 5/ 6/16ths. Assorted, 2/ to 6/16ths.
Per Dozen, $

No. 301, B Lip Bits.

Inches, 2/ 3/ 4/ 5/ 6/16ths. Assorted, 2/ to 6/16ths.
Per Dozen, $

No. 305, A Spoon Bits.

Inches, 2/ 3/ 4/ 5/ 6/16ths. Assorted, 2/to 6/16ths.
Per Dozen, $

No. 309, Centre Bits.

Inches, $\frac{1}{4}$ to $\frac{3}{4}$ 1 $1\frac{1}{8}$ $1\frac{1}{4}$ $1\frac{3}{8}$ $1\frac{1}{2}$ $1\frac{5}{8}$ $1\frac{3}{4}$ $1\frac{7}{8}$ 2
Per Dozen, $
Assorted, $\frac{1}{4}$ to $1\frac{1}{4}$ $\frac{1}{2}$ to $1\frac{1}{2}$
Per Dozen, $

ONE DOZEN IN A BOX.

German Bits.

Countersinks.

No.		PER DOZEN.
28	Flat, Extra Cast-Steel,	$
29	Bent, " "	

30 Rose, Extra Cast-Steel, $

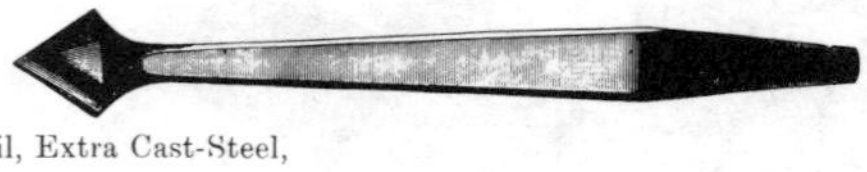

32 Snail, Extra Cast-Steel, $

Reamers.

342	Square, Extra Cast-Steel,	$
343	Half Round," "	
344	Octagon, " "	

Wheeler's Patent Countersinks.

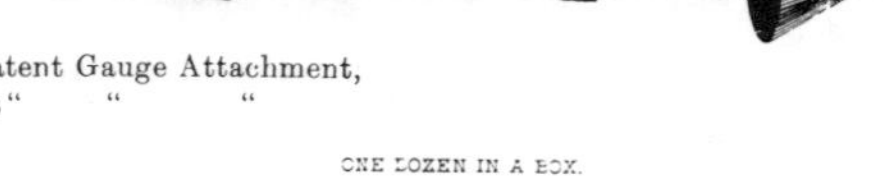

With Patent Gauge Attachment, $
Without " " "

ONE DOZEN IN A BOX.

SAP BITS

All Sap Bits Are Made of Crucible Tool Steel and Well Finished

COOK'S DOUBLE LIP

COOK'S SINGLE LIP

No. 93 [illegible] in. .... Per Dozen, $4.50 **4.50**
No. 93 [illegible] in. .... Per Dozen, 5.00 **5.00**
No. 94 $\frac{3}{8}$ in. .... Per Dozen, $4.25 **4.25**
No. 94 [illegible] in. .... Per Dozen, 4.50 **4.50**

One Dozen in a Box.

SNELL PATTERN

IRWIN

No. 74 [illegible] in. .... Per Dozen, $4.00 **3.60**
No. 74 [illegible] in. .... Per Dozen, 4.50 **4.00**
No. 21T $\frac{3}{8}$ in.; Single Lip .... Per Dozen, $4.00 **4.00**
No. 91T $\frac{3}{8}$ in.; Double Lip .... Per Dozen, 4.00 **4.00**

One Dozen in a Box.

ELECTRICIANS' OR BELL HANGER BITS

Crucible Tool Steel; Extra Length; for Wood or Metal

No. 155					
Diameter .... Inches,	$\frac{1}{4}$	$\frac{3}{16}$	$\frac{3}{16}$	$\frac{3}{8}$	$\frac{3}{8}$
Length .... Inches,	24	18	24	18	24
Per Dozen	9.00	7.50	9.50	8.00	10.00
	10.80	**9.00**	**11.40**	**9.60**	**12.00**

Half Dozen in a Package.

WOOD BORING BRACE DRILLS

No. 109B Size ....No.	2	3	4	5	6	7	8	9	10	11	12	13	14	15	16	17	18	19	20
Size .... Inches,	[illegible]	[illegible]	[illegible]	[illegible]	[illegible]	[illegible]	[illegible]	[illegible]	[illegible]	[illegible]	[illegible]	[illegible]	[illegible]	[illegible]	[illegible]	[illegible]	[illegible]	[illegible]	[illegible]
Per Dozen	$1.60	1.60	1.60	1.75	2.00	2.50	3.00	3.50	3.50	4.00	4.00	4.50	4.50	5.00	5.00	5.50	5.50	6.00	6.00
	1.92	**1.92**	**1.92**	**2.10**	**2.40**	**3.00**	**3.60**	**4.20**	**4.20**	**4.80**	**4.80**	**5.40**	**5.40**	**6.00**	**6.00**	**6.60**	**6.60**	**7.20**	**7.20**

One Dozen in a Box.

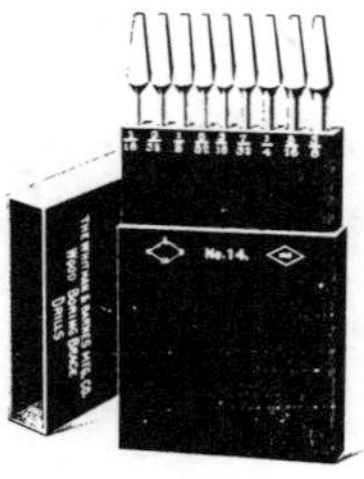

In Sets

Packed in Flat Black Leatherette Boxes; Size of Each Drill Stamped on Case in Gold

No. 14 Set Containing One Each [illegible] and $\frac{3}{8}$ in. .... Per Set, **$2.40**
No. 14A Set Containing One Each [illegible] and $\frac{3}{8}$ in. .... Per Set, **2.28**

COUNTERSINK GIMLET BITS

No. 8

[illegible] o Bore, $\frac{3}{4}$ in. for 1 in. Screw .... Per Dozen, **$3.00**
[illegible] o Bore, 1 in. for $1\frac{1}{4}$ in. Screw .... Per Dozen, **3.00**
No. 8 [illegible] to Bore, $1\frac{1}{4}$ in. for $1\frac{1}{2}$ in. Screw .... Per Dozen, **$3.00**
No. 8 [illegible] to Bore, $1\frac{1}{2}$ in. for 2 in. Screw .... Per Dozen, **3.00**

One Dozen in a Box.

Hibbard, Spencer & Co.'s Winooski Gouges.

Tanged Firmer Gouges.

Inches,	1/8	1/4	3/8	1/2	5/8	3/4	7/8	1	1 1/4	1 1/2	1 3/4	2
Per Dozen,	$2 25	2 50	2 63	2 88	3 00	3 25	3 50	4 50	6 00	7 50	10 00	12 00

In Sets of Twelve, one each of above, — Per Set. $6 00

Turning Gouges.

Inches,	1/8 & 1/4	3/8	1/2	5/8	3/4	7/8	1	1 1/4	1 1/2	1 3/4	2
Per Dozen,	$3 00	3 50	4 00	4 50	5 50	6 00	7 00	8 50	12 75	14 00	18 00

In Sets of Twelve, one each of above, — Per Set. $8 50

Hibbard, Spencer & Co.'s Winooski Chisels.

Socket Firmer Chisels.

Inches,	1/8, 1/4 & 3/8	1/2	5/8	3/4	7/8	1	1 1/4	1 1/2	1 3/4	2
Per Dozen,	$8 00	9 00	10 00	11 00	11 00	12 00	13 00	14 00	15 00	16 00

In Sets of Twelve, one each of above, — Per Set.

Hibbard, Spencer & Co.'s Winooski Gouges.

Tanged Firmer Gouges.

Inches,	1/8	1/4	3/8	1/2	5/8	3/4	7/8	1	1 1/4	1 1/2	1 3/4	2
Per Dozen,	$2 25	2 50	2 63	2 88	3 00	3 25	3 50	4 50	6 00	7 50	10 00	12 00

In Sets of Twelve, one each of above, — Per Set. $6 00

Turning Gouges.

Inches,	1/8 & 1/4	3/8	1/2	5/8	3/4	7/8	1	1 1/4	1 1/2	1 3/4	2
Per Dozen,	$3 00	3 50	4 00	4 50	5 50	6 00	7 00	8 50	12 75	14 00	18 00

In Sets of Twelve, one each of above, — Per Set. $8 50

Hibbard, Spencer & Co.'s Winooski Chisels.

Socket Firmer Chisels.

Inches,	1/8, 1/4 & 3/8	1/2	5/8	3/4	7/8	1	1 1/4	1 1/2	1 3/4	2
Per Dozen,	$8 00	9 00	10 00	11 00	11 00	12 00	13 00	14 00	15 00	16 00

In Sets of Twelve, one each of above, — Per Set. $11 25

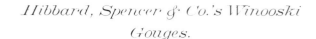

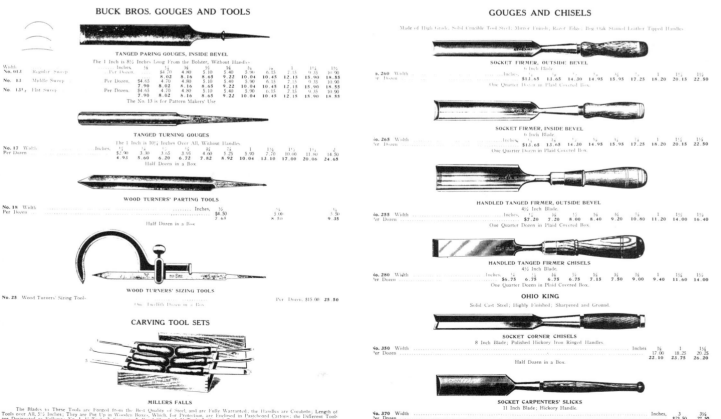

BUCK BROS. GOUGES AND TOOLS

TANGED PARING GOUGES, INSIDE BEVEL

The 1 Inch is 8½ Inches Long From the Bolster, Without Handles

Width		Inches,	1/8	1/4	3/8	1/2	5/8	3/4	7/8	1	1 1/4	1 1/2
No. 013	Regular Sweep	Per Dozen,	....	$4.70	4.80	5.10	5.40	5.90	6.15	7.15	9.35	10.90
			....	**8.02**	**8.16**	**8.65**	**9.22**	**10.04**	**10.45**	**12.15**	**15.90**	**18.55**
No. 13	Middle Sweep	Per Dozen,	$4.65	4.70	4.80	5.10	5.40	5.90	6.15	7.15	9.35	10.90
			7.90	**8.02**	**8.16**	**8.65**	**9.22**	**10.04**	**10.45**	**12.15**	**15.90**	**18.55**
No. 13½	Flat Sweep	Per Dozen,	$4.65	4.70	4.80	5.10	5.40	5.90	6.15	7.15	9.35	10.90
			7.90	**8.02**	**8.16**	**8.65**	**9.22**	**10.04**	**10.45**	**12.15**	**15.90**	**18.55**

The No. 13 is for Pattern Makers' Use

TANGED TURNING GOUGES

The 1 Inch is 10¼ Inches Over All, Without Handles

No. 17 Width ... Inches,	1/4	3/8	1/2	5/8	3/4	7/8	1	1 1/4	1 1/2	1 3/4	2
Per Dozen	$2.90	3.30	3.65	3.95	4.60	5.25	5.90	7.70	10.00	11.80	14.50
	4.93	**5.60**	**6.20**	**6.72**	**7.82**	**8.92**	**10.04**	**13.10**	**17.00**	**20.06**	**24.65**

Half Dozen in a Box

WOOD TURNERS' PARTING TOOLS

No. 18 Width ... Inches,	1/2	5/8	3/4
Per Dozen	$4.50	5.00	5.50
	7.65	8.50	**9.35**

Half Dozen in a Box

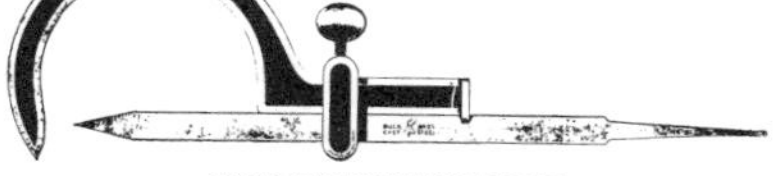

WOOD TURNERS' SIZING TOOLS

No. 25 Wood Turners' Sizing Tools ... Per Dozen, $15.00 **25.50**

One Twelfth Dozen in a Box

CARVING TOOL SETS

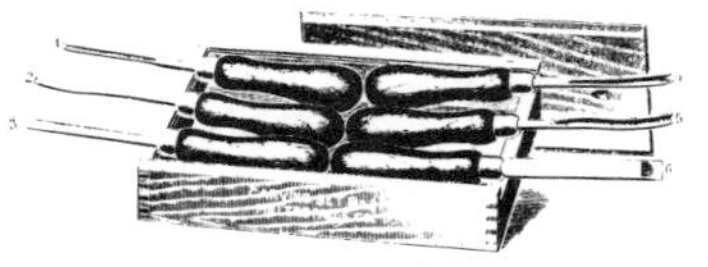

MILLERS FALLS

The Blades to These Tools are Forged from the Best Quality of Steel, and are Fully Warranted; the Handles are Cocobolo; Length of Tools over All, 5½ Inches; They are Put Up in Wooden Boxes, Which, for Protection, are Enclosed in Pasteboard Cartons; the Different Tools are Designated as Follows: No. 1, U Tool; 2, Scraper; 3, Bevel Chisel; 4, V Tool; 5, Curved Gouge; 6, Straight Chisel.

No. 1 Millers Falls ... Per Dozen Sets, **$20.00**

GOUGES AND CHISELS

Made of High Grade, Solid Crucible Tool Steel; Mirror Finish; Razor Edge; Bog Oak Stained Leather Tipped Handles

SOCKET FIRMER, OUTSIDE BEVEL

6 Inch Blade

No. 260 Width ... Inches,	1/4	3/8	1/2	5/8	3/4	7/8	1	1 1/4	1 1/2
Per Dozen	**$13.65**	**13.65**	**14.30**	**14.95**	**15.95**	**17.25**	**18.20**	**20.15**	**22.50**

One Quarter Dozen in Plaid Covered Box.

SOCKET FIRMER, INSIDE BEVEL

6 Inch Blade.

No. 265 Width ... Inches,	1/4	3/8	1/2	5/8	3/4	7/8	1	1 1/4	1 1/2
Per Dozen	**$13.65**	**13.65**	**14.30**	**14.95**	**15.95**	**17.25**	**18.20**	**20.15**	**22.50**

One Quarter Dozen in Plaid Covered Box.

HANDLED TANGED FIRMER, OUTSIDE BEVEL

4½ Inch Blade.

No. 255 Width ... Inches,	1/4	3/8	1/2	5/8	3/4	7/8	1	1 1/4	1 1/2
Per Dozen	**$7.20**	**7.20**	**8.00**	**8.40**	**9.20**	**10.80**	**11.20**	**14.00**	**16.40**

One Quarter Dozen in Plaid Covered Box.

HANDLED TANGED FIRMER CHISELS

4½ Inch Blade.

No. 280 Width ... Inches,	1/8	1/4	3/8	1/2	5/8	3/4	7/8	1	1 1/4	1 1/2
Per Dozen	**$6.75**	**6.75**	**6.75**	**6.75**	**7.15**	**7.50**	**9.00**	**9.40**	**11.60**	**14.00**

One Quarter Dozen in Plaid Covered Box.

OHIO KING

Solid Cast Steel; Highly Finished; Sharpened and Ground.

SOCKET CORNER CHISELS

8 Inch Blade; Polished Hickory Iron Ringed Handles.

No. 350 Width ... Inches	7/8	1	1 1/4
Per Dozen	17.00	18.25	20.25
	22.10	**23.75**	**26.20**

Half Dozen in a Box.

SOCKET CARPENTERS' SLICKS

11 Inch Blade; Hickory Handle.

No. 370 Width ... Inches,	3	3 1/2
Per Dozen	$23.50	27.50
	30.60	**35.75**

One Sixth Dozen in a Box.

Beam Scales 1200 lbs.

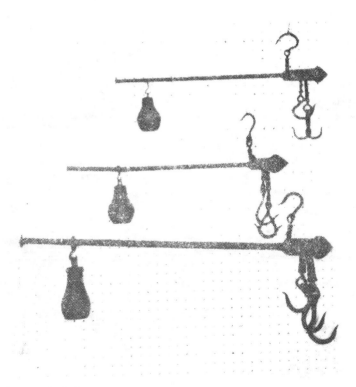

Steel Yards
Top two 40 lb. range; Bottom one has 100 lb.

170

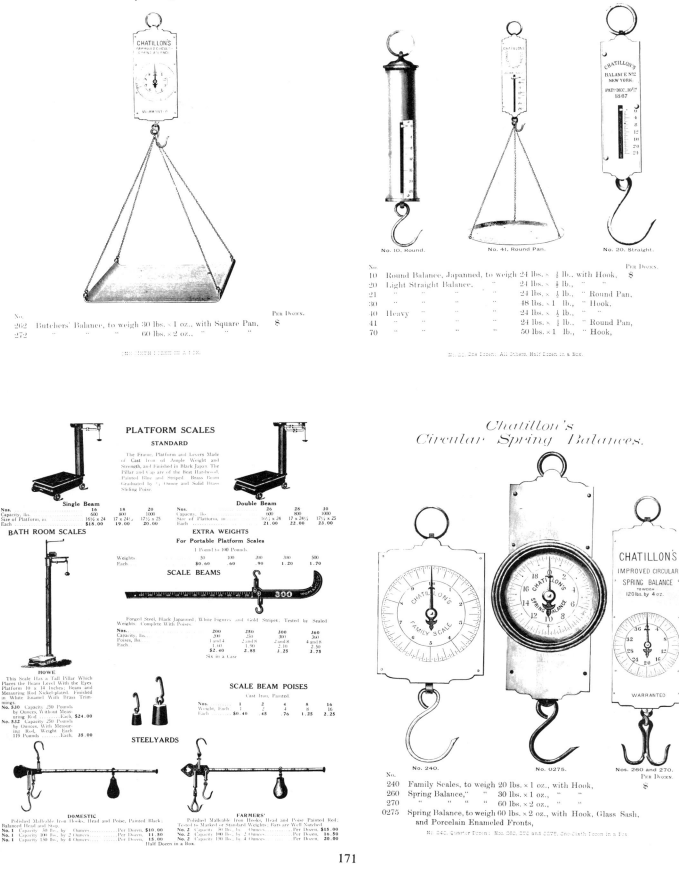

No. 262 Butchers' Balance, to weigh 30 lbs. × 1 oz., with Square Pan, $
No. 272 " " " 60 lbs. × 2 oz., " " "

PER DOZEN.

No. 10. Round. No. 41. Round Pan. No. 20. Straight.

No.				PER DOZEN.
10	Round Balance, Japanned, to weigh 24 lbs. × ⅛ lb., with Hook,			$
20	Light Straight Balance. " " 24 lbs. × ½ lb., " "			
21	" " " 24 lbs. × ⅛ lb., " Round Pan,			
30	" " " 48 lbs. × 1 lb., " Hook,			
40	Heavy " " 24 lbs. × ⅛ lb., " "			
41	" " " 24 lbs. × ⅛ lb., " Round Pan,			
70	" " " 50 lbs. × 1 lb., " Hook,			

No. 20, One Dozen; All Others, Half Dozen in a Box.

PLATFORM SCALES
STANDARD

The Frame, Platform and Levers Made of Cast Iron of Ample Weight and Strength, and Finished in Black Japan. The Pillar and Cap are of the Best Hardwood, Painted Blue and Striped. Brass Beam Graduated by ½ Ounce and Solid Brass Sliding Poise.

Single Beam

Nos.	16	18	20
Capacity, lbs.	600	800	1000
Size of Platform, in.	16½ x 24	17 x 24½	17½ x 25
Each	$18.00	19.00	20.00

Double Beam

Nos.	26	28	30
Capacity, lbs.	600	800	1000
Size of Platform, in.	16½ x 24	17 x 24½	17½ x 25
Each	21.00	22.00	23.00

BATH ROOM SCALES

EXTRA WEIGHTS
For Portable Platform Scales

1 Pound to 100 Pounds

Weights	50	100	200	300	500
Each	$0.60	.60	1.00	1.20	1.70

SCALE BEAMS

300

Forged Steel, Black Japanned, White Figures and Gold Stripes. Tested by Sealed Weights. Complete With Poises.

Nos.	200	250	300	360
Capacity, lbs.	200	250	300	360
Poises, lbs.	1 and 4	2 and 8	2 and 8	4 and 8
Each	1.60	1.90	2.10	2.50
	$2.40	2.85	3.25	3.75

Six in a Case

HOWE

This Scale Has a Tall Pillar Which Places the Beam Level With the Eyes. Platform 10 x 14 Inches; Beam and Measuring Rod Nickel-plated. Finished in White Enamel With Brass Trimmings.
No. 530 Capacity 250 Pounds by Ounces, Without Measuring Rod .... Each, $24.00
No. 532 Capacity 250 Pounds by Ounces, With Measuring Rod, Weight Each 119 Pounds .... Each, 35.00

SCALE BEAM POISES
Cast Iron, Painted

Nos.	1	2	4	8	16
Weight, Each	1	2	4	8	16
Each	$0.40	.45	.76	1.25	2.25

STEELYARDS

DOMESTIC
Polished Malleable Iron Hooks, Head and Poise, Painted Black; Balanced Head and Stop.
				Per Dozen,
No. 1	Capacity 50 lbs., by Ounces			$10.00
No. 1	Capacity 100 lbs., by 2 Ounces			11.50
No. 1	Capacity 150 lbs., by 4 Ounces			15.00

Half Dozen in a Box.

FARMERS'
Polished Malleable Iron Hooks, Head and Poise Painted Red. Tested to Marked or Standard Weights; Bars are Well Notched.
				Per Dozen,
No. 2	Capacity 50 lbs., by Ounces			$15.00
No. 2	Capacity 100 lbs., by 2 Ounces			16.50
No. 2	Capacity 150 lbs., by 4 Ounces			20.00

CHATILLON'S IMPROVED CIRCULAR SPRING BALANCE TO WEIGH 120 lbs. by 4 oz.

WARRANTED

No. 240. No. 0275. Nos. 260 and 270.

PER DOZEN.

No.		PER DOZEN.
240	Family Scales, to weigh 20 lbs. × 1 oz., with Hook,	$
260	Spring Balance," " 30 lbs. × 1 oz., " "	
270	" " " 60 lbs. × 2 oz., " "	
0275	Spring Balance, to weigh 60 lbs. × 2 oz., with Hook, Glass Sash, and Porcelain Enameled Fronts,	

No. 240, Quarter Dozen; Nos. 260, 270 and 0275, One-Sixth Dozen in a Box.

171

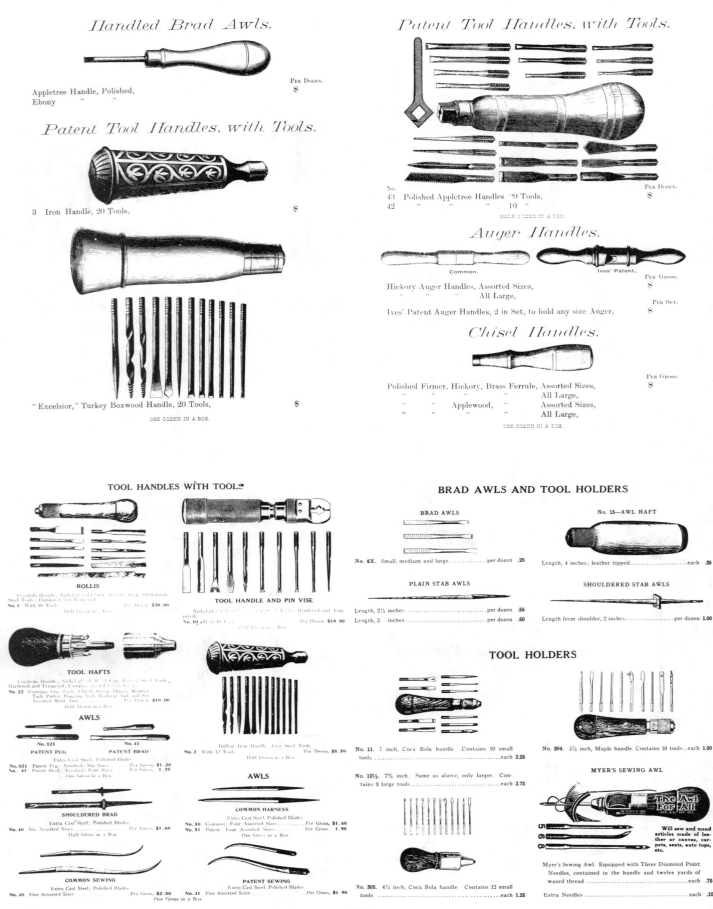

Handled Brad Awls.

Appletree Handle, Polished,
Ebony   "   "

Patent Tool Handles, with Tools.

3 Iron Handle, 20 Tools,

$

"Excelsior," Turkey Boxwood Handle, 20 Tools, $

ONE DOZEN IN A BOX.

Patent Tool Handles, with Tools.

No.
43   Polished Appletree Handles 20 Tools,   Per Dozen.
42   "   "   "   10 " $

HALF DOZEN IN A BOX.

Auger Handles.

Common.   Ives' Patent,

Hickory Auger Handles, Assorted Sizes,   Per Gross.
"   "   "   All Large, $

Ives' Patent Auger Handles, 2 in Set, to hold any size Auger,   Per Set.
$

Chisel Handles.

Polished Firmer, Hickory, Brass Ferrule, Assorted Sizes,   Per Gross.
"   "   "   "   All Large, $
"   "   Applewood,   "   Assorted Sizes,
"   "   "   "   All Large,

ONE DOZEN IN A BOX.

TOOL HANDLES WITH TOOLS.

ROLLIS

Cocobolo Handle, Nickel plated Chuck, Positive Grip, Best Grade
Steel Tools, Hardened and Tempered.
No. 1 With 10 Tools   Per Dozen $10.00
Half Dozen in a Box.

TOOL HANDLE AND PIN VISE

Nickel plated Chuck, Forged Steel Tools, Hardened and Tem-
pered.
No. 10 . With 10 Tools   Per Dozen $18.00
Half Dozen in a Box.

TOOL HAFTS

Cocobolo Handle, Nickel plated Metal Chuck, Forged Steel Tools,
Hardened and Tempered; Complete Tool Chest for Use.
No. 22 Contains One Each, Chisel, Screw Driver, Reamer,
Tack Puller, Pegging Awl, Marking Awl and Six
Assorted Brad Awls   Per Dozen $10.00
Half Dozen in a Box.

AWLS

No. 021   No. 41
PATENT PEG   PATENT BRAD
Extra Cast Steel; Polished Blades
No. 021 Patent Peg; Assorted; Six Sizes   Per Gross, $1.20
No. 41 Patent Brad; Assorted; Four Sizes   Per Gross, 1.70
One Gross in a Box.

SHOULDERED BRAD
Extra Cast Steel; Polished Blades
No. 40 Six Assorted Sizes   Per Gross, $1.60
Half Gross in a Box.

COMMON SEWING
Extra Cast Steel; Polished Blades
No. 30 Five Assorted Sizes   Per Gross, $2.00
One Gross in a Box.

No. 2 With 12 Tools   Per Dozen, $5.50
Half Dozen in a Box.

AWLS

COMMON HARNESS
Extra Cast Steel; Polished Blades
No. 50 Common; Four Assorted Sizes   Per Gross, $1.60
No. 51 Patent; Four Assorted Sizes   Per Gross, 1.90
One Gross in a Box.

PATENT SEWING
Extra Cast Steel; Polished Blades
No. 31 Five Assorted Sizes   Per Gross, $1.90
One Gross in a Box.

BRAD AWLS AND TOOL HOLDERS

BRAD AWLS

No. 4X. Small, medium and large   per dozen .25

PLAIN STAB AWLS

Length, 2½ inches   per dozen .55
Length, 3   inches   per dozen .60

No. 15—AWL HAFT

Length, 4 inches; leather tipped   each .35

SHOULDERED STAB AWLS

Length from shoulder, 2 inches   per dozen 1.00

TOOL HOLDERS

No. 11. 7 inch, Coca Bola handle. Contains 10 small
tools   each 2.25

No. 12½. 7¾ inch. Same as above, only larger. Contains 9 large tools   each 2.75

No. 305. 4½ inch, Coca Bola handle. Contains 12 small
tools   each 1.25

No. 304. 5¾ inch, Maple handle. Contains 10 tools . . each 1.00

MYER'S SEWING AWL

Will sew and mend
articles made of lea-
ther or canvas, car-
pets, seats, auto tops,
etc.

Myer's Sewing Awl. Equipped with Three Diamond Point
Needles, contained in the handle and twelve yards of
waxed thread   each .75

Extra Needles   each .10

FARM
TOOL
SECTION

Early Primitive Vise

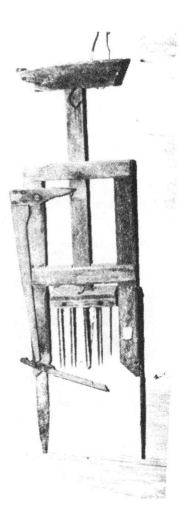

Mole Trap

Well Wheels.

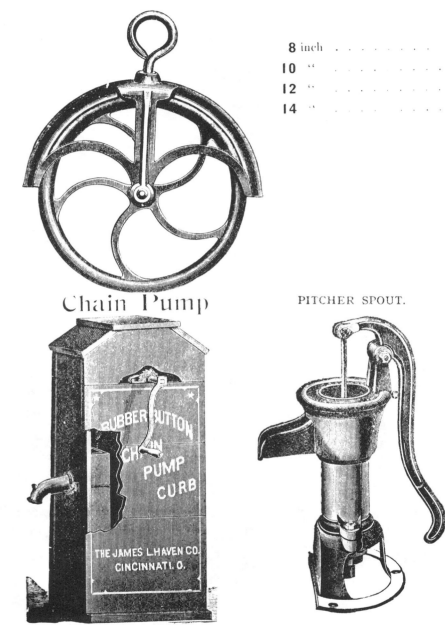

8 inch	. . . .	
10 "	. . . .	
12 "	. . . .	
14 "	. . . .	

Chain Pump

PITCHER SPOUT.

Calf Yoke

Single Ox Yoke

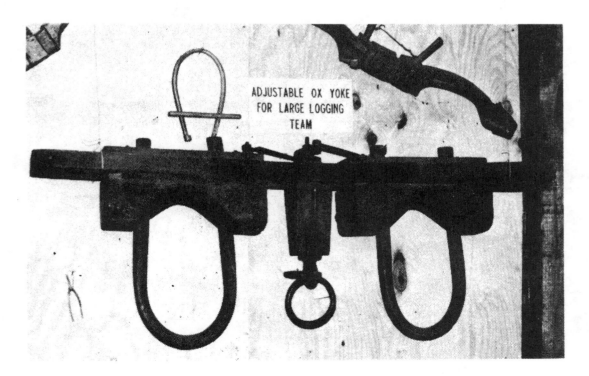

Adjustable Ox Yoke for Large Logging Team

176

Farm Tools

Many of the tools in this section were found both on the farm and in the city.

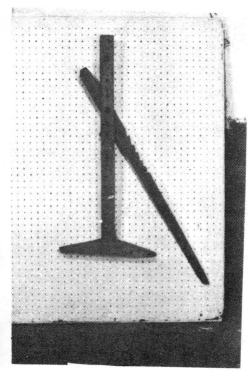

Buggy Jack

Wooden Rake
Wooden Snow Shovel

Ice Tongs, Butchering Hooks,
Hog Spreaders

Fodder Chopper

Grain Grader

Rocker Churn

Corn Planters.

Planet.

Chautauqua.

Cyclone.

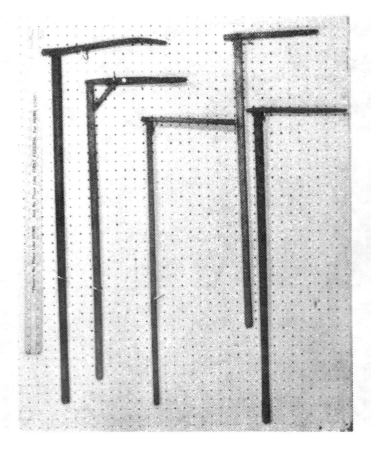

Butchering Stirrers

Gem Pump Curb for Dug Well or Cistern

CUTTER COMPLETE.

BED OF KNIVES.
Showing manner in which
potato is cut.

This is a seldom seen item, only found in potato
growing areas. In good shape, worth up to $300.

180

Avery Plows
"NEW CLIPPER" SERIES STEEL PLOWS

Painted red. An extra high grade of plow, embracing the qualities of the "general purpose" with that of the superior sod and stubble plow. Suited for any and all work in any secion of country, particularly in clay and stiff lands. Has our patent adjustable chilled heel, very strongly made and braced. In every particular an A No. 1 plow. Mold boards are double shin. Finest and strongest plow made. Extra hardened soft center mold board, landside and point.

WOOD BEAM
NUMBER OF PLOW INDICATES THE CUT

Numbers	Weight	Plow, no Extra Point
10	81	$13.50
12	101	15.75
14	106	18.25
16	110	20.50

In 1978 a display model very similar to this one was sold at the National Advertising Show in Indianapolis, Indiana. Randy Rhonemus (the seller) reported a sale price of over $700. Today I'm sure this same plow would sell for around $1000. Sorry, but in used condition only $100+.

Avery's "Wing Shovel" Plow

Avery's Combination Scraper and
Sweep, No. 1

181

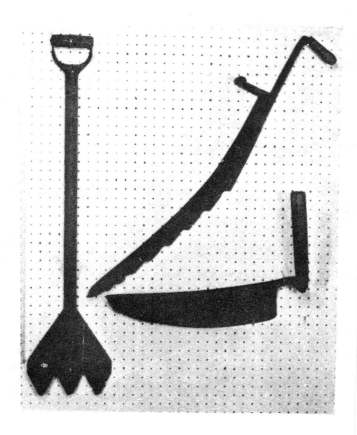

Forks
Three Tined Wood
Barley Fork
Six Tined Wood

Hay Knives

Forks Two at Left
Other Forks   Seeder

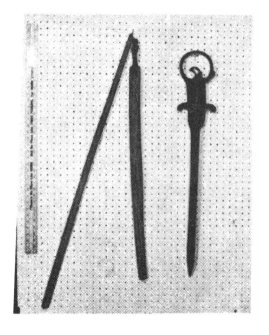

Right, Hay Harpoon
Left, Grain Flailer

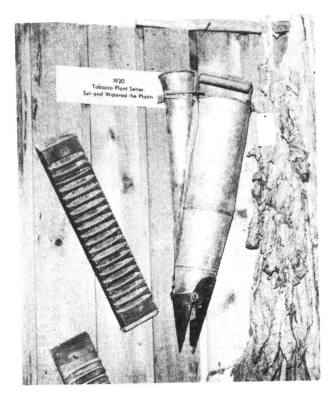

Tobacco Plant Setter
Cigar Molds

Fodder Chopper

Cider Press (in good shape)

183

One Man Wheat Drill

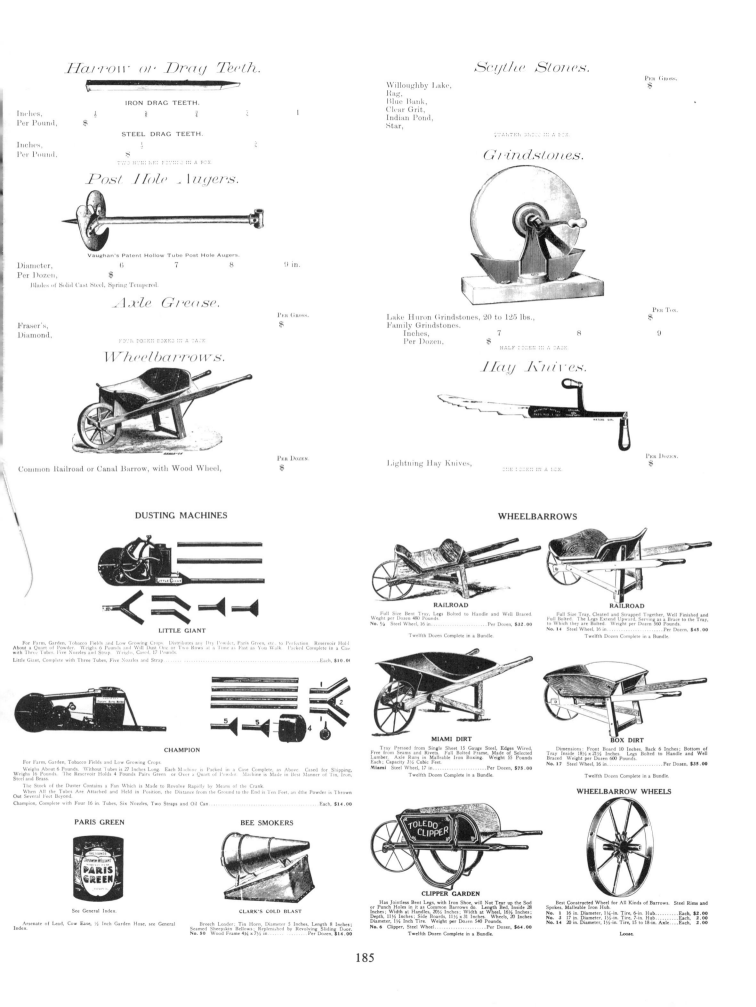

Harrow or Drag Teeth.

IRON DRAG TEETH.

Inches,	¼	⅜	¾	⅞	1
Per Pound,	$				

STEEL DRAG TEETH.

Inches,				⅝
Per Pound.	$			

TWO HUNDRED POUNDS IN A BOX.

Post Hole Augers.

Vaughan's Patent Hollow Tube Post Hole Augers.

Diameter,	6	7	8	9 in.
Per Dozen,	$			

Blades of Solid Cast Steel, Spring Tempered.

Axle Grease.

		Per Gross.
Fraser's,		$
Diamond,		

FOUR DOZEN BOXES IN A CASE.

Wheelbarrows.

	Per Dozen.
Common Railroad or Canal Barrow, with Wood Wheel,	$

Scythe Stones.

Per Gross. $

Willoughby Lake,
Rag,
Blue Bank,
Clear Grit,
Indian Pond,
Star,

QUARTER GROSS IN A BOX.

Grindstones.

			Per Ton.
Lake Huron Grindstones, 20 to 125 lbs.,			$
Family Grindstones.			

Inches,	7	8	9
Per Dozen,	$		

HALF DOZEN IN A CASE.

Hay Knives.

		Per Dozen.
Lightning Hay Knives,	ONE DOZEN IN A BOX.	$

DUSTING MACHINES

LITTLE GIANT

For Farm, Garden, Tobacco Fields and Low Growing Crops. Distributes any Dry Powder, Paris Green, etc., to Perfection. Reservoir Holds About a Quart of Powder. Weighs 6 Pounds and Will Dust One or Two Rows at a Time as Fast as You Walk. Packed Complete in a Case with Three Tubes, Five Nozzles and Strap. Weighs, Cased, 17 Pounds.

Little Giant, Complete with Three Tubes, Five Nozzles and Strap........Each, $10.00

CHAMPION

For Farm, Garden, Tobacco Fields and Low Growing Crops.

Weighs About 6 Pounds. Without Tubes is 27 Inches Long. Each Machine is Packed in a Case Complete, as Above. Cased for Shipping, Weighs 16 Pounds. The Reservoir Holds 4 Pounds Paris Green or Over a Quart of Powder. Machine is Made in Best Manner of Tin, Iron, Steel and Brass.

The Stock of the Duster Contains a Fan Which is Made to Revolve Rapidly by Means of the Crank.

When All the Tubes Are Attached and Held in Position, the Distance from the Ground to the End is Ten Feet, and the Powder is Thrown Out Several Feet Beyond.

Champion, Complete with Four 16 in. Tubes, Six Nozzles, Two Straps and Oil Can...............Each, $14.00

PARIS GREEN

See General Index.

Arsenate of Lead, Cow Ease, ½ Inch Garden Hose, see General Index.

BEE SMOKERS

Breech Loader; Tin Horn, Diameter 5 Inches, Length 8 Inches; Seamed Sheepskin Bellows; Replenished by Revolving Sliding Door.
No. 50 Wood Frame 4¾ x 7½ in....... Per Dozen, $14.00

WHEELBARROWS

RAILROAD

Full Size Bent Tray, Legs Bolted to Handle and Well Braced. Weght per Dozen 480 Pounds.
No. ½ Steel Wheel, 16 in........................Per Dozen, $32.00

Twelfth Dozen Complete in a Bundle.

RAILROAD

Full Size Tray, Cleated and Strapped Together, Well Finished and Full Bolted. The Legs Extend Upward, Serving as a Brace to the Tray, to Which they are Bolted. Weight per Dozen 360 Pounds.
No. 14 Steel Wheel, 16 in........................Per Dozen, $45.00

Twelfth Dozen Complete in a Bundle.

MIAMI DIRT

Tray Pressed from Single Sheet 15 Gauge Steel, Edges Wired, Free from Seams and Rivets. Full Bolted Frame, Made of Selected Lumber. Axle Runs in Malleable Iron Boxing. Weight 55 Pounds Each; Capacity 3½ Cubic Feet.
Miami Steel Wheel, 17 in........................Per Dozen, $75.00

Twelfth Dozen Complete in a Bundle.

BOX DIRT

Dimensions: Front Board 10 Inches, Back 6 Inches; Bottom of Tray Inside 18½ x 21½ Inches. Legs Bolted to Handle and Well Braced. Weight per Dozen 600 Pounds.
No. 17 Steel Wheel, 16 in........................Per Dozen, $35.00

Twelfth Dozen Complete in a Bundle.

WHEELBARROW WHEELS

Best Constructed Wheel for All Kinds of Barrows. Steel Rims and Spokes, Malleable Iron Hub.
No. 1 16 in. Diameter, 1½-in. Tire, 6-in. Hub..........Each, $2.00
No. 3 17 in. Diameter, 1½-in. Tire, 7-in. Hub..........Each, 2.00
No. 14 20 in. Diameter, 1½-in. Tire, 15 to 18-in. Axle....Each, 2.00

Loose.

CLIPPER GARDEN

Has Jointless Bent Legs, with Iron Shoe, will Not Tear up the Sod or Punch Holes in it as Common Barrows do. Length Bed, Inside 28 Inches; Width at Handles, 20½ Inches; Width at Wheel, 16½ Inches; Depth, 11½ Inches; Side Boards, 11½ x 31 Inches. Wheels, 20 Inches Diameter, 1½ Inch Tire. Weight per Dozen 540 Pounds.
No. 6 Clipper, Steel Wheel........................Per Dozen, $64.00

Twelfth Dozen Complete in a Bundle.

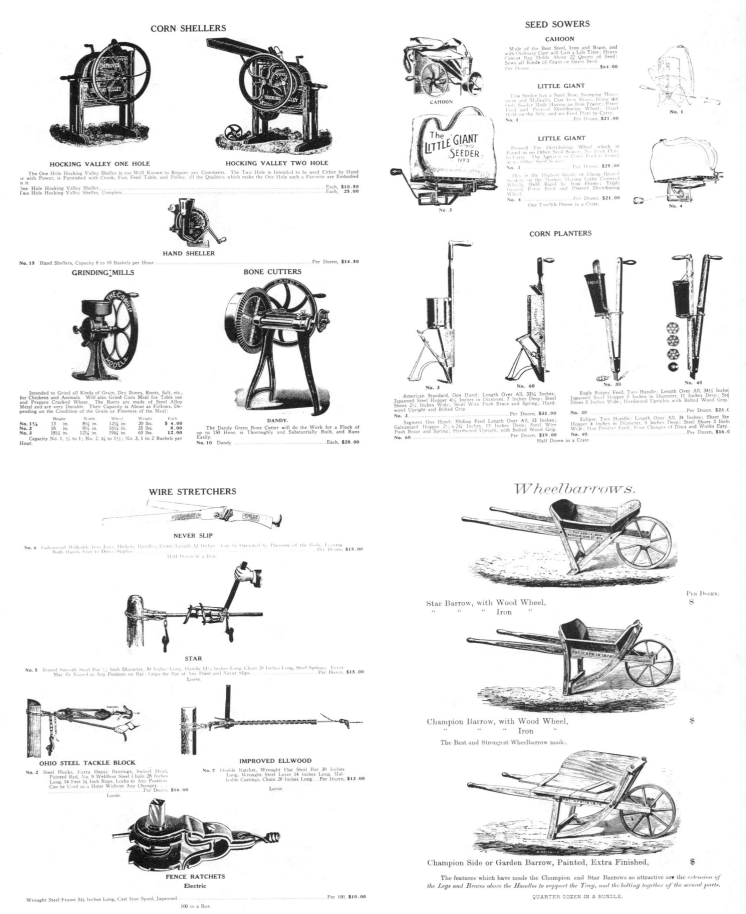

CORN SHELLERS

HOCKING VALLEY ONE HOLE

HOCKING VALLEY TWO HOLE

The One Hole Hocking Valley Sheller is too Well Known to Require any Comments. The Two Hole is Intended to be used Either by Hand or with Power, is Furnished with Crank, Fan, Feed Table, and Pulley, all the Qualities which make the One Hole such a Favorite are Embodied in it.

One Hole Hocking Valley Sheller.......................................Each, **$10.50**
Two Hole Hocking Valley Sheller, Complete.......................................Each, **25.00**

HAND SHELLER

No. 15 Hand Shellers, Capacity 8 to 10 Bushels per Hour.......................................Per Dozen, **$14.50**

GRINDING MILLS

Intended to Grind all Kinds of Grain, Dry Bones, Roots, Salt, etc., for Chickens and Animals. Will also Grind Corn Meal for Table use and Prepare Cracked Wheat. The Burrs are made of Steel Alloy Metal and are very Durable. Their Capacity is About as Follows, Depending on the Condition of the Grain or Fineness of the Meal:

	Height	Width	Wheel	Weight	Each
No. 1½	13 in.	8¼ in.	12¼ in.	20 lbs.	**$ 4.00**
No. 2	16 in.	9½ in.	16½ in.	35 lbs.	**8.00**
No. 3	18½ in.	12¼ in.	19¾ in.	63 lbs.	**12.00**

Capacity No. 1, ½ to 1; No. 2, ¾ to 1½; No. 3, 1 to 2 Bushels per Hour.

BONE CUTTERS

DANDY.

The Dandy Green Bone Cutter will do the Work for a Flock of up to 150 Hens, is Thoroughly and Substantially Built, and Runs Easily.

No. 10 Dandy.......................................Each, **$28.00**

SEED SOWERS

CAHOON

No. 3

CAHOON

Made of the Best Steel, Iron and Brass, and with Ordinary Care will Last a Life Time; Heavy Canvas Bag Holds About 22 Quarts of Seed; Sows all Kinds of Grain or Grass Seed.

Per Dozen.......................................**$64.00**

LITTLE GIANT

This Seeder has a Steel Bow, Swinging Movement and Malleable Cast Iron Brace, Being the Only Seeder Made Having an Iron Frame; Force Feed and Pressed Distributing Wheel; Hand Hold on the Side, and no Feed Plate to Carry.

No. 1.......................................Per Dozen, **$21.00**

LITTLE GIANT

Pressed Tin Distributing Wheel which is Found in no Other Seed Sower; No Feed Plate to Carry. The Agitator or Force Feed is Found in no Other Seed Sower.

No. 3.......................................Per Dozen, **$25.00**

This is the Highest Grade of Cheap Geared Seeders on the Market, Having Lathe Centered Wheels, Held Rigid by Iron Frame; Triple Geared, Force Feed and Pressed Distributing Wheel.

No. 4.......................................Per Dozen, **$21.00**

One Twelfth Dozen in a Crate.

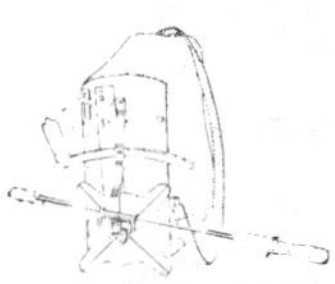

No. 1

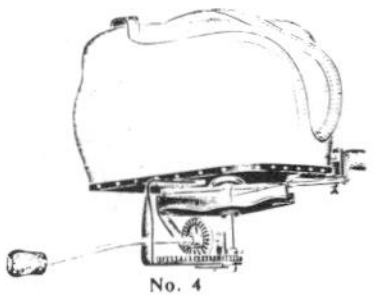

No. 4

CORN PLANTERS

No. 3

No. 60

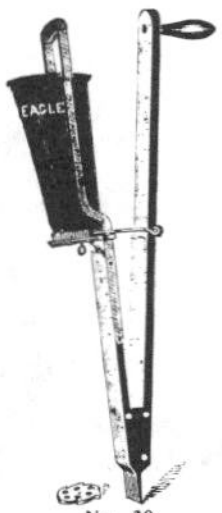

No. 30

No. 40

American Standard, One Hand; Length Over All, 33½ Inches; Japanned Steel Hopper 4½ Inches in Diameter, 7 Inches Deep; Steel Shoes 2½ Inches Wide; Steel Wire Push Brace and Spring; Hardwood Upright and Bolted Grip.

No. 3.......................................Per Dozen, **$31.00**

Segment One Hand; Sliding Feed Length Over All, 33 Inches; Galvanized Hopper 2½ x 2¾ Inches, 13 Inches Deep; Steel Wire Push Brace and Spring; Hardwood Upright, with Bolted Wood Grip.

No. 60.......................................Per Dozen, **$19.00**

Eagle Rotary Feed, Two Handle; Length Over All, 34½ Inches; Japanned Steel Hopper 5 Inches in Diameter, 11 Inches Deep; Steel Shoes 3 Inches Wide; Hardwood Uprights with Bolted Wood Grip.

No. 30.......................................Per Dozen, **$23.0**

Eclipse, Two Handle; Length Over All, 34 Inches; Sheet Steel Hopper 4 Inches in Diameter, 9 Inches Deep; Steel Shoes 3 Inches Wide; Has Positive Feed; Four Changes of Discs and Works Easy.

No. 40.......................................Per Dozen, **$16.0**

Half Dozen in a Crate.

WIRE STRETCHERS

NEVER SLIP

No. 6 Galvanized Malleable Iron Jaws, Hickory Handles, Entire Length 32 Inches. Can be Operated by Pressure of the Body, Leaving Both Hands Free to Drive Staples.......................................Per Dozen, **$15.00**

Half Dozen in a Box.

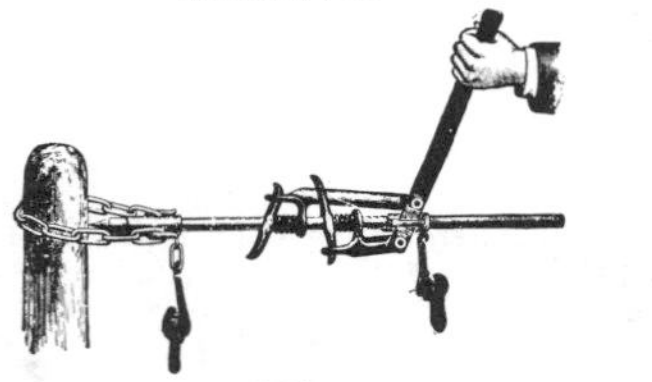

STAR

No. 5 Round Smooth Steel Bar ½ Inch Diameter, 30 Inches Long, Handle 13¾ Inches Long, Chain 28 Inches Long, Steel Springs. Lever May Be Raised in Any Position on Bar; Grips the Bar at Any Point and Never Slips.......................................Per Dozen, **$15.00**

Loose.

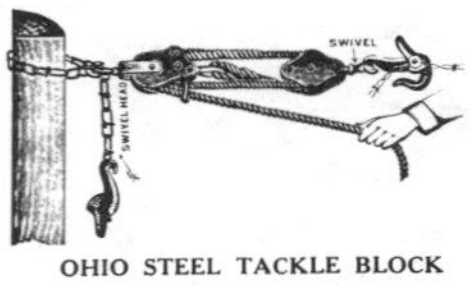

OHIO STEEL TACKLE BLOCK

No. 2 Steel Blocks, Extra Heavy Bearings, Swivel Head, Painted Red, No. 9 Weldless Steel Chain 28 Inches Long, 14 Feet ⅜ Inch Rope, Locks in Any Position. Can be Used as a Hoist Without Any Changes.......................................Per Dozen, **$16.00**

Loose.

IMPROVED ELLWOOD

No. 7 Double Ratchet, Wrought Flat Steel Bar 30 Inches Long, Wrought Steel Lever 14 Inches Long, Malleable Castings, Chain 28 Inches Long...Per Dozen, **$12.00**

Loose.

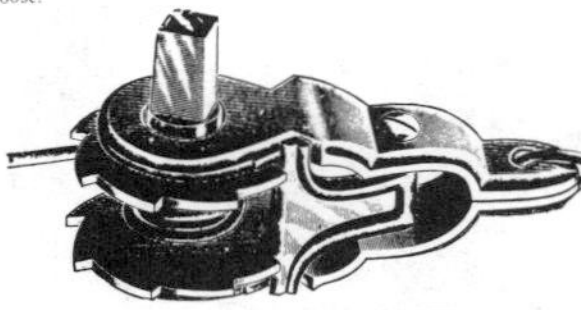

FENCE RATCHETS

Electric

Wrought Steel Frame 3¼ Inches Long, Cast Iron Spool, Japanned.......................................Per 100, **$10.00**

100 in a Box.

Wheelbarrows.

Per Dozen.

Star Barrow, with Wood Wheel, $
" " " Iron "

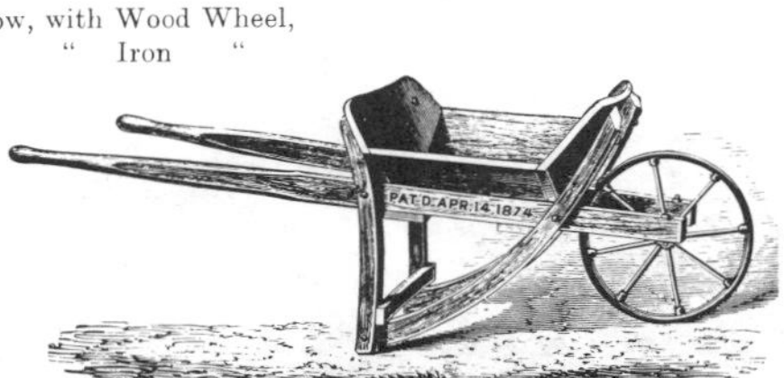

Champion Barrow, with Wood Wheel, $
" " " Iron "

The Best and Strongest Wheelbarrow made.

Champion Side or Garden Barrow, Painted, Extra Finished, $

The features which have made the Champion and Star Barrows so attractive are the *extension of the Legs and Braces above the Handles to support the Tray, and the bolting together of the several parts.*

QUARTER DOZEN IN A BUNDLE.

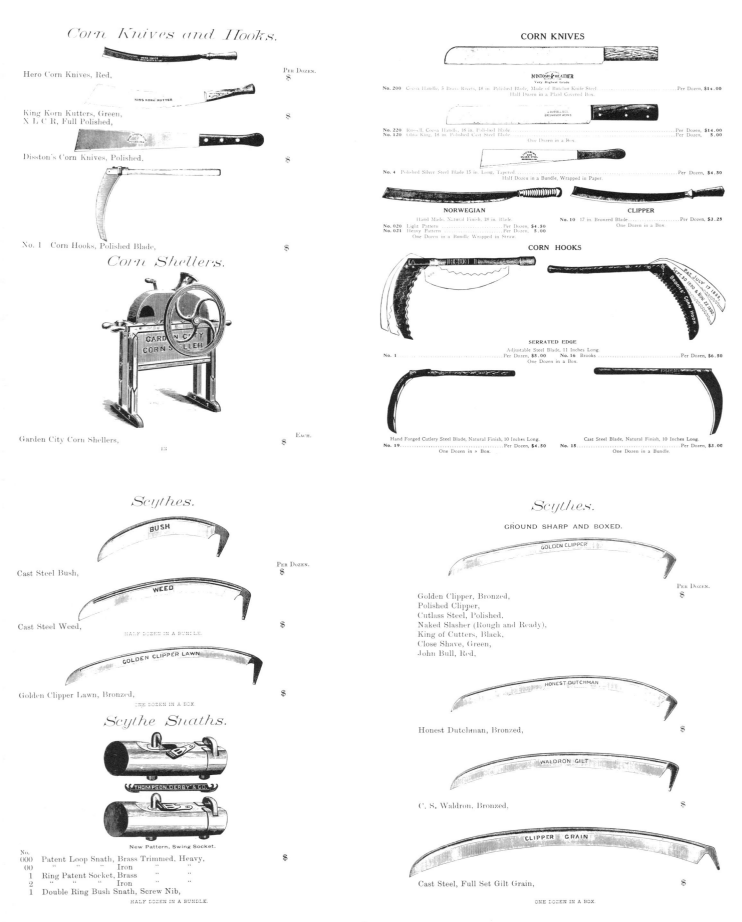

Corn Knives and Hooks.

	Per Dozen.
Hero Corn Knives, Red,	$
King Korn Kutters, Green, X L C R, Full Polished,	$
Disston's Corn Knives, Polished,	$
No. 1 Corn Hooks, Polished Blade,	$

Corn Shellers.

Garden City Corn Shellers,   Each. $

13

CORN KNIVES

No. 200 Cocoa Handle, 5 Brass Rivets, 18 in. Polished Blade, Made of Butcher Knife Steel. .... Per Dozen, $14.00
Half Dozen in a Plaid Covered Box.

M·INTOSH & HEATHER
Very Highest Grade

No. 220 Russell, Cocoa Handle, 18 in. Polished Blade. .... Per Dozen, $14.00
No. 120 Ohio King, 18 in. Polished Cast Steel Blade. .... Per Dozen, 5.00
One Dozen in a Box.

No. 4 Polished Silver Steel Blade 15 in. Long, Tapered. .... Per Dozen, $4.50
Half Dozen in a Bundle, Wrapped in Paper.

NORWEGIAN
Hand Made, Natural Finish, 18 in. Blade.
No. 020 Light Pattern .... Per Dozen, $4.50
No. 021 Heavy Pattern .... Per Dozen, 5.00
One Dozen in a Bundle Wrapped in Straw.

CLIPPER
No. 10 17 in. Bronzed Blade. .... Per Dozen, $3.25
One Dozen in a Box.

CORN HOOKS

SERRATED EDGE
Adjustable Steel Blade, 11 Inches Long.
No. 1 .... Per Dozen, $5.00   No. 16 Brooks .... Per Dozen, $6.50
One Dozen in a Box.

Hand Forged Cutlery Steel Blade, Natural Finish, 10 Inches Long.
No. 19 .... Per Dozen, $4.50
One Dozen in a Box.

Cast Steel Blade, Natural Finish, 10 Inches Long.
No. 15 .... Per Dozen, $3.00
One Dozen in a Bundle.

Scythes.

	Per Dozen.
Cast Steel Bush,	$
Cast Steel Weed,	$
Golden Clipper Lawn, Bronzed,	$

HALF DOZEN IN A BUNDLE.

ONE DOZEN IN A BOX.

Scythe Snaths.

New Pattern, Swing Socket.

No.		Per Dozen
000	Patent Loop Snath, Brass Trimmed, Heavy,	$
00	" " " Iron	
1	Ring Patent Socket, Brass " "	
2	" " " Iron " "	
1	Double Ring Bush Snath, Screw Nib,	

HALF DOZEN IN A BUNDLE.

Scythes.

GROUND SHARP AND BOXED.

	Per Dozen.
Golden Clipper, Bronzed,	$
Polished Clipper,	
Cutlass Steel, Polished,	
Naked Slasher (Rough and Ready),	
King of Cutters, Black,	
Close Shave, Green,	
John Bull, Red,	
Honest Dutchman, Bronzed,	$
C. S. Waldron, Bronzed,	$
Cast Steel, Full Set Gilt Grain,	$

ONE DOZEN IN A BOX.

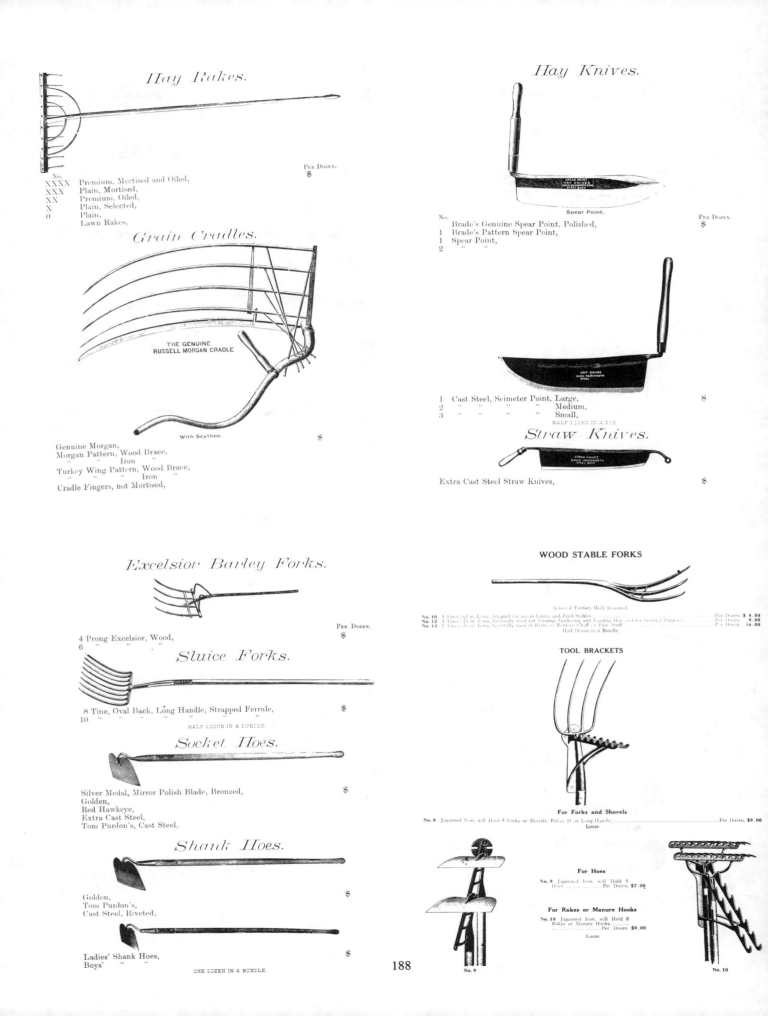

Hay Rakes.

PER DOZEN.
$

No.
XXXX   Premium, Mortised and Oiled,
XXX   Plain, Mortised,
XX   Premium, Oiled,
X   Plain, Selected,
0   Plain,
       Lawn Rakes,

Grain Cradles.

THE GENUINE
RUSSELL MORGAN CRADLE

With Scythes.

Genuine Morgan,
Morgan Pattern, Wood Brace,
   "   "   Iron
Turkey Wing Pattern, Wood Brace,
   "   "   "   Iron
Cradle Fingers, not Mortised,

$

Hay Knives.

Spear Point.

No.   PER DOZEN.
       Brade's Genuine Spear Point, Polished, $
1   Brade's Pattern Spear Point,
1   Spear Point,
2   "   "

1   Cast Steel, Scimeter Point, Large, $
2   "   "   "   "   Medium,
3   "   "   "   "   Small,
                      HALF DOZEN IN A BOX.

Straw Knives.

Extra Cast Steel Straw Knives, $

Excelsior Barley Forks.

                                                    PER DOZEN.
4 Prong Excelsior, Wood, $
6   "   "   "

Sluice Forks.

8 Tine, Oval Back, Long Handle, Strapped Ferrule, $
10 "   "   "   "   "
              HALF DOZEN IN A BUNDLE.

Socket Hoes.

Silver Medal, Mirror Polish Blade, Bronzed, $
Golden,
Red Hawkeye,
Extra Cast Steel,
Tom Purdon's, Cast Steel.

Shank Hoes.

Golden,
Tom Purdon's,
Cast Steel, Riveted, $

Ladies' Shank Hoes, $
Boys'   "   "
              ONE DOZEN IN A BUNDLE.

WOOD STABLE FORKS

Selected Timber, Well Seasoned.

No. 10   3 Tines, 62 in. Long, Adapted for use in Livery and Feed Stables .... Per Dozen $ 8.50
No. 12   3 Tines, 76 in. Long, Generally used for Tossing, Gathering and Loading Hay and for General Purposes .... Per Dozen   9.00
No. 13   3 Tines, 76 in. Long, Generally used in Barns to Remove Chaff or Fine Stuff .... Per Dozen 16.00
                        Half Dozen in a Bundle.

TOOL BRACKETS

For Forks and Shovels

No. 8   Japanned Iron, will Hold 8 Forks or Shovels, Either D or Long Handle .... Per Dozen $9.00
                        Loose.

For Hoes

No. 9   Japanned Iron, will Hold 8 Hoes .... Per Dozen, $7.00

For Rakes or Manure Hooks

No. 10   Japanned Iron, will Hold 8 Rakes or Manure Hooks .... Per Dozen $9.00
                        Loose.

No. 9   No. 10

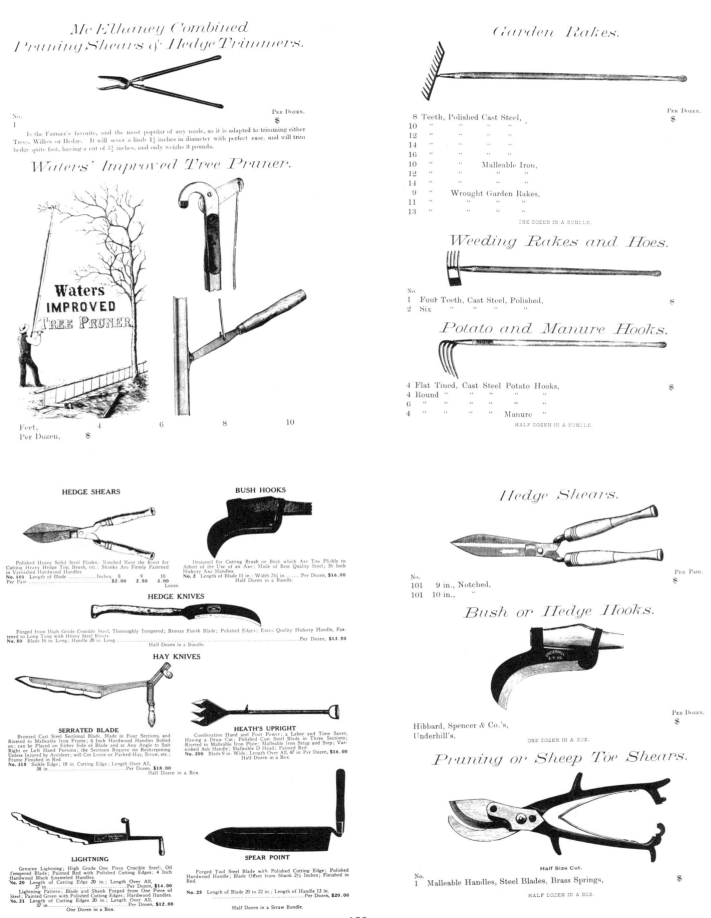

McElhaney Combined
Pruning Shears & Hedge Trimmers.

No.   Per Dozen.
1 $

Is the Farmer's favorite, and the most popular of any made, as it is adapted to trimming either Trees, Willow or Hedge. It will sever a limb 1½ inches in diameter with perfect ease, and will trim hedge quite fast, having a cut of 5½ inches, and only weighs 3 pounds.

Waters' Improved Tree Pruner.

Waters IMPROVED TREE PRUNER.

Feet,   4   6   8   10
Per Dozen, $

Garden Rakes.

				Per Dozen.
8 Teeth, Polished Cast Steel,				$
10 " " " "				
12 " " " "				
14 " " " "				
16 " " " "				
10 " " Malleable Iron,				
12 " " " "				
14 " " " "				
9 " Wrought Garden Rakes,				
11 " " " "				
13 " " " "				

ONE DOZEN IN A BUNDLE.

Weeding Rakes and Hoes.

No. $
1   Four Teeth, Cast Steel, Polished,
2   Six   "   "   "

Potato and Manure Hooks.

4   Flat Tined, Cast Steel Potato Hooks, $
4   Round   "   "   "   "
6   "   "   "   "
4   "   "   "   "   Manure   "

HALF DOZEN IN A BUNDLE.

HEDGE SHEARS

Polished Heavy Solid Steel Blades; Notched Near the Rivet for Cutting Heavy Hedge Top, Brush, etc.; Shanks Are Firmly Fastened in Varnished Hardwood Handles.
No. 101 Length of Blade ....Inches. 8   9   10
Per Pair $2.00   2.50   3.00
                                                            Loose.

BUSH HOOKS

Designed for Cutting Brush or Bush which Are Too Pliable to Admit of the Use of an Axe; Made of Best Quality Steel; 36 Inch Hickory Axe Handles.
No. 2 Length of Blade 11 in.; Width 2¾ in.......Per Dozen, **$16.00**
                                            Half Dozen in a Bundle.

HEDGE KNIVES

Forged from High Grade Crucible Steel, Thoroughly Tempered; Bronze Finish Blade; Polished Edges; Extra Quality Hickory Handle, Fastened to Long Tang with Heavy Steel Rivets.
No. 50 Blade 16 in. Long; Handle 20 in. Long ....Per Dozen, **$13.50**
                                            Half Dozen in a Bundle.

HAY KNIVES

SERRATED BLADE
Bronzed Cast Steel Sectional Blade, Made in Four Sections, and Riveted to Malleable Iron Frame; 6 Inch Hardwood Handles Bolted on; can be Placed on Either Side of Blade and at Any Angle to Suit Right or Left Hand Persons; the Sections Require no Resharpening Unless Injured by Accident; will Cut Loose or Packed Hay, Straw, etc.; Frame Finished in Red.
No. 315 Sickle Edge; 18 in. Cutting Edge; Length Over All,
38 in. ....Per Dozen, **$18.00**
                                            Half Dozen in a Box.

HEATH'S UPRIGHT
Combination Hand and Foot Power; a Labor and Time Saver, Having a Draw Cut; Polished Cast Steel Blade in Three Sections; Riveted to Malleable Iron Plate; Malleable Iron Strap and Step; Varnished Ash Handle; Malleable D Head; Painted Red.
No. 300 Blade 9 in. Wide; Length Over All, 47 in. Per Dozen, **$16.00**
                                            Half Dozen in a Box.

LIGHTNING
Genuine Lightning; High Grade One Piece Crucible Steel; Oil Tempered Blade; Painted Red with Polished Cutting Edges; 4 Inch Hardwood Black Enameled Handle.
No. 20 Length of Cutting Edge 20 in.; Length Over All,
37 in. ....Per Dozen, **$14.00**
Lightning Pattern; Blade and Shank Forged from One Piece of Steel; Painted Green with Polished Cutting Edges; Hardwood Handles.
No. 21 Length of Cutting Edges 20 in.; Length Over All,
37 in. ....Per Dozen, **$12.00**
                                            One Dozen in a Box.

SPEAR POINT
Forged Tool Steel Blade with Polished Cutting Edge; Polished Hardwood Handle; Blade Offset from Shank 2½ Inches; Finished in Red.
No. 25 Length of Blade 20 to 22 in.; Length of Handle 13 in.
................................Per Dozen, **$20.00**
                                            Half Dozen in a Straw Bundle.

Hedge Shears.

No.   Per Pair.
101   9 in., Notched, $
101   10 in.,   "

Bush or Hedge Hooks.

Per Dozen.
Hibbard, Spencer & Co.'s, $
Underhill's,
                            ONE DOZEN IN A BOX.

Pruning or Sheep Toe Shears.

Half Size Cut.

No. $
1   Malleable Handles, Steel Blades, Brass Springs,
                            HALF DOZEN IN A BOX.

LOG MEASURING STICKS

Left, Primitive Cant Hook
(used to roll logs)
Right, Post Hole Digger
Pat. March 28, 1880

Diameter 7 inches.

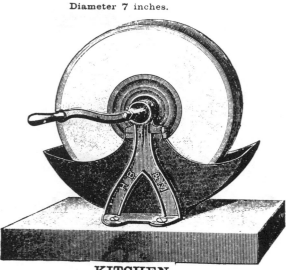

KITCHEN.

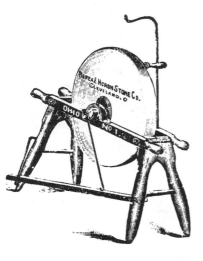

MOUNTED.

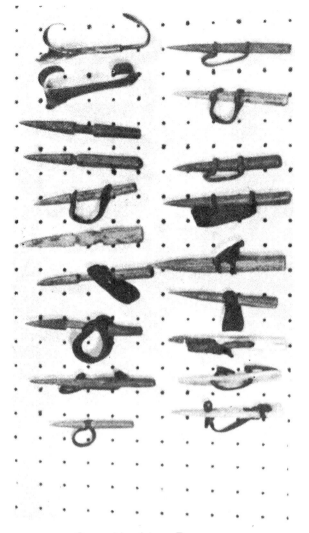

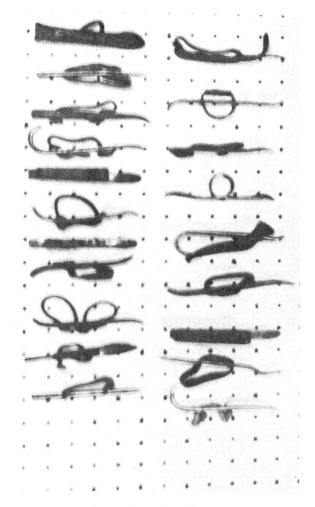

Corn Husking Pegs
(All Metal & Homemade)

Corn Husking Pegs
All above are handmade except two on top left
which are brass and dated 1862-1882.

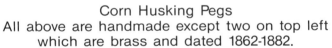

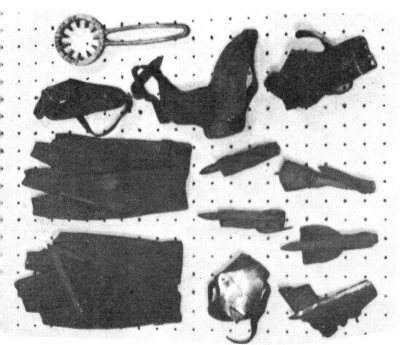

Corn Husking Gloves & Pegs
Upper Left, Corn Sheller

191

Fence and Barb Staples.

No. 9, Annealed Fence Staples, 1, 1¼, 1½, 1¾ and 1⅜ in.,
No. 12, Coppered Barb Staples, ¾ in.,

ONE HUNDRED POUNDS IN A KEG.

Jayne & Hill's Patent Barb Formers.

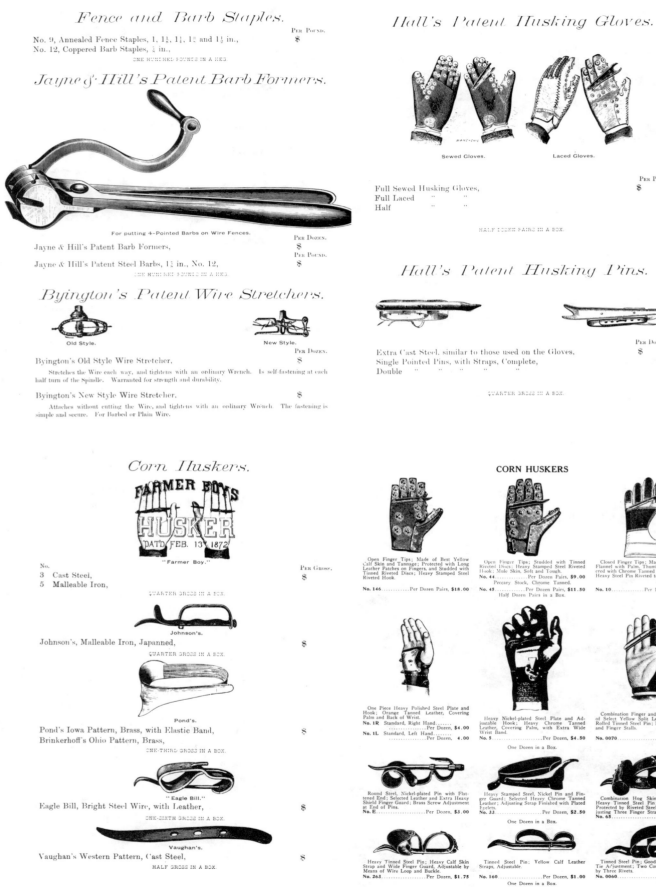

For putting 4-Pointed Barbs on Wire Fences.

PER DOZEN.
$

Jayne & Hill's Patent Barb Formers,

PER POUND.
$

Jayne & Hill's Patent Steel Barbs, 1⅜ in., No. 12,

ONE HUNDRED POUNDS IN A KEG.

Byington's Patent Wire Stretchers.

Old Style.

New Style.

PER DOZEN.
$

Byington's Old Style Wire Stretcher,

Stretches the Wire each way, and tightens with an ordinary Wrench. Is self-fastening at each half turn of the Spindle. Warranted for strength and durability.

PER DOZEN.
$

Byington's New Style Wire Stretcher,

Attaches without cutting the Wire, and tightens with an ordinary Wrench. The fastening is simple and secure. For Barbed or Plain Wire.

Corn Huskers.

FARMER BOYS HUSKER
PAT'D FEB. 13™ 1872.

"Farmer Boy."

No.

PER GROSS.
$

3   Cast Steel,
5   Malleable Iron,

QUARTER GROSS IN A BOX.

Johnson's.

Johnson's, Malleable Iron, Japanned,

$

QUARTER GROSS IN A BOX.

Pond's.

Pond's Iowa Pattern, Brass, with Elastic Band,
Brinkerhoff's Ohio Pattern, Brass,

$

ONE-THIRD GROSS IN A BOX.

"Eagle Bill."

Eagle Bill, Bright Steel Wire, with Leather,

$

ONE-SIXTH GROSS IN A BOX.

Vaughan's.

Vaughan's Western Pattern, Cast Steel,

$

HALF GROSS IN A BOX.

Hall's Patent Husking Gloves.

Sewed Gloves.   Laced Gloves.

PER PAIR.
$

Full Sewed Husking Gloves,
Full Laced   "   "
Half   "   "

HALF DOZEN PAIRS IN A BOX.

Hall's Patent Husking Pins.

Extra Cast Steel, similar to those used on the Gloves,
Single Pointed Pins, with Straps, Complete,
Double   "   "

PER DOZEN.
$

QUARTER GROSS IN A BOX.

CORN HUSKERS

Open Finger Tips; Made of Best Yellow Calf Skin and Tannage; Protected with Long Leather Patches on Fingers, and Studded with Tinned Riveted Discs; Heavy Stamped Steel Riveted Hook.
No. 146 .... Per Dozen Pairs, $18.00

Open Finger Tips; Studded with Tinned Riveted Discs; Heavy Stamped Steel Riveted Hook; Mule Skin, Soft and Tough.
No. 44 .... Per Dozen Pairs, $9.00
Peccary Stock, Chrome Tanned.
No. 45 .... Per Dozen Pairs, $11.50
Half Dozen Pairs in a Box.

Closed Finger Tips; Made of Heavy Cotton Flannel with Palm, Thumb and Fingers Covered with Chrome Tanned Mule Skin Leather; Heavy Steel Pin Riveted to Glove.
No. 10 .... Per Dozen Pairs, $4.50

One Piece Heavy Polished Steel Plate and Hook; Orange Tanned Leather, Covering Palm and Back of Wrist.
No. 1R Standard, Right Hand ....
No. 1L Standard, Left Hand ....
.... Per Dozen, $4.00

Heavy Nickel-plated Steel Plate and Adjustable Hook; Heavy Chrome Tanned Leather, Covering Palm, with Extra Wide Wrist Band.
No. 5 .... Per Dozen, $4.50
One Dozen in a Box.

Combination Finger and Thumb Cot; Made of Select Yellow Split Leather; Heavy Cold Rolled Tinned Steel Pin; Buckled Wrist Band and Finger Stalls.
No. 0070 .... Per Dozen, $2.30

Round Steel, Nickel-plated Pin with Flattened End; Selected Leather and Extra Heavy Shield Finger Guard; Brass Screw Adjustment at End of Pins.
No. E .... Per Dozen, $3.00

Heavy Stamped Steel, Nickel Pin and Finger Guard; Adjusting Strap Finished with Plated Eyelets.
No. 33 .... Per Dozen, $2.50
One Dozen in a Box.

Combination Hog Skin Finger Cot with Heavy Tinned Steel Pin; Open Tip Finger Protected by Riveted Steel Washers; Tie Adjusting Three Finger Strap.
No. 65 .... Per Dozen, $1.50

Heavy Tinned Steel Pin; Heavy Calf Skin Strap and Wide Finger Guard, Adjustable by Means of Wire Loop and Buckle.
No. 263 .... Per Dozen, $1.75

Tinned Steel Pin; Yellow Calf Leather Straps, Adjustable.
No. 160 .... Per Dozen, $1.00
One Dozen in a Box.

Tinned Steel Pin; Good Leather Strapping; Two Compartments Secured by Three Rivets.
No. 0060 .... Per Dozen, $0.70

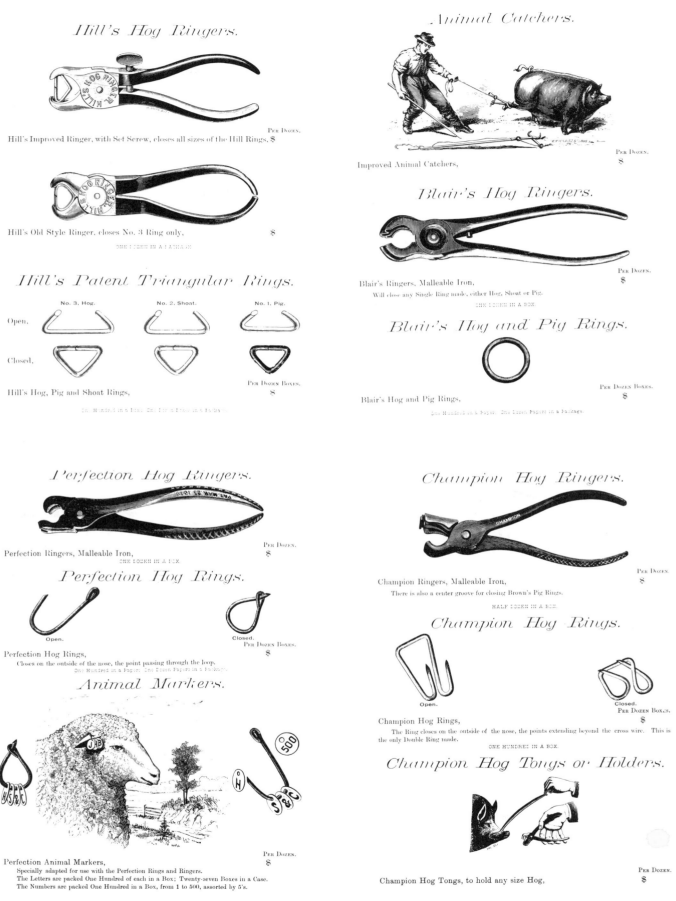

Hill's Hog Ringers.

Hill's Improved Ringer, with Set Screw, closes all sizes of the Hill Rings, $

PER DOZEN.

Hill's Old Style Ringer, closes No. 3 Ring only, $

ONE DOZEN IN A PACKAGE.

Hill's Patent Triangular Rings.

No. 3, Hog.　　No. 2, Shoat.　　No. 1, Pig.

Open,

Closed,

Hill's Hog, Pig and Shoat Rings, $

PER DOZEN BOXES.

One Hundred in a Box. One Dozen Boxes in a Package.

Animal Catchers.

Improved Animal Catchers, $

PER DOZEN.

Blair's Hog Ringers.

Blair's Ringers, Malleable Iron, $

Will close any Single Ring made, either Hog, Shoat or Pig.

ONE DOZEN IN A BOX.

PER DOZEN.

Blair's Hog and Pig Rings.

Blair's Hog and Pig Rings, $

PER DOZEN BOXES.

One Hundred in a Paper. One Dozen Papers in a Package.

Perfection Hog Ringers.

Perfection Ringers, Malleable Iron, $

ONE DOZEN IN A BOX.

PER DOZEN.

Perfection Hog Rings.

Open.　　　Closed.

Perfection Hog Rings, $

PER DOZEN BOXES.

Closes on the outside of the nose, the point passing through the loop.

One Hundred in a Paper. One Dozen Papers in a Package.

Animal Markers.

Perfection Animal Markers, $

PER DOZEN.

Specially adapted for use with the Perfection Rings and Ringers.
The Letters are packed One Hundred of each in a Box; Twenty-seven Boxes in a Case.
The Numbers are packed One Hundred in a Box, from 1 to 500, assorted by 5's.

Champion Hog Ringers.

Champion Ringers, Malleable Iron, $

PER DOZEN.

There is also a center groove for closing Brown's Pig Rings.

HALF DOZEN IN A BOX.

Champion Hog Rings.

Open.　　　Closed.

Champion Hog Rings, $

PER DOZEN BOXES.

The Ring closes on the outside of the nose, the points extending beyond the cross wire. This is the only Double Ring made.

ONE HUNDRED IN A BOX.

Champion Hog Tongs or Holders.

Champion Hog Tongs, to hold any size Hog, $

PER DOZEN.

193

Ox Bow Pins.

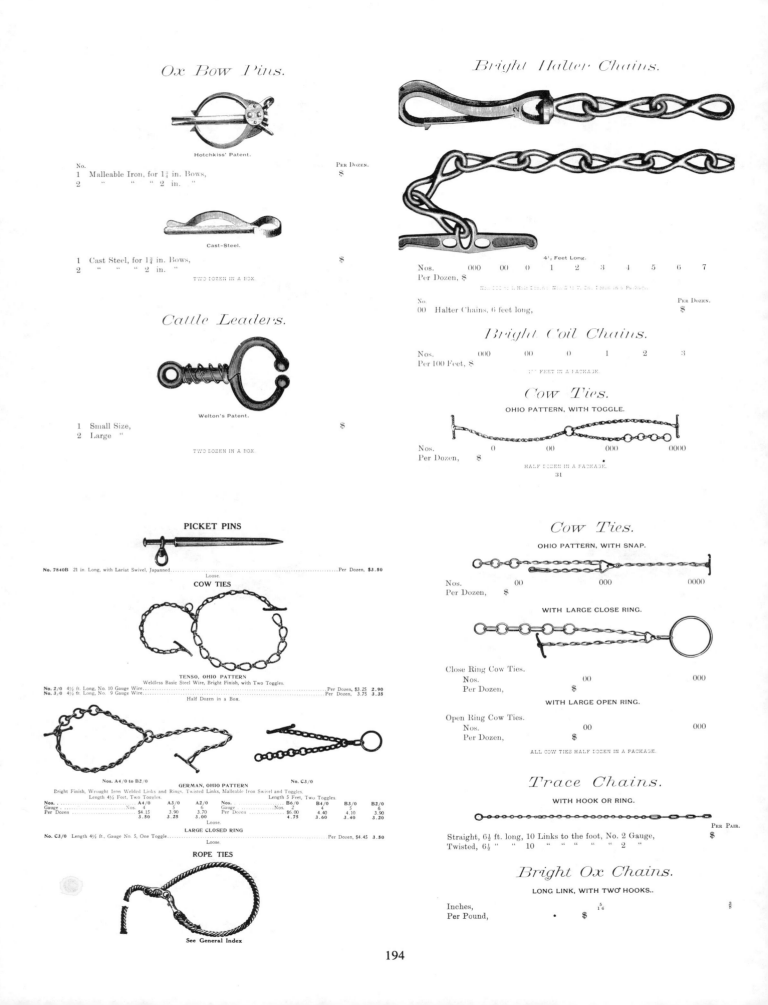

Hotchkiss' Patent.

No.		Per Dozen.
1	Malleable Iron, for 1¾ in. Bows,	$
2	" " " 2 in. "	

Cast-Steel.

| 1 | Cast Steel, for 1¾ in. Bows, | $ |
| 2 | "   "   " 2 in. " | |

TWO DOZEN IN A BOX.

Cattle Leaders.

Welton's Patent.

| 1 | Small Size, | $ |
| 2 | Large " | |

TWO DOZEN IN A BOX.

Bright Halter Chains.

4½ Feet Long.

Nos.	000	00	0	1	2	3	4	5	6	7
Per Dozen, $										

No.		Per Dozen.
00	Halter Chains, 6 feet long,	$

Bright Coil Chains.

Nos.	000	00	0	1	2	3
Per 100 Feet, $						

100 FEET IN A PACKAGE.

Cow Ties.

OHIO PATTERN, WITH TOGGLE.

Nos.	0	00	000	0000
Per Dozen, $				

HALF DOZEN IN A PACKAGE.
31

PICKET PINS

No. 7840B 21 in. Long, with Lariat Swivel, Japanned..Per Dozen, $3.50
Loose.

COW TIES

TENSO, OHIO PATTERN

No. 2/0 4½ ft. Long, No. 10 Gauge Wire...........Per Dozen, $3.25 2.90
No. 3/0 4½ ft. Long, No. 9 Gauge Wire.............Per Dozen, 3.75 3.35
Weldless Basic Steel Wire, Bright Finish, with Two Toggles.
Half Dozen in a Box.

Nos. A4/0 to B2/0   No. C3/0

GERMAN, OHIO PATTERN
Bright Finish, Wrought Iron Welded Links and Rings, Twisted Links, Malleable Iron Swivel and Toggles.
Length 4½ Feet, Two Toggles.   Length 5 Feet, Two Toggles.

Nos.	A4/0	A3/0	A2/0		Nos.	B6/0	B4/0	B3/0	B2/0
Gauge ....Nos.	4	5	6	Gauge ....Nos.	2	4	5	6
Per Dozen	$4.15	3.90	3.70	Per Dozen	$6.00	4.40	4.10	3.90
	3.50	3.25	3.00		4.75	3.60	3.40	3.20

Loose.

LARGE CLOSED RING
No. C3/0 Length 4½ ft. Gauge No. 5, One Toggle..................................Per Dozen, $4.45 3.50
Loose.

ROPE TIES

See General Index

Cow Ties.

OHIO PATTERN, WITH SNAP.

Nos.	00	000	0000
Per Dozen, $			

WITH LARGE CLOSE RING.

Close Ring Cow Ties.
Nos.	00	000
Per Dozen, $		

WITH LARGE OPEN RING.

Open Ring Cow Ties.
Nos.	00	000
Per Dozen, $		

ALL COW TIES HALF DOZEN IN A PACKAGE.

Trace Chains.

WITH HOOK OR RING.

Per Pair.
Straight, 6½ ft. long, 10 Links to the foot, No. 2 Gauge, $
Twisted, 6½ "   " 10 "   "   "   "   " 2 "

Bright Ox Chains.

LONG LINK, WITH TWO HOOKS..

Inches,		$\frac{5}{16}$	
Per Pound,	$		

194

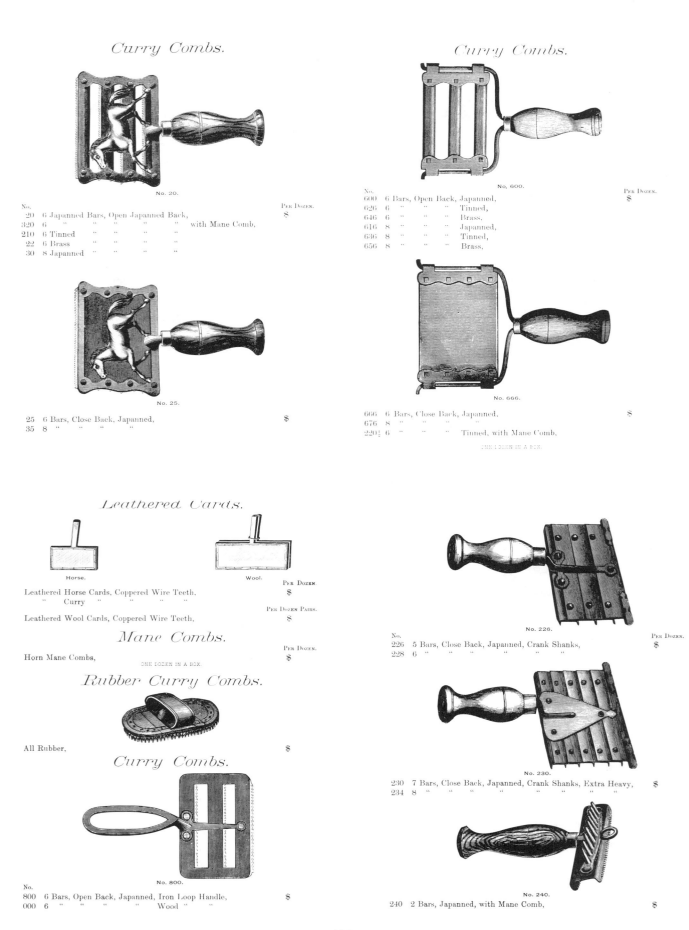

Curry Combs.

No. 20.

No.								Per Dozen.
20	6 Japanned Bars, Open Japanned Back,							$
320	6	"	"	"	"	"	with Mane Comb,	
210	6 Tinned	"	"	"				
22	6 Brass	"	"	"				
30	8 Japanned	"	"	"				

No. 25.

25	6 Bars, Close Back, Japanned,			$
35	8	"	"	"

Curry Combs.

No. 600.

No.					Per Dozen.
600	6 Bars, Open Back, Japanned,				$
626	6	"	"	Tinned,	
646	6	"	"	Brass,	
616	8	"	"	Japanned,	
636	8	"	"	Tinned,	
656	8	"	"	Brass,	

No. 666.

666	6 Bars, Close Back, Japanned,					$
676	8	"	"	"		
220½	6	"	"	"	Tinned, with Mane Comb,	

ONE DOZEN IN A BOX.

Leathered Cards.

Horse.   Wool.

	Per Dozen.
Leathered Horse Cards, Coppered Wire Teeth,	$
" Curry " " " "	
	Per Dozen Pairs.
Leathered Wool Cards, Coppered Wire Teeth,	$

Mane Combs.

	Per Dozen.
Horn Mane Combs,	$

ONE DOZEN IN A BOX.

Rubber Curry Combs.

All Rubber,	$

Curry Combs.

No. 800.

No.						Per Dozen.
800	6 Bars, Open Back, Japanned, Iron Loop Handle,					$
000	6	"	"	"	Wood " "	

No. 226.

No.					Per Dozen.
226	5 Bars, Close Back, Japanned, Crank Shanks,				$
228	6	"	"	"	" "

No. 230.

230	7 Bars, Close Back, Japanned, Crank Shanks, Extra Heavy,					$
234	8	"	"	"	" " " "	

No. 240.

240	2 Bars, Japanned, with Mane Comb,	$

195

Curry Combs.

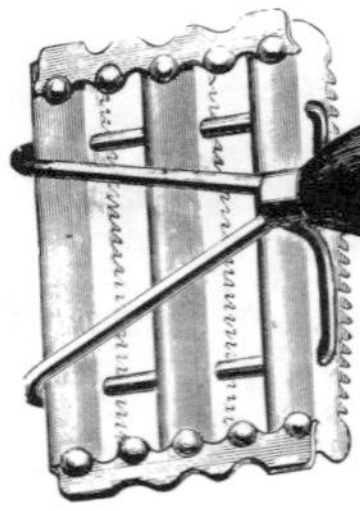

No.		Per Dozen.
200	6 Bars, Open Back, Japanned,	$
120	6 " " " Tinned,	
220	6 " " " Brass,	

21	8 Bars, Open Back, Japanned,	$
121	8 " " " Tinned,	
221	8 " " " Brass,	

ONE DOZEN IN A BOX.

Curry Combs.

No. 6000.

No.		Per Dozen.
6000	6 Bars, Open Back, Japanned, Light,	$
604	6 " " " " Heavy,	
605	6 " " " Tinned, "	
608	8 " " " " "	

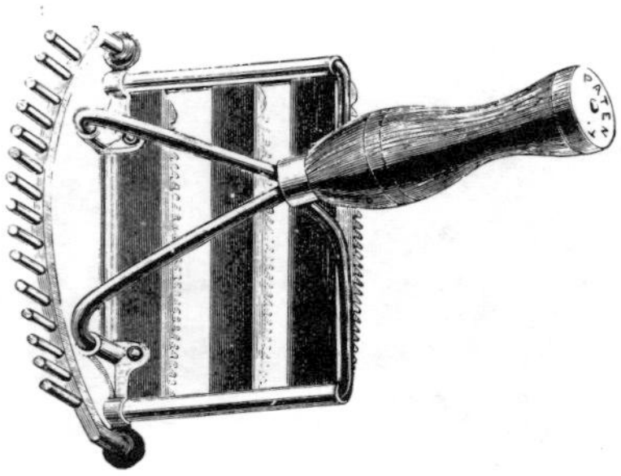

No. 80.

80	6 Bars, Open Back, Japanned, with Tinned Mane Comb,	$
180	6 " " " Tinned, " " " "	

ONE DOZEN IN A BOX.

Curry Combs.

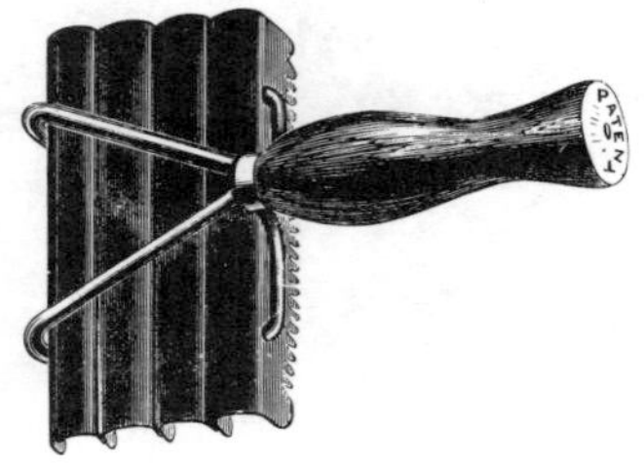

No.		Per Dozen.
1	5 Bars, Close Back, Japanned,	$
300	6 " " " "	
2300	6 " " " Brass,	

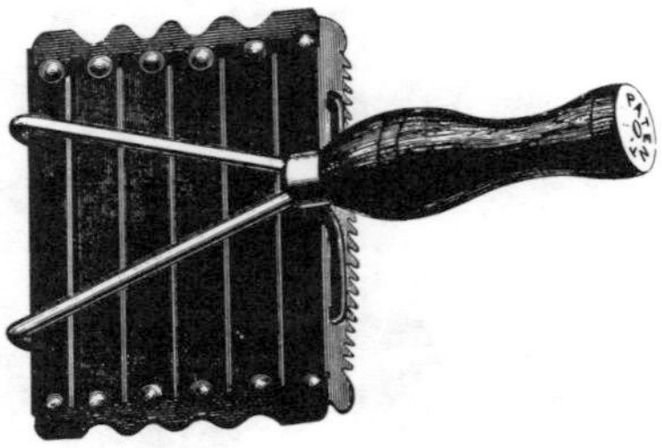

31	8 Bars, Close Back, Japanned,	$
131	8 " " " Tinned,	

ONE DOZEN IN A BOX.

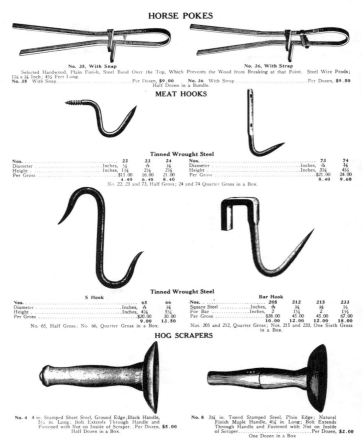

HORSE POKES

No. 35, With Snap

No. 36, With Strap

Selected Hardwood. Plain Finish, Steel Band Over the Top, Which Prevents the Wood from Breaking at that Point. Steel Wire Prods; 1⅞ x ⅞ Inch; 4½ Feet Long.

No. 35 With Snap........Per Dozen, **$9.00** **No. 36** With Strap........Per Dozen, **$9.50**

Half Dozen in a Bundle.

MEAT HOOKS

Tinned Wrought Steel

Nos.	22	23	24
Diameter ....Inches,	¼	5/16	⅜
Height ....Inches,	1⅞	2⅛	2⅞
Per Gross	$11.00	16.00	21.00
	4.40	**6.40**	**8.40**

Nos.	73	74
Diameter ....Inches,	5/16	⅜
Height ....Inches,	3⅞	4½
Per Gross	$21.00	24.00
	8.40	**9.60**

No. 22, 23 and 73, Half Gross; 24 and 74 Quarter Gross in a Box.

Tinned Wrought Steel

S Hook

Nos.	65	66
Diameter ....Inches,	5/16	⅜
Height ....Inches,	4⅞	5¼
Per Gross	$20.00	30.00
	9.00	**13.50**

No. 65, Half Gross; No. 66, Quarter Gross in a Box.

Bar Hook

Nos.	205	212	215	233
Square Steel ....Inches,	5/16	⅜	⅜	½
For Bar ....Inches,	2	1¼	2	1½
Per Gross	$38.00	45.00	45.00	67.00
	10.00	**12.00**	**12.00**	**18.00**

Nos. 205 and 212, Quarter Gross; Nos. 215 and 233, One Sixth Gross in a Box.

HOG SCRAPERS

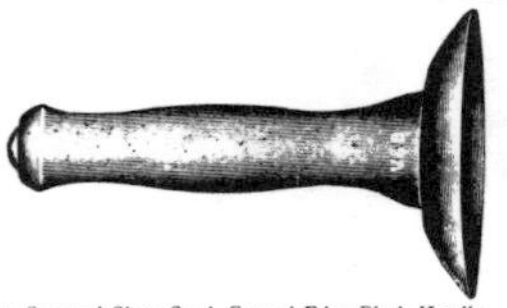

No. 4 4 in. Stamped Sheet Steel, Ground Edge; Black Handle, 5½ in. Long; Bolt Extends Through Handle and Fastened with Nut on Inside of Scraper..Per Dozen, **$5.00**

Half Dozen in a Box.

No. 8 3¼ in. Tnned Stamped Steel, Plain Edge; Natural Finish Maple Handle, 4¼ in. Long; Bolt Extends Through Handle and Fastened with Nut on Inside of Scraper........Per Dozen, **$2.00**

One Dozen in a Box

Price Guide

Price Guide

Price Guide

Price Guide

Price Guide

Price Guide

Price Guide

Price Guide

Price Guide

INDEX

LOCKS, KEYS, AND
CLOSURES W PRICES

LOCKS, KEYS, AND CLOSURES

CONTENTS

Padlocks.

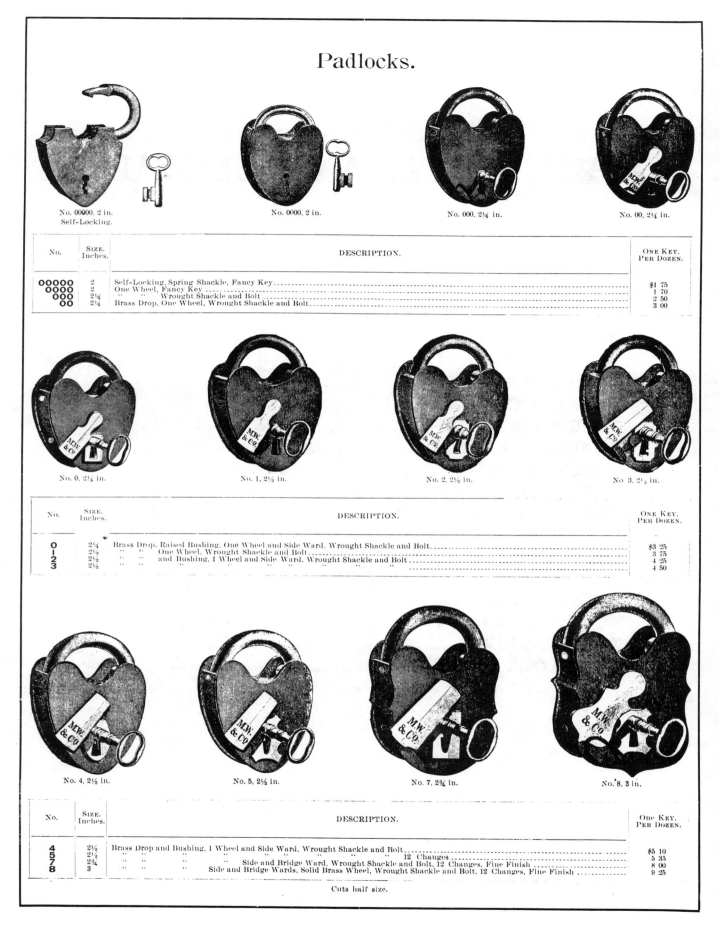

No. 00000, 2 in.
Self-Locking.

No. 0000, 2 in.

No. 000, 2¼ in.

No. 00, 2¼ in.

No.	Size. Inches.	DESCRIPTION.	One Key. Per Dozen.
00000	2	Self-Locking, Spring Shackle, Fancy Key	$1 75
0000	2	One Wheel, Fancy Key	1 70
000	2¼	" " Wrought Shackle and Bolt	2 50
00	2¼	Brass Drop, One Wheel, Wrought Shackle and Bolt	3 00

No. 0, 2¼ in.

No. 1, 2½ in.

No. 2, 2½ in.

No 3, 2½ in.

No.	Size. Inches.	DESCRIPTION.	One Key. Per Dozen.
0	2¼	Brass Drop, Raised Bushing, One Wheel and Side Ward, Wrought Shackle and Bolt	$3 25
1	2½	" " " One Wheel, Wrought Shackle and Bolt	3 75
2	2½	" " and Bushing, 1 Wheel and Side Ward, Wrought Shackle and Bolt	4 25
3	2½	" " " " " " " "	4 50

No. 4, 2½ in.

No. 5, 2½ in.

No. 7, 2¾ in.

No. 8, 3 in.

No.	Size. Inches.	DESCRIPTION.	One Key. Per Dozen.
4	2½	Brass Drop and Bushing, 1 Wheel and Side Ward, Wrought Shackle and Bolt	$5 10
5	2½	" " " " " " " " 12 Changes	5 35
7	2¾	" " " " Side and Bridge Ward, Wrought Shackle and Bolt, 12 Changes, Fine Finish	8 00
8	3	" " " Side and Bridge Wards, Solid Brass Wheel, Wrought Shackle and Bolt, 12 Changes, Fine Finish	9 25

Cuts half size.

2

Padlocks.

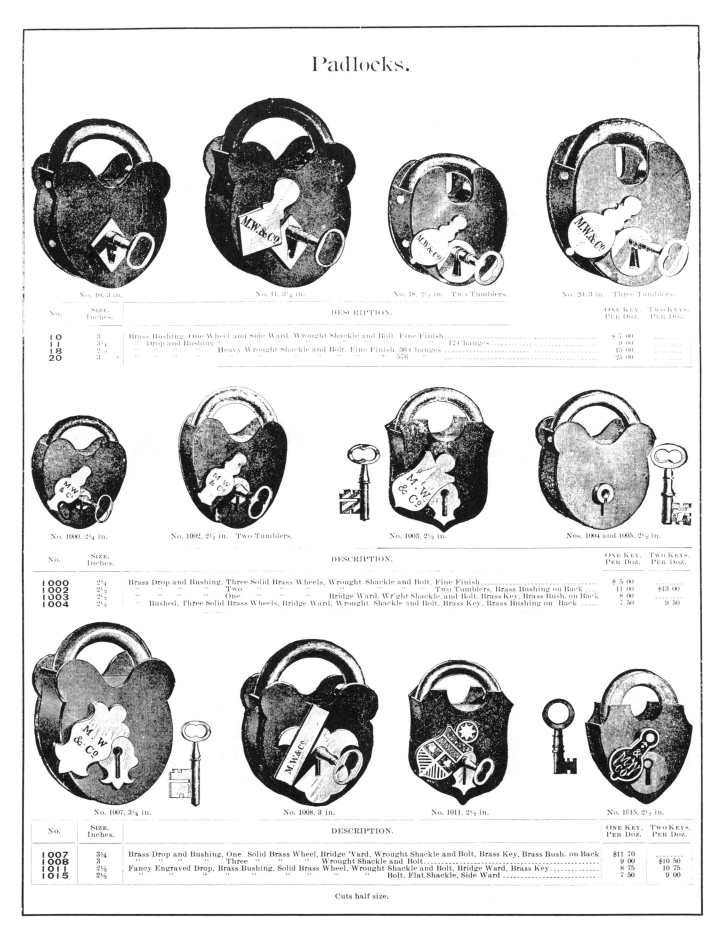

No. 10, 3 in.   No. 11, 3¼ in.   No. 18, 2½ in. Two Tumblers.   No. 20, 3 in. Three Tumblers.

No.	Size. Inches.	Description.	One Key. Per Doz.	Two Keys. Per Doz.
10	3	Brass Bushing, One Wheel and Side Ward, Wrought Shackle and Bolt, Fine Finish	$7 00	......
11	3¼	" Drop and Bushing " " " " " " " " 12 Changes	9 00	......
18	2½	" " " " " " " Heavy Wrought Shackle and Bolt, Fine Finish, 36 Changes	15 00	......
20	3	" " " " " " " " " " " 576 "	25 00	......

No. 1000, 2¼ in.   No. 1002, 2½ in. Two Tumblers.   No. 1003, 2½ in.   Nos. 1004 and 1005, 2½ in.

No.	Size. Inches.	Description.	One Key. Per Doz.	Two Keys. Per Doz.
1000	2¼	Brass Drop and Bushing, Three Solid Brass Wheels, Wrought Shackle and Bolt, Fine Finish	$5 00	......
1002	2½	" " " " Two " " " " " " Two Tumblers, Brass Bushing on Back	11 00	$13 00
1003	2½	" " " " One " " " Bridge Ward, Wr'ght Shackle, and Bolt, Brass Key, Brass Bush. on Back	8 00	......
1004	2½	" Bushed, Three Solid Brass Wheels, Bridge Ward, Wrought Shackle and Bolt, Brass Key, Brass Bushing on Back	7 50	9 50

No. 1007, 3¼ in.   No. 1008, 3 in.   No. 1011, 2½ in.   No. 1015, 2½ in.

No.	Size. Inches.	Description.	One Key. Per Doz.	Two Keys. Per Doz.
1007	3¼	Brass Drop and Bushing, One Solid Brass Wheel, Bridge Ward, Wrought Shackle and Bolt, Brass Key, Brass Bush. on Back	$11 70	......
1008	3	" " " " Three " " " " Wrought Shackle and Bolt	9 00	$10 50
1011	2½	Fancy Engraved Drop, Brass Bushing, Solid Brass Wheel, Wrought Shackle and Bolt, Bridge Ward, Brass Key	8 75	10 75
1015	2½	" " " " " " " " Bolt, Flat Shackle, Side Ward	7 50	9 00

Cuts half size.

Padlocks.

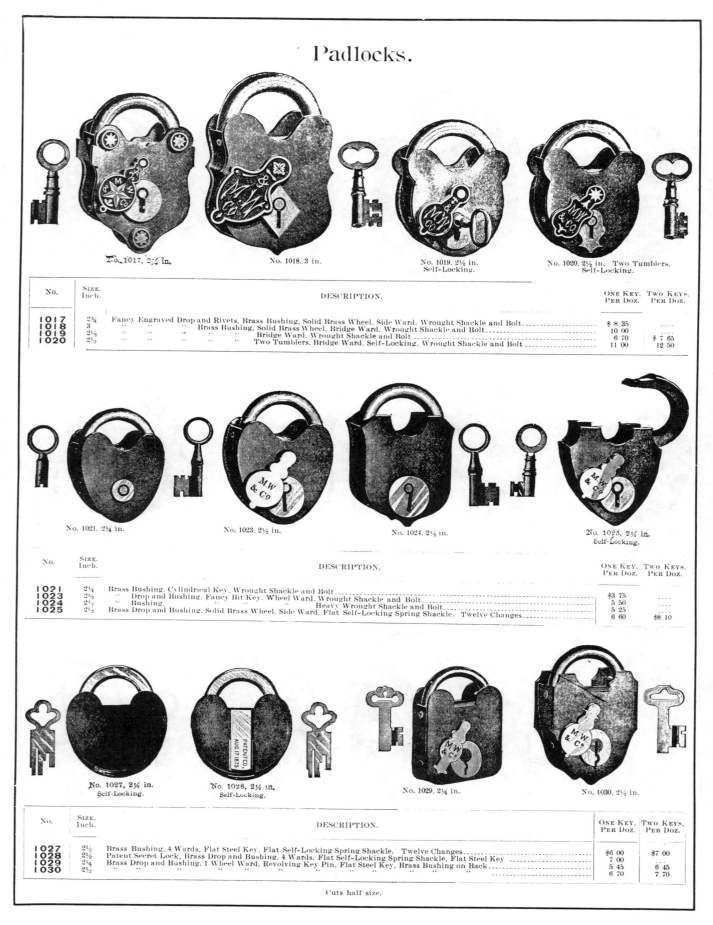

No. 1017, 2¾ in.

No. 1018. 3 in.

No. 1019. 2½ in.
Self-Locking.

No. 1020. 2½ in. Two Tumblers.
Self-Locking.

No.	Size. Inch.	DESCRIPTION.	One Key. Per Doz.	Two Keys. Per Doz.
1017	2¾	Fancy Engraved Drop and Rivets, Brass Bushing, Solid Brass Wheel, Side Ward, Wrought Shackle and Bolt	$ 8 35	....
1018	3	" " " " Brass Bushing, Solid Brass Wheel, Bridge Ward, Wrought Shackle and Bolt	10 00	....
1019	2½	" " " " Bridge Ward, Wrought Shackle and Bolt	6 70	$ 7 65
1020	2½	" " " " Two Tumblers, Bridge Ward, Self-Locking, Wrought Shackle and Bolt	11 00	12 50

No. 1021, 2¼ in.

No. 1023. 2½ in.

No. 1024. 2½ in.

No. 1025, 2½ in.
Self-Locking.

No.	Size. Inch.	DESCRIPTION.	One Key. Per Doz.	Two Keys. Per Doz.
1021	2¼	Brass Bushing, Cylindrical Key, Wrought Shackle and Bolt	$3 75	....
1023	2½	" Drop and Bushing, Fancy Bit Key, Wheel Ward, Wrought Shackle and Bolt	5 50	....
1024	2½	" Bushing, Heavy Wrought Shackle and Bolt	5 25	....
1025	2½	Brass Drop and Bushing, Solid Brass Wheel, Side Ward, Flat Self-Locking Spring Shackle, Twelve Changes	6 60	$8 10

No. 1027, 2½ in.
Self-Locking.

No. 1028, 2½ in.
Self-Locking.

No. 1029, 2¼ in.

No. 1030, 2½ in.

No.	Size. Inch.	DESCRIPTION.	One Key. Per Doz.	Two Keys. Per Doz.
1027	2½	Brass Bushing, 4 Wards, Flat Steel Key, Flat Self-Locking Spring Shackle, Twelve Changes	$6 00	$7 00
1028	2½	Patent Secret Lock, Brass Drop and Bushing, 4 Wards, Flat Self-Locking Spring Shackle, Flat Steel Key	7 00	....
1029	2¼	Brass Drop and Bushing, 1 Wheel Ward, Revolving Key Pin, Flat Steel Key, Brass Bushing on Back	5 45	6 45
1030	2½	" " " " " " " " " "	6 70	7 70

Cuts half size.

4

Padlocks.

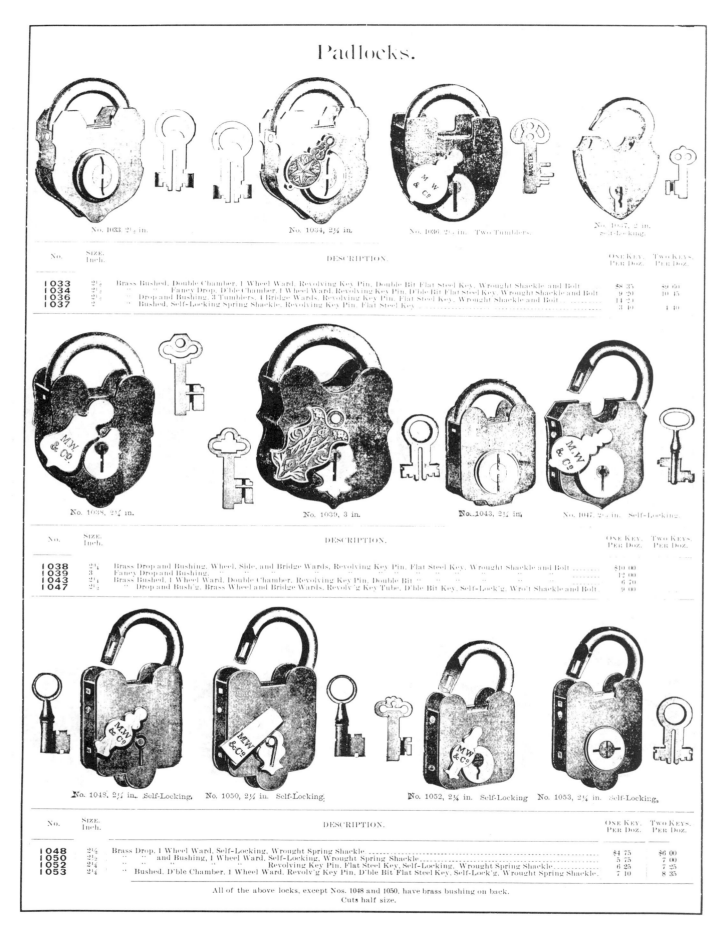

No. 1033, 2½ in.   No. 1034, 2½ in.   No. 1036, 2½ in. Two Tumblers.   No. 1037, 2 in. Self-Locking.

No.	SIZE. Inch.	DESCRIPTION.	ONE KEY. PER DOZ.	TWO KEYS. PER DOZ.
1033	2½	Brass Bushed, Double Chamber, 1 Wheel Ward, Revolving Key Pin, Double Bit Flat Steel Key, Wrought Shackle and Bolt	$8 35	$9 60
1034	2½	" Fancy Drop, D'ble Chamber, " " " " D'ble Bit Flat Steel Key, Wrought Shackle and Bolt	9 20	10 45
1036	2½	" Drop and Bushing, 3 Tumblers, 4 Bridge Wards, Revolving Key Pin, Flat Steel Key, Wrought Shackle and Bolt	14 20	
1037	2	" Bushed, Self-Locking Spring Shackle, Revolving Key Pin, Flat Steel Key	3 40	4 40

No. 1038, 2¾ in.   No. 1039, 3 in.   No. 1043, 2¾ in.   No. 1047, 2¾ in. Self-Locking.

No.	SIZE. Inch.	DESCRIPTION.	ONE KEY. PER DOZ.	TWO KEYS. PER DOZ.
1038	2¾	Brass Drop and Bushing, Wheel, Side, and Bridge Wards, Revolving Key Pin, Flat Steel Key, Wrought Shackle and Bolt	$10 00	
1039	3	" Fancy Drop and Bushing, " " " " " " " " " " " " "	12 00	
1043	2¾	Brass Bushed, 1 Wheel Ward, Double Chamber, Revolving Key Pin, Double Bit " " " " " "	6 70	
1047	2½	" Drop and Bush'g, Brass Wheel and Bridge Wards, Revolv'g Key Tube, D'ble Bit Key, Self-Lock'g, Wro't Shackle and Bolt	9 00	

No. 1048, 2½ in. Self-Locking.   No. 1050, 2½ in. Self-Locking.   No. 1052, 2¼ in. Self-Locking   No. 1053, 2¼ in. Self-Locking.

No.	SIZE. Inch.	DESCRIPTION.	ONE KEY. PER DOZ.	TWO KEYS. PER DOZ.
1048	2½	Brass Drop, 1 Wheel Ward, Self-Locking, Wrought Spring Shackle	$4 75	$6 00
1050	2½	" " and Bushing, 1 Wheel Ward, Self-Locking, Wrought Spring Shackle	5 75	7 00
1052	2¼	" " " " Revolving Key Pin, Flat Steel Key, Self-Locking, Wrought Spring Shackle	6 25	7 25
1053	2¼	" Bushed, D'ble Chamber, 1 Wheel Ward, Revolv'g Key Pin, D'ble Bit Flat Steel Key, Self-Lock'g, Wrought Spring Shackle	7 10	8 35

All of the above locks, except Nos. 1048 and 1050, have brass bushing on back.
Cuts half size.

Padlocks.

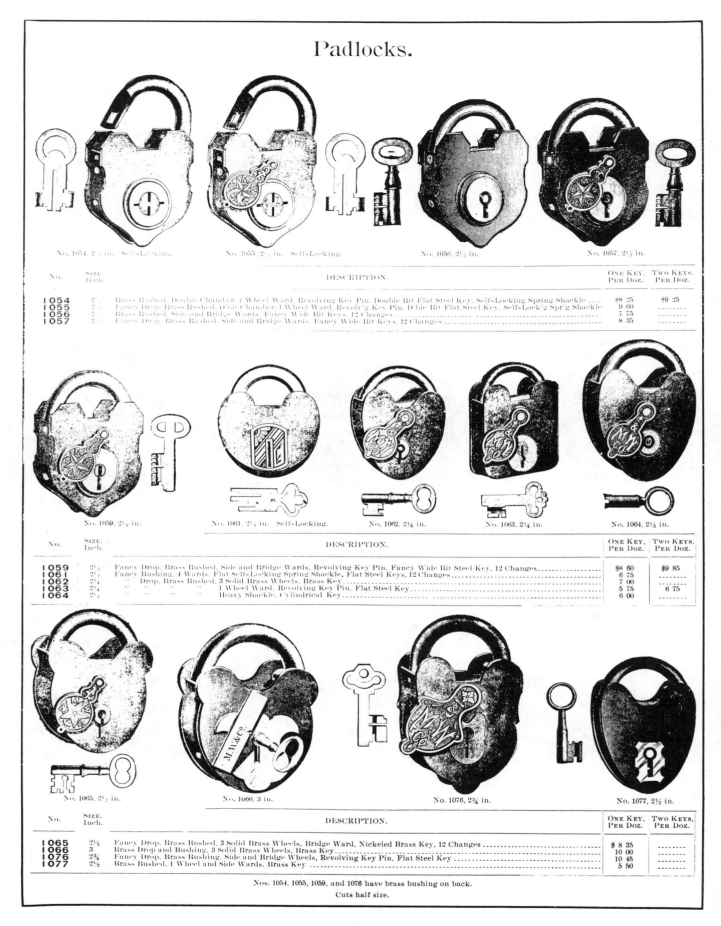

No. 1054, 2 in. Self-Locking. No. 1055, 2½ in. Self-Locking. No. 1056, 2½ in. No. 1057, 2½ in.

No.	SIZE. Inch.	DESCRIPTION.	ONE KEY, PER DOZ.	TWO KEYS, PER DOZ.
1054	2½	Brass Bushed, Double Chamber, 1 Wheel Ward, Revolving Key Pin, Double Bit Flat Steel Key, Self-Locking Spring Shackle	$8 25	$9 25
1055	2½	Fancy Drop, Brass Bushed, D'ble Chamber, 1 Wheel Ward, Revolv'g Key Pin, D'ble Bit Flat Steel Key, Self-Lock'g Spr'g Shackle	9 60	....
1056	2½	Brass Bushed, Side and Bridge Wards, Fancy Wide Bit Keys, 12 Changes	7 75	....
1057	2½	Fancy Drop, Brass Bushed, Side and Bridge Wards, Fancy Wide Bit Keys, 12 Changes	8 35	....

No. 1059, 2½ in. No. 1061, 2½ in. Self-Locking. No. 1062, 2¼ in. No. 1063, 2¼ in. No. 1064, 2½ in.

No.	SIZE. Inch.	DESCRIPTION.	ONE KEY, PER DOZ.	TWO KEYS, PER DOZ.
1059	2½	Fancy Drop, Brass Bushed, Side and Bridge Wards, Revolving Key Pin, Fancy Wide Bit Steel Key, 12 Changes	$8 60	$9 85
1061	2½	Fancy Bushing, 4 Wards, Flat Self-Locking Spring Shackle, Flat Steel Keys, 12 Changes	6 75	....
1062	2¼	'' Drop, Brass Bushed, 3 Solid Brass Wheels, Brass Key	7 00	....
1063	2¼	'' '' 1 Wheel Ward, Revolving Key Pin, Flat Steel Key	5 75	6 75
1064	2½	'' '' Heavy Shackle, Cylindrical Key	6 00	....

No. 1065, 2½ in. No. 1066, 3 in. No. 1076, 2¾ in. No. 1077, 2½ in.

No.	SIZE. Inch.	DESCRIPTION.	ONE KEY, PER DOZ.	TWO KEYS, PER DOZ.
1065	2½	Fancy Drop, Brass Bushed, 3 Solid Brass Wheels, Bridge Ward, Nickeled Brass Key, 12 Changes	$8 35	....
1066	3	Brass Drop and Bushing, 3 Solid Brass Wheels, Brass Key	10 00	....
1076	2¾	Fancy Drop, Brass Bushing, Side and Bridge Wheels, Revolving Key Pin, Flat Steel Key	10 45	....
1077	2½	Brass Bushed, 1 Wheel and Side Wards, Brass Key	5 50	....

Nos. 1054, 1055, 1059, and 1076 have brass bushing on back.

Cuts half size.

6

Padlocks.

WITH CHAIN.

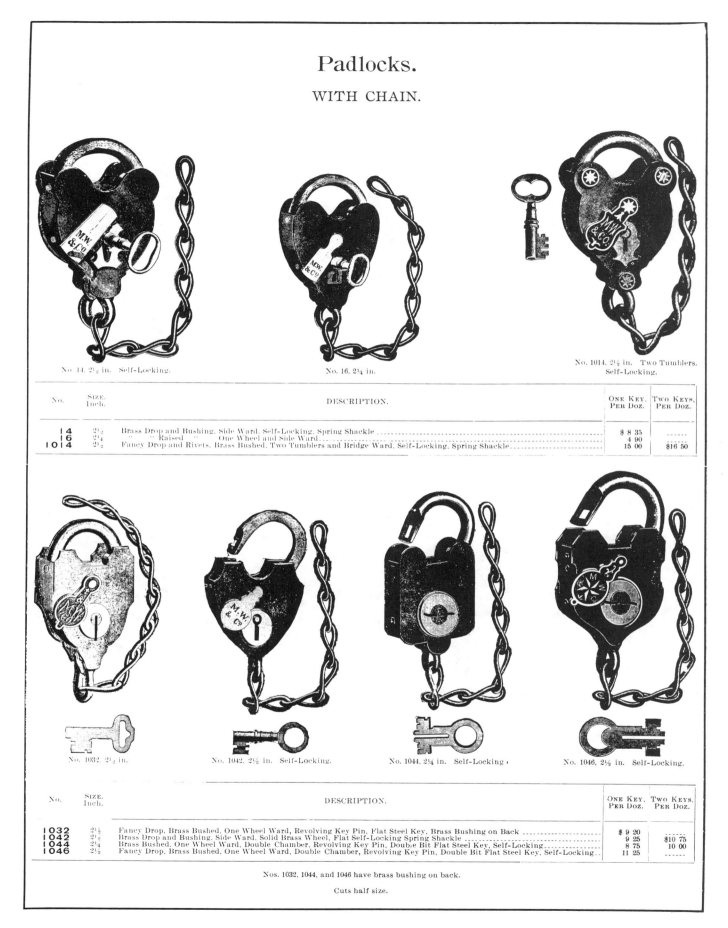

No. 14, 2½ in. Self-Locking.

No. 16, 2¼ in.

No. 1014, 2½ in. Two Tumblers.
Self-Locking.

No.	SIZE. Inch.	DESCRIPTION.	ONE KEY, PER DOZ.	TWO KEYS, PER DOZ.
14	2½	Brass Drop and Bushing, Side Ward, Self-Locking, Spring Shackle	$ 8 35	------
16	2¼	" Raised " One Wheel and Side Ward	4 90	
1014	2½	Fancy Drop and Rivets, Brass Bushed, Two Tumblers and Bridge Ward, Self-Locking, Spring Shackle	15 00	$16 50

No. 1032, 2½ in.

No. 1042, 2½ in. Self-Locking.

No. 1044, 2¼ in. Self-Locking.

No. 1046, 2½ in. Self-Locking.

No.	SIZE. Inch.	DESCRIPTION.	ONE KEY, PER DOZ.	TWO KEYS, PER DOZ.
1032	2½	Fancy Drop, Brass Bushed, One Wheel Ward, Revolving Key Pin, Flat Steel Key, Brass Bushing on Back	$ 9 20	------
1042	2½	Brass Drop and Bushing, Side Ward, Solid Brass Wheel, Flat Self-Locking Spring Shackle	9 25	$10 75
1044	2¼	Brass Bushed, One Wheel Ward, Double Chamber, Revolving Key Pin, Double Bit Flat Steel Key, Self-Locking	8 75	10 00
1046	2½	Fancy Drop, Brass Bushed, One Wheel Ward, Double Chamber, Revolving Key Pin, Double Bit Flat Steel Key, Self-Locking	11 25	------

Nos. 1032, 1044, and 1046 have brass bushing on back.

Cuts half size.

Padlocks.
WITH CHAINS.

No. 1051, 2½ in. Self-Locking No. 1060, 2½ in. Self-Locking No. 1069, 2½ in.

No.	Size Inches.	DESCRIPTION	ONE KEY, PER DOZ.	TWO KEYS, PER DOZ.
1051	2½	Brass Drop and Bushing, One Wheel Ward, Self-Locking, Wrought Spring Shackle	$7 50	$8 50
1060	2½	.... Revolving Key Pin	8 00	9 00
1069	2½	Bushed, Three Solid Brass Wheels, Bridge Ward, Brass Key, Twelve Changes	9 50	11 75

No. 1072, 2½ in. No. 1073, 2½ in No. 1074, 2½ in. No. 1075, 2½ in.

No.	Size. Inches.	DESCRIPTION.	ONE KEY, PER DOZ.	TWO KEYS, PER DOZ.
1072	2½	Brass Bushed, Wheel, Side and Bridge Wards, Fancy Wide Bit Key, Twelve Changes	$10 00	....
1073	2½	Fancy Drop, Brass Bushed, Wheel, Side and Bridge Wards, Fancy Wide Bit Key, Twelve Changes	11 00	$12 25
1074	2½	Brass Bushed, Wheel, Side and Bridge Wards, Revolving Key Pin, Fancy Wide Bit Steel Key, Twelve Changes	10 25	....
1075	2½	Fancy Drop, Brass Bushed, Wheel, Side and Bridge Wards, Revolving Key Pin, Fancy Wide Bit Steel Key	11 00	....

Nos. 1060, 1074, and 1075 have brass bushing on back.

Cuts half size.

PADLOCKS.

Half Size Cuts.

No. 270.

Cast Brass Case, Self-Locking Brass Spring Shackle. **Two Nickel** Plated Steel Keys.

No. 270—1⅝ inch, Highly Polished......Per Dozen, $4.50

Half Dozen in a Box.

No. 272.

Cast Brass Case, Self-Locking Brass Spring Shackle. **Two Nickel** Plated Steel Keys.

No. 272—2 inch, Highly Polished........Per Dozen, $8.00

Half Dozen in a Box.

No. 172.

Cast Iron Case, Self-Locking Cast Iron Spring Shackle, Brass Interior Works. **Two Flat Steel Keys.**

No. 172—2⅛ inch, Nickel Plated........Per Dozen, $3.00

Half Dozen in a Box.

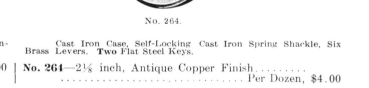

No. 264.

Cast Iron Case, Self-Locking Cast Iron Spring Shackle, Six Brass Levers. **Two Flat Steel Keys.**

No. 264—2⅛ inch, Antique Copper Finish.........
................................Per Dozen, $4.00

Half Dozen in a Box.

No. 174.

Cast Brass Case, Self-Locking Brass Spring Shackle. **Two Flat** Steel Keys.

No. 174—1⅝ inch, Polished Raised Parts, Maroon
Depressed Parts ....Per Dozen, $3.50

Half Dozen in a Box.

No. 507.

Cast Brass Case, Self-Locking Brass Spring Shackle. **Two Flat** Steel Keys.

No. 507—2¼ inch, Polished Edges and Raised Parts
................................Per Dozen, $8.00

Half Dozen in a Box.

9

PADLOCKS.

Half Size Cuts.

No. 505.

Cast Brass Case, Self-Locking Spring Shackle, Four Levers. Two Nickel Plated Flat Steel Keys.

No. 505—1¾ inch, Polished Surface and Shackle
.................................Per Dozen, $6.50

Half Dozen in a Box.

No. 502.

Cast Brass Case, Self-Locking Spring Shackle, Six Levers. Two Nickel Plated Flat Steel Keys.

No. 502—2¼ inch, Polished Surface and Shackle
.................................Per Dozen, $7.20

Half Dozen in a Box.

No. 262CH.

Steel Case, Self-Locking Malleable Iron Spring Shackle. Two Flat Steel Keys.

No. 262CH—1¾ inch, Brass Finish with 8 inch Steel Chain...........................Per Dozen, $3.20

One Dozen in a Box.

No. 261.

Steel Case, Self-Locking Steel Spring Shackle. Two Flat Steel Keys.

No. 261—1 inch, Nickel Plated.........Per Dozen, $3.60

One Dozen in a Box.

No. 506.

Steel Case, Self-Locking Steel Spring Shackle. Two Nickel Plated Steel Keys.

No. 506—2 inch, Dark Gun Steel Finish..Per Dozen, $9.00

Half Dozen in a Box.

No. 271.

Cast Brass Case, Self-Locking Brass Spring Shackle. Two Nickel Plated Flat Steel Keys.

No. 271—2 inch, Polished Relief Finish...Per Dozen, $7.20

Half Dozen in a Box.

R. F. D. PADLOCKS.

Half Size Cuts

No. 268.

Brass Case, Self-Locking Brass Spring Shackle, Heavy Slotted Key Cylinder. Galvanized Anti-Rust Steel Springs. **Two** Corrugated Steel Keys to each lock. One **Master Key** with each Dozen.

No. 268—1⅝ inch, Polished............Per Dozen, $4.00

One Dozen in a Box.

SWITCH PADLOCKS.

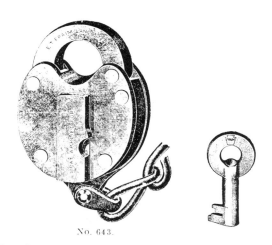

No. 643.

Solid Cast Bronze Gun Metal, Self-Locking Spring Shackle, Three Tumblers, Spring Drop Cover. Made to fit any Special Key.

No. 643—2½x3¾x1¹¹⁄₁₆ inch, Unpolished, with 10 inch Steel Chain......................Per Dozen, $10.00

Half Dozen in a Box.

DOG COLLAR PADLOCKS.

Full Size Cuts.

No. 176.

Cast Bronze Metal Case and Shackle. **One** Flat Steel Key.

No. 176—⅝ inch, Nickel Plated........Per Dozen, $1.50

One Dozen in a Box.

No. 183.

Cast Brass Case and Shackle, Self-Locking. Secret Lock, **No Key.**

No. 183—⅝ inch, Nickel Plated........Per Dozen, $1.50

One Dozen in a Box.

No. 175.

Cast Bronze Metal, Self-Locking Spring Shackle. **One** Brass Key.

No. 175—¾ inch, Nickel Plated........Per Dozen, $2.50

One Dozen in a Box.

No. 182.

Cast Bronze Metal, Self Locking Spring Shackle. **One** Brass Key.

No. 182—⅞ inch, Nickel Plated........Per Dozen, $4.00

One Dozen in a Box.

11

YALE PADLOCKS.

Half Size Cuts.

No. 830.

Cast Bronze Metal Case, Self-Locking Steel Spring Shackle, Five Pin Tumblers. Two Nickel Plated, Coined, Gold Plated Bow Paracentric Keys, Unlimited Changes.

No. 830—1½ inch, Cast Bronze Metal...Per Dozen, $28.80

Half Dozen in a Box.

No. 830½.

Cast Bronze Metal Case, Self-Locking Steel Spring Shackle, Five Pin Tumblers. Two Nickel Plated, Coined, Gold Plated Bow Paracentric Keys, Unlimited Changes.

No. 830½—1½ inch, Cast Bronze Metal, with 9 inch Bronze Chain....................Per Dozen, $31.80

Half Dozen in a Box.

No. 840.

Cast Bronze Metal Case, Self-Locking Steel Spring Shackle, Five Pin Tumblers. Two Nickel Plated, Coined, Gold Plated Bow Paracentric Keys, Unlimited Changes.

No. 840—1¾ inch, Cast Bronze Metal...Per Dozen, $35.75

Half Dozen in a Box.

No. 840½.

Cast Bronze Metal Case, Self-Locking Steel Spring Shackle, Five Pin Tumblers. Two Nickel Plated, Coined, Gold Plated Bow Paracentric Keys, Unlimited Changes.

No. 840½—1¾ inch, Cast Bronze Metal, with 9 inch Bronze Chain ....Per Dozen, $38.75

Half Dozen in a Box.

No. 850.

Note—All Locks on this page can be furnished with **Master Key** at additional price, if so desired.

Cast Bronze Metal Case, Self-Locking Steel Spring Shackle, Five Pin Tumblers. Two Nickel Plated, Coined, Gold Plated Bow Paracentric Keys, Unlimited Changes.

No. 850—2 inch, Cast Bronze Metal.....Per Dozen, 43.70

Half Dozen in a Box.

No. 850½.

Cast Bronze Metal Case, Self-Locking Steel Spring Shackle, Five Pin Tumblers. Two Nickel Plated, Coined, Gold Plated Bow Paracentric Keys, Unlimited Changes.

No. 850½—2 inch, Cast Bronze Metal, with 9 inch Bronze Chain ....Per Dozen, $47.70

Half Dozen in a Box.

12

YALE PADLOCKS.

Half Size Cuts.

No. 813.

Cast Bronze Metal Case, Self-Locking Bronze Metal Spring Shackle, Three Lever Tumblers. Two Nickel Bronze, Coined, Gold Plated Bow Fluted Keys, all different in a dozen. 48 Changes.

No. 813—1 inch, Cast Bronze Metal......Per Dozen, $20.00

Half Dozen in a Box.

No. 813½.

Cast Bronze Metal Case, Self-Locking Bronze Metal Spring Shackle, Three Lever Tumblers. Two Nickel Bronze, Coined, Gold Plated Bow Fluted Keys, all different in a dozen. 48 Changes.

No. 813½—1 inch, Cast Bronze Metal, with 9 inch Bronze Chain....................Per Dozen, $22.40

Quarter Dozen in a Box.

No. 823.

Cast Bronze Metal Case, Self-Locking Bronze Metal Spring Shackle, Three Lever Tumblers. Two Nickel Bronze, Coined, Gold Plated Bow Fluted Keys. All different in a dozen. 48 Changes.

No. 823—1¼ inch, Cast Bronze Metal...Per Dozen, $22.00

Half Dozen in a Box.

No. 823½.

Cast Bronze Metal Case, Self-Locking Bronze Metal Spring Shackle, Three Lever Tumblers. Two Nickel Bronze, Coined, Gold Plated Bow Fluted Keys, all different in a dozen. 48 Changes.

No. 823½—1¼ inch, Cast Bronze Metal, with 9 inch Bronze Chain....................Per Dozen, $24.40

Quarter Dozen in a Box.

No. 833.

Cast Bronze Metal Case, Self-Locking Bronze Metal Spring Shackle, Three Lever Tumblers. Two Nickel Bronze, Coined, Gold Plated Bow Fluted Keys, all different in a dozen. 48 Changes.

No, 833—1½ inch, Cast Bronze Metal...Per Dozen, $25.00

Half Dozen in a Box.

No. 833½.

Cast Bronze Metal Case, Self-Locking, Bronze Metal Spring Shackle, Three Lever Tumblers. Two Nickel Bronze, Coined, Gold Plated Bow Fluted Keys, all different in a dozen. 48 Changes.

No. 833½—1½ inch, Cast Bronze Metal, with 9 inch Bronze Chain....................Per Dozen, $29.20

Quarter Dozen in a Box.

YALE PADLOCKS.

Half Size Cuts.

No. 843.

Cast Bronze Metal Case, Self-Locking Bronze Metal Spring Shackle, Four Lever Tumblers. Two Nickel Bronze, Coined, Gold Plated Bow Fluted Keys, all different in a Dozen. 72 Changes.

No. 843—1¾ inch, Cast Bronze Metal...Per Dozen, $28.05

Half Dozen in a Box.

No. 843½.

Cast Bronze Metal Case, Self-Locking Bronze Metal Spring Shackle, Four Lever Tumblers. Two Nickel Bronze, Coined, Gold Plated Bow Fluted Keys, all different in a Dozen. 72 Changes.

No. 843½—1¾ inch, Cast Bronze Metal, with 9 inch Bronze Chain......................Per Dozen, $32.25

Quarter Dozen in a Box.

No. 853.

Cast Bronze Metal Case, Self-Locking Bronze Metal Spring Shackle, Four Lever Tumblers. Two Nickel Bronze, Coined, Gold Plated Bow Fluted Keys, all different in a Dozen. 144 Changes.

No. 853—2 inch, Cast Bronze Metal.....Per Dozen, $31.00

Half Dozen in a Box.

No. 853½.

Cast Bronze Metal Case, Self-Locking Bronze Metal Spring Shackle, Four Lever Tumblers. Two Nickel Bronze, Coined, Gold Plated Bow Fluted Keys, all different in a Dozen. 144 Changes.

No. 853½—2 inch, Cast Bronze Metal, with 9 inch Bronze Chain......................Per Dozen, $35.20

Quarter Dozen in a Box.

No. 726.

Heavy Iron Case, Steel Discs, Self-Locking Steel Spring Shackle, Four Pin Tumblers, Bronze Metal Inside Parts. Two Nickel Plated, Coined, Gold Plated Bow Paracentric Keys. Unlimited Changes.

No. 726—2¼ inch, Bower-Barffed Case, Bronze Plated Discs and Shackle.........Per Dozen, $31.75

Half Dozen in a Box.

No. 726½.

Heavy Iron Case, Steel Discs, Self-Locking Steel Spring Shackle, Four Pin Tumblers, Bronze Metal Inside Parts. Two Nickel Plated, Coined, Gold Plated Bow Paracentric Keys. Unlimited Changes.

No. 726½—2¼ inch, Bower-Barffed Case, Bronze Plated Discs and Shackle, with 9 inch Bronze Chain.........................Per Dozen, $35.75

Half Dozen in a Box.

YALE PADLOCKS.

Half Size Cuts

No. 526.

Heavy Iron Case, Steel Discs, Self-Locking Steel Spring Shackle, Four Lever Tumblers, Brass Inside Parts. Two Nickel Plated Flat Steel Keys, 144 Changes.

No. 526—2¼ inch, Brass Plated Case and Shackle, Oxidized Discs................Per Dozen, $19.85

Half Dozen in a Box.

No. 526½.

Heavy Iron Case, Steel Discs, Self-Locking Steel Spring Shackle, Four Lever Tumblers, Brass Inside Parts. Two Nickel Plated Flat Steel Keys, 144 Changes.

No 526½—2¼ inch, Brass Plated Case and Shackle, Oxidized Discs, with 9 inch Steel Chain ......
......................Per Dozen, $22.25

Half Dozen in a Box.

No. 326.

Heavy Iron Case, Steel Discs, Self-Locking Steel Spring Shackle, Warded, Steel Inside Parts. Two Nickel Plated Flat Steel Keys, 6 Changes.

No. 326—2¼ inch, Nubian Finish Case, Copper Plated Discs and Shackle........Per Dozen, $11.95

Half Dozen in a Box.

No. 326½.

Heavy Iron Case, Steel Discs, Self-Locking Steel Spring Shackle, Warded, Steel Inside Parts. Two Nickel Plated Flat Steel Keys, 6 Changes.

No. 326½—2¼ inch, Nubian Finish Case, Copper Plated Discs and Shackle, with 9 inch Steel Chain..........................Per Dozen, $14.35

Half Dozen in a Box.

No. 735.

Wrought Bronze Metal Case, Self-Locking Bronze Metal Spring Shackle, Five Pin Tumblers. Two Nickel Plated, Coined, Gold Plated Bow Paracentric Keys, unlimited Changes.

No. 735— 2 inch, Wrought Bronze Metal. Per Dozen, $37.75

Half Dozen in a Box.

No. 585.

Cast Bronze Metal Case, Self-Locking Bronze Metal Spring Shackle, Three Lever Tumblers, Brass Inside Parts. Two Nickel Plated Flat Steel Keys, 12 Changes.

No. 585—2 inch, Wheel Finish Case, Buffed Shackle
......................Per Dozen, $13.90

Half Dozen in a Box.

15

YALE PADLOCKS.

Half Size Cuts.

No. 435. **Master Keyed.**

Wrought Brass Case, Self-Locking Brass Spring Shackle, Four Lever Tumblers Each for change and Master Key. Brass Inside Parts. Two Flat Steel Change Keys. Master Keys as ordered. 618 Changes.

No. 435—2 inch, Brass, Bright Finish....Per Dozen, $20.85

Half Dozen in a Box.

No. 435½.

Wrought Brass Case, Self-Locking Brass Spring Shackle, Four Lever Tumblers Each for change and Master Key. Brass Inside Parts. Two Flat Steel Change Keys. Master Keys as ordered. 618 Changes.

No. 435½—2 inch, Brass, Bright Finish, with 9 inch Bronze Chain...................Per Dozen, $23.85

Half Dozen in a Box.

Note—The above Locks have Two Separate Keyways, one for the Change Key and the other for the Master Key, either of which controls the Bolt.

No. 803F.

Cast Iron Case, Self-Locking Bronze Metal Spring Shackle, Three Pin Tumblers. Two Flat Steel Keys. 144 Changes.

No. 803F—1½ inch, Bower-Barffed Case, Buffed Shackle.........................Per Dozen, $17.90

Half Dozen in a Box.

No. 803½F.

Cast Iron Case, Self-Locking Bronze Metal Spring Shackle, Three Pin Tumblers. Two Flat Steel Keys, 144 Changes.

No. 803½F—1½ inch, Bower-Barffed Case, Buffed Shackle, with 9 inch Bronze Chain..Per Dozen, $20.90

Quarter Dozen in a Box.

No. 805F.

Cast Iron Case, Self-Locking Bronze Metal Spring Shackle. Four Pin Tumblers. Two Flat Steel Keys. 144 Changes.

No. 805F—2 inch, Bower-Barffed Case, Buffed Shackle.........................Per Dozen, $17.90

Half Dozen in a Box.

No. 805½F.

Cast Iron Case, Self-Locking Bronze Metal Spring Shackle, Four Pin Tumblers. Two Flat Steel Keys. 144 Changes.

No. 805½F—2 inch, Bower-Barffed Case, Buffed Shackle, with 9 inch Bronze Chain..Per Dozen, $20.90

Half Dozen in a Box.

16

YALE PADLOCKS.

Half Size Cuts.

No. 225.

Cast Iron Case, Wrought Steel Panels, Self-Locking Steel Spring Shackle. Two Flat Steel Keys, 6 Changes.
No. 225—2 inch, Bower-Barffed Case, Brass Plated
Panels and Shackle...............Per Dozen, $7.95

Half Dozen in a Box.

No. 225½.

Cast Iron Case, Wrought Steel Panels, Self-Locking Steel Spring Shackle. Two Flat Steel Keys, 6 Changes.
No. 225½—2 inch, Bower-Barffed Case, Brass Plated
Panels and Shackle, with 9 inch Steel Chain
.... Per Dozen, $10.35

Half Dozen in a Box.

Nos. 9645J, 9645C and 9645V.

Self-Locking Spring Shackle, Three Lever Tumblers. Two Malleable Iron Barrel Keys, 12 Changes.
No. 9645J—2 inch, **Steel,** Ivory Black Case, Sanded,
Brass Plated Shackle...........Per Dozen, $4.80
No. 9645C—2 inch, **Steel,** Old Copper Case and
Shackle...............Per Dozen, 5.20
No. 9645V—2 inch, **Wrought Brass** Case and
Shackle, Buffed................Per Dozen, 8.55
Half Dozen in a Box.

Nos. 647J, 647C and 647V.

Self-Locking Spring Shackle, Three Lever Tumblers. Two Flat Steel Keys, 12 Changes.
No. 647J—2½ inch, **Steel,** Ivory Black Case, Sanded,
Brass Plated Shackle............Per Dozen, $ 8.95
No. 647C—2½ inch, **Steel,** Old Copper Case and
Shackle......................Per Dozen, 9.95
No. 647V—2½ inch, **Wrought Brass** Case and
Shackle, Buffed................Per Dozen, 14.90
Half Dozen in a Box.

No. 563.

Seamless Steel Case, Self-Locking Steel Spring Shackle, Three Lever Tumblers. Two Flat Steel Keys, 48 Changes.
No. 563—1½ inch, Bower-Barffed Case, Nickel Plated
Shackle......................Per Dozen, $11.35
Half Dozen in a Box.

No. 565.

Seamless Steel Case, Self-Locking Steel Spring Shackle, Three Lever Tumblers. Two Flat Steel Keys, 48 Changes.
No. 565—2 inch, Bower-Barffed Case, Nickel Plated
Shackle......................Per Dozen, $13.90
Half Dozen in a Box.

YALE PADLOCKS.

Half Size Cuts.

No. 453X.

Steel Case, Self-Locking Malleable Iron Spring Shackle. Two Flat Steel Keys, 6 Changes.

No. 453X—1½ inch, Brass Plated Case and Shackle,
....Per Dozen, $2.60

Half Dozen in a Box.

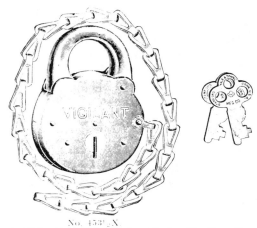

No. 453½X.

Steel Case, Self-Locking Malleable Iron Spring Shackle. Two Flat Steel Keys, 6 Changes.

No. 453½X—1½ inch, Brass Plated Case and Shackle, with 9 inch Steel Chain............Per Dozen, $5.00

Half Dozen in a Box.

No. 455X.

Steel Case, Self-Locking Malleable Iron Spring Shackle. Two Flat Steel Keys, 6 Changes.

No. 455X—2 inch, Brass Plated Case and Shackle,
.... Per Dozen, $3.80

Half Dozen in a Box.

No. 455½X.

Steel Case, Self-Locking Malleable Iron Spring Shackle. Two Flat Steel Keys, 6 Changes.

No. 455½X—2 inch, Brass Plated Case and Shackle, with 9 inch Steel Chain............Per Dozen, $6.20

Half Dozen in a Box.

No. 457X.

Steel Case, Self-Locking Malleable Iron Spring Shackle. Two Flat Steel Keys, 6 Changes.

No. 457X—2½ inch, Brass Plated Case and Shackle,
....Per Dozen, $5.20

Half Dozen in a Box.

No. 457½X.

Steel Case, Self-Locking Malleable Iron Spring Shackle. Two Flat Steel Keys, 6 Changes.

No. 457½X—2½ inch, Brass Plated Case and Shackle, with 9 inch Steel Chain............Per Dozen, $7.60

Half Dozen in a Box.

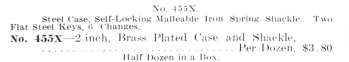

YALE PADLOCKS.

Half Size Cuts.

No. 297.

Steel Case, Self-Locking Malleable Iron Spring Shackle. Two Flat Steel Keys. 6 Changes.

No. 297—2½ inch, Bower-Barffed Case, Brass Plated Shackle.. .... Per Dozen, $6.00

Half Dozen in a Box.

No. 674N.

Steel Case, Self-Locking Steel Spring Shackle. Two Lever Tumblers. Two Flat Steel Keys. 6 Changes.

No. 674N—1¾ inch, Nickel Plated Case and Shackle ....Per Dozen, $3.00

Half Dozen in a Box.

No. 8414.

Seamless Steel Case, Self-Locking Steel Spring Shackle, Three Lever Tumblers. Two Corrugated Steel Keys. 48 Changes.

No. 8414—1 inch, Bower-Barffed Case and Shackle ....Per Dozen, $12.90

Half Dozen in a Box.

No 8434.

Seamless Steel Case, Self-Locking Steel Spring Shackle, Three Lever Tumblers. Two Corrugated Steel Keys. 48 Changes.

No. 8434—1½ inch, Bower-Barffed Case and Shackle ....Per Dozen, $16.90

Half Dozen in a Box.

No. 8454.

Seamless Steel Case, Self-Locking Steel Spring Shackle, Four Lever Tumblers. Two Corrugated Steel Keys. 144 Changes.

No. 8454—2 inch, Bower-Barffed Case and Shackle ....Per Dozen, $20.85

Half Dozen in a Box.

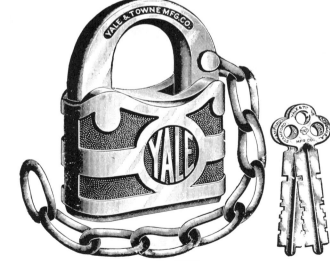

No. 897½.

Malleable Iron Case, Self-Locking Steel Spring Shackle, Four Lever Tumblers. Two Flat Steel Keys. 144 Changes.

No. 897½—3½ inch, Bower-Barffed Case, with 9 inch Welded Iron Curb Chain.....Per Dozen, $105.80

One-twelfth Dozen in a Box.

19

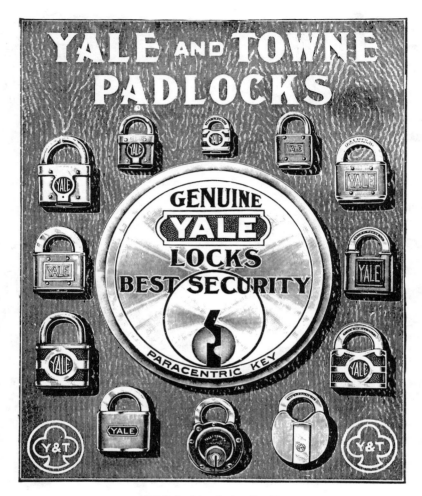

All Self-Locking Spring Shackles.

Handsome Sample Board, containing 12 of the Best Selling Yale Padlocks. The Board is stoutly built with Wood Easel and makes a handsome display either in the window or on the counter.

Beginning with the small one at the Top and reading to the Right they are as follows:

No. 813 —1 inch, Cast Bronze Metal.	No. 645J —2 inch, Steel Ivory Black.
No. 563 —1½ inch, Steel, Bower-Barffed.	No. 735 —2 inch, Wrought Bronze Metal.
No. 8454V—2 inch, Brass, Sand Blasted.	No. 850 —2 inch, Cast Bronze Metal.
No. 805F—2 inch, Iron, Bower-Barffed.	No. 8454 —2 inch, Steel, Bower-Barffed.
No. 853 —2 inch, Cast Bronze Metal.	No. 745V—2 inch, Brass, Bright Finish.
No. 625 —2⅛ inch, Cast Bronze Metal.	No. 743S—1½ inch, Steel, Bower-Barffed.

No. 20—Yale Assortment, One Dozen Assorted Padlocks on a Card as illustrated·.................Per Assortment, $20.00

Each Assortment, One Card, in a Box.

20

PADLOCKS.

No. 300.

Cast Bronze Metal Case, Self Locking Spring Shackle, New Improved Tumbler. **Two Keys.**

No. 300—2 inch................Per Dozen, $8.00
Half Dozen in a Box.

No. 310.

Cast Bronze Metal Case, Self Locking Spring Shackle, New Improved Tumbler. **Two Keys.**

No. 310—2¼ inch..............Per Dozen, $9.25
Half Dozen in a Box.

No. 530.

Malleable Iron Case, Self Locking Spring Shackle, Brass Inside Works, Three Tumblers. **Two Flat Steel Keys.**

No. 530—2¼ inch, Japanned............Per Dozen, $8.25
Half Dozen in a Box.

No. 531.

Malleable Iron Case, Self Locking Spring Shackle, Brass Inside Works, Three Tumblers. **Two Flat Steel Keys.**

No. 531—2¼ inch, Japanned, with Chain..Per Dozen, $9.25
Half Dozen in a Box.

No. 116.

Malleable Iron Case, Self Locking Spring Shackle, Spring Cover, Heavy Tumbler. **Two Keys.** Especially adapted for R. R. Cars and Switches.

No. 116—2½ inch, Tinned, with Chain...Per Dozen, $11.75
Half Dozen in a Box.

No. 311.

Cast Bronze Metal Case, Self Locking Spring Shackle, Improved Tumbler. **Two Keys.**

No. 311—2¼ inch with Chain..........Per Dozen, $10.50
Half Dozen in a Box.

PADLOCKS.

Half Size Cuts.

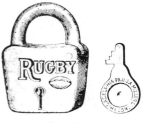

No. 101.

Steel Case, Self-Locking Malleable Iron Spring Shackle. **Two Flat Steel Keys.**

No. 101—1⁹⁄₁₆ inch, Black Enameled Case, Nickel Plated Shackle....................Per Dozen, $1.50

One Dozen in a Box.

No. 102.

Steel Case, Self-Locking Malleable Iron Spring Shackle. **Two Flat Steel Keys.**

No. 102—1⁵⁄₁₆ inch, Nickel Plated.......Per Dozen, $1.80

One Dozen in a Box.

No. 104.

Steel Case, Self-Locking Malleable Iron Spring Shackle. **Two Flat Steel Keys**

No. 104—1½ inch, Brass Finish........Per Dozen, $2.16

One Dozen in a Box.

No. 103.

Steel Case, Self-Locking Malleable Iron Spring Shackle. **Two Nickeled Steel Keys.**

No. 103—1½ inch, Nickel Plated.......Per Dozen, $1.50

One Dozen in a Box.

Nos. 253 and 254.

Steel Case, Self-Locking Malleable Iron Spring Shackle. **Two Nickeled Steel Keys.**

No. 253—2¼ inch, Nickel Plated.......Per Dozen, $4.80
No. 254—2¼ inch, Brass Finish........Per Dozen, 4.80

Half Dozen in a Box.

No. 152. Style of No. 263.

Steel Case, Self-Locking Malleable Iron Spring Shackle. **Two Strong Flat Keys.**

No. 152—2 inch, Brass Finish..........Per Dozen, $3.00
No. 263—Same as above, with 8 inch **Steel Chain**....
................................Per Dozen, 4.20

Half Dozen in a Box.

No. 153.

Steel Case, Self-Locking Malleable Iron Spring Shackle. **Two** Flat Steel Keys.

No. 153—1¾ inch, Black Enameled Case, Nickel Plated Shackle....................Per Dozen, $2.40

One Dozen in a Box.

No. 155.

Steel Case, Self-Locking Malleable Iron Spring Shackle. **Two** Flat Steel Keys.

No. 155—2 inch, Brass Finish...........Per Dozen, $3.60

Half Dozen in a Box.

No. 255.

Steel Case, Self-Locking Malleable Iron Spring Shackle. **Two** Flat Steel Keys.

No. 255—2⅝ inch, Black Enameled Case, Nickel Plated Shackle....................Per Dozen, $4.20

Half Dozen in a Box.

No. 154.

Steel Case, Self-Locking Double Action Malleable Iron **Spring** Shackle. **Two** Flat Steel Keys.

No. 154—1⅞ inch, Brass Finish.........Per Dozen, $2.50

One Dozen in a Box.

No. 252.

Wrought Steel Case, Self-Locking Malleable Iron Spring Shackle. **Two** Flat Steel Keys.

No. 252—2 inch, Brass Finish..........Per Dozen, $4.80

Half Dozen in a Box.

No. 260.

Wrought Steel Case, Self-Locking Malleable Iron **Spring** Shackle. **Two** Flat Steel Keys.

No. 260—2½ inch, Brass Finish.........Per Dozen, $5.40

Half Dozen in a Box.

PADLOCKS.

Half Size Cuts.

No. 151.

Wrought Steel Case, Self-Locking Malleable Iron Spring Shackle. **Two** Flat Steel Keys.

No. 151—2¼ inch, Brass Finish.........Per Dozen, $4.20

Half Dozen in a Box.

No. 251.

Steel Case, Self-Locking Malleable Iron Spring Shackle, Three Levers. **Two** Flat Steel Keys.

No. 251—2 inch, Black Enameled Case, Nickel Plated Hook Shackle.....................Per Dozen, $3.00

Half Dozen in a Box.

No. 259.

Cast Brass Case, Self-Locking Spring Shackle. **Two** Flat Steel Keys.

No. 259—1½ inch, Bright relief design, Bright Shackle ....Per Dozen, $3.50

Half Dozen in a Box.

No. 501.

Cast Brass Case, Self-Locking Spring Shackle. **Two** Flat Steel Keys.

No. 501—2 inch, Bright relief design, Bright Shackle.. ....Per Dozen, $4.00

Half Dozen in a Box.

No. 503.   Style of No. 504.

Heavy Wrought Steel Case, Self-Locking, Malleable Iron Spring Shackle, Eight Levers. **Two** Brass Plated Double Bitted Keys.

No. 503—2½ inch, Bright Finish........Per Dozen, $5.40

No. 504—2½ inch, Brass Finish, with 8 inch **Steel Chain**.........................Per Dozen, 7.20

Half Dozen in a Box.

Nos. 256, 257 and 258.

Heavy Wrought Steel Case, Self-Locking, Malleable Iron Spring Shackle, Six Levers. **Two** Brass Plated Double Bitted Keys.

No. 256—2 inch, Bright Finish..........Per Dozen, $3.00

No. 257—2 inch, Red and Blue Finish....Per Dozen, 3.25

No. 258—2 inch, Brass Finish..........Per Dozen, 3.60

Half Dozen in a Box.

Padlocks.

SMALL BRASS PADLOCKS.

Polished Brass. No.	Polished Brass. Per Doz.	Inch.	Description.	Nickel Plated. No.	Nickel Plated. Per Doz.
40	$4 50	$\frac{5}{8}$	Wrought Shackle and Bolts, Bit Key	51	$5 75
41	4 50	$\frac{3}{4}$	" " " "	52	5 75
42	5 00	1	" " " "	53	6 25
43	5 50	$1\frac{1}{8}$	" " " "	54	6 75
44	6 00	$1\frac{1}{4}$	" " " "	55	7 25
45	6 50	$1\frac{1}{2}$	" " " "	56	7 75

One dozen in a box.

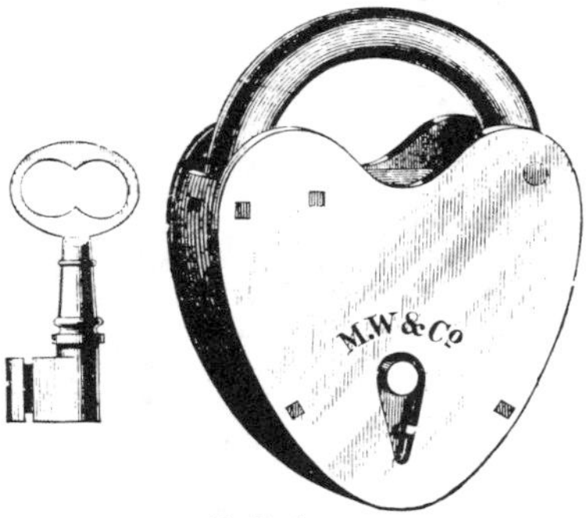

Full size cut of No. 45.

CAST BRONZE PADLOCKS.

BRASS INSIDE WORK.

SELF-LOCKING—SPRING SHACKLE.

No.	Inch.	Description.	Per Doz.
209	$1\frac{5}{8}$	1 Tumbler, Bridge and Wheel Wards, 1 Brass Key	$17 00
211	$1\frac{7}{8}$	1 " " "	19 50
213	$2\frac{1}{8}$	1 " " "	22 00
229	$1\frac{5}{8}$	2 " " "	19 50
231	$1\frac{7}{8}$	2 " " "	22 00
233	$2\frac{1}{8}$	2 " " "	24 50

Half dozen in a box.

CAST BRONZE PADLOCKS, WITH CHAIN.

BRASS INSIDE WORK.

SELF-LOCKING—SPRING SHACKLE.

No.	Inch.	Description.	Per Doz.
409	$1\frac{5}{8}$	1 Tumbler, Bridge and Wheel Wards, 1 Brass Key	$21 00
411	$1\frac{7}{8}$	1 " " "	23 50
413	$2\frac{1}{8}$	1 " " "	26 00
429	$1\frac{5}{8}$	2 " " "	23 50
431	$1\frac{7}{8}$	2 " " "	26 00
433	$2\frac{1}{8}$	2 " " "	28 50

Half dozen in a box.

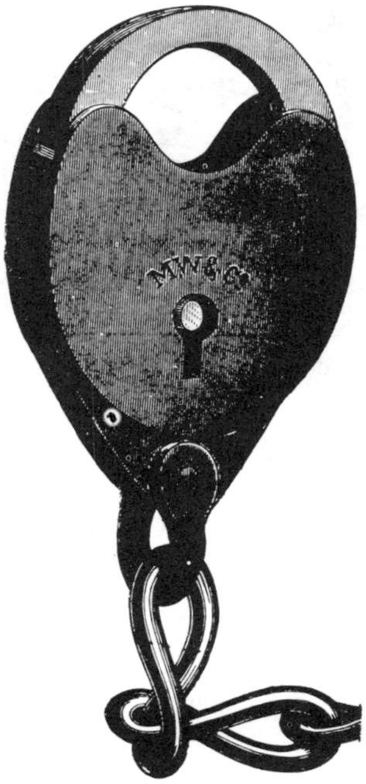

Champion Padlocks.

GUN METAL.

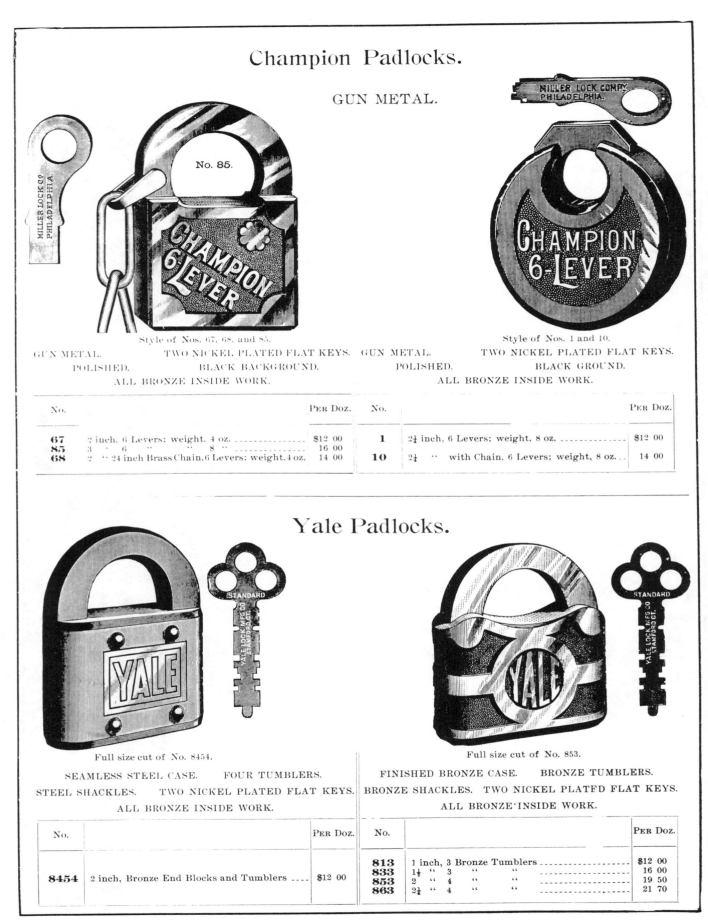

No. 85.

Style of Nos. 67, 68, and 85.

Style of Nos. 1 and 10.

GUN METAL.	TWO NICKEL PLATED FLAT KEYS.	GUN METAL.	TWO NICKEL PLATED FLAT KEYS.
POLISHED.	BLACK BACKGROUND.	POLISHED.	BLACK GROUND.
ALL BRONZE INSIDE WORK.		ALL BRONZE INSIDE WORK.	

No.		Per Doz.	No.		Per Doz.
67	2 inch, 6 Levers; weight, 4 oz.	$12 00	**1**	2¼ inch, 6 Levers; weight, 8 oz.	$12 00
85	3 " 6 " " 8 "	16 00			
68	2 " 24 inch Brass Chain, 6 Levers; weight, 4 oz.	14 00	**10**	2¼ " with Chain, 6 Levers; weight, 8 oz.	14 00

Yale Padlocks.

Full size cut of No. 8454.

Full size cut of No. 853.

SEAMLESS STEEL CASE.	FOUR TUMBLERS.	FINISHED BRONZE CASE.	BRONZE TUMBLERS.
STEEL SHACKLES.	TWO NICKEL PLATED FLAT KEYS.	BRONZE SHACKLES.	TWO NICKEL PLATED FLAT KEYS.
ALL BRONZE INSIDE WORK.		ALL BRONZE INSIDE WORK.	

No.		Per Doz.	No.		Per Doz.
8454	2 inch, Bronze End Blocks and Tumblers	$12 00	**813**	1 inch, 3 Bronze Tumblers	$12 00
			833	1½ " 3 " "	16 00
			853	2 " 4 " "	19 50
			863	2¼ " 4 " "	21 70

Padlocks.

BRONZE.

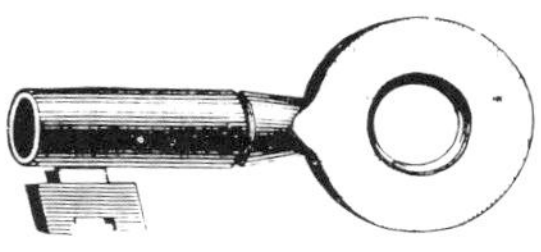

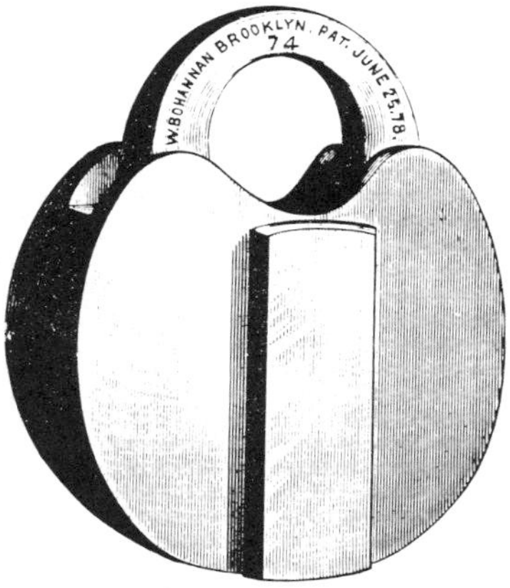

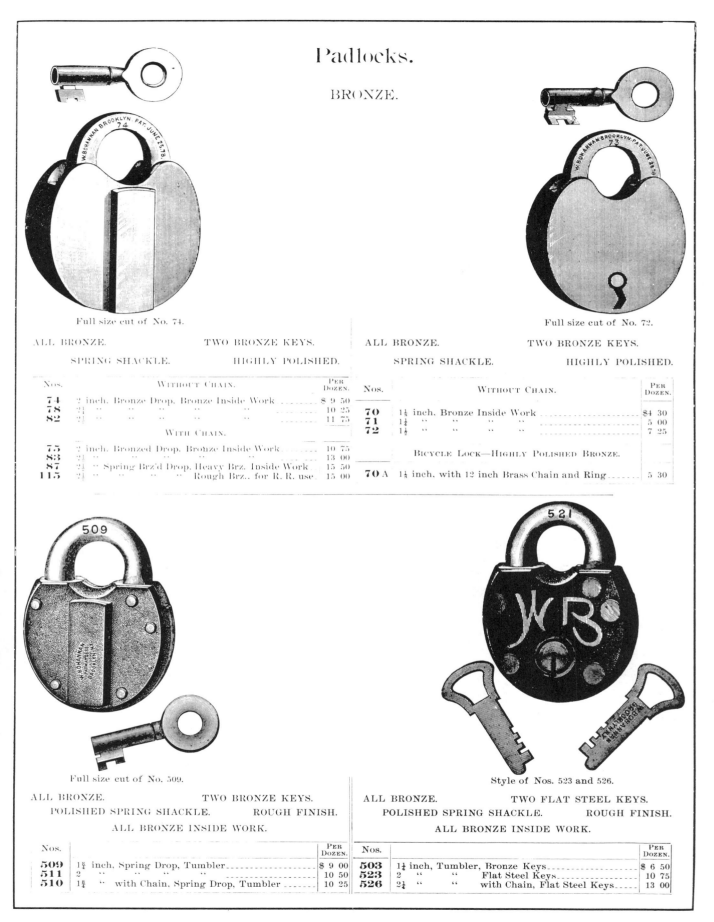

Full size cut of No. 74.

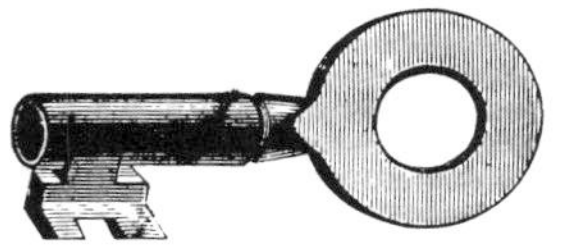

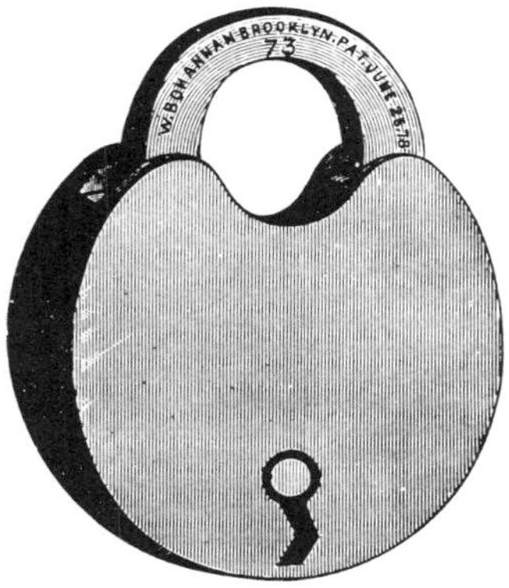

Full size cut of No. 72.

ALL BRONZE. TWO BRONZE KEYS.

SPRING SHACKLE. HIGHLY POLISHED.

Nos.	Without Chain.	Per Dozen.
74	2 inch, Bronze Drop, Bronze Inside Work	$ 9 50
78	2¼ " " " " "	10 25
82	2½ " " " " "	11 75
	With Chain.	
75	2 inch, Bronzed Drop, Bronze Inside Work	10 75
83	2½ " " " " "	13 00
87	2½ " Spring Brz'd Drop, Heavy Brz. Inside Work	15 50
115	2½ " " " " Rough Brz., for R. R. use	15 00

ALL BRONZE. TWO BRONZE KEYS.

SPRING SHACKLE. HIGHLY POLISHED.

Nos.	Without Chain.	Per Dozen.
70	1⅛ inch, Bronze Inside Work	$4 30
71	1¼ " " " " "	5 00
72	1½ " " " " "	7 25
	Bicycle Lock—Highly Polished Bronze.	
70 A	1⅛ inch, with 12 inch Brass Chain and Ring	5 30

Full size cut of No. 509.

ALL BRONZE. TWO BRONZE KEYS.

POLISHED SPRING SHACKLE. ROUGH FINISH.

ALL BRONZE INSIDE WORK.

Nos.		Per Dozen.
509	1¾ inch, Spring Drop, Tumbler	$ 9 00
511	2 " " " "	10 50
510	1¾ " with Chain, Spring Drop, Tumbler	10 25

Style of Nos. 523 and 526.

ALL BRONZE. TWO FLAT STEEL KEYS.

POLISHED SPRING SHACKLE. ROUGH FINISH.

ALL BRONZE INSIDE WORK.

Nos.		Per Dozen.
503	1¼ inch, Tumbler, Bronze Keys	$ 6 50
523	2 " " Flat Steel Keys	10 75
526	2¼ " " with Chain, Flat Steel Keys	13 00

Eagle Padlocks.

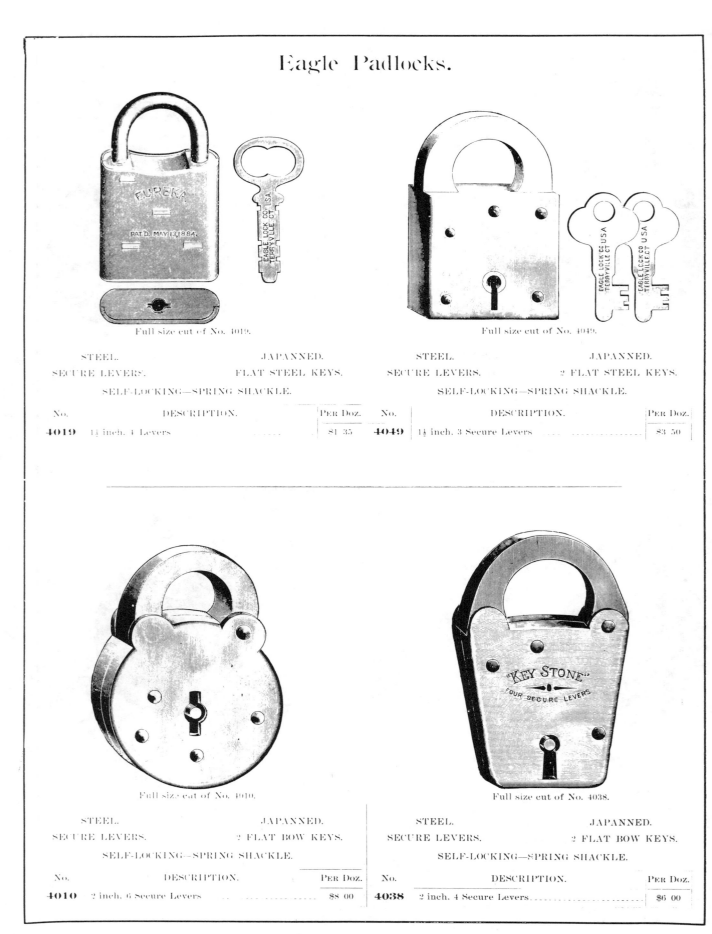

Full size cut of No. 4019.

STEEL.		JAPANNED.	
SECURE LEVERS.		FLAT STEEL KEYS.	
SELF-LOCKING—SPRING SHACKLE.			
No.	DESCRIPTION.		Per Doz.
4019	1¼ inch. 4 Levers		$1 35

Full size cut of No. 4049.

STEEL.		JAPANNED.	
SECURE LEVERS.		2 FLAT STEEL KEYS.	
SELF-LOCKING—SPRING SHACKLE.			
No.	DESCRIPTION.		Per Doz.
4049	1½ inch. 3 Secure Levers		$3 50

Full size cut of No. 4010.

STEEL.		JAPANNED.	
SECURE LEVERS.		2 FLAT BOW KEYS.	
SELF-LOCKING—SPRING SHACKLE.			
No.	DESCRIPTION.		Per Doz.
4010	2 inch. 6 Secure Levers		$8 00

Full size cut of No. 4038.

STEEL.		JAPANNED.	
SECURE LEVERS.		2 FLAT BOW KEYS.	
SELF-LOCKING—SPRING SHACKLE.			
No.	DESCRIPTION.		Per Doz.
4038	2 inch. 4 Secure Levers		$6 00

Fancy Padlocks.

No. 999.   No. 303.   No. 1304.

No. **999**.	Fancy Bronze, Black Background, Raised Figures, 4 Tumblers, 2 Flat Steel Keys; weight, ½ lb.	...... Per dozen,	$8 00
No. **99**.	" " " " " " 2 " " " ¼ "	"	6 00
No. **303**.	Solid Brass, Round Shackle, 2 Flat Steel Keys, Self-Locking Spring Shackle		"	2 50
No. **1304**.	" " " 2 " " " " "		"	2 15

No. 420.   Nos. 806 and 807.

SOLID RUSTLESS STEEL CASE.

REVOLVING KEY CYLINDER DUST PROOF PLUNGER.

ALL BRASS INSIDE WORK.

DOUBLE LOCKING TUMBLERS. FLAT STEEL KEYS.

	Per Doz.
No. **420**. Steel Self-Locking Spring Shackle, 1¼ in. wide	$3 25
No. **421**. " " " " 1½ "	4 15
No. **425**. Bronze " " " 1½ "	4 75

AUTOMATIC.

Turn the key to the left, and the shackle will unlock and automatically spring into position shown by dotted lines.

FLAT STEEL KEYS.

		Per Dcz.
No. **806**.—Rustless Steel Case and Shackle,	1¾ in.	$4 35
No. **807**.—Highly Finished Bronze Case and Shackle, 1¾ "	5 60
No. **808**.—Rustless Steel Case and Shackle,	2 "	4 90
No. **809**.—Highly Finished Bronze Case and Shackle, 2 "	6 60

Scandinavian Padlocks.

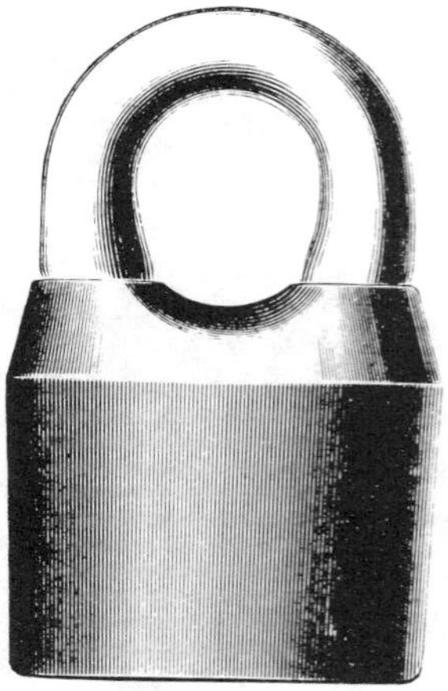

FAST SHACKLE.

TWO KEYS EACH. RED FINISH.

No.	Inch.	Description.	Per Doz.
1010	1½	Wrought Caps. Malleable Shackles. Interlocking Tumblers	$ 9 00
1011	1⅝	" " " "	11 00
1012	1⅞	" " " "	13 00

Half dozen in a box.

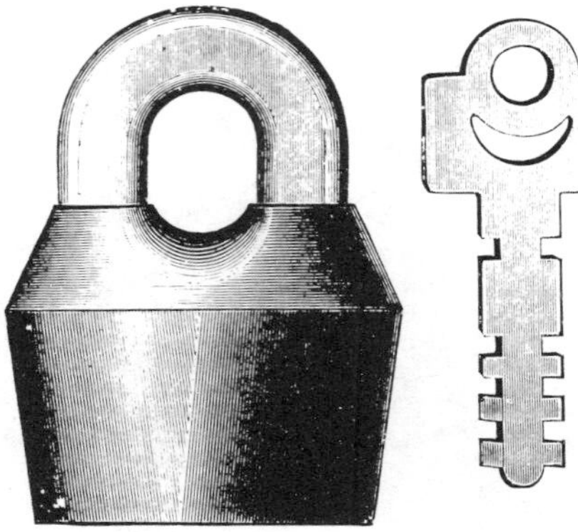

IRON.

POLISHED SHACKLES. TWO FLAT STEEL KEYS.

JAPANNED. FINE FINISH.

No.	Inch.	Description.	Per Doz.
2010	1½	Wrought Iron Caps and Tumblers. Malleable Shackles	$7 00
2011	1⅝	" " " "	7 85
2012	1⅞	" " " "	9 25

BRONZE.

POLISHED SHACKLES. TWO FLAT STEEL KEYS.

HIGHLY POLISHED.

No.	Inch.	Description.	Per Doz.
2110	1½	All Brass Inside Works	$20 00
2111	1⅝	" "	22 00

Half dozen in a box.

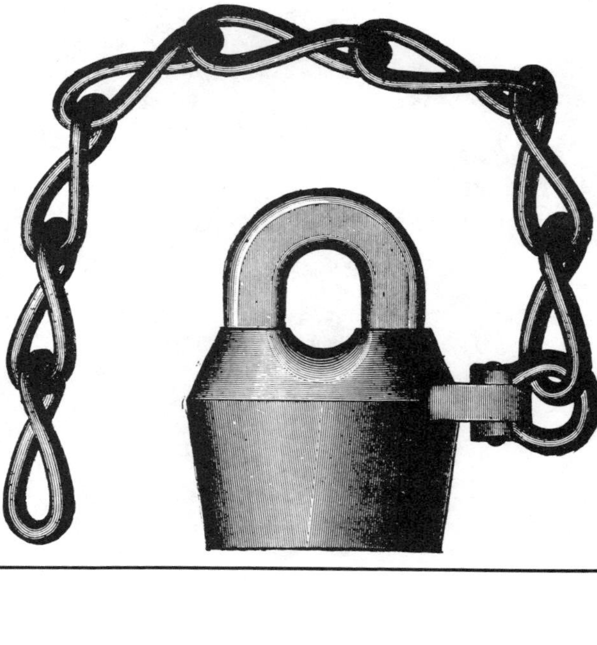

IRON. WITH CHAIN.

POLISHED SHACKLES. TWO FLAT STEEL KEYS.

JAPANNED. FINE FINISH.

No.	Inch.	Description.	Per Doz.
2050	1½	Wrought Caps and Tumblers. Malleable Shackles	$ 8 70
2051	1⅝	" " " "	10 35
2052	1⅞	" " " "	11 75

BRONZE.

POLISHED SHACKLES. TWO FLAT STEEL KEYS.

HIGHLY POLISHED. FINE FINISH.

No.	Inch.	Description.	Per Doz.
2150	1½	All Brass Inside Works	$22 50
2151	1⅝	" "	24 50

Half dozen in a box.

Padlocks.

CAST BRONZE METAL.

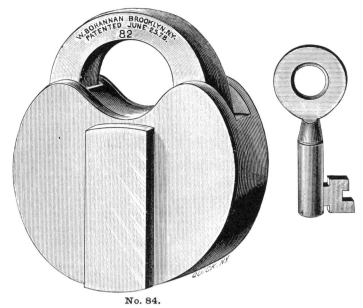

No. 84.

TUMBLER LOCK—SPRING COVER.

No. 84, 2½ inch . . . . . per dozen, ...

One-half dozen in a box.

TUMBLER LOCK—SPRING COVER.

No. 85, 2½ inch . . . . per dozen, ...

One-half dozen in a box.

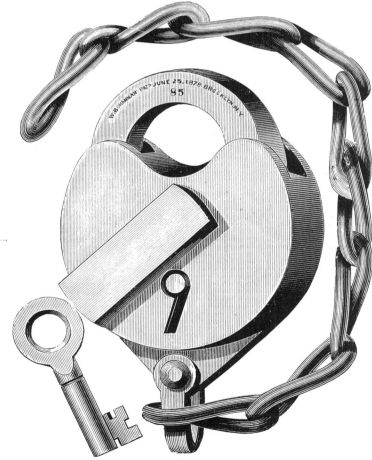

No. 85.

Padlocks.

No. 1013.

No. 1016.

WROUGHT IRON SHACKLES AND BOLTS.

No. 1013, Size, 3 inch, Fancy Engraved Drop and Bushings, 3 Solid Brass Wheels, Fine Finish.

1 Key, per dozen, ... 2 Keys, per dozen, ...

No. 1016, Size, 2¾ inch, Fancy Engraved Drop and Bushings, Secret Key Hole, Side Ward, Solid Brass Wheel, assorted, 12 Changes to dozen, Extra Fine Finish.

1 Key, per dozen, ... 2 Keys, per dozen, ...

Padlocks.

BRASS.

Plain Finish, Self-locking, Heavy Spring Shackle,
6 Secure Levers, 2 Double-bitted Flat Steel
Keys each, all different in a dozen.

No. 4034, 2 inch . . . . per dozen, ...

4034

4023

4027

Self-locking Spring Shackle, Flat Steel Keys.

IRON.—Black Japanned.

No. 4023, 2 in. . . . . per dozen, ...
" 4027, 2¼ in. . . . . . . " ....

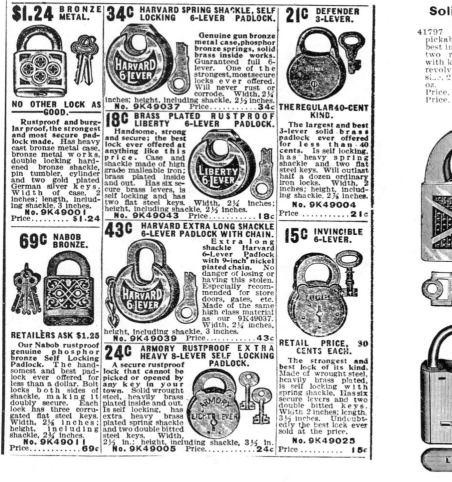

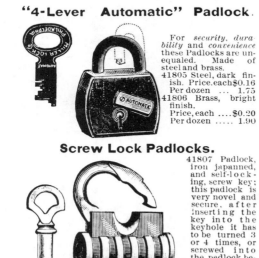

34

SMALL BRASS PADLOCKS.

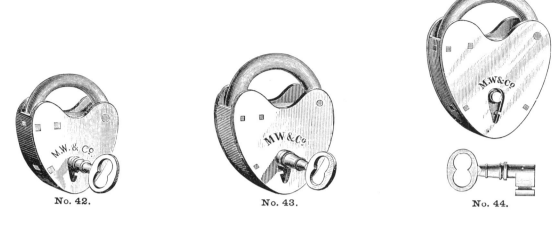

No. 42.   No. 43.   No. 44.

AMERICAN PATTERN.

No. 42, 1 inch . . . . per dozen, ...

" **43**, 1⅛ inch . . . . " ....

" **44**, 1¼ inch, with Bang-up Closing Key-hole . . . . " ....

"REX" TIRE LOCK

4K9280—36 in., ¼ in. chain, saw and fileproof, patent finish duck cover, heavy duty lock, 2 keys. 1 in carton.

"CORBIN"
2 Inch Padlock
A big padlock for you to profitably retail at a "dime!"

2H1298—"Corbin," 2 in. steel case, **(2 finishes,** brass plated and black japanned), nickel plated and brass plated steel shackles, swivel keyway, 2 flat keys. Asstd. 1 doz. in box

2H1213—"Eagle" mail **box lock,** 1¼ in. black japanned steel case, nickel plated steel shackle, swivel keyway, 2 flat keys. 1 doz. in

2H1309—"Segal," 2⅛ in. cast iron case, bower barffed finish, brassed panels, brassed steel shackle, swivel keyways. 2 flat keys.

"THE BIG THREE"
Stimulate sales by using price tickets on these big value 10c, 25c and 50c padlocks!

RETAIL 10¢   RETAIL 25¢   RETAIL 50¢

2H7558—Fraim "Security," 2 in. steel case, **brassed and black japanned,** brassed shackle, swivel keyway, 2 flat keys.

2H1265—"Corbin Hercules," 2 in. black japanned steel case, **rustproof,** steel shackle, swivel keyway, 2 flat keys.

2H1240—"Fraim," 2⅛ in. polished cast brass case, nickel plated steel shackle, swivel keyway, 2 corrugated keys. ½ doz.

2H10673—2 in. galvanized steel case, **dustproof** keyway cover, aluminum shackle, 2 barrel keys.

2H1274—2½ in., highly polished **nickel plated** steel case and shackle, stippled relief, swivel keyway, 2 corrugated keys. 1 doz. in box.

2H1218—"Reese," **locker lock,** 1½ in. cast bronze case, polished panels, red, blue and green enameled relief, nickel plated spring steel shackle, 2 corrugated keys. ½ doz. in box.

35

"YALE" PADLOCKS IN DISPLAY CARTONS

Selections from the famous "Yale" line of better padlocks—packed in the attractive counter display carton

DISPLAY THESE "YALE" NUMBERS IN "CARTONS OF 12"

2H51—"Yale," 1½ in. steel case, 2 finishes, black japanned and brass plated, nickel plated and brass plated malleable shackles, warded mechanism, brass swivel keyway, 2 flat keys. Asstd. 1 doz. in display carton with easel....Doz **$2.10**

2H54—"Yale," 1½ in. iron case, bower-barffed, brass plated steel panels, brass plated steel shackles, warded mechanism, bottom brass swivel keyway, 2 flat keys. 1 doz. in display carton with easel back..............Doz **$4.10**

2H8—"Yale," 1¾ in. iron case, bower-barffed, copper plated steel discs, bronzed steel shackles, warded mechanism, bottom brass swivel keyway, 2 flat keys. 1 doz. in display carton with easel back. Doz **$5.40**

"YALE" PADLOCKS IN "CARTONS OF 6"—READY FOR YOUR COUNTER

2H57—"Yale," 2¼ in. iron case, bower-barffed, nickel plated steel shackles, warded mechanism, bottom brass swivel keyway. 2 flat keys. 6 in counter display carton with easel back. CARTON of 6 **$2.50**

2H58—"Yale," 2 in. iron case, bower-barffed, brass plated steel panels, brass plated steel shackles, warded mechanism, bottom brass swivel keyway, 2 flat keys. 6 in display carton with easel back. CARTON of 6 **$2.50**

2H59—"Yale," 2¼ in. iron case, bower-barffed, copper plated steel discs, bronzed steel shackles, warded mechanism, bottom brass swivel keyway, 2 flat keys. 6 in counter display carton. CARTON of 6 **$3.25**

A "YALE"
6-Lever Padlock

This padlock formerly retailed for 50c. You can now sell it for 25c.

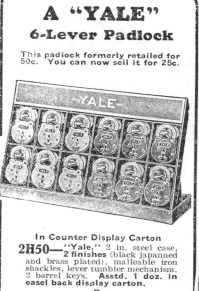

In Counter Display Carton
2H50—"Yale," 2 in. steel case, 2 finishes (black japanned and brass plated), malleable iron shackles, lever tumbler shackles. 2 barrel keys. Asstd. 1 doz. in easel back display carton.
Doz

$2.10

Laminated Case

2H1271—(Mfrs 40) "Master," 1¾ in., built up from 20 plates cold rolled steel, cadmium rustproof finish, riveted 7 times, steel shackle, swivel keyway, 2 paracentric keys, 6 on varnished walnut board in carton, 5 lbs.
Board of 6 **$3.00**

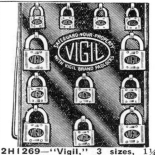

2H1269—"Vigil," 3 sizes, 1¼, 1¾ and 2¼ in. polished cast brass cases, red enameled centers, nickel plated steel shackles, 2 corrugated keys. Asstd. 1 doz. on easel metal display board. Doz **$3.60**

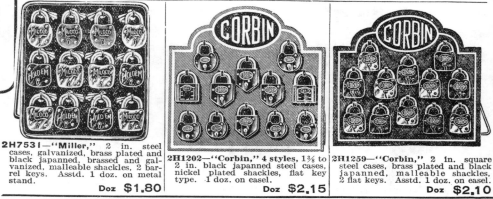

2H7531—"Miller," 2 in. steel cases, galvanized, brass plated and black japanned, brassed and galvanized, malleable shackles, 2 barrel keys. Asstd. 1 doz. on metal stand. Doz **$1.80**

2H1202—"Corbin," 4 styles, 1¾ to 2 in. black japanned steel cases, nickel plated shackles, flat key type. 1 doz. on easel. Doz **$2.15**

2H1259—"Corbin," 2 in. square steel cases, brass plated and black japanned, malleable shackles, 2 flat keys. Asstd. 1 doz. on easel. Doz **$2.10**

YALE ASSORTED PADLOCKS.

No. 10.

With the following Assortment for Stock:

⅙ Dozen No.	840	Padlocks, retailing at	$1.50 each	½ Dozen No.	225	Padlocks, retailing at	$0.40 each
⅙ Dozen No.	843	Padlocks, retailing at	1.25 each	½ Dozen No.	615S	Padlocks, retailing at	.35 each
⅙ Dozen No.	8454	Padlocks, retailing at	.85 each	½ Dozen No.	453J	Padlocks, retailing at	.15 each
¼ Dozen No.	805F	Padlocks, retailing at	.85 each	½ Dozen No.	645C	Padlocks, retailing at	.30 each
¼ Dozen No.	585	Padlocks, retailing at	.60 each	½ Dozen No.	115	Padlocks, retailing at	.25 each
¼ Dozen No.	605V	Padlocks, retailing at	.60 each	½ Dozen No.	671V	Padlocks, retailing at	.25 each
½ Dozen No.	326	Padlocks, retailing at	.50 each	½ Dozen No.	674N	Padlocks, retailing at	.15 each
¼ Dozen No.	563	Padlocks, retailing at	.50 each	½ Dozen No.	9645J	Padlocks, retailing at	.30 each

Total Retail Value... $ 30.75

No. 10--Yale Padlock Sample Board and Assortment as above...Each, ...

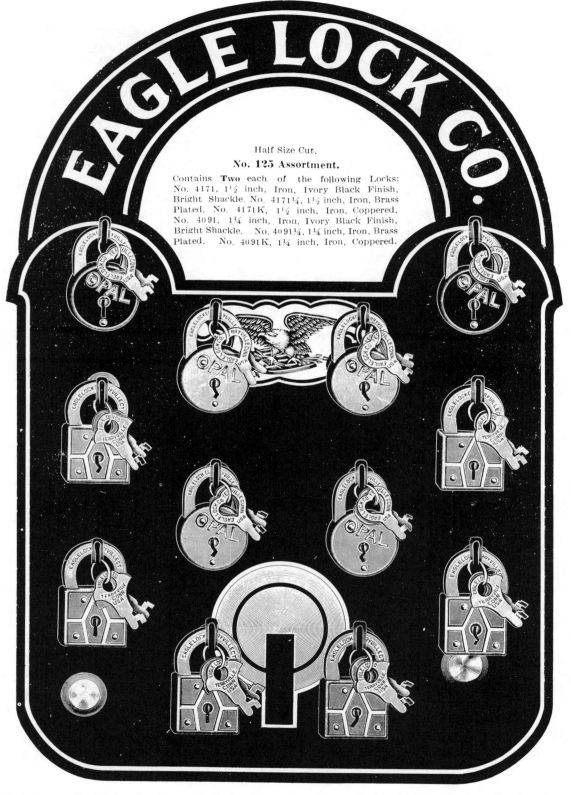

Half Size Cut.

No. 125 Assortment.

Contains **Two** each of the following Locks: No. 4171, 1½ inch, Iron, Ivory Black Finish, Bright Shackle. No. 4171¼, 1½ inch, Iron, Brass Plated. No. 4171K, 1½ inch, Iron, Coppered. No. 4091, 1¼ inch, Iron, Ivory Black Finish, Bright Shackle. No. 4091¼, 1¼ inch, Iron, Brass Plated. No. 4091K, 1¼ inch, Iron, Coppered.

No. 125—Assortment, Containing One Dozen Padlocks, Mounted on Fancy Cards with Easel Backs . Per Assortment, $1.70
Each Assortment, One Card, in a Box.

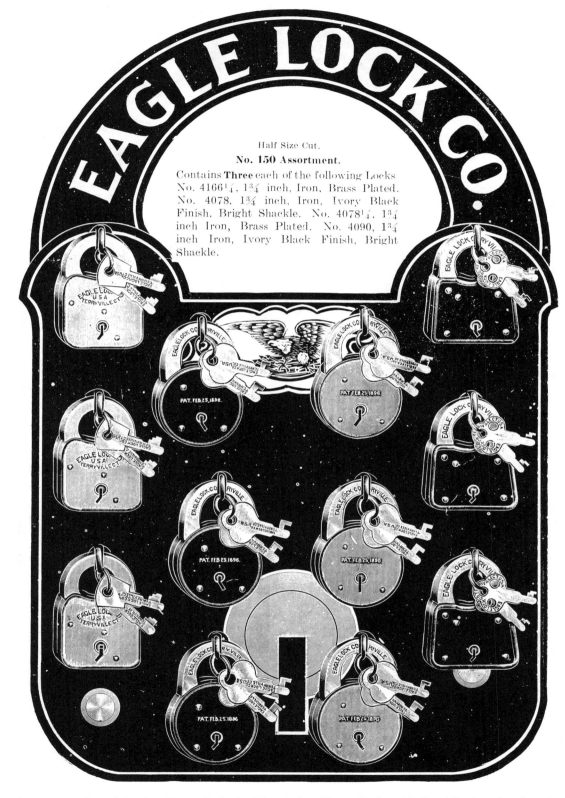

Half Size Cut.

No. 150 Assortment.

Contains **Three** each of the following Locks No. 4166¼, 1¾ inch, Iron, Brass Plated. No. 4078, 1¾ inch, Iron, Ivory Black Finish, Bright Shackle. No. 4078¼, 1¾ inch Iron, Brass Plated. No. 4090, 1¾ inch Iron, Ivory Black Finish, Bright Shackle.

No. 150—Assortment, Containing One Dozen Padlocks, Mounted on Fancy Cards, with Easel Backs . . Per Assortment, $2.00

Each Assortment, One Card, in a Box.

EAGLE LOCK CO.

Half Size Cut.

No. 175 Assortment.

Contains **Two** each of the following Locks:—No. 4127, 2 inch, Iron, Bright Finish. No. 4127¼, 2 inch, Iron, Brass Plated. No. 4128, 2 inch, Iron, Ivory Black Finish, Bright Shackle. No. 4158, 2 inch, Iron, Bright Finish. No. 4158¼, 2 inch, Iron, Brass Plated. No. 4159, 2 inch, Iron, Ivory Black Finish, Bright Shackle.

No. 175—Assortment, containing One Dozen Padlocks, Mounted on Fancy Cards with Easel Backs. Per Assortment, $4.00 Each Assortment, One Card, in a Box.

YALE, Brass shackle, Iron body, 2″ body
Embossed Stanford, Connecticut, U.S.A.,

ALL BRASS,
Left to right, 3¾″, 3¾″, 3¾″, 4½″

MOTOR, Brass body, 1⅝″,
STABILITY, Brass body, 2″ diameter,
SARGENT, 2⅛″, Iron body,

WINCHESTER, Solid brass,

Left, B & O,

Middle, U.P.,

Right, I.H.B., ADLAKE,

Left, G. R. & I. R.R.,

Middle, CCC & STL R.R.,

Right, TSTL & W R.R.,

Top Row (left to right)

NYNH & H R.R.
(New York, New Haven and Hartford)

MOPAC R.R. (Missouri, Pacific),

MC (Michigan Central),

DNH (Delaware and Hartford),

B & O (Baltimore and Ohio),

NYC (New York Central),

Bottom Row

L & N (Louisville and Nashville),

PC R.R. (Penn Central R.R.),

NKP (Nickel Plate),

C & O (Chesapeake and Ohio),

E (Erie R.R.),

Left, N.Y.C.S., Steel,

Middle, Back showing in picture, L.G.,
Front Penn. Sys.,

Right C & W. I.,

RAILROAD KEYS

As it would serve no useful purpose to illustrate locks from many different railroads we have illustrated a few to serve as identification. Most railroad locks with key sell from $30 to $50. If the railroad has been out of business or is a small line then the price will be higher. Here again a collector that needs a certain lock for his collection may be willing to pay above market price to complete his collection.

Left, ADLAKE, steel,

Right, B & O R.R., steel,

Left, CIRR (Central Indiana Railroad), steel,

Right, NYC (MOON), steel,

CCC & STL
XLCR (with Arrow) Trade Mark
Mfg., Corbin,

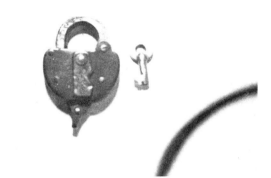

CCC & STL
Train Lock Co., Lancaster
Steel body, Brass shackle,

Left, ADLAKE, solid brass,

Right. B & O R.R., F.S. Hdw. Co., solid brass.

Left, L & N R.R., steel,

Right, Wabash R.R., steel,

Locks.

TUBULAR STORE DOOR DEAD LOCK.

Swivel Escutcheon.

A. E. DEITZ'S.

For Doors 1½ to 2⅞-inches Thick.

EXTRA HEAVY AND POSITIVELY SAFE.

Heavy Japanned Iron Case ; Heavy Brass Bolt ; Brass Knob ; Four Tumblers ; Two
Flat Steel Keys ; Bronze Metal Swivel Escutcheons.

No. 172, Size 6 x 2⅞ inches . . . .

Door Keys.

TINNED MALLEABLE IRON.

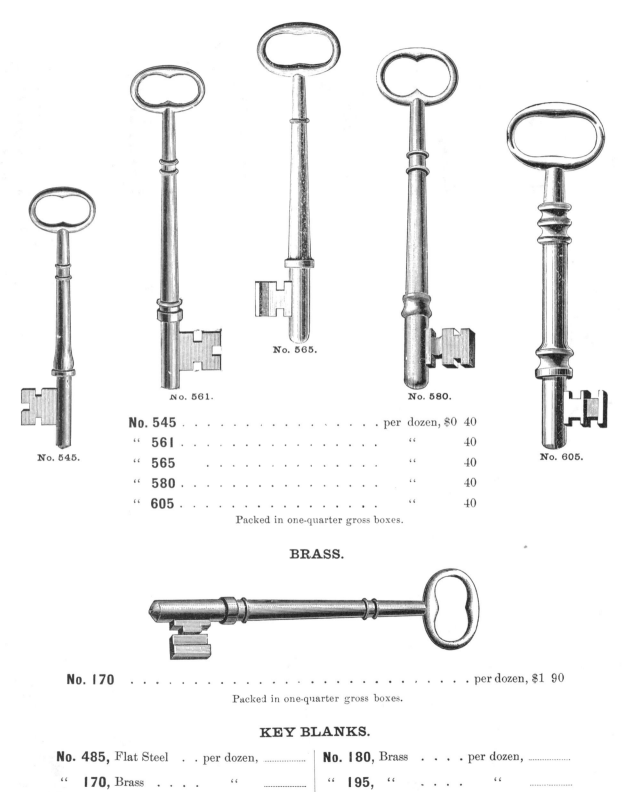

No. 565.

No. 561.

No. 580.

No. 545.

No. 605.

No. 545	per dozen, $0	40
" **561**	"	40
" **565**	"	40
" **580**	"	40
" **605**	"	40

Packed in one-quarter gross boxes.

BRASS.

No. 170 . . . . per dozen, $1 90

Packed in one-quarter gross boxes.

KEY BLANKS.

No. 485, Flat Steel . . per dozen, _____	**No. 180**, Brass . . . . per dozen, _____
" **170**, Brass . . . . " _____	" **195**, " . . . . " _____

45

Padlock Keys.

Nos. 44 and 55.   Nos. 4 O and 5 O.   No. 3 O.   Nos. O, 2 O, and 16.   Nos. 1 and 2.   No. 3.   No. 4.

No. 1052.

No. 1058.

No. 1043.

No. 1054.

Nos.	FOR LOCKS.	Per Gross.
44	44, 55	$ 8 25
4 O	4-O, 5-O	2 50
3-O	3-O	4 60
O	O, 2-O, 16	4 60
1	1, 2	4 60
3	3	8 50
4	4	8 25
1052	1052, 1029, 1060	12 00
1043	1043, 1044, 1053	15 00
1058	1058, 1059	12 00
1054	1054, 1055, 1033, 1034, 1045, 1046	15 00
16	16	4 60
1000	1000	12 50
1001	1001	12 50
1003	1003, 1011	21 00
1015	1015, 1025, 1042	16 00
1024	1024, 1050, 1051, 1048, 1049	12 50
1056	1056, 1057	20 00
	Assorted Keys, 5-O to 4	5 75

No. 16.   No. 1000.   No. 1001.   Nos. 1003 and 1011.   Nos. 1015, 1025, and 1042.   Nos. 1024, 1048.   Nos. 1056 and 1057.

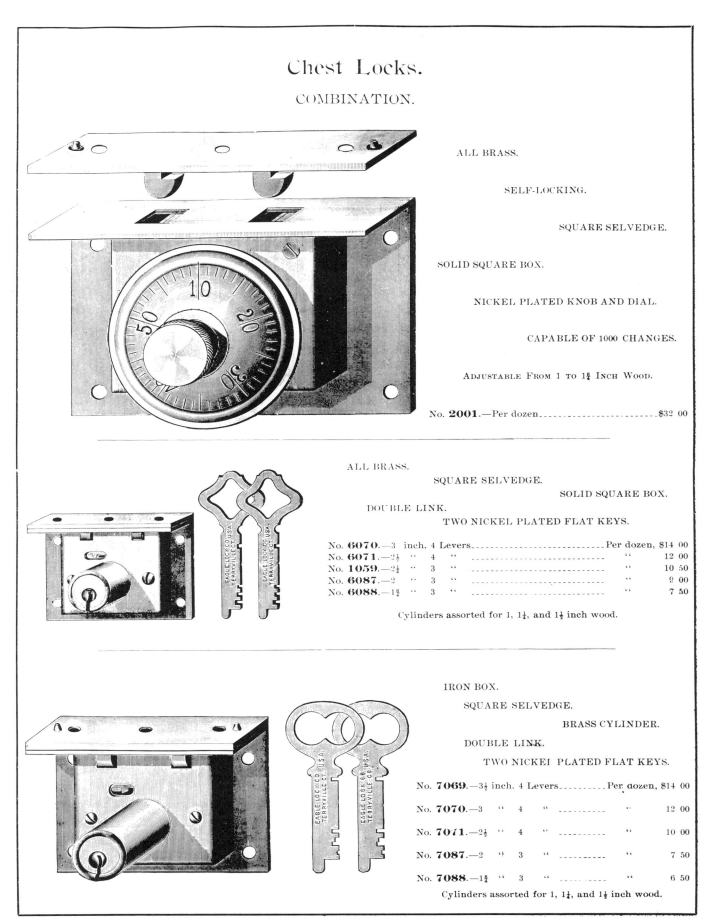

Chest Locks.

COMBINATION.

ALL BRASS.

SELF-LOCKING.

SQUARE SELVEDGE.

SOLID SQUARE BOX.

NICKEL PLATED KNOB AND DIAL.

CAPABLE OF 1000 CHANGES.

ADJUSTABLE FROM 1 TO 1½ INCH WOOD.

No. **2001.**—Per dozen........................$32 00

ALL BRASS.

SQUARE SELVEDGE.

SOLID SQUARE BOX.

DOUBLE LINK.

TWO NICKEL PLATED FLAT KEYS.

No. **6070.**—3 inch, 4 Levers......................Per dozen, $14 00
No. **6071.**—2½ " 4 " ...." 12 00
No. **1059.**—2¼ " 3 " ...." 10 50
No. **6087.**—2 " 3 " ...." 9 00
No. **6088.**—1¾ " 3 " ...." 7 50

Cylinders assorted for 1, 1¼, and 1½ inch wood.

IRON BOX.

SQUARE SELVEDGE.

BRASS CYLINDER.

DOUBLE LINK.

TWO NICKEL PLATED FLAT KEYS.

No. **7069.**—3½ inch. 4 Levers..........Per dozen, $14 00
No. **7070.**—3 " 4 " ...." 12 00
No. **7071.**—2½ " 4 " ...." 10 00
No. **7087.**—2 " 3 " ...." 7 50
No. **7088.**—1¾ " 3 " ...." 6 50

Cylinders assorted for 1, 1¼, and 1½ inch wood.

Chest Locks.

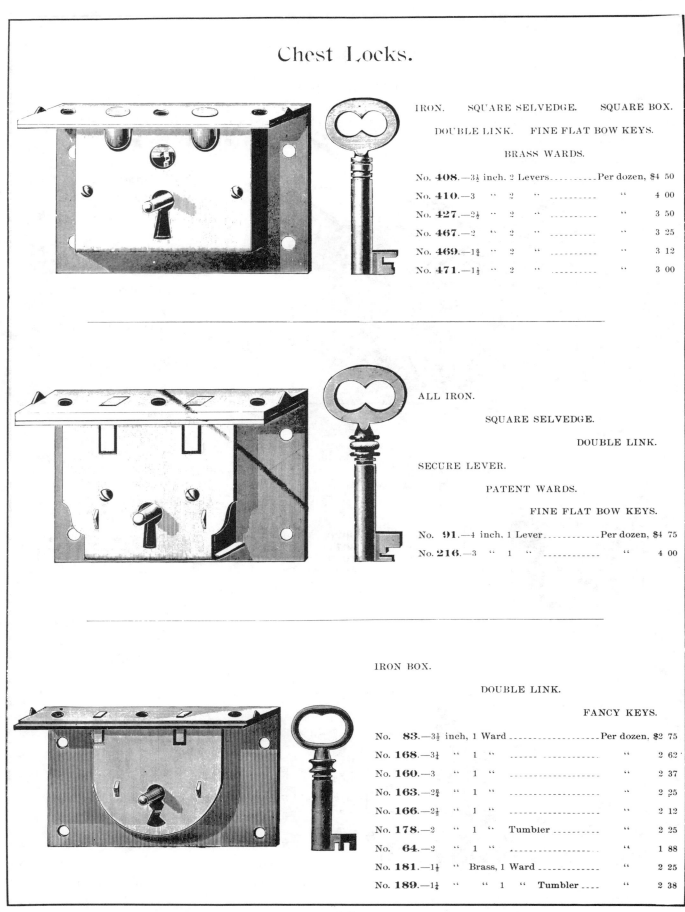

IRON.   SQUARE SELVEDGE.   SQUARE BOX.

DOUBLE LINK.   FINE FLAT BOW KEYS.

BRASS WARDS.

No. **408**.—3½ inch. 2 Levers............Per dozen, $4 50	
No. **410**.—3 " 2 " .... " 4 00	
No. **427**.—2½ " 2 " .... " 3 50	
No. **467**.—2 " 2 " .... " 3 25	
No. **469**.—1¾ " 2 " .... " 3 12	
No. **471**.—1½ " 2 " .... " 3 00	

ALL IRON.

SQUARE SELVEDGE.

DOUBLE LINK.

SECURE LEVER.

PATENT WARDS.

FINE FLAT BOW KEYS.

No. **91**.—4 inch. 1 Lever............Per dozen, $4 75	
No. **216**.—3 " 1 " .... " 4 00	

IRON BOX.

DOUBLE LINK.

FANCY KEYS.

No. **83**.—3½ inch, 1 Ward..................Per dozen. $2 75	
No. **168**.—3¼ " 1 " .... " 2 62	
No. **160**.—3 " 1 " .... " 2 37	
No. **163**.—2¾ " 1 " .... " 2 25	
No. **166**.—2½ " 1 " .... " 2 12	
No. **178**.—2 " 1 " Tumbler .... " 2 25	
No. **64**.—2 " 1 " .... " 1 88	
No. **181**.—1½ " Brass, 1 Ward............. " 2 25	
No. **189**.—1¼ " " 1 " Tumbler .... " 2 38	

Secure Lever Chest Locks.

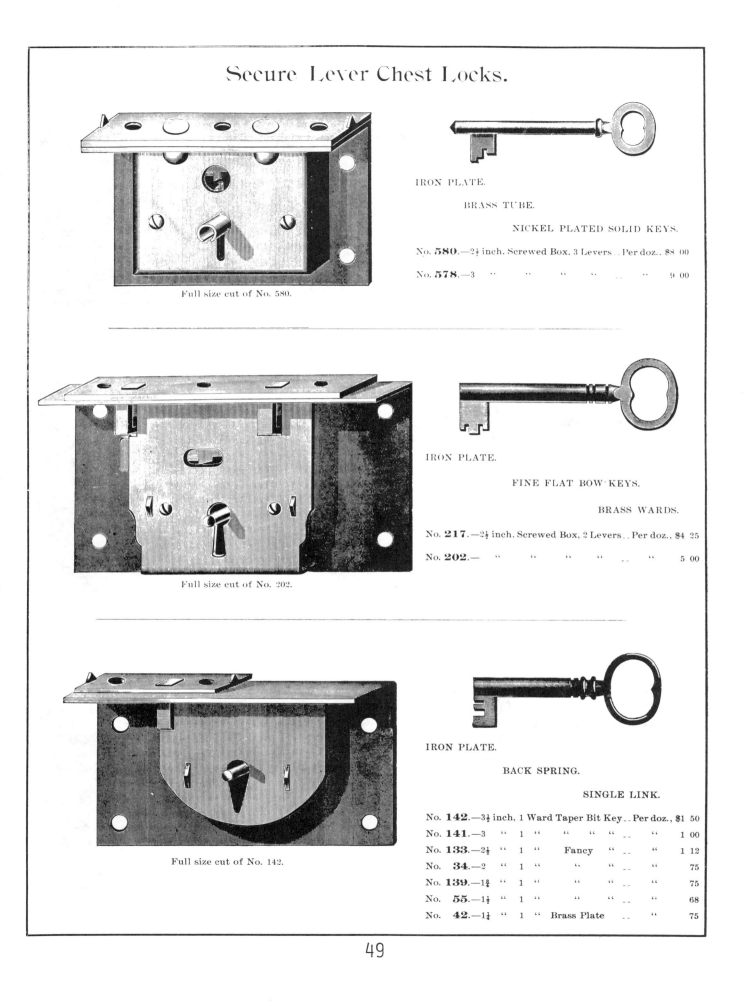

Full size cut of No. 580.

IRON PLATE.

BRASS TUBE.

NICKEL PLATED SOLID KEYS.

No. **580.**—2½ inch. Screwed Box, 3 Levers .. Per doz., $8 00

No. **578.**—3   "   "   "   "   .. "   9 00

Full size cut of No. 202.

IRON PLATE.

FINE FLAT BOW KEYS.

BRASS WARDS.

No. **217.**—2½ inch. Screwed Box, 2 Levers .. Per doz., $4 25

No. **202.**—   "   "   "   "   .. "   5 00

Full size cut of No. 142.

IRON PLATE.

BACK SPRING.

SINGLE LINK.

No. **142.**—3½ inch, 1 Ward Taper Bit Key .. Per doz., $1 50

No. **141.**—3   "   1   "   "   "   "   .. "   1 00

No. **133.**—2½ "   1   "   Fancy   "   .. "   1 12

No. **34.**—2   "   1   "   "   "   .. "   75

No. **139.**—1¾ "   1   "   "   "   .. "   75

No. **55.**—1½ "   1   "   "   "   .. "   68

No. **42.**—1¼ "   1   "   Brass Plate   .. "   75

49

Chest Locks.

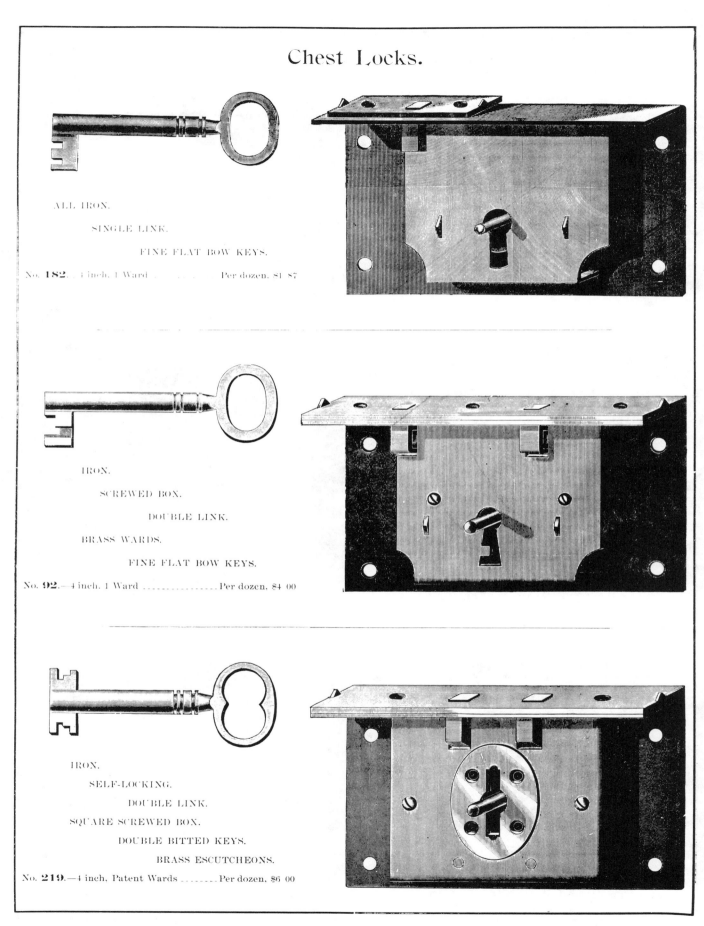

ALL IRON.

SINGLE LINK.

FINE FLAT BOW KEYS.

No. **182**.—4 inch, 1 Ward .... Per dozen, $1 87

IRON.

SCREWED BOX.

DOUBLE LINK.

BRASS WARDS.

FINE FLAT BOW KEYS.

No. **92**.—4 inch, 1 Ward .... Per dozen, $4 00

IRON.

SELF-LOCKING.

DOUBLE LINK.

SQUARE SCREWED BOX.

DOUBLE BITTED KEYS.

BRASS ESCUTCHEONS.

No. **219**.—4 inch, Patent Wards .... Per dozen, $6 00

Cash Box Locks.

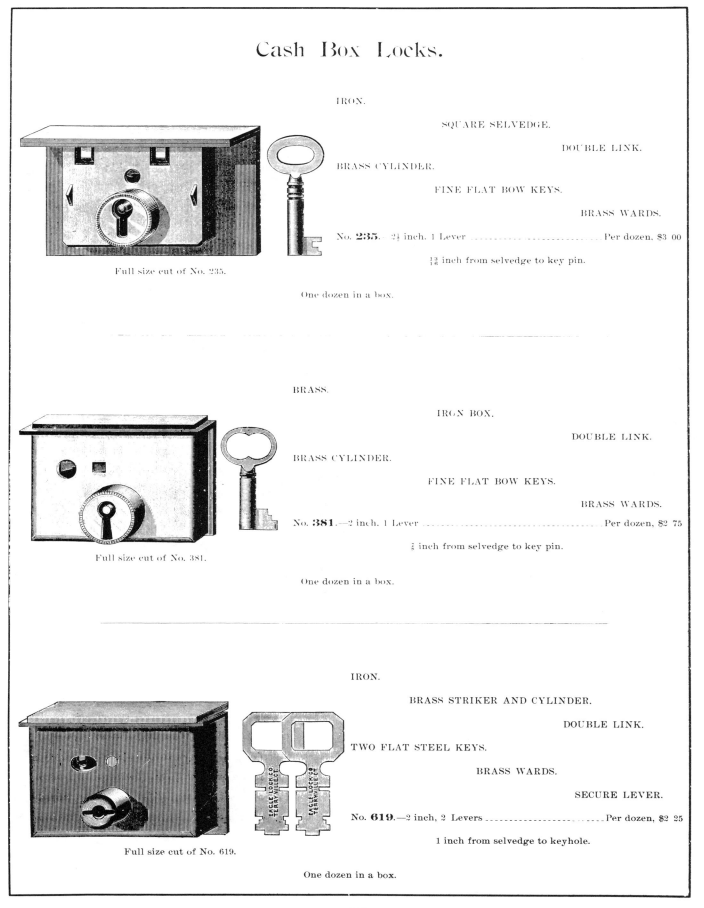

IRON.

SQUARE SELVEDGE.

DOUBLE LINK.

BRASS CYLINDER.

FINE FLAT BOW KEYS.

BRASS WARDS.

No. **235**.—2¼ inch. 1 Lever .... Per dozen, $3 00

$\frac{13}{16}$ inch from selvedge to key pin.

One dozen in a box.

Full size cut of No. 235.

BRASS.

IRON BOX.

DOUBLE LINK.

BRASS CYLINDER.

FINE FLAT BOW KEYS.

BRASS WARDS.

No. **381**.—2 inch. 1 Lever .... Per dozen, $2 75

⅞ inch from selvedge to key pin.

One dozen in a box.

Full size cut of No. 381.

IRON.

BRASS STRIKER AND CYLINDER.

DOUBLE LINK.

TWO FLAT STEEL KEYS.

BRASS WARDS.

SECURE LEVER.

No. **619**.—2 inch, 2 Levers .... Per dozen, $2 25

1 inch from selvedge to keyhole.

One dozen in a box.

Full size cut of No. 619.

Drawer and Cupboard Locks.

COMBINATION.

ALL BRASS.

SQUARE SELVEDGE.

SQUARE SCREWED BOX.

HEAVY LATCH BOLT.

NICKEL PLATED KNOB AND DIAL.

CAPABLE OF 1,000 CHANGES.

ADJUSTABLE FROM ⅞ TO 1½ INCH WOOD.

No. **2011.**—3 inch .... Per dozen, $17 00

1¼ inch from selvedge to center of knob

One in a box.

Full size cut of No. 2011.

ALL BRASS.

SQUARE SELVEDGE.

SQUARE SCREWED BOX.

BROAD. HEAVY BOLT.

TWO NICKEL PLATED FLAT KEYS.

SECURE LEVERS.

No. **6002.**—2½ inch, 3 Levers .... Per dozen, $8 50

No. **6001.**—2¼ " 3 " .... " 7 50

Cylinders for ⅞ inch wood.

One dozen in a box.

Full size cut of No. 6002.

IRON.

SQUARE SELVEDGE.

SQUARE SCREWED BOX.

BROAD. HEAVY BOLT.

TWO NICKEL PLATED FLAT KEYS.

BRASS CYLINDER.

No. **6017.**—2¼ inch, 3 Levers .... Per dozen, $6 50

No. **1079.**—2 " 2 " .... " 4 50

No. **6090.**—1⅞ " 2 " .... " 4 50

Cylinder for ⅞ inch wood.

One dozen in a box.

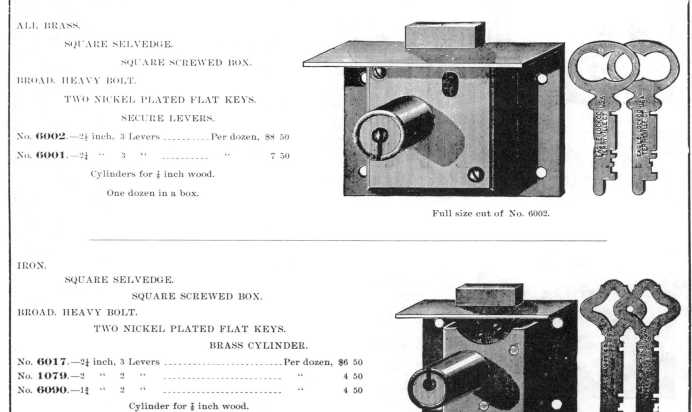

Full size cut of No. 6090.

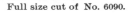

Drawer Locks.

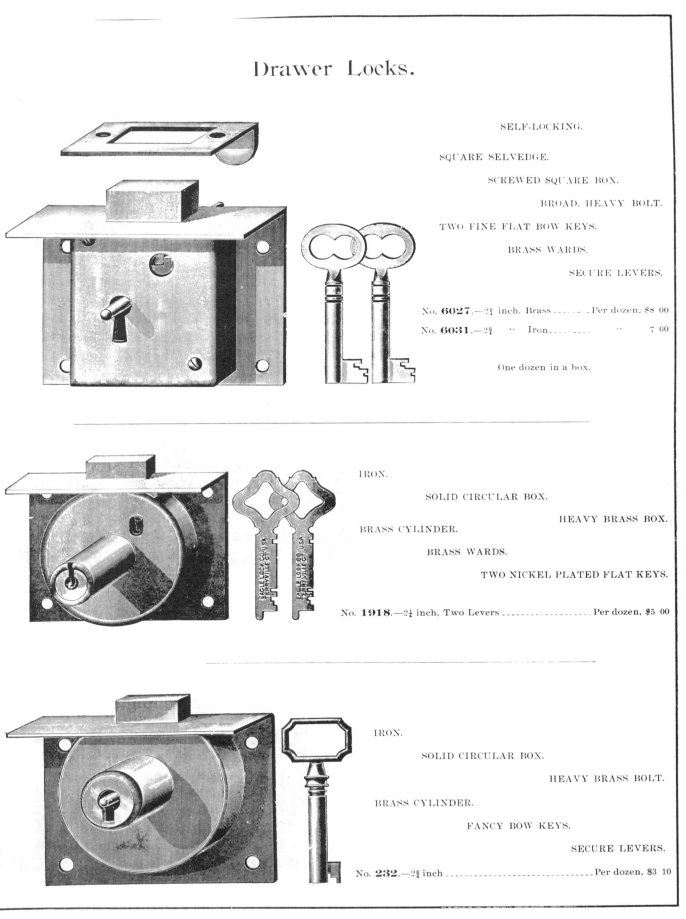

SELF-LOCKING.

SQUARE SELVEDGE.

SCREWED SQUARE BOX.

BROAD, HEAVY BOLT.

TWO FINE FLAT BOW KEYS.

BRASS WARDS.

SECURE LEVERS.

No. **6027**.—2⅜ inch, Brass .... Per dozen, $8 00

No. **6031**.—2⅜ " Iron .... " 7 00

One dozen in a box.

IRON.

SOLID CIRCULAR BOX.

HEAVY BRASS BOX.

BRASS CYLINDER.

BRASS WARDS.

TWO NICKEL PLATED FLAT KEYS.

No. **1918**.—2¼ inch, Two Levers .... Per dozen, $5 00

IRON.

SOLID CIRCULAR BOX.

HEAVY BRASS BOLT.

BRASS CYLINDER.

FANCY BOW KEYS.

SECURE LEVERS.

No. **232**.—2¾ inch .... Per dozen, $3 10

53

Drawer Locks.

BRASS.

SCREWED, SQUARE BOX.

SQUARE SELVEDGE.

BROAD, HEAVY BOLT.

TWO FINE FLAT BOW KEYS.

ALL DIFFERENT.

No. **266**.—2¼ inch, 2 Levers ....Per dozen, $10 00

No. **276**.—2 " 2 " .... " 8 75

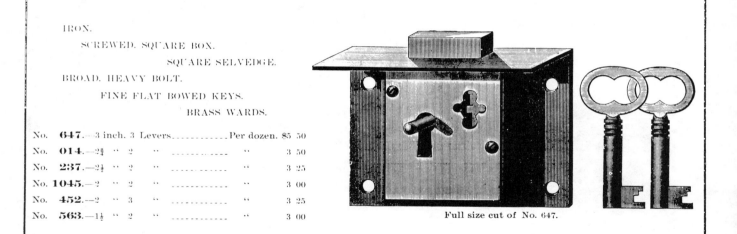

Full size cut of No. 266.

IRON.

SCREWED, SQUARE BOX.

SQUARE SELVEDGE.

BROAD, HEAVY BOLT.

FINE FLAT BOWED KEYS.

BRASS WARDS.

No. **647**.—3 inch, 3 Levers............Per dozen, $5	50
No. **014**.—2⅜ " 2 " .... " 3	50
No. **237**.—2¼ " 2 " .... " 3	25
No. **1045**.—2 " 2 " .... " 3	00
No. **452**.—2 " 3 " .... " 3	25
No. **563**.—1½ " 2 " .... " 3	00

Full size cut of No. 647.

IRON.

SCREWED, SQUARE BOX.

SQUARE SELVEDGE.

BROAD, HEAVY BOLT.

SOLID NICKEL PLATED KEYS.

BRASS BARREL AND WARDS.

No. **558**.—2½ inch, 3 Levers ....Per dozen, $5 00

No. **561**.—2¼ " 2 " .... " 4 25

No. **1221**.—2 " 2 " .... " 4 00

Full size cut of No. 1221.

Drawer and Till Locks.

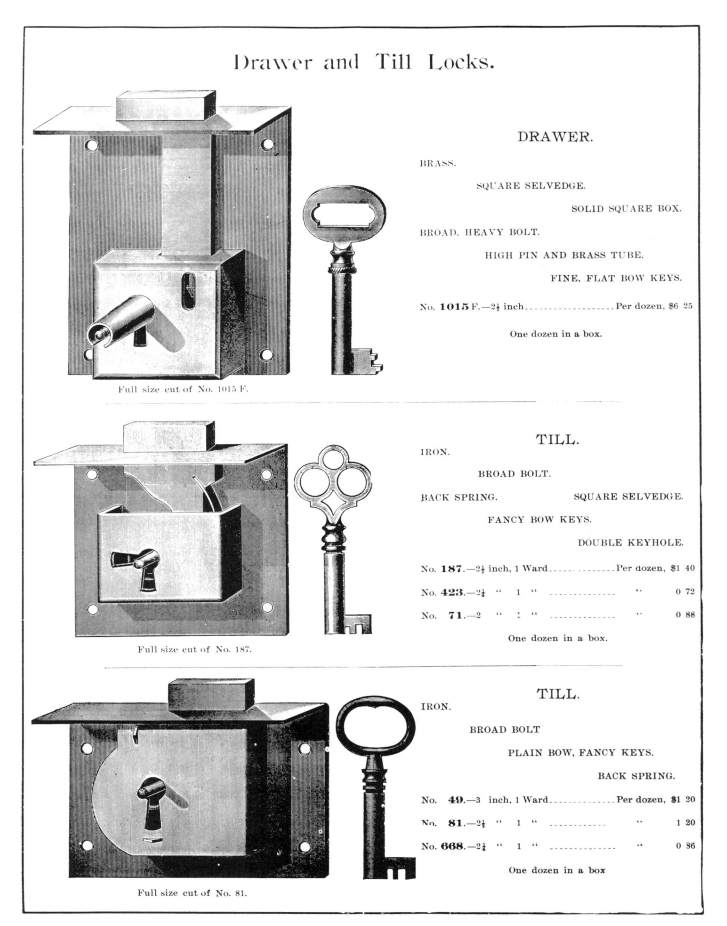

DRAWER.

BRASS.

SQUARE SELVEDGE.

SOLID SQUARE BOX.

BROAD. HEAVY BOLT.

HIGH PIN AND BRASS TUBE.

FINE, FLAT BOW KEYS.

No. **1015** F.—2½ inch.................Per dozen, $6 25

One dozen in a box.

Full size cut of No. 1015 F.

TILL.

IRON.

BROAD BOLT.

BACK SPRING.   SQUARE SELVEDGE.

FANCY BOW KEYS.

DOUBLE KEYHOLE.

No. **187.**—2½ inch, 1 Ward............Per dozen, $1 40

No. **423.**—2¼ "   1 "   ....   "   0 72

No. **71.**—2 "   1 "   ....   "   0 88

One dozen in a box.

Full size cut of No. 187.

TILL.

IRON.

BROAD BOLT

PLAIN BOW, FANCY KEYS.

BACK SPRING.

No. **49.**—3 inch, 1 Ward.............Per dozen, $1 20

No. **81.**—2¼ "   1 "   ....   "   1 20

No. **668.**—2¼ "   1 "   ....   "   0 86

One dozen in a box

Full size cut of No. 81.

Cupboard Locks.

Full size cut of No. 1061.

IRON.   TWO NICKEL PLATED FLAT KEYS.

HEAVY BOLT.   BRASS CYLINDERS.

No. **1069.**—2¾ inch. 2 Levers................Per dozen, $5 50

No. **1061.**—2½ "   2   " .... "   5 00

¾ inch from selvedge to center of cylinder.

One dozen in a box.

Full size cut of No. 450.

IRON.   FINE FLAT BOW KEYS.

HEAVY BOLT.   BRASS WARDS.

No. **406.**—3 inch, 3 Levers ....Per dozen, $4 50

No. **450.**—2½ "   3   " .... "   3 50

No. **503.**—2 "   all Brass, 1 Lever .... "   4 00

One dozen in a box.

Full size cut of No. 116.

IRON.   FANCY BOW KEYS.

BROAD BOLT.   BACK SPRING.

No. **116.**—3 inch, 1 Ward ....Per dozen, $1 25

No. **117.**—2¾ "   1   " .... "   1 00

No. **58.**—2½ "   1   " .... "   0 87

No. **57.**—2¼ "   1   " .... "   0 75

One dozen in a box.

Full size cut of No. 473.

IRON, BRASS SELVEDGE.   FLAT BOW KEYS.

BROAD BOLT.   MORTISE.

No. **350.**—3 inch, 1 Ward...................Per dozen, $3 50

No. **473.**—2¼ "   1   " .... "   2 75

One dozen in a box.

Wardrobe Locks.

Full size cut of No. 7098.

IRON.

SQUARE SCREWED BOX.

BROAD. HEAVY BOLTS.

BRASS CYLINDERS.

TWO NICKEL PLATED FLAT KEYS.

SECURE LEVERS.

No. **7074**.—3×1¾ inch. 2 Levers. Iron Bolt............ Per dozen, $7 00

No. **7098**. 2¾×1¾ " 2 " Brass " .... " 6 00

One dozen in a box.

IRON.

SQUARE SCREWED BOX.

HEAVY BRASS BOLTS.

BRASS BARREL.

SOLID NICKEL PLATED STEEL KEYS.

SECURE LEVERS.

No. **567**.—3½×2 inch. 2 Levers............... Per dozen, $6 00

No. **569**.—3 ×1¾ " 2 " .... " 5 25

No. **571**.—2½×1¾ " 2 " .... " 4 75

One dozen in a box.

Full size cut of No. 567.

IRON.

SQUARE SCREWED BOX.

HEAVY BRASS BOLTS.

FINE FLAT BOW KEYS.

SECURE LEVERS.

ALL DIFFERENT.

No. 147.—3½×2 inch. 2 Levers............... Per dozen, $4 75

No. **6065**.—3 ×1¾ " 2 " .... " 4 00

No. **6067**.—2¾×1¾ " 2 " .... " 3 50

No. **1801**.—2½×1⅜ " 2 " .... " 3 50

No. **1205**.—2 ×⅞ " 2 " .... " 4 00

One dozen in a box.

Full size cut of No. 6067.

Wardrobe Locks.

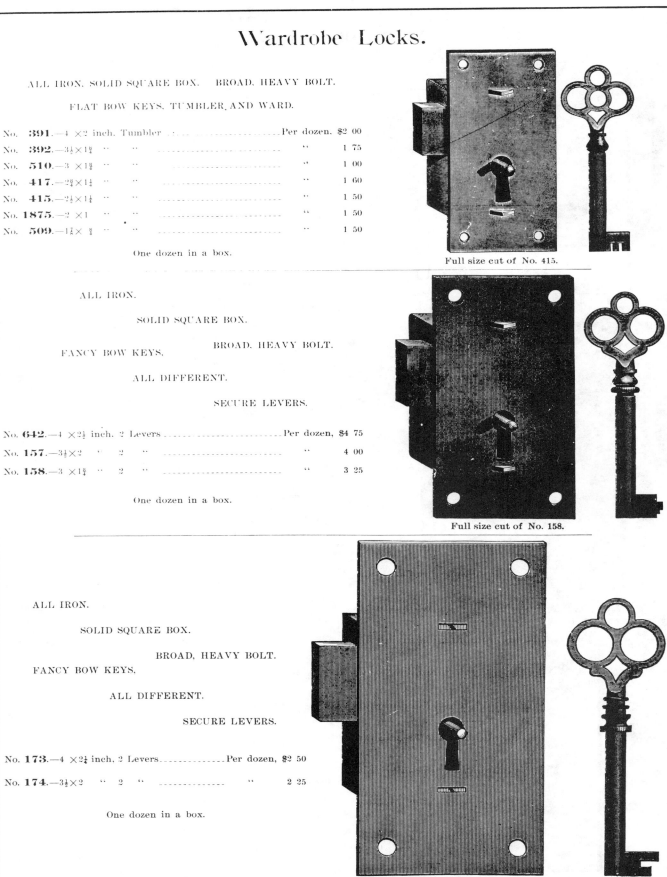

ALL IRON. SOLID SQUARE BOX. BROAD, HEAVY BOLT.

FLAT BOW KEYS, TUMBLER, AND WARD.

No. **391.**—4 ×2 inch. Tumbler ....Per dozen $2 00
No. **392.**—3½×1¾ " " .... " 1 75
No. **510.**—3 ×1¼ " " .... " 1 00
No. **417.**—2⅝×1¼ " " .... " 1 60
No. **415.**—2½×1¼ " " .... " 1 50
No. **1875.**—2 ×1 " " .... " 1 50
No. **509.**—1⅞× ⅞ " " .... " 1 50

One dozen in a box.

Full size cut of No. 415.

ALL IRON.

SOLID SQUARE BOX.

FANCY BOW KEYS.   BROAD, HEAVY BOLT.

ALL DIFFERENT.

SECURE LEVERS.

No. **642.**—4 ×2½ inch. 2 Levers ....Per dozen, $4 75
No. **157.**—3½×2 " 2 " .... " 4 00
No. **158.**—3 ×1¾ " 2 " .... " 3 25

One dozen in a box.

Full size cut of No. 158.

ALL IRON.

SOLID SQUARE BOX.

BROAD, HEAVY BOLT.

FANCY BOW KEYS,

ALL DIFFERENT.

SECURE LEVERS.

No. **173.**—4 ×2¼ inch, 2 Levers ....Per dozen, $2 50
No. **174.**—3½×2 " 2 " .... " 2 25

One dozen in a box.

Full size cut of No. 173.

Roller Top Desk Locks.

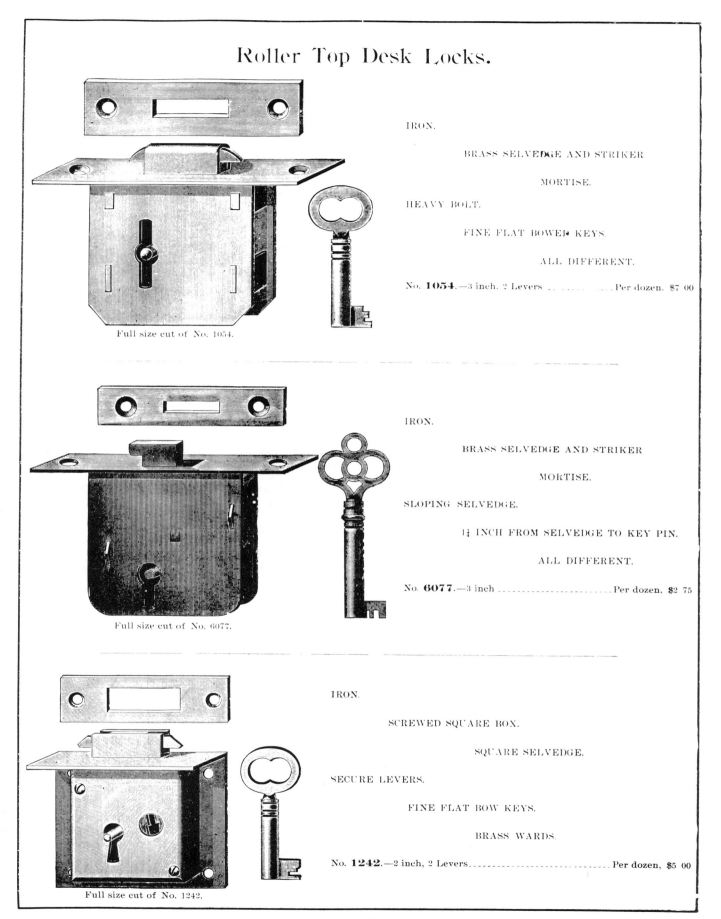

IRON.

BRASS SELVEDGE AND STRIKER

MORTISE.

HEAVY BOLT.

FINE FLAT BOWED KEYS.

ALL DIFFERENT.

No. **1054**.—3 inch. 2 Levers ....Per dozen. $7 00

Full size cut of No. 1054.

IRON.

BRASS SELVEDGE AND STRIKER

MORTISE.

SLOPING SELVEDGE.

1¼ INCH FROM SELVEDGE TO KEY PIN.

ALL DIFFERENT.

No. **6077**.—3 inch ....Per dozen, $2 75

Full size cut of No. 6077.

IRON.

SCREWED SQUARE BOX.

SQUARE SELVEDGE.

SECURE LEVERS.

FINE FLAT BOW KEYS.

BRASS WARDS.

No. **1242**.—2 inch, 2 Levers.....................Per dozen, $5 00

Full size cut of No. 1242.

Sub-Treasury Locks.

FOR INSIDE SAFE DOORS.

JAPANNED IRON.

 WROUGHT SCREWED BOX.

  HEAVY BRASS LATCH BOLT.

BRASS CYLINDER.

 2 NICKEL PLATED FLAT KEYS.

  BRASS WARDS.

No. **1807.**—1½ inch, 3 Levers................Per dozen, $6 00

 ⅞ inch from selvedge to center of key cylinder.

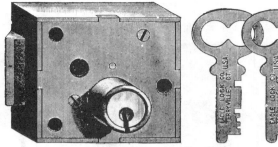

Full size cut of No. 1807.

JAPANNED IRON.

 WROUGHT SCREWED BOX.

  HEAVY BRASS BOLT.

BRASS CYLINDER.

 2 NICKEL PLATED FLAT KEYS.

  BRASS WARDS.

No. **1807½.**—1½ inch, 3 Levers................Per dozen, $6 00

 ⅞ inch from selvedge to center of key cylinder.

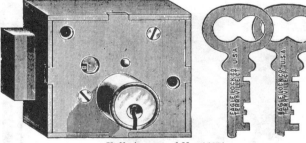

Full size cut of No. 1807½.

IRON.

 SQUARE SELVEDGE.

  WROUGHT SCREWED BOX.

BRASS CYLINDER.

 2 NICKEL PLATED FLAT KEYS.

  BRASS WARDS.

No. **1048¾.**—1½ inch, 2 Levers................Per dozen, $5 00

 ⅞ inch from selvedge to center of key cylinder.

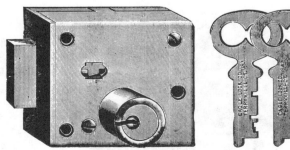

Full size cut of No. 1048¾.

Trunk Locks.

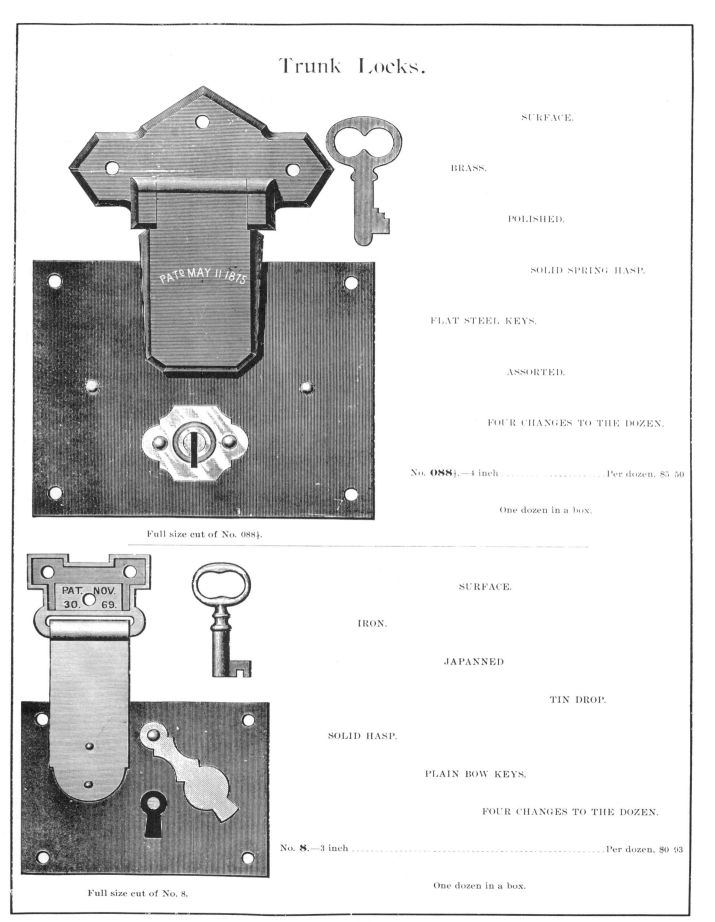

PAT? MAY 11 1875

SURFACE.

BRASS.

POLISHED.

SOLID SPRING HASP.

FLAT STEEL KEYS.

ASSORTED.

FOUR CHANGES TO THE DOZEN.

No. **088½.**—4 inch ....Per dozen, $5 50

One dozen in a box.

Full size cut of No. 088½.

PAT. NOV.
30. 69.

SURFACE.

IRON.

JAPANNED

TIN DROP.

SOLID HASP.

PLAIN BOW KEYS.

FOUR CHANGES TO THE DOZEN.

No. **8.**—3 inch ....Per dozen, $0 93

One dozen in a box.

Full size cut of No. 8.

Cabinet Keys and Blanks.

NUMBERS.	FOR LOCKS, NUMBERS.	KEYS. PER DOZEN.	BLANKS, PER DOZEN.
6075	1807½, 1807, 1048⅞	$1 50	$0 75
6069	6070, 1059, 6088, 7070, 7071, 7087	1 50	0 75
550	558, 561, 1221	1 50	1 00
566	567, 569, 571, 580, 578	1 50	1 00
0228	406, 450, 503, 350, 473, 266, 276		0 30
650	647, 014, 237, 1045, 452, 563	1 10	0 32
411	408, 410, 427, 467, 469, 471	1 10	0 35
254	202, 217	1 50	0 38
133	133	0 25	
99½	088½	0 30	
142	34, 142, 141, 133, 139, 42, 55	0 25	
10	189, 168, 160, 163, 166, 178, 64, 181		0 35
15	232	1 00	0 25
216	91, 216	1 00	0 38
219	219	1 25	0 75
1480	642, 157, 158		0 50
76½	391, 392, 510, 417, 415, 1875, 509		0 25
1001	1015	0 35	
93	93	1 00	
....	Cabinet Keys, Assorted .... Per gross		3 75

6075. ¾ in. 6069. 1 in. 550. 566. 0228. 650. 411. 254.

133. St. 99½. S. 142. 10.

15. 216. 219. 1480. 76½. 1001. 93.

Trunk Locks.

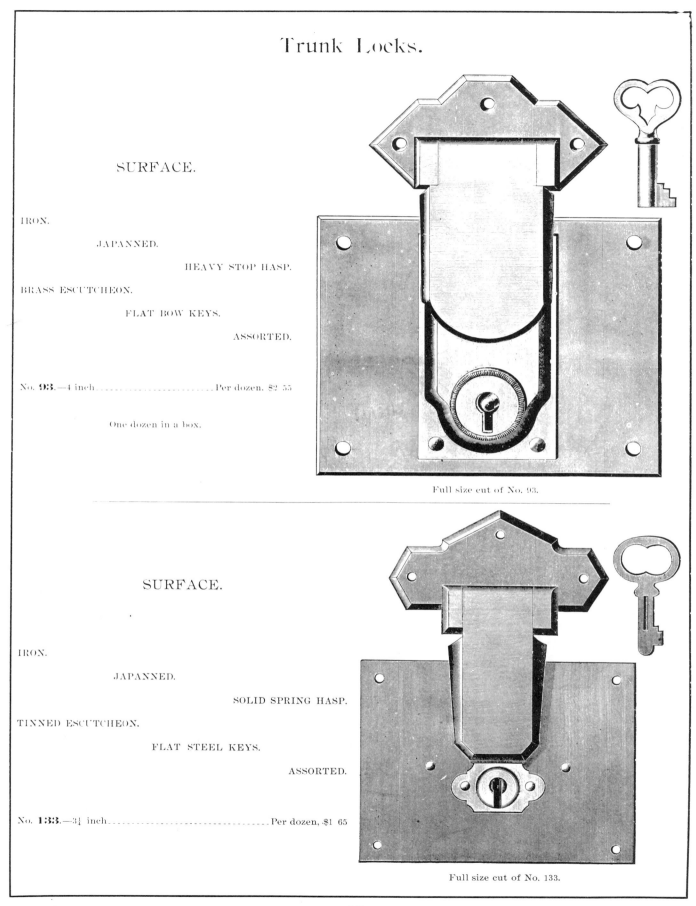

SURFACE.

IRON.

JAPANNED.

HEAVY STOP HASP.

BRASS ESCUTCHEON.

FLAT BOW KEYS.

ASSORTED.

No. **93**.—4 inch................................Per dozen, $2 55

One dozen in a box.

Full size cut of No. 93.

SURFACE.

IRON.

JAPANNED.

SOLID SPRING HASP.

TINNED ESCUTCHEON.

FLAT STEEL KEYS.

ASSORTED.

No. **133**.—3¼ inch................................Per dozen, $1 65

Full size cut of No. 133.

Cupboard Catches.

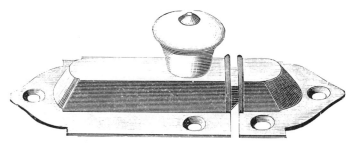

JAPANNED—PORCELAIN KNOBS.

No. 4, 2½ inch . . . .

" 6, 3 " . . . .

ENAMELED.

Bronze Metal Knobs.

No. 327, 2 inch . . . . . ,

Porcelain Knobs.

No. 427, 2 inch . . . . .

Two dozen in a box, with Screws.

GENEVA BRONZE.

Bronze Metal Knobs.

No. 369 . . . .

Two dozen in a box, with Screws.

Cupboard Turns.

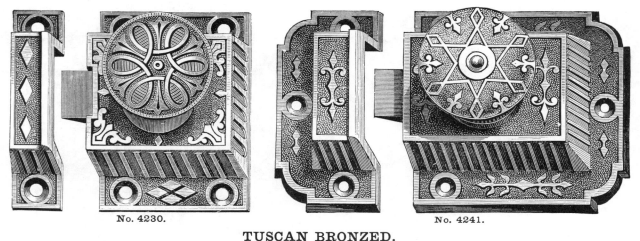

No. 4230.   No. 4241.

TUSCAN BRONZED.

Triangular Bolt, with Screws.

No. 4230, Tuscan Bronze Knob . . . .

" 424!, Bronze Metal Knob . . . .

Transom Catches.

GENEVA BRONZED.

No. 404 . . . .

Two dozen in a box, with Screws.

Door Buttons.

JAPANNED—RAISED.

No. 35, { Inch 1½ 1¾ 2 2¼
Per gross . . . .
Half gross in a box.

DOOR BUTTONS ON PLATES.

Japanned.

No. 20, 2 inch . . . .

Half gross in a box.

Tuscan Bronzed.

No. 32, 2 inch . . . . . .

Quarter gross in a box, with Screws.

No. 20.

No. 32.

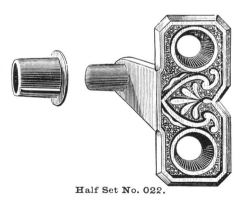

Half Set No. 022.

No. 022 . . . . . .

Wollensak's

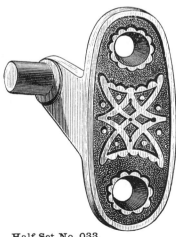

Half Set No. 033.

65

Sun Latch.

For Screen and Light Doors.

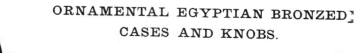

ORNAMENTAL EGYPTIAN BRONZED CASES AND KNOBS.

Iron Bolts, Stop on Latch Bolt.

Size 3½ x 2¼ . . . .

PERSIAN BRONZED CASE.

Complete with Bronzed Screws.

No. 747, 2½ x 3¾ inches, Brass Bolt, Brass Slide Bolt, Brass Flush Thumb Piece, Without Knobs . . . .

Store Door Handles.

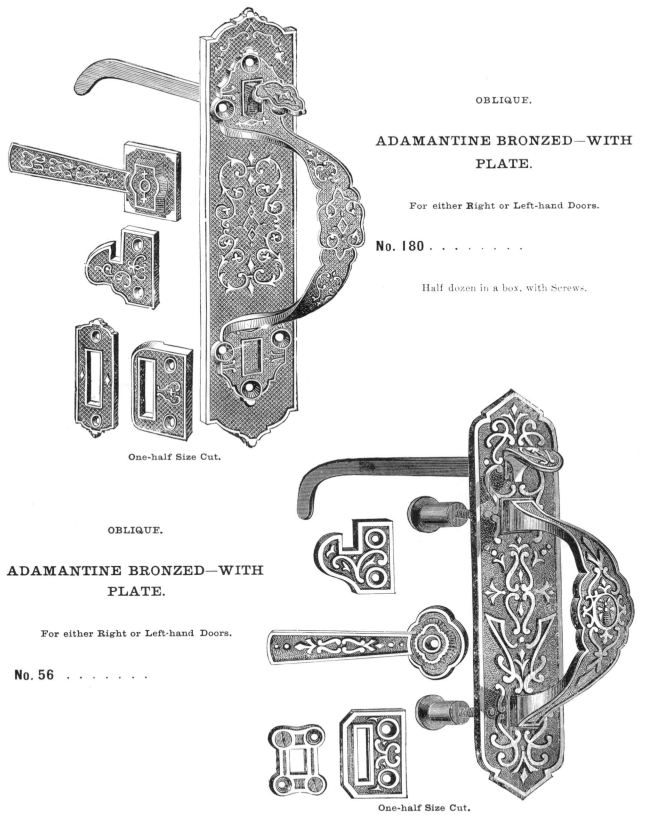

OBLIQUE.

ADAMANTINE BRONZED—WITH PLATE.

For either Right or Left-hand Doors.

No. 180 . . . .

Half dozen in a box, with Screws.

One-half Size Cut.

OBLIQUE.

ADAMANTINE BRONZED—WITH PLATE.

For either Right or Left-hand Doors.

No. 56 . . . .

One-half Size Cut.

Store Door Handles.

GENEVA BRONZED.

Oblique Handle, Right or Left Hand.

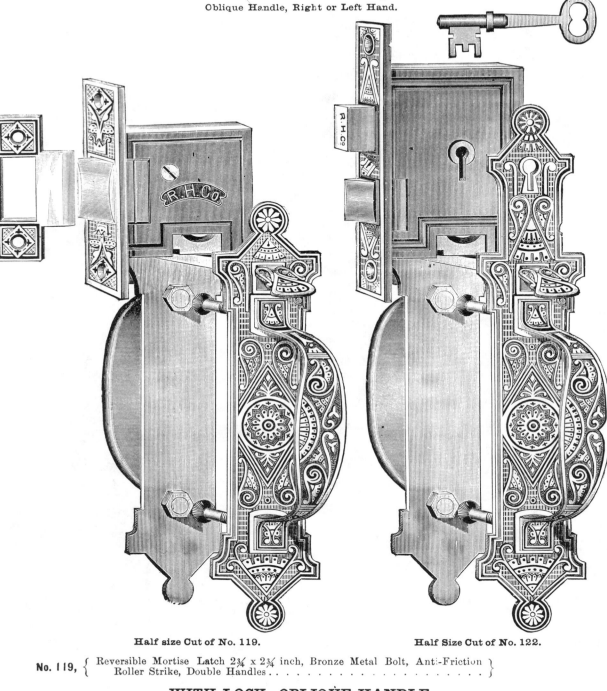

Half size Cut of No. 119.   Half Size Cut of No. 122.

No. 119, { Reversible Mortise Latch 2¾ x 2¾ inch, Bronze Metal Bolt, Anti-Friction } Roller Strike, Double Handles . . . . }

WITH LOCK—OBLIQUE HANDLE.

Geneva Bronzed Lock with Bronze Metal Bolts, Double Handle, 2 Nickel-Plated Steel Keys.

No. 122, { Reversible, 1 Tumbler, Mortise Lock 4 x 3 inch, Flat Front, Anti-Friction Rol- } ler Strike, Right or Left Hand . . . . }

No. 124, { 1 Tumbler Mortise Lock, 4 x 3 inch, Full Rabbet, Front Anti-Friction Roller } Strike, Right or Left Hand . . . . }

Escutcheons.

ORNAMENTAL GOLD BRONZE METAL.

Rose and Escutcheon Combined.

No. 1235½.   No. 1234½.

No. 1234½, ⅝-inch Key Hole . . . .

" **1235**½, ⅝ " " . . . .

Packed with Screws made from the same metal.

69

Mortise Front Door Sets.

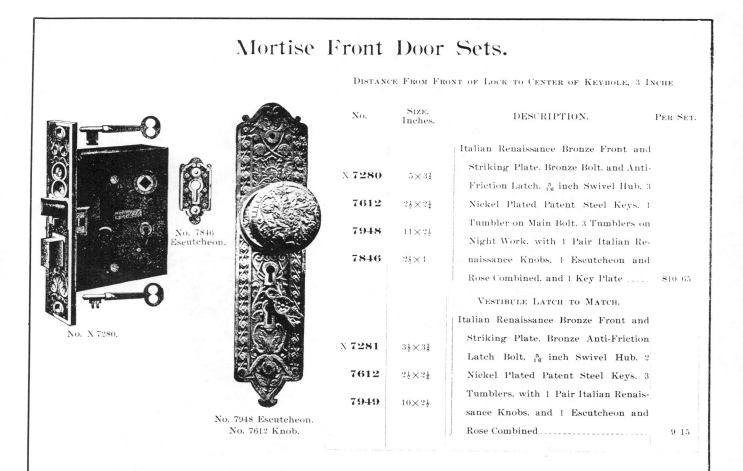

Distance From Front of Lock to Center of Keyhole, 3 Inches.

No. X 7280.

No. 7846 Escutcheon.

No. 7948 Escutcheon.
No. 7612 Knob.

No.	Size. Inches.	Description.	Per Set.
X 7280	5×3¾	Italian Renaissance Bronze Front and Striking Plate, Bronze Bolt, and Anti-Friction Latch, 5/16 inch Swivel Hub, 3 Nickel Plated Patent Steel Keys, 1 Tumbler on Main Bolt, 3 Tumblers on Night Work, with 1 Pair Italian Renaissance Knobs, 1 Escutcheon and Rose Combined, and 1 Key Plate	$10 65
7612	2½×2¼		
7948	11×2½		
7846	2½×1		
		Vestibule Latch to Match.	
X 7281	3½×3⅞	Italian Renaissance Bronze Front and Striking Plate, Bronze Anti-Friction Latch Bolt, 5/16 inch Swivel Hub, 2 Nickel Plated Patent Steel Keys, 3 Tumblers, with 1 Pair Italian Renaissance Knobs, and 1 Escutcheon and Rose Combined	9 15
7612	2½×2¼		
7949	10×2½		

Distance From Front of Lock to Center of Keyhole, 3 Inches.

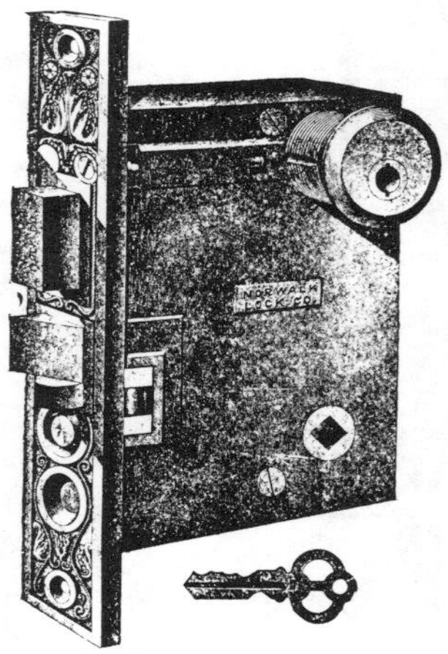

No. X 7404 R.

No. 7475 R. Escutcheon.
No. 7602 R. Knob.

No.	Size. Inches.	Description.	Per Set.
X 7404 R.	5¼×4	Italian Renaissance Bronze Front and Striking Plate, Bronze Bolt, and Anti-Friction Latch, ⅜ inch Swivel Hub, 3 Keys, Plain Bronze Turn Knob for inside, with 1 Pair Italian Renaissance Bronze Knobs, and 1 Escutcheon and Rose Combined	$21 15
7602 R.	2½×2¼		
7475 R.	12½×3		
		Vestibule Latch to Match.	
X 7405	5¼×4	Italian Renaissance Bronze Front and Striking Plate, Bronze Anti-Friction Latch Bolt, ⅜ inch Swivel Hub, 3 Keys, with 1 Pair Italian Renaissance Bronze Knobs, and 1 Escutcheon and Rose Combined	19 40
7602 R.	2½×2¼		
7475 R.	12½×3		

In ordering, state Hand and Thickness of Door.

Operated by Key from outside and Knob from inside.

"ARABIAN."

ANTIQUE COPPER FINISH.

Illustration ¾ size.

No.	SIZE, IN.	DESCRIPTION.	PER DOZEN SETS.
7124	4⅜×3¼	"Arabian." Bronzed Front and Striking Plate, Bronzed Bolts,	
7687	2¼×2¼	Japanned Case ⅜ inch thick. Nickle Plated Patent Steel Keys, Night Work, one Tumbler, one pair Bronzed Knobs, and two	
7851½	11×2¼	Escutcheons and Roses Combined to Each Set	$24 00

Locks.

UPRIGHT RIM KNOB.

For Right or Left-hand Doors.   Reverse by simply pulling Latch Bolt forward and turning half around.

No. 2000.

No.	Size, Inches.	5-16 Inch Hub—Thin-bit Key—Wrought Iron Inside Work.
1997	5 x 3½	Ornamental English Bronzed Case, Iron Bolts, Brass Key, 1 Rack Tumbler, 24 Changes . . . .
2000	5 x 3½	Ornamental English Bronzed Case, Brass Bolts and Thumb Bolt, Brass Key, 1 Rack Tumbler, 24 Changes . . . .

Locks.

HORIZONTAL RIM KNOB LOCKS.

Reversible for Right or Left-hand Doors, by simply pulling Latch Bolt forward and turning half around.

ORNAMENTAL ENGLISH BRONZED CASE.

No.	Size. Inches.	5-16 Inch Hub, with Thin-bit Key. Wrought Iron Inside Work.
1935	5 x 3½	Iron Bolts, Brass Key, 1 Rack Tumbler, 24 Changes . . . .
1936	5 x 3½	Brass Bolts and Key, 1 " " 24 " . . . .

Packed with English Bronzed Key Escutcheons.

Locks.

SLIDING DOOR, WITH PULL COMBINED.

For Doors sliding in flush with the wall. Complete with Elongated Flush Cup Escutcheons, Door
Stop, and Bronze Screws. Double Lock. Flat Front.

5½ x 3½ inches, { **Bronze Metal** Fronts, Bolt and Pulls, Drop Key and Escutcheons . .

No. 01288, { **Royal Bronze**   "   "   "   "   "   . .

RABBETED MORTISE FRONT DOOR.

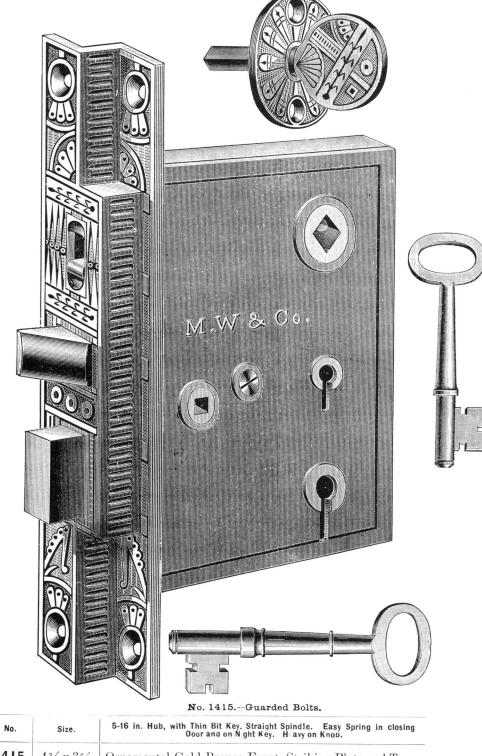

M.W & Co.

No. 1415.--Guarded Bolts.

No.	Size.	5-16 in. Hub, with Thin Bit Key. Straight Spindle. Easy Spring in closing Door and on Night Key. Heavy on Knob.
1415	4¾ x 3⅝	Ornamental Gold Bronze Front, Striking Plate and Turn-knob and Plate, Brass Bolts, Nickel Key, 1 Tumbler on both Bolts, 2 small Nickel Night Keys, 12 Changes.

Locks.

REVERSIBLE MORTISE KNOB LOCK.

To Reverse, Take off Cap and Turn Over Latch.

ORNAMENTAL BRONZE METAL FRONT AND STRIKE, BRONZE METAL BOLTS.

Patent Steel Keys, Nickel-Plated, 1 Steel Tumbler, 24 Changes.

No. 3408, 3¾ x 3¼ inch . . . .

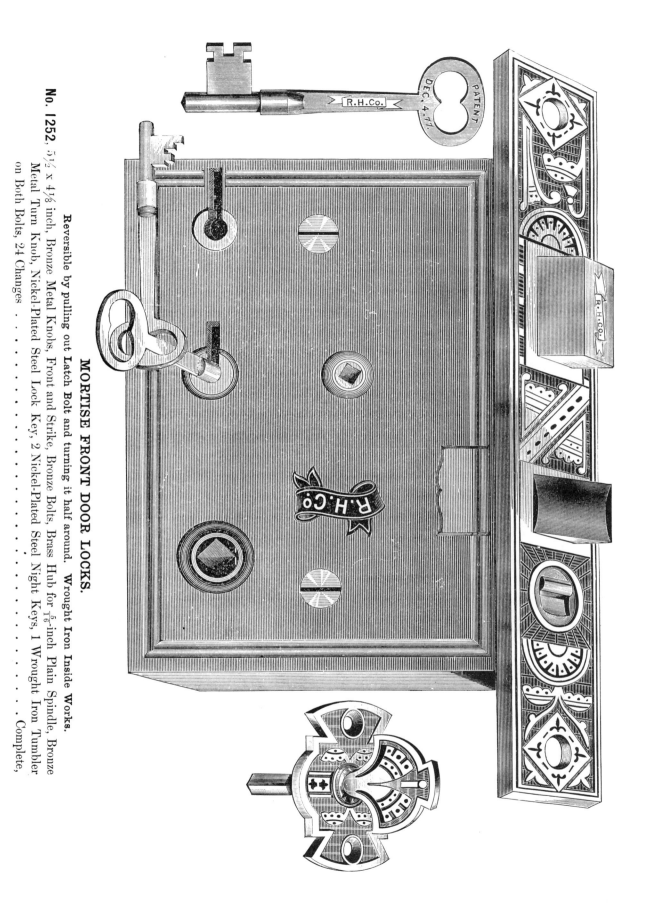

MORTISE FRONT DOOR LOCKS.

No. 1252. $5\frac{1}{2}$ x $4\frac{1}{8}$ inch, Bronze Metal Knobs, Front and Strike, Bronze Bolts, Brass Hub for $\frac{5}{16}$-inch Plain Spindle, Bronze Metal Turn Knob, Nickel-Plated Steel Lock Key, 2 Nickel-Plated Steel Night Keys, 1 Wrought Iron Tumbler on Both Bolts, 24 Changes . . . . Complete,

Reversible by pulling out Latch Bolt and turning it half around. Wrought Iron Inside Works.

Locks.

MORTISE FRONT DOOR.—REVERSIBLE.

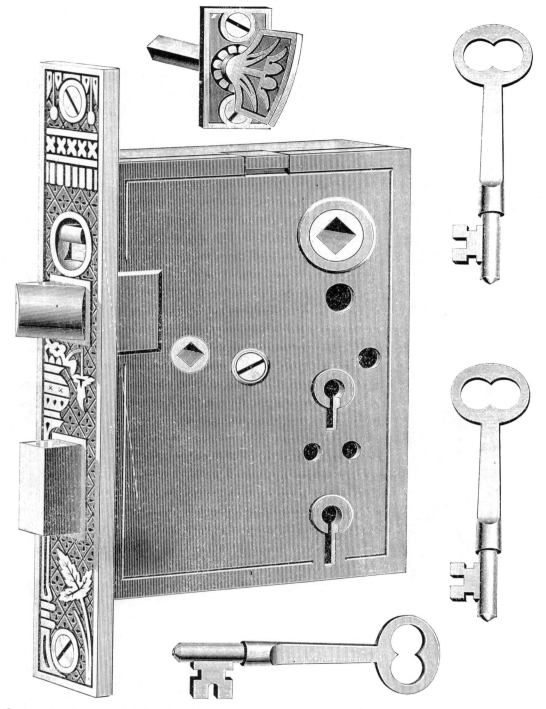

Ornamental Bronze Metal Front and Strike; two Nickel-Plated Steel Keys for Night Bolt, and one for Dead Bolt.

No. 580, 3¾ x 4¾ inch . . . . `

One Wrought Tumbler on both Bolts, 12 Changes.   Complete with Knobs, Escutcheons, and Roses, and finished—No. 1, Natural Color, Light Bronze, Polished Surface.   No. 3, Light Bronze, Polished Surface, with Black Background.

Latches.

TUBULAR RIM NIGHT LATCHES.
A. E. DEITZ'S.

For Doors 1 to 2-inch Thick.

Heavy Japanned Iron Case, Iron Bolt, Bronze Slide and Stop Knobs, Ornamental Bronze
Escutcheon, Two Tumblers, Two Flat Steel Keys.

No. 1103 . . . . per dozen, $11 40

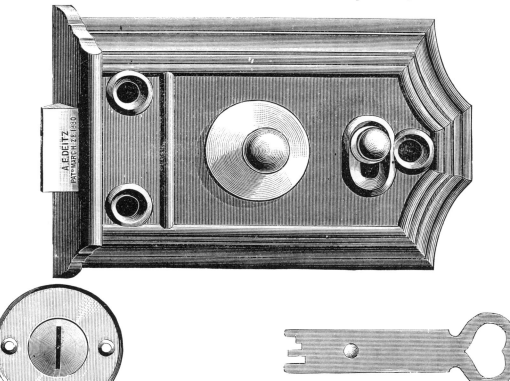

For Doors 1 to 2⅜-inches Thick.

Heavy Japanned Iron Case, Heavy Bronze Bolt, Bronze Slide and Stop Knobs, Four Tumblers,
Two Flat Steel Keys, Bronze Metal Swivel Escutcheon.

No. 108, 2⅜ x 3¾ . . . .

79

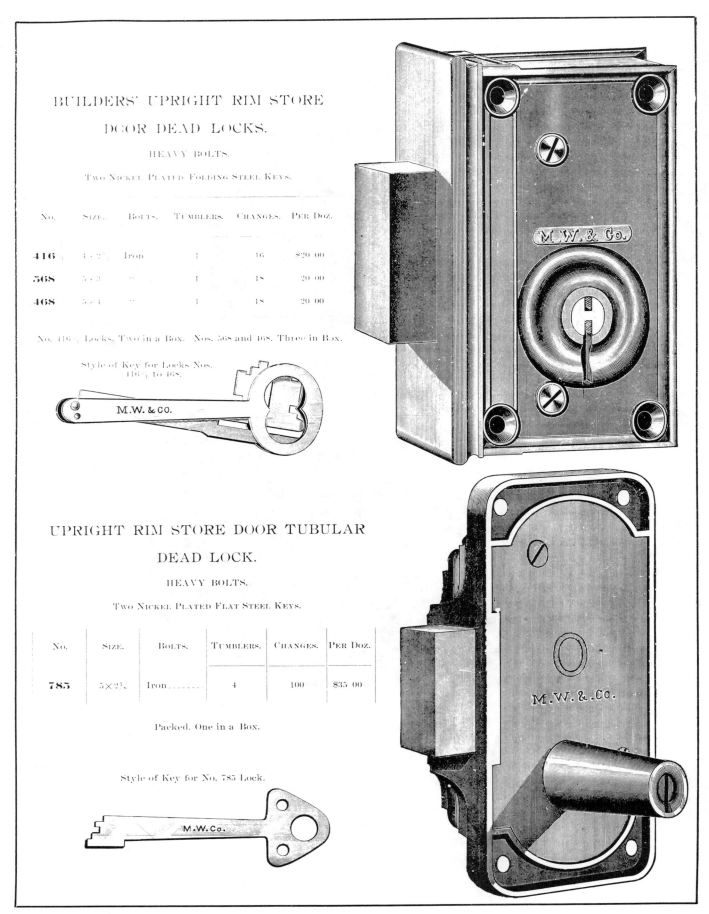

BUILDERS' UPRIGHT RIM STORE
DOOR DEAD LOCKS.

HEAVY BOLTS.

Two Nickel Plated Folding Steel Keys.

No.	Size.	Bolts.	Tumblers.	Changes.	Per Doz.
416	4 x 2½	Iron	1	16	$20 00
568	5 x 3	"	1	18	20 00
468	5 x 3	"	1	18	20 00

No. 416½ Locks. Two in a Box. Nos. 568 and 468, Three in Box.

Style of Key for Locks Nos.
416½ to 468.

UPRIGHT RIM STORE DOOR TUBULAR
DEAD LOCK.

HEAVY BOLTS.

Two Nickel Plated Flat Steel Keys.

No.	Size.	Bolts.	Tumblers.	Changes.	Per Doz.
785	5 x 2½	Iron........	4	100	$35 00

Packed. One in a Box.

Style of Key for No. 785 Lock.

PRICE GUIDE

All prices are for locks complete with keys, in good condition. Locks or keys in less than good shape will be priced less. Therefore it is wise to remember this when building your collection. Prices may vary from one location to the next so this price guide is just a price comparison and it will vary somewhat in your area. This is not an offer to buy or sell. It is only a guide.

Page 2
No. 00000 - $20-25
No. 0000 - $20-25
No. 000 - $25-30
No. 00 - $25-30
No. 0 - $25-30
No. 1 - $45-50
No. 2 - $45-50
No. 3 - $45-50
No. 4 - $45-50
No. 5 - $45-50
No. 7 - $45-50
No. 8 - $60-70

Page 3
No. 10 - $40-50
No. 11 - $40-50
No. 18 - $40-50
No. 20 - $40-50
No. 1000 - $40-50
No. 1002 - $40-50
No. 1003 - $40-50
No. 1004 - $40-50
No. 1007 - $40-50
No. 1008 - $40-50
No. 1011 - $25-35
No. 1015 - $20-30

Page 4
No. 1017 - $40-50
No. 1018 - $40-50
No. 1019 - $40-50
No. 1020 - $40-50
No. 1021 - $20-25
No. 1023 - $20-25
No. 1024 - $20-25
No. 1025 - $20-25
No. 1027 - $20-25
No. 1028 - $20-25
No. 1029 - $20-25
No. 1030 - $20-25

Page 5
No. 1033 - $60-70
No. 1034 - $60-70
No. 1036 - $40-50
No. 1037 - $40-50
No. 1038 - $25-35
No. 1039 - $50-60
No. 1043 - $40-50
No. 1047 - $40-50
No. 1048 - $40-50
No. 1050 - $40-50
No. 1052 - $40-50
No. 1053 - $40-50

Page 6
No. 1054 - $40-50
No. 1055 - $40-50
No. 1056 - $40-50
No. 1057 - $40-50
No. 1059 - $40-50
No. 1061 - $40-50
No. 1062 - $40-50
No. 1063 - $40-50
No. 1064 - $25-30
No. 1065 - $40-50
No. 1066 - $40-50
No. 1076 - $40-50
No. 1077 - $40-50

Page 7
No. 14 - $40-50
No. 15 - $40-50
No. 1014 - $40-50
No. 1032 - $60-70
No. 1042 - $50-60
No. 1044 - $50-60
No. 1046 - $60-70

Page 8
No. 1051 - $40-50
No. 1060 - $40-50
No. 1069 - $40-50
No. 1072 - $40-50
No. 1073 - $40-50
No. 1074 - $40-50
No. 1075 - $40-50

Page 9
No. 270 - $50-65
No. 272 - $50-65
No. 172 - $55-65
No. 264 - $40-50
No. 174 - $40-50
No. 507 - $50-65

Page 10
No. 505 - $60-70
No. 502 - $60-70
No. 262CH - $10-20
No. 261 - $10-20
No. 506 - $10-20
No. 271 - $50-60

Page 11
No. 268 - $30-40
No. 643 - $70-80
No. 176 - $20-25
No. 183 - $20-25
No. 175 - $20-25
No. 182 - $20-25

Page 12
No. 830 - $15-20
No. 830 1/2 - $20-30
No. 840 - $10-20
No. 840 1/2 - $10-20
No. 850 - $10-20
No. 850 1/2 - $10-20

Page 13
No. 813 - $10-20
No. 813 1/2 - $15-25
No. 823 - $10-20
No. 823 1/2 - $10-20
No. 833 - $10-20
No. 833 1/2 - $20-30

Page 14
No. 843 - $15-25
No. 843 1/2 - $25-30
No. 853 - $10-15
No. 853 1/2 - $25-30
No. 726 - $10-15
No. 726 1/2 - $25-30

Page 15
No. 526 - $10-15
No. 526 1/2 - $20-25
No. 326 - $10-15
No. 326 1/2 - $20-25
No. 735 - $20-30
No. 585 - $25-35

Page 16
No. 435 - $20-30
No. 435 1/2 - $20-30
No. 803F - $20-30
No. 803 1/2F - $35-45
No. 805F - $20-30
No. 805 1/2F - $20-30

Page 17
No. 225 - $10-20
No. 225 1/2 - $10-20
No. 9645J - $10-20
No. 9645C - $10-20
No. 9645V - $10-20
No. 647J - $10-20
No. 647C - $10-20
No. 647V - $10-20
No. 563 - $10-15
No. 565 - $10-15

Page 18
No. 453X - $10-20
No. 453 1/2X - $10-20
No. 455X - $10-20
No. 455 1/2X - $10-20
No. 457X - $10-20
No. 457 1/2X - $10-20

Page 19
No. 297 - $10-20
No. 674N - $10-20
No. 8414 - $10-20
No. 8434 - $10-20
No. 8454 - $10-20
No. 897 1/2 - $55-70

Page 20
Complete card $700+

Page 21
No. 300 - $25-35
No. 310 - $25-35
No. 530 - $25-35
No. 531 - $25-35
No. 116 - $25-35
No. 311 - $60-70

Page 22
No. 101 - $20-30
No. 102 - $10-15
No. 104 - $10-15
No. 103 - $30-40
No. 253 - $10-15
No. 254 - $40-50
No. 152 - $10-15
No. 263 - $10-15

Page 23
No. 153 - $15-25
No. 155 - $15-25
No. 255 - $15-25
No. 154 - $15-25
No. 252 - $20-25
No. 260 - $20-25

Page 24
No. 151 - $20-25
No. 251 - $20-25
No. 259 - $20-30
No. 501 - $25-35
No. 503 - $25-35
No. 504 - $25-35
No. 256 - $20-25
No. 257 - $20-25
No. 258 - $20-25

Page 25
No. 40 - $25-30
No. 41 - $25-30
No. 42 - $25-30
No. 43 - $25-30
No. 44 - $25-30
No. 45 - $25-30
No. 51 - $25-30
No. 52 - $25-30
No. 53 - $25-30
No. 54 - $25-30

Price Guide

Page 25 continued
No. 55 - $25-30
No. 56 - $25-30
No. 209 - $25-30
No. 211 - $25-30
No. 213 - $25-30
No. 229 - $25-30
No. 231 - $25-30
No. 233 - $25-30
No. 409 - $25-35
No. 411 - $25-35
No. 413 - $25-35
No. 429 - $25-35
No. 431 - $25-35
No. 433 - $25-35

Page 26
All $60-70

Page 27
No. 74 - $40-50
No. 72 - $40-50
No. 509 - $40-50
No. 521 - $40-50

Page 28
No. 4019 - $20-25
No. 4049 - $20-25
No. 4010 - $20-25
No. 4038 - $20-25

Page 29
No. 999 - $35-45
No. 303 - $50-70
No. 1304 - $35-45
No. 420 - $15-20
No. 806 - $20-25

Page 30
No. 1010 - $40-50
No. 1011 - $40-50
No. 1012 - $40-50
No. 2010 - $40-50
No. 2011 - $40-50
No. 2012 - $40-50
No. 2050 - $40-50
No. 2051 - $40-50
No. 2052 - $40-50

Page 31
No. 84 - $60-70
No. 85 - $60-80

Page 32
No. 1013 - $40-50
No. 1016 - $40-50

Page 33
No. 4034 - $25-30
No. 4023 - $20-25
No. 4027 - $40-50

Page 34
Brass Locks - $20-25
Bronze Locks - $20-25
Screw Lock - $40-50
Bicycle Lock - $15-25
Sprocket Lock - $25-35

Page 35
No. 42 - $20-25
No. 43 - $20-25
No. 44 - $20-25
Rex - $20-30
Big Three - $10-15
Corbin - $10-15
2H1213 - $10-15
2H1309 - $10-15
2H10673 - $15-25
2H1274 - $20-25
2H1218 - $20-25

Page 36
Reference Only

Page 37
Reference Only

Page 38
Reference Only

Page 39
Reference Only

Page 40
Reference Only

Page 41
Yale - $50-60
Brass Keys - $10-15
Motor - $15-20
Stability - $15-20
Sargent - $15-20
Winchester - $125-175

Page 42
All Brass RR Keys with
Company Letters - $40-55
scarcer one much more
Steel - $10-15

Page 43
Adlake Steel - $10-15
B & O Steel - $60-70
Cirr Steel - $65-80
NYC (Moon) Steel - $50-70
CCC & STL (XLCR) w-Arrow) - $70-80
CCC & STL (Steel Body Brass Shackle) - $60-70
Adlake (Brass) - $25-30
B&O F.S. Howe Co. - $60-70
L & N Steel - $60-70
Wabash - $75-100

Page 44
No. 172 - $25-30

Page 45
No. 545 - 561 - 565 - 580 - 605 - $5-10 each
No. 170 - $10-15
No. 485 - $2-5
No. 180 - $10-15
No. 195 - $10-15

Page 46
All Keys - $10-15

Page 47
No. 2001 - $45-55
All Others - $10-15

Page 48
All - $15-25

Page 49
All - $15-25

Page 50
No. 182 - $15-25
No. 92 - $15-25
No. 219 - $15-25

Page 51
All - $5-10 each

Page 52
No. 2011 - $15-20
Others - $10-15

Page 53
All - $10-15

Page 54
All - $10-15

Page 55
No. 1015 - $20-30
All Others - $10-15

Page 56
All - $10-15

Page 57
All - $10-20

Page 58
All - $10-20

Page 59
All - $20-30

Page 60
All - $15-20

Page 61
All - $45-50

Page 62
All - $10-15

Page 63
All - $40-50

Page 64
No. 4 - $10-20
No. 6 - $10-20
No. 327 - $10-20
No. 427 - $10-20
No. 369 - $15-25
No. 4230-No. 4241 - $10-20

Page 65
No. 404 - $15-20
No. 35 - $3
No. 20 - $3
No. 32 - $5-10
No. 022 - $3-5
No. 033 - $5-10

Page 66
Sun Latch - $25-35
Egyptian - $40-45
No. 747 - $25-35

Page 67
No. 180 - $60-70
No. 56 - $60-70

Page 68
No. 119 - $60-70
No. 122 - $60-70
No. 124 - $60-70

Page 69
No. 1234 - $20-30
No. 1234 - $20-30

Page 70
Upper Set - $60-70
Lower Set - $60-70

Page 71
Set - $60-70

Page 72
No. 1997 - $20-40
No. 2000 - $40-60

Page 73
No. 1935 - $20-30
No. 1936 - $60-70

Page 74
No. 01288 - $75-85

Page 75
No. 1415 - $60-70

Page 76
No. 3408 - $40-50

Page 77
No. 1252 - $60-70

Page 78
No. 580 - $50-60

Page 79
No. 1103 - $20-30
No. 108 - $40-50

Page 80
Top - $50-60
Bottom - $60-70

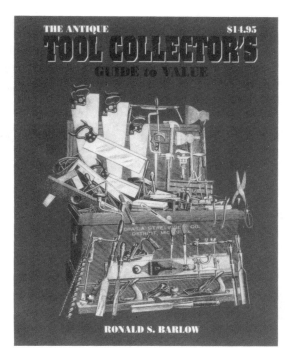

Item #1114
Only $14.95 + $3.00 Shipping

THE ANTIQUE TOOL
COLLECTOR'S GUIDE TO VALUE
by Ronald S. Barlow

Old tools are hot collectibles. The items in this book are described and priced for dealers and collectors alike. Items such as: Wooden Plow Planes, Axes, Adzes, Anvils, Chisels, Hammers, Hatchets, Pocket Knives, levels, Pliers, Rules, Saws, Screwdrivers, Shaves, Tinsmith's Tools, Wrenches and Blacksmith Tools just to name a few.

This book is 9" x 12" with 240 pages includes hundreds of illustrations and has many addresses of major antique tool auctioneers, dealers and collectors clubs.

TO ORDER CALL:
1-800-777-6450 for VISA & MASTERCARD Orders Only

OR SEND CHECK OR MONEY ORDER TO:
L-W BOOK SALES • P.O. BOX 69 • GAS CITY, IN 46933

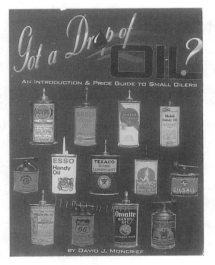